SERIALS ON BRITISH TELEVISION 1950–1994

Serials on British Television 1950–1994

Ellen Baskin

SCOLAR PRESS

©Ellen Baskin, 1996

All rights reserved. No part of this publication may be reproduced, stored in a retrieval system, or transmitted in any form or by any means, electronic, mechanical, photocopying, recording, or otherwise without the prior permission of the publisher.

Published by
SCOLAR PRESS
Gower House
Croft Road
Aldershot
Hants GU11 3HR
England

Ashgate Publishing Company
Old Post Road
Brookfield
Vermont 05036-9704
USA

British Library Cataloguing-in-Publication data.

Baskin, Ellen
 Serials on British Television, 1950–1994
 I. Title
 791.45750941

Library of Congress Cataloging-in-Publication Data

Baskin, Ellen
 Serials on British Television, 1950–1994 / Ellen Baskin.
     p.   cm.
  Includes indexes.
  ISBN 1-85928-015-3 (hc)
  1. Television serials–Great Britain–Catalogs. 2. Television serials–Great Britain–History and criticism. I. Title.
 PN1992.8.S4B37 1995
 016.79145'S--dc20   95-13808
                                                                    CIP

ISBN 1 85928 015 3

Typset in Plantin by Cappella, Ipswich and printed in Great Britain by Hartnoll Ltd, Bodmin.

Contents

Preface	vii
Introduction	ix
How to use this book	xiii
1950–1959	3
1960–1969	47
1970–1979	101
1980–1989	169
1990–1994	249
Index of titles of serials	285
Index of original works	291
Index of serial writers	292
Index of authors of original works	296
Index of producers	299
Index of directors	302
Index of players	306
Index of genres	331

Preface

This volume presents the first ever comprehensive anthology of dramatic television serials produced from 1950 to 1994. Exactly what is a serial? In a standard television series, each individual episode tells a different story about the same group of regular characters. By the time the credits roll, the issues, problems or mystery presented have been resolved. This is not the case in a serial, where each episode answers questions left unresolved from prior segments, while presenting new narrative threads to be woven into subsequent episodes. By the end of the serial, all loose ends have been tied up and the fabric of the story woven into a unified whole.

For the purposes of this book, a serial is defined as a multi-part, self-contained drama. A television serial is broadcast in a number of episodes (as few as 3, as many as 26), telling one connected story, always with a view towards the end. In this regard, *The Forsyte Saga* is a serial; the soap opera *Coronation Street*, which does not seem ever to have a view to an end, is not. A serial can be an original idea developed for television or an adaptation of previously-published material.

In the early years of television, most programmes, including serials, were a half-hour in duration; for dramatic programmes, the one-hour time period became the standard in the 1960s. The majority of the programmes in this book were presented as one-hour-long episodes (at times the premiere or concluding episode ran longer), on the same night over a period of weeks. This is different from the 'miniseries' format, made popular in the 1970s, in which a programme aired for two or three hours a night over several consecutive nights. A miniseries is not a serial. (In the U.S., however, anything that is not in standard weekly series format is referred to as a miniseries, including the British serials which have been aired in the States.)

Multi-part programmes such as *The Six Wives of Henry VIII* and *Number 10*, whose individual episodes are limited in number and linked by a singular, specific theme, are also included here. But an anthology programme about a single character, such as *The Adventures of Sherlock Holmes*, is not a serial, as each segment tells its own, self-contained story, and thus is not included in this book.

Three-part detective thrillers became quite popular in the 1980s; perhaps due to the popularity of miniseries, many of these aired in hourly segments over three consecutive nights, such as *Harry's Game*, broadcast on ITV starting 25 October 1982. Recognizing this as a standardized format change, these programmes have been included, as have the first three *Prime Suspect* serials, whose four parts were broadcast on two nights.

A number of multi-part thrillers has also served to introduce detectives who have then returned to solve more crimes. We have included only the story which introduced the protagonist, such as 1983's *Killer*, where we first met the character of Detective Chief Inspector Jim Taggart, portrayed for the next decade by the late Mark McManus, except for instances where each story is based on an individual book, such as the Lord Peter Wimsey and Adam Dalgliesh mysteries.

Admittedly, there are gray areas when we attempt to define what is a serial and what might instead be considered a series or a soap opera. In the 1970s and 1980s a number of serially-structured dramatic programmes were broadcast, perhaps with the intent of acting as a springboard for a new set of episodes, but at the same time offering a self-contained narrative arc. We have attempted here to be as comprehensive as possible, as the 950+ programme listings indicate. Any additions or corrections from readers would be welcome.

The book is complete until the end of 1994, but during production of the book the opportunity was taken to include as many as possible of the 1995 serials. British video availability was kindly supplied by *VideoLog* magazine; note that this status changes as certain titles are pulled from circulation and others are newly put into distribution.

Most of the research for this book was done at the British Film Institute in London, using the London editions of the *Radio Times* and *TV Times* to verify specific programme listings. A special thanks to the Second Floor Cataloguing Department staff at the BFI, who so graciously welcomed me into their midst.

Tony Mechele was instrumental to the development of this book and his guidance and assistance were invaluable at every phase. I am most grateful to him for his generous help, without which the book could not have been completed.

Ellen Baskin
October 1995

Introduction

BRITISH TELEVISION DRAMA

BBC Television began regular transmissions on 2 November 1936 from studios at the Alexandra Palace. From the outset drama was a basic of programming; in 1937, more than 100 dramas were aired, most of them adaptations of stage plays and shorter than 30 minutes in length. These early, live broadcasts came to a halt in September 1939, and were suspended for the duration of the Second World War.

Transmission resumed on 7 June 1946, setting the stage for television to overwhelm popular culture in the post-war years, fulfilling the mission stated in a paper to the BBC Board of Governors in 1948 that television was to be 'an instrument of education and information as well as of public entertainment'.

Programming at that time, virtually all of which was live, was aired for just a few hours during the day, and listings relegated to a few short pages at the back of the *Radio Times*. By the end of 1952, of 12.8 million broadcast licences issued by the BBC, 1.8 million were for both radio and television. London viewers alone numbered more than 600,000. In June 1953, the coronation of Queen Elizabeth II was televised live by the BBC; it was the first time more people 'saw' than 'listened to' a major news event. More than 50 per cent of the adult population of Great Britain is estimated to have watched the broadcast, although far less than that percentage owned televisions at the time. By 1955, nearly five million combined licences were being issued. (Not coincidentally, cinema attendance in Great Britain dropped from over 900 million in 1954 to 450 million in 1959.)

Independent, commercial television was inaugurated in Great Britain on 22 September 1955, when the ITV went on the air, branching out regionally from the London area until it extended across the nation. Offering an alternative to the more sophisticated BBC offerings, ITV's programming aimed at popular formats, which included imported American television shows. In fact, the cover of the first issue of *TV Times*, ITV's programme publication, featured American television personality Lucille Ball, along with Patricia Dainton, one of the featured stars of ITV's first soap opera, *Sixpenny Opera*.

By the late 1950s, a majority of people in the United Kingdom had televisions or access to viewing. Competition between the BBC and ITV was fierce. Starting in 1956, ITV's *Armchair Theatre*, produced by ATV (Associated TeleVision), telecast 'one-off' plays which had been either adapted or written and produced exclusively for television, introducing a new format of dramatic writing. The BBC counter-attacked with an increase in its output of drama; in 1963, Sydney Newman was hired away from the commercial network and named BBC Head of Drama. Newman subdivided the department into three sections: Plays, Series, and Serials, ushering in what has been called the 'Golden Age' of BBC Drama.

In the early 1960s, while broadcasts of feature films and American programmes continued to be a staple of television broadcasting, drama productions were flourishing. Anthology programmes became popular, such as *The Somerset Maugham Hour*, where a different Maugham story was presented each week and *Out of this World*, a supernatural anthology hosted by Boris Karloff. Episodic drama series were also being developed, some based on historical or literary characters such as Richard the Lionheart, Robin Hood or the Scarlet Pimpernel. At the same time, originally-developed series whose weekly episodes revolved around doctors or lawyers or police officers were introduced, and remain a standard programming format.

By the late 1960s, there was notably less dominance of American programming on British television sets. Even more significant, both ITV and BBC began airing some programmes in colour in December, 1968 and both were fully operational in colour by the end of 1969. BBC2, which first aired on 20 April 1964, had already begun transmitting in colour in July 1967. A fourth commercial television network, aptly called Channel 4, began airing on 2 November 1982.

The technology of videotape, which allowed programmes to be recorded for later, non-live broadcast, was introduced in 1958, and by the 1960s, pre-recorded productions began to predominate over live drama broadcasts. In addition to expanding and enhancing production values, videotape made it easier for programmes to be re-broadcast (and sold to other markets) and, since tapes of programmes were often archived by the networks, laid the preliminary foundation for the home video revolution which was to explode in the 1980s.

THE TELEVISION SERIAL

Whatever its format – Scheherezade weaving tales to last a thousand and one nights, Charles Dickens writing in instalments for Victorian magazines, or ever-periled Pauline left hanging from cinematic cliffs week after week – the serial has long been a favourite narrative form, with one consistent, crucial mandate: keep the audience coming back for more.

Since its inception, television has faced this challenge on a daily, even an hourly basis, and one of the standard formats for maintaining a hold on the viewing audience has been the drama serial. British television's first drama serial, an adaptation of Louisa May Alcott's *Little Women*, was broadcast in six parts beginning 12 December 1950.

Serials have remained a staple of television programming since the 1950s. In the medium's early years, most of the serials aired by the BBC, either for an adult or children's audience, were adaptations of recognized works. Adult-oriented thrillers written exclusively for television were soon added to the programme roster, when Francis Durbridge made his television writing debut in 1952 with *The Broken Horseshoe*. The science fiction classic *Quatermass* enthralled its first audience in 1953. When ITV went on the air, it, too, quickly adopted the serial form, focusing almost exclusively in its premiere months on the thriller, even promoting some of its multi-part programmes under the attention-getting *Suspense* banner.

The BBC continued overwhelmingly to dominate serial programming in the 1960s, adapting many classic literary works on both its channels. In time, BBC2 offered more adult-oriented adaptations, while BBC1 tended to broadcast those aimed at a family audience. At the same time, BBC1 began offering original multi-part contemporary dramas aimed at an adult audience. ITV got into the adaptation business as well, offering, in 1966, one of the longest adaptations to date, a 26-part serial which combined three Arnold Bennett novels under the title of *Clayhanger*.

In addition to its focus on classic adaptations, BBC2 began to develop historical dramas, and throughout the 1970s it offered multi-part looks at the lives of significant figures in political and cultural history in such works as *The First Churchills* (which aired at the end of 1969), *The Six Wives of Henry VIII* and *Notorious Woman*, based on the life of writer George Sand. ITV caught on to this trend as well, with biographical programmes including *Dickens of London*, *Edward & Mrs. Simpson*, and *Jennie: Lady Randolph Churchill*. The majority of the adaptations the commercial network produced in the 1970s were contemporary adult works.

Breaking the BBC stranglehold on long-form drama adaptations, it was ITV which offered the two most highly-acclaimed serials of the 1980s: *Brideshead Revisited* and *The Jewel in the Crown*, both produced by Granada Television. These lavish productions offered viewers an alternative to the miniseries format which had first been popularized in the United States.

Channel 4 also featured a number of adaptations, beginning with its four-part presentation of the Royal Shakespeare Company's production of *The Life and Adventures of Nicholas Nickleby*; the new network stepped forward assertively in terms of contemporary drama as well, notably in 1989's *Traffik*, acclaimed worldwide for its cutting-edge look at the illegal drugs trade.

Production of multi-part thrillers had waned somewhat in the 1970s, but came back strongly in the 1980s. A number of detective stories were adapted from novels, including P.D. James' Adam Dalgliesh intrigues, which were produced by ITV. And many new sleuthing characters were introduced to the television audience via the serialized thriller form. The three-part detective serial, at times broadcast on three consecutive nights, became common in the 1980s and remains a regular form of dramatic presentation.

These detective thrillers seemed almost to have taken over the serial form for a number of years, with the 1990s introducing compelling characters such as *Prime Suspect*'s Jane Tennison to the fold. But this decade has also seen the elaborate, once-standard classic adaptation making an enthusiastic comeback, in such recent serials as *Middlemarch* and *Martin Chuzzlewit*. Late in 1995, a new adaptation of *Pride and Prejudice* was screened; this was the fifth serialized television production of Jane Austen's classic, making it the most often adapted drama on television.

How to use this book

Entries are arranged chronologically; by decade, year, month and date of first episode. A sample entry is shown below.

Serial title	**THE FORSYTE SAGA**	
No. of episodes, genre, story setting, time period	7 January 1967, Saturday, 8:15–9:05pm, BBC2, 26 episodes, drama, classic, British, 19th–20th century	Date and time of first episode, broadcast channel
	BBCtv	Production company
	Video: available in UK	
	Pr: Donald Wilson	Producer
	Dir: David Giles, James Cellan Jones	Director(s)*
Writer	Wtr: Constance Cox, Laurie Craig, Anthony Steven, Vincent Tilsley, Donald Wilson	
Based on (if adaptation)	Based on *The Man of Property*, *In Chancery* and *To Let* by John Galsworthy	
	Cast: June – June Barry Marjorie Ferrar – Caroline Blakiston Val – Jonathan Burn **Fleur – Susan Hampshire** **Jon – Martin Jarvis** **Jo – Kenneth More** Helene – Lana Morris Jolyon Forsyte – Joseph O'Conor Annette – Dallia Penn Michael Mont – Nicholas Pennell **Soames – Eric Porter** **Irene – Nyree Dawn Porter** Winifred – Margaret Tyzack James – John Welsh Jolly – Michael York	Characters and players (main characters in **bold**)
Synopsis	Beginning in 1879 and concluding in 1926, the story of the wealthy, respectable Forsyte family spans three generations, the Victorian and Edwardian eras, and focuses most specifically on the individual lives of Jo and Soames Forsyte, the women they love, and their children, culminating in the ill-fated love of Jo's son Jon and Soames' daughter Fleur.	
Notes	A broadcasting phenomenon on both sides of the Atlantic, *The Forsyte Saga* aired on public television in the United States beginning 5 October 1969.	

*Or 'designed by' or 'settings by' in early entries, where directors are not listed.

1950–1959

LITTLE WOMEN

12 December 1950, Tuesday,
5:30–6:00pm, BBC, 6 episodes, drama,
classic, family, American, 19th century
BBCtv
Pr: Pamela Brown
Settings by Stephen Taylor and Lawrence Broadhouse
Wtr: Winifred Oughton, Brenda R. Thompson
Based on Louisa May Alcott
Cast: John Brooke – Alan Bromly
    Mrs. March – Barbara Everest
    Beth – Nora Gaussen
    Meg – Sheila Shand Gibbs
    Jo – Jane Hardie
    Laurie – David Jacobs
    Mr. March – Arthur Ridley
    Amy – Susan Stephen

In New England during the 1860s, the four daughters in the March family – Meg, Jo, Beth and Amy – come of age in the years surrounding the American Civil War. Jo takes charge of the family in the absence of her father, and the March girls, along with their beloved mother, experience both triumph and tragedy.

Based on the RADA stage adaptation of the classic novel, this was British television's first serialized drama, the initial "For the Children" presentation of the BBC.

THE RAILWAY CHILDREN

6 February 1951, Tuesday, 5:30–6:00pm, BBC, 8 episodes, drama, classic, family, British, 20th century
BBCtv
Pr: Dorothea Brooking
Settings by Lawrence Broadhouse
Wtr: Dorothea Brooking
Based on E.E. Nesbit
Cast: Mother – Jean Anderson
    Roberta – Marian Chapman
    Ruth – Ysanne Churchman
    Peter – Michael Croudson
    The Stationmaster – David Duncan
    Phyllis – Carole Lorimer
    Father – John Stuart

After their father is mysteriously called away, Roberta, Peter and Phyllis move with their mother from London to the country. They live near a remote railway station, and the children find a world of adventure and new friends in their new surroundings.

TREASURE ISLAND

1 May 1951, Tuesday, 5:30–6:00pm, BBC, 8 episodes, drama, classic, adventure, British, 18th century
BBCtv
Pr: Joy Harington
Settings by Richard Henry
Wtr: Joy Harington
Based on Robert Louis Stevenson
Cast: Captain Billy Bones – Ernest Barrow
    Tom Redruth – Howell Davies
    Dr. Livesay – Valentine Dyall
    Captain Smollett, Narrator – Brian Haines
    Black Dog – Peter Jones
    Long John Silver – Bernard Miles
    Jim Hawkins – John Quayle
    Squire Trelawney – Raymond Rollett

After Jim Hawkins finds a map leading to a buried treasure, the boy, accompanied by Squire Trelawney and Dr. Livesay, sets out on the Hispaniola for the island where the treasure is buried. But mutinous crewman Long John Silver wants the riches for himself, and endeavours to foil the search, leading to swashbuckling adventures for young Jim Hawkins and the rest.

This production was re-broadcast with a different cast on Saturday evenings starting 25 August 1951, an early form of television "rerun".

THE WARDEN

12 May 1951, Saturday, 8:00–8:30pm, BBC, 6 episodes, drama, British, 19th century
BBCtv
Pr: Campbell Logan
Settings by Roy Oxley
Wtr: Cedric Wallis
Based on Anthony Trollope
Cast: Eleanor Harding – Thea Holme
    Mrs. Grantly – Alice Landone
    John Bold – David Markham

Reverend Septimus Harding – J.H. Roberts
Narrator – Leonard Sachs
Dr. Theophilus Grantly – Lockwood West

Reverend Septimus Harding, honourable Warden of Hiram's Hospital, becomes a pawn in a power struggle between Dr. Theophilus Grantly, the Archdeacon of Barchester Rectory, and priggish physician John Bold, who challenges Harding's monetary allowance from the hospital – while at the same time courting Harding's daughter Eleanor.

This was the first program broadcast as a "classic serial," a banner heading used by the BBC for decades to come.

PUCK OF POOK'S HILL

25 September 1951, Tuesday, 5:30–6:00pm, BBC, 6 episodes, drama, British, 19th century
BBCtv
Pr: Matthew Forsyth
Settings by Lawrence Broadhouse
Wtr: Vere Shepstone
Based on story by Rudyard Kipling
Cast: Maximus – Basil Dignam
　　　　Weland – Archie Duncan
　　　　Una – Carole Lorimer
　　　　Dan – Barry Macgregor
　　　　Puck – Georgie Wood
　　　　Sir Richard – John Wyse

After acting in *A Midsummer Night's Dream*, young Dan and Una meet a real-life Puck, who takes them on a series of magical adventures across time to old English history, where they meet the long-ago inhabitants of Pook's Hill.

HUCKLEBERRY FINN

4 November 1951, Tuesday, 5:30–6:00pm, BBC, 7 episodes, drama, classic, family, American, 19th century
BBCtv
Pr: Vivian Milroy
Settings by Stephen Taylor
Wtr: W.S. Merwin
Based on *Adventures of Huckleberry Finn* by Mark Twain
Cast: **Huckleberry Finn – Colin Campbell**

　　　　Pap Finn – Kenneth Connor
　　　　Aunt Polly – Noel Dyson
　　　　Aunt Sally – Megs Jenkins
　　　　Widow Douglas – Janet Joye
　　　　Jim – Orlando Martins
　　　　Tom Sawyer – Jeremy Spenser

Set in the mid-19th century, the tale of young American Huck Finn begins with Huck's escape from his drunken, abusive father, then follows his adventurous raft trip down the Mississippi River, accompanied by runaway slave Jim.

The seven-week span of this serial lasted about as long as Huck and Jim's trip down the Mississippi!

SARA CREWE

6 November 1951, Tuesday, 5:15–5:45pm, BBC, 6 episodes, drama, classic, family, British, 19th century
BBCtv
Pr: Naomi Capon
Settings by Stephen Taylor
Wtr: Penelope Knox
Based on *A Little Princess* by Frances Hodgson Burnett
Cast: Captain Crewe – David Aylmer
　　　　Sara Crewe – Patricia Fryer
　　　　Miss Amelia – Mary Lincoln
　　　　Winnie – Joan Plowright
　　　　Mr. Carrisford – John Southworth
　　　　Miss Minchin – Helen Stirling

Young Sara Crewe is brought to London by her father and enrolled in Miss Minchin's posh school for young ladies. But when Captain Crewe dies and his fortune is gone, Sara is allowed to remain there only as a servant, all her earlier status stripped away by the cruel schoolmistress. The appearance of a mysterious benefactor improves Sara's circumstances, and she is at last able to resume her rightful, privileged place in the world.

This early television production was staged in deliberately theatrical terms, suggesting to the audience a plush Victorian theatre with the characters framed within the proscenium arch.

PRIDE AND PREJUDICE

2 February 1952, Saturday, 8:00–8:30pm,
BBC, 6 episodes, drama, classic, British,
19th century
BBCtv
Pr: Campbell Logan
Dir: Campbell Logan
Wtr: Cedric Wallis
Based on Jane Austen
Cast: **Jane Bennet – Ann Baskett**
Mr. Darcy – Peter Cushing
Lady Catherine de Bourgh – Helen Haye
Mr. Wickham – Richard Johnson
Mrs. Bennet – Gillian Lind
Mr. Bingley – David Markham
Mr. Bennet – Milton Rosmer
Lydia Bennet – Prunella Scales
Elizabeth Bennet – Daphne Slater
Mr. Collins – Lockwood West

The classic tale of marriage and mores in Regency England focuses on the five marriageable Bennet daughters, and most notably on the developing love between Elizabeth Bennet and the aristocratic Mr. Darcy, an attachment which is severely impeded by circumstances of class and personality.

Each episode was introduced by "Jane Austen," portrayed by Thea Holme.

THE BROKEN HORSESHOE

15 March 1952, Saturday, 8:00–8:30pm,
BBC, 6 episodes, thriller, British,
contemporary
BBCtv
Pr: Martyn C. Webster
Designed by Frederick Knapman
Wtr: Francis Durbridge
Cast: Inspector George Bellamy – John Byron
Della Freeman – Barbara Lott
Mark Fenton – John Robinson
Charles Constance – Michael Yannis

After Charles Constance is knocked down by a car, taken to a London hospital and operated on by surgeon Mark Fenton, the mysterious circumstances surrounding the accident are investigated, leading to many unexpected questions . . . and even more surprising answers.

Durbridge, already well known for his radio writing, was to become a major presence in television writing, and wrote in *Radio Times* in 1952 of the difference in writing for the relatively new medium of television: "Every radio writer develops his own tricks for catching the listener's interest and holding it. In television he . . . has to discard some of these while others have to be reshaped to utilize the extra possibilities offered by a visual medium. However . . . in writing a show for television the main object is precisely the same as in writing a radio show, a stage play, or a film – namely, to entertain."

THE SECRET GARDEN

29 April 1952, Tuesday, 5:00–5:30pm,
BBC, 8 episodes, drama, classic, family,
British, 20th century
BBCtv
Pr: Dorothea Brooking
Settings by Lawrence Broadhouse
Wtr: Alice de Gray
Based on Frances Hodgson Burnett
Cast: Colin – Dawson France
Archibald Craven – James Raglan
Mrs. Medlock – Nancy Roberts
Dickon – Brian Roper
Mary Lennox – Elizabeth Saunders
Ben Weatherstaff – Herbert Smith
Martha – Billie Whitelaw

In 1911, young Mary Lennox, orphaned after her parents' death in India, is sent to live with her reclusive uncle, Archibald Craven, and her invalided cousin Colin, at their Yorkshire estate. One day she stumbles upon a long-neglected garden, and, with the help of local lad Dickon, Mary brings the garden back to glorious life, which has a magical effect on the entire household.

THE THREE HOSTAGES

21 June 1952, Saturday, 8:30–9:00pm,
BBC, 6 episodes, thriller, British,
contemporary
BBCtv

Pr: Ian Atkins
Dir: Julian Amyes
Wtr: C.A. Lejeune
Based on John Buchan
Cast: **Sir Richard Hannay – Patrick Barr**
　　　The Thin Grey Man – Alan Gordon
　　　Inspector MacGillivray – John Laurie
　　　Lady Mary Hannay – Carla Lehmann

Recently-knighted Sir Richard Hannay is retired from the espionage game and happily married and settled down. But when Inspector MacGillivray visits with the story of three people who have been mysteriously kidnapped, Hannay finds himself drawn back into the world of international intrigue.

The Three Hostages was the fourth in a series of books about the adventures of Richard Hannay (the first was *The 39 Steps*). In adapting the story for television, writer Lejeune moved the action from its original post-World War I setting to shortly after World War II.

KIDNAPPED

7 July 1952, Monday, 8:45–9:15pm, BBC, 6 episodes, drama, classic, adventure, Scottish, 18th century
BBCtv
Pr: Joy Harington
Settings by Stephen Taylor
Wtr: Joy Harington
Based on Robert Louis Stevenson
Cast: 　Ransome – Robert Dickens
　　　David Balfour – John Fraser
　　　Ebenezer Balfour – Willoughby Gray
　　　Narrator – James McKechnie
　　　Alan Breck – Patrick Troughton

After being cheated of his birthright by his uncle and forced onto a slave ship, young David Balfour is befriended by daredevil Highlander Alan Breck. The two make it back to shore and are pursued by both law and outlaw before Balfour finally outwits his uncle and claims what is rightfully his.

HAPPY AND GLORIOUS

13 September 1952, Saturday, 8:30–9:30pm, BBC, 6 episodes, drama, biographical, historical, British, 19th century
BBCtv
Pr: Desmond Davis
Asst Pr: Tony Richardson
Designed by Stephen Bundy
Wtr: Desmond Davis
Based on play by Laurence Housman
Cast: **Prince Albert/Prince Edward – Michael Aldridge**
　　　Queen Victoria – Renee Asherson
　　　Archbishop of Canterbury – Graveley Edwards
　　　Benjamin Disraeli – Ernest Milton
　　　Mr. Gladstone – Edmund Willard

The biography of Queen Victoria, from her youthful ascension to the throne in 1837 to the years following her Diamond Jubilee in 1897.

Housman's play is also known as *Victoria Regina*.

ANNE OF GREEN GABLES

16 September 1952, Tuesday, 5:00–5:30pm, BBC, 6 episodes, drama, classic, family, Canadian, 19th century
BBCtv
Pr: Pamela Brown
Settings by Lawrence Broadhouse
Wtr: Pamela Brown
Based on L.M. Montgomery
Cast: 　Mr. Lynde – Robert Irvine
　　　Anne Shirley – Carole Lorimer
　　　Anne Shirley (as an adult) – Shirley Lorimer
　　　Marilla Cuthbert – Joan Miller
　　　Matthew Cuthbert – Charles Richardson
　　　Diana Barry – Phyllis Shumway
　　　Gilbert Blythe – Jeremy Spenser
　　　Gilbert Blythe (as an adult) – David Spenser
　　　Mrs. Rachel Lynde – Joan Young

During the late part of the 19th century, orphaned Anne Shirley is adopted by bachelor farmer Matthew Cuthbert and his sister Marilla and brought to live in their scenic farmhouse, known as Green Gables in the village of Avonlea on Prince Edward Island, Canada. Anne grows from a girl to a young woman, and ultimately decides to stay on in Avonlea as a teacher.

The role of Anne was played by two

sisters, showing the character at different ages in her life; similarly, two brothers played Anne's friend Gilbert.

OPERATION DIPLOMAT

25 October 1952, Saturday, 8:30–9:00pm, BBC, 6 episodes, thriller, British, contemporary
BBCtv
Pr: Martyn C. Webster
Settings by Frederick Knapman
Wtr: Francis Durbridge
Cast: Detective Inspector Austin – Raymond Huntley
Detective Sergeant Lewis – Alun Okun
Sir Oliver Peters – Arthur Ridley
Mark Fenton – Hector Ross
Colonel Wyman – Ivan Samson

Surgeon Mark Fenton reads that Sir Oliver Peters, a prominent diplomat, has mysteriously disappeared – and has supposedly been spotted behind the Iron Curtain. Fenton had operated on Peters several years earlier, and so is drawn into the investigation surrounding Peters' disappearance.

Principal character Mark Fenton (portrayed by a different actor) was also featured in *The Broken Horseshoe*, but Durbridge specifically noted that this was not a sequel to the early drama. Durbridge also noted in *Radio Times* that "the story is not based on any actual incident and was not suggested or even inspired by the mysterious disappearance of Guy Burgess or Donald Maclean."

THE PICKWICK PAPERS

6 December 1952, Saturday, 8:15–8:45pm, BBC, 7 episodes, drama, classic, British, 19th century
BBCtv
Pr: Douglas Allen
Settings by Richard R. Greenough
Wtr: Robert Christie
Based on Charles Dickens
Cast: Mr. Snodgrass – Robert Beaumont
Tony Weller – Peter Bull
Sergeant Snubbin – Erik Chitty
Arabella – Petra Davies
Mr. Wardle – David Horne
Mr. Samuel Pickwick – George Howe
Sam Weller – Sam Kydd
Rachel Wardle – Betty Marsden
Mr. Winkle – Geoffrey Sumner

Benevolent Samuel Pickwick, chairman of the Pickwick Club, travels about with his servant Sam Weller and fellow club members, serving as their advisor on a series of mishaps and (mostly) benign adventures, which ultimately find Pickwick defending himself against an unjust charge of breach of contract.

THE SILVER SWAN

30 December 1952, Tuesday, 5:30–6:00pm, BBC, 6 episodes, drama, family, British, 17th–20th century
BBCtv
Pr: Rex Tucker
Settings by John Cooper
Wtr: C.E. Webber
Cast: Oliver Cromwell – Oliver Burt
Gerald Gresham – Randal Herley
Francis/Timothy/Robert Gresham – Robert Irvine
Elsa Gresham – Peggy Livesay
Lucy – Carole Maybank
Jenny Lind – Elsie Morison

When Lucy visits her aunt, the housekeeper at Gresham Hall, she picks up the Silver Swan, a violin she finds in the music room . . . and is then magically transported back in time through the past 400 years – tracing the history of the violin, the Gresham family, and England itself.

This was the first originally written "For the Children" serial; previous productions were adaptations of classic stories.

LITTLE RED MONKEY

24 January 1953, Saturday, 8:30–9:00pm, BBC, 6 episodes, mystery, British, contemporary
BBCtv
Pr: W. Lyon-Shaw
Settings by Richard Wilmot
Wtr: Eric Maschwitz

Cast: Williams – Basil Appleby
Jocelyn Cullum – Honor Blackman
Colin Currie – Donald Houston
Commander Hilliard – Philip Lennard
Superintendant Harington – Arthur Rigby

During the course of one day, from 9:00am until midnight, an investigation ensues when an attempted murder takes place – but the circumstances are so vague that the police cannot draw any clear conclusions. In fact, it is possible that there was no murder attempt at all, but the police must nevertheless continue their search, in case the alleged killer decides to strike again.

EPITAPH FOR A SPY

14 March 1953, Saturday, 8:30–9:00pm, BBC, 6 episodes, thriller, British, 20th century
BBCtv
Pr: Stephen Harrison
Dir: Patrick Harvey
Wtr: Giles Cooper
Based on Eric Ambler
Cast: Major Clandon-Hartley – Maurice Colbourne
Josef Vadassy – Peter Cushing
Frau Vogel – Lislott Goettinger
M. Beghin – Philip Leaver
Herr Vogel – Meinhart Maur
Warren Skelton – Warren Stanhope
Mary Skelton – Joan Winmill

While on holiday in France in 1937, teacher Josef Vadassy is arrested and charged with espionage by M. Beghin, an agent of French Naval Intelligence. In order to prove his innocence, Vadassy must reveal the real spy, who is among his fellow guests at the posh Hotel de la Reserve. Is it the shifty English Major? His Italian wife? The American brother-and-sister team? The Swiss tourist couple? Any and all fall under suspicion, and Vadassy must, despite his lack of experience with such matters, uncover the truth, in order to clear his own name.

ROBIN HOOD

17 March 1953, Tuesday, 5:00–5:30pm, BBC, 6 episodes, drama, classic, adventure, British, 12th century
BBCtv
Pr: Joy Harington
Settings by Richard Henry
Wtr: Max Kester
Cast: **Sheriff of Nottingham – David Kossoff**
Little John – Kenneth Macintosh
Friar Tuck – Wemsley Pitney
Maid Marian – Josee Richard
Robin Hood – Patrick Troughton

The story of the legendary medieval hero Robin of Locksley, who, aided by his faithful Merry Men, keeps the greedy, nasty Sheriff of Nottingham at bay, "stealing from the rich to give to the poor".

STRICTLY PERSONAL

25 April 1953, Saturday, 9:00–9:30pm, BBC, 6 episodes, thriller, British, contemporary
BBCtv
Pr: Bryan Sears
Dir: Alvin Rakoff
Wtr: Michael Pertwee
Cast: **Richard Williams – John Bentley**
Edward Jackson – Grey Blake
Diana Wilson – Anne Crawford
Wilfred Wainwright – Geoffrey Sumner

Unemployed ex-RAF officer Richard Williams is hired by gangsters to smuggle a suitcase to Dublin. Before the plane takes off Williams decides not to go through with the job; the plane then crashes and Williams is reported dead. When he returns the suitcase to the gangsters, Williams accidentally kills one of the crooks. Now both the police and the other gangsters are after him and, in order to save his life, Williams must discover the contents of the suitcase. He enlists the aid of newspaper reporter Diana Wilson, and together they travel to Dublin where they come face to face with those who are trying to kill Williams.

SEVEN LITTLE AUSTRALIANS

28 April 1953, Tuesday, 5:00–5:30pm, BBC, 5 episodes, drama, family, Australian, 19th century
BBCtv
Pr: Pamela Brown
Asst Pr: Shaun Sutton
Wtr: Pamela Brown
Based on *Seven Little Australians* and *The Family at Misrule* by Ethel S. Turner
Cast: Meg – Margaret Anderson
       Captain Woolcot – Gerald Case
       Esther Woolcot – Sheila Shand Gibbs
       Nell – Adele Long
       Judy – Pixie Murphy
       Pip – Barry Macgregor

The adventures of the Woolcot family, who live just outside Sydney in the 1890s.

STAND BY TO SHOOT

6 June 1953, Saturday, 9:00–9:30pm, BBC, 6 episodes, mystery, British, contemporary
BBCtv
Pr: Dennis Vance
Settings by Stephen Taylor
Wtr: Donald Wilson
Cast: **Jamieson White – Cyril Chamberlain**
       Ruth Andrews – Anne Cullen
       Clive Dunstan – Ian Fleming
       Stirling Carr – Kenneth MacLeod
       Inspector Acheson – Duncan McIntyre
       Yvonne Jouvert – Betty Paul

At a motion picture studio, shooting on the film *The Patriot* is interrupted by the murder of lead actor Stirling Carr. The mystery is compounded when everyone, it seems, had a motive to kill the unpleasant egoist, including co-star Yvonne Jouvert, has-been actor Clive Dunstan, director Jamieson White, and assistant Ruth Andrews, among others.

THE HEIR OF SKIPTON

9 June 1953, Tuesday, 5:00–5:30pm, BBC, 4 episodes, drama, British, 15th century
BBCtv
Pr: Naomi Capon
Settings by Michael Yates
Wtr: Phyllis Bentley
Cast: Edward, Duke of York – Robert Desmond
       Earl of Rutland – Alan Dobie
       Lady Clifford – Rachel Gurney
       John Lord Clifford/Henry Clifford – Richard Johnson
       Thomas, Steward of Skipton Castle – Peter Sallis
       Henry Clifford (as a boy) – Jimmy Verner

Skipton Castle in Yorkshire has been home to the Clifford family for 100 years. Henry, son of the ninth Earl of Clifford, born in 1454, is caught in the middle of the War of the Roses when Yorkists swear vengeance on the Clifford family after Henry's father kills a Yorkist prisoner. Henry manages to escape from the castle, but then must live in hiding for more than 20 years before he can attempt to return home.

Although the characters directly involved in the story are fictional, the basic elements of *The Heir of Skipton* are true.

THE STORY OF THE TREASURE SEEKERS

14 July 1953, Tuesday, 5:00–5:30pm, BBC, 6 episodes, drama, classic, family, British, 19th century
BBCtv
Pr: Dorothea Brooking
Settings by Richard Henry
Wtr: Dorothea Brooking
Based on E.E. Nesbit
Cast: Father – Oliver Burt
       Albert-next-door – Christopher Cresswell
       Alice Bastable – Caroline Denzil
       Horace Octavius – Sonny Doran
       Dicky Bastable – Ernest Downing
       Oswald Bastable – Wilfrid Downing
       Noel Bastable – Anthony Land
       Dora Bastable – Isla Richardson

In 1899, the Bastable children decide to search for treasure to improve their family's troubled financial circumstances, which leads to a series of adventures.

THE QUATERMASS EXPERIMENT

18 July 1953, Saturday, 8:15–8:45pm (subsequent episodes aired from 8:45–9:15pm), BBC, 6 episodes, science fiction, British, future
BBCtv
Pr: Rudolph Cartier
Settings by Richard R. Greenough, Stewart Marshall
Wtr: Nigel Kneale
Cast: Chief Inspector Lomax – Ian Colin
Judith Carroon – Isabel Dean
Blair – W. Thorp Devereux
Dr. Gordon Briscoe – John Glen
John Paterson – Hugh Kelly
Victor Carroon – Duncan Lamont
Professor Bernard Quatermass – Reginald Tate
Peter Marsh – Moray Watson

Under the earthbound leadership of Professor Quatermass, the British Experimental Rocket Group launches an observational rocket thousands of miles above the Earth. The rocket is meant to return after just a few hours, but it mysteriously veers off course and travels hundreds of thousands of miles into the unknown before control is regained and the rocket returns – with only one crew member left alive. This survivor is unable to remember what happened, but, while supervised by Quatermass and his crew – including chief assistant Carroon and engineers John Paterson and Peter Marsh – he transforms into a monstrous being who can reproduce infinitely . . . and who must be destroyed in order to prevent worldwide catastrophe.

The first of the now-legendary *Quatermass* serials, this is one of the earliest and most potent television memories of those old enough to remember where they were when it first aired.

A PLACE OF EXECUTION

26 September 1953, Saturday, 9:00–9:30pm, BBC, 6 episodes, thriller, British, contemporary
BBCtv
Pr: Alvin Rakoff
Settings by Stewart Marshall
Wtr: Alfred Shaughnessy
Cast: **Paul Farrell – Derek Bond**
Lady Harper – Barbara Couper
Dr. Main – William Devlin
General Sir John Harper – Wyndham Goldie
Caroline Harper – Ann Hanslip
Zorab – Michael Mellinger
Inspector Clifford – Bruce Seton

In a fictitious Near East British colony, the leader of a terrorist group is sentenced to hang. The Governor of the Colony, General Harper, rejects an appeal to save the terrorist's life, and the terrorist group retaliates by kidnapping Harper's daughter, Caroline, from her London home, vowing to kill her at the same time as the hanging. Caroline's fiancé, Paul Farrell, searches London for her as the minutes tick away to the hour of the dual executions.

HEIDI

6 October 1953, Tuesday, 5:00–5:30pm, BBC, 6 episodes, drama, classic, family, Swiss, 19th century
BBCtv
Pr: Joy Harington
Settings by Michael Yates
Wtr: Joy Harington
Based on Johanna Spyri
Cast: Aunt Dete – Vari Falconer
Heidi – Julia Lockwood
Grandfather – Roger Maxwell
Brigitta – Dorothy Primrose
Clara – Hilary Rennie
Peter – Lance Sevretan

After being cared for by her Aunt Dete, orphaned Heidi is sent to live with her grandfather, who lives alone on top of a mountain. Many worry that the reclusive old man will not welcome the young girl, but Heidi finds a new world of adventure and happiness with him, makes a good friend with local lad Peter, and is brokenhearted when Aunt Dete insists Heidi return to Frankfurt to be a companion for invalided Clara. Finally, Heidi is able to return to her beloved home in the Alps.

JOHNNY, YOU'RE WANTED!

7 November 1953, Saturday, 9:20–9:50pm, BBC, 6 episodes, thriller, British, contemporary
BBCtv
Pr: Douglas Moodie
Designed by Lawrence Broadhouse
Wtr: Maurice McLoughlin
Cast: **Ferrari – Theodore Bikel**
Sonia – Diana Graves
Beryl – Elspet Gray
Joan – Joan Newell
Johnny – John Slater
Inspector Markham – Martin Wyldeck

After Johnny offers a ride to Sonia, whom he just met, she is suddenly killed. Johnny escapes and visits a local music hall where Sonia had worked as assistant to illusionist Ferrari, who now has a new assistant, Beryl. Johnny offers Beryl a ride and has another near-bout with death. Johnny discovers that Ferrari is involved with a narcotics ring and then finds himself and his wife Joan in danger from the drug dealers.

THE TECKMAN BIOGRAPHY

26 December 1953, Saturday, 9:30–10:00pm, BBC, 6 episodes, thriller, British, contemporary
BBCtv
Pr: Alvin Rakoff
Settings by Richard Henry
Wtr: Francis Durbridge
Cast: Helen Teckman – Pamela Alan
Philip Chance – Patrick Barr
Maurice Miller – Peter Coke
Andrew Garvin – John Laurie
David Jefferies – James Raglan
Detective Inspector Hilton – Ivan Samson

Novelist Philip Chance is hired to write the biography of famous test pilot Martin Teckman, who was reported killed during a test flight of a new jet plane. What appears at first to be a straightforward assignment turns out to be anything but, involving Chance in a suspenseful search for the truth behind Teckman's fate.

CLEMENTINA

6 February 1954, Saturday, 8:00–8:35pm, BBC, 6 episodes, drama, British, 18th century
BBCtv
Pr: Joy Harington
Settings by Frederick Knapman
Wtr: C.A. Lejeune
Based on A.E.W. Mason
Cast: **James Stuart – Michael Ashwin**
Prince of Poland – Beckett Bould
Sir John Hay – Raymond Francis
Clementina – Elizabeth Henson
Charles Wogan – Patrick Troughton

In the early part of the 18th century the House of Hanover has succeeded to the British throne; James Stuart, living in exile in Italy, still retains hope of regaining the monarchy for his family. To fund his campaign he decides to marry wealthy Polish Princess Clementina Sobieski. But the Hanovers learn of the plan and Clementina is kidnapped on the way to her wedding and imprisoned by the Emperor of Austria, who is working with the Hanovers. Loyal Jacobite Charles Wogan devises a daring rescue plan.

THE CABIN IN THE CLEARING

16 February 1954, Tuesday, 5:00–5:30pm, BBC, 5 episodes, drama, American, 18th century
BBCtv
Pr: Rex Tucker
Settings by Richard Henry
Wtr: Susan Ashman, Felix Felton
Based on E.S. Ellis
Cast: **Brayton Ripley – Derek Aylward**
Chief Haw-hu-da – Carl Duering
Alice Sutherland – Ann Hanslip
Polly Sutherland – Peggy Mount
Mul-keep-mo – Ewen Solon
Silas Sutherland – Shaun Sutton

American pioneer Silas Sutherland settles with his family in a log cabin in the Ohio wilderness. The family is warned of an Indian uprising making its way towards their cabin, and they prepare to fight against the Shawnee Indians, hoping help will come from soldiers who are 50 miles away. But frontiersman Brayton Ripley and friendly Miami Indian Mul-keep-mo are the only ones close enough to help the Sutherlands . . . will their help be enough to keep the Shawnee at bay?

THE WIDE, WIDE WORLD

30 March 1954, Tuesday, 5:00–5:30pm, BBC, 6 episodes, drama, family, American, 19th century
BBCtv
Pr: Naomi Capon
Settings by Michael Yates
Wtr: Penelope Fitzgerald
Based on Susan Warner
Cast: Mrs. Montgomery – Fiona Clyne
Fortune Emerson – Helen Horton
Mr. Van Brunt – Paul Whitsun-Jones
Ellen Montgomery – Carol Wolveridge

In the mid-1800s, Ellen Montgomery travels from New York to New England to stay with her aunt, Fortune Emerson. Ellen's journey from the city is a lonely one, and it doesn't seem as though things will improve when she arrives at the Emerson farm. Her aunt is not expecting her and greets the girl coldly; Ellen is left wondering whether anyone in the whole, wide world wants her at all.

GRAVELHANGER

31 March 1954, Wednesday, 7:50–8:20pm, BBC, 6 episodes, drama, British, contemporary
BBCtv
Pr: Ayton Whitaker
Designed by Barry Learoyd
Wtr: Val Gielgud
Based on Val Gielgud
Cast: Agatha Pleeze – Jean Cadell
Tony Havilland – Peter Coke
Monica Hervey – Ursula Howells
Francis Grayle – Esme Percy
Charles Hartopp – Olaf Pooley
Captain Rudiger Maltzan – Christopher Rhodes

On his way to visit Charles Hartopp at his Suffolk home, Tony Havilland gets lost and instead ends up at the large Tudor mansion called Gravelhanger – where he is knocked unconscious. When he comes to, Tony discovers two dead bodies. Enlisting the aid of Hartopp (who is in fact a British secret agent), Tony investigates the mysterious owner of Gravelhanger and helps prevent a Fascist revolution in Britain.

THE WINDMILL FAMILY

11 May 1954, Tuesday, 5:00–5:30pm, BBC, 5 episodes, drama, family, British, contemporary
BBCtv
Pr: Pamela Brown
Settings by Richard Henry
Wtr: Pamela Brown
Cast: Mrs. Channing – Barbara Cochran
Kate Channing – Diana Day
Colin Channing – Glyn Dearman
Mr. Channing – Clement Lister
Puffin – Ronald Moody
Uncle Porteous – George Skillan

The Channing family, living in a windmill on the border of Essex and Suffolk, is threatened with having to sell their home by greedy Uncle Porteous. Kate and Colin, the Channing children, come upon a plan to make money by hiding their friend, the runaway heir to an Oriental state, Prince Suresh of Ranistan, nicknamed Puffin. But Puffin's government becomes suspicious of his whereabouts, as do enemies of the Ranistan throne, and Kate and Colin find themselves in the center of action and danger.

THE DANCING BEAR

12 May 1954, Wednesday, 8:55–9:25pm, BBC, 6 episodes, thriller, European, contemporary
BBCtv
Pr: Dennis Vance
Dir: David Macdonald
Wtr: Richard Wade, John Wiles
Cast: E. Robertson Caldwell – Willoughby Goddard
Sir Ronald Glasgow – Clive Morton
Mansfield Potter – Geoffrey Sumner
Helga Froehlich – Ingeborg Weeks
Captain Peter Trueman – Norman Wooland

The treachery of an underground organization provides the setting for intrigue surrounding a group of people in Austria.

THE GENTLE FALCON

15 June 1954, Tuesday, 5:00–5:30pm, BBC, 7 episodes, drama, historical, British, 14th–15th century
BBCtv
Pr: Dorothea Brooking
Designed by Eileen Diss
Wtr: Hilda Lewis
Based on Hilda Lewis
Cast: **Isabella – Glen Alyn**
   King Richard II – Dennis Edwards
   Giles Cobham – Patrick Horgan
   Isabella (as a child) – Victoria Nolan
   Sir Geoffrey Cobham – James Raglan
   Isabella's Nurse – Vi Stevens

Isabella of Valois, daughter of the King of France, is wed to Richard II when she is just seven years old, in order to make peace between France and England. Richard is 30 years older than his child bride; this is the story of ten years in their life together, from 1395–1406.

THE SIX PROUD WALKERS

14 July 1954, Wednesday, 8:25–8:55pm, BBC, 6 episodes, thriller, British, contemporary
BBCtv
Pr: Leonard Brett
Designed by John Clements and Brandon Acton-Bond
Wtr: Donald Wilson
Cast: **Polly Arden – Anne Crawford**
   Bertie Walker – Peter Croft
   Sally Walker – Lisa Daniely
   Joey Walker – Walter Fitzgerald
   Detective Inspector Roger Stanton – Andrew Osborn

The Walker gang, led by Joey Walker, steals a valuable diamond necklace, which accidentally ends up in the possession of aspiring actress Polly Arden, who has mistaken it for a paste necklace she is to wear on a television show. Joey follows Polly, determined to get the necklace back, but he repeatedly shows up just a moment too late to snare the gems. Complicating matters further is Polly's close friendship with Detective Inspector Roger Stanton, who is assigned to track down the Walker gang.

CRIME ON OUR HANDS

25 August 1954, Wednesday, 8:10–8:40pm, BBC, 6 episodes, thriller, British, contemporary
BBCtv
Pr: Bryan Sears
Designed by John Cooper
Wtr: Edward Boyd
Cast: Mrs. Curzon – Sonia Dresdel
   Charles Dingle – George Howe
   Kay Martin – Geraldine McEwan
   Inspector Johnston – William Mervyn
   Cecil Davenport – Dennis Price
   Ken Martin – Jack Watling

Radio personality Ken Martin, who specializes in solving crimes over the airwaves, stumbles across an actual crime when neighbour Mrs. Curzon is murdered. With the help of his wife Kay, Ken investigates the crime, aggravating their other neighbours, all of whom come under hasty suspicion, along with Inspector Johnston, the detective assigned to the case . . . and the actual murderer, who threatens the Martins' lives when they get too close for his comfort.

HEIDI GROWS UP

28 September 1954, Tuesday, 5:00–5:30pm, BBC, 6 episodes, drama, classic, family, Swiss, 19th century
BBCtv
Pr: Joy Harington
Designed by Donald Horne
Wtr: Joy Harington
Based on Charles Tritten
Cast: **Heidi – Julia Lockwood**
   Grandfather – Roger Maxwell
   Miss Smith – Susan Richmond
   Peter – William Simons
   Mademoiselle Larbey – Gladys Young

The further adventures of Johanna Spyri's young heroine, as she grows into adulthood in the Swiss Alps where she has lived so happily with her grandfather.

THE THREE MUSKETEERS

24 November 1954, Wednesday, 7:45–8:45pm, BBC, 6 episodes, drama, classic, adventure, French, 17th century
BBCtv
Pr: Rex Tucker
Designed by Richard Henry
Wtr: Susan Ashman, Felix Felton
Based on Alexandre Dumas
Cast: Milady de Winter – Adrienne Corri
Athos – Roger Delgado
Cardinal Richelieu – William Devlin
Louis XIII – Garard Green
Aramis – Paul Hansard
D'Artagnan – Laurence Payne
D'Artagnan the Elder – James Raglan
Porthos – Paul Whitsun-Jones

Determined to become a guardsman to Louis XIII, young D'Artagnan becomes involved with three of the most well-regarded swordsmen of the time – musketeers Athos, Porthos and Aramis – and joins them in their noble and adventurous escapades and exploits.

Given the universal appeal of Dumas' classic, this was also performed at 5:00pm for children's viewing; film sequences produced by the BBCtv Film Unit were added to studio material to expand the scope of the project.

MUSIC AND MACARONI

11 January 1955, Tuesday, 5:00–5:30pm, BBC, 6 episodes, drama, family, Italian, 19th century
BBCtv
Pr: Pamela Brown
Designed by Gordon Roland
Wtr: Eileen Blackburn
Based on story by Louisa May Alcott
Cast: Stella – Renate Brent
Tino – Gwyn James
Mario d'Algero – Harold Kasket
Luigi – John Mansi
Grandmother – Eileen Way

Young singer Tino leaves his small Italian village to seek fame and fortune in France, under the tutelage of corrupt impresario Mario, but disillusionment soon sets in, and Tino then seeks to make his way back home to his sister Stella.

PORTRAIT OF ALISON

16 February 1955, Wednesday, 7:45–8:15pm, BBC, 6 episodes, mystery, British, contemporary
BBCtv
Pr: Alan Bromly
Designed by Roy Oxley
Wtr: Francis Durbridge
Cast: **Tim Forester – Patrick Barr**
Major Colby – Anthony Nicholls
Alison Ford – Helen Shingler
Detective Inspector Layton – Lockwood West
David Forester – Brian Wilde

Artist Tim Forester learns that one of his brothers has been killed in an automobile accident in Italy. Forester sets out to learn all the facts behind his brother's death, including what happened to the other person in the car, an actress named Alison who was reportedly killed as well, but whose body has not been found . . . in fact, the only glimpse of her which can be found is in an intriguing portrait.

BENBOW AND THE ANGELS

22 February 1955, Tuesday, 5:00–5:30pm, BBC, 6 episodes, drama, family, British, contemporary
BBCtv
Pr: Dorothea Brooking
Designed by Frederick Knapman
Wtr: Dorothea Brooking, Donald Masters
Based on Margaret J. Baker
Cast: **Timandra – Patricia Garwood**
Benbow Taylor – Bunny May
Reverend Simon Angel – Joseph O'Conor
Philadelphia Smith – Sally Pearce
Andrew – William Simons
Lindsay Jane – Valerie Turner
Wren – Jane Whitehead

The four Angel children – Timandra, Lindsay Jane, Andrew and Wren – seek refuge with their uncle, the Reverend Simon Angel, after their parents are reported missing from a medical mission in Manchuria. After a summer of adventure and discovery shared with their new friends, Benbow Taylor and Philadelphia Smith, the children are reconciled to the loss of their parents and ready to start a new life with their uncle.

CHILDREN OF THE NEW FOREST

5 April 1955, Tuesday, 5:00–5:30pm, BBC, 6 episodes, drama, family, British, 17th century
BBCtv
Pr: Douglas Hurn
Designed by Stephen Bundy
Wtr: Tom Twigge
Based on Captain Frederick Marryat
Cast: **Edward Beverley – John Charlesworth**
Alice Beverley – Shirley Cooklin
Edith Beverley – Gillian Gale
Jacob Armitage – Harold Scott
Humphrey Beverley – Anthony Valentine

In 1647, the four Beverley children must flee for their lives when their father, a Cavalier Colonel, is killed during the struggle between King Charles I and Oliver Cromwell. The children are rescued by forester Jacob Armitage, who hides them in his cottage, which is hidden in the depths of the forest. There, the Beverleys begin a new life as Armitage's grandchildren. Many adventures ensue, but none are as exciting as what faces Edward Beverley when he is able to leave the forest and fight at the side of newly-crowned monarch Charles II, whom he follows into exile in France.

THE MULBERRY ACCELERATOR

16 April 1955, Saturday, 8:15–8:45pm, BBC, 6 episodes, thriller, British, contemporary
BBCtv
Pr: Rex Tucker
Designed by Richard Henry, Lawrence Broadhouse
Wtr: Donald Wilson
Cast: **Polly Arden – Anne Crawford**
Joey Walker – Andrew Cruickshank
Willie Walker – Dan Cunningham
Martha Barlow – Diane Hart
Roger Stanton – Andrew Osborn
Lady Barlow – Frances Rowe

Polly Arden and detective Roger Stanton met and fell in love when she was caught in the middle of a jewel theft. They are due to marry shortly, as are Willie Walker (one of the instigators of the original robbery) and Martha Barlow. But intrusive family members and other, more sinister elements get in the way and threaten everyone's plans for happily-ever-after endings.

This sequel to Wilson's earlier serial, *The Six Proud Walkers*, featured Anne Crawford and Andrew Osborn reprising their roles.

THE EXPLORER

17 May 1955, Tuesday, 5:00–5:30pm, BBC, 5 episodes, drama, biographical, British, 19th century
BBCtv
Pr: Naomi Capon
Designed by Stewart Marshall
Wtr: Estelle Holt
Cast: **Henry Morton Stanley – Michael Aldridge**
James Gordon Bennett – Robert Ayres
Dr. Livingstone – Andrew Cruickshank
Aunt Mary – Mary Jones
Stanley (as a child) – Roy Sone

The life of explorer Sir Henry Morton Stanley, beginning with his school days in Wales and Liverpool in the mid-1800s, and culminating with the discoveries of Stanley and Livingstone.

THE GORDON HONOUR

5 July 1955, Tuesday, 5:00–5:30pm, BBC, 7 episodes, drama, family, British, 6th–20th century
BBCtv
Pr: Shaun Sutton
Designed by Richard Henry, Stephen Taylor
Wtr: Shaun Sutton
Cast: Gezir Mohammed – Patrick Cargill
Sir James Fitzwilliam – Colin Douglas

Lord Freddie Gordon – Bruce Gordon
Ronald Fitzwilliam – Barry Letts
Poppy – Sheila Shand Gibbs
King Richard the Lion Heart – Robert Raikes
Colonel Mainwaring – Campbell Singer
Don Jose – Ewen Solon
King Charles the First – Derek Waring
Admiral the Duke of Tyburne – Paul Whitsun-Jones
King Arthur – Richard Wordsworth

The "Gordon Honour" is a magnificent candlestick with 14 branches, one for each 100 years of its life; it has been owned by the Gordons for those 14 centuries and witnesses, along with family members, much of England's history, from the Court of King Arthur to the Crusade of Richard the Lionheart, to the West Indies, to the Civil War and beyond, often playing a significant role in Gordon family adventure and survival – most notably against the rival Fitzwilliam family, which in each generation seeks to steal the candlestick.

Each recurring cast member played a number of different roles as the story moved through the centuries; noted here are the characters portrayed in the first episode.

THE PRINCE AND THE PAUPER

21 August 1955, Sunday, 5:00–6:00pm, BBC, 6 episodes, drama, classic, family, British, 16th century
BBCtv
Pr: Dorothea Brooking
Designed by Gordon Roland
Wtr: Rhoda Power
Based on Mark Twain
Cast: Mistress Canty – Vera Cook
John Canty – Colin Douglas
Miles Hendon – Alan Edwards
King Henry VIII – Leslie Kyle
Tom Canty – Dwyryd Wyn Jones
Prince Edward – Tegid Wyn Jones

Young beggar Tom Canty finds his way into the courtyard of Henry VIII's palace and meets Prince Edward, who looks just like him. The two boys playfully change clothes, but when the Prince, in beggar's clothes, is chased from the palace grounds, Tom is treated as though he is the Prince – and nothing either boy can say or do will convince those around them of the truth. When Henry VIII dies and the Prince is about to be crowned as King, Edward must somehow get back into the palace and prevent Tom from sitting on the throne.

THE BLAKES

2 October 1955, Sunday, 5:00–6:00pm, BBC, 4 episodes, drama, British, contemporary
BBCtv
Pr: Pamela Brown
Designed by Claude Whatham
Wtr: Muriel Levy
Based on Alison Wright
Cast: Bill Blake – Martyn Anderson
Micky Blake – Douglas Hankin
Jim Blake – Robert Raglan
Jean Blake – Anneke Willys
Ellen Blake – Betty Woolfe

When Jim Blake loses his factory job, he impulsively buys an old bus and turns it into a "home on wheels" for his family. The Blakes then set out on an adventurous journey from Herefordshire to Sussex.

This family drama, written under the pseudonym "Alison Wright" by Douglas and Daphne Holmes (who took this kind of a journey with their children) was first adapted by Muriel Levy as a serial for radio, and later revised for television.

QUATERMASS II

22 October 1955, Saturday, 8:00–8:30pm, BBC, 6 episodes, science fiction, British, future
BBCtv
Pr: Rudolph Cartier
Designed by Stephen Taylor
Wtr: Nigel Kneale
Cast: Vincent Broadhead – Rupert Davies
Paula – Monica Grey
Dr. Leo Pugh – Hugh Griffith
Captain John Dillon – John Stone

Professor Bernard Quatermass – John Robinson

Several years after his first Experiment, Professor Bernard Quatermass continues his work of exploring outer space, testing prototypes of a second space rocket. Although his equipment and assistants are all new, the discoveries Quatermass makes are as terrifying as the earlier ones, as alien objects land on earth, inhabiting human bodies and spreading a dangerous "frenzy."

ST. IVES

30 October 1955, Sunday, 5:00–6:00pm, BBC, 6 episodes, drama, classic, adventure, British/French, 19th century
BBCtv
Pr: Rex Tucker
Designed by John Cooper
Wtr: Rex Tucker
Based on Robert Louis Stevenson
Cast: Clausel – Gerald Lawson
　　　Ronald – Francis Matthews
　　　Flora Gilchrist – Noelle Middleton
　　　St. Ives – William Russell
　　　Mr. Romaine – Arthur Young

French aristocrat Anne de Keroual de Saint-Yves (better known as St. Ives) fights with Napoleon's army, but is captured by British forces and held prisoner in an Edinburgh castle. St. Ives makes the startling discovery that he is heir to a Buckinghamshire fortune, and escapes from prison, travelling across hundreds of miles of enemy territory in order to claim his inheritance.

SPACE SCHOOL

8 January 1956, Sunday, 5:30–6:00pm, BBC, 4 episodes, science fiction, family, British, future
BBCtv
Pr: Kevin Sheldon
Designed by Gordon Roland
Wtr: Gordon Ford
Cast: **Winnie Winter – Ann Cooke**
　　　Humphrey Soames – David Drummond
　　　Wilfred Winter – Meurig Jones
　　　Space Captain Michael O'Rorke – Matthew Lane
　　　Wallace Winter – Michael Maguire
　　　Tubby Thompson – Donald McCorkindale
　　　Space Commodore Sir Hugh Sterling – John Stuart
　　　Miss Osborne – Julie Webb

While their father is surveying possible landing sites on the moons of Mars, the three Winter children live with their mother in a house on the rim of "Earth Satellite One," which rotates in space. The children attend classes led by Miss Osborne, where they learn about the universe which surrounds them as their satellite turns slowly in space against the background of the Earth.

JANE EYRE

24 February 1956, Friday (final episode broadcast on Thursday because of Good Friday), 9:15–9:45pm, BBC, 6 episodes, drama, classic, British, 19th century
BBCtv
Pr: Campbell Logan
Designed by Stephen Bundy
Wtr: Constance Cox, Ian Dallas
Based on Charlotte Brontë
Cast: **Mr. Rochester – Stanley Baker**
　　　Mrs. Fairfax – Barbara Everest
　　　Blanche Ingram – Jane Hardie
　　　Grace Poole – Jane Henderson
　　　St. John Rivers – Eric Lander
　　　Jane Eyre – Daphne Slater
　　　Adele – Valerie Smith

Shy orphan Jane Eyre takes a job as governess at Thornfield, where she falls in love with her employer, the mysterious, intense Mr. Rochester. Their attachment is severed when it is revealed that Mr. Rochester is already married; Jane flees Thornfield, but eventually Rochester's situation is resolved and he and Jane are lovingly reunited.

Excerpts from a theatrical version of *Jane Eyre* were first televised on the BBC on 8 March 1937; this live production incorporated pre-recorded film inserts of exterior locations and the fire at Thornfield.

MY FRIEND CHARLES

10 March 1956, Saturday, 8:30–9:00pm, BBC, 6 episodes, mystery, British, contemporary
BBCtv
Pr: Alan Bromly
Designed by Roy Oxley
Wtr: Francis Durbridge
Cast: **Detective Inspector Dane – John Arnatt**
Geoffrey Windsor – Bryan Coleman
Charles Kaufmann – Marvin Kane
Dr. Howard Latimer – Stephen Murray
Laura James – Gillian Raine
Nurse Kay – Anne Ridler

Film producer Charles asks his friend, Dr. Howard Latimer, to meet a girl at the airport. Latimer does the favor, but quickly regrets it, as the girl is killed and he finds himself at the center of a murder investigation.

REX MILLIGAN

15 April 1956, Sunday, 5:00–6:00pm, BBC, 6 episodes, comedy, family, British, contemporary
BBCtv
Pr: Pharic Maclaren
Designed by Donald Horne
Wtr: Anthony Buckeridge
Cast: **Jigger Johnson – Anthony Bryant**
Mr. Milligan – Anthony Marlowe
Headmaster Hunter – Anthony Sharp
Rex Milligan – Paul Streather
J.O. Stagg – Anthony Valentine
Mrs. Milligan – Margaret Ward

Sheldrake Grammar School student Rex Milligan and his best friend, Jigger Johnson, seem always to be in the middle when there is any trouble brewing, whether in school or elsewhere in the market town of Whitbury where they live.

OPPORTUNITY MURDER

21 April 1956, Saturday, 8:20–8:50pm, BBC, 6 episodes, mystery, British, contemporary
BBCtv
Pr: Julian Amyes
Designed by Guy Sheppard
Wtr: Raymond Bowers
Cast: Miss Baxter – Adrienne Corri
Vera Lewis – Anne Crawford
Malcolm Lewis – Alexander Knox
Detective Inspector Truff – Duncan Lamont
Peter Hobley – Roderick Lovell

Malcolm and Vera Lewis, along with their neighbor, Peter Hobley, are caught in a web of mystery and murder after they meet the unscrupulous and attractive Miss Baxter. When Miss Baxter is murdered, Detective Inspector Truff is on the case, and the trio finds itself the focus of his investigation.

THE BLACK BRIGAND

10 June 1956, Sunday, 5:00–6:00pm, BBC, 8 episodes, drama, classic, Spanish, 18th century
BBCtv
Pr: Dorothea Brooking
Designed by Richard Wilmot
Wtr: J. Potter Brown
Based on *The Brigand* by Alexandre Dumas
Cast: Jaco – Gerald Blake
Don Rogano – Laidman Browne
Karl, the White King – William Devlin
Janella – Catherine Feller
Fernando – Anthony Newlands
Slago – John Woodnutt

The mysterious Brigand leads a group of rough-and-tough outlaws in Spain, battling against the corrupt King Karl, the crusade taking the Brigand and his followers from the open country to the mountains, to the Royal Court and back again.

Because of the many exterior sword-fighting scenes in the story, a number of sequences were filmed in advance and inserted into the live broadcast.

THE CRIMSON RAMBLERS

31 July 1956, Tuesday, 9:00–9:30pm, ITV, 7 episodes, thriller, British, contemporary
Associated-Rediffusion Network
Pr: Robert Evans

Dir: Robert Evans
Wtr: Gerald Verner
Cast: Howard Gilbert – Warwick Ashton
  Sharon Roy – Sally Bazely
  Detective Sergeant Soames – Gordon Bell
  Tony Wayne – John Horsley
  Zoe Manners – Betty McDowall
  Simon Beatal – Raymond Rollett
  Vera Lee – Margaret Tyzack
  Andy McKay – Eric Woodburn

The Crimson Ramblers concert party comes into possession of a mysterious packet, which enmeshes the group in a web of intrigue and terror. After the packet is stolen and a young woman is murdered, Tony Wayne and Sharon Roy lead the others in solving the mystery, but several other bodies fall before all questions are answered.

The Crimson Ramblers was the first ITV night-time serial, airing during ITV's first broadcast year. Novelist Gerald Verner had previously written radio serials for the BBC; this was his first television venture.

DEATH TO THE FIRST LADY

11 August 1956, Saturday, 9:00–9:30pm, ITV, 5 episodes, mystery, British, contemporary
ABC Television Network
Pr: John Knight
Designed by Bertram Tyrer
Wtr: Peter Key
Cast: **Kim Abel – Maureen Connell**
  Dave Craddock – Kenneth Hyde
  Tom Abel – John Loder
  John Bridger – John Ruddock
  Prime Minister Sturgess – Grahame Stuart
  Bill Anderson – Dermot Walsh

Tom Abel, President of the powerful Pacific Federation, travels to Britain to sign a strategic agreement. As part of a plot to undermine the agreement, his daughter Kim is kidnapped. Kim's boyfriend Bill Anderson is instrumental in the efforts to rescue Kim, who is being held somewhere in London, and the seconds are ticking away.

THE BLACK TULIP

21 August 1956, Tuesday, 5:00–6:00pm, BBC, 5 episodes, drama, classic, French, 17th century
BBCtv
Pr: Naomi Capon
Designed by Charles Lawrence
Wtr: Estelle Holt
Based on Alexandre Dumas
Cast: William, Prince of Orange – Henry Davies
  Rosa – Sheila Shand Gibbs
  Isaac Boxtel – Anthony Jacobs
  Cornelius van Baerle – Douglas Wilmer

In 1672, William, Prince of Orange, seeks to defeat France with military force. When two statesmen who wish to negotiate a settlement with France are killed, it is up to Cornelius van Baerle to attempt to convince William to make peace. But Cornelius is branded a traitor and imprisoned; while behind bars, Cornelius decides to grow the black tulip, the rarest and most lovely tulip in the world, but his attempt to find something of beauty while trapped in a squalid prison is nearly thwarted by jealous tulip grower Isaac Boxtel, who tries to claim the black tulip as his own.

THE STRANGE WORLD OF PLANET X

15 September 1956, Saturday, 7:30–8:00pm, ITV, 6 episodes, science fiction, British, future
ATV Network
Pr: Arthur Lane, Quentin Lawrence
Dir: Arthur Lane, Quentin Lawrence
Wtr: Rene Ray
Cast: Fenella Laird – Helen Cherry
  Pollie Boulter – Maudie Edwards
  Gavin Laird – David Garth
  Professor Kollheim – Paul Hardmuth
  David Graham – William Lucas

A group of scientists' discovery of a new formula, "Magnetic Field X," gives them the opportunity to smash the Fourth Dimension, time, and they are transported to the bizarre, abstract world of Planet X.

DAVID COPPERFIELD

28 September 1956, Friday, 8:45–9:15pm, BBC, 13 episodes, drama, classic, British, 19th century
BBCtv
Pr: Douglas Allen
Dir: Stuart Burge
Wtr: Vincent Tilsley
Based on Charles Dickens
Cast: **David Copperfield (as a child) – Leonard Cracknell**
Mr. Murdstone – William Devlin
Betsey Trotwood – Sonia Dresdel
Mr. Micawber – Hilton Edwards
Dora – Sheila Shand Gibbs
Richard Babley – Richard Goolden
David Copperfield – Robert Hardy
Mrs. Emma Micawber – Olga Lindo
Uriah Heep – Maxwell Shaw
Rosa Dartle – Gwen Watford
Agnes Wickfield – Mary Watson

After his mother's death and mistreatment by his cruel stepfather, David Copperfield is taken in by the kindly but impoverished Micawber family. Afterwards, David spends time with his aunt, Betsey Trotwood, who becomes his guardian. Unaware that he is loved by warmhearted Agnes Wickfield, David marries frivolous Dora Spenlow, but their union is shortlived. When David realizes that he truly loves Agnes, their attachment is threatened by Uriah Heep, who has a financial hold over Agnes and her father; David strives to foil Heep's nefarious schemes so that he and Agnes can find true happiness.

The longest classic adaptation to date, running 13 episodes; even within this lengthy space a number of Dickens' characters had to be eliminated.

THE OTHER MAN

20 October 1956, Saturday, 8:00–8:30pm, BBC, 6 episodes, mystery, British, contemporary
BBCtv
Pr: Alan Bromly
Designed by Roy Oxley
Wtr: Francis Durbridge
Cast: Harry Vincent – John Arnatt
David Henderson – Tony Britton
Detective Sergeant Broderick – Victor Brooks
Katherine Walters – Patricia Driscoll
Detective Inspector Ford – Duncan Lamont
Roger Ford – David Tilley

In the small town of Medlow, public school housemaster David Henderson is caught in the middle of a murder investigation headed by Detective Inspector Ford, whose son is one of Henderson's pupils.

KIDNAPPED

28 October 1956, Sunday, 5:00–6:10pm, BBC, 6 episodes, drama, classic, adventure, Scottish, 18th century
BBCtv
Pr: Joy Harington
Designed by Lawrence Broadhouse
Wtr: Joy Harington
Based on Robert Louis Stevenson
Cast: Ebenezer Balfour – John Laurie
David Balfour – Leo Maguire
Ransome – Ian Thompson
Alan Breck – Patrick Troughton

After David Balfour is tricked by his greedy uncle and kidnapped onto a slave ship, Highlander Alan Breck comes to his rescue. Together the two survive a shipwreck, make their way to shore and embark on a series of adventures before Balfour is able to confront his uncle and be restored to his rightful position.

An earlier production of Harington's adaptation aired in 1952; Patrick Troughton revised here his portrayal of Alan Breck.

DR. JEKYLL AND MR. HYDE

11 November 1956, Saturday, 8:30–9:00pm, ITV, 6 episodes, thriller, classic, British, 19th century
ABC Network
Pr: Philip Saville
Dir: Philip Saville
Wtr: James Parish
Based on Robert Louis Stevenson
Cast: Dr. Lanyon – Ian Fleming
Dr. Henry Jekyll – Dennis Price

Utterson – Philip Ray
Katherine – Paddy Webster

Respectable Dr. Henry Jekyll performs an experiment on himself which transforms him into the malevolent and murderous Mr. Hyde. Despite his use of an antidote, Jekyll loses control of his alter ego and increasingly descends into Hyde's world of evil.

THE CRIME OF THE CENTURY

1 December 1956, Saturday, 7:30–8:00pm, BBC, 6 episodes, thriller, British, contemporary
BBCtv
Pr: Andrew Osborn
Designed by John Cooper
Wtr: Michael Gilbert
Cast: Clare Pinnock – Gene Anderson
   Mr. Brakewell – Edward Chapman
   Abbie – Sidney James
   Charlton Bradbury – William Lucas
   M. Bernard – Patrick Westwood

Charlton Bradbury and Mr. Brakewell find themselves unwittingly at the center of an intrigue which leads them on a labrynthine trail across the streets of London.

THE TROLLENBERG TERROR

15 December 1956, Saturday, 8:00–8:30pm, ITV, 6 episodes, thriller, British/European, contemporary
ATV Network
Pr: Quentin Lawrence
Dir: Quentin Lawrence
Wtr: Peter Key
Cast: Mr. Petitjean – Michael Anthony
   Sarah Pilgrim – Sarah Lawson
   Ann Pilgrim – Rosemary Miller
   Albert – Roland O'Casey
   George Brett – Glyn Owen
   Philip Truscott – Laurence Payne
   Dr. Dewhurst – Stuart Saunders

High on the slopes of the Trollenberg Mountain in the Alps, George Brett is encamped for the night when he is mysteriously called out into the darkness. Meanwhile, in a small hotel nestled at the foot of the mountain, mind-reader Ann Pilgrim knows that Brett has disappeared. Philip Truscott goes out in search of him. When Brett finally returns to the hotel, it is apparent that a weird, deadly influence has affected his brain, and the dangerous power must be discovered and stopped before more victims fall.

VANITY FAIR

28 December 1956, Friday, 9:00–9:30pm, BBC, 6 episodes, drama, classic, British, 19th century
BBCtv
Pr: Campbell Logan
Designed by Stephen Bundy
Wtr: Constance Cox, Ian Dallas
Based on William Makepeace Thackeray
Cast: **Rawdon Crawley – Alan Badel**
   Major Dobbin – Derek Blomfield
   Amelia Sedley Osborne – Petra Davies
   Joseph Sedley – Jack May
   Sir Pitt Crawley – Lloyd Pearson
   George Osborne – David Peel
   Becky Sharp – Joyce Redman

Poor but clever Becky Sharp leaves Miss Pinkerton's academy to enter society, along with her best friend, Amelia Sedley. Their subsequent lives and loves propel the story forward, from English drawing rooms to balls in Brussels and the battlefield at Waterloo.

THE ADVENTURES OF PETER SIMPLE

13 January 1957, Sunday, 5:20–5:45pm, BBC, 6 episodes, drama, family, British, 19th century
BBCtv
Pr: Naomi Capon
Designed by John Cooper
Wtr: Naomi Capon
Based on Captain Frederick Marryat
Cast: **Peter Simple – Timothy Bateson**
   Peter's Father – Peter Bull
   Peter's Uncle – Michael Goodliffe
   Terence O'Brien – Thomas Heathcote
   Captain Savage, R.N. – John Phillips

Young Peter travels to Portsmouth and goes to sea on the frigate Diomede, under Captain Savage. Peter is inexperienced and taunted by his fellow shipmates, but fortunately taken under wing by O'Brien, an older midshipman, who teaches Peter all there is to know about being at sea.

THE MAN WHO WAS TWO

26 January 1957, Saturday, 8:00–8:30pm, ITV, 6 episodes, mystery, British, contemporary
ABC Network
Pr: John Nelson Burton
Designed by Rex Spencer
Wtr: Lester Powell
Cast: Ann – Jennifer Browne
   Brigadier Dickerson – Alan Cuthbertson
   John Fairburn – William Devlin
   The Man – Ronald Howard
   Lieutenant Naismith – Morris Perry
   Willi Bloch – Maxwell Shaw

The Man walks into the Western Zone of Berlin from the East, where he is met by an officer from Scotland Yard. Before anyone can ask The Man a question, he has one himself: "Who am I?" The Man returns to London, where he is met by people who claim to know him as David Metcalf, an antiques dealer. But others claim he is David Raglaw, a thief and murderer. The Man must delicately choose whom he can trust as he searches for the truth about his identity.

KENILWORTH

8 February 1957, Friday, 9:00–9:30pm, BBC, 6 episodes, drama, classic, British, 16th century
BBCtv
Pr: Chloe Gibson
Designed by Fanny Taylor
Wtr: Vincent Tilsley
Based on Sir Walter Scott
Cast: **Elizabeth I – Maxine Audley**
   Robert Dudley, Earl of Leicester – Robin Bailey
   Amy Robsart – Ann Firbank
   Richard Varney – Anthony Newlands

To remain in the good graces of Queen Elizabeth, Robert Dudley, the Earl of Leicester, must keep his marriage to Amy Robsart a secret. When the monarch learns of the marriage she is furious, and the ambitious Leicester finds himself in the middle of a court intrigue which leads to the tragic death of his beloved wife.

THE RAILWAY CHILDREN

3 March 1957, Sunday, 5:20–5:50pm, BBC, 8 episodes, drama, classic, family, British, 20th century
BBCtv
Pr: Dorothea Brooking
Designed by Eileen Diss
Wtr: Dorothea Brooking
Based on E.E. Nesbit
Cast: Mother – Jean Anderson
   Peter – Cavan Kendall
   Phyllis – Sandra Michaels
   Mr. Gill, the Stationmaster – Donald Morley
   Father – John Richmond
   Perks, the porter – Richard Warner
   Bobbie – Anneke Willys

In 1906, Bobbie, Peter and Phyllis move to Yorkshire with their mother, following the unexpected and unexplained departure of their father. They live near a railway station and become involved with the people who work there and those who travel through, ultimately learning the truth behind their father's absence and helping to bring him back home.

THE GENTLE KILLERS

9 March 1957, Saturday, 9:45–10:15pm, ITV, 6 episodes, thriller, British, contemporary
ATV Network
Pr: Quentin Lawrence
Dir: Quentin Lawrence
Wtr: Lewis Greifer, Leigh Vance
Cast: Inspector Fellowes – Tony Church
   Stella Manning – Hazel Court
   Sergeant Maybrick – Frank Hawkins
   Dr. Julian Goldsworthy – Sydney Tafler
   Paul Donaldson – Dermot Walsh

Engineer Paul Donaldson finds himself caught in the middle of international espionage and murder when he witnesses a kidnapping. The hunted becomes the hunter when Donaldson joins forces with

Stella Manning to track down "The Gentle Killers," a gang of skilled assassins who are awaiting instructions on who is to be their next victim.

DESTINATION DOWNING STREET

25 March 1957, Monday, 8:00–8:30pm, ITV, 5 episodes, thriller, British, contemporary
Associated-Rediffusion Network
Designed by Michael Yates
Dir: Robert Tronson
Wtr: St. John Curzon
Cast: Romaine – John Bailey
    Colin – Graham Crowden
    Phoebe – Diana Lambert
    Sylva – Sylva Langova
    Tony Machiavelli – Richard Molinas
    Jacques – Donald Morley
    Mike Anson – John Stone

Mike Anson and his team does battle with ARKAB, a menacing organization which strikes suddenly and dangerously at the heart of the free world. Reporting directly and only to Downing Street, Anson and the others travel to Paris, enlisting the aid of Tony Machiavelli to break into a safe to gain access to much needed information in their fight against the ARKAB crime lords.

This serial, subtitled "The Machiavelli Touch," was the first in a series of six *Destination Downing Street* thrillers, all of which were written by St. John Curzon and featured the exploits of Mike Anson and his colleagues. The sequels were entitled "The Green Patch," "Mr. Crazy," "Two Faces East," "The Empty Man," and "Danger's End".

JOYOUS ERRAND

30 March 1957, Saturday, 7:30–8:00pm, BBC, 6 episodes, mystery, British, contemporary
BBCtv
Pr: Peter Lambert
Designed by Lawrence Broadhouse
Wtr: Ian Dallas
Based on Denis Wylie
Cast: **Richard Kendal – Peter Arne**
    Carrie Dean – Jacqueline Hill
    Ruth Blair – Ursula Howells
    Mr. Skaife – Ernest Thesiger
    Max Parrot – Michael Warre

Ruth Blair searches for answers about her husband's mysterious death, a quest which leads her across England. She is accompanied and aided by Richard Kendal, a man with secrets of his own. On their journey, Ruth and Richard learn the truth they are seeking, and ultimately are able to sort out their futures as well as their pasts.

ELECTRODE 93

20 April 1957, Saturday, 9:45–10:15pm, ITV, 7 episodes, science fiction, British, contemporary
ABC Network
Pr: John Knight
Designed by Rex Spencer
Wtr: Douglas Riley
Cast: Dr. Bill Herrick – Richard Bebb
    Carol Quorum – Greta Gynt
    Hugo Canning – David Langton
    David Williams – David Markham
    Dr. Quorum – George Pravda

Distinguished scientist Dr. Quorum conducts a secret experiment which results in the discovery of mysterious Electrode 93, which has magical curative powers . . . but can be used to do great harm as well. Hugo Canning steals the secret formula from Dr. Quorum, kills those who get in his way, uses Electrode 93 to gain access to government secrets – and must be stopped before he goes too far.

SARA CREWE

30 April 1957, Tuesday, 5:00–5:25pm, BBC, 6 episodes, drama, classic, family, British, 19th century
BBCtv
Pr: Naomi Capon
Designed by Gordon Roland
Wtr: Penelope Knox
Based on *A Little Princess* by Frances Hodgson Burnett
Cast: Captain Crewe – David Aylmer
    Miss Minchin – Peggy Livesay

Miss Amelia – Rosamund Greenwood
Indian Gentleman – Barry Letts
Sara Crewe – Carol Wolveridge
Ram Dass – John Woodnutt

Sara Crewe is sent from India to Miss Minchin's girls' school in England; when her father dies and leaves her penniless, Sara must work as a servant for the cruel schoolmistress. Sara bears her suffering with grace, pretending to herself that she is actually a princess . . . and her dreams come true when a mysterious benefactor comes to her rescue.

THE MACHINE BREAKERS

19 May 1957, Sunday, 5:35–6:05pm, BBC, 3 episodes, drama, British, 20th century
BBCtv
Pr: Barbara Hammond
Designed by Edwin Florence
Wtr: Phyllis Bentley
Cast: Tom Thorpe – Peter Hawkins
Will Oldroyd – David Higson
Joe Bamforth – Stuart Hutchinson
Dick Bamforth – Cavan Kendall
George Mellor – Simon Merrick

At the turn of the century, brothers Joe and Dick Bamforth become involved with a band of Luddites, an association which leads to violence and tragedy.

PRECIOUS BANE

29 May 1957, Wednesday, 8:30–9:00pm, BBC, 6 episodes, drama, British, 19th century
BBCtv
Pr: Campbell Logan
Designed by Stephen Bundy
Wtr: Constance Cox
Based on Mary Webb
Cast: Mr. Sarn – Beckett Bould
Mrs. Beguildy – Olga Lindo
Mrs. Sarn – Nora Nicholson
Mr. Beguildy – Henry Oscar
Prue Sarn – Daphne Slater
Gideon Sarn – Patrick Troughton

In 1812, Shropshire farmer Gideon Sarn is driven to self-destruction by greed, pride and ruthless ambition; tragically, his sister Prue, a gentle, good-hearted soul who is deformed by a harelip and shunned by superstitious villagers because of it, is also a victim of the family's gloomy destiny.

THE ASSASSIN

7 June 1957, Saturday, 8:00–8:30pm, ITV, 6 episodes, thriller, British, contemporary
ATV Network
Pr: Leonard Brett
Designed by Anthony Waller
Wtr: Jimmy Sangster
Cast: Dr. Peter Wingrove – Peter Cellier
Assassin – Carl Duering
Mrs. Lunt – Lucy Griffiths
Julie Clayton – Helen Lindsay
Superintendent Blackthorne – John Loder
Dr. Michael Clayton – Glyn Owen
Mr. Lunt – Llewellyn Rees
Kadar – Barry Shawzin

An Assassin is sent to England to kill a statesman who is on a state visit. The assassin's assistant dies accidentally, and it is the discovery of his death that sets Dr. Michael Clayton and Superintendent Blackthorne on the Assassin's trail, in an attempt to keep the murder from taking place.

The first of several dramas promoted in *TV Times* as "The Saturday Serial".

MOTIVE FOR MURDER

15 June 1957, Saturday, 9:00–9:30pm, ITV, 6 episodes, mystery, British, contemporary
ATV Network
Pr: Leonard Brett
Dir: Leonard Brett
Wtr: Jimmy Sangster
Cast: **Jean Blackmoor – Gene Anderson**
Dr. Meinster – Michael Ashwin
John Blackmoor – Vincent Ball
Detective Inspector Wrigley – Victor Brooks
Harry Manners – Geoffrey Chater
Miss Douglas – Barbara Lott

John and Jean Blackmoor return to London after two years abroad. In two days John is due to collect a large sum of money . . . a situation which implicates him in the investigation of his twin sister's murder. Since circumstantial evidence points to John as the police's prime suspect, John must try to clear his name.

WIDEAWAKE

15 June 1957, Saturday, 7:30–8:00pm, BBC, 6 episodes, mystery, British, contemporary
BBCtv
Pr: Gerard Glaister
Designed by John Cooper
Wtr: Michael Gilbert
Cast: **Shelley Stayman – Jill Adams**
Oliver Male – Terence Alexander
Hagen – Danny Green
Inspector Hodsell – Jack Lambert
Mr. Male, Snr. – Patrick Waddington
Frank Stayman – Charles Workman

Frank Stayman, the jewel thief known as "Wideawake" because he seemed to scarcely sleep at all during his 20 years in prison, is released – and many people, including his daughter Shelley and solicitor Oliver Male, for whom Stayman had once worked, are interested in tracing his newly-freed steps, since the seven priceless diamonds he had stolen just before being arrested were never found.

HUNTINGTOWER

16 June 1957, Sunday, 5:35–6:05, BBC, 6 episodes, mystery, Scottish, 20th century
BBCtv
Pr: Shaun Sutton
Designed by Eileen Diss
Wtr: Judith Kerr
Based on John Buchan
Cast: **Dickson McCunn – James Hayter**
Thomas Yownie – Roy Hines
Peter Patterson – Bernard Livesay
Dougal – Leo Maguire
Princess Saskia – Dudy Nimmo
Dobson – Paul Whitsun-Jones
John Heritage – Richard Wordsworth

A deserted house on a peninsula is the stage for a mystery which finds a number of Glasgow residents banding together to uncover the secrets they are certain are held in its high tower. The group, known as the Gorbals Diehards and led by retired grocer Dickson McCunn, finds that a princess is being held in the tower and, after a series of adventures, is finally able to rescue her.

VILLETTE

17 July 1957, Wednesday, 8:30–9:00pm, BBC, 6 episodes, drama, classic, British, 19th century
BBCtv
Pr: Barbara Burnham
Designed by Frederick Knapman
Wtr: Ada F. Kay
Based on Charlotte Brontë
Cast: **Lucy Snowe – Jill Bennett**
Mrs. Bretton – Lally Bowers
Dr. Graham Bretton – Michael David
Mademoiselle Zelie St. Pierre – Hazel Hughes
Rosine – Mairhi Russell
Madame Beck – Marda Vanne
Professor Paul Emmanuel – Michael Warre

Impoverished gentlewoman Lucy Snowe arrives in the Belgian village of Villette, where she is trained as a governess by Madame Beck, who runs a boarding school for girls. Lucy suffers from unrequited love for a young doctor, but ultimately realizes her true feelings lie with the school's headmaster, Professor Emmanuel.

A TALE OF TWO CITIES

28 July 1957, Sunday, 5:35–6:05pm, BBC, 8 episodes, drama, classic, British/French, 18th century
BBCtv
Pr: Kevin Sheldon
Designed by Gordon Roland
Wtr: John Keir Cross
Based on Charles Dickens
Cast: **Charles Darnay – Edward de Souza**
Dr. Manette – Fred Fairclough
Lucie Manette – Wendy Hutchinson
Madame Defarge – Margaretta Scott
Defarge – Kenneth Thorne
Sydney Carton – Peter Wyngarde

In Paris during the French Revolution, dissolute lawyer Sydney Carton finds redemption through his unrequited love for Lucie Manette and self-sacrifice, as he valiantly offers up his own life in exchange for that of the man whom Lucie loves, aristocrat Charles Darnay.

THE SCHIRMER INHERITANCE

3 August 1957, Saturday, 9:00–9:30pm, ITV, 6 episodes, thriller, British, contemporary
ABC Network
Pr: Stuart Latham
Dir: Philip Dale
Wtr: Kenneth Hyde
Based on Eric Ambler
Cast: Robert Moreton – Jefferson Clifford
Hacker – Colin Croft
John Sistrom – James Dyrenforth
Kolin – Vera Fusek
Kathy Moreton – Laurie Garner
Frau Gresser – Irene Handl
Captain Streftaris – Paul Stassino
George Carey – William Sylvester
Harry Budd – Roger Winton

Attorney George Carey sets out to find the rightful heir to the $4 million Schirmer inheritance. Assisted by attractive Kolin, Carey heads from New York to Bonn, where a number of false claims must be dealt with before Carey's search reaches its dramatic end in the bandit-infested mountains of Greece.

LITTLE LORD FAUNTLEROY

3 September 1957, Tuesday, 5:00–5:25pm, BBC, 5 episodes, drama, classic, family, British, 19th century
BBCtv
Pr: Dorothea Brooking
Designed by Lawrence Broadhouse
Wtr: Josephine Smith Wright
Based on Frances Hodgson Burnett
Cast: **Earl of Dorincourt – Laidman Browne**
Mr. Havisham – John N. Gordon
Mrs. Errol – Mary Holland
Mr. Hobbs – Gerald James
Dick – Michael Maguire
Cedric Errol – Richard O'Sullivan

American street urchin Cedric Errol goes from rags to riches when it is discovered that he is in fact of British aristocratic extraction; the boy travels to England, where he has inherited a stately home and title from his father's estate, but he does not live happily ever after until he is reunited with his mother, who had initially been rejected by the Little Lord's newfound relations.

FIVE NAMES FOR JOHNNY

14 September 1957, Saturday, 9:30–10:00pm, ITV, 7 episodes, thriller, British, contemporary
ATV Network
Pr: Quentin Lawrence
Dir: Quentin Lawrence
Wtr: Lewis Greifer
Cast: Detective Constable Bill Wright – Anthony Doonan
Peter Haigue – David Langford
Carol Haigue – Patricia Marmont
David Haigue – Conrad Phillips
Inspector Mason – Victor Platt
Dr. Mark Willoughby – Norman Wooland

David Haigue is accused of killing his brother Johnny, whom he had not seen nor spoken to for eight years. In trying to learn the truth of what happened to Johnny, Haigue must piece together the missing years in his brother's life, leading to a number of unsettling discoveries, including another corpse, and nearly forcing Haigue to commit the very crime he is trying to prove himself innocent of: murder.

TREASURE ISLAND

29 September 1957, Sunday, 5:35–6:05pm, BBC, 7 episodes, drama, classic, adventure, British, 18th century
BBCtv
Pr: Joy Harington
Designed by Susan Spence
Wtr: Joy Harington
Based on Robert Louis Stevenson
Cast: Captain Smollett – Derek Birch
Ben Gunn – Clive Dunn
Dr. Livesay – Valentine Dyall
Narrator – Peter Hawkins
Long John Silver – Bernard Miles
Jim Hawkins – Richard Palmer
Captain Billy Bones – Ronald Radd

Squire Trelawney – Raymond Rollett

Young Jim Hawkins sets out to sea on the Hispaniola, searching for the treasure outlined on a mysterious map. Jim is aided by some on his journey, but hindered by greedy ship crewman Long John Silver, a mutinous blackguard who seeks the bounty of Treasure Island for himself.

THUNDER IN THE WEST

5 October 1957, Saturday, 5:15–5:45pm, BBC, 6 episodes, drama, British, 17th century
BBCtv
Pr: Desmond O'Donovan
Designed by Lawrence Broadhouse
Wtr: Constance Cox
Cast: Sarah Drummond – Barbara Brown
Mr. Drummond – Joseph Conor
Jonathan Carey – John Forrest
Anthony Drummond – Barry Foster
King James II – Desmond Llewellyn
Mrs. Drummond – Hilary Mason
Joshua Benton – Alan Robinson
Duke of Monmouth – John Westbrook
Simon Woodall – Meadows White

The Drummond and Carey families are caught up in a feud at the time of the Battle of Sedgemoor – one supporting Monmouth, the other King James II.

THE ROYALTY

16 October 1957, Wednesday, 9:30–10:00pm, BBC, 4 episodes, drama, British, contemporary
BBCtv
Pr: Campbell Logan
Designed by Richard Wilmot
Wtr: Michael Voysey, Donald Wilson
Cast: Miss Plimm – Joan Hickson
Mollie Miller – Margaret Lockwood
Carol – Carol Marsh
Lord Charters – A.E. Matthews
Maisie – Lana Morris
Fred Potter – Richard Pearson
Richard Manning – Hugh Sinclair

The fictional Royalty Hotel in London is the setting for intrigue involving both the staff and guests, all overseen by the imperious hotel owner, Mollie Miller. Mollie is aided in her stewardship of the Royalty by the advice of her friend and lawyer, Richard Manning.

Margaret Lockwood revised her role as Mollie Miller in 1958 for a second series at the Royalty; this time Lockwood's own daughter, Julia, played the role of Mollie's daughter Carol.

NICHOLAS NICKLEBY

18 October 1957, Friday, 8:00–8:30pm, BBC, 10 episodes, drama, classic, British, 19th century
BBCtv
Pr: Douglas Allen
Dir: Eric Taylor
Wtr: Vincent Tilsley
Based on Charles Dickens
Cast: Alfred Mantalini – Carl Bernard
Madame Mantalini – Fabia Drake
Ralph Nickleby – Malcolm Keen
Wackford Squeers – Esmond Knight
Fanny Squeers – Rosalind Knight
Mrs. Nickleby – Gillian Lind
Smike – Brian Peck
Nicholas Nickleby – William Russell
Kate Nickleby – Jennifer Wilson
Newman Noggs – Richard Wordsworth

Following the death of his father, Nicholas Nickleby is sent by his cruel uncle Ralph out into the world, in order to support his mother and sister. Unfortunately, Nicholas' first contact is with malevolent schoolmaster Wackford Squeers. Accompanied by Smike, the much-abused brunt of much of Squeers' cruelty, Nicholas flees, embarking on a series of adventures before a final, revelatory confrontation with his uncle wherein the fortunes and misfortunes of all involved are resolved.

McCREARY MOVES IN

2 November 1957, Saturday, 9:30–10:00pm, ITV, 7 episodes, thriller, British, contemporary
ABC Network
Pr: John Knight
Dir: John Knight, Guy Verney

Wtr: Michael East
Cast: Raeburn – David Davies
 Wilson – Harry Moore
 Captain Raka – George Pastell
 Brandon – Robert Raglan
 Van Gelder – André Van Gyseghem
 Mike McCreary – Alan White
 Lian Shin – Lian-Shin Yang

Adventurer Mike McCreary joins with Captain Raka to investigate the death of oil surveyor Wilson and find the missing pieces of the vital survey plan Wilson was working on. The search leads him to exotic locales and into dangerous situations with a number of people. Whom can he trust? Beautiful Lian Shin? His contact Raeburn? Captain Raka?

Mike McCreary first came to life on Australian radio, where his serialized adventures ran for nearly two years.

A TIME OF DAY

13 November 1957, Wednesday, 8:30–9:00pm, BBC, 6 episodes, mystery, British, contemporary
BBCtv
Pr: Alan Bromly
Designed by Roy Oxley
Wtr: Francis Durbridge
Cast: **Lucy Freeman – Dorothy Alison**
 Roy Pelford – Gerald Cross
 Detective Inspector Kenton –
  Raymond Huntley
 Clive Freeman – Stephen Murray
 Janet Freeman – Angela Ramsden
 Laurence Hudson – John Sharplin

Lucy and Clive Freeman are on the verge of divorcing, but their marital problems are quickly put aside when their daughter Janet is kidnapped and they must join forces with the police in order to ensure Janet's safe return.

THE SILVER SWORD

24 November 1957, Sunday, 5:40–6:10pm, BBC, 7 episodes, drama, family, European, 20th century
BBCtv
Pr: Shaun Sutton
Designed by Lawrence Broadhouse
Wtr: C.E. Webber

Based on Ian Serraillier
Cast: Mrs. Wolff – Brenda Dunrich
 Edek Balicki – Melvyn Hayes
 Jan – Frazer Hines
 Joseph Balicki – Barry Letts
 Ruth Balicki – Pat Pleasance
 Bronia Balicki – Ingrid Sylvester
 Magrit Balicki – Gwen Watford
 Mr. Wolff – George Woodbridge

The Balickis, a Polish family, are rendered homeless when the Nazis invade their country. Soon separated from their parents, the three Balicki children must depend on each other for survival, and journey together to Switzerland in search of their father.

WEB

13 December 1957, Saturday, 9:30–10:00pm, ITV, 6 episodes, mystery, British, contemporary
ATV Network
Pr: Quentin Lawrence
Dir: Quentin Lawrence
Wtr: Lewis Greifer
Cast: **Harry Warren – Lyndon Brook**
 Detective Sergeant Prebble –
  Richard Burrell
 Doctor Evans – Leslie Handford
 Rose Warren – Betty McDowall
 Inspector Mason – Victor Platt
 Lena Jennings – Mary Webster

Salesman and respectable family man Harry Warren is shocked when the police show up at his door with conclusive proof linking him to the murder of a woman he swears he has never met. Warren has no idea who would try to frame him in this manner, until he learns that he and his family are caught in the middle of a dangerous game of chess which uses real people as expendable pawns.

Victor Platt played the same character in an earlier Quentin Lawrence-Lewis Greifer serial, *Five Names for Johnny*.

ANGEL PAVEMENT

27 December 1957, Friday, 8:00–8:30pm, BBC, 4 episodes, drama, British, 20th century

BBCtv
Pr: John Jacobs
Designed by Frederick Knapman
Wtr: Constance Cox
Based on J.B. Priestley
Cast: **Mr. Smeeth – Maurice Denham**
　　　Lena Golspie – Catherine Feller
　　　Turgis – Alec McCowen
　　　Mrs. Smeeth – Maureen Pryor
　　　Mr. Golspie – Sydney Tafler
　　　Miss Matfield – Margaret Tyzack

A group of people works at a furniture company in the City of London in 1930, and their normally very quiet and predictable daily routine is interrupted by the sudden appearance in their midst of a bandit, one rather talkative Mr. Golspie.

THE BLACK ARROW

19 January 1958, Sunday, 5:35–6:05pm, BBC, 6 episodes, drama, classic, adventure, British, 15th century
BBCtv
Pr: Naomi Capon
Designed by Frederick Knapman
Wtr: John Blatchley
Based on Robert Louis Stevenson
Cast: **Richard Shelton – Patrick Blackwell**
　　　Ellis Duckworth – Patrick Crean
　　　Joanna Sedley – Anne Dickins
　　　Bennett Hatch – Alan Dobie
　　　Sir Daniel Brackley – Barry Letts
　　　Selden – Ralph Nossek
　　　Richard, Duke of Gloucester – Eric Thompson
　　　Will Lawless – Patrick Wymark

The Fellowship of the Black Arrow is a band of 15th-century Yorkshire outlaws, led by Ellis Duckworth, who seek vengeance against the villains who have wronged them and their families. Chief among the villains is Sir Daniel Brackley, whose innocent ward, Richard Shelton, is caught in the middle of the intrigue, and must decide on whose side he stands.

PRIDE AND PREJUDICE

24 January 1958, Friday, 9:00–9:30pm, BBC, 6 episodes, drama, classic, British, 19th century
BBCtv
Pr: Barbara Burnham
Designed by Stephen Bundy
Wtr: Cedric Wallis
Based on Jane Austen
Cast: **Mr. Darcy – Alan Badel**
　　　Mary Bennet – Pamela Binns
　　　Elizabeth Bennet – Jane Downs
　　　Jane Bennet – Susan Lyall Grant
　　　Lydia Bennet – Vivienne Martin
　　　Mr. Collins – Jack May
　　　Lady Catherine de Bourgh – Phyllis Neilson-Terry
　　　Mr. Bennet – Hugh Sinclair
　　　Mrs. Bennet – Marian Spencer
　　　Mr. Bingley – William Squire
　　　Caroline Bingley – Greta Watson

Jane Austen's classic tale of marriage and manners unfolds in Hertfordshire during the Regency period, telling of Mr. Bennet's five eligible daughters, who will never inherit his money, which is entailed to a male nephew – and most notably presenting the developing relationship between Bennet daughter Elizabeth and haughty Mr. Darcy, where each must overcome pride and prejudice before they can be happily united.

This was the second production of Cedric Wallis' adaptation of *Pride and Prejudice*, but this time there was no "introduction by Jane Austen" at the start of each episode.

THE MAN WHO SOLD DEATH

1 February 1958, Saturday, 8:00–8:30pm, ITV, 6 episodes, thriller, British, contemporary
ABC Network
Pr: Andrew Osborn
Dir: Andrew Osborn
Wtr: Ingram D'Abbes
Cast: Diana – Margaret Anderson
　　　Inspector Gray – Ballard Berkeley
　　　Adam Krane – Edward Chapman
　　　Chief Inspector Marshall – David Davies
　　　Sir Frank Egerton – John Longden
　　　Grubbe – Cyril Shaps
　　　Harman – Malcolm Watson

Adam Krane is a professional contract killer, so adept at his perverse talent that Scotland Yard has not been able to solve the murders for which he is responsible. After carrying out his latest "job," he awaits payment, but his client unexpectedly dies. When Krane attempts to collect from Diana, the dead man's heir, the police finally get a break in the case, and the net begins slowly to close around "The Man Who Sold Death."

The Man Who Sold Death was one of the first ITV shows to include out-of-studio location shoots, in the third and fourth episodes.

THE RIDDLE OF THE RED WOLF

1 February 1958, Saturday, 5:10–5:40pm, BBC, 6 episodes, mystery, family, Ancient Rome
BBCtv
Pr: Desmond O'Donovan
Designed by Marilyn Roberts
Wtr: C.E. Webber
Based on *Detectives In Togas* by Henry Winterfield
Cast: **Xanthos – Oliver Burt**
       Caius – Paul Cole
       Rufus – Kevin Kelly
       Antonius – Michael Maguire
       Mucius – Vernon Morris
       Lukos – John Salew

In Rome in the year AD 100, a group of Roman schoolboys seeks to clear one of their fellows, who has been charged with desecrating a sacred temple.

RUN TO EARTH

11 February 1958, Tuesday, 5:00–5:30pm, BBC, 5 episodes, drama, family, Scottish, contemporary
BBCtv
Pr: David Goddard
Designed by Lawrence Broadhouse
Based on Elizabeth Kyle
Cast: Captain Gaunt – Michael Balfour
       Mr. Fairbairn – James Cairncross
       Mrs. Almond – Barbara Cavan
       Mick Fairbairn – Frazer Hines
       Archie Almond – Andrew Irvine
       Mrs. Fairbairn – Katharine Page

Glasgow youths Mick and Archie are looking for adventure, but get more than they bargained for when they meet embittered American Merchant Navy Captain Gaunt, who has journeyed to Scotland seeking revenge against a former crewmate.

MORE THAN ROBBERY

12 February 1958, Wednesday, 9:00–9:30pm, BBC, 6 episodes, thriller, British, contemporary
BBCtv
Pr: Shaun Sutton
Designed by Richard Henry
Wtr: Raymond Bowers
Cast: **Norma Tredford – Helen Cherry**
       Miss Li – Patricia Cree
       Morley – Owen Holder
       Dr. Nesbitt – David Horne
       Durbin – Terence Morgan

A thriller serial involving British citizens travelling in Malaya.

THE DIARY OF SAMUEL PEPYS

7 March 1958, Friday, 9:00–9:30pm, BBC, 13 episodes, drama, biographical, British, 17th century
BBCtv
Pr: Chloe Gibson
Designed by Fanny Taylor
Wtr: A.R. Rawlinson
Based on Samuel Pepys
Cast: Deb Willett – Rosemarie Anderson
       Nell Gwynne – Sheila Brennan
       Lady Castlemaine – Diana Fairfax
       Elizabeth Pepys – Susan Maryott
       Samuel Pepys – Peter Sallis
       Lord Clarendon – Peter Stephens
       King Charles II – Douglas Wilmer
       Lord Sandwich – Manning Wilson

A chronicle of the life and times of diarist Samuel Pepys, covering the years 1660––1669, and including some of London's most turbulent times, such as the siege of the Plague, the Great Fire, and major upheaval in Pepys' personal life as well.

THE INVISIBLE ARMIES

9 March 1958, Sunday, 5:30–6:00pm, BBC,

4 episodes, drama, biographical, French, 19th century
BBCtv
Pr: Rex Tucker
Designed by Susan Spence
Wtr: Nesta Pain
Cast: **Marie Laurent Pasteur – Margaret Barton**
Professor Colin – Oliver Burt
Louis Pasteur – Hugh David
M. Dumas – Philip Hay

The story of French scientist Louis Pasteur, whose 19th-century research in the field of microbes was considered revolutionary, and which changed the practice of medical science.

CAPTAIN MOONLIGHT – MAN OF MYSTERY

22 March 1958, Saturday, 5:10–5:40pm, BBC, 6 episodes, thriller, British, contemporary
BBCtv
Pr: Kevin Sheldon
Designed by Gordon Foster
Wtr: Kevin Sheldon
Cast: Les – Terry Baker
Forrest – Anthony Bate
Jimmy Bell – Leonard Jeffrey
Ken – Donald Masters
Alice – Lorraine Peters
Captain Moonlight (Tony) – Jeremy White

On the radio, Captain Moonlight deals bravely with international spies and other villains, but in real life, the man who portrays him is shy and mild-mannered . . . until he finds himself involved in a number of dangerous escapades which require him to call upon his experience as Captain Moonlight!

THE MONEY MAN

5 April 1958, Saturday, 7:30–8:00pm, BBC, 6 episodes, thriller, British, contemporary
BBCtv
Pr: Alan Bromly
Designed by Stephen Taylor
Wtr: Iain MacCormick
Cast: **George Henry – James Bree**
Major Sanders – Gerald Case
Viola Church – Jacqueline Ellis
Carlo – Stewart Guidotti
Inspector Gluckli – Alec Mango

While on holiday in Switzerland, George Henry becomes caught up in intrigue involving the European currency racket.

LITTLE WOMEN

13 April 1958, Sunday, 5:35–6:05pm, BBC, 6 episodes, drama, classic, family, American, 19th century
BBCtv
Pr: Joy Harington
Designed by Eileen Diss
Wtr: Constance Cox
Based on Louisa May Alcott
Cast: John Brooke – Michael Aldridge
Mrs. March – Phyllis Calvert
Meg – Kate Cameron
Laurie – David Cole
Amy – Sylvia Davies
Beth – Diana Day
Mr. March – Tom Fleming
Jo – Andrée Melly

The four March sisters – Meg, Jo, Beth and Amy – share one another's joys and sorrows before and during the American Civil War, vivacious Jo working with Mrs. March to hold the family together in the absence of the girls' father.

THE TRUTH ABOUT MELANDRINOS

26 April 1958, Saturday, 8:00–8:30pm, ITV, 6 episodes, thriller, British, contemporary
ABC Network
Designed by Rex Spencer
Dir: James Ferman
Wtr: James Parish
Cast: **David Westbrook – George Baker**
Melandrinos – George Eugeniou
Stavros – Arnold Marle
Joanna Westbrook – Ellen McIntosh

News editor David Westbrook accidentally takes the wrong overcoat from a cloakroom and discovers a cryptic letter in the pocket. Westbrook's well-meaning attempt to return the coat to its rightful owner leads him to search through newspaper files, which suggest that the letter refers to a crime for which a young Greek, Melandrinos, is serving a prison sentence. Westbrook is further led into a number of dangerous situations before a climactic meeting in a remote Oxfordshire village reveals long-buried facts about Melandrinos' heritage.

THE DANGEROUS GAME

13 May 1958, Tuesday, 5:00–5:30pm, BBC, 4 episodes, drama, family, British, contemporary
BBCtv
Pr: David Goddard
Designed by Marilyn Roberts
Wtr: David Carr
Cast: Mrs. Hunter – Betty Cooper
George Clayton – Colin Douglas
Joe Hunter – Patrick Ellis
Major Seton – Tim Hudson
Max Brett – Bryan Kendrick
Philip Baker – Patrick Troughton
Pete Hunter – Anthony Wilson

Brothers Joe and Pete Hunter find themselves involved in espionage which at first seems exciting but quickly becomes dangerous.

THE ADVENTURES OF BEN GUNN

1 June 1958, Sunday, 5:35–6:05pm, BBC, 6 episodes, drama, adventure, British, 18th century
BBCtv
Pr: Desmond O'Donovan
Designed by Frederick Knapman
Wtr: R.F. Delderfield
Based on R.F. Delderfield
Cast: Gabriel Pew – Nigel Arkwright
Nick Allardyce – Richard Coleman
Captain Flynt – Rupert Davies
Israel Hands – Sean Lynch
Ben Gunn – John Moffatt
Jim Hawkins – John H. Watson
Ben Gunn (as an old man) –
   Meadows White
John Silver – Peter Wyngarde

A "prequel" to *Treasure Island*, telling the story of how Ben Gunn, Long John Silver, and the rest of the crew of the Hispaniola came to be pirates on the high seas.

THE FIRM OF GIRDLESTONE

24 June 1958, Tuesday, 5:00–5:30pm, BBC, 6 episodes, drama, British, 19th century
BBCtv
Pr: Naomi Capon
Designed by Susan Spence
Wtr: C.E. Webber
Based on Sir Arthur Conan Doyle
Cast: John Girdlestone – Andrew
   Cruickshank
Ezra Girdlestone – Alan Dobie
Gilray – Toke Townley
Kate Harston – Elaine Usher

Victorian merchant John Girdlestone runs his firm with his son, Ezra. John's dishonest financial doings threaten the business and the family is near ruin, so Ezra must find some means of raising enough money to save the family name.

QUEEN'S CHAMPION

20 July 1958, Sunday, 5:35–6:05pm, BBC, 8 episodes, drama, British, 16th century
BBCtv
Pr: Shaun Sutton
Designed by Eileen Diss
Wtr: Shaun Sutton
Cast: **Roger Penlynden – Michael Anderson**
Master Fidian – Patrick Cargill
Sir Henry Penlynden – William Devlin
Ralph – Colin Douglas
Toby – Frazer Hines
Sir Thomas Wycherley – Barry Letts
Queen Elizabeth I – Peggy
   Thorpe-Bates
Master Allan – John Woodnutt

During the reign of Elizabeth I, a British naval column, under the leadership of Roger Penlynden, must protect the country against the danger of a Spanish invasion.

CHAMPION ROAD

12 September 1958, Friday, 9:15–9:45pm,

BBC, 8 episodes, drama, British, 20th century
BBCtv
Pr: Hal Burton
Designed by Fanny Taylor
Wtr: Constance Cox
Based on Frank Tilsley
Cast: Mrs. Briggs – Violet Carson
Geraldine Forbes – Jennifer Hales
Jonathan Briggs (as a boy) – Roy Hines
Mr. Briggs – Jack Howarth
Steven Briggs – Bryan Hulme
Jonathan Briggs – William Lucas
Nellie Greenhaigh Briggs – Anna Turner

In Lancashire in 1906, Mrs. Briggs' 13-year-old son Jonathan sets out on the road which takes him over the years from humble beginnings to a rich and prosperous, but not always happy, future.

GOOD WIVES

14 September 1958, Sunday, 5:40–6:10pm, BBC, 5 episodes, drama, classic, American, 20th century
BBCtv
Pr: Dorothea Brooking
Designed by Lawrence Broadhouse
Wtr: Constance Cox
Based on Louisa May Alcott
Cast: **Mrs. March – Phyllis Calvert**
Meg – Kate Cameron
Laurie – David Cole
Amy – Jill Dixon
John Brooke – Harvey Hall
Mr. Laurence – Noel Howlett
Mr. March – Edward Jewesbury
Jo – Annabelle Lee
Professor Bhaer – George Pravda

A sequel to *Little Women*, which takes place three years after the end of that story and finds the March daughters grown and contemplating families of their own.

LEAVE IT TO TODHUNTER

29 September 1958, Monday, 8:30–9:00pm, BBC, 6 episodes, mystery, British, contemporary
BBCtv

Pr: Andrew Osborn
Designed by Barry Learoyd
Wtr: Patrick Campbell
Based on *Trial And Error* by Anthony Berkeley
Cast: **Detective Chief Inspector Moresby – Ballard Berkeley**
Marcia Loraine – Helen Cherry
Sir Ernest Prettiboy – Campbell Cotts
Felicity Farroway – Ann Firbank
Lawrence Todhunter – Mervyn Johns
Ambrose Chitterwick – Kynaston Reeves

Lawrence Todhunter is mortally ill; since he is going to die anyway, he decides to take the opportunity to murder someone the world will not miss. Detective Chief Inspector Moresby and meek, wealthy Ambrose Chitterwick work together to solve the ensuing mystery.

THE LOST KING

2 November 1958, Sunday, 5:40–6:10pm, BBC, 6 episodes, drama, adventure, French, 18th century
BBCtv
Pr: Naomi Capon
Designed by John Cooper
Wtr: Constance Cox
Based on Rafael Sabatini
Cast: Marie-Therese – Sheila Burrell
Baron Jean de Batz – Patrick Cargill
Charles Deslys – Alan Dobie
Fouche, Duke of Otranto – Michael Goodliffe
LaSalle – Barry Letts
Louis-Charles – Ronnie Raymond
Justine Perrin – Jeannette Sterke

Louis-Charles, son of Louis XVI and Marie Antoinette, was supposedly spared the guillotine and rescued by an underground royalist organization – and then whisked away to Switzerland for a life of secrecy and adventure.

THE MAD O'HARAS

4 November 1958, Tuesday, 5:00–5:30pm, BBC, 6 episodes, drama, Irish, contemporary
BBCtv

Pr: Richard West
Designed by Frederick Knapman
Wtr: Pamela Brown
Based on Patricia Lynch
Cast: Desmond Burke – Sean Barrett
　　　Terry O'Hara – John Hussey
　　　Judy O'Hara – Diana Lambert
　　　Eily O'Hara – Pauline Letts
　　　Phil O'Hara – James Neylin
　　　Grania O'Hara – Jacqueline Ryan
　　　Mrs. O'Hara – Gladys Young

Grania O'Hara, a young Irish girl who is a talented painter, is taken from her aunt's home and transported to remote Castle O'Hara. There she is to live with her dour, unruly relatives, who are dominated by matriarch grandmother Mrs. O'Hara, and all of whom are transformed by Grania's warm personality.

OUR MUTUAL FRIEND

7 November 1958, Friday, 9:00–9:30pm, BBC, 12 episodes, drama, classic, British, 19th century
BBCtv
Pr: Douglas Allen
Dir: Eric Taylor
Wtr: Freda Lingstrom
Based on Charles Dickens
Cast: John Rokesmith – Paul Daneman
　　　Miss Lavinia Wilfer – Jill Dixon
　　　George Sampson – Bruce Gordon
　　　Reginald Wilfer – George Howe
　　　'Rogue' Riderhood – Richard Leech
　　　Mrs. Wilfer – Daphne Newton
　　　Nicodemus Boffin – Richard Pearson
　　　Bradley Headstone – Alex Scott
　　　Mrs. Henrietta Boffin – Marda Vanne
　　　Miss Bella Wilfer – Zena Walker

The body of a man discovered in the Thames is presumed to be that of John Harmon, last heir to a vast fortune – which is then inherited by former servant Nicodemus Boffin. Good-natured Boffin gradually comes to assume the greed and arrogance great wealth can bring, as does his young ward Bella Wilfer. When John Rokesmith arrives on the scene as Boffin's secretary, the situation takes a decidedly strange and mysterious turn, as things and people are not what they at first appear to be.

SOLO FOR CANARY

10 November 1958, Monday, 8:30–9:00pm, BBC, 6 episodes, thriller, British, contemporary
BBCtv
Pr: George R. Foa
Designed by Guy Sheppard
Wtr: Ken Hughes
Cast: Chief Superintendent Drew – David Davies
　　　Ruth Maddern – Lana Morris
　　　Superintendent Maddern – Andrew Osborn
　　　Marie Vazzani – Barbara Shelley

Superintendent Maddern of the C.I.D. is known for "getting his man," which has earned him many enemies in London's underworld – and his present case is no different from all his others.

THE REBEL HEIRESS

15 November 1958, Saturday, 5:25–5:55pm, BBC, 6 episodes, drama, British, 19th century
BBCtv
Pr: David Goddard
Designed by Fanny Taylor
Wtr: David Goddard
Based on *Mistress Nancy Molesworth* by Joseph Hocking
Cast: Uncle Anthony – Nigel Arkwright
　　　Clement Killigrew – Terry Baker
　　　Nancy Molesworth – Mary Holland
　　　Old Peter Trevisa – Anthony Jacobs
　　　Young Peter Trevisa – Derek Smer
　　　Roger Trevanion – Patrick Troughton
　　　Otho Killigrew – John Woodnutt

Cornish gentleman Roger Trevanion inherits a heavily mortgaged estate on the death of his father. He is persuaded by Old Peter Trevisa, to whom the money is owed, to rescue beautiful heiress Nancy Molesworth, in exchange for which the debt will be cancelled. Trevanion charges around Cornwall, enduring false imprisonment, hold-ups and other attacks, ultimately winning the favour of the Crown, the return of his estate, and the hand of the fair Nancy.

QUATERMASS AND THE PIT

22 December 1958, Monday, 8:00–8:35pm, BBC, 6 episodes, science fiction, British, future
BBCtv
Video: compilation available in UK, US
Pr: Rudolph Cartier
Dir: Clifford Hatts
Wtr: Nigel Kneale
Cast: Colonel Breen – Anthony Bushell
Barbara Judd – Christine Finn
Corporal Gibson – Harold Goodwin
Dr. Matthew Roney – Cec Linder
Professor Quatermass – André Morell
Sergeant – Michael Ripper
Captain Potter – John Stratton

Professor Quatermass is called in when an ordinary-seeming excavation at Knightsbridge uncovers an alien spacecraft. What started as a simple construction site is soon overrun with scientists and government agents, but even they seem unable to make a conclusive determination as to the Pit's contents . . . which emit a powerful form of energy that appears to have the ability to enslave all of mankind.

On 2 January 1960 a two-part compilation of *Quatermass and The Pit* was broadcast, the original having been transferred to film.

THE CABIN IN THE CLEARING

4 January 1959, Sunday, 5:40–6:10pm, BBC, 5 episodes, drama, American, 18th century
BBCtv
Pr: Rex Tucker
Dir: Patrick Dowling
Wtr: Susan Ashman, Felix Felton
Based on E.S. Ellis
Cast: **Brayton Ripley – Derek Aylward**
Polly Sutherland – Brenda Dunrich
Alice Sutherland – Ann Hanslip
Silas Sutherland – Thomas Heathcote
Mul-keep-mo – Ewen Solon
Haw-hu-da – John Woodnutt

Settler Silas Sutherland builds a cabin for his family in the Ohio wilderness, but soon hears of an Indian uprising which could threaten their safety. Frontiersman Brayton Ripley and Miami Indian warrior Mul-keep-mo befriend the Sutherlands and endeavour to protect them in the event of a Shawnee Indian attack.

This was the second production of the Ashman/Felton adaptation; Derek Aylward, Ann Hanslip and Ewen Solon reprised their roles from that earlier telecast.

THE HONEY SIEGE

17 January 1959, Saturday, 5:10–5:40pm, BBC, 6 episodes, drama, family, French, contemporary
BBCtv
Pr: Kevin Sheldon
Designed by Marilyn Roberts
Wtr: Antonia Ridge, Adrian Thomas
Based on *Le Chevalier Pierrot* by Gil Buhet
Cast: Maria – Jill Booty
M. Grillon – Peter Cloughton
Tatave – Martin Cox
Cisco – Nicky Edmett
Pierrot – Sam Jephcott
Georget – Leonard Monaghan
Riquet – Anthony Richmond
Victor – Dudley Singleton

Six young boys in a French village are angry when they are accused of stealing honey from their schoolmaster. Determined to hold out for real justice, they lock themselves in an old castle on the outskirts of the village and refuse to come out until the charges are dropped.

THE LAST CHRONICLE OF BARSET

30 January 1959, Friday, 9:30–10:00pm, BBC, 6 episodes, drama, classic, British, 19th century
BBCtv
Pr: Stephen Harrison
Designed by Richard Wilmot
Wtr: Peter Black
Based on Anthony Trollope
Cast: **Reverend Josiah Crawley – Hugh Burden**
Mr. Harding – Maurice Colbourne
Mr. Toogood – James Hayter

Lady Lufton – Marie Lohr
Mrs. Proudie – Beryl Measor
Archdeacon Grantly – Clive Morton
Bishop Proudie – Redmond Phillips
Mrs. Crawley – Maureen Pryor
Mrs. Grantly – Frances Rowe

The final installment in Trollope's Barsetshire series concerns Reverend Josiah Crawley, who is unjustly accused of theft and finds himself in direct conflict with imperious Mrs. Proudie, who seeks to replace him in his own church.

JO'S BOYS

8 February 1959, Sunday, 5:40–6:10pm, BBC, 7 episodes, drama, classic, American, 19th century
BBCtv
Pr: Joy Harington
Designed by Susan Spence
Wtr: Constance Cox
Based on *Little Men* and *Jo's Boys* by Louisa May Alcott
Cast: Meg – Kate Cameron
Ned Barker – Michael Caridia
Laurie – David Cole
Tommy Bangs – Kenneth Collins
John Brooke – Harvey Hall
Nat Bake – Cavan Kendall
Jo – Annabelle Lee
Amy – Susan Maryott
Professor Bhaer – George Pravda
Jack Ford – Donald Wilson

Now-married Jo March and her husband, Professor Bhaer, open their Plumfield home as a school for boys and girls; in time the students grow into young men and women who face problems and good times not unlike those experienced years earlier by Jo and her sisters.

THE SCARF

9 February 1959, Monday, 8:00–8:30pm, BBC, 6 episodes, mystery, British, contemporary
BBCtv
Pr: Alan Bromly
Designed by Roy Oxley
Wtr: Francis Durbridge
Cast: John Hopedean – Leo Britt

Alistair Goodman – Bryan Coleman
Marian Hastings – Diana King
Clifton Morris – Stephen Murray
Detective Inspector Yates – Donald Pleasence
Edward Collins – Patrick Troughton
The Rev. Nigel Matthews – Lockwood West

When young Fay Collins is strangled, Detective Inspector Yates investigates the crime, journeying from the seemingly-idyllic country town of Littleshaw to the darker side of London. Among the prime suspects is Clifton Morris, who is being blackmailed by a mysterious figure who claims that Morris owns the scarf with which Fay was killed.

THE BUDDS OF PARAGON ROW

17 February 1959, Tuesday, 5:30–6:00pm, BBC, 4 episodes, drama, family, British, contemporary
BBCtv
Pr: Barbara Hammond
Designed by Frederick Knapman
Wtr: Rosemary Hill
Based on Marjorie A. Sindall
Cast: Snipe Coster – Pearson Dodd
Vicky Budd – Mary Hewing
Mrs. Budd – Mary Hignett
Mrs. Parkin – Patricia Kneale
Mr. Cody – Paul Lorraine
Malcolm Budd – Robin Ranson
Rudge Ellis – Anthony Singleton

Malcolm Budd, his sister Vicky and their mother live on Paragon Row in a close-knit community outside London, their lives and adventures always connected with those of their friends and neighbors.

GARRY HALLIDAY

28 February 1959, Saturday, 5:15–5:40pm, BBC, 6 episodes, drama, family, British, contemporary
BBCtv
Pr: Richard West
Designed by Stewart Marshall
Wtr: Justin Blake
Cast: Bill Dodds – Terence Alexander

The Voice – Elwyn Brook-Jones
Jean Wills – Ann Gudrun
Kurt – Maurice Kaufmann
Garry Halliday – Terence Longdon

Commercial pilot Garry Halliday spots unusual sights in the sky as he flies from England to Amsterdam and back. No one believes his claims, but "The Voice," a mysterious figure behind the goings-on, knows that Garry is up to something and seeks to ground him . . . permanently.

Halliday proved a very popular television figure and returned for several other serialized adventures; in 1962, with its eighth run, the show became an episodic series, with a new story each week.

LOVE AND MR. LEWISHAM

3 April 1959, Friday, 9:30–10:00pm, BBC, 6 episodes, drama, British, 20th century
BBCtv
Pr: Douglas Allen
Designed by Stephen Bundy
Wtr: Denis Constanduros
Based on H.G. Wells
Cast: Miss Heydinger – Annette Carell
Mr. Bonover – Hilton Edwards
Mr. Lagune – Leslie French
Ethel Henderson – Sheila Shand Gibbs
Mr. Lewisham – Alec McCowen

Schoolmaster Lewisham is focused solely on his professional ambitions – until he meets Ethel Henderson, the cousin of one of his pupils. He attempts to balance romance with his career, which is no mean feat, as his time courting Ethel cuts into the hours he can devote to work and his dates with Ethel strain his already too-tight budget.

GREAT EXPECTATIONS

5 April 1959, Sunday, 5:40–6:10pm, BBC, 13 episodes, drama, classic, British, 19th century
BBCtv
Pr: Dorothea Brooking
Designed by Richard Henry
Wtr: P.D. Cummings
Based on Charles Dickens
Cast: Joe Gargery – Michael Gwynn

Miss Havisham – Marjory Hawtrey
Mr. Wemmick – Ronald Ibbs
Herbert Pocket – Colin Jeavons
Pip – Dinsdale Landen
Estella – Helen Lindsay
Estella (as a child) – Sandra Michaels
Pip (as a boy) – Colin Spaull
Mr. Jaggers – Kenneth Thornett
Mrs. Gargery – Margot van der Burgh
Magwitch – Jerold Wells

Orphan Pip meets escaped convict Magwitch, for whom he performs a kindness which will have unexpected ramifications on Pip's life in the future. When his fortunes begin to improve, Pip assumes it is due to his acquaintance with Miss Havisham and Estella, with whom Pip falls in love. But Magwitch is revealed as the one responsible for Pip's prosperity, and other truths, some of them pleasant, others quite painful, come to the surface before Pip's destiny is fully determined and resolved.

THE INFAMOUS JOHN FRIEND

6 April 1959, Monday, 8:00–8:30pm, BBC, 8 episodes, drama, British, 19th century
BBCtv
Pr: Chloe Gibson
Designed by Fanny Taylor
Wtr: A.R. Rawlinson
Based on Mrs. R.S. Garnett
Cast: **William North – Barry Foster**
John Friend – William Lucas
François Sauvignac – David Peel
Susan North – Pat Pleasance
Lord Mountstephen – Raymond Rollett
Mrs. Friend – Margaret Tyzack

In 1805, when England is under threat of invasion by Napoleon, John Friend helps devise a plan to divert the English forces just as the French Emperor launches his plan to attack.

THE POCKET LANCER

7 April 1959, Tuesday, 5:30–6:00pm, BBC, 4 episodes, drama, family, British, 19th century
BBCtv
Pr: Shaun Sutton

Designed by John Cooper
Wtr: Shaun Sutton
Cast: Old Joey – Nigel Arkwright
Timothy Bretwyn – Nigel Lambert
Rosie Trimmer – Barbara Leslie
Captain Fanshawe-Bellingham – Barry Letts
Captain Bretwyn – John Paul
Countess of Clarencourt – Joan Sanderson
Sergeant Finch – Paul Whitsun-Jones

Timothy Bretwyn awaits the return of his father, a Captain in the 43rd Light Lancers, who has been away for three years, serving in the war against the Russians in the Crimea. At the same time, Timothy waits anxiously for the day when he can ride with the Lancers . . . a day which comes sooner than he thinks.

THE WANDERER

9 May 1959, Saturday, 5:25–5:55pm, BBC, 4 episodes, drama, European, 20th century
BBCtv
Pr: Rex Tucker
Designed by Frederick Knapman
Wtr: C.E. Webber
Cast: **Julia – Anne Castaldini**
Mrs. Vargas – Ellen Dane
Erica Vargas – Karen Glazer
Janos Zoltan – Endre Muller
Matyas Vargas – Gordon Pleasant

In 1941, Julia, a young Hungarian girl, searches for her father, from whom she has been separated by the advent of World War II. Her search continues for more than a decade, culminating in Budapest at the time of the Hungarian uprising in 1956.

HILDA LESSWAYS

15 May 1959, Friday, 9:30–10:00pm, BBC, 6 episodes, drama, British, 19th century
BBCtv
Pr: Peter Dews
Designed by Margaret Peacock
Wtr: Michael Voysey
Based on *Clayhanger* and *Hilda Lessways* by Arnold Bennett
Cast: Maggie Clayhanger – Eileen Atkins
Auntie Hamps – Violet Carson
Hilda Lessways – Judi Dench
Darius Clayhanger – Chris Gittins
Edwin Clayhanger – Brian Smith
George Cannon – William Squire
Mrs. Lessways – Beatrice Varley

When Hilda Lessways meets Edwin Clayhanger a triangle develops between the two of them and solicitor George Cannon. Also drawn into the romantic intrigue are Hilda's mother and the other members of the Clayhanger family, especially Edwin's dominating father. Hilda becomes engaged to Edwin, but breaks off the relationship when she finds she is expecting Cannon's child. But Cannon loses all of Hilda's money in unwise, speculative investments, is himself jailed, and Hilda's downfall is complete.

HEIDI

19 May 1959, Tuesday, 5:30–6:00pm, BBC, 6 episodes, drama, classic, family, Swiss, 19th century
BBCtv
Pr: Joy Harington
Designed by Susan Spence
Wtr: Joy Harington
Based on Johanna Spyri
Cast: **Grandfather – Mark Dignam**
Brigitta – Olive Gregg
Clara – Leslie Judd
Heidi – Sarah O'Connor
Aunt Dete – Anne Padwick
Peter – Colin Spaull

Swiss orphan Heidi is taken to live with her grandfather, a hermit who lives in a mountaintop cottage; Heidi quickly learns to love both her grandfather and living in the Alps, and when she is forced to leave, she remains unhappy until once again able to return to her beloved Alpine cottage.

A new production of the Harington adaptation that was first aired by the BBC in 1953.

THE WIDOW OF BATH

1 June 1959, Monday, 9:30–10:00pm, BBC, 6 episodes, mystery, British, contemporary
BBCtv

Pr: Gerard Glaister
Designed by Roy Oxley
Wtr: Margot Bennett
Based on Margot Bennett
Cast: Mrs. Leonard – Fay Compton
    Detective Inspector Leigh –
    Andrew Cruickshank
    Hugh Everton – John Justin
    Lucy Bath – Barbara Murray
    Charles Atkinson – Guy Rolfe
    Cady – Peter Sallis
    Jan Deverill – Jennifer Wright

A number of people come to a small seaside resort town, each for his or her own mysterious reason; when a murder occurs, it is up to Detective Inspector Leigh to solve the crime, in order to salvage the good name and reputation of the town.

THE EUSTACE DIAMONDS

26 June 1959, Friday, 9:30–10:00pm, BBC, 6 episodes, drama, classic, British, 19th century
BBCtv
Pr: Naomi Capon
Designed by John Cooper
Wtr: Marjorie Deans
Based on Anthony Trollope
Cast: Lady Glencora Palliser – Jessica Dunning
    Lord Fawn – Robert Eddison
    Frank Greystock – David McCallum
    Lucy Morris – Perlita Neilson
    Duke of Omnium – Kynaston Reeves
    Lady Linlithgow – Marda Vanne
    Lady Lizzie Eustace – Wendy Williams

London's Mayfair district in the 1860s is rife with titles and gossip; the arrival of beautiful young widow Lizzie Eustace, wearing an heirloom necklace worth thousands of pounds, is enough to ensure a barrage of intrigue and scandal . . . especially when the necklace mysteriously disappears.

THE GOLDEN SPUR

5 July 1959, Sunday, 5:40–6:10pm, BBC, 6 episodes, drama, adventure, British, 15th century

BBCtv
Pr: Kevin Sheldon
Designed by Susan Spence
Wtr: Constance Cox
Cast: Sir Edmund Fenton – John Brooking
    Edward IV – Michael Kilgarriff
    Duke of Clarence – Donald Oliver
    Richard of Gloucester – Oliver Reed
    Gillian – Jill Tracey
    Tom Fenton – Edward Vaughan-Scott

Set during the Wars of the Roses, young Tom Fenton helps King Edward IV and Richard of Gloucester in their quest to win back the Crown of England and defeat the villainous Duke of Clarence – during the course of which Tom also finds true love and regains his lost inheritance.

THE NAKED LADY

13 July 1959, Monday, 9:30–10:00pm, BBC, 4 episodes, thriller, British, contemporary
BBCtv
Pr: Campbell Logan
Designed by Guy Sheppard
Wtr: Duncan Ross
Cast: Kitty Cusack – Daphne Anderson
    Sylvia Craig – Lana Morris
    Detective Inspector Bill Burroughs – Andrew Osborn
    Jim Larkins – Richard Pearson
    Miss LeRoy – Janet Rowsell
    Bob Dyson – Patrick Troughton
    Dr. Gordon – Robert Urquhart

A quiet weekend at a small hotel in a fishing village on the South Coast is interrupted by the arrival of two army officers looking only for a few holes of uninterrupted golf, but whose discovery of a woman's body leads to a mystery involving everyone at the hotel – especially Sylvia Craig, the self-designated assistant to Detective Inspector Burroughs, who is investigating the crime.

DANCERS IN MOURNING

10 August 1959, Monday, 9:30–10:00pm,

BBC, 6 episodes, mystery, British, contemporary
BBCtv
Pr: John Harrison
Designed by Reece Pemberton
Wtr: John Hopkins
Based on Margery Allingham
Cast: Linda Sutane – Sheila Shand Gibbs
  Albert Campion – Bernard Horsfall
  William Faraday – Noel Howlett
  Lugg – Wally Patch
  Sock Petrie – David Phethean
  Jimmy Sutane – Denis Quilley

Detective Albert Campion is involved with backstage intrigue while investigating a murder committed at a London theatre which seems to have been the result of an escalating series of practical jokes. The likely suspects involve the cast and crew at the theatre, led by world-famous musical comedy star Jimmy Sutane.

THE MOONSTONE

23 August 1959, Sunday, 5:35–6:05pm, BBC, 7 episodes, mystery, classic, British, 19th century
BBCtv
Pr: Shaun Sutton
Designed by Eileen Diss
Wtr: A.R. Rawlinson
Based on Wilkie Collins
Cast: Godfrey Ablewhite – Derek Aylward
  Sergeant Cuff – Patrick Cargill
  Rosanna Spearman – Dorothy Gordon
  Lady Verinder – Rachel Gurney
  Gabriel Betteredge – James Hayter
  Ezra Jennings – Philip Latham
  Penelope Betteredge – Annabelle Lee
  Colonel Herncastle – Barry Letts
  Franklin Blake – James Sharkey
  Rachel Verinder – Mary Webster

Indian Brahmins try to regain possession of a huge diamond that has been feloniously removed from the forehead of an Indian god and has ended up in the possession of Rachel Verinder. But it disappears again, and no one's life is safe until the stone is returned to its rightful place.

Long considered the first English detective story, *The Moonstone* was based on a true story, the Road Hill Murder Case.

THE HISTORY OF MR. POLLY

28 August 1959, Friday, 8:00–8:30pm, BBC, 6 episodes, drama, British, 19th century
BBCtv
Pr: Douglas Allen
Designed by Stephen Bundy
Wtr: Constance Cox
Based on H.G. Wells
Cast: Annie – Daphne Anderson
  Harold Johnson – Richard Caldicott
  Alfred Polly – Emrys Jones
  Miriam – Mary Mackenzie
  Grace Johnson – Edna Morris
  Uncle Jim – Patrick Troughton
  Mr. Platt – Aubrey Woods

Tradesman Mr. Polly attempts to escape from his dreary life by setting his house on fire and committing suicide. He does not die, but is presumed dead, and so sets out across the countryside, enjoying his new freedom and settling down with a newfound love to run an inn.

THE MAN WHO FINALLY DIED

12 September 1959, Saturday, 7:30–8:00pm, ITV, 7 episodes, thriller, British, contemporary
ATV Network
Pr: Quentin Lawrence
Designed by Vic Symonds
Wtr: Lewis Greifer
Cast: Frank Robb – Peter Hughes
  Lisa Deutsch – Delphi Lawrence
  Marta Gellman – Ruth Lodge
  Joe Newman – Richard Pasco
  Madge Robb – Myrtle Reed

Joe Newman heads from England to Germany, where he had grown up, after learning that his father, whom Joe had thought was dead for 17 years, has only recently died. He turns to his young stepmother, Lisa, to help solve the mystery. But then Joe discovers that his father is not dead after all, and he must find the man he had believed lost to him all those years ago, discover his father's dangerous secret . . . and manage to stay alive in the process.

Featured as part of the "Suspense" series of thriller serials.

A MASK FOR ALEXIS

21 September 1959, Monday, 8:05–8:35pm, BBC, 6 episodes, thriller, British, contemporary
BBCtv
Pr: Eric Fawcett
Designed by Roy Oxley
Wtr: Lindsay Hardy
Cast: **Brenda Carpenter – Gene Anderson**
Alexis Brant – Kevin Brennan
Detective Sergeant Edwards – Edward Cast
Elaine Brant – Harriette Johns
Christopher March – David Knight
Henri Clouzot – Harold Robert
Detective Inspector Fenner – Ewen Solon

Christopher March is assigned to go to Paris on business for his boss, Alexis Brant. But before March gets on the plane he learns that his employer has been murdered, and March is quickly targeted as the prime suspect. On the run from the police, March enlists the aid of Brenda Carpenter in seeking out the real killer.

REDGAUNTLET

11 October 1959, Sunday, 5:00–5:30pm, BBC, 6 episodes, drama, British, 18th century
BBCtv
Pr: Kevin Sheldon
Designed by Fanny Taylor
Wtr: E.J. Bell
Based on Sir Walter Scott
Cast: **Alan Fairford – John Cairney**
Prince Charles Edward – Brown Derby
Arthur Darsie Redgauntlet – Donald Douglas
Sir Edward Redgauntlet – Tom Fleming
Lilias – Claire Isbister
Mr. Fairford – Leonard Maguire
Captain Nanty Ewart – Roddy McMillan

Fanatical Jacobite Sir Edward Redgauntlet kidnaps his nephew, Sir Arthur Darsie Redgauntlet, as part of his plan for helping Young Pretender Prince Charles Edward. Darsie's friend Alan Fairford endeavours to rescue Darsie, and the two are then caught up in a series of adventures which ultimately lead to Sir Edward's fleeing abroad and serve a crushing blow to the planned Jacobite revolt.

BLEAK HOUSE

16 October 1959, Friday, 8:00–8:30pm, BBC, 11 episodes, drama, classic, British, 19th century
BBCtv
Pr: Eric Taylor
Designed by Stephen Bundy
Wtr: Constance Cox
Based on Charles Dickens
Cast: William Guppy – Timothy Bateson
Mademoiselle Hortense – Annette Carell
John Jarndyce – Andrew Cruickshank
Esther Summerson – Diana Fairfax
Sir Leicester Dedlock – David Horne
Richard Carstone – Colin Jeavons
Mr. Inspector Bucket – Richard Pearson
Mr. Tulkinghorn – John Phillips
Lady Honoria Dedlock – Iris Russell
Ada Clare – Elizabeth Shepherd
Allan Woodcourt – Jerome Willis

Orphaned Esther Summerson is entrusted by her guardian, John Jarndyce, with the running of Bleak House, while he is ensnared in a seemingly-endess lawsuit. Also residing at Bleak House are Ada Clare and Richard Carstone, who enter into an ill-fated marriage, only one of the dire circumstances to come along Esther's way before her own fate is more pleasantly resolved, in happy marriage to surgeon Allan Woodcourt.

EPILOGUE TO CAPRICORN

31 October 1959, Saturday, 7:30–8:00pm, ITV, 6 episodes, thriller, British, contemporary
ATV Network
Pr: John Nelson Burton
Designed by Eric Shedden
Wtr: John Roddick
Cast: **Jill Howard – Adrienne Corri**
Lewis Osborne – Alan Cuthbertson
Robert Faulkner – Richard Johnson
Maxie Lehmann – Maxwell Shaw
Peter Vauxhall – Peter Wyngarde
Pamela Warren – Pauline Yates

Foreign correspondent Robert Faulkner is called in by the War Office to compile a dossier on a disastrously unsuccessful top-secret World War II mission – Operation Capricorn. It soon becomes clear that the operation was not a failure because of bad luck, but because of treachery, and it is up to Faulkner to uncover the truth.

Featured as part of the "Suspense" series of thriller serials.

ASK FOR KING BILLY

3 November 1959, Tuesday, 5:30–6:00pm, BBC, 5 episodes, thriller, British, contemporary
BBCtv
Pr: Tony Halfpenny
Designed by Susan Spence
Wtr: C.E. Webber
Based on Henry Treece
Cast: **Man in Black – Peter Bull**
Gordon Stewart – Donald Churchill
Sergeant Baines – Richard Sharp

Fledgling London private detective Gordon Stewart is about to give up his new career when he is hired on a case which brings him to the city of Hull, involves him with a gang of ruthless crooks, and finds Gordon himself the suspect in a murder investigation.

THREE GOLDEN NOBLES

11 November 1959, Saturday, 5:25–5:50pm, BBC, 7 episodes, drama, family, British, 14th century
BBCtv
Pr: David Goddard
Designed by Eileen Diss
Wtr: David Goddard
Based on Christine Price
Cast: John Bellinger – Nigel Arkwright
Roger Bailiff – Colin Douglas
Stephen Bellinger – Cavan Kendall
Marian – Victoria Watts

In 1357, young Stephen Bellinger, son of a serf, escapes to London and is apprenticed to a master painter. When his father becomes involved in the rebellion of the serfs back in his home village, Stephen is able to save him by using three golden coins which had been given to him personally by King Edward.

THE YOUNG LADY FROM LONDON

22 November 1959, Sunday, 5:00–5:30pm, BBC, 6 episodes, drama, family, British/European, contemporary
BBCtv
Pr: Rex Tucker
Designed by Frederick Knapman
Wtr: Rex Tucker
Cast: **Jane Holland/Anna Kortzeroth – Anne Castaldini**
Prince Laszlo – Sandor Eles
Robert – Barry MacGregor
Kortzeroth – Kenneth Thornett

Sixteen-year-old Jane wins a newspaper competition and a trip to Paris – where she discovers that she has an exact double, Eastern European pianist Anna. Anna is in love with an exiled Prince, who confuses Anna with Jane, leading to a series of high-spirited adventures for the young English girl.

THE VOODOO FACTOR

12 December 1959, Saturday, 8:25–8:55pm, ITV, 6 episodes, thriller, British, contemporary
ATV Network
Pr: Quentin Lawrence
Designed by Tom Lingwood
Wtr: Lewis Greifer

Cast: **Marion Whittaker – Maxine Audley**
Dr. David Whittaker – Maurice Kaufmann
Dr. Sam Newman – Trevor Reid
The Goddess – Anna May Wong

London physician David Whittaker sees a patient who is suffering from a mysterious disease which is similar to one Whittaker had once studied on a South Indian Ocean island. Despite everything his logical reasoning tells him, Whittaker begins to wonder if the illness may be the result of a deadly 2000-year-old curse, and Whittaker is forced into a confrontation with a woman who may be an innocent victim of the curse . . . or the evil Goddess responsible for the mayhem which now threatens to overcome Whittaker, his wife Marion, and those around them.

Featured as part of the "Suspense" series of thriller serials.

1960–1969

HOW GREEN WAS MY VALLEY

1 January 1960, Friday, 8:00–8:30pm, BBC, 8 episodes, drama, classic, Welsh, 19th–20th century
BBCtv/Wales
Pr: Dafydd Gruffydd
Designed by Alan Taylor
Wtr: Barry Thomas
Based on Richard Llewellyn
Cast: **Gwilym Morgan – Eynon Evans**
Huw Morgan (as a boy) – Islwyn Maelor Evans
Davy Morgan – Glyn Houston
Reverend Merddyn Gruffydd – William Squire
Huw Morgan – Henley Thomas
Beth Morgan – Rachel Thomas

The Morgan family lives in a small Welsh mining valley; the story, told from the point of view of Huw Morgan as he comes of age, follows the family's lives and fortunes from the last decade of Victoria's reign until just before the outbreak of World War I, when the Morgans are forced to abandon their home in order to avoid being buried by the dangerously approaching mountain of sludge.

THE SECRET GARDEN

3 January 1960, Sunday, 5:00–5:30pm, BBC, 8 episodes, drama, classic, family, British, 20th century
BBCtv
Pr: Dorothea Brooking
Settings by Richard Henry
Wtr: Dorothea Brooking
Based on Frances Hodgson Burnett
Cast: **Mary Lennox – Gillian Ferguson**
Ben Weatherstaff – Fred Fairclough
Colin – Peter Hempson
Mrs. Medlock – Hilary Mason
Martha – Prunella Scales
Archibald Craven – Frank Shelley
Dickon – Colin Spaull

In the early part of the 20th century, orphaned Mary Lennox is sent to Misselthwaite Manor in Yorkshire to live with her uncle, embittered widower Archibald Craven, and her invalided cousin, Colin. The mood in the house is dour and dismal – until Mary discovers a long-neglected garden, which she brings back to life . . . and in so doing, restores faith, love and joy to all at the Manor.

EMMA

26 February 1960, Friday, 8:00–8:30pm, BBC, 6 episodes, drama, classic, British, 19th century
BBCtv
Pr: Campbell Logan
Settings by Stephen Bundy
Wtr: Vincent Tilsley
Based on Jane Austen
Cast: Robert Martin – David Cole
Mr. Knightley – Paul Daneman
Jane Fairfax – Petra Davies
Emma Woodhouse – Diana Fairfax
Mr. Woodhouse – Leslie French
Frank Churchill – David McCallum
Harriet Smith – Perlita Neilson
Mr. Elton – Raymond Young

Vain Emma Woodhouse takes great pleasure in manipulating the lives of those around her. Her machinations go too far when she tries, against the advice of her good friend Mr. Knightley, to turn simple Harriet Smith into a lady, and Emma's own life is dealt a nearly catastrophic blow when it appears Harriet might steal away Knightley's affections.

THE SPLENDID SPUR

28 February 1960, Sunday, 5:00–5:30pm, BBC, 6 episodes, drama, British, 17th century
BBCtv
Pr: David Goddard
Designed by Stewart Marshall
Wtr: David Tutaev
Based on Arthur Quiller-Couch
Cast: Tingcomb – Nigel Arkwright
Black Dick – Michael Balfour
Jack Marvel – Kenneth Farrington
King Charles I – Elton Hayes
Anthony Killigrew – Derek Smer
Captain Luke Settle – Patrick Troughton
Delia Killigrew – Victoria Watts

In 1642, with the Civil War raging, King Charles I moves his court to Oxford. Villainous adventurer Captain Luke Settle kills royal messenger Anthony Killigrew – but the letter Anthony was carrying is still safely held by Jack Marvel. Marvel sets out to deliver the letter, which has an important message for one of the King's generals, and also seeks to protect Anthony's sister Delia from the murderous Settle and his dangerous henchmen.

CAPTAIN MOONLIGHT – MAN OF MYSTERY

12 March 1960, Saturday, 5:25–5:50pm, BBC, 6 episodes, thriller, British, contemporary
BBCtv
Pr: Kevin Sheldon
Designed by Susan Spence
Wtr: E.J. Bell
Cast: Maggie Hart – Pamela Buck
The Imposter – Heron Carvic
"Baron Otto Brodnick" – Peter Claughton
Stephen Sycamore/Captain Moonlight – Bernard Horsfall
"Count Manfred von Betelstein" – Frank Partington

Captain Moonlight is the hero of a weekly television espionage serial who every week foils the sinister plans of his arch-enemies, Count Manfred von Betelstein and Baron Otto Brodnick. The actor who plays Moonlight, Stephen Sycamore, becomes involved in a genuine mystery and employs the aid of reporter Maggie Hart in its solution. He also uses some of Captain Moonlight's methods to try to vanquish his enemies, but finds there's a vast difference between solving reel-life and real-life crimes.

THE PEN OF MY AUNT

12 April 1960, Tuesday, 5:30–6:00pm, BBC, 6 episodes, mystery, family, British, contemporary
BBCtv
Pr: Barbara Hammond
Designed by Richard Wilmot
Wtr: Eric Allen
Cast: **Dennis Harper – Jonathan Bergman**
Madame Blitskaya – Nicolette Bernard
Mr. Ash – Eric Dodson
Hotel Detective Perichon – Michael Hitchman
Susan Harper – Hilary Wyce

English sister and brother Dennis and Susan Harper, on holiday in Paris, find a mysterious object in their hotel which causes an uproar for everyone there, and plunges the children into an adventurous chase.

THE LONG WAY HOME

24 April 1960, Sunday, 5:00–5:30pm, BBC, 7 episodes, drama, British, 20th century
BBCtv
Pr: Shaun Sutton
Designed by Frederick Knapman
Wtr: Shaun Sutton
Cast: **Captain Gill – Nigel Arkwright**
Herr Grosnitz – Patrick Cargill
Gaston Rondeur – Derek Francis
Colonel von Stretzhelm – Laurence Hardy
Lieutenant Anson, R.N.V.R. – Barry Letts
Captain Miller – James Sharkey
Commissioned Gunner Parks, R.N. – Neil Wilson

During World War II, four English officers tunnel their way out of a prisoner-of-war camp in occupied France. The main reason they are successful is because the Germans are aware of the escape and actually allow it to take place. But what is the motivation for this and, more significantly, will the Gestapo permit the officers to remain free?

THE SECRET KINGDOM

6 May 1960, Friday, 8:00–8:30pm, BBC, 8 episodes, drama, British, 20th century
BBCtv
Pr: Chloe Gibson
Designed by Fanny Taylor
Wtr: Walter Greenwood, Sheila Hodgson
Based on Walter Greenwood
Cast: Viola Byron – Anne Godfrey
William Byron – Malcolm Keen
Anne Byron – Sheila Manahan
Paula Byron – Maureen Pryor

Bert Treville – John Stratton

At the start of the 20th century, Paula Byron watches as her craftsman father William's career is undermined by the advent of mass production. Paula is further confronted with the drab life of workers in the industrialized north through her sisters' romances with two men who work in the pits. Paula marries a new arrival in the village, shopkeeper Bert Treville, and in the years which follow she continues to struggle against a hostile world, both outside and inside her own home.

A MATTER OF DEGREE

16 May 1960, Monday, 9:00–9:30pm, BBC, 6 episodes, drama, British, contemporary
BBCtv/Wales
Pr: David J. Thomas
Designed by Alan Taylor
Wtr: Elaine Morgan
Cast: Glyn Morris – Hugh David
Emlyn Powell – Meredith Edwards
Lil Thomas – Jessie Evans
Leslie Bates – Peter Gill
Doreen Powell – Anita Morgan

Welsh miner's daughter Doreen Powell wins a scholarship to Oxford, and once she begins her studies Doreen attempts to find a balance between the two very separate and different worlds in which she lives.

THE DAYS OF VENGEANCE

8 June 1960, Wednesday, 9:10–9:45pm, BBC, 6 episodes, thriller, British, contemporary
BBCtv
Pr: Harry Carlisle
Settings by Richard Wilmot
Wtr: Edward J. Mason, Ted Willis
Cast: Narrator – Peter Hawkins
Detective Inspector Mitchell – William Lucas
Ann Mitchell – Betty McDowall
Agnes Cranwell – Katherine Parr
Detective Sergeant West – Richard Pearson

Detective Inspector Mitchell and his wife Ann are both caught up in the intrigue of his latest investigation.

ST. IVES

12 June 1960, Sunday, 5:05–5:35pm, BBC, 6 episodes, drama, classic, adventure, British/French, 19th century
BBCtv
Pr: Richard West
Designed by Stewart Marshall
Wtr: Rex Tucker
Based on Robert Louis Stevenson
Cast: Viscount Alain – Denis Goacher
Flora Gilchrist – Audrey Nicholson
Mr. Romaine – Leslie Perrins
St. Ives – William Russell

French Viscount Anne de Keroual de Saint-Yves, better known as St. Ives, fought with Napoleon's Army, but is captured and held prisoner in an Edinburgh Castle. St. Ives is visited by a solicitor who tells him that he is the heir to a Buckinghamshire fortune – if he can claim it. St. Ives must somehow escape from the castle and make his way across 400 miles of enemy English countryside to claim his birthright.

DEATH OF A GHOST

27 June 1960, Monday, 8:45–9:15pm, BBC, 6 episodes, mystery, British, contemporary
BBCtv
Pr: John Harrison
Designed by Norman James
Wtr: John Hopkins
Based on Margery Allingham
Cast: Superintendent Oates – Arthur Brough
Albert Campion – Bernard Horsfall
Belle Lafcadio – Mary Merrall
Lisa Capella – Hira Talfrey
Max Fustian – André Van Gyseghem

Albert Campion visits his old friend Belle Lafcadio, a widow whose late husband was an artist. One of her husband's last pictures is to be shown for the first time, 18 years after his death, but the excitement over this is cut short when a murder occurs. The police are called in, and Campion helps them with their investigation.

THE HERRIES CHRONICLE

1 July 1960, Friday, 8:45–9:15pm, BBC,
7 episodes, drama, British, 18th century
BBCtv
Pr: Joan Craft
Designed by Charles Lawrence
Wtr: Constance Cox
Based on *Rogue Herries* by Hugh Walpole
Cast: David Herries – Philip Bond
    Mirabell – Zoe Caldwell
    Francis Herries – Ronald Leigh-Hunt
    Deborah Herries – Rosemary Miller
    Deborah Herries (as a child) – Susan Purdy
    David Herries (as a child) – Ronnie Raymond
    Mary Herries – Delene Scott
    Margaret Herries – Margot van der Burgh

Francis Herries settles with his wife Margaret and three children in Cumberland in 1730, determined to start a new life for them all in his own ancestral home. The family is quickly involved with the people in the region and are caught up in love, intrigue, and the Jacobite uprising of 1745, before their chronicle ends in 1762.

THE ADVENTURES OF TOM SAWYER

24 July 1960, Sunday, 5:05–5:35pm, BBC,
7 episodes, drama, classic, American, 19th century
BBCtv
Pr: Dorothea Brooking
Settings by Archie Clark
Wtr: C.E. Webber
Based on Mark Twain
Cast: Injun Joe – John Bennett
    Widow Douglas – Barbara Cavan
    Becky Thatcher – Janina Faye
    Aunt Polly – Betty Hardy
    Tom Sawyer – Fred Smith
    Huckleberry Finn – Mike Strotheide

Tom Sawyer and his friend Huckleberry Finn entertain themselves in a small Missouri town in the mid-1800s, their adventures culminating in their witnessing a murder, pretending they themselves are dead, and Tom's attending his own funeral. The truth is ultimately revealed and all is made right, with Tom returning home with Aunt Polly, and Huck being taken in by kindly Widow Douglas.

The roles of Tom and Huck were played by American boys, neither of whom had acted professionally before.

GOLDEN GIRL

27 July 1960, Wednesday, 9:15–9:45pm,
BBC, 6 episodes, drama, British, contemporary
BBCtv
Pr: Ronald Marsh
Settings by Harry Smith
Wtr: Michael Pertwee
Cast: **Katie Johnson – Catherine Boyle**
    Joe Francis – Peter Dyneley
    Barstow – Noel Howlett

Katie Johnson unexpectedly inherits an enormous fortune, becoming the richest girl in the world. Katie thoroughly enjoys the privileges of her new position, travelling to a number of the world's capitals, but also finds she must deal carefully with these new situations and the people she meets.

HERE LIES MISS SABRY

8 August 1960, Monday, 8:00–8:30pm,
BBC, 6 episodes, thriller, British, contemporary
BBCtv
Pr: Dennis Vance
Dir: Ronald Mason
Wtr: Raymond Bowers
Cast: Tony – John Cairney
    Clare Talbot – Petra Davies
    Jason – Patrick Magee
    Felice Sabry – Sydonie Platt
    Cracker Talbot – Sebastian Shaw
    Paul Sterne – Derrick Sherwin

Rakish James "Cracker" Talbot finds himself embroiled in mystery when Miss Sabry, with whom he had been romantically involved, is kidnapped. Cracker's daughter Clare and stepson Paul help him arrange a ransom payment, finding their own lives in jeopardy.

THE SMALL HOUSE AT ALLINGTON

19 August 1960, Friday, 8:00–8:30pm, BBC, 6 episodes, drama, British, 19th century
BBCtv
Pr: Michael Leeston-Smith
Designed by Daphne Shortman
Wtr: Marjorie Deans
Based on Anthony Trollope
Cast: **Bell Dale – Miranda Connell**
Lady Alexandrina – Patricia Heneghan
Adolphus Crosbie – Frederick Jaeger
John Eames – Colin Jeavons
Dr. James Crofts – Desmond Jordan
Lily Dale – Shirley Lawrence
Captain Bernard Dale – Barry Letts
Squire Dale – John Robinson
Mrs. Dale – Nora Swinburne

The small house at Allington belongs to Squire Dale, and its story follows the fortunes and misfortunes of the Squire's nieces, Bell and Lily Dale, who live there with their widowed mother. Lily falls in love with civil servant Adolphus Crosbie, but he jilts her to marry someone of rank, leaving Lily alone and brokenhearted. Bell is encouraged to make a financially advantageous match, but instead marries for love, joining happily with struggling local physician James Crofts.

SHEEP'S CLOTHING

18 September 1960, Sunday, 5:05–5:35pm, BBC, 4 episodes, mystery, British, contemporary
BBCtv
Pr: David Goddard
Designed by Frederick Knapman
Wtr: A.R. Rawlinson
Cast: **Derek Orr – Leonard Cracknell**
Policeman – Frank Sieman
Petra Carew – Katy Wild

Young Derek Orr lives a quiet life in a small countryside village, but even there he discovers a wellspring of intrigue and mystery which leads Derek down a path to adventure and romance.

NO WREATH FOR THE GENERAL

19 September 1960, Monday, 8:45–9:15pm, BBC, 6 episodes, thriller, British, contemporary
BBCtv
Pr: Julian Amyes
Designed by Fanny Taylor
Wtr: Donald Wilson
Cast: Alison Campbell – Rona Anderson
Dr. Roger Kenyon – William Franklyn
General Campbell – Maurice Hedley
Isobel Gilmour – Lana Morris
Johnny Brookman – Moray Watson

Shortly after retired General Campbell submits his war memoirs to the authorities for security clearance he disappears, and when it is discovered that a vital chapter is missing, a search ensues not only for the General and the pages, but for whoever is behind their theft . . . and what threat this presents to the national security.

THE MYSTERY OF EDWIN DROOD

29 September 1960, Wednesday, 8:00–8:30pm, ITV, 8 episodes, mystery, classic, British, 19th century
Associated-Rediffusion Network
Designed by Henry Federer
Dir: Mark Lawton
Wtr: John Keir Cross, from an idea by John Dickson Carr
Based on Charles Dickens
Cast: Rosa Bud – Barbara Brown
Mr. Grewgious – Laidman Browne
Old Opium Woman – Sonia Dresdel
Neville Landless – Clifford Elkin
Crisparkle – Richard Pearson
Edwin Drood – Tim Seely
John Jasper – Donald Sinden
Helena Landless – Catherine Woodville

Dickens' final, unfinished novel is set in an English cathedral town at Christmas time. Edwin Drood is engaged to marry pretty orphan girl Rosa. Everyone approves of the match, except Edwin's uncle, John Jasper, who wants Rosa for himself. But before the wedding can take place a sinister web of intrigue forms around Edwin, who then suddenly vanishes. Many think he has been murdered, although there is no trace of a body. John Jasper swears that he will devote his life to unmasking his nephew's killer . . . but is he covering up for his own guilt?

Dickens died before completing *Edwin Drood*; mystery writer John Dickson Carr (also known by his pen name Carter Dickson) devised a resolution to Dickens' story, which was then adapted into a teleplay by John Kier Cross. The serial also featured appearances by mystery writers Ngaio Marsh and Raymond Francis, who offered their own theories on solving the mystery.

BARNABY RUDGE

30 September 1960, Friday, 8:00–8:30pm, BBC, 13 episodes, drama, classic, British, 18th century
BBCtv
Pr: Douglas Allen
Dir: Morris Brady
Wtr: Michael Voysey
Based on Charles Dickens
Cast: Mr. Rudge – Nigel Arkwright
    Gabriel Varden – Newton Blick
    Edward Chester – Bernard Brown
    Dolly Varden – Jennifer Daniel
    Mrs. Rudge – Isabel Dean
    Joe Willet – Alan Haywood
    Emma Haredale – Eira Heath
    Mrs. Varden – Joan Hickson
    Dennis – Esmond Knight
    Hugh – Neil McCarthy
    Barnaby Rudge – John Wood

At the time of the anti-Papist riots of 1780, locksmith Gabriel Varden finds himself caught in the wake of a decades-old murder which inadvertently results in the kidnapping of his daughter Dolly. The murder, it is revealed, was committed by Mr. Rudge, the victim's former steward; Rudge is caught and hanged, and his half-crazed son Barnaby narrowly escapes the gallows himself.

KIPPS

14 October 1960, Friday, 7:00–7:30pm, ITV, 8 episodes, drama, British, 19th century
Granada Television
Pr: Jack Williams
Dir: Stuart Latham
Wtr: Clive Exton
Based on H.G. Wells
Cast: Helen Walshingham – Diana Fairfax
    Ann – Renny Lister
    Sid – Barry Lowe
    Kipps – Bryan Murray
    Mr. Shalford – Lloyd Pearson
    Mrs. Kipps – Beatrice Varley

Victorian-era drapery assistant Kipps inherits a fortune and tries to crash into the upper classes. He marries an upper-class woman, but discovers that sophisticated society is not for him and, after a number of misfortunes, gladly returns to his old ways and his old friends.

On the Friday following the final episode of *Kipps*, 9 December 1960, this same time slot was filled with the debut appearance of *Coronation Street*, an ongoing dramatic serial which continues to air at this time over 30 years later.

THE ODD MAN

19 October 1960, Wednesday, 7:00–7:30pm, ITV, 8 episodes, thriller, British, contemporary
Granada Television
Pr: Jack Williams
Dir: Gordon Flemyng
Wtr: Edward Boyd
Cast: Bernard Berridge – Roger Delgado
    Miss Croy – Judith Furse
    Dorothy Berridge – Lisa Gastoni
    Judy Gardiner – Jan Holden
    Viccy – Jemma Hyde
    Chief-Inspector Gordon – Moultrie Kelsall
    Detective Sergeant MacBride – Alan Tilvern
    Steve Gardiner – Geoffrey Toone
    Charles Ormiston – Richard Vernon

When Dorothy Berridge, a friend of jazz impresario Steve Gardiner and his actress wife Judy, is attacked by an unknown assailant, Gardiner is Detective Sergeant MacBride's prime suspect. It is then up to Gardiner to clear his name; he finds two more likely suspects than himself – Dorothy's estranged husband Bernard and mystery man Charles Ormiston – but Dorothy dies before being able to name her attacker, and the race is on to find the killer before Gardiner is formally charged with the crime.

In 1962, a second *The Odd Man* serial was produced, this time featuring Edwin Richfield as Steve Gardiner.

THE WORLD OF TIM FRAZER

15 November 1960, Tuesday,
8:00–8:30pm, BBC, 6 episodes, thriller, British, contemporary
BBCtv
Pr: Alan Bromly
Designed by Roy Oxley
Wtr: Francis Durbridge, Clive Exton
Cast: Helen Baker – Heather Chasen
Dr. Killick – Gerald Cross
Harry Denston – John Dearth
Tim Frazer – Jack Hedley
Charles Ross – Ralph Michael
Donald Edwards – Redmond Phillips

Engineer Tim Frazer is surprised when Henry Denston, his business partner, mysteriously disappears, especially since Denston owes him a good deal of money. In pursuit of the money and Denston, Frazer travels to the fishing village of Henton, where he finds himself involved in a series of enterprises which are notably more dangerous than engineering.

Introduced under the "Francis Durbridge Presents . . . " banner, this was the first of three serials about Tim Frazer, a character Durbridge created especially for television. For the first time on television, Durbridge shared writing credit.

THE CITADEL

23 November 1960, Wednesday,
8:00–8:30pm, ITV, 9 episodes, drama, British, 20th century
Associated-Rediffusion Network
Pr: Peter Graham Scott
Dir: John Frankau

Wtr: Kenneth Hyde
Based on A.J. Cronin
Cast: **Dr. Andrew Manson – Eric Lander**
Dr. Philip Denny – Jack May
Frances LeRoy – Elizabeth Shepherd
Dr. Ivory – Richard Vernon
Christine Barlow – Zena Walker

In 1924, young doctor Andrew Manson arrives at a mining village to work as a general practitioner. He works eagerly and marries local schoolmistress Christine Barlow, but finds it impossible to make a living, and eventually moves on to another post. Manson soon becomes a fashionable doctor who takes care of the wealthy and neglects the more needy cases who had been his original patients. He also becomes estranged from Christine. After a serious crisis of confidence, Manson realizes that his work as a doctor is more important than making money, and endeavours to return to the older, more simple practice of medicine with which he had begun his career.

PERSUASION

30 December 1960, Friday, 9:30–10:00pm, BBC, 4 episodes, drama, classic, British, 19th century
BBCtv
Pr: Campbell Logan
Designed by Stephen Bundy
Wtr: Barbara Burnham, Michael Voysey
Based on Jane Austen
Cast: Mrs. Clay – Daphne Anderson
William Elliot – Derek Blomfield
Sir Walter Elliot – George Curzon
Captain Frederick Wentworth – Paul Daneman
Lady Russell – Fabia Drake
Elizabeth Elliot – Jane Hardie
Mrs. Croft – Thea Holme
Anne Elliot – Daphne Slater
Charles Hayter – Timothy West

Anne Elliot had jilted her lover, Frederick Wentworth, eight years ago, under pressure from her family, who deemed him unworthy. Now Wentworth returns, a distinguished officer . . . who seems attached to another woman. Gentle, sensitive Anne still loves Wentworth, and endeavours not to lose another chance to declare her feelings, but fate seems determined to put still more obstacles in the lovers' path before they can be happily reunited.

PARADISE WALK

15 January 1961, Sunday, 5:00–5:30pm, BBC, 4 episodes, drama, family, British, contemporary
BBCtv
Pr: Shaun Sutton
Designed by Frederick Knapman
Wtr: Shaun Sutton
Cast: Mr. Collis – George A. Cooper
    Sammy – Dudley Hunt
    Uncle Joshua – Errol John
    Aunt Jubilee – Gladys Taylor

West Indian boy Sammy has emigrated to England, where he lives with his Uncle Joshua and great-Aunt Jubilee. Not long after his arrival, Sammy gets involved in an adventure which seems exciting to him, but in the end threatens to disgrace his family and friends.

THE HOUSE UNDER THE WATER

27 January 1961, Friday, 9:00–9:30pm, BBC, 8 episodes, drama, British, 19th century
BBCtv/Wales
Pr: Dafydd Gruffydd
Designed by David Butcher
Wtr: Barry Thomas
Based on Francis Brett Young
Cast: Evan Vaughan – Richard Bebb
    Sir Arthur Weldon – Ian Colin
    Lucrezia Tregaron – Margaret Courtenay
    Colonel Tregaron – Desmond Llewellyn
    Philippa – Carole Mowlam
    Gerald – Ray Smith
    Griffith Tregaron – William Squire

Ruthless and arrogant Griffith Tregaron lives in 1887 on a small farm in the Midlands with his Italian wife and their children. He is summoned to his family's property in a mountain-surrounded valley in Wales, where a clash of will between the power of Man, symbolized by the North Bromwich Corporation which seeks to develop the area, and the forces of Nature ensues, with cataclysmic results.

THE TREASURE SEEKERS

19 February 1961, Sunday, 5:00–5:30pm, BBC, 6 episodes, drama, classic, family, British, 19th century
BBCtv
Pr: Dorothea Brooking
Designed by Susan Spence
Wtr: Dorothea Brooking
Based on *The Story of the Treasure Seekers* by E.E. Nesbit
Cast: **Dicky Bastable – Jonathan Collins**
    Oswald Bastable – Anthony Klouda
    Mr. Bastable – Philip Latham
    H.O. Bastable – Mark Mileham
    Alice Bastable – Sarah O'Connor
    Mrs. Leslie – Noel Streatfeild
    Albert-next-door – Christopher Williams
    Noel Bastable – Richard Williams
    Dora Bastable – Hilary Wyce

The Bastable family has fallen on somewhat hard times, and the children set out to find a way to improve the family fortunes, digging in the back garden for buried treasure, which leads to a series of adventurous mishaps for the group.

THE FIFTH FORM AT ST. DOMINIC'S

21 February 1961, Tuesday, 5:00–5:30pm, BBC, 4 episodes, drama, family, British, contemporary
BBCtv
Pr: Barbara Hammond
Designed by Richard Wilmot
Wtr: Mary Cathcart Borer, C.E. Webber
Based on Talbot Baines Reed
Cast: Pembury – James Beck
    Dr. Senior – Maurice Colbourne
    Oliver Greenfield – Peter Marden
    Bramble – Kenneth Gough
    Paul – Nigel Jenkins
    Wraysford – Richard Palmer
    Stephen Greenfield – Lindsay Scott-Patton
    Tom Senior – Julian Yardley

Thanks to the generosity of a wealthy relative, Stephen Greenfield is able to attend the posh public school St. Dominic's – where he is regularly bullied by the other, richer boys enrolled there. But Stephen becomes involved with the traditional public school pursuits – "fagging" for seniors and sport – and gets by cheerfully and manages to turn out well.

ROB ROY

9 April 1961, Sunday, 5:00–5:30pm, BBC, 7 episodes, drama, classic, adventure, Scottish, 18th century
BBCtv
Pr: Kevin Sheldon
Designed by Fanny Taylor
Wtr: E.J. Bell
Based on Sir Walter Scott
Cast: **Frank Osbaldistone – Donald Douglas**
Diana Vernon – Samantha Eggar
Rob Roy – Tom Fleming
William Osbaldistone – George Hagan
Dougal – Roddy McMillan
Rashleigh Osbaldistone – Gabriel Woolf

Frank Osbaldistone is summoned by his father to return from Bordeaux to London, leading then to a journey rife with intrigue and romance to Glasgow, where outlaw hero Rob Roy, head of the McGregor clan, is embroiled in a rivalry between dueling dukes beyond the Highland Line.

AMELIA

14 April 1961, Friday, 9:20–9:50pm, BBC, 7 episodes, drama, British, 18th century
BBCtv
Pr: Chloe Gibson
Designed by Stephen Bundy
Wtr: A.R. Rawlinson
Based on Henry Fielding
Cast: **Will Booth – Frederick Jaeger**
Dr. Harrison – Malcolm Keen
Colonel James – David Peel
William Hogarth – Peter Sallis
Amelia – Elizabeth Shepherd
Henry Fielding – André van Gyseghem

Penniless army officer Will Booth marries heiress Amelia, to the great annoyance of her mother and other suitors, most notably Colonel James, who is attracted in large part to Amelia's money and attempts to take advantage of the situation when Booth is unjustly thrown into prison.

Each episode began in Hogarth's studio, where Fielding was sitting for a portrait; Fielding then began narrating Amelia's story.

TRITON

4 June 1961, Sunday, 5:00–5:30pm, BBC, 4 episodes, drama, historical, British, 19th century
BBCtv
Pr: Rex Tucker
Designed by Frederick Knapman
Wtr: Rex Tucker
Cast: Lord Nelson – Robert James
Lieutenant Lamb – Francis Matthews
Lieutenant Singleton – Peter Mayock
Captain Belwether – William Russell

In 1800, as Napoleon prepares to invade England, two English officers, Captain Belwether and Lieutenant Lamb, are sent on a dangerous mission to France, where they are to find out what they can about a new secret weapon the French are supposedly developing.

MAGNOLIA STREET

16 June 1961, Friday, 8:55–9:25pm, BBC, 6 episodes, drama, British, 20th century
BBCtv
Pr: Vivian A. Daniels
Designed by Richard Henry
Wtr: Allan Prior
Based on Louis Golding
Cast: Mrs. Shulman – Golda Casimir
Maggie Tawnie – Vanda Godsell
Mr. Emmanuel – Carl Jaffe
Rose Berman Cooper – Susan Maryott
Mick Shulman – Timothy Pearce

Rabbi Shulman – Michael Poole
Steve Tawnie – Leonard Williams
John Cooper – Edward Woodward

The Manchester-based story of a neighborhood in the years 1910–1926, where one side of the street is occupied entirely by Jewish families, and the other side all by Gentiles. At times the two sides are united as one community; at other times their differences seem overwhelming.

WALK A CROOKED MILE

20 June 1961, Tuesday, 8:15–8:45pm, BBC, 6 episodes, thriller, British, contemporary
BBCtv
Pr: David E. Rod
Designed by Roy Oxley
Wtr: Lindsay Hardy
Cast: Gillian – Doreen Aris
Fergus Ryder – Philip Bond
Adrian Charles – Raymond Huntley
Commander Anthony Gardiner – David Langton
Detective Superintendent Faulkner – Peter Madden
Arthur Boone – Patrick Newell
Gordon Cheviot – Anthony Newlands

Film star Gordon Cheviot is under suspicion of murder when a member of the crew of his current project is killed. Producer Adrian Charles assigns his assistant director, Fergus Ryder, to investigate the murder, but what Ryder uncovers leads to tumult in many lives . . . including his own.

HURRICANE

2 July 1961, Sunday, 5:00–5:30pm, BBC, 6 episodes, drama, British, contemporary
BBCtv
Pr: Joy Harington
Designed by Richard Henry
Wtr: C.E. Webber
Cast: Mrs. de Boissiere – Nadia Cattouse
Winston Churchill Robinson – Dudley Hunt
Jessica de Boissiere – Dolores Mantez
Midge Lammerton – Suzanne Neve

Young nurses Midge Lammerton and Jessica de Boissiere complete their training in London and go on assignment to the West Indies, where they are trapped on a tiny island during a devastating hurricane.

THE RACKETTY STREET GANG

13 August 1961, Sunday, 5:00–5:30pm, BBC, 6 episodes, mystery, family, Australian, contemporary
BBCtv
Pr: Dorothea Brooking
Designed by Robert MacGowan
Wtr: Dorothea Brooking
Based on L.H. Evers
Cast: Stephan Smertzer – John Abineri
Ben – Geoffrey Bettenay
Spider – Edwin Finn
Stanley – Peter Hempson
The Professor – Michael Luckie
Anton Smertzer – Michael Meier
Frau Smertzer – Stella Textor

Four boys – good-natured Ben, the inventive "Professor," unreliable Stanley, and German Anton – turn detectives on the waterfront of Sydney Harbour, investigating the strange goings on behind locked boatyard doors; meanwhile, Anton, whose family has just recently emigrated to Australia, learns that his father is keeping a secret, which adds to the boys' intrigue.

FRONTIER DRUMS

22 September 1961, Friday, 5:00–5:30pm, ITV, 6 episodes, drama, British, 19th century
Associated-Rediffusion Network
Designed by Sylva Nadolny
Dir: Jim Pople
Wtr: Peter Hayes
Cast: Major Neville Chrichton – Bernard Brown
Abu Singh – Joseph Cuby
Captain Nigel Chrichton – Ronnie Raymond
Kardar Khan – Derek Sidney
Azim Khan – David Spenser

In 1870, Kardar Khan, the Maharajah of Ghurkistan, plots against the British Raj. The Government is unprepared for the uprising, and Captain Nigel Chrichton hastily begins training the tribesmen in gunnery. Chrichton, aided by informant Abu Singh, is able to learn some facts of Khan's plot, but it might be too late to stop the Maharajah from realizing his deadly ambitions.

PLATEAU OF FEAR

24 September 1961, Sunday, 4:00–4:30pm, ITV, 6 episodes, science fiction, British, contemporary
ABC Network
Pr: Guy Verney
Dir: Kim Mills
Wtr: Malcolm Stuart Fellows, Sutherland Ross
Cast: Ralph Morton – Richard Coleman
       Mark Bannerman – Gerald Flood
       Julietta Aranda – Maureen Lindholm
       General Villagran – Ferdy Mayne

Scientific journalist Mark Bannerman journeys to Potencia-One, a nuclear research station in South America, to investigate the mysterious creatures which have been attacking the station. Nefarious General Villagran is behind the efforts to stop the work being done at Potencia-One, and Bannerman and his new friends at the station struggle to keep the reactor working under desperate, life-threatening measures.

STRANGER ON THE SHORE

24 September 1961, Sunday, 4:45–5:15pm, BBC, 5 episodes, drama, family, British, contemporary
BBCtv
Pr: Kevin Sheldon
Settings by Raymond Cusick
Wtr: Sheila Hodgson
Cast: **Marie-Helene Ronsin – Jeanne le Bars**
       Penelope Gough – Amanda Grinling
       Mrs. Gough – Beatrix Mackey
       David Gough – Richard Vernon

Marie-Helene Ronsin is on her first trip to England, staying with a family in Brighton. Although she speaks some English, Marie-Helene is very shy, and must overcome many personal challenges as she learns to adjust to her new seaside surroundings.

"A" FOR ANDROMEDA

3 October 1961, Tuesday, 8:30–9:15pm, BBC, 7 episodes, science fiction, British, future
BBCtv
Pr: Michael Hayes, Norman James
Designed by Norman James
Wtr: John Elliot, Fred Hoyle
Cast: Andromeda – Julie Christie
       John Fleming – Peter Halliday
       J.M. Osborne – Noel Johnson
       Judy Adamson – Patricia Kneale
       Professor Reinhart – Esmond Knight

In the not-very distant future (1970!), a group of scientists working on a powerful new radio-telescope picks up a strange message from the constellation Andromeda; this proof of alien intelligence is ultimately put into human form through the efforts of brilliant physicist John Fleming. But Fleming and his creation, the beautiful, womanly Andromeda, are pursued by dangerous elements whose threats extend to all of mankind, leading them to flee to a remote Scottish island . . . where Andromeda falls into an underground pool and disappears.

FLOWER OF EVIL

11 October 1961, Wednesday, 8:45–9:15pm, BBC, 6 episodes, thriller, European, contemporary
BBCtv
Pr: Harry Carlisle
Dir: Robin Nash
Wtr: Edward J. Mason, Ted Willis
Cast: **Detective Inspector Mitchell – William Lucas**
       Ann Mitchell – Betty McDowall
       Otto Schneider – Aubrey Morris
       Dr. Mylanos – Anthony Newlands
       Greta Lessing – Felicity Young

The Austrian Alps provide the setting for

the search for a missing fortune left behind by fleeing Nazis at the end of World War II. Among those searching for the treasure are ex-S.S. guards who somehow escaped capture, local residents who have heard of the legendary riches, and British Detective Inspector Mitchell.

OPERATION FANTAIL

14 October 1961, Saturday, 5:25–5:50pm, BBC, 2 episodes, drama, non-fiction, British, 20th century
BBCtv
Pr: Gerald Wiltshire
Designed by Frederick Knapman
Wtr: Keith Latham
Cast:　Lieutenant Roger Lewis – Douglas Blackwell
　　　　Antonio Thomar – Paul Bogdan
　　　　Susan Forest – Michele Dotrice
　　　　Neil Forest – Kenneth Gouge
　　　　Lieutenant-Commander W.J. Kingsford – Alan White

The World War II exploits of the Tarrant, one of His Majesty's submarines, focusing on the leadership of Lieutenant-Commander W.J. Kingsford and his crew's rescue of civilians from a crashed airliner in 1942.

GAMBLE FOR A THRONE

4 November 1961, Saturday, 5:25–5:50pm, BBC, 6 episodes, drama, British, 17th century
BBCtv
Pr: David Goddard
Designed by Frederick Knapman
Wtr: Barbara S. Harper
Based on Henry Garnett
Cast:　Stephen Elkin – John Bonney
　　　　Colonel Rushwick – Colin Douglas
　　　　Peter Marshall – Barry Letts
　　　　Jeremy Rushwick – Richard Palmer
　　　　Damaris – Katy Wild
　　　　Kaye Chance – Annika Wills
　　　　Colonel Habbakuk Capstick – John Woodnutt

A group of loyalists committed to exiled King Charles II works to undermine Oliver Cromwell. Unfortunately, one among them is secretly an agent for Cromwell, which leads to danger for the rest of the group, doom to their planned rebellion, and major upheaveal in the lives of the Rushwick family, which is sympathetic to the loyalist cause.

THE POCKET LANCER

5 November 1961, Sunday, 4:45–5:15pm, BBC, 4 episodes, drama, family, British, 19th century
BBCtv
Pr: Shaun Sutton
Designed by Susan Spence
Wtr: Shaun Sutton
Cast:　Old Joey – Nigel Arkwright
　　　　Timothy Bretwyn – Nicholas Clay
　　　　Sergeant Finch – Derek Francis
　　　　Rosie Trimmer – Barbara Leslie
　　　　Captain Court-Bellingham – Barry Letts
　　　　Countess of Clarencourt – Joan Sanderson
　　　　Captain Bretwyn – Ian Shand

Timothy Bretwyn's father is a Captain in the 43rd Light Lancers, and Timothy hopes to one day be as brave a soldier as the man he hasn't seen in three years, as the Captain has been off fighting the Crimean War – and gets his chance when Timothy finds himself called into service.

This was the second production of Sutton's story, first broadcast in April 1959, with several cast members reprising their original roles.

THE ESCAPE OF R.D.7

21 November 1961, Tuesday, 8:30–9:15pm, BBC, 5 episodes, science fiction, British, contemporary
BBCtv
Pr: James Ormerod
Designed by Stephen Bundy
Wtr: Thomas Clarke
Based on original idea by James Parish
Cast:　Patrice Constantine – Patrick Cargill
　　　　David Cardosa – Derek Croucher
　　　　Peter Warner – Roger Croucher
　　　　Dr. Anna Hastings – Barbara Murray
　　　　Dr. Mary Carter – Ellen Pollock
　　　　Peggy Butler – Jennifer Wright

Dr. Anna Hastings is researching the strange and deadly virus R.D.7, but becomes so obsessed with the project that conventional authority cuts off her funding. She continues on her own, but in her zeal jeopardizes the sanctity of the laboratory . . . and is nearly responsible for a nationwide epidemic.

A CHANCE OF THUNDER

22 November 1961, Wednesday, 8:45–9:15pm, BBC, 6 episodes, thriller, British, contemporary
BBCtv
Designed by Roy Oxley
Dir: Peter Hammond
Wtr: John Hopkins
Cast: **Steven Prador – Clifford Evans**
Martin – John Meillon
Wilson – Godfrey Quigley
Yardley – Peter Vaughan
Pam Marchant – Catherine Woodville

Writer Steven Prador is set to address a writers' conference, but three men are trying to kill him, each for a different reason, and Prador must elude a variety of traps and doublecrosses if he is to escape with his life, much less be able to make his appearance at the conference.

VICE VERSA

3 December 1961, Sunday, 4:45–5:15pm, BBC, 3 episodes, comedy, family, British, 19th century
BBCtv
Pr: Stephen Harrison
Wtr: C.E. Webber
Based on F. Anstey
Cast: **Dick Bultitude – Graham Aza**
Marmaduke Paradine – Richard Caldicott
Dr. Grimstone – William Devlin
Paul Bultitude – William Mervyn

Young Dick Bultitude's complaints about his mistreatment at school fall on deaf ears at home, where his Victorian father offers little sympathy . . . until a bizarre switch occurs, with Dick assuming power of his father's body, while the older Bultitude is trapped in the form of a young man, and subject to the terrors of boarding school.

OLIVER TWIST

7 January 1962, Sunday, 5:00–5:25pm, BBC, 13 episodes, drama, classic, British, 19th century
BBCtv
Pr: Eric Taylor
Designed by Stephen Bundy
Wtr: Constance Cox
Based on Charles Dickens
Cast: **Fagin – Max Adrian**
Harry Maylie – John Breslin
Rose Maylie – Gay Cameron
Monks – John Carson
Mr. Brownlow – George Curzon
Old Sally – Aimée Delamain
Mr. Sowerberry – Donald Eccles
Mr. Bumble – Willoughby Goddard
Artful Dodger – Melvyn Hayes
Nancy – Carmel McSharry
Oliver Twist – Bruce Prochnik
Mrs. Bumble – Peggy Thorpe-Bates
Bill Sikes – Peter Vaughan

Orphaned Oliver Twist runs away from indentured workhouse servitude to London, where he falls into the company of young thieves led by the evil Fagin. Fate seems to smile kindly on Oliver when he is taken in by Mr. Brownlow, but a happily-ever-after destiny for the boy is sorely threatened on a number of fronts before all can be triumphantly resolved.

The serial's depiction of the brutal murder of Nancy by Bill Sikes caused a debate in the House of Commons about violence on television, leading the BBC to shorten the programme's final scene, which showed a shadowy view of Sikes' hanged corpse.

CRYING DOWN THE LANE

8 January 1962, Monday, 8:00–8:30pm, BBC, 6 episodes, thriller, British, contemporary
BBCtv
Pr: Prudence FitzGerald
Designed by Lawrence Broadhouse
Wtr: Ivan Roe

Cast: **Joe Kovacs – Edward Cast**
Carol Miller – Elvi Hale
Louisa – Delphi Lawrence
Danny – Gregory Phillips
Champion – Peter Sallis
Fernandes – Paul Stassino

Canadian Joe Kovacs journeys to London to seek custody of his young son; the situation becomes critical when young Danny is kidnapped, and Joe finds himself in deep conflict with his estranged wife Louisa as the search for their son escalates in tension and danger.

BARBARA IN BLACK

19 February 1962, Monday, 8:00–8:30pm, BBC, 6 episodes, thriller, Welsh, contemporary
BBCtv/Wales
Pr: David J. Thomas
Designed by Alan Taylor
Wtr: Elaine Morgan
Cast: Chief Inspector – Douglas Blackwell
Dr. Dave Sharland – John Cairney
Superintendent – Edward Evans
Brachet – John Gill
Barbara Griffiths – Tracey Lloyd
Cobley – Neil McCarthy

A lorry crash in the mountains of Wales sets off a dangerous chain of events involving a number of people in a small community, including Barbara Griffiths, who believes her father's sudden disappearance is somehow connected to the accident. Or was it really an accident at all?

THE SIX PROUD WALKERS

10 March 1962, Saturday, 6:30–7:00pm, BBC, 13 episodes, thriller, British, contemporary
BBCtv
Pr: Douglas Allen
Designed by Robert Macgowan
Wtr: Donald Wilson
Cast: **Detective Inspector Roger Stanton – Tony Britton**
Bertie Walker – Terence Alexander
Freddie Walker – Scot Finch
Joey Walker – Derek Francis
Sally Walker – Jacqueline Hill
Martha Barlow – Julia Lockwood
Polly Arden – Lana Morris
Willie Walker – Andrew Sachs

Aspiring actress Polly Arden gets her first big break, but it is thwarted when she is caught in the middle of a jewel robbery that goes awry. The Walker family is behind the heist, and soon Polly finds herself involved with the Walker gang – and the Detective Inspector in charge of the case.

This remake of Wilson's 1954 serialized treatment of the Walker family combines two stories: *The Six Proud Walkers* and *The Mulberry Accelerator*.

STRANGER IN THE CITY

8 April 1962, Sunday, 5:00–5:25pm, BBC, 6 episodes, drama, family, British, contemporary
BBCtv
Pr: Kevin Sheldon
Settings by Fanny Taylor
Wtr: Sheila Hodgson
Cast: **Marie-Helene Ronsin – Jeanne le Bars**
Podger Gough – Denis Gilmore
Mrs. Gough – Beatrix Mackey
Edie Croucher – Joy Osborne
Mr. Gough – Richard Vernon
Penelope Gough – April Wilding
Syd Croucher – Henry Woolf

In this follow-up to *Stranger on the Shore*, Marie-Helene moves with the Gough family to London, where life in a fifth-floor flat proves quite different from the quiet seaside life to which Marie-Helene had finally become accustomed.

PARBOTTLE SPEAKING

30 April 1962, Monday, 5:30–5:55pm, BBC, 6 episodes, thriller, family, British, contemporary
BBCtv
Pr: Rex Tucker
Dir: Gerald Wiltshire
Wtr: Rex Tucker
Cast: Bill Paley – Harvey Hall
Inspector Hoggins – Tim Hudson
Mustapha Manalik – Anthony Jacobs

Horatio Parbottle – Toke Townley

Soft-spoken, retired Intelligence agent Horatio Parbottle becomes involved in intrigue once again when a mysterious Middle Easterner collapses across the threshold of Parbottle's front door.

THE FRANCHISE AFFAIR

21 May 1962, Monday, 8:00–8:30pm, BBC, 6 episodes, mystery, British, 20th century
BBCtv
Pr: George R. Foa
Dir: Mervyn Pinfield
Wtr: Constance Cox
Based on Josephine Tey
Cast:　Robert Blair – Michael Aldridge
　　　Aunt Lin – Gladys Boot
　　　Marion Sharpe – Rosalie Crutchley
　　　Detective Inspector Grant – Clifford Earl
　　　Mr. Heseltine – Leslie French
　　　Betty Kane – Meg Wynn Owen
　　　Mrs. Wynn – Peggy Thorpe-Bates
　　　Mrs. Sharpe – Veronica Turleigh

Betty Kane tells the police that she has been held prisoner and brutally mistreated in a remote country house by Marion Sharpe and her mother, and the fearful truth of what happened comes out during the trial which follows her charges.

THE MASTER OF BALLANTRAE

27 May 1962, Sunday, 4:55–5:25pm, BBC, 6 episodes, drama, classic, Scottish, 18th century
BBCtv/Scotland
Pr: Pharic Maclaren
Designed by Stanley Morris
Wtr: Constance Cox
Based on Robert Louis Stevenson
Cast:　**Henry Durie – John Breslin**
　　　James Durie, Master of Ballantrae – John Cairney
　　　Ephraim Mackellar – Paul Kermack
　　　Lord Durrisdeer – David Steuart
　　　Alison Graeme – Hilary Thomson

In Scotland in 1745, James Durie, the Master of Ballantrae, joins Prince Charles Edward's uprising against the House of Hanover, and is reported killed at Culloden. His brother Henry, who has remained loyal to King George, remains behind, succeeding to James' title and estate – and marrying James' sweetheart, Alison Graeme. But James returns home, and the bitter feud between the brothers erupts in a duel, after which Henry and Alison flee to America. James follows them, reappearing from the (supposed) dead more than once more, but ultimately the conflict brings death to both brothers, and they are buried in a common grave.

THE BIG PULL

9 June 1962, Saturday, 7:00–7:30pm, BBC, 6 episodes, science fiction, British, future
BBCtv
Pr: Terence Dudley
Designed by Lionel Radford
Wtr: Robert Gould
Cast:　Dr. Weatherfield – Felix Deebank
　　　Sir Robert Nailer – William Dexter
　　　Pam – Laura Graham
　　　Mrs. Weatherfield – Helen Horton
　　　Lady Nailer – June Tobin

25 years after an astronaut died after orbiting around the earth, researcher Sir Robert Nailer is confronted with the frightening possibility that the dead man somehow returned to Earth contaminated by radioactivity from space, and that the contamination has begun to spread. Is this a direct assault from creatures from outer space? And what can be done to prevent the danger from spreading any further?

THE ANDROMEDA BREAKTHROUGH

28 June 1962, Thursday, 8:00–8:45pm, BBC, 6 episodes, science fiction, British, future
BBCtv
Pr: John Elliot
Designed by Norman James
Wtr: John Elliot, Fred Hoyle
Cast:　Mademoiselle Gamboule – Claude Farell
　　　John Fleming – Peter Halliday
　　　Andromeda – Susan Hampshire
　　　J.M. Osborne – Noel Johnson

Madeleine Dawnay – Mary Morris

Physicist John Fleming and biochemist Madeleine Dawney follow the trail of Andromeda, Fleming's computer-generated "woman" who had supposedly been destroyed. The search leads them to the Middle East, where they discover the true power behind the messages from space which have been picked up by the computer Fleming built.

This sequel to *"A" For Andromeda*, which aired beginning 3 October 1961, found Peter Halliday and Noel Johnson reprising their roles, but the part of Andromeda was recast.

THE DARK ISLAND

8 July 1962, Sunday, 5:25–5:55pm, BBC, 6 episodes, thriller, Scottish, contemporary
BBCtv/Scotland
Pr: Gerard Glaister
Designed by Douglas Duncan
Wtr: Robert Barr
Cast: Mary Somers – Angela Browne
Nicolson – Robert Hardy
Brigadier – Cyril Luckham
Grant – Francis Matthews
Ian McLeod – Bryden Murdoch

When a strange, unidentifiable torpedo is found washed up on shore of a small, nearly uninhabited island, local officials are called in to try to defuse it. But disturbing discoveries about a long-standing Soviet espionage ring are made, and many lives are endangered before the keys to the dangerous mystery are finally unlocked.

OUTBREAK OF MURDER

21 July 1962, Saturday, 6:30–7:00pm, BBC, 7 episodes, mystery, British, contemporary
BBCtv
Pr: Harry Carlisle
Settings by Richard Wilmot
Wtr: Edward J. Mason, Ted Willis
Cast: Ken Mitchell – Christopher Beeny
Chief Superintendent Ruger – John Gabriel
Detective Inspector Mitchell – Glyn Houston
Ann Mitchell – Betty McDowall

Detective Inspector Mitchell investigates a number of murders at the Hot Piano Club, where he is a member, which appear to have no motive, but all end up being quite closely linked.

KATY

19 August 1962, Sunday, 5:00–5:25pm, BBC, 8 episodes, drama, family, American, 19th century
BBCtv
Pr: Dorothea Brooking
Dir: Edward Barnes
Wtr: Constance Cox
Based on *What Katy Did*, *What Katy Did At School* by Susan Coolidge
Cast: Clover Carr – Michele Dotrice
Cousin Helen – Rachel Gurney
Katy Carr – Susan Hampshire
Aunt Izzie – Betty Hardy
Dorry Carr – Paul Large
Elsie Carr – Elspeth Pairie
Dr. Carr – John Welsh

In New England in the 1870s, tomboy Katy must take over as "mother" to her brothers and sisters after the death of her widowed father's housekeeper, but does not take any of life's responsibilities seriously until she sustains a temporarily crippling injury, which helps Katy learn several valuable lessons. Later, Katy is sent to the very proper Seminary for Young Ladies, where she is quite rebellious and unhappy – until she is allowed to come home once again.

THE LAST MAN OUT

6 October 1962, Saturday, 5:25–5:55pm, BBC, 6 episodes, drama, adventure, British/European, 20th century
BBCtv
Pr: Shaun Sutton
Designed by Barry Newbury
Wtr: Shaun Sutton
Cast: Herr Straffen – Patrick Cargill
Professor Servillon – Richard Hurndall
Captain Stuart – Barry Letts
Captain Lord Tenborough – Francis Matthews
Sergeant Hardacre – Anthony Sagar
The Colonel – Richard Vernon

Colonel von Hertz – John Welsh

In 1940, three British soldiers are sent into German-occupied France to locate and bring back a French scientist who is working on a secret weapon.

THE RIVER FLOWS EAST

14 October 1962, Sunday, 5:00–5:25pm, BBC, 6 episodes, thriller, family, British, contemporary
BBCtv
Pr: Brian Bell
Designed by Norman James
Wtr: Terence Dudley
Cast: Mrs. Cowie – Sheila Burrell
    Susan Melford – Judy Cornwell
    John Farrance – Richard Gale
    Big Willie Holmes – Harold Innocent
    Professor Irving – Charles Leno
    Gerald Farrance – Anthony Nicholls
    Ann Farrance – Meg Wynn Owen
    Andrew Giddings – Gary Watson

One square mile of the Thames, and the shops on its banks, is the scene of kidnappings and chases, focusing on the abduction of the daughter of a renowned scientist and the young people who become involved in solving the dangerous mystery.

THE MONSTERS

8 November 1962, Thursday, 8:00–8:45pm, BBC, 4 episodes, science fiction, British, contemporary
BBCtv
Pr: George R. Foa
Dir: Mervyn Pinfield
Wtr: Evelyn Frazer, Vincent Tilsley
Cast: Hopkins – Mark Dignam
    Wilf Marner – Howard Douglas
    Van Halloran – Alan Gifford
    John Brent – William Greene
    Professor Cato – Robert Harris
    Esmee Pulford – Helen Lindsay
    Felicity Brent – Elizabeth Weaver

Wilf Marner swears he's seen the "monster on Lake Kingswater," but no one takes his claim seriously – except zoology professor John Brent, who happens to be honeymooning nearby. When a dead body is found floating in the water, Brent wonders if there is a connection between the murder and whatever it is that lies beneath the murky waters of the lake.

THE OLD CURIOSITY SHOP

25 November 1962, Sunday, 5:00–5:30pm, BBC, 13 episodes, drama, classic, British, 19th century
BBCtv
Pr: Douglas Allen
Dir: Joan Craft
Wtr: Constance Cox
Based on Charles Dickens
Cast: Mrs. Jiniwin – Peggyann Clifford
    Kit Nubbles – Ronald Cunliffe
    Nell Trent – Michele Dotrice
    Mrs. Quilp – Sheila Shand Gibbs
    Grandfather – Oliver Johnston
    Dick Swiveller – Anton Rodgers
    Daniel Quilp – Patrick Troughton

Orphaned Nell Trent is devoted to her Grandfather, who borrows money from evil Daniel Quilp to see to Nell's needs. When Grandfather gambles away all he owns, Quilp takes over the elderly man's Old Curiosity Shop, leaving Nell and her Grandfather to roam the countryside as beggars. Grandfather's brother, Kit Nubbles, searches for the pair and eventually finds them, but it is not soon enough to save Nell and Grandfather from coming to tragic ends.

DIMENSION OF FEAR

5 January 1963, Saturday, 10:10–10:55pm, ITV, 4 episodes, science fiction, British, future
ABC Network
Pr: Guy Verney
Dir: Don Leaver
Wtr: John Lucarotti
Based on story by Berkley Mather
Cast: **Colonel Alan Renton – Robin Bailey**
    Dr. Barbara Finch – Katharine Blake
    Inspector Truick – Richard Coleman
    Professor Meredith – Peter Copley
    Astronaut – Michael Graham Cox
    Dr. Read – Peter Vaughan

A space flight gone awry leads to the

sudden death of an astronaut, whose brain apparently has been taken over by a strange force . . . leading him to plummet his capsule in a small English village. There, the power again asserts its dangerous force, this time on Earth, and it is up to a group of scientists to contain the power and keep word of its presence from leaking to the public, in order to avert wide-scale panic.

THE CHEM. LAB. MYSTERY

5 January 1963, Saturday, 5:25–5:55pm, BBC, 6 episodes, mystery, family, British, contemporary
BBCtv
Pr: Joy Harington
Designed by Stewart Marshall
Wtr: David Turner
Cast: Bugs – Roy Holder
　　　Mrs. Dukes – Dandy Nichols
　　　Mad Willy – Peter Sallis
　　　Headmaster – Kevin Stoney
　　　Twink – Derek Williams
　　　Mr. Lions – Manning Wilson

During a science lesson being given by Mr. Lions in a Midlands comprehensive school, one of the students, form dunce Twink in fact, finds gold among the mixture in his test tube. Has the lad discovered a secret formula . . . or are there more sinister elements in the mix?

THE DESPERATE PEOPLE

24 February 1963, Sunday, 4:55–5:20pm, BBC, 6 episodes, thriller, British, contemporary
BBCtv
Pr: Alan Bromly
Designed by Roy Oxley
Wtr: Francis Durbridge
Cast: **Detective Inspector Hyde – Hugh Cross**
　　　Vanessa Curtis – June Ellis
　　　Philip Martin – Philip Guard
　　　Dr. Linderhof – Gerard Heinz
　　　Ruth Sanders – Renny Lister
　　　Larry Martin – Denis Quilley

Photographer Larry Martin's brother Philip arrives for a visit while on leave from the Armed Forces in Germany. But soon after his brother's arrival, Larry Martin is thrust into a series of mysterious adventures which may or may not involve international espionage . . . and murder.

Featured under the program banner of "Francis Durbridge Presents . . ."

JANE EYRE

7 April 1963, Sunday, 5:45–6:10pm, BBC, 6 episodes, drama, classic, British, 19th century
BBCtv
Pr: Douglas Allen
Dir: Rex Tucker
Wtr: Constance Cox
Based on Charlotte Brontë
Cast: Mrs. Fairfax – Elsie Arnold
　　　Jane Eyre – Ann Bell
　　　Jane Eyre (as a child) – Rachel Clay
　　　Mr. Rochester – Richard Leech
　　　Blanche Ingram – Justine Lord
　　　Grace Poole – Nan Marriott-Watson
　　　Adele – Elaine Pratt
　　　St. John Rivers – William Russell

After eight years at the grim Lowood orphanage, Jane Eyre is hired as governess at Thornfield Hall, where she falls in love with her employer, the formidable Mr. Rochester. Fate intervenes in a number of painful ways – most notably in the revelation that Rochester is already married – before Jane and Rochester are able to be happily united.

EPITAPH FOR A SPY

19 May 1963, Sunday, 5:40–6:10pm, BBC, 4 episodes, thriller, British, contemporary
BBCtv
Pr: Dorothea Brooking
Dir: Dorothea Brooking
Wtr: Elaine Morgan
Based on Eric Ambler
Cast: Major Clandon-Hartley – William Fox
　　　Joseph Vadassy – Colin Jeavons
　　　Mary Skelton – Janet McIntire
　　　M. Duclos – Henry Oscar
　　　Mrs. Clandon-Hartley – Hana Pravda
　　　Warren Skelton – Burnell Tucker

Language teacher Joseph Vadassy arrives

in the South of France on holiday, and soon unwittingly finds himself caught up in the espionage and intrigue surrounding several of the guests at the hotel where he is staying.

To update the story from both the 1938 novel and the 1953 serial, the action here was moved to the 1960s.

LORNA DOONE

16 June 1963, Sunday, 5:45–6:10pm, BBC, 11 episodes, drama, classic, British, 17th century
BBCtv
Pr: Douglas Allen
Dir: Brandon Acton-Bond
Wtr: Constance Cox, from a treatment by A.R. Rawlinson
Based on R.D. Blackmore
Cast: Mrs. Ridd – Jean Anderson
       Tom Faggus – John Bennett
       Sir Ensor Doone – Carl Bernard
       Counsellor Doone – Terence de Marney
       Carver Doone – Andrew Faulds
       Lorna Doone – Jane Merrow
       Jeremy Stickles – Nigel Stock
       John Ridd – Bill Travers

In Exmoor in the 17th century, the Doones, an outlaw clan, have long been known to terrorize the surrounding country. Moorland farmer John Ridd seeks to crush the wild brigands, who were responsible for the death of his father, but in the meantime he falls in love with Lorna, "queen" of the Doones.

NO CLOAK – NO DAGGER

1 September 1963, Sunday, 5:40–6:10pm, BBC, 6 episodes, thriller, British, contemporary
BBCtv
Pr: Christopher Barry
Dir: Christopher Barry
Wtr: Duncan Ross
Cast: **Pat Penmore – Caroline Blakiston**
       Ian Lambart – William Franklyn
       Detective Chief Superintendent Gage – Cyril Luckham
       Emma Cresswell – Lana Morris
       Professor Penmore – Keith Pyott
       Trev – Patrick Troughton

When physicist Penmore is imprisoned for selling scientific secrets to the East Germans, his daughter Pat and assistant Emma set out to prove his innocence. Pat's fiancé, writer Ian Lambart, gets all-too involved when he is approached to join an undercover Special Forces branch of the police, leading him to follow a dangerous spy trail which ends at ancient caves in Cornwall.

SWALLOWS AND AMAZONS

3 September 1963, Tuesday, 5:00–5:25pm, BBC, 6 episodes, drama, family, British, 20th century
Windsor Films Production for BBCtv
Pr: John Robins
Dir: Peter Saunders
Wtr: Anthony Steven
Based on Arthur Ransome
Cast: Peggy Blackett – Paula Boyd
       Nancy Blackett – Amanda Coxell
       Kitty Walker – Susan George
       Mrs. Walker – Mary Kenton
       John Walker – David Lott
       Captain Flint – John Paul
       Susan Walker – Siobhan Taylor
       Roger Walker – Shane Younger

The Walker family goes on a camping and sailing holiday in the Lake District in 1929, where they encounter the aggressive Blackett girls who are travelling with their uncle, and whose sailboat is appropriately named the Amazon; together the children have sailing adventures which cause no small amount of concern for the adults.

KIDNAPPED

13 October 1963, Sunday, 5:00–5:25pm, BBC, 12 episodes, drama, classic, adventure, Scottish, 18th century
BBCtv
Pr: Campbell Logan
Dir: Gerard Glaister
Wtr: Joy Harington
Based on *Kidnapped* and *Catriona* by Robert Louis Stevenson
Cast: **David Balfour – Ian Cullen**
       Catriona – Gay Hamilton

Ebenezer Balfour – Duncan Macrae
James More Drummond – Leonard Maguire
Alan Breck – Roddy McMillan
Captain Hoseason – Ewan Roberts
Ransome – John Wainwright

Young David Balfour is cheated of his birthright and cast adrift in Scotland in the middle of the 18th century, when Jacobite feelings are still easily stirred. Mercurial Highlander Alan Breck takes David under his wing, and the two are pursued by both law and outlaw until David is finally able to outwit his uncle. Then the tables are turned and David must step forward and rescue Breck, jeopardizing his new romance with the beautiful Catriona.

This was the third production of Joy Harington's dramatization, this time combining both *Kidnapped* and its sequel, *Catriona*.

MARTIN CHUZZLEWIT

19 January 1964, Sunday, 4:55–5:20pm, BBC, 13 episodes, drama, classic, British, 19th century
BBCtv
Pr: Campbell Logan
Dir: Joan Craft
Wtr: Constance Cox
Based on Charles Dickens
Cast: Mrs. Gamp – Angela Baddeley
Montague Tigg – Peter Bayliss
Anthony Chuzzlewit – Carl Bernard
John Westlock – Jeremy Burnham
Martin Chuzzlewit the elder – Barry Jones
Charity – Rosalind Knight
Mercy – Anna Middleton
Pecksniff – Richard Pearson
Tom Pinch – John Quentin
Martin Chuzzlewit – Gary Raymond
Mary Graham – Ilona Rodgers
Jonas Chuzzlewit – Alex Scott
Ruth Pinch – Fern Warner

Selfish young Martin Chuzzlewit comes of age and learns valuable lessons, best summed up in the novel's full title: *The Life and Adventures of Martin Chuzzlewit, His relatives, friends and enemies, Comprising all His Wills and His Ways, with a Historical record of what he did and what he didn't, Shewing moreover who inherited the Family Plate, who came in for the Silver Spoons, and who for the Wooden Ladles, The Whole forms a complete guide to the House of Chuzzlewit.*

RUPERT OF HENTZAU

19 April 1964, Sunday, 5:30–5:55pm, BBC, 6 episodes, drama, European, 19th century
BBCtv
Pr: Campbell Logan
Dir: Gerald Blake
Wtr: Donald Wilson
Based on Anthony Hope
Cast: King Rudolf/Rudolf Rassendyll – George Baker
Fritz von Tarlenheim – Tristram Jellinek
Colonel Sapt – John Phillips
Queen Flavia – Barbara Shelley
Rupert of Hentzau – Peter Wyngarde

In this sequel to *The Prisoner of Zenda*, Rupert of Hentzau returns secretly to his home of Ruritania after being banished for treason, where he again attempts to overthrow the monarch. Rupert fails in his attempt and is himself killed by Rudolf Rassendyll, thus enabling Ruritania to return to its former, now stable monarchy.

MADAME BOVARY

25 April 1964, Saturday, 8:00–8:45pm, BBC2, 4 episodes, drama, classic, French, 19th century
BBCtv
Pr: Douglas Allen
Dir: Rex Tucker
Wtr: Giles Cooper
Based on Gustave Flaubert
Cast: Homsais – Gerald Cross
Rodolphe – Nigel Davenport
Charles Bovary – Glynn Edwards
L'heureux – Anthony Jacobs
Leon Dupuis – Peter Kriss
Madame Bovary – Nan Marriott-Watson
Emma Bovary – Nyree Dawn Porter

Emma Bovary, bored and frustrated with

life in provincial Normandy with her staid physician husband, dreams of a life of luxury and romance, feeding this fantasy with extravagant purchases the family cannot afford. While wending her way to backruptcy Emma also courts disaster as she attempts to hold on to successive lovers. In the end it is all too much for her, and Emma commits suicide.

The first serial telecast on the BBC2 network, which began broadcasting on 21 April.

MELISSA

26 April 1964, Sunday, 9:55–10:20pm, BBC2, 6 episodes, thriller, British, contemporary
BBCtv
Pr: Alan Bromly
Dir: Alan Bromly
Wtr: Francis Durbridge
Cast: **Guy Foster – Tony Britton**
Paula Hepburn – Helen Christie
Melissa Foster – Petra Davies
Felix Hepburn – Kerry Jordan
Don Page – Brian McDermott
Chief Inspector Carter – Brian Wilde

Journalist Guy Foster wants nothing more than to settle down quietly and write books, but this dream is quickly shattered when Foster is swept up in a wave of crime and intrigue after his wife Melissa is killed in an "accident" that may well have been directed at someone else.

Featured under the program banner of "Francis Durbridge Presents . . . "

ANN VERONICA

23 May 1964, Saturday, 8:00–8:45pm, BBC2, 4 episodes, drama, British, 20th century
BBCtv
Pr: Douglas Allen
Dir: Christopher Barry
Wtr: Denis Constanduros
Based on H.G. Wells
Cast: Mr. Stanley – Laurence Hardy
Hubert Manning – Barrie Ingham
Miss Stanley – Gillian Lind
Ann Veronica – Rosemary Nicols

This Edwardian drama, set against the backdrop of the suffragette movement, finds young and vivacious Ann Veronica resenting the circumstances which force a woman to be economically dependent on marriage to a man chosen for her; she subsequently shocks society and convention by making her own, independent choices.

SILAS MARNER

31 May 1964, Sunday, 5:35–6:00pm, BBC1, 6 episodes, drama, classic, British, 19th century
BBCtv
Pr: Campbell Logan
Dir: Harold Clayton
Wtr: Constance Cox
Based on George Eliot
Cast: Sarah Weston – Anna Cropper
Deacon Anderson – Julian d'Albie
Brother Eben – Colin Douglas
Molly – Camilla Hasse
Silas Marner – David Markham
Eppie – Natasha Pyne
Godfrey Cass – Moray Watson
Elder Johnson – Lockwood West

Weaver Silas Marner, a shy and religious man in the rural Midlands, is betrayed by those he thought were his friends just as he is to become engaged and embark on a lifetime of simple contentment. These cruel acts turn Marner into a recluse and a miser, but his life turns around yet again when he loses his gold and finds an abandoned baby girl.

MARY BARTON

20 June 1964, Saturday, 8:15–9:50pm, BBC2, 4 episodes, drama, British, 19th century
BBCtv
Pr: Douglas Allen
Dir: Michael Imison
Wtr: Elaine Morgan
Based on Mrs. Elizabeth Gaskell
Cast: **John Barton – George A. Cooper**
Mary Barton – Lois Daine
Mrs. Carson – Eileen Dale
Mr. Carson – Cyril Luckham
Harry Carson – Patrick Mower
Will – Brian Peck

Jem Wilson – Barry Warren

Mary Barton comes of age in Manchester in the mid-19th century, when famine rages in Ireland and England is in the midst of the rise and fall of the Chartist movement. Mary is caught in the middle of love affairs in and out of her own class and her Chartist father's tragic stand for workers' rights.

THE MIDNIGHT MEN

21 June 1964, Sunday, 9:55–10:25pm, BBC2, 6 episodes, thriller, European, 20th century
BBCtv
Pr: Rudolph Cartier
Dir: Rudolph Cartier
Wtr: Victor Canning
Cast: **General Plaski, Chief of Police – Bernard Archard**
Veronique Vranja – Eva Bartok
Tillio Grunditz – Derek Francis
King Alexander – Joseph Furst
Mayo Khunz – Andrew Keir

In the Balkans in 1913, a group of underground freedom fighters sets out to overthrow the tyrannical police state. Farmer Mayo Khunz, who has never before been involved in anything political, is approached to play a key role in the plot, and the naïve man is unaware until too late of the danger of his assignment.

The Midnight Men was novelist Canning's first serial written expressly for television.

SMUGGLER'S BAY

12 July 1964, Sunday, 5:35–6:05pm, BBC1, 6 episodes, drama, British, 18th century
BBCtv
Pr: Campbell Logan
Dir: Christopher Barry
Wtr: Bob Stuart
Based on *Moonfleet* by J. Meade Falkner
Cast: Magistrate Maskew – Paul Curran
John Trenchard – Frazer Hines
Grace Maskew – Suzanne Neve
Elzevir Block – John Phillips
Ratsey – Patrick Troughton

In 18th-century Dorset, orphaned John Trenchard finds a locket in the Moonfleet churchyard. Searching for the answer to the locket's mysterious inscription, John, accompanied by kindly innkeeper Elzevir Block, sets out on a series of adventures on land and sea, which culminate in the discovery of a coffin buried beneath Moonfleet Church.

WITCH WOOD

18 July 1964, Saturday, 8:15–9:45pm, BBC2, 4 episodes, thriller, Scottish, 17th century
BBCtv
Pr: Douglas Allen
Dir: Michael Leeston-Smith
Wtr: Donald Wilson
Based on John Buchan
Cast: Katrine Yester – Isobel Black
David Sempill – Donald Douglas
King Charles I – Stephen MacDonald
Marquis of Montrose – Fulton Mackay
Nicholas Hawkshaw – Roddy McMillan
Mark Kerr – Tom Watson

In Scotland during the Civil War, David Sempill, a young minister of the Presbyterian Kirk newly arrived in the area, must do battle against the forces of black magic which threaten his congregants. At the same time, the Marquis of Montrose embarks on his desperate mission to reclaim Scotland for the royalist cause.

THE SLEEPER

2 August 1964, Sunday, 10:25–10:50pm, BBC2, 6 episodes, thriller, British/European, contemporary
BBCtv
Pr: Alan Bromly
Dir: Alan Bromly
Wtr: Lindsay Hardy
Cast: Colonel Welenski – Alexis Chesnakov
Anne Romilly – Jennifer Daniel
General Zukoyan – Michael Gover
Peter Dibden – Gerald Harper
Sir John – Cyril Luckham
Simon Romilly – Anthony Parker

Peter Dibden is a "sleeper" – a top-level secret agent who is kept inactive until a major incident develops. Dibden is called into action when an airplane *en route* to Moscow crashes in Poland, and the diaries of the American admiral on board disappear. Architect Simon Romilly is innocently caught in the middle of the intrigue by virtue of his unfortunate choice of a holiday locale – Warsaw.

JUDITH PARIS

15 August 1964, Saturday, 8:15–9:30pm, BBC2, 4 episodes, drama, British, 19th century
BBCtv
Pr: Douglas Allen
Dir: Joan Craft
Wtr: Constance Cox
Based on Hugh Walpole
Cast: **Georges Paris – Edward Brayshaw**
Osbaldistone – Bryon O'Leary
Judith Paris – Nyree Dawn Porter
David Herries – John Sharp
Sarah Herries – Peggy Thorpe-Bates

Judith Paris is the daughter of Rogue Herries, but her father dies when Judith is born. She marries young, to gambler Georges Paris, and has a haphazard existence in Cumberland and London. This climaxes in Judith's long exile from Cumberland and her return to further chances and changes, the most unforeseen of which sends Judith to Paris and gives her life new direction and purpose.

THE CHILDREN OF THE NEW FOREST

23 August 1964, Sunday, 5:35–6:00pm, BBC1, 6 episodes, drama, family, British, 17th century
BBCtv
Designed by Desmond Chinn
Dir: Brandon Acton-Bond
Wtr: Anthony Coburn
Based on Captain Frederick Marryat
Cast: Roundhead Heatherstone – Bernard Archard
Edward Beverley – Richard Arthure
King Charles II – David Cargill
Humphrey Beverley – Brendan Collins
Alice Beverley – Petra Markham
Edith Beverley – Melanie Parr
Jacob Armitage – Norman Tyrrell
Patience Heatherstone – Kara Wilson

During the Civil War, the four orphaned children of famed Cavalier leader Colonel Beverley are forced to live in hiding in the New Forest, where they are disguised as peasants and sheltered by old and loyal forester Jacob Armitage, who shields the youngsters by pretending they are his grandchildren. Eldest Beverley son Edward grows to become a great fighter himself, and falls in love with Patience Heatherstone, daughter of the Intendant of the New Forest.

THE ORDEAL OF RICHARD FEVEREL

12 September 1964, Saturday, 8:40–9:20pm, BBC2, 4 episodes, drama, British, 19th century
BBCtv
Pr: Douglas Allen
Dir: Rex Tucker
Wtr: Rosemary Anne Sisson
Based on George Meredith
Cast: **Sir Austin Feverel – Hugh Burden**
Adrian Harley – David Cargill
Lucy – Anna Carteret
Clare Forey – Anne Castaldini
Bessy Berry – Betty Hardy
Richard Feverel – Barry Justice
Richard Feverel (as a child) – Nicholas Roylance

Richard Feverel is brought up in sheltered manner by his eccentric and misogynistic father, Sir Austin, who fully expects his educational methods to produce a "perfect" adult specimen. But human nature interjects when Richard falls in love with Lucy, a girl seen as beneath his station; their union has profound and tragic effects on all involved.

THE MASSINGHAM AFFAIR

12 September 1964, Saturday, 10:05–10:35pm, BBC2, 6 episodes, thriller, British, 19th century
BBCtv
Pr: Paddy Russell

Dir: Paddy Russell
Wtr: Rex Tucker
Based on Edward Grierson
Cast: Charlotte Verney – Eileen Atkins
Justin Derry – Lyndon Brook
Superintendent Blair – Andrew Keir
Jean Kelly – Renny Lister
Pat Milligan – George Little
Mr. Gilmore – Norman Rodway
Georgina Deverel – Patsy Rowlands
Mick Kelly – Barry Wilsher

In rural Yorkshire in the 1890s, a policeman is killed by a gang of poachers. Soon afterwards, in the same area, a clergyman is shot and wounded. Two men are arrested and charged with both crimes, but Justin Derry, a young law clerk, doubts the evidence and endeavours to learn the entire truth, a decision which leads to great upheaval in Derry's own life.

THE COUNT OF MONTE CRISTO

4 October 1964, Sunday, 5:30–5:55pm, BBC1, 12 episodes, drama, classic, French, 19th century
BBCtv
Pr: Campbell Logan
Dir: Peter Hammond
Wtr: Anthony Steven
Based on Alexandre Dumas
Cast: **Edmond Dantes – Alan Badel**
Madame Danglars – Rosalie Crutchley
de Villefort – Michael Gough
Fernand Mondego – Philip Madoc
Morrel – Anthony Newlands
Valentine – Anna Palk
Mercedes – Natasha Parry
Danglars – Morris Perry
Haydee – Valerie Sarruf

Seaman Edmond Dantes returns home, where he is charged falsely with treason and sentenced to life imprisonment. Dantes escapes and travels to the island of Monte Cristo, where he discovers a great fortune – funds he uses to return home as the mysterious Count and seek revenge against those who had sought to destroy him.

THE OLD WIVES' TALE

8 October 1964, Saturday, 8:45–9:30, BBC2, 5 episodes, drama, British, 19th–20th century
BBCtv
Pr: Douglas Allen
Dir: David Giles
Wtr: Michael Voysey
Based on Arnold Bennett
Cast: Gerald Scales – Philip Bond
Samuel Povey – John Carson
Constance Baines – Frances Cuka
Cyril – Frazer Hines
Mrs. Baines – Alison Leggatt
Sophia Baines – Lana Morris
Mr. Baines – Clifford Parrish

Constance and Sophia Baines are the daughters of a draper in the Potteries town of Bursley in the mid-nineteenth century. Constance is steady, has a common-sense approach to life and remains in Bursley after she marries Samuel Povey. But Sophia, who has a more romantic nature, elopes to Paris, where she is jilted; Sophia settles in Paris and runs a *pension*, but ultimately returns to Bursley in her retirement, where she and widowed Constance are reunited for the remainder of their lives.

CURTAIN OF FEAR

28 October 1964, Wednesday, 10:05–10:35pm, BBC2, 6 episodes, thriller, British, contemporary
BBCtv
Pr: Gerald Blake
Dir: Gerald Blake
Wtr: Victor Canning
Cast: **Stewart Caxton – George Baker**
Peter Linton – John Breslin
Hans Liebert – William Franklyn
Tannikov – George Pravda
Clare Linton – Colette Wilde

Brother and sister Peter and Clare Linton perform a hypnotism act, but one night, while performing in a cabaret, they unwittingly become centrally involved in an espionage dragnet when a man is murdered, a coded message disappears . . . and Clare somehow has all the answers locked in her mind. Still in a hypnotic state, Clare is kidnapped, and it is up to Peter and Clare's fiancé, Stewart Caxton, to find and save her before it is too late.

VICTORIA REGINA

13 November 1964, Friday, 9:10–10:00pm, ITV, 4 episodes, drama, biographical, historical, British, 19th century
Granada Television
Pr: Peter Wildeblood
Dir: Stuart Latham
Wtr: Peter Wildeblood
Based on play by Laurence Housman
Cast: Benjamin Disraeli – Max Adrian
Archbishop of Canterbury – Geoffrey Dunn
Prince Albert – Joachin Hansen
Queen Victoria – Patricia Routledge

Based on the collected plays by Housman, an illustration of four pivotal chapters of Victoria's life: as teenaged Queen ascending the throne in 1837, adoring wife of Prince Albert, young widow devastated by the death of her consort in 1861, and celebrated monarch at her Diamond Jubilee in 1887.

ESTHER WATERS

14 November 1964, Saturday, 8:40–9:25pm, BBC2, 4 episodes, drama, British, 19th century
BBCtv
Pr: Douglas Allen
Dir: James Cellan Jones
Wtr: Harry Green
Based on George Moore
Cast: **William Latch – John Bennett**
Fred Parsons – Gordon Gostelow
Mrs. Barfield – Pauline Letts
Esther Waters – Meg Wynn Owen
Miss Rice – Anne Ridler
Margaret Gale – Gwendolyn Watts

Esther Waters flees her drunken stepfather and enters service as a kitchen maid at the Barfield racing stables. Illiterate and innocent, she is caught between the influence of the servants and her strict, religious mistress, Mrs. Barfield, and is also caught between two men: William Latch, the disreputable-but-disarming father of her illegitimate son, and Fred Parsons, the Salvation Army trumpeter who offers Esther a secure, if unspectacular future. Esther eventually marries Latch, but he dies, leaving Esther penniless; she returns to Mrs. Barfield, who is also impoverished, but with whom Esther finds at last a measure of peace.

RING OUT AN ALIBI

25 November 1964, Wednesday, 6:30–6:55pm, BBC2, 6 episodes, mystery, Welsh, contemporary
BBCtv/Wales
Pr: Arthur Williams
Designed by Colin Shaw
Wtr: Eynon Evans
Cast: Sergeant Bowen – D.L. Davies
Detective Inspector Enoch Probert – Eynon Evans
Rhys Charles – David Garfield
Hannah Mathias – Nesta Harris
Elinor Charles – Patricia Mort
Watty – Ray Smith

Detective Inspector Enoch Probert is called to the Welsh village of Pandymawr to investigate a series of shootings which are, unknown as yet to Probert, linked with the murderous plan of Rhys and Elinor Charles – who are behind the shootings and are deliberately creating a fictional shooter, in order to provide themselves with an alibi when they commit their intended killing.

THE BROTHERS KARAMAZOV

13 December 1964, Sunday, 10:05–10:50pm, BBC2, 6 episodes, drama, classic, Russian, 19th century
BBCtv/Scotland
Pr: Douglas Allen
Dir: Alan Bridges
Wtr: Frederick Gotfurt
Based on Fyodor Dostoevsky
Cast: Lise – Jane Asher
Mitya Karamazov – Ray Barrett
Fyodor Karamazov – John Barrie
Ivan Karamazov – Lyndon Brook
Alyoska Karamazov – Nicholas Pennell
Father Zossima – Frederick Piper
Smerdyakov – Alan Rowe

Grushenka – Judith Stott

Tsarist Russia in the middle of the 19th century is the home of the Karamazovs. Mitya, the eldest son of Fyodor Karamazov, is an arrogant ex-officer; his half-brothers Ivan and Alyoska are more serious minded. Mitya competes with his father, Fyodor, for the attentions of Grushenka, a beautiful prostitute, and Ivan attempts to mediate between the two. When Fyodor is murdered, Mitya is tried for the crime, although it seems clear that all the sons had reasons to wish their father dead.

HIT AND RUN

18 January 1965, Monday, 10:00–10:30pm, BBC2, 4 episodes, thriller, British, contemporary
BBCtv
Pr: Paddy Russell
Dir: Paddy Russell
Wtr: Evelyn Frazer
Based on Jeffrey Ashford
Cast: Georgina Prestley – Rosalie Crutchley
Detective Inspector Kleenan – William Dexter
Gerald Prestley – Joseph O'Conor
Steve Prestley – John Tillinger

Solicitor Gerald Prestley discovers that his car was used to commit a crime – and not only is he being blackmailed by a witness, he's also considered a suspect by the police.

NIGHT TRAIN TO SURBITON

27 January 1965, Wednesday, 9:15–9:40pm, BBC2, 6 episodes, thriller, British, contemporary
BBCtv
Pr: Bryan Sears
Designed by Richard Hunt
Wtr: John Chapman
Cast: Mrs. Banks – Fabia Drake
Stella Craine – Christine Finn
Matthew Pilbeam – Peter Jones
Guy Bretherton – Nicholas Parsons
Chief Inspector – Robert Raglan
Esther Pilbeam – Eleanor Summerfield

Businessmen Matthew Pilbeam and Guy Bretherton discover a corpse on the night train to Surbiton. When the body mysteriously disappears no one believes the men's claims about the corpse. Later, they discover that Guy has mistakenly picked up the dead man's briefcase, and their quest to find out his identity gets them unwittingly involved with a master criminal's quest to destroy the world.

THE AMBASSADORS

31 January 1965, Sunday, 10:05–10:50pm, BBC2, 3 episodes, drama, classic, American, 20th century
BBCtv
Pr: Douglas Allen
Dir: James Cellan Jones
Wtr: Denis Constanduros
Based on Henry James
Cast: Waymarsh – David Bauer
Lambert Strether – Alan Gifford
Miss Maria Gostrey – Bethel Leslie
Sarah Pocock – Lois Maxwell
Chadwick Newsome – Harvey Spencer
Little Bilham – Roy Stephens
Madame de Vionnet – Lila Valmere

New Englander Lambert Strether journeys to Paris at the height of the "belle epoque" on a mission to deliver Chadwick Newsome back to his mother in the States. Strether meets expatriate American Miss Maria Gostrey, who introduces him to European society – and soon Strether is none-too enthusiastic about his assignment. But ultimately Strether remains detached from personal involvement, unable to participate fully in life on either shore, and returns to his solitary existence in Massachusetts.

RELUCTANT BANDIT

15 February 1965, Monday, 10:00–10:30pm, BBC2, 5 episodes, thriller, British/Italian, contemporary
BBCtv
Pr: Paddy Russell
Dir: Paddy Russell
Wtr: Colin Morris
Cast: Luigi – Michael Balfour
Robert North – William Dexter
Diana Craven – Patricia Haines

Mr. Carson – **William Mervyn**
Peppino – George Pastell
Prince Giorgio – Derek Sydney

Ex-British Army Officer Robert North returns on holiday to the Sicilian village he helped liberate after World War II and unwittingly becomes embroiled in Mafia intrigue.

THE MILL ON THE FLOSS

21 February 1965, Sunday, 8:50–9:35pm, BBC2, 4 episodes, drama, classic, British, 19th century
BBCtv
Pr: Douglas Allen
Dir: Rex Tucker
Wtr: Rosemary Anne Sisson
Based on George Eliot
Cast: Lucy Deane – Annette Andre
    Maggie Tulliver – Jane Asher
    Stephen Guest – Edward de Souza
    Mrs. Tulliver – Betty Hardy
    Tom Tulliver – Barry Justice
    Philip Wakem – Peter Kriss
    Mr. Tulliver – Joseph O'Conor

In the early Victorian countryside, sensitive Maggie Tulliver is devoted to her rigid brother Tom, who does not respond in kind. Hurt by his rejection, she turns to Philip Wakem, the son of her father's enemy, but is forced away from him by family pressure. Another attempt at romance fails, and an unhappy Maggie is estranged from all – until she and brother Tom are reunited in death, when the river Floss floods and both are drowned.

ALEXANDER GRAHAM BELL

28 February 1965, Sunday, 5:35–6:00pm, BBC1, 6 episodes, drama, biographical, historical, Scottish, 19th century
BBCtv
Pr: Campbell Logan
Dir: Julia Smith
Wtr: Alistair Bell
Based on Lyon Todd
Cast: Mabel Hubbard – Francesca Annis
    Mrs. Bell – Barbara Cavan
    Thomas Watson – Clive Endersby
    Alexander Graham Bell – **Alec McCowen**
    Professor Bell – John Phillips

The story of the man who invented the telephone begins in Edinburgh in 1870 when Alexander Graham Bell gets his first start in communications by training deaf people to speak, read and write. Bell himself suffers from ill health, but overcomes his personal difficulties to change for all time the way people communicate with one another.

A MAN CALLED HARRY BRENT

22 March 1965, Monday, 9:15–9:40pm, BBC2, 6 episodes, thriller, British, contemporary
BBCtv
Pr: Alan Bromly
Dir: Alan Bromly
Wtr: Francis Durbridge
Cast: **Harry Brent – Edward Brayshaw**
    Eric Vyner – Bernard Brown
    Carol Vyner – Jennifer Daniel
    Detective Inspector Alan Milton – Gerald Harper
    Barbara Smith – Audine Leith
    Jacqueline Dawson – Judy Parfitt
    Harold Tolly – Brian Wilde

When travel agent Harry Brent meets Carol Vyner, the mutual attraction is so strong that Carol soon breaks off her engagement to Detective Inspector Alan Milton. But Carol's encounters with Brent become increasingly dangerous, which arouses the suspicions of Milton as to Brent's true motives.

Featured under the program banner of "Francis Durbridge Presents . . . "

A TALE OF TWO CITIES

11 April 1965, Sunday, 5:35–6:00pm, BBC1, 10 episodes, drama, classic, British/French, 18th century
BBCtv
Pr: Campbell Logan
Dir: Joan Craft
Wtr: Constance Cox
Based on Charles Dickens
Cast: Madame Defarge – Rosalie Crutchley
    Lucie Manette – Kika Markham

Charles Darnay – Nicholas Pennell
Dr. Manette – Patrick Troughton
Sydney Carton – John Wood

Dickens' classic of the French Revolution tells of dissolute barrister Sydney Carton's discovery of his own idealism and his redemption through self-sacrifice, when he gives his own life in order to save that of aristocrat Charles Darnay.

CONTRACT TO KILL

3 May 1965, Monday, 9:15–9:40pm, BBC2, 6 episodes, thriller, British, contemporary
BBCtv
Pr: Alan Bromly
Dir: Peter Hammond
Wtr: Victor Canning
Cast: Maria Galen – Pauline Boty
       Madame Charlustin – Violet Farebrother
       Luke Childs – Jeremy Kemp
       Pierre Heradot – Godfrey Quigley

Madame Charlustin remains bent on revenge against the Nazi who killed her son during World War II. S.S. Officer Carl Buhler is officially dead, but Madame does not believe this, so she hires British freelance undercover agent Luke Childs to find him. He discovers that others are also seeking the truth about Buhler, a situation which quickly escalates in intrigue and danger.

THE SCARLET AND THE BLACK

9 May 1965, Sunday, 9:15–10:00pm, BBC2, 5 episodes, drama, classic, French, 19th century
BBCtv/Scotland
Pr: Douglas Allen
Dir: James Cellan Jones
Wtr: Michael Barry
Based on Stendhal
Cast: Father Pirard – Hamilton Dyce
       Mathilde de la Mole – Karin Fernald
       Monsieur de Renal – Emrys Jones
       Julien Sorel – John Stride
       Louise de Renal – June Tobin

In post-Napoleonic France, Julien Sorel, the younger son of a carpenter, sets out to climb the social ladder, despite his lack of hereditary advantages, relying solely on his intelligence and ambition. Julien determines to rise through the army (the "scarlet") and the church (the "black"), at the same time seducing the most eligible young women in Paris . . . and some who are not so eligible.

THE RISE AND FALL OF CESAR BIROTTEAU

13 June 1965, Sunday, 7:55–8:40pm, BBC2, 4 episodes, drama, classic, French, 19th century
BBCtv
Pr: Douglas Allen
Dir: Michael Barry
Wtr: Anthony Steven
Based on Honoré de Balzac
Cast: Césarine Birotteau – Isobel Black
       Anselme Popinot – John Noakes
       César Birotteau – Morris Perry
       Ferdinand du Tillet – Alan Rowe
       Constance Birotteau – Gwen Watford

In 1816, perfumier César Birotteau is the proprietor of a shop in the fashionable Rue St. Honoré. But one of his assistants, Ferdinand du Tillet, is dishonest and plots against his trusting employer, with devastating results. Birotteau has many faults, but his goodness and probity and tragic end make him a sympathetic character, even though he begs and borrows money from all directions in order to fund speculative obligations and is left penniless in the process.

THE MIND OF THE ENEMY

14 June 1965, Monday, 9:15–9:40pm, BBC2, 5 episodes, thriller, British, contemporary
BBCtv
Pr: Alan Bromly
Dir: Paddy Russell
Wtr: Michael Gilbert
Cast: Anthea Fairside – Anna Cropper
       Fortescue – Mark Dignam
       John Craven – Charles Hill
       Sir Henry Blake – Cyril Luckham
       Brian Calder – Mike Pratt
       General Fairside – John Welsh
       Gerald Gould – Manning Wilson

Solicitor Brian Calder also writes crime stories and is called upon to investigate real-life intrigue when a murdered barrister is revealed to have been working on security leakages which threaten fundamental British policies.

POISON ISLAND

20 June 1965, Sunday, 5:35–6:00pm, BBC1, 6 episodes, mystery, British, contemporary
BBCtv
Pr: Campbell Logan
Dir: Brandon Acton-Bond
Wtr: Bob Stuart
Based on Arthur Quiller-Couch
Cast: Jack Rogers – Terence Alexander
George Goodfellow – John Bown
Captain Branscombe – Michael Gwynn
Major Brooks – David Phethean
Captain Coffin – Billy Russell
Dr. Beauregard – Austin Trevor
Harry Brooks – Kit Williams

Harry Brooks begins his formal education at Mr. Stimcoe's Falmouth Academy for Backward Boys, but his real learning starts when he fortuitously assists drunken old Captain Coffin, who spins wondrous tales of the treasure which lies hidden on Poison Island.

LEGEND OF DEATH

19 July 1965, Monday, 9:30–9:55pm, BBC2, 5 episodes, thriller, British, contemporary
BBCtv
Pr: Alan Bromly
Dir: Gerald Blake
Wtr: Brian Hayles
Cast: Theodore – David Andrews
Finn – Victor Brooks
Myra Gargan – Sarah Lawson
Edward Gargan – John Phillips
Dr. Zemouron – Andrew Sachs

In a modern-day telling of the legend of Theseus, industrial tycoon Edward Gargan is surrounded by rivals determined to bring about his downfall. Gargan has been working on developing the first nuclear-powered aircraft, but the project's cost in human lives has come to sicken him: volunteers journey every year to his atomic plant on the remote island of Mitremos, but none has ever returned. Gargan decides to end the experiment, but others have more nefarious plans . . . including bringing about the end of Edward Gargan himself.

HEIRESS OF GARTH

1 August 1965, Sunday, 5:35–6:00pm, BBC1, 6 episodes, drama, British, 19th century
BBCtv
Pr: Campbell Logan
Dir: Paddy Russell
Wtr: Anthony Coburn
Based on *Ovington's Bank* by Stanley J. Weyman
Cast: **Charles Ovington – Bernard Archard**
Squire Griffin – William Mervyn
Josina Griffin – June Ritchie
Sir Charles Woosenham – John Wentworth
Clement Ovington – David Weston

In the earliest days of the Industrial Revolution, as England quickly tools up its workshops, Midland banker Charles Ovington wants to install a railway link with Manchester. But the tracks will have to pass over the land of Squire Griffin, who has little use for the new ways. The conflict between the two men becomes even more pointed when Griffin's daughter Josina falls in love with Ovington's son Clement.

MOULDED IN EARTH

26 August 1965, Thursday, 7:00–7:30pm, BBC1, 5 episodes, drama, Welsh, 19th century
BBCtv/Wales
Pr: Dafydd Gruffydd
Designed by David Butcher
Wtr: Barry Thomas
Based on Richard Vaughan
Cast: Daniel Peele – David Davies
Edwin Peele – Emrys James
Grett Ellis – Anne Lloyd
Justin Peele – Philip Madoc
Rhys Blacksmith – John Rees
Jeff Ellis – Ray Smith

John Ellis – Ieuan Rhys Williams

The story of a Welsh family feud, set in the foothills of the Black Mountains in Carmarthenshire, finds the Peele and Ellis families arguing about disputed grazing rights; their battles have split much of the parish into two factions. Tension between the two families comes to a breaking point when Edwin Peele and Grett Ellis fall in love, but what should be cause for celebration and peacemaking instead leads to tragedy.

First telecast on BBC Wales in 1964.

HEREWARD THE WAKE

12 September 1965, Sunday, 5:35–6:00pm, BBC1, 16 episodes, drama, British, 11th century
BBCtv
Pr: Campbell Logan
Dir: Peter Hammond
Wtr: Anthony Steven
Based on Charles Kingsley
Cast: William, Duke of Normandy – John Carson
        Edward the Confessor – George Howe
        Hereward the Wake – Alfred Lynch
        Martin Lightfoot – Bryan Pringle
        Lady Godiva – Dorothy Reynolds
        Earl Leofric – Tony Steedman
        Herluin – David Swift

Anglo-Saxon nobleman Hereward the Wake, son of Lady Godiva, is made an outlaw at the end of the reign of Edward the Confessor. He wanders the world on a series of adventures, but returns from his journeying to Cornwall, Ireland and Flanders to lead a gallant stand against Duke William of Normandy.

FOR WHOM THE BELL TOLLS

2 October 1965, Saturday, 8:00–8:45pm, BBC2, 4 episodes, drama, classic, American, 20th century
BBCtv
Pr: Douglas Allen
Dir: Rex Tucker
Wtr: Giles Cooper
Based on Ernest Hemingway
Cast: **Maria – Ann Bell**
        Pablo – Glynn Edwards
        Pilar – Joan Miller
        Robert Jordan – John Ronane

The Spanish Civil War seen through the eyes of idealistic American Robert Jordan, who volunteers to fight with a band of Republican forces – led by Pablo and his wife Pilar – and goes on a treacherous mission to destroy a strategically-placed bridge.

AN ENEMY OF THE STATE

17 October 1965, Sunday, 10:00–10:25pm, BBC2, 6 episodes, thriller, British, contemporary
BBCtv
Pr: Alan Bromly
Dir: James Cellan Jones
Wtr: Ken Hughes
Cast: Colonel Rykov – James Maxwell
        Henderson – Robert Mill
        Karin – Dallia Penn
        Jennifer Sutton – Veronica Strong
        Harry Sutton – Charles Tingwell
        Harley Brooks – Frederick Treves

Electronics engineer Harry Sutton travels to Moscow on business and is drawn into an espionage plot which ends up with Harry on trial for his life, charged with stealing top-secret information.

BUDDENBROOKS

30 October 1965, Saturday, 8:30–9:15pm, BBC2, 7 episodes, drama, classic, German, 19th century
BBCtv
Pr: Douglas Allen
Dir: Michael Imison
Wtr: Jack Pulman
Based on Thomas Mann
Cast: Frau Consul – Jean Anderson
        Gerda – Annette Carrell
        Grunlich – Roger Croucher
        Consul Johann Buddenbrooks – William Fox
        Christian Buddenbrooks – Kenneth Griffith
        Hanno – Martin Norton
        Toni Buddenbrooks – Elizabeth Shepherd

Thomas Buddenbrooks – Nigel Stock

The North German Buddenbrooks family makes its fortune in the merchant trade in the 19th century, using its money to gain commercial and political influence. Johann Buddenbrooks and his three children, Thomas, Christian and Toni become involved in personal and philosophical struggles as the business changes hands and the society in which they live and work changes with the times, leading ultimately to the family's financial and spiritual decline.

THE BIG SPENDER

5 December 1965, Sunday, 10:10–10:35pm, BBC2, 6 episodes, thriller, British, contemporary
BBCtv
Pr: Alan Bromly
Dir: Richard Martin
Wtr: Margot Bennett
Cast: **Tom Masefield – John Brown**
Polly – Sheila Fearn
Chief Superintendent – Eric Longworth
Barney Simms – Henry Manning
Tessa – Suzanne Neve
Hamud Faizi – Ian Thompson

Inspector Tom Masefield becomes involved in a colleague's robbery case, and then finds himself defending his girlfriend Polly against a number of accusations. These actions bring Masefield himself under suspicion, and he seeks to clear himself before his career and his life are cut short.

EUGENIE GRANDET

18 December 1965, Saturday, 8:30–9:15pm, BBC2, 3 episodes, drama, French, 19th century
BBCtv
Pr: Douglas Allen
Dir: Rex Tucker
Wtr: John Elliot, Elizabeth Holford
Based on Honoré de Balzac
Cast: M. des Grassins – Carl Bernard
Felix Grandet – Mark Dignam
Eugénie Grandet – Valerie Gearon
Madame des Grassins – Mary Kerridge
Madame Grandet – Beatrix Lehmann
Charles Grandet – David Sumner

Rich timber merchant Felix Grandet is a miser whose personal and emotional stinginess affects not only Grandet himself, but also his wife and, most particularly, his daughter Eugénie, whose happiness, embodied in a romance with her cousin Charles, is destroyed by Grandet's tyranny.

CLAYHANGER

1 January 1966, Thursday, 9:00–10:00pm, ITV, 26 episodes, drama, British, 19th century
ATV Network
Pr: David Reid, Douglas Livingstone
Dir: John Davies, David Reid
Wtr: Douglas Livingstone
Based on *Clayhanger*, *Hilda Lessways* and *These Twain* by Arnold Bennett
Cast: **Darius Clayhanger – Harry Andrews**
Clara Clayhanger – Rosemary Blake
Tertius Ingpen – Denholm Elliott
Edwin Clayhanger – Peter McEnery
Big James – Bruce Purchase
Janet Orgreave – Louise Purnell
George Cannon – Denis Quilley
Auntie Hamps – Joyce Redman
Edwin Clayhanger (as a boy) – William Relton
Hilda Lessways – Janet Suzman
Maggie Clayhanger – Thelma Whiteley

In 1872, when Edwin Clayhanger leaves school, he is pressured by his domineering father to join the family business in the Staffordshire Potteries, but Edwin would rather pursue his dreams of being an architect. Edwin falls in love with sensual liberated woman Hilda Lessways, who is involved in a bigamous marriage to businessman George Cannon. These difficult and complicated relationships are traced over the next 25 years, as Edwin and Hilda strive to make a life together.

THE IDIOT

11 January 1966, Tuesday, 9:35–10:20pm,
BBC2, 5 episodes, drama, Russian, 19th century
BBCtv
Pr: Douglas Allen
Dir: Alan Bridges
Wtr: Leo Lehman
Based on Fyodor Dostoevsky
Cast: Rogojin – Anthony Bate
  Hypolite – Hywel Bennett
  Prince Myshkin – David Buck
  Nastasia – Adrienne Corri
  Aglaia – Suzan Farmer
  General Epanchin – Michael Goodliffe
  Gavrili – John Kelland
  Lebediev – Patrick Newell
  Lizaveta Epanchin – Ambrosine Phillpotts

Prince Myshkin, long nicknamed "the idiot" because of his idealistic, kind-hearted nature, returns to St. Petersburg after four years, where he soon finds himself caught up in the ways and means of a corrupt society, leading ultimately to his descent into genuine idiocy.

THE MAN IN THE MIRROR

15 January 1966, Saturday, 8:15–8:40pm,
BBC2, 6 episodes, thriller, British, contemporary
BBCtv
Pr: Alan Bromly
Dir: Gerald Blake
Wtr: Lindsay Hardy
Cast: Edmund Beatty – John Barron
  Maggie Jones – Wendy Gifford
  Gregor Sanders/Beaumont Sutton – Frederick Jaeger
  Stern – Philip Locke
  Peter Gilbey – Ralph Michael
  Melitza Konradis – Dallia Penn
  Nicholas Cheverski – George Pravda

Master forger Gregor Sanders is at the center of "The Ring," an international counterfeit scheme. Treasury agents recruit unemployed airline pilot Beaumont Sutton, who is a dead ringer for Sanders, to impersonate the counterfeiter as the cornerstone of a plot to undermine the illegal operation.

DAVID COPPERFIELD

16 January 1966, Sunday, 5:30–5:55pm,
BBC1, 13 episodes, drama, classic, British, 19th century
BBCtv
Pr: Campbell Logan
Dir: Joan Craft
Wtr: Vincent Tilsley
Based on Charles Dickens
Cast: Mr. Peggotty – Joss Ackland
  Mr. Micawber – Bill Fraser
  Agnes Wickfield – Hannah Gordon
  David Copperfield (as a child) – Christopher Guard
  Uriah Heep – Colin Jeavons
  Peggotty – Lila Kaye
  Mr. Murdstone – Richard Leech
  Mrs. Gummidge – Olga Lindo
  David Copperfield – Ian McKellen
  Dora – Tina Packer
  Rosa Dartle – Judy Parfitt
  Betsey Trotwood – Flora Robson
  Little Emily – Suzanne Togni

After his mother dies and he is persecuted by stepfather Mr. Murdstone, David Copperfield is on his own in London, where he meets, among others, the endearing, eccentric Mr. Micawber and the cruel, greedy Uriah Heep, all this leading to a series of adventures and misfortunes.

A FAREWELL TO ARMS

15 February 1966, Tuesday, 9:40–10:25pm,
BBC2, 3 episodes, drama, classic, American, 20th century
BBCtv
Pr: Douglas Allen
Dir: Rex Tucker
Wtr: Giles Cooper
Based on Ernest Hemingway
Cast: **Lieutenant Frederic Henry – George Hamilton**
  Lieutenant Rinaldi – Laurence Payne
  Catherine Barkley – Vanessa Redgrave
  Nurse Ferguson – Ann Rye

American Lieutenant Frederic Henry fights on the Italian front during World War I, where he meets and falls in love with English nurse Catherine Barkley. After Catherine becomes pregnant, Henry deserts in order to be with her; the two escape to Switzerland, but the child is stillborn and Catherine dies in childbirth.

A GAME OF MURDER

26 February 1966, Saturday, 8:15–8:40pm, BBC2, 6 episodes, thriller, British, contemporary
BBCtv
Pr: Alan Bromly
Dir: Alan Bromly
Wtr: Francis Durbridge
Cast: Cathy White – June Barry
Detective Inspector Ed Royce – David Burke
Detective Inspector Jack Kerry – Gerald Harper
Charles Bannister – John Harvey
Chief Superintendent Bromford – Conrad Phillips

When a once-famous athlete suddenly dies, his son Jack, a police Detective Inspector, cannot believe the death was accidental. Jack sets out on his own to follow up on his suspicions, making uncomfortable – and dangerous – discoveries about his father's private life.

Featured under the program banner of "Francis Durbridge Presents . . . "

THE HUNCHBACK OF NOTRE DAME

8 March 1966, Tuesday, 9:50–10:15pm, BBC2, 7 episodes, drama, classic, French, 15th century
BBCtv
Pr: Douglas Allen
Dir: James Cellan Jones
Wtr: Vincent Tilsley
Based on Victor Hugo
Cast: Captain Phoebus – Alex Davion
Esmeralda – Gay Hamilton
Archdeacon Frollo – James Maxwell
Pierre Gringoire – Gary Raymond
Quasimodo – Peter Woodthorpe

In Medieval Paris, Quasimodo, the deformed bellringer at the cathedral of Notre Dame, falls tragically in love with beautiful gypsy dancer Esmeralda.

TAKE A PAIR OF PRIVATE EYES

10 April 1966, Sunday, 7:25–7:50pm, BBC2, 6 episodes, mystery, British, contemporary
BBCtv
Pr: Alan Bromly
Dir: Christopher Barry
Wtr: Peter O'Donnell
Cast: **Ambrose Frayne – Derek Fowlds**
Hector Frayne – Sam Kydd
Charles Charles – Henry McGee
Dominique Frayne – Jeanne Roland

Perky Frenchwoman Dominique assists her British husband, private eye Ambrose, as he tries to track down a missing set of valuable pearls.

LORD RAINGO

26 April 1966, Tuesday, 9:50–10:35pm, BBC2, 4 episodes, drama, British, 20th century
BBCtv
Pr: Douglas Allen
Dir: Peter Hammond
Wtr: Jeremy Paul
Based on Arnold Bennett
Cast: Tom Hogarth – Joss Ackland
Adela – Diana Churchill
Sam Raingo – Kenneth More
Andy Clyth – Joseph O'Conor
Geoffrey Raingo – Tim Preece
Delphine – Janet Suzman

In 1918, business tycoon Sam Raingo accepts a cabinet post as Minister of Records from Prime Minister Andy Clyth, who is, oddly enough, a long-time rival of Sam's. Raingo's idea is to compel all government propaganda to be under one sole director, and intrigue abounds through the corridors of power as he faces opposition to his goal.

DEATH IS A GOOD LIVING

22 May 1966, Sunday, 7:25–7:50pm, BBC2, 4 episodes, thriller, British/European, contemporary
BBCtv
Pr: Alan Bromly
Dir: Gerald Blake

Wtr: Brian Degas, Tudor Gates
Based on Philip Jones
Cast: Peter Virtanen – Don Borisenko
Tim Barton – Jeremy Burnham
Bartolome Salias – Henry Gilbert
Ramon Aguirre – Michael Godfrey
Maria Salvedor – Dallia Penn
Norman Lynch – Leonard Rossiter
Jim Prescott – Geoffrey Toone

Deposed dictator Salias seeks to regain control of his former country and sends his friend Ramon Aguirre to Europe to seek funds for the anticipated uprising. The opposition hires assassin Norman Lynch to kill Aguirre. British security agents Prescott and Barton follow Aguirre, hoping to nab Lynch, all this leading to the unfolding of many sinister plots and counter-plots.

WATCH THE BIRDIES

19 June 1966, Sunday, 10:10–10:35pm, BBC2, 5 episodes, thriller, British, contemporary
BBCtv
Pr: Alan Bromly
Dir: Douglas Camfield
Wtr: Peter Yeldham
Cast: **Bill Page – Nicholas Courtney**
Frank Crawford – Edward Dentith
Anna Bergmann – Karin Fernald
Detective Inspector Clayton – Nicholas Selby
Irene Grant – Wanda Ventham

Photographer Bill Page gets a call for help from a friend, and is quickly and unexpectedly swept up into the violent sphere of the London underworld.

THE HEART OF MIDLOTHIAN

9 July 1966, Saturday, 8:00–9:00pm, BBC2, 2 episodes, drama, classic, Scottish, 18th century
BBCtv
Pr: Douglas Allen
Dir: Michael Barry
Wtr: Alistair Bell
Based on Sir Walter Scott
Cast: Reuben Butler – Peter Clay
Effie Deans – Gay Hamilton
Madge Wildfire – Elizabeth MacLennan
Geordie Robertson – Patrick Mower
Sharpitlaw – David Steuart
Jeanie Deans – Amanda Walker

In Scotland in 1736, Effie Deans is imprisoned in the old Midlothian jail for concealing her pregnancy. Worse yet, Effie's baby is snatched away from her. Thanks to the efforts of her sister Jeanie, Effie gets out of jail and marries the baby's father, Geordie Robertson, but their union, while happy, is brief and ill-fated.

RANSOM FOR A PRETTY GIRL

10 September 1966, Saturday, 10:05–10:30pm, BBC2, 6 episodes, thriller, British, contemporary
BBCtv
Pr: Alan Bromly
Dir: Richard Martin
Wtr: Ian Stuart Black
Cast: **Princess Nadia – Nike Arrighi**
Sophia – Maxine Audley
Colonel Caron – David Bailie
Inspector McRoberts – James Copeland
Charlie – James Cosmo

Teenaged Princess Nadia is about to be delivered to her estranged father for a visit, but is kidnapped at Glasgow airport. Nadia's extremely wealthy family hastily attempts to rescue the girl, but some of the mobsters who are holding her have different ideas, as the line between good guys and bad guys is vaguely drawn.

NORTH AND SOUTH

20 September 1966, Tuesday, 10:10–10:55pm, BBC2, 5 episodes, drama, British, 19th century
BBCtv
Pr: David Conroy
Dir: Hugh David
Wtr: David Turner
Based on Mrs. Elizabeth Gaskell
Cast: Mrs. Thornton – Sonia Dresdel
John Thornton – Richard Leech

The Reverend Richard Hale – David Markham
Margaret Hale – Wendy Williams

Culture clashes between the North and South of England come to a head in the mid-19th century, focusing on the troubled love affair between gentle Margaret Hale, who moves North to a manufacturing district with her father, and John Thornton, the hard-driving master of a cotton mill.

THE WOMAN IN WHITE

2 October 1966, Sunday, 5:30–5:55pm, BBC1, 6 episodes, mystery, British, 19th century
BBCtv
Pr: David Conroy
Dir: Brandon Acton-Bond
Wtr: Michael Voysey
Based on Wilkie Collins
Cast: Sir Percival Glyde – John Barron
Frederick Fairlie – Geoffrey Bayldon
Marian Halcombe – Alethea Charlton
Count Fosco – Francis de Wolff
Madame Fosco – Daphne Heard
Laura Fairlie/Anne Catherick – Jennifer Hilary
Professor Pesca – Louis Mansi
Walter Hartright – Nicholas Pennell

Teacher Walter Hartright gets a job in Cumberland and falls in love with Laura Fairlie, one of his charges, but is troubled by her uncanny resemblance to Anne Catherick, a mysterious "Woman in White" he had met briefly in London. When Laura is forced into an asylum in place of Anne, who has died, it is up to Hartright to figure out what is going on in time to come to her rescue.

BREAKING POINT

22 October 1966, Saturday, 10:00–10:25pm, BBC2, 5 episodes, thriller, British, contemporary
BBCtv
Pr: Alan Bromly
Dir: Douglas Camfield
Wtr: Victor Canning
Cast: Sir Alfred – Richard Hurndall
Max Stevens – Bernard Kay
Hellman – Terence Longdon
Diana Maxwell – Rosemary Nicols
Martin Kennedy – William Russell

Professor Max Stevens has discovered a new form of steel which is virtually indestructible; security agent Martin Kennedy is ordered to contact Stevens and keep news of the discovery a protected state secret. But others, with more nefarious and selfish interests, get wind of Stevens' work, and both his work and life are soon in serious jeopardy.

BROOME STAGES

25 October 1966, Tuesday, 9:05–9:50pm, BBC2, 8 episodes, drama, biographical, British, 18th–19th century
BBCtv
Pr: Michael Barry
Dir: Michael Barry
Wtr: Michael Barry
Based on Clemence Dane
Cast: Richard Broome – Edmund Bailey
William Broome – Anthony Bate
Harry Broome – Paul Daneman
Hilaret – Eileen Helsby
Robert Broome – Richard Pasco
Lettice – Gwen Watford

The fortunes and misfortunes of the Broomes, an English theatrical family, led first by 18th-century patriarch Richard, a contemporary of the legendary Garrick, and ultimately focusing on his great-granddaughter Lettice, whose experiences bring the story to its conclusion in 1871.

THE THREE MUSKETEERS

13 November 1966, Sunday, 5:30–5:55pm, BBC1, 10 episodes, drama, classic, adventure, French, 17th century
BBCtv
Pr: William Sterling
Dir: Peter Hammond
Wtr: Anthony Steven
Based on Alexandre Dumas
Cast: **Porthos – Brian Blessed**
Rochefort – Edward Brayshaw
D'Artagnan – Jeremy Brett
King Louis XIII – John Carlin
Cardinal Richelieu – Richard Pasco

Milady de Winter – Mary Peach
Anne of Austria – Carole Potter
D'Artagnan the Elder – Roy Purcell
Aramis – Gary Watson
Athos – Jeremy Young

In the years 1625-1628, Louis XIII is on the throne, but much of the power in France is held by ambitious Cardinal Richelieu. The Musketeers, members of the King's select guard, are joined by eager young d'Artagnan as they come dashingly to the aid of the monarch and his Queen, Anne of Austria.

BAT OUT OF HELL

26 November 1966, Saturday, 10:05–10:30pm, BBC2, 5 episodes, thriller, British, contemporary
BBCtv
Pr: Alan Bromly
Dir: Alan Bromly
Wtr: Francis Durbridge
Cast: Inspector Clay – Dudley Foster
Geoffrey Stewart – Noel Johnson
Diana Stewart – Sylvia Syms
Mark Paxton – John Thaw

Diana Stewart discovers that her father's death was no accident, and searches for answers, aided by boyfriend Mark Paxton – but her quest for the truth brings Diana into grave danger.

Featured under the program banner of "Francis Durbridge Presents . . . "

THE DARK NUMBER

31 December 1966, Saturday, 9:50–10:15pm, BBC2, 5 episodes, thriller, British, contemporary
BBCtv
Pr: Alan Bromly
Dir: Michael Ferguson
Wtr: Eddie Boyd
Cast: **Johnny Maxen – Patrick Allen**
Helen Duncan – Madeleine Christie
Torquil MacIlvanney – Archie Duncan
Bill Ferguson – John Junkin
Dorothy Havergal – Anne Kristen
Inspector Wardlaw – Roddy McMillan
Alistair Dodds – Simon Ward

When Johnny Maxen's estranged wife disappears, he is summoned back to Glasgow from Paris to assist in the search; then, when her body is discovered, Johnny finds himself the prime suspect in a murder investigation.

SWORD OF HONOUR

2 January 1967, Monday, 9:05–10:35pm, BBC2, 3 episodes, drama, British, 20th century
BBCtv
Pr: Michael Bakewell
Dir: Donald McWhinnie
Wtr: Giles Cooper
Based on *Men At Arms*, *Officers And Gentlemen* and *Unconditional Surrender* by Evelyn Waugh
Cast: Apthorpe – Ronald Fraser
Ritchie-Hook – Paul Hardwick
Virginia Troy – Vivian Pickles
Ian Kilbannock – James Villiers
Guy Crouchback – Edward Woodward

Guy Crouchback, a withdrawn man, goes off to fight in World War II, in search of the chivalry he feels is lacking in day-to-day life; instead he finds first disillusionment and then a deeper sense of human understanding, leading him to perform acts of heroism on and off the battlefield.

THE FORSYTE SAGA

7 January 1967, Saturday, 8:15–9:05pm, BBC2, 26 episodes, drama, classic, British, 19th–20th century
BBCtv
Video: available in UK
Pr: Donald Wilson
Dir: David Giles, James Cellan Jones
Wtr: Constance Cox, Laurie Craig, Anthony Steven, Vincent Tilsley, Donald Wilson
Based on *The Man of Property*, *In Chancery* and *To Let* by John Galsworthy
Cast: June – June Barry
Marjorie Ferrar – Caroline Blakiston
Val – Jonathan Burn
Fleur – Susan Hampshire
Jon – Martin Jarvis
Jo – Kenneth More
Helene – Lana Morris

Jolyon Forsyte – Joseph O'Conor
Annette – Dallia Penn
Michael Mont – Nicholas Pennell
Soames – Eric Porter
Irene – Nyree Dawn Porter
Winifred – Margaret Tyzack
James – John Welsh
Jolly – Michael York

Beginning in 1879 and concluding in 1926, the story of the wealthy, respectable Forsyte family spans three generations, the Victorian and Edwardian eras, and focuses most specifically on the individual lives of Jo and Soames Forsyte, the women they love, and their children, culminating in the ill-fated love of Jo's son Jon and Soames' daughter Fleur.

A broadcasting phenomenon on both sides of the Atlantic, *The Forsyte Saga* aired on public television in the United States beginning 5 October 1969.

GREAT EXPECTATIONS

22 January 1967, Sunday, 5:25–5:50pm, BBC1, 10 episodes, drama, classic, British, 19th century
BBCtv
Pr: Campbell Logan
Dir: Alan Bridges
Wtr: Hugh Leonard
Based on Charles Dickens
Cast: **Estella – Francesca Annis**
Miss Havisham – Maxine Audley
Pip – Gary Bond
Pip (as a child) – Christopher Guard
Herbert Pocket – Derek Lamden
Joe Gargery – Neil McCarthy
Magwitch – John Tate
Mr. Jaggers – Peter Vaughan

Pip, an orphan, is suddenly and mysteriously transformed into a monied, educated young gentleman. He thinks thanks are due to eccentric Miss Havisham, whose ward, Estella, holds the key to Pip's heart. But in truth Pip's anonymous benefactor is escaped convict Magwitch, for whom Pip had once done a kindness – and when Pip learns the humble truth of his good fortune, he is torn between obligation to his sponsor and the snobbish privilege of his new position.

GIRL IN A BLACK BIKINI

4 February 1967, Saturday, 10:45–11:10pm, BBC2, 6 episodes, thriller, British, contemporary
BBCtv
Pr: Alan Bromly
Dir: Gerald Blake
Wtr: John Roddick
Cast: **Robert Sheridan – John Carson**
Alan Ramsey – John Cater
Grace Heager – Jean Harvey
Detective Sergeant Napier – Glyn Houston
Lee Anderson – Calvin Lockhart
Kathy Sheridan – Angela Scoular

A year after the death of a young woman, new evidence is discovered concerning the unsolved case, which quickly – and dangerously – involves barrister Robert Sheridan, Detective Sergeant Napier, and a number of others before matters are finally resolved.

THE PARADISE MAKERS

18 March 1967, Saturday, 10:20–10:45pm, BBC2, 6 episodes, thriller, British, contemporary
BBCtv
Pr: Alan Bromly
Dir: Rex Tucker
Wtr: Arden Winch
Cast: **James Crieg – Michael Bryant**
Inga Swynnerton – Rosalie Crutchley
DeLacelle – Richard Hurndall
Colonel Sparrow – Joseph O'Conor

Ex-spy James Crieg returns to the world of international espionage in an attempt to undermine a corrupt organization's quest for world domination.

ST. IVES

9 April 1967, Sunday, 5:25–5:50pm, BBC1, 6 episodes, drama, classic, adventure, British/French, 19th century
BBCtv
Pr: Campbell Logan
Dir: Christopher Barry

Wtr: Rex Tucker
Based on Robert Louis Stevenson
Cast: Miss Gilchrist – Jean Anderson
Romaine – Hamilton Dyce
Alain – Mark Eden
Flora Gilchrist – Gay Hamilton
St. Ives – David Sumner
Clausel – Talfryn Thomas

Towards the end of the Napoleonic Wars, Frenchman Vicomte St. Ives escapes his captivity in an Edinburgh castle and embarks on a dangerous journey to Buckinghamshire, in order to claim a fortune which has been bequeathed to him.

SPINDOE

23 April 1967, Tuesday, 10:30–11:30pm, ITV, 6 episodes, drama, British, contemporary
Granada Television
Pr: Robin Chapman
Dir: Cyril Coke, Cormac Newell
Wtr: Robin Chapman
Cast: **Eddie Edwards – Anthony Bate**
Detective Inspector Tierney – Basil Dignam
Billy Humphries – Glynn Edwards
Renata – Rachel Herbert
Henry Mackleson – Richard Hurndall
Detective Sergeant Peach – Bryan Marshall
Alec Spindoe – Ray McAnally
Shelagh – Colette O'Neil

Gangster Alec Spindoe is released from prison and returns to South London, where he discovers that he has been betrayed by former partner Eddie Edwards. Edwards, now working with Henry Mackleson, has not only cheated Spindoe out of his money, he's stolen his wife, too. Spindoe fights a dangerous battle to regain the criminal kingdom which was once his, a struggle which leaves many bodies in its wake and both the police and other criminals hot on Spindoe's trail.

WITCH HUNT

29 April 1967, Saturday, 10:25–10:50pm, BBC2, 5 episodes, thriller, British, contemporary
BBCtv
Pr: Alan Bromly
Dir: Peter Duguid
Wtr: Jon Manchip White
Cast: Cass Russell – Peter Blythe
Colonel Cooper – Derek Francis
Maggie Lowther – Sally Home
Rex Fordham – Patrick Kavanagh
Shelby Jones – Robert MacLeod
Nancy Jones – Anna Palk
Harvey Collier – John Paul
Reverend Philip Nyren – Morris Perry

Rex Fordham considers buying Brookthorne, a farm, from his friend Shelby Jones, but reconsiders when he senses something sinister in the air, and discovers that Shelby and his wife Nancy have been accused by some locals of practising witchcraft.

FURTHER ADVENTURES OF THE MUSKETEERS

21 May 1967, Sunday, 5:25–5:50pm, BBC1, 16 episodes, drama, classic, adventure, French, 17th century
BBCtv
Pr: William Sterling
Dir: Christopher Barry, Hugh David
Wtr: Alexander Baron
Based on *Twenty Years After* by Alexandre Dumas
Cast: **D'Artagnan – Joss Ackland**
Rochefort – Edward Brayshaw
Porthos – Brian Blessed
Cardinal Mazarin – William Dexter
Anne, Queen Regent – Carole Potter
Prince de Beaufort – John Quentin
King Louis XIV – Louis Selwyn
Aramis – John Woodvine
Athos – Jeremy Young

This sequel to *The Three Musketeers* finds D'Artagnan and his comrades older, wiser . . . but still ready and eager to leap into swashbuckling action, this time to defend the boy king. Set in the reign of Louis XIV, D'Artagnan, a chivalrous captain in the King's Musketeers, is now a mature figure, a clear-sighted, gallant swordsman whose chivalry and courage make him a commanding presence. He is a quick-witted, lovable soldier, in contrast to his companions – Porthos, the giant of a man, Athos, the gentleman of honour, and Aramis, the cunning schemer.

THIS WAY FOR MURDER

3 June 1967, Saturday, 10:05–10:30pm, BBC2, 6 episodes, thriller, British, contemporary
BBCtv
Pr: Alan Bromly
Dir: Eric Hills
Wtr: Victor Canning
Cast: Worth – Peter Arne
Sandra – Isobel Black
Chairman – Hugh Cross
Rawlings – Hamilton Dyce
Hendrix – Noel Johnson
Raikes – Terence Longdon
Inspector Frant – Peter Vaughan

Ex-con Raikes is persuaded by C.I.D. Inspector Frant to infiltrate Tintoc Ltd., a development company which is really a front for organized crime, in the hopes of discovering who is responsible for the murder of Raikes' wife.

RAINBOW CITY

5 July 1967, Wednesday, 7:30–7:55pm, BBC1, 6 episodes, drama, British, contemporary
BBCtv/Midlands
Pr: John Elliot
Dir: John Elliot
Wtr: John Elliot, Horace James
Cast: Dennis Jackson – Horace James
John Steele – Errol John
Mary Steele – Gemma Jones
Inspector – Frank Veasay

Lawyer John Steele is one of a group of West Indians living in and around Birmingham. He is married to a white woman, but many of his cases involve fellow immigrants and their problems in being accepted into mainstream British society.

THE SECRET AGENT

8 July 1967, Saturday, 9:15–10:00pm, BBC2, 2 episodes, drama, classic, British, 19th century
BBCtv
Pr: David Conroy
Dir: Gerald Blake
Wtr: Alexander Baron
Based on Joseph Conrad
Cast: The Professor – John Cater
Mr. Vladimir – David Collings
Adolph Verloc – Nigel Green
Michaelis – George Pravda
Stevie – Dennis Waterman
Winnie Verloc – Mary Webster
The Minister – Llewellyn Rees

Double agent Adolph Verloc works for both the Tsarists in Moscow and Scotland Yard in London. He persuades his dimwitted brother-in-law Stevie to blow up the Greenwich Royal Observatory, but when Stevie is accidentally killed in the attempt, Verloc's wife Winnie is so infuriated that she kills Verloc, and subsequently commits suicide.

Conrad's novel was based on an actual anarchist attempt to blow up the Observatory which took place in 1894.

THE LION, THE WITCH AND THE WARDROBE

9 July 1967, Sunday, 6:15–6:35pm, ITV, 10 episodes, drama, classic, family, fantasy, British, 20th century
ABC Network
Pr: Pamela Lonsdale
Dir: Helen Standage
Wtr: Trevor Preston
Based on C.S. Lewis
Cast: **Lucy – Elizabeth Crowther**
Mr. Tumnus – Angus Lennie
Aslan – Bernard Kay
Edmund – Edward McMurray
Susan – Zuleika Robson
White Witch – Elizabeth Wallace
Peter – Paul Waller
Professor – Jack Woolgar

Four children who have been evacuated from London in 1940 discover a magical wardrobe in the country home of an aged professor which leads to the fantastic land of Narnia. There the children meet a strange gathering of people and animals ruled by the cruel White Witch. The children help gentle Aslan the Lion regain the throne of Narnia, embarking on a series of adventures before the children re-emerge from the wardrobe back into the English countryside.

ANGEL PAVEMENT

19 August 1967, Saturday, 9:20–10:05pm, BBC2, 4 episodes, drama, British, 20th century
BBCtv
Pr: David Conroy
Dir: Paddy Russell
Wtr: David Turner
Based on J.B. Priestley
Cast: **Mr. Golspie – Anthony Bate**
Lena Golspie – Jane Bond
Smeeth – Cyril Luckham
Turgis – Murray Melvin
Lilian Matfield – Judy Parfitt
Goath – Tony Steedman

In London in 1930, furniture dealer Twigg and Dersingham has its offices in the City, and the generally uneventful lives of those employed there are turned upside down by the sudden appearance of fast-talking bandit, Mr. Golspie.

THE QUEEN'S TRAITOR

28 August 1967, Monday, 5:20–5:50pm, BBC1, 5 episodes, thriller, British, 16th century
BBCtv
Pr: Brandon Acton-Bond
Dir: Campbell Logan
Wtr: John Hale
Cast: Mary, Queen of Scots – Stephanie Beacham
Queen Elizabeth – Susan Engel
Lord Burleigh – Derek Francis
John Hawkins – Nigel Green
George Fitzwilliam – Norman Jones
Duke of Norfolk – Conrad Phillips

The Ridolfi Plot, a conspiracy against the reign of Elizabeth I, is hatched, and seaman John Hawkins, mingling amidst royalty and nobility, plays an instrumental role in foiling its nefarious ends.

THE BIG M

29 August 1967, Tuesday, 10:00–10:25pm, BBC2, 6 episodes, thriller, British, contemporary
BBCtv
Pr: Alan Bromly
Dir: Alan Bromly
Wtr: Lester Powell
Cast: Inspector Spain – Victor Brooks
Johnny Treherne – Michael Bryant
Inspector Scott – Barry Linehan
Tancred – Reginald Marsh
Verity Hassett – Mitzi Rogers
Stratton – Michael Wynne

Johnny Treherne is involved with a protection gang in Southwest Britain, but things go too far when people's lives are first jeopardized, then brought to vicious ends. In order to save his own skin, Johnny must take decisive action . . . but is it too little too late?

PRIDE AND PREJUDICE

10 September 1967, Sunday, 5:30–5:55pm, BBC1, 6 episodes, drama, classic, British, 19th century
BBCtv
Pr: Campbell Logan
Dir: Joan Craft
Wtr: Nemone Lethbridge
Based on Jane Austen
Cast: **Jane Bennet – Polly Adams**
Elizabeth Bennet – Celia Bannerman
Lady Catherine de Bourgh – Sylvia Coleridge
Mr. Collins – Julian Curry
Mr. Darcy – Lewis Fiander
Lydia Bennet – Lucy Fleming
Mr. Bennet – Michael Gough
Mr. Wickham – Richard Hampton
Charlotte Lucas – Kate Lansbury
Mrs. Bennet – Vivian Pickles
Mr. Bingley – David Savile
Kitty Bennet – Sarah Taunton
Caroline Bingley – Georgina Ward

Marriage in Regency England is the focus of this classic tale which tells most notably of the romance between easygoing Jane Bennet and Mr. Bingley and the developing love between strong-willed Elizabeth Bennet and arrogant, aristocratic Mr. Darcy.

THE WHITE RABBIT

16 September 1967, Saturday,
8:45–9:30pm, BBC2, 4 episodes, drama,
biographical, British, 20th century
BBCtv
Pr: David Conroy
Dir: Peter Hammond
Wtr: Michael Voysey
Based on Bruce Marshall
Cast: Barbara – Denise Buckley
       Jose Dupuis – Annette Crosbie
       Rudi – Alan MacNaughtan
       Wing Commander Yeo-Thomas – Kenneth More

The wartime biography of Wing Commander F.F. Yeo-Thomas, G.C., M.C., a hero of the French Resistance during World War II. Under his code name, "The White Rabbit," British Officer Yeo-Thomas, who had been brought up in France, journeys a number of times into occupied France to contact the Resistance, and is captured by the Germans and imprisoned and tortured in Buchenwald before war's end brings about his liberation.

AFTER MANY A SUMMER

14 October 1967, Saturday, 7:55–8:40pm,
BBC2, 2 episodes, drama,
American/British, 20th century
BBCtv
Pr: David Conroy
Dir: Douglas Camfield
Wtr: Rex Tucker
Based on Aldous Huxley
Cast: Virginia – Judith Arthy
       Jo Stoyte – Stubby Kaye
       Dr. Obispo – Zia Mohyeddin
       Jeremy Portage – Frank Williams

American millionaire Jo Stoyte is deathly afraid of . . . death. When Jeremy Portage discovers a manuscript of a centuries-old British elixir, he and Stoyte travel to England, where Stoyte spends a good deal of his fortune in search of the magical potion which will promise eternal life.

LES MISERABLES

22 October 1967, Sunday, 5:30–5:55pm,
BBC1, 10 episodes, drama, classic,
French, 19th century
BBCtv
Pr: Campbell Logan
Dir: Alan Bridges
Wtr: Giles Cooper, Harry Green
Based on Victor Hugo
Cast: **Javert – Anthony Bate**
       Eponine – Elizabeth Counsell
       Bishop of Digne – Finlay Currie
       Cosette – Michele Dotrice
       Jean Valjean – Frank Finlay
       Marius – Vivian Mackerrel

Jean Valjean steals a loaf of bread in order to feed his family. His arrest and subsequent escape set the scene for the life-long cat-and-mouse game between him and Inspector Javert, who is obsessed with Valjean's capture.

WUTHERING HEIGHTS

28 October 1967, Saturday, 7:55–8:40pm,
BBC2, 4 episodes, drama, classic, British,
19th century
BBCtv
Pr: David Conroy
Dir: Peter Sasdy
Wtr: Hugh Leonard
Based on Emily Brontë
Cast: Hareton – Keith Buckley
       Isabella Linton – Angela Douglas
       Joseph – John Garrie
       Heathcliff (as a child) – Dennis Golding
       Edgar Linton – Drewe Henley
       Cathy (as a child) – June Liversidge
       Hindley – William Marlowe
       Heathcliff – Ian McShane
       Cathy/Catherine – Angela Scoular
       Ellen – Anne Stallybrass
       Linton – Michael Wennink

The fierce and passionate connection between Cathy Earnshaw and Heathcliff begins when the orphaned Heathcliff is adopted into the Earnshaw home and does not lose any of its intensity even after Cathy gives in to her vanity and ambition and marries local aristocrat Edgar Linton. But the love Cathy and Heathcliff share transcends even her death, and Heathcliff's determination for revenge has severe repercussions for Heathcliff's son, Cathy's daughter, and Hareton, the son of Cathy's brother Hindley.

THE PILGRIM'S PROGRESS

29 October 1967, Sunday, 6:35–7:25pm, ITV, 3 episodes, drama, classic, religious allegory
ABC Network
Pr: Voytek
Dir: Voytek
Wtr: Trevor Preston
Based on John Bunyan
Cast: **Christian – George Innes**
Interrogator/Worldly Wiseman – Philip Locke
Woman Official/Passion/Presumption/Mistrust – Colette O'Neil
Jailor/Help/Goodwill/Watchful – Michael Robbins
Evangelist/Doctor – Tony Steedman
The Prisoner – William Squire

This adaptation of Bunyan's religious allegory finds The Prisoner dreaming of Christian, a God-fearing man who tries to escape from the City of Destruction in order to make his way to the Celestial City, encountering both friends and enemies along the way.

VANITY FAIR

2 December 1967, Saturday, 7:55–8:40pm, BBC2, 5 episodes, drama, classic, British, 19th century
BBCtv
Pr: David Conroy
Dir: David Giles
Wtr: Rex Tucker
Based on William Makepeace Thackeray
Cast: Lord Steyne – Robert Flemyng
Becky Sharp – Susan Hampshire
Rawdon Crawley – Dyson Lovell
George Osborne – Roy Marsden
Captain Dobbin – Bryan Marshall
Jos Sedley – John Moffatt
Amelia – Marilyn Taylerson
Sir Pitt Crawley – John Welsh

Poor, orphaned Becky Sharp sets out to climb the social ladder, no matter what the cost to convention and kindness. She sets her cap on a profitable marriage, but her husband, Rawdon Crawley, is a gambler and a rake. In contrast to Becky's wheedling and needling is her close friend Amelia, who idealizes her (undeserving) husband George Osborne – and is loved from afar by noble Captain Dobbin. By story's end Becky is alone and destitute, and does perhaps the one unselfish act of her life, enabling Amelia and Dobbin to finally share their love.

This was the BBC's first colour serial.

THE PORTRAIT OF A LADY

6 January 1968, Saturday, 7:55–8:40pm, BBC2 (colour), 6 episodes, drama, classic, American, 19th century
BBCtv
Video: available in US
Pr: David Conroy
Dir: James Cellan Jones
Wtr: Jack Pulman
Based on Henry James
Cast: Caspar Goodwood – Edward Bishop
Ralph Touchett – Richard Chamberlain
Lord Warburton – Edward Fox
Madame Merle – Rachel Gurney
Mrs. Touchett – Beatrix Lehmann
Gilbert Osmond – James Maxwell
Isabel Archer – Suzanne Neve

The innocence of America, as personified by idealistic Isabel Archer, is set against the corrupt experience of Europe, when she comes to live with her aunt in England. Her ailing, supportive cousin Ralph attempts to help Isabel spread her wings, but the results are disastrous, most notably in Isabel's mismatched marriage with dishonourable Gilbert Osmond.

NICHOLAS NICKLEBY

11 February 1968, Sunday, 5:25–5:50pm, BBC1, 13 episodes, drama, classic, British, 19th century
BBCtv
Pr: Campbell Logan
Dir: Joan Craft
Wtr: Hugh Leonard

Based on Charles Dickens
Cast: **Kate Nickleby – Susan Brodrick**
Miss La Creevy – Hazel Coppen
Ralph Nickleby – Derek Francis
Ned Cheeryble – John Gill
Newman Noggs – Gordon Gostelow
Madeleine Bray – Sharon Gurney
Mrs. Nickleby – Thea Holme
Nicholas Nickleby – Martin Jarvis
Charles Cheeryble – Edward Palmer
Wackford Squeers – Ronald Radd
Frank Cheeryble – Paul Shelley
Smike – Hugh Walters

Mistreated by his greedy uncle after the death of his father, poor but honest Nicholas Nickleby sets off on the road seeking a fortune suitable enough to provide for his sister and mother. Accompanied by faithful friend Smike, Nicholas is pursued by cruel schoolmaster Squeers, from whose miserable establishment he and Smike had fled. Adventures, both good and bad, abound, and several fateful and even tragic hands are dealt before all is resolved.

THE GAMBLER

17 February 1968, Saturday, 8:00–8:45pm, BBC2 (colour), 2 episodes, drama, classic, Russian, 19th century
BBCtv
Pr: David Conroy
Dir: Michael Ferguson
Wtr: John Hopkins
Based on Fyodor Dostoevsky
Cast: **Grandmamma – Edith Evans**
The General – John Phillips
Marquis de Grieux – Philip Madoc
Mr. Astley – Corin Redgrave
Alexei – Maurice Roeves
Polina – Georgina Ward

Russian nobleman Alexei is obsessed with gambling at roulette and loses all of his money, then greedily awaits his expected inheritance from rich old Grandmamma. Not only does she not die, the old woman regains her strength, tries her hand at roulette, and greatly increases her fortune – all wagered on one last spin of the wheel.

THE FLIGHT OF THE HERON

28 February 1968, Wednesday, 5:25–5:55pm, ITV, 8 episodes, drama, Scottish, 18th century
Scottish Television Network
Pr: Brian Mahoney
Dir: Brian Mahoney
Wtr: Moultrie R. Kelsall
Based on D.K. Broster
Cast: Captain Greening – Tom Conti
Angus MacMartin – Finlay Currie
Captain Scott – Brown Derby
Neil MacMartin – Robert Doherty
Lachlan MacMartin – Bill Henderson
Captain Windham – Jon Laurimore
Ewen Cameron – Ian McCulloch
Lochiel – Leonard Maguire
Aunt Margaret – Sophie Stewart
Alison Grant – Sheila Whittingham

Soothsayer Angus McMartin prophesies that a flying heron will bring about the meeting of Highland chieftain Ewen Cameron and English Officer Captain Windham. Although enemies at the battle of Culloden, the final stand of Bonnie Prince Charlie and his Jacobites, the two learn from one another, becoming wiser from the experience.

POINT COUNTER POINT

2 March 1968, Saturday, 8:00–8:45pm, BBC2 (colour), 5 episodes, drama, satire, British, 20th century
BBCtv
Pr: David Conroy
Dir: Rex Tucker
Wtr: Simon Raven
Based on Aldous Huxley
Cast: John Bidlake – Max Adrian
Philip Quarles – Lyndon Brook
Mark Rampion – Edward Caddick
Eleanor Quarles – Patricia English
Lucy Tantamount – Valerie Gearon
Mrs. Marjorie Carling – Sheila Grant
Walter Bidlake – Tristram Jellinek
Everard Webley – Edward Judd

Set between the two World Wars, this satirical look at decadent upper-class society in the 1920s is seen from the point of view of novelist Philip Quarles, who plans to write a novel about his intellectual but spiritually empty acquaintances.

THE SPANISH FARM

6 April 1968, Saturday, 7:50–8:35pm, BBC2 (colour), 4 episodes, drama, British, 20th century
BBCtv
Pr: David Conroy
Dir: Gerald Blake
Wtr: Lennox Phillips
Based on R.H. Mottram
Cast: Colonel Birchin – Maurice Hedley
Captain Dormer – Bernard Hepton
Baron D'Archeville – Cyril Luckham
Madeleine – Caroline Mortimer
Georges D'Archeville – Carl Rigg
Jerome – Jack Woolgar

The story of Madeleine, the Spanish Farm located in French Flanders close to the Front in World War I . . . and the British troops billeted there. The life and atmosphere in France during the War are conveyed as Madeleine struggles to keep the farm which has belonged to her family for generations.

PERE GORIOT

4 May 1968, Saturday, 7:50–8:35pm, BBC2 (colour), 4 episodes, drama, classic, French, 19th century
BBCtv
Pr: David Conroy
Dir: Paddy Russell
Wtr: David Turner
Based on Honoré de Balzac
Cast: Anastasie – Angela Browne
Victorine – Anna Cropper
Eugène de Rastignac – David Dundas
Monsieur Goriot – Michael Goodliffe
Vautrin – Andrew Keir
Madame Vauquer – Pat Nye
Madame de Beauseant – Moira Redmond
Delphine – June Ritchie
Sylvie – Patsy Rowlands

In Paris in 1819, formerly prosperous Goriot is among those living in the seedy boarding house owned by Madame Vauquer, having squandered his entire fortune in order to assure the social climb of his two ungrateful daughters who now find their father an embarrassment – and yet continue to expect him to help them out of financial difficulties.

THE RAILWAY CHILDREN

12 May 1968, Sunday, 5:25–5:50pm, BBC1, 7 episodes, drama, classic, family, British, 20th century
BBCtv
Pr: Campbell Logan
Dir: Julia Smith
Wtr: Denis Constanduros
Based on E.E. Nesbit
Cast: **Bobbie – Jenny Agutter**
Signalman – Bart Allison
Phyllis – Gillian Bailey
Mother – Ann Castle
Stationmaster – Brian Hayes
Old Gentleman – Joseph O'Conor
Peter – Neil McDermot
Father – Frederick Treves

At the turn of the century, the lives of Bobbie, Peter and Phyllis are turned upside down when their father mysteriously leaves and they go to live with their mother close to a Yorkshire railway station. Disappointed at first, the children soon discover a new world of friends and adventures, all culminating with the eventual happy return of their father.

WHAT MAISIE KNEW

1 June 1968, Saturday, 7:50–8:35pm, BBC2 (colour), 3 episodes, drama, American, 19th century
BBCtv
Pr: David Conroy
Dir: Derek Martinus
Wtr: Denis Constanduros
Based on Henry James
Cast: Susan Ash – Yvonne Antrobus
Ida Farange – Maxine Audley
Beale Farange – Paul Hardwick
Miss Overmore – Penelope Horner
Sir Claude – Gary Raymond
Maisie – Sally Thomsett
Mrs. Wix – Ann Way

After the divorce of her parents, 13-year-old Maisie finds herself being shuttled between one and the other and their new spouses. Maisie discovers that her stepfather and stepmother are each having extramarital affairs, and in the end she elects to live with her governess instead of either of her parents.

DEVIL-IN-THE-FOG

21 June 1968, Friday, 5:25–5:55pm, ITV, 6 episodes, drama, British, 18th century
Rediffusion Network
Pr: Michael Currier-Briggs
Dir: Michael Currier-Briggs
Wtr: Stanley Miller
Based on Leon Garfield
Cast: Lady Dexter – Stephanie Bidmead
Salathiel Treet – Martin Dempsey
Stranger – Valentine Dyall
George Treet – Nicholas Evans
Rose Treet – Verina Greenlaw
Sir John Dexter – Richard Leech
Hotspur Treet – John Moulder-Brown
Jane Treet – Diana Simpson
Edward Treet – Keith Skinner

Fourteen-year-old actor George Treet, one of a family of 18th-century strolling players, discovers he is the heir to baronet Sir John Dexter. The revelation delivers young George into a world of riches and privilege, but no joy; instead, he finds himself the victim of attempted murder and family treachery.

COLD COMFORT FARM

22 June 1968, Saturday, 7:50–8:35pm, BBC2 (colour), 3 episodes, drama, British, 20th century
BBCtv
Pr: David Conroy
Dir: Peter Hammond
Wtr: David Turner
Based on Stella Gibbons
Cast: **Flora Poste – Sarah Badel**
Aunt Ada Doom – Fay Compton
Judith – Rosalie Crutchley
Seth – Peter Egan
Elphine – Sharon Gurney
Urk – Freddie Jones
Adam Lambsbreath – Billy Russell
Amos – Alastair Sim

Orphaned 20-year-old Flora Poste goes to live with her relatives in Sussex, meeting a gallery of eccentric characters, dominated by tyrannical matriarch Aunt Ada Doom, far unlike the more cultured, mannered types she has known until then – and Flora takes it upon herself to reform them.

TRITON

30 June 1968, Sunday, 5:25–5:50pm, BBC1, 4 episodes, drama, British, 19th century
BBCtv
Pr: John McRae
Dir: Michael Ferguson
Wtr: Rex Tucker
Cast: **Captain Julius Belwether – Jonathan Adams**
Napoleon Bonaparte – Tony Boyd
Robert Fulton – Robert Cawdron
Earl St. Vincent – Hamilton Dyce
Lieutenant Simon Lamb – Paul Grist
Lord Nelson – Terry Scully

Lord Nelson assigns two young officers, Captain Belwether and Lieutenant Lamb, to a secret mission, which leads the duo to infiltrate Napoleon's forces and discover the threat of a secret weapon being designed for the French . . . a rocket-launching submarine!

A sequel to this production of *Triton*, titled *Pegasus* and featuring the same principal cast members, aired beginning 17 November 1969.

MIDDLEMARCH

13 July 1968, Saturday, 7:50–8:35pm, BBC2 (colour), 7 episodes, drama, classic, British, 19th century
BBCtv
Pr: David Conroy
Dir: Joan Craft
Wtr: Michael Voysey
Based on George Eliot
Cast: **Dorothea – Michele Dotrice**
Dr. Tertius Lydgate – Donald Douglas
Fred Vincy – Clive Francis
Mr. Brooke – Derek Francis

Mary Garth – Hannah Gordon
Sir James Chettam – Clive Graham
Celia – Gillian Hawser
The Reverend Mr. Farebrother – Bernard Hepton
The Reverend Mr. Casaubon – Philip Latham
Mr. Bulstrode – Richard Pearson
Will Ladislaw – Michael Pennington
Rosamund Vincy Lydgate – Marilyn Taylerson

In the 1830s, the provincial village of Middlemarch is reluctant to adapt to the changing industrial tides of the century. New physician Dr. Lydgate hopes to have a positive, progressive impact on the community's health, but his imprudent marriage to the vain and materialistic Rosamond changes his fortunes for the worse in every respect. At the same time, idealistic Dorothea Brooke seeks only a life of service and self-sacrifice for the good of others, but gets more than she bargained for when she marries much-older, pedantic scholar Casaubon.

KENILWORTH

22 July 1968, Saturday, 9:20–10:05pm, BBC2, 4 episodes, drama, classic, British, 16th century
BBCtv
Pr: David Conroy
Dir: Tristan de Vere Cole
Wtr: Anthony Steven
Based on Sir Walter Scott
Cast: Edmund Tressilian – Jeremy Brett
Richard Varney – John Fraser
Elizabeth I – Gemma Jones
Earl of Sussex – David Langton
Earl of Leicester – Graham Lines
Amy Robsart – Prunella Ransome

In order to avoid provoking the jealous wrath of Elizabeth I, the ambitious Earl of Leicester hides his marriage to Amy Robsart from the monarch, who expects complete and total loyalty and devotion from Leicester, one of her court favourites. Leicester later wrongfully believes that Amy has been unfaithful to him, and ultimately is responsible for her death.

THE MAN IN THE IRON MASK

28 July 1968, Sunday, 5:30–5:55pm, BBC1, 9 episodes, drama, classic, French, 17th century
BBCtv
Pr: Campbell Logan
Dir: Hugh David
Wtr: Anthony Steven
Based on Alexandre Dumas
Cast: **Philippe/King Louis XIV – Nicolas Chagrin**
Duchesse de Chevreuse – Sonia Dresdel
Athos – Jack Gwillim
Porthos – Roger Livesay
Louise de la Valliere – Susan Macready
D'Artagnan – Edwin Richfield
The Queen Mother – Daphne Slater
Aramis – Noel Willman

Late in the 17th century, a mysterious prisoner in the Bastille, kept in an iron mask which completely covers his face, is revealed to be the twin brother of reigning monarch Louis XIV. It is up to the loyal musketeers and D'Artagnan to help the mysterious prisoner escape, survive many attempts on his life, and claim his rightful place in the royal hierarchy.

RAMSHACKLE ROAD

19 August 1968, Monday, 5:15–5:40pm, BBC1, 4 episodes, thriller, family, British, contemporary
BBCtv
Pr: Brian Miller
Dir: Brian Miller
Wtr: Peter J. Hammond
Cast: Timothy Bateson
Christopher Benjamin
Denis Gilmore
Linda Jolliff
Trevor Martin
Malcolm McFee

Three teenagers use an abandoned old house as their own private hideaway, but their sanctuary – and possibly their lives – is interrupted by the sudden appearance of mysterious intruders.

Producer Miller invited viewers to

contribute to the serial plot following episode one, asking *Radio Times* readers to submit story ideas which were incorporated into further developing plot and characters as the serial progressed; character names were not made available.

NANA

31 August 1968, Saturday, 9:05–9:50pm, BBC2 (colour), 5 episodes, classic, drama, French, 19th century
BBCtv
Pr: David Conroy
Dir: John Davies
Wtr: Robert Muller
Based on Emile Zola
Cast: Steiner – John Bryans
       Fauchery – Roland Curram
       Countess Muffat – Nancie Jackson
       Count Muffat – Freddie Jones
       Bordenave – Barry Linehan
       Nana – Katharine Schofield

In Paris at the height of the decadent 1860s, Nana, a woman who loves luxury, becomes a famous actress, the toast of the city . . . until entering into a tragic love affair which leads to her subsequent painful, disastrous fall from favour.

THE £1,000,000 BANK NOTE

29 September 1968, Sunday, 5:30–5:55pm, BBC1, 4 episodes, drama, American/British, 19th century
BBCtv
Pr: Campbell Logan
Dir: Rex Tucker
Wtr: John Hawkesworth
Based on Mark Twain
Cast: **Henry Adams – Stuart Damon**
       Bertie – Arthur Hewlett
       Algernon – George Howe
       Lady Portia – Bonnie Hurren

American Henry Adams finds himself stranded penniless in London . . . until he is taken under the wing of two eccentric brothers, whose unusual and quite generous gift to Henry changes his life radically, but not altogether for the better.

TREASURE ISLAND

3 November 1968, Sunday, 5:30–5:55pm, BBC1, 9 episodes, drama, classic, adventure, British, 18th century
BBCtv
Pr: Campbell Logan
Dir: Peter Hammond
Wtr: David Turner
Based on Robert Louis Stevenson
Cast: Dr. Livesay – Anthony Bate
       Black Dog – George Coulouris
       Squire Trelawney – Michael Gough
       Ben Gunn – Freddie Jones
       Jim Hawkins – Michael Newport
       Billy Bones – Bill Owen
       Long John Silver – Peter Vaughan

After an encounter with Billy Bones at the Admiral Benbow Inn, Jim Hawkins sets out on a seafaring adventure in search of a map and the hidden treasure to which it leads, but mutinous pirate Long John Silver has other plans for the boy and the fortune.

RESURRECTION

16 November 1968, Saturday, 8:15–9:00pm, BBC2 (colour), 4 episodes, drama, Russian, 19th century
BBCtv
Pr: David Conroy
Dir: David Giles
Wtr: Alexander Baron
Based on Leo Tolstoy
Cast: **Prince Dmitri Nekhlyudov – Alan Dobie**
       Princess Sophia – Constance Lorne
       Maslennikov – John Stratton
       Katerina Maslova – Bridget Turner

Prince Dmitri and Katerina fall in love, but after seducing her, Dmitri abandons Katerina. By chance, they meet again years later, when Dmitri is on the jury trying the case of a prostitute – Katerina, who fell into disrepute after Dmitri's betrayal. When Katerina is unjustly sentenced, Dmitri devotes himself in vain to making things right for Katerina, ultimately following her into exile in Siberia.

THE TENANT OF WILDFELL HALL

28 December 1968, Saturday, 8:15–9:00pm, BBC2 (colour), 4 episodes, drama, British, 19th century
BBCtv
Pr: David Conroy
Dir: Peter Sasdy
Wtr: Christopher Fry
Based on Anne Brontë
Cast: Arthur – Jeremy Burring
Lawrence – William Gaunt
Gilbert – Bryan Marshall
Helen Graham – Janet Munro
Huntingdon – Corin Redgrave

The arrival of widowed painter Helen Graham and her son at Wildfell Hall, accompanied by just one servant, causes much speculation in a small Yorkshire village – particularly since Helen is, in fact, still married, having fled her abusive husband to save herself and her child.

SCOBIE IN SEPTEMBER

14 January 1969, Tuesday, 9:55–10:20pm, BBC1, 6 episodes, thriller, Scottish, contemporary
BBCtv/Scotland
Pr: Pharic Maclaren
Designed by Tim Harvey
Wtr: Bill Craig
Cast: Pandorus – Anton Diffring
Judy – Hannah Gordon
Sir James Thorne – David Langton
Scobie – Maurice Roeves

Set in Edinburgh at festival time, painter Scobie is on the run from mysterious pursuers – is he fleeing for his life, or on the run from the police?

Scobie became caught up in another intrigue, this time involving arson fires at an art gallery, beginning 11 February 1972, in the sequel *The Scobie Man*.

THE POSSESSED

25 January 1969, Saturday, 8:15–9:00pm, BBC2 (colour), 6 episodes, drama, Russian, 19th century
BBCtv
Pr: David Conroy
Dir: Naomi Capon
Wtr: Hugh Leonard
Based on Fyodor Dostoevsky
Cast: Nikolay Stavrogin – Keith Bell
Shatov – James Caffrey
Pyotr Verhovensky – David Collings
Varvara Stavrogin – Rosalie Crutchley
Narrator – Laurence Hardy
Madame Drosdov – Joan Hickson
Stepan Verhovensky – Joseph O'Conor
Dasha – Anne Stallybrass

A provincial Russian town in the middle of the 19th century is the setting for this tale of a group of middle-class liberals, into whose midst arrives a determined revolutionary, whose actions foreshadow the real Revolution in 1917.

LETTERS FROM THE DEAD

20 February 1969, Thursday, 9:00–9:30pm, ITV, 6 episodes, thriller, British, contemporary
Southern Independent Television
Pr: James Gatward
Designed by John Dilly
Wtr: Ian Kennedy Martin
Cast: **Peter Allery – Norman Bowler**
Herrick – Richard Coleman
Sergeant Maitland – Michael Graham
Chief Inspector Reaygo – Glyn Owen
Pippa Hales – Jayne Sofiano
Damian Anthony – John Stratton

Boatyard owner Peter Allery visits a small village and suddenly finds himself involved in the brutal murder of a young girl. When a postman begins to deliver letters apparently written by the dead girl, a conspiracy of silence falls over the village, frustrating the police in their investigation, which ultimately points in the direction of a strange religious sect, the cult of Space Spirit Meditation.

IMPERIAL PALACE

8 March 1969, Saturday, 8:15–9:00pm,

BBC2 (colour), 4 episodes, drama, British, 20th century
BBCtv
Pr: David Conroy
Dir: Paddy Russell
Wtr: Michael Voysey
Based on Arnold Bennett
Cast: Violet Powler – Anna Cropper
Evelyn Orcham – Roy Dotrice
Sir Henry Savott – Cyril Luckham
Gracie Savott – Hildegard Neil

The Imperial Palace Hotel, overseen by autocratic Managing Director Evelyn Orcham, is the most luxurious hotel in the world, but life within its plush walls in the 1930s undergoes a severe and traumatic change when he becomes involved with Gracie Savott – whose millionaire father, Sir Henry Savott, seeks to buy the hotel.

THE WAY WE LIVE NOW

5 April 1969, Saturday, 8:25–9:10pm, BBC2 (colour), 5 episodes, drama, British, 19th century
BBCtv
Pr: David Conroy
Dir: James Cellan Jones
Wtr: Simon Raven
Based on Anthony Trollope
Cast: **Augustus Melmotte – Colin Blakely**
Lady Carbury – Rachel Gurney
Henrietta Carbury – Sharon Gurney
Sir Felix Carbury – Cavan Kendall
Madame Melmotte – Irene Prador
Marie Melmotte – Angharad Rees

In the 1890s, London heiress Marie Melmotte is pursued by a number of greedy suitors, principal among whom is Sir Felix Carbury, egged on by his ambitious mother. Meanwhile, Marie's father Augustus becomes involved in a grandiose financial speculation scheme, which changes things for all involved.

THE ELUSIVE PIMPERNEL

20 April 1969, Sunday, 5:30–5:55pm, BBC1, 10 episodes, drama, classic, French, 18th century
BBCtv
Pr: Campbell Logan
Dir: Gerald Blake
Wtr: John Hawkesworth
Based on *The Elusive Pimpernel, Eldorado* by The Baroness Orczy
Cast: **Marguerite Blakeney – Diane Fletcher**
Juliette de Marny – Tamara Fuerst
Robespierre – Jimmy Gardner
Chauvelin – Bernard Hepton
Charles de Marny – David Reynalds
Armand St. Just – Malcolm Reynolds
Sir Percy Blakeney/The Scarlet Pimpernel – Anton Rodgers
Desiree Candeille – Norma West

In a tale of derring-do and intrigue, foppish Sir Percy Blakeney is really the dashing Scarlet Pimpernel, rescuing aristocrats who are victims of the Reign of Terror during the French Revolution, to the dismay of revolutionary agent Chauvelin. Chauvelin finally captures Sir Percy and seems to have broken his spirit, and it is up to Marguerite Blakeney to help rescue her husband.

THE PRIOR COMMITMENT

22 April 1969, Tuesday, 9:55–10:20pm, BBC1, 6 episodes, thriller, Scottish, contemporary
BBCtv/Scotland
Pr: Pharic Maclaren
Designed by David McKenzie
Wtr: Bill Craig
Cast: Cadwaller – Peter Copley
Helen Prior – Libby Glenn
Shaw – John Grieve
Eddie Prior – William Lucas
Sergeant Forbes – Callum Mill
Spinner – Aubrey Morris
Liz Elliot – Claire Nielson

Television reporter Eddie Prior journeys to a remote Scottish island in search of his missing wife, Helen. She is not found, but the corpse of a man is discovered, and Prior becomes caught up in solving the murder, a dangerous intrigue which is ultimately revealed to involve Helen Prior . . . and national security.

SINISTER STREET

10 May 1969, Saturday, 7:30–8:15 pm,

BBC2, 6 episodes, drama, British, 20th
century
BBCtv
Pr: David Conroy
Dir: Rex Tucker
Wtr: Ray Lawler
Based on Compton Mackenzie
Cast: Nanny – Angela Baddeley
       Michael Fane (as a child) – Kim
         Burfield
       Stella Fane (as a child) –
         Sarah-Juliette Dejey
       Stella Fane – Gillian Hawser
       Miss Carthew – Jo Kendall
       Mrs. Fane – Jeanne Moody
       Lily – Elaine Taylor
       Michael Fane – Brett Usher

The old world and the new come into crashing conflict in the days before World War I, seen through the eyes of Stella and Michael Fane, the illegitimate children of well-to-do parents, as they progress from early childhood through university.

CHRIST RECRUCIFIED

16 August 1969, Saturday, 7:30–8:15pm,
BBC2 (colour), 6 episodes, drama, Greek,
20th century
BBCtv
Pr: David Conroy
Dir: Hugh David
Wtr: Jack Pulman
Based on Nikos Kazantzakis
Cast: Michelis – Michael da Costa
       **Pope Fotis – John
         Franklyn-Robbins**
       Manolios – Aharon Ipale
       Pope Grigoris – John Phillips
       The Agha – George Pravda
       Lenio – Diana Quick
       Yannakos – Edwin Richfield
       Youssoufaki – Yasmin Singh
       Katerina – Monica Vassiliou

As a village in Greece makes plans for its annual Passion Play about the life and death of Christ, those chosen for the leading parts are expected to conduct themselves as befits their sacred roles – a practice which in 1920 has serious consequences, as the area is under cruel Turkish occupation. When a group of refugees comes to the village seeking help, Manolios and Katerina, the chosen Christ and Mary Magdalene figures, offer assistance, but they are among the only ones, and, tragically, faith and love lose out to mob violence.

DOMBEY AND SON

17 August 1969, Sunday, 5:30–5:55pm,
BBC1, 13 episodes, drama, classic, British,
19th century
BBCtv
Pr: Campbell Logan
Dir: Joan Craft
Wtr: Hugh Leonard
Based on Charles Dickens
Cast: **Mr. Dombey – John Carson**
       Fanny Dombey – Maude Foster
       Susan Nipper – Helen Fraser
       Edith Dombey – Sally Home
       Captain Cuttle – William Moore
       Paul Dombey – Roland Pickering
       James Carker – Gary Raymond
       Walter Gay – Derek Seaton
       Major Bagstock – Clive Swift
       **Florence Dombey Gay – Kara
         Wilson**

Cold-hearted businessman Mr. Dombey focuses his attentions solely on Paul, his son and heir, ignoring his daughter Florence. Dombey's antipathy towards Florence grows stronger when Paul dies; he marries again, but selfish new wife Edith runs off with another man. Meanwhile, Florence marries happily, and when Dombey loses his money and is left alone and miserable, Florence has the opportunity to repay her father for his bad treatment of her. Instead, she takes him into her home, and the family is reconciled.

THE CONTENDERS

5 September 1969, Friday, 9:00–10:00pm,
ITV, 4 episodes, drama, British,
contemporary
Granada Television
Pr: Dennis Woolf
Dir: Graham Evans
Wtr: Dennis Woolf
Based on John Wain
Cast: Justin Cartridge – John Bryans
       Ned Mitchell – Keith Drinkel

Robert Lamb – Victor Henry
Celia Rathbone – Betty
  Huntley-Wright
Tom Stocker – Alan Lake
Myra Chetwynd – Jocelyne Sbath
Mrs. Shaw – Joan Scott
Joe Shaw – Peter Sproule

Childhood friends Robert Lamb, now an artist, and Ned Mitchell, a successful businessman, try over the course of 20 years to outdo each other in their respective careers and their efforts to win the love of beautiful model Myra Chetwynd.

A HANDFUL OF THIEVES

22 September 1969, Monday, 5:20–5:45pm, BBC1, 4 episodes, drama, family, British, contemporary
BBCtv
Pr: John McRae
Dir: Barry Letts
Wtr: Rosemary Anne Sisson
Based on Nina Bawden
Cast: **Algy – John Gugolka**
  Gran – Barbara Leake
  Clio – Juliet Marshall
  Mr. Gribble – Frank Mills
  Fred McAlpine – Martin Ratcliffe
  Sid – Martin Skinner
  Rosie – Helen Worth

When Fred's Gran discovers that the money she'd been saving in an old teapot is missing, Fred and his friends are immediately suspicious of Mr. Gribble, the strange new lodger at Gran's Lilac House. The youngsters then endeavour to steal the money back from the presumed thief, but are in for suspense and surprises before all is resolved.

THE FIRST CHURCHILLS

27 September 1969, Saturday, 10:00–10:45pm, BBC2 (colour), 13 episodes, drama, biographical, historical, British, 18th century
BBCtv
Pr: Donald Wilson
Dir: David Giles
Wtr: Donald Wilson
Cast: Henrietta Churchill Godolphin – Polly Adams
  Sarah Jennings Churchill – Susan Hampshire
  Duke of Monmouth – James Kerry
  John Churchill – John Neville
  Robert Harley – Richard Pearson
  Louis XIV – Robert Robinson
  Sidney Godolphin – John Standing
  Queen Anne – Margaret Tyzack
  Charles II – James Villiers
  Francis Godolphin – Richard Warwick
  James II – John Westbrook

The story of John Churchill, 1st Duke of Marlborough, and his wife Sarah, two strong characters who brought the family to the forefront of British social and political life in the 18th century (a tradition which continued through the centuries and perhaps culminated with the worldwide prominence of their 20th-century descendant Sir Winston Churchill).

On 10 January 1971, *The First Churchills* was the first program aired in the United States on public television's *Masterpiece Theatre*, an anthology series which continues to be the country's primary outlet for the broadcast of British television drama.

SPECIAL PROJECT AIR

16 November 1969, Sunday, 5:10–5:55pm, BBC1 (colour), 4 episodes, thriller, British, contemporary
BBCtv
Pr: Peter Bryant
Dir: Philip Dudley
Wtr: Ben Williams
Cast: **Wing Commander Routledge – Peter Barkworth**
  Flight Lieutenant Jo Foster – Elizabeth Bell
  Saunders – Tenniel Evans
  Chappie Smith – Alex Scott

When an attempt is made on the life of a Foreign Officer in Singapore, the Special Project Air team, under the leadership of Wing Commander Routledge, is called in to investigate.

This was the first serial on BBC1 to be broadcast in colour.

THE BATTLE OF ST. GEORGE WITHOUT

15 December 1969, Monday, 5:20–5:45pm, BBC1, 3 episodes, drama, family, British, contemporary
BBCtv
Pr: Dorothea Brooking
Designed by Oliver Bayldon
Wtr: John Tully
Based on Janet McNeill
Cast: Mrs. McGinley – Beth Boyd
       Henry – Stephen Brassett
       Ma Flint – Jean Challis
       The Flint Twins – David Littleton, Kenneth Littleton
       Madge – Caroline North
       Matt McGinley – Stephen Shipp
       Sidney Lumba – Norman Sweeney

Matt McGinley and his friends who live in Dove Square in a rundown part of the city focus their attentions on the long-neglected church of St. George Without at the center of the Square's untended park. The children use the tower as their private hideaway, but when it is threatened by a sinister gang, they are determined to protect their special place.

THE OWL SERVICE

21 December 1969, Sunday, 4:15–4:45pm, ITV, 8 episodes, thriller, family, Welsh, contemporary
Granada Television
Pr: Peter Plummer
Dir: Peter Plummer
Wtr: Alan Garner
Based on Alan Garner
Cast: Nancy – Dorothy Edwards
       Alison Bradley – Gillian Hills
       Gwyn – Michael Holden
       Huw – Raymond Llewellyn
       Clive Bradley – Edwin Richfield
       Roger Bradley – Francis Wallis

When Roger's father marries Alison's mother the new family travels on holiday to a house in a Welsh valley. But far from being a peaceful refuge, strange and frightening things are seen and heard. A set of flower-patterned plates – the Owl Service – is discovered by Gwyn, the local boy helping the Bradley family, and Alison becomes obsessed with the china, unwittingly unearthing the terrifying power of the ancient mythic spirit Blodeuwedd.

1970–1979

THE SIX WIVES OF HENRY VIII

1 January 1970, Thursday, 9:10–10:40pm, BBC2, 6 episodes, drama, historical, British, 16th century
BBCtv
Video: available in UK, US
Pr: Ronald Travers, Mark Shivas
Dir: John Glenister, Naomi Capon
Wtr: Beverley Cross, Nick McCarty, Jean Morris, John Prebble, Rosemary Anne Sisson, Ian Thorne
Based on an idea by Maurice Cowan
Cast: Lady Rochford – Sheila Burrell
Catherine of Aragon – Annette Crosbie
Catherine Parr – Rosalie Crutchley
Princess Mary – Alison Frazer
Will Somers – Howard Goorney
Anne of Cleves – Elvi Hale
Archbishop Cranmer – Bernard Hepton
Henry VIII – Keith Michell
Catherine Howard – Angela Pleasence
Sir Thomas Seymour – John Ronane
Princess Elizabeth – Jody Schaller
Jane Seymour – Anne Stallybrass
Duke of Norfolk – Patrick Troughton
Anne Boleyn – Dorothy Tutin

The marital sagas of Henry VIII, focusing on each of his six wives – from the deeply religious Catherine of Aragon to Anne Boleyn, who bore the daughter destined to be Elizabeth I, to Jane Seymour, whose son Edward succeeded Henry to the throne, to the political choice of Anne of Cleves, to Catherine Howard, the daughter of his chief advisor, to his last wife, Catherine Parr, who served as his nurse and companion in his waning years – outlining an epic tale of passion, intrigue, corruption, loyalty and even treachery.

IVANHOE

4 January 1970, Sunday, 5:30–5:55pm, BBC2 (colour), 10 episodes, drama, classic, British, 12th century
BBCtv
Pr: Campbell Logan, John McRae
Dir: David Maloney
Wtr: Alexander Baron
Based on Sir Walter Scott
Cast: **Sir Brian de Bois Guilbert – Anthony Bate**
Rebecca – Vivian Brooks
Ivanhoe – Eric Flynn
Locksley – Clive Graham
Black Knight – Bernard Horsfall
Rowena – Clare Jenkins
Prince John – Tim Preece

Ivanhoe returns home from the Crusades, ready to claim both his inheritance and the woman he loves, Rowena. But instead he is caught in the middle of intrigue and adventure, becomes involved with the beautiful Rebecca, and must do fierce battle with Sir Brian de Bois Guilbert before all circumstances can be resolved.

GERMINAL

11 January 1970, Sunday, 10:30–11:10pm, BBC2 (colour), 5 episodes, drama, French, 19th century
BBCtv
Pr: David Conroy
Dir: John Davies
Wtr: David Turner
Based on Emile Zola
Cast: Mme. Gregoire – Nancie Jackson
Etienne Lantier – Mark Jones
M. Hennebeau – Charles Morgan
Catherine – Annette Robertson
M. Gregoire – John Wentworth

The story of the harsh world of coal miners in Northern France in the late 19th century, focusing on the personal struggles of Etienne Lantier and the brutal labor struggles between the miners and their bosses.

A STRANGER ON THE HILLS

2 February 1970, Monday, 5:20–5:50pm, BBC1, 3 episodes, drama, family, British, 15th century
BBCtv
Pr: Brian Miller
Designed by Desmond Chinn, Chris Robillard
Wtr: John Elliot, Brian Miller
Based on *Nicholas and The Woolpack* by Cynthia Harnett
Cast: Mistress Fetterlock – Thelma Barlow

Master Richard – Adrian Cairns
Nicholas Fetterlock – Raymond Millross
Cecily Bradshaw – Karen Newport
Thomas Fetterlock – Godfrey Quigley
Antonio de Bari – Julian Sherrier

In 1493, teenaged Nicholas Fetterlock works with his father in the family wool business and is engaged to Cecily Bradshaw, the daughter of a famous weaver. Nicholas and Cecily find their lives turned upside down by the sudden arrival in their Cotswold village of a man from Lombardy, who has been buying large quantities of wool, and who nearly gets away with a plan to ruin the Fetterlock family business.

THE WOODLANDERS

15 February 1970, Sunday,
10:05–10:50pm, BBC2 (colour),
4 episodes, drama, British, 19th century
BBCtv
Pr: Martin Lisemore
Dir: John Davies
Wtr: Harry Green
Based on Thomas Hardy
Cast: Edred Fitzpiers – Ralph Bates
Giles Winterborne – David Burke
George Melbury – Michael Goodliffe
Grace Melbury – Felicity Kendal
Marty South – Annette Robertson
Mrs. Charmond – Angela Thorne

Grace Melbury evolves from a simple country girl to an educated young woman, and when she returns to her Dorset home from boarding school she enters into an ill-fated relationship with Giles Winterborne, her childhood sweetheart.

DANIEL DERONDA

15 March 1970, Sunday, 10:15–11:00pm, BBC2 (colour), 6 episodes, drama, British, 19th century
BBCtv
Pr: David Conroy
Dir: Joan Croft
Wtr: Alexander Baron
Based on George Eliot
Cast: Mordechai – John Bennett

Mrs. Gascoigne – Elizabeth Bradley
Henleigh Grandcourt – Robert Hardy
Gwendolen Harleth – Martha Henry
Mirah – Vanessa Miles
Daniel Deronda – John Nolan
Isabel Davilow – Annemarie Reed
Alice Davilow – Louise Rush

To avoid a life of destitution, Gwendolen Harleth marries tyrannical Henleigh Grandcourt. After his death (for which she blames herself), Gwendolen is drawn to idealistic Daniel Deronda, a relationship which helps to develop Gwendolen's finer qualities, but which comes to an end when Daniel discovers the hidden truths of his heritage.

A FAMILY AT WAR

14 April 1970, Tuesday, 9:00–10:00pm,
ITV, 17 episodes, drama, British, 20th century
Granada Television
Pr: Richard Doubleday
Dir: Michael Cox, Richard Doubleday, June Howson, Tim Jones, Gerry Mill
Wtr: Alexander Baron, Stan Barstow, John Finch, H.V. Kershaw, Elaine Morgan, Leslie Sands
Devised by John Finch
Cast: Sheila Ashton – Coral Atkins
Tony Briggs – Trevor Bowen
David Ashton – Colin Campbell
Robert Ashton – David Dixon
Edwin Ashton – Colin Douglas
Philip Ashton – Keith Drinkel
Freda Ashton – Barbara Flynn
Jean Ashton – Shelagh Fraser
Sefton Briggs – John McKelvey
Margaret Ashton Porter – Lesley Nunnerley
John Porter – Ian Thompson

The lives of the Ashton family – Edwin, his wife Jean, and their children, David, Margaret, Philip, Robert and Freda – are changed forever in 1938 when the first word of impending war creeps into their consciousness. Their story is told against a background of the homefront in Liverpool and the battlefields of World War II. Eldest son David joins the RAF, leaving behind his wife Sheila; Philip, too, becomes involved. Margaret's husband

John Porter is reported missing in action after the retreat to Dunkirk. By December 1940, youngest son Robert is 16, and the family worries that he will be called to serve.

First of three self-contained *A Family at War* serials; the saga totalled more than 50 hours when completed in February 1972.

THE SPOILS OF POYNTON

26 April 1970, Sunday, 10:00–10:40pm, BBC2 (colour), 4 episodes, drama, British, 19th century
BBCtv
Pr: Martin Lisemore
Dir: Peter Sasdy
Wtr: Denis Constanduros
Based on Henry James
Cast: Mrs. Brigstock – June Ellis
       Mona Brigstock – Diane Fletcher
       Mrs. Gereth – Pauline Jameson
       Fleda Vetch – Gemma Jones
       Owen Gereth – Ian Ogilvy

The "spoils" of Poynton are furniture and other objects which have been willed to Owen Gereth by his father. His mother, who had lovingly collected them over the years, leaves Poynton, but takes the spoils for herself to a small house when Owen plans to marry an artless young woman. Mrs. Gereth finds a kindred spirit in sensitive Fleda Vetch, to whom she offers any item from the collection, but fate intervenes destructively, literally spoiling both objects and lives.

VILLETTE

31 May 1970, Sunday, 10:35–11:20pm, BBC2 (colour), 5 episodes, drama, classic, British, 19th century
BBCtv
Pr: Martin Lisemore
Dir: Moira Armstrong
Wtr: Lennox Phillips
Based on Charlotte Brontë
Cast: **Madame Beck – Mona Bruce**
       Rosine – Mary Healey
       Mrs. Bretton – Joan Heath
       Paul Emmanuel – Peter Jeffrey
       Dr. John Graham Bretton – Bryan Marshall
       Lucy Snowe – Judy Parfitt
       Ginevra Fanshawe – Angela Richards

Self-reliant Lucy Snowe moves to the Belgian village of Villette, where she takes up a teaching position under the formidable Madame Beck. In Villette, Lucy is reunited with people from her past, suffers the pangs of an unhappy romance, and ultimately finds happiness with headmaster Paul Emmanuel.

SENTIMENTAL EDUCATION

9 August 1970, Sunday, 10:20–11:05pm, BBC2 (colour), 4 episodes, drama, French, 19th century
BBCtv
Pr: Martin Lisemore
Dir: David Maloney
Wtr: Hugh Leonard
Based on Gustave Flaubert
Cast: Rosanette – Stephanie Beacham
       Madame Dambreuse – Wendy Gifford
       Arnoux – Glyn Owen
       Frederic Moreau – Robert Powell
       Dambreuse – André Van Gyseghem
       Marthe – Victoria Williams
       Madame Arnoux – Pauline Yates

In 1848, ambitious, self-centered Frederic Moreau returns home from Paris, intent on living the life of a romantic hero. He gallantly suffers unrequited love for Madame Arnoux, while at the same time involving himself in a number of more down-to-earth yet ultimately disillusioning affairs of the heart.

THE BLACK TULIP

13 September 1970, Sunday, 5:40–6:05pm, BBC1, 6 episodes, drama, classic, French, 17th century
BBCtv
Pr: John McRae
Dir: Derek Martinus
Wtr: Alexander Baron
Based on Alexandre Dumas
Cast: Dirk – John Cater
       Van Systens – David Dodimead
       Colonel van Deken – Leon Eagles

Isaac Boxtel – **Wolfe Morris**
Gryphus – John Stratton
Cornelius van Baerle – Simon Ward
Prince William – Eric Woofe
Rosa – Tessa Wyatt

In Holland during the 17th century, during the conflict between Prince William of Orange and France, Cornelius van Baerle is unjustly branded a traitor. While imprisoned, van Baerle endeavours to grow the rare and beautiful black tulip, but his noble efforts are the target of a jealous rival, tulip grower Isaac Boxtel, who aims to claim the precious bloom as his own.

THE ROADS TO FREEDOM

4 October 1970, Sunday, 10:05–10:50pm, BBC2 (colour), 13 episodes, drama, French, 20th century
BBCtv
Pr: David Conroy
Dir: James Cellan Jones
Wtr: David Turner
Based on *The Age of Reason*, *The Reprieve*, and *Iron In The Soul* by Jean-Paul Sartre
Cast: Lola – Georgia Brown
Mathieu Delarue – Michael Bryant
Brunet – Donald Burton
Ivich – Alison Fiske
Marcelle – Rosemary Leach
Daniel – Daniel Massey
Pinette – Norman Rossington

In Paris in 1938, philosophy professor Mathieu and his friend Daniel struggle for love, friendship and commitment, their experiences paralleled with a Europe heading towards disaster, everything culminating in the fall of France in 1940.

LITTLE WOMEN

25 October 1970, Sunday, 5:35–6:00pm, BBC1 (colour), 9 episodes, drama, classic, family, American, 19th century
BBCtv
Video: available in UK, US
Pr: John McRae
Dir: Paddy Russell
Wtr: Alistair Bell, Denis Constanduros
Based on *Little Women* and *Good Wives* by Louisa May Alcott
Cast: Mrs. March – Stephanie Bidmead
Beth – Sarah Craze
Jo – Angela Down
Amy – Janina Faye
Professor Bhaer – Frederick Jaeger
John Brooke – Martin Jarvis
Meg – Jo Rowbottom
Mr. March – Patrick Troughton
Laurie – Stephen Turner
Mr. Laurence – John Welsh

The March sisters grow from young women into adulthood in New England in the 1860s; after their father returns to the family following the American Civil War, Jo, Amy and Meg begin to think of having families of their own.

A FAMILY AT WAR (second series)

11 November 1970, Wednesday, 9:00–10:00pm, ITV, 20 episodes, drama, British, 20th century
Granada Television
Pr: Michael Cox, Richard Doubleday
Dir: Les Chatfield, Bob Hird, Tim Jones, Richard Martin, Gerry Mill, James Ormerod, Baz Taylor, Oscar Whitbread
Wtr: Alexander Baron, James Brabazon, John Finch, Geoffrey Lancashire, Susan Pleat, Philip Purser, Jack Ronder, John Stevenson
Devised by John Finch
Cast: **Sheila Ashton – Coral Atkins**
Tony Briggs – Trevor Bowen
David Ashton – Colin Campbell
Dennis Pringle – Mark Dignam
Robert Ashton – David Dixon
Edwin Ashton – Colin Douglas
Owen Thomas – Mark Edwards
Freda Ashton – Barbara Flynn
Jean Ashton – Shelagh Fraser
Michael Armstrong – Mark Jones
Stashek – Bryan Marshall
Sefton Briggs – John McKelvey
Dr. Ian Mackenzie – John Nettles
Margaret Porter – Lesley Nunnerley
Sergeant Hazard – Maurice Roeves
Peggy Drake – Amelia Taylor

Picking up the story of the Ashton family in January 1941, with Edwin in conflict with his brother-in-law, Sefton Briggs, for whom he works. Briggs' son Tony returns home on leave. Margaret's husband is still presumed dead; she becomes romantically involved with conscientious objector Michael Armstrong. Sheila and David's children have been evacuated to the countryside. The Ashton sons are all away from home; even youngest son Robert has gone to sea, to his mother's horror. Liverpool is bombed and the Ashtons are directly affected. Then Robert is killed, which serves a devastating blow to the marriage of Edwin and Jean.

SENSE AND SENSIBILITY

9 January 1971, Saturday, 10:05–10:50pm
BBC2, 4 episodes, drama, classic, British, 19th century
BBCtv
Pr: Martin Lisemore
Dir: David Giles
Wtr: Denis Constanduros
Based on Jane Austen
Cast: **Elinor Dashwood – Joanna David**
Mrs. Dashwood – Isabel Dean
Edward Ferrars – Robin Ellis
John Willoughby – Clive Francis
Fanny Dashwood – Kay Gallie
John Dashwood – Milton Johns
Charlotte Palmer – Jo Kendall
Marianne Dashwood – Ciaran Madden
Colonel Brandon – Richard Owens

The lives of the Dashwood sisters, impetuous Marianne and conventional Elinor, are radically altered following the death of their father when they must move from the family home, which has been entailed to their half-brother. Elinor falls in love with Edward Ferrars, who is promised to another, and Marianne, who is loved by staid Colonel Brandon, loses her heart to roguish John Willoughby, who jilts her. Their mutual suffering brings a deeper understanding to each sister of the other's temperament, and in the end both are happily married.

As of 1971, programs are no longer specifically notated as being in colour.

THE LAST OF THE MOHICANS

17 January 1971, Sunday, 5:20–6:05pm, BBC1, 8 episodes, drama, classic, American, 18th century
BBCtv
Pr: John McRae
Dir: David Maloney
Wtr: Harry Green
Based on James Fenimore Cooper
Cast: **Chingachgook – John Abineri**
Colonel Munro – Andrew Crawford
Alice Munro – Joanna David
Major Heyward – Tim Goodman
Hawkeye – Kenneth Ives
Magua – Philip Madoc
Cora Munro – Patricia Maynard
Uncas – Richard Warwick

During the French-Indian Wars of the 1750s, colonial scout Hawkeye, a white man raised by Mohican Chingachgook, intervenes with Chingachcook's son Uncas to protect the daughters of British Colonel Munro, whose lives are repeatedly threatened by Magua, a Huron warrior aligned with the French.

JUDE THE OBSCURE

6 February 1971, Saturday, 9:35–10:20pm, BBC2, 6 episodes, drama, classic, British, 19th century
BBCtv
Video: available in US
Pr: Martin Lisemore
Dir: Hugh David
Wtr: Harry Green
Based on Thomas Hardy
Cast: Richard Phillotson – John Franklyn-Robbins
Arabella Donn – Alex Marshall
Young Jude – Mark Praid
Jude Fawley – Robert Powell
Juey – Gary Rich
Sue Bridehead – Fiona Walker

In Victorian England, poorly educated country stonemason Jude Fawley dreams of going to university. Instead, he is seduced into an unhappy marriage to Arabella, who subsequently abandons him. Jude falls in love with his cousin, free-thinking Sue Bridehead, but when he is finally free to marry her she has tired of waiting for him and has married another. Ultimately the two ill-fated lovers decide to live together, and for this they are persecuted, leading to unhappiness and tragedy for them both.

ELIZABETH R

17 February 1971, Wednesday, 9:20–10:50pm, BBC2, 6 episodes, drama, biographical, historical, British, 16th century
BBCtv
Video: available in UK, US
Pr: Roderick Graham
Dir: Roderick Graham, Richard Martin, Donald McWhinnie, Claude Whatham, Herbert Wise
Wtr: John Hale, Julian Mitchell, John Prebble, Ian Rodger, Rosemary Anne Sisson, Hugh Whitemore
Cast: Catherine Parr – Rosalie Crutchley
Bishop Gardiner – Basil Dignam
Earl of Essex – Robin Ellis
Robert Dudley, Earl of Leicester – Robert Hardy
Archbishop Cranmer – Bernard Hepton
William Cecil, Lord Burghley – Ronald Hines
Elizabeth I – Glenda Jackson
Philip II – Peter Jeffrey
Edward VI – Jason Kemp
Kay Ashley – Rachel Kempson
Sir Francis Walsingham – Stephen Murray
Francis Bacon – John Nettleton
Mary, Queen of Scots – Vivian Pickles
Catherine de Medici – Margaretta Scott
Sir Walter Raleigh – Nicholas Selby
Earl of Sussex – John Shrapnel
Mary Tudor – Daphne Slater
Sir Francis Drake – John Woodvine

A biographical drama tracing the life and personality of Elizabeth I, daughter of Henry VIII and Anne Boleyn, from her early teens until her death in 1603 at the age of 69, demonstrating her ferocity as a monarch despite the then-lowly status of being a woman. First viewed during the brief reigns of her brother Edward and sister Mary, when Elizabeth becomes Queen she is soon caught up in her great but ill-fated romance with Robert Dudley, Earl of Leicester, highlighting the conflict between the personal and public interests of the Queen. Elizabeth's duel with Mary, Queen of Scots is also examined, as is the Spanish Armada, portraying the Queen at her glory . . . a glory that is to fade in her later years, when Elizabeth is out of touch with the social and economic developments around her.

The characters of Bishops Cranmer and Gardiner and Elizabeth's fourth stepmother, Catherine Parr, were portrayed by the same actors who played these roles in *The Six Wives of Henry VIII*.

Winner, Emmy Awards, Outstanding Dramatic Series, Outstanding New Series 1971–1972.

JOE AND THE GLADIATOR

22 February 1971, Monday, 5:20–5:45pm, BBC1, 3 episodes, drama, British, contemporary
BBCtv
Pr: Anna Home
Dir: Anna Home
Wtr: Anna Home
Based on Catherine Cookson
Cast: Mr. Prodhurst – James Garbutt
Joe Darling – Dennis Lingard
Willie Styles – Ken Purvis
Mrs. Darling – Ursula Smith
Mr. Darling – Richard Steele

Life is bleak for young Joe Darling, what with trouble at home between his parents and trouble with a bully at the Tyneside shipyard where he works. A friendship with rag-and-bone man Mr. Prodhurst leads Joe into the challenge of his life when Prodhurst entails his horse, "The Gladiator," to Joe – but only provides sufficent funds for a few weeks' food. Joe is determined to continue to look after the horse, which will otherwise have to be put down, and turns his life around in order to provide for "The Gladiator."

SUNSET SONG

26 March 1971, Friday, 9:50–10:35pm, BBC2, 6 episodes, drama, Scottish, 20th century
BBCtv/Scotland

Pr: Pharic Maclaren
Dir: Moira Armstrong
Wtr: Bill Craig
Based on Lewis Grassic Gibbon
Cast: Rob Duncan – Derek Anders
Chae Strachan – Victor Carin
Ewan Tavendale – James Grant
Chris Guthrie – Vivien Heilbron
John Guthrie – Andrew Keir
Jean Guthrie – Edith Macarthur
Will Guthrie – Paul Young

Set in the years just before World War I, young Scottish girl Chris Guthrie develops both intellectually and emotionally, as opposed to the rigid, repressive peasant community in which she lives.

PERSUASION

18 April 1971, Sunday, 10:15–11:15pm, ITV, 5 episodes, drama, classic, British, 19th century
Granada Television
Video: available in UK
Pr: Howard Baker
Dir: Howard Baker
Wtr: Julian Mitchell
Based on Jane Austen
Cast: Charles Musgrove – Rowland Davies
Sir Walter Elliot – Basil Dignam
Anne Elliot – Ann Firbank
Elizabeth Elliot – Valerie Gearon
Mary Musgrove – Morag Hood
Captain Wentworth – Bryan Marshall
Henrietta Musgrove – Mel Martin
Mrs. Clay – Charlotte Mitchell
Mrs. Smith – Polly Murch
Louisa Musgrove – Zhivila Roche
Mr. Elliot – David Savile
Lady Russell – Marian Spencer

Anne Elliot, unmarried daughter of the pompous but nearly penniless Sir Walter Elliot, learns that the man she was once engaged to, Captain Wentworth, is about to return to the area, a successful and wealthy officer. Anne, who has not cared for another man in the eight years since she was pressurised to break off her engagement, wonders whether Wentworth might still care for her, or if his affections are now directed elsewhere.

Broadcast as part of ITV's "Sunday Night Theatre," this was the first Theatre presentation to present a multi-part adaptation of a classic novel.

BEL AMI

8 May 1971, Saturday, 8:10–8:55pm, BBC2, 5 episodes, drama, French, 19th century
BBCtv
Pr: Martin Lisemore
Dir: John Davies
Wtr: Robert Muller
Based on Guy de Maupassant
Cast: Suzanne Walter – Wendy Allnutt
Monsieur Walter – John Bryans
Madame Walter – Margaret Courtenay
Georges Duroy – Robin Ellis
Clotilde de Marelle – Elvi Hale
Madeleine Forestier – Suzanne Neve
Comte de Vaudrec – John Wentworth

In Paris in the 1890s, Georges Duroy returns from the colonial wars in North Africa destitute and with no prospects, but through the force of his charm and a series of unscrupulous dealings manages to develop a position of social power and wealth, wooing a number of women along the way.

COUSIN BETTE

7 August 1971, Saturday, 8:30–9:15pm, BBC2, 5 episodes, drama, French, 19th century
BBCtv
Pr: Martin Lisemore
Dir: Gareth Davies
Wtr: Ray Lawler
Based on Honoré de Balzac
Cast: Steinbock – Colin Baker
Adeline – Ursula Howells
General Hulot – Esmond Knight
Valerie – Helen Mirren
Cousin Bette – Margaret Tyzack
Hector – Thorley Walters

The Hulot family has risen to prominence in French society during the time of Napoleon I. But Baroness Hulot's cousin, embittered, never married Bette, is the only member of the family who has not shared in their good fortune. When Bette's protégé, a young sculptor, falls in love with Hulot's daughter, Bette's all-consuming jealousy leads to a series of revenges against the family.

THE SILVER SWORD

22 August 1971, Sunday, 5:15–5:40pm, BBC1, 8 episodes, drama, family, European, 20th century
BBCtv
Pr: John McRae
Dir: Joan Craft
Wtr: Alexander Baron
Based on Ian Serraillier
Cast: Joseph Balicki – Philip Brack
Margrit Balicki – Elizabeth Burger
Bronia Balicki – Cherrald Butterfield
Edek Balicki – Rufus Frampton
Emma Wolff – Lila Kaye
Kurt Wolff – Peter Schofield
Ruth Balicki – Joanna Shelley
Jan – Simon Turner

The Polish Balicki children are forced from their home following the German invasion at the start of World War II, and a series of adventures takes them across the devastated European continent as they struggle to survive and hopefully reunite with their parents.

EYELESS IN GAZA

12 September 1971, Sunday, 9:00–9:45pm, BBC2, 5 episodes, drama, British, 20th century
BBCtv
Pr: Martin Lisemore
Dir: James Cellan Jones
Wtr: Robin Chapman
Based on Aldous Huxley
Cast: Mary Amberley – Adrienne Corri
Miller – John Laurie
Anthony Beavis – Ian Richardson
Anthony (as a boy) – Jeremy Richardson

During the 1930s, philosopher Anthony Beavis carries on an ongoing debate with those around him about pacifism, violence and the individual need for action.

THE SEARCH FOR THE NILE

22 September 1971, Wednesday, 9:20–10:20pm, BBC2, 6 episodes, drama, historical, British, 19th century
BBCtv
Video: available in US
Pr: Christopher Ralling
Dir: Fred Burnley, Richard Marquand, Christopher Ralling
Wtr: Michael Hastings, Derek Marlowe
Cast: **Henry Morton Stanley – Keith Buckley**
Dr. David Livingstone – Michael Gough
Richard Burton – Kenneth Haigh
Isabel Burton – Barbara Leigh-Hunt
Narrator – James Mason
James Grant – Ian McCulloch
John Hanning Speke – John Quentin
Samuel Baker – Norman Rossington
Florence Baker – Catherine Schell
Sir Roderick Murchison – André van Gyseghem

The quest for the source of the Nile, long considered the ultimate prize in global exploration, based in large part on the diaries of and focusing on the attempts of six British explorers – Richard Burton, John Hanning Speke, James Grant, Samuel Baker, Henry Morton Stanley and Dr. David Livingstone – during the latter half of the 19th century.

THE WITCH'S DAUGHTER

4 October 1971, Monday, 5:20–5:45pm, BBC1, 4 episodes, drama, family, Scottish, 20th century
BBCtv
Pr: John McRae
Dir: David Maloney
Wtr: Alistair Bell
Based on Nina Bawden
Cast: Mr. Smith – John Abineri
Janey – Gillian Bailey
Tim – Spencer Banks
Will Campbell – James Garbutt
Perdita – Fiona Kennedy
Jones – Barry Linehan

Orphaned Perdita lives on a remote island in the Hebrides with her foster mother, who is housekeeper for secretive Mr. Smith. Perdita makes her first friend when blind Janey comes to the island for a visit. With Janey and her brother Tim, Perdita uncovers a mystery on the island which involves Mr. Smith, and which involves the children in a great deal of danger.

A FAMILY AT WAR (third series)

6 October 1971, Wednesday, 9:00–10:00pm, ITV, 20 episodes, drama, British, 20th century
Granada Television
Pr: Michael Cox
Dir: Les Chatfield, Richard Doubleday, David Giles, Bob Hird, Quentin Lawrence, Richard Martin, Gerry Mill, Baz Taylor
Wtr: Alexander Baron, John Ellison, John Finch, John Foster, Robert Furnival, Jonathan Powell, Roy Russell, David Weir, John Wiles
Devised by John Finch
Cast: **Sheila Ashton – Coral Atkins**
Grace Gould – Adrienne Corri
Edwin Ashton – Colin Douglas
Freda Ashton Mackenzie – Barbara Flynn
Barbara – Mel Martin
Sefton Briggs – John McKelvey
Dr. Ian Mackenzie – John Nettles
Margaret Porter – Lesley Nunnerley
John Porter – Ian Thompson
Harry Porter – Patrick Troughton

Picking up the story of the Ashton and Briggs families in June 1943, followng the deaths of Robert and Jean Ashton. Edwin is still in conflict with Sefton Briggs, and remains focused on the lives of his children. David's freewheeling ways, particularly his affair with Grace Gould, have shattered his marriage to Sheila, but they ultimately reconcile when he finally comes home from the war. Margaret's husband John has returned alive and safe and attempts to pick up the threads of civilian life in Liverpool. Freda marries Dr. Ian Mackenzie. By spring of 1945, the war in Europe is drawing to an end and the Ashtons attempt to return to a normal life. In December 1945, the remaining members of the Briggs and Ashton families gather together, looking forward to a world at peace.

FATHERS AND SONS

17 October 1971, Sunday, 9:15–10:00pm, BBC2, 4 episodes, drama, classic, Russian, 19th century
BBCtv
Pr: Martin Lisemore
Dir: Paddy Russell
Wtr: Denis Constanduros
Based on Ivan Turgenev
Cast: Princess Natasha – Jean Anderson
Nikolai Kirsanov – Anthony Bate
Pavel Kirsanov – John Bennett
Doctor Bazarov – Basil Dignam
Yevgeny Bazarov – James Laurenson
Anna Sergeyevna – Rosemary Nicols
Arina Bazarov – Anna Wing

When Russian Yevgeny Bazarov arrives at his physician father's farm in the 1860s, his nihilistic attitudes wreak tragic havoc on those around him.

THE PASSENGER

23 October 1971, Saturday, 8:55–9:40pm, BBC1, 3 episodes, mystery, British, contemporary
BBCtv
Pr: Gerard Glaister
Dir: Michael Ferguson
Wtr: Francis Durbridge
Cast: **Detective Inspector Denson – Peter Barkworth**
Christine Bodley – Mona Bruce
Sue Denson – Joanna Dunham
Detective Sergeant Kennedy – Paul Grist
David Walker – David Knight

Detective Inspector Martin Denson is called in to investigate a complicated murder case involving the death of wealthy Company Director David Walker.

Featured under the program banner of "Francis Durbridge Presents . . . "

THE RUNAWAY SUMMER

8 November 1971, Monday, 5:20–5:45pm,

BBC1, 4 episodes, drama, family, British, 20th century
BBCtv
Pr: John McRae
Dir: Mary Ridge
Wtr: Rosemary Anne Sisson
Based on Nina Bawden
Cast: Simon – Stephen Bone
Aunt Alice – Beryl Cooke
Mary – Carol Davis
Grandfather – John Welsh

After her parents' marriage breaks up, 11-year-old Mary goes to live with her Grandfather and Aunt Alice at their seaside home. Mary is at first angry and embittered and considers running away, but a series of adventures which soon turn dangerous lead to Mary's realization that she cannot run away from reality, but instead must adjust to it.

TOM BROWN'S SCHOOLDAYS

14 November 1971, Sunday, 5:20–6:05pm, BBC1, 5 episodes, drama, classic, British, 19th century
BBCtv
Pr: John McRae
Dir: Gareth Davies
Wtr: Anthony Steven
Based on Thomas Hughes
Cast: **Dr. Arnold – Iain Cuthbertson**
Sir Richard Flashman – Gerald Flood
Gerald Flashman – Richard Morant
Tom Brown – Anthony Murphy
Squire Brown – John Paul
Mrs. Brown – Christine Pollon
Ned East – Simon Turner

This most enduring English schoolboy adventure, somewhat autobiographical in nature, relates the adventures of "average boy" Tom Brown and his days at public school under the progressive leadership of Dr. Arnold . . . and under the constant threat of haughty bully Gerald Flashman.

Winner, Emmy Award, Outstanding Drama (Limited Episodes) 1972–1973.

WIVES AND DAUGHTERS

14 November 1971, Sunday, 9:05–9:55pm, BBC2, 6 episodes, drama, British, 20th century

BBCtv
Pr: Martin Lisemore
Dir: Hugh David
Wtr: Michael Voysey
Based on Mrs Elizabeth Gaskell
Cast: Lady Harriet – Caroline Blakiston
Osborne Hamley – Stephan Chase
Clare Kirkpatrick Gibson – Helen Christie
Lord Cumnor – Roland Culver
Roger Hamley – Rowland Davies
Lady Cumnor – Sonia Dresdel
Miss Dorothy Browning – Sheila Fay
Miss Phoebe Browning – Gabrielle Hamilton
Cynthia Kirkpatrick – Rosalind Lloyd
Dr. Gibson – Alan MacNaughtan
Squire Hamley – Clive Morton
Molly Gibson – Zhivila Roche

In rural Hollingford in the middle of the 19th century people live their lives unaffected as yet by the major changes being brought about elsewhere by the Industrial Revolution . . . but for Molly Gibson and others in her small village, all that is about to change, in a tale of marriage and manners which finds Molly at its center, developing from an insecure girl into a self-assured young woman who wins the affections of scientist Roger Hamley.

CASANOVA

16 November 1971, Tuesday, 9:20–10:15pm, BBC2, 6 episodes, drama, biographical, Italian, 18th century
BBCtv
Pr: Mark Shivas
Dir: Mark Cullingham, John Glenister
Wtr: Dennis Potter
Cast: The Uncle – George Benson
Casanova – Frank Finlay
Pauline – Valerie Gearon
Caroline – Gillian Hills
Cristina – Zienia Merton
Schalon – Patrick Newell
Capitani – Frederick Peisley
Lorenzo – Norman Rossington
Genoveffa – Lyn Yeldham

The life story of Casanova, the notorious 18th-century adventurer, lover, soldier, and voluminous memoir writer, covering his experiences from age 30 through to his death at 73 of a heart attack.

THE INTRUDER

2 January 1972, Sunday, 5:35–6:05pm, ITV, 8 episodes, thriller, British, contemporary
Granada Television
Pr: Peter Plummer
Designed by Peter Caldwell
Wtr: Mervyn Haisman, Peter Plummer
Based on John Rowe Townsend
Cast: Miss Binns – Jean Alexander
Arnold Haithwaite – James Bates
Sonny – Milton Johns
Jane Ellison – Sheila Ruskin
Peter Ellison – Simon Turner
Ernest Haithwaite – Jack Woolgar

Pilot Arnold Haithwaite is used to being a solitary figure along the sands of Cumberland, but intruder Sonny suddenly appears on the landscape – claiming to be the real Arnold Haithwaite. Arnold's search for the truth involves his friends, Jane and Peter Ellison, but in the end it is just Arnold and Sonny, struggling together in the marshy seas.

MAN DOG

3 January 1972, Monday, 5:20–5:45pm, BBC1, 6 episodes, thriller, family, British, contemporary
BBCtv
Pr: Anna Home
Dir: Paul Stone
Wtr: Peter Dickinson
Cast: **Sammy – Jane Anthony**
Miss Thorne – Valerie Georgeson
Kate – Carol Hazell
Levin – Christopher Owen
Duncan – Adrian Shergold

Kate and Sammy happen upon a mystery when they are kept in after school. As they investigate further, accompanied by Kate's brother Duncan, the children are confronted with a strange, dangerous situation at the headquarters of an organization involved in time travel.

THE SHADOW OF THE TOWER

6 January 1972, Thursday, 8:30–9:20pm, BBC2, 13 episodes, drama, biographical, historical, British, 15th century
BBCtv
Pr: Jordan Lawrence
Dir: Moira Armstrong, Darrol Blake, Anthea Browne-Wilkinson, Prudence Fitzgerald, Joan Kemp-Welch, Peter Moffatt, Keith Williams
Wtr: John Elliot, John Gould, Julian Mitchell, John Peacock, Brian Rawlinson, Alun Richards, Rosemary Anne Sisson, Ian Thorne, Hugh Whitemore
Cast: James IV – Derek Anders
Catherine of Aragon – Adrienne Byrne
Sir William Stanley – John Franklyn-Robbins
Sir Robert Clifford – Colin Jeavons
Lord Lovell – Michael Johnson
Prince Arthur – Jason Kemp
Margaret of Burgundy – Rachel Kempson
Earl of Lincoln – James Laurenson
Henry VII – James Maxwell
Earl of Warwick – Christopher Neame
Humphrey Stafford – Maurice Roeves
Earl of Devon – Nicholas Selby
Margaret Beaufort – Marigold Sharman
Perkin Warbeck – Richard Warwick
Elizabeth of York – Norma West

The story of Henry VII, England's first Tudor king, whose reign gets off to a troubling start, as he must deal with insurgent rebels and three other claimants to the throne. Once accepted as the rightful King, he devotes his time and energy to faithful service, despite a number of efforts to dethrone him over the years.

THE MOONSTONE

16 January 1972, Sunday, 5:20–6:05pm, BBC1, 5 episodes, mystery, classic, British, 19th century
BBCtv
Pr: John McRae
Dir: Paddy Russell
Wtr: Hugh Leonard
Based on Wilkie Collins
Cast: Major Frayne – Colin Baker
Rosanna Spearman – Anna Cropper
Gabriel Betteredge – Basil Dignam

Franklin Blake – Robin Ellis
Ezra Jennings – Christopher Hancock
Rachel Verinder – Vivien Heilbron
Godfrey Ablewhite – Martin Jarvis
Sergeant Cuff – John Welsh

The fabulous Moonstone diamond is said to bring misfortune – and even death – to all who possess it, a legend which fascinates Victorian woman Rachel Verinder, who has been given the diamond as a birthday present . . . unaware that it has been stolen from the forehead of an Indian god. When the diamond disappears, Sergeant Cuff considers everyone a suspect, and no stone is left unturned in the search for the true culprit.

MAN OF STRAW

30 January 1972, Sunday, 9:05–9:50pm, BBC2, 6 episodes, drama, German, 19th century
BBCtv
Pr: Martin Lisemore
Dir: Herbert Wise
Wtr: Robert Muller
Based on Heinrich Mann
Cast: Emmi Hessling – Elizabeth Bell
Frau Hessling – Sheila Brennan
Wolfgang Buck – Ian Ogilvy
Rosa – Valerie Holliman
Diederich Hessling – Derek Jacobi
Herr Hessling – Graham Leaman
Magda Hessling – Karin MacCarthy

In Imperial Germany at the end of the 19th century, pompous and ambitious Diederich Hessling journeys from a provincial town to Berlin, where he plans to study. He uses what he has learned to later assume control of the town, his brutish methods appealing to the same sympathies the Nazis were to exploit several decades later.

CLOCHEMERLE

18 February 1972, Friday, 10:05–10:35pm, BBC2, 9 episodes, comedy, French, 19th century
BBCtv/co-production with Bavaria Atelier GMBH, Munich
Pr: Michael Mills
Designed by Spencer Chapman
Wtr: Ray Galton, Alan Simpson
Based on Gabriel Chevallier
Cast: **Mayor Barthelemy Piechut – Cyril Cusack**
Cure Ponosse – Roy Dotrice
Francois Toumignon – Freddie Earlle
Senator Bourdillat – Hugh Griffith
Ernest Tafardel – Kenneth Griffith
Adele Torbayon – Cyd Hayman
Justine Putet – Wendy Hiller
Arthur Torbayon – Barry Linehan
Rose Bivaque – Georgina Moon
Baroness Courtebiche – Micheline Presle
Foncimagne – Christian Roberts
Judith Toumignon – Catherine Rouvel
Claudius Brodequin – James Wardroper

An army detachment is called into the small Beaujolais village of Clochemerle after controversy is stirred up over the unlikely subject of the construction of a public urinal for men . . . which happens to be located just under the window of the village spinster. But what appears to be a quiet town is revealed as anything but, as the uproar over the urinal exposes uproarious scandal at every level amongst the townspeople.

ANNE OF GREEN GABLES

20 February 1972, Sunday, 5:20–6:05pm, BBC1, 5 episodes, drama, classic, family, Canadian, 19th century
BBCtv
Pr: John McRae
Dir: Joan Craft
Wtr: Julia Jones
Based on L.M. Montgomery
Cast: **Anne Shirley – Kim Braden**
Rachel Lynde – Avis Bunnage
Diana Barry – Jan Francis
Gilbert Blythe – Robin Halstead
Marilla Cuthbert – Barbara Hamilton
Matthew Cuthbert – Elliott Sullivan

In the late 19th century, imaginative orphan Anne Shirley is adopted by Canadian farmer Matthew Cuthbert and his sister Marilla and brought to live at their home, Green Gables. Anne grows into young womanhood, deciding to postpone her university studies in order to remain in the community of Avonlea as a teacher.

PRETENDERS

27 February 1972, Sunday, 5:35–6:05pm, ITV, 13 episodes, drama, British, 17th century
HTV
Pr: Patrick Dromgoole, Leonard White
Dir: Bill Bain, David Boisseau, Fred Burnley, Terry Delacey, Patrick Dromgoole, Terry Harding, Leonard White
Wtr: Bob Baker, Ivan Benbrook, Carole Boyer, Denis Constanduros, Dave Martin, Paul Nicholson, Eric Pringle, Christopher Robinson, Martin C. Rogers, A.C.H. Smith
Cast: **Elam – Curtis Arden**
　　　Joachim – Frederick Jaeger
　　　Monmouth – Jonathan Newth
　　　Perfect – Elizabeth Robillard

In 1685, children Elam and Perfect are caught up in the conflict of the Protestant Rebellion when, after their mother's death, they set off in search of their father. The children fall into Royalist hands, but are protected by prisoner Joachim, with whom they escape, seeking refuge in Monmouth's camp. Elam and Perfect are witness to the climactic battle of Sedgmoor, which decides the future of the Crown, and discover the identity of their father, who is of royal blood.

NAPOLEON AND LOVE

5 March 1972, Tuesday, 9:00–10:00pm, ITV, 9 episodes, drama, biographical, historical, French, 19th century
Thames Television
Pr: Reginald Collin
Dir: Jonathan Alwyn, Derek Bennett, Reginald Collin, Don Leaver
Wtr: Philip Mackie
Cast: Captain Charles – Tony Anholt
　　　Madame Duchatel – Stephanie Beacham
　　　La Grassini – Adrienne Corri
　　　Desiree – Karen Dotrice
　　　Caroline – Janina Faye
　　　Napoleon – Ian Holm
　　　Pauline – Cheryl Kennedy
　　　Captain Junot – Christopher Neame
　　　Georgina – Nicola Pagett
　　　Eleonore – Diana Quick
　　　Marie Walewska – Catherine Schell
　　　Josephine – Billie Whitelaw
　　　Marie-Louise – Susan Wooldridge

Beginning with Napoleon at age 25, already a general in the French army, and tracing his life through his romantic rather than military conquests. In Marseilles he woos wealthy young Desiree, but must make his fortune before her family will allow them to marry. In Paris, he meets Josephine, falls madly in love, and marries her, unaware of his wife's fickle, unfaithful nature. Napoleon has a succession of mistresses, including Josephine's lady-in-waiting, Madame Duchatal, and Georgina, the star of the *Comédie Française*. Eventually, after several more amorous liaisons, Napoleon divorces Josephine and marries Marie-Louise, the daughter of the Austrian Emperor, who bears him a son. After his military defeat in Russia, Napoleon is forced into exile on Elba, but his wife and child are taken to Vienna by the Austrian Emperor. Josephine dies. A year later, Napoleon fights once more . . . at Waterloo.

IT'S MURDER, BUT IS IT ART?

23 March 1972, Thursday, 8:00–8:30pm, BBC2, 6 episodes, thriller, British, contemporary
BBCtv
Pr: Graeme Muir
Designed by Gillian Howard, Valerie Warrender
Wtr: David Pursall, Jack Seddon
Cast: Inspector Hook – Dudley Foster
　　　Stillitoe – Arthur Howard
　　　Brigadier Austin Binghop – Richard Hurndall
　　　Phineas Drake – Arthur Lowe
　　　Detective Sergeant Watson – Anthony Sagar

Eccentric amateur detective Mr. Drake intrudes in Inspector Hook's investigation into the murder of attractive blond Tina Kent, even going so far as to endanger his own life in order to clear Brigadier Binghop, who has been accused of the crime, and to bring the real killer to justice.

LORD PETER WIMSEY: CLOUDS OF WITNESS

5 April 1972, Wednesday, 8:15–9:00pm, BBC1, 5 episodes, mystery, British, 20th century
BBCtv
Pr: Richard Beynon
Dir: Hugh David
Wtr: Anthony Steven
Based on Dorothy L. Sayers
Cast: **Lord Peter Wimsey – Ian Carmichael**
Helen, Duchess of Denver – Georgina Cookson
Detective Inspector Parker – Mark Eden
Lady Mary – Rachel Herbert
Bunter – Glyn Houston
Duke of Denver – David Langton

Not long after the end of World War I, erudite Lord Peter Wimsey works hand in hand with the Yorkshire police in solving an unusual murder case with strong personal ramifications for Wimsey: the victim was his sister's fiancé, and the finger of guilt is pointed at Wimsey's brother, the Duke of Denver.

Clouds of Witness marked the first television appearance of Lord Peter Wimsey.

THE GOLDEN BOWL

4 May 1972, Thursday, 8:30–9:20pm, BBC2, 6 episodes, drama, classic, American, 20th century
BBCtv
Pr: Martin Lisemore
Dir: James Cellan Jones
Wtr: Jack Pulman
Based on Henry James
Cast: Fanny Assingham – Kathleen Byron
Bob Assingham – Cyril Cusack
Charlotte Stant – Gayle Hunnicutt
Prince Amerigo – Daniel Massey
Adam Verver – Barry Morse
Maggie Verver – Jill Townsend

American Maggie Verver lives in turn-of-the-century London with her wealthy widowed father, Adam, with whom she is very close. Maggie marries impoverished Italian Prince Amerigo; complications ensue when Adam marries Maggie's beautiful friend Charlotte, who, unbeknownst to the Ververs, was once engaged to Amerigo. The subsequent events are seen through the eyes of the couples' cynical and jaded acquaintance, Bob Assingham.

THE VISITORS

15 June 1972, Thursday, 8:30–9:20pm, BBC2, 5 episodes, drama, British, 20th century
BBCtv
Pr: Martin Lisemore
Dir: Ronald Wilson
Wtr: Ray Lawler
Based on Mary McMinnies
Cast: **Milly Purdoe – Sarah Badel**
Olga Wragg – Diane Fletcher
Larry Purdoe – Edward Hardwicke
Herbert Wragg – David Hargreaves
Abe Schulman – James Maxwell
Gisela – Susan Penhaligon

In 1951, Milly Purdoe, whose husband is a member of a British Mission, travels with her family to live behind the Iron Curtain.

EMMA

20 July 1972, Thursday, 8:30–9:10pm, BBC2, 6 episodes, drama, classic, British, 19th century
BBCtv
Video: available in UK
Pr: Martin Lisemore
Dir: John Glenister
Wtr: Denis Constanduros
Based on Jane Austen
Cast: Robert Martin – John Alkin
Harriet Smith – Debbie Bowen
Mr. Knightley – John Carson
Frank Churchill – Robert East
Mr. Woodhouse – Donald Eccles
Emma Woodhouse – Doran Godwin
Jane Fairfax – Ania Marson
Mr. Elton – Timothy Peters

Emma Woodhouse takes it upon herself to educate Harriet Smith in the ways of the world – but seems to have done her work too well when it appears that Harriet has captured the affections of

Emma's good friend Mr. Knightley, with whom Emma realizes she herself is in love. Ultimately Harriet reveals that she loves another, and Emma and Knightley declare their true feelings for one another and are married.

LOVE AND MR. LEWISHAM

31 August 1972, Thursday, 8:30–9:15pm, BBC2, 4 episodes, drama, British, 20th century
BBCtv
Pr: Martin Lisemore
Dir: Christopher Barry
Wtr: Alun Richards
Based on H.G. Wells
Cast: **Ethel Henderson – Carolyn Courage**
Mr. Lewisham – Brian Deacon
Mr. Bonover – Robert James
Miss Heydinger – Jane Lapotaire

Mr. Lewisham arrives to begin his job as assistant master at a boys' school in Sussex. His clearly-drawn plans for an intellectual future change when he meets and falls in love with the beautiful but not very intelligent Ethel Henderson.

HOLLY

1 September 1972, Friday, 9:00–10:00pm, ITV, 6 episodes, thriller, British, contemporary
Granada Television
Pr: Michael Cox
Dir: Gareth Davies, Brian Mills
Wtr: Robin Chapman
Cast: **Tom Prentiss – David Burke**
Mr. Elliot – Richard Butler
Holly Elliot – Brigit Forsyth
Gordon Godolphin – William Gaunt
Mrs. Elliot – Elizabeth Kelly
David Elliot – Paul Moriarty

Shortly after Holly and David Elliot celebrate their second anniversary, Holly, an art teacher, suddenly disappears. Holly has been kidnapped by one of her students, Tom Prentiss, but she manages to escape and return to David. However, the time away has amplified for Holly the basic differences between her and her husband. Moreover, Holly feels herself drawn to Tom, who is arrested and tried for abduction. David is devastated when Holly leaves him and testifies in Tom's defense. His entire world is turned upside down and David feels powerless to do anything about it.

THE STRAUSS FAMILY

7 September 1972, Tuesday, 9:00–10:00pm (first episode ran from 8:30–10:00pm), ITV, 8 episodes, drama, biographical, Austrian, 19th century
ATV Network
Pr: David Reid
Dir: David Giles, Cyril Ornadel, Peter Potter, David Reid
Wtr: Anthony Skene, David Butler
Cast: Adele – Lynn Farleigh
Lili – Georgina Hale
Josef Lanner – Derek Jacobi
Josef Strauss – Louis Selwyn
Karoline – Jane Seymour
Anna – Anne Stallybrass
Hetti – Margaret Whiting
Johann Strauss, the son – Stuart Wilson
Johann Strauss, the father – Eric Woofe

The Strauss musical legacy begins with Johann Strauss, the father, who embarks on a musical career at the same time as his friend Josef Lanner. Strauss' eldest son, Johann, seeks the same path, but the family suffers great upheaval when fighting breaks out in Vienna and Strauss is exiled. He returns, but things after the revolution are never the same for the Strauss Orchestra. The younger Strauss falls in love and marries Hetti. They live happily until her untimely death, and Johann marries twice more. His third wife, Adele, inspires Johann to new musical heights, and the Strauss name regains its popularity and influence.

Music for *The Strauss Family*, which drew upon the two Strauss' over 750 published works, was performed by the London Symphony Orchestra.

THE MAN WHO WAS HUNTING HIMSELF

14 September 1972, Thursday,

9:25–10:15pm, BBC1, 3 episodes, thriller, British/European, contemporary
BBCtv
Pr: Bill Sellars
Dir: Terence Williams
Wtr: N.J. Crisp
Cast: Caroline Foster – Carol Austin
Ruth Faraday – Lois Baxter
David Foster/Gregory – Donald Burton
Anton – Robin Hawdon
The Planner – Garfield Morgan
Captain Mason – David Savile

Businessman David Foster is stopped and interrogated as he attempts to return to West Germany from behind the Iron Curtain, as authorities suspect that he may actually be an imposter. Foster is then forced to find his replica, and enters into a cat-and-mouse game where he is both the hunter and the hunted.

SIX FACES

24 September 1972, Sunday, 9:25–10:10pm, BBC2, 6 episodes, drama, British, contemporary
BBCtv
Pr: Stella Richman
Dir: Alastair Reid
Wtr: Julian Bond
Cast: Harry Mellor – Joss Ackland
Margaret – Pamela Brown
Kate – Catherine Lacey
Lucy Walters – Kika Markham
Richard Drew – Kenneth More
Mary Drew – Zena Walker

Businessman Richard Drew is able to present an almost entirely different persona to each person he meets; these variant sides to Drew are revealed from several points of view, including those of his wife, mistress and boss.

WAR AND PEACE

28 September 1972, Thursday, 8:30–9:15pm, BBC2, 20 episodes, drama, classic, Russian, 19th century
BBCtv
Video: available in UK
Pr: David Conroy
Dir: John Davies
Wtr: Jack Pulman
Based on Leo Tolstoy
Cast: Anatole Kuragin – Colin Baker
Countess Rostova – Faith Brook
Dolohov – Donald Burton
Sonya – Joanna David
Count Rostov – Rupert Davies
Andrei Bolkonsky – Alan Dobie
Maria – Angela Down
Helene – Fiona Gaunt
Prince Vasili Kuragin – Basil Henson
Natasha Rostova – Morag Hood
Pierre Bezukov – Anthony Hopkins
Prince Bolkinsky – Anthony Jacobs
Nikolai – Sylvester Morand
Petya – Barnaby Shaw
Napoleon – David Swift

Set during the Napoleonic wars and covering 15 years, Tolstoy's epic tale focuses most specifically on the lives of the Rostov, Bolkonsky and Bezukov families, and tells, among other things, the ill-fated love story of Andrei and Natasha.

THE HOLE IN THE WALL

8 October 1972, Sunday, 5:40–6:05pm, BBC1, 7 episodes, drama, family, British, 19th century
BBCtv
Pr: John McRae
Dir: Joan Craft
Wtr: Arthur Morrison
Based on P.J. Hammond
Cast: Aunt Martha – Brenda Kempner
Nathaniel Kemp – Joseph O'Conor
Stephen – Nigel Rathbone
Uncle – Frank Treagear

Set in London's dockland in 1860, a close relationship develops between Nathaniel Kemp and his grandson Stephen, who comes to live with Kemp after the death of his mother.

SCOOP

8 October 1972, Sunday, 9:00–9:30pm, BBC2, 7 episodes, comedy, British, 20th century
BBCtv
Pr: Michael Mills
Designed by Roger Murray-Leach

Wtr: Barry Took
Based on Evelyn Waugh
Cast: Corker – James Beck
    Prime Minister – C. Kenneth Benda
    Katchen – Sinead Cusack
    Uncle Theodore – Meredith Edwards
    Mrs. Stitch – Sheila Hancock
    Dr. Benito – Dan Jackson
    Mr. Baldwin – John Junkin
    Cuthbert – Hugh Latimer
    Mr. Salter – Brian Oulton
    Lord Copper – Kenneth J. Warren
    William Boot – Harry Worth

Disaster-prone nature correspondent William Boot is mistakenly sent on assignment to cover a civil war in a mythical African Republic.

CRANFORD

26 November 1972, Sunday, 5:20–6:05pm, BBC1, 4 episodes, drama, British, 19th century
BBCtv
Pr: John McRae
Dir: Hugh David
Wtr: Michael Voysey
Based on Mrs. Elizabeth Gaskell
Cast: Captain Brown – Roland Culver
    Mrs. Jamieson – Fabia Drake
    Martha – Sarah Grazebrook
    The Reverend Hayter – George Hagan
    Miss Matty Jenkyns – Gabrielle Hamilton
    Lady Glenmire – Mollie Maureen
    Mr. Holbrook – Clifford Parrish
    Peter Jenkyns – John Richmond
    Miss Jenkyns – Margery Withers

In the village of Cranford in the early 19th century, all the wealthy householders are women, who, under the leadership of pompous Mrs. Jamieson, design the social image of the village. At the center of things is Miss Matty Jenkyns, a warm-hearted, tender soul whose minor crises escalate into serious adversity before all is restored to calm and order.

THE BLACK ARROW

4 December 1972, Monday, 4:25–4:55pm, ITV, 7 episodes, drama, classic, adventure, British, 15th century
Southern Television
Pr: Peter Croft
Wtr: Ben Healy
Based on Robert Louis Stevenson
Cast: Bennet Hatch – Ivan Beavis
    Will Lawless – Eric Flynn
    Nicholas Appleyard – Charles Lamb
    Richard Shelton – Robin Langford
    Mistress Hatch – Dorothea Phillips
    Father Oates – Gordon Rollings
    Sir Daniel Brackley – William Squire
    Joanna Sedley – Helen Stronge
    Richard of Gloucester – Charles Waite

Ravaged by the Wars of the Roses, 15th-century England is subjugated by the tyranny of corrupt noblemen who use their power to take advantage of the poor. But one man, the mysterious masked archer known as "The Black Arrow," leads the fight for righteousness, rescuing honest citizens from exploitation at the hands of cruel Sir Daniel Brackley, whose ward, Richard Shelton, discovers that Brackley was responsible for the death of his father.

In 1973 a regular television series was developed from this novel, featuring the "continuing adventures" of the Black Arrow.

THURSDAY'S CHILD

27 December 1972, Wednesday, 4:35–5:05pm, BBC1, 6 episodes, drama, family, British, 20th century
BBCtv
Pr: Dorothea Brooking
Designed by Antony Thorpe
Wtr: John Tully
Based on Noel Streatfeild
Cast: Lavinia Beresford – Gillian Bailey
    Peter Beresford – Simon Gipps-Kent
    Matron – Althea Parker
    Horatio Beresford – David Tully
    Margaret Thursday – Claire Walker

Margaret Thursday is sent to an orphanage, where she becomes close with the Beresford children. As Margaret's story progresses, her exploits take her to a canal boat and a theatre tent as well as the orphanage.

FISH

8 January 1973, Monday, 5:15–5:40pm, BBC1, 4 episodes, drama, family, Welsh, 20th century
BBCtv
Pr: Anna Home
Dir: Anna Home
Wtr: Alison Morgan
Cast: Pete – Robert Fellowes
Mr. Barnes – Jimmy Gardner
Fish – David Hogarth
Jimmy Price – Alan Jones
Cary – Leslie Mitchell

Jimmy Barnes, better known as "Fish," is somewhat of an outsider in his small Welsh village, but when he adopts a stray dog, whom he names Floss, things start to change.

WOODSTOCK

14 January 1973, Sunday, 5:20–6:05pm, BBC1, 5 episodes, drama, classic, adventure, British, 17th century
BBCtv
Pr: John McRae
Dir: David Maloney
Wtr: Anthony Steven
Based on Sir Walter Scott
Cast: Roger Wildrake – John Baddeley
Joceline Joliffe – Michael Beint
Markham Everard – David Buck
Alice Lee – Judy Loe
Trusty Tomkins – Philip Madoc
Albert Lee – Stephen Moore
Charles Stuart – Richard Morant
Sir Henry Lee – Clive Morton
Oliver Cromwell – Jerome Willis

A swashbuckling tale of Roundheads and Cavaliers set in 1651, which finds Oliver Cromwell in supreme command of the Commonwealth, and young Charles Stuart, son of Charles I, a fugitive; caught in the middle of their battles are Cromwellian Markham Everard and the woman he loves, Alice Lee, whose father, Sir Henry Lee, is a staunch Cavalier.

LORD PETER WIMSEY: THE UNPLEASANTNESS AT THE BELLONA CLUB

1 February 1973, Thursday, 9:25–10:10pm, BBC1, 4 episodes, mystery, British, 20th century
BBCtv
Pr: Richard Beynon
Dir: Ronald Wilson
Wtr: John Bowen
Based on Dorothy L. Sayers
Cast: Robert Fentiman – Terence Alexander
Lord Peter Wimsey – Ian Carmichael
Ann Dorland – Anna Cropper
Detective Inspector Parker – Mark Eden
Sheila Fentiman – Vivien Heilbron
Bunter – Derek Newark
Dr. Penberthy – Donald Pickering
George Fentiman – John Quentin
Pritchard – Clifford Rose
Mr. Murbles – John Welsh

On Armistice Day in 1922, 90-year-old General Fentiman is found dead in his favourite armchair at the Bellona Club. It appears to be natural causes, but Lord Peter Wimsey thinks otherwise, and sets out to expose the death as murder.

THE VIADUCT

13 February 1973, Tuesday, 4:50–5:10pm, BBC1, 3 episodes, drama, family, British, contemporary
BBCtv
Pr: Dorothea Brooking
Exec. Pr: Claire Chovil
Wtr: John Tully
Based on Ron Brown
Cast: **Phil Benson – David Arnold**
Mrs. Partridge – Julie May
Grandad – Michael Raghan
Andy Smith – Jeffrey Segal

Phil lives with his grandfather, who entertains the boy with tales of their ancestor, railway engineer and brilliant inventor Ebenezer. When Phil discovers that Grandad has a secret in the attic, Phil thinks it may be a hidden treasure left there by Ebenezer . . . but ultimately Grandad is revealed as being Ebenezer himself!

WEIR OF HERMISTON

15 February 1973, Thursday, 8:30–9:15pm, BBC2, 4 episodes, drama, Scottish, 19th century
BBCtv/Scotland
Pr: Pharic Maclaren
Dir: Tina Wakerell
Wtr: Tom Wright
Based on unfinished novel by Robert Louis Stevenson
Cast: Frank Innes – David Dundas
Adam Weir – Tom Fleming
Kirstie Eliott – Edith Macarthur
Lord Glenalmond – Leonard Maguire
Lord Glenkindie – Callum Mill
Archie Weir – David Rintoul
Dand Elliott – Paul Young

Strict judge Adam Weir banishes his son Archie to a life of solitude in the village of Hermiston. Archie finds love instead, but all does not go smoothly, leading to a fateful confrontation between father and son.

A LITTLE PRINCESS

18 February 1973, Sunday, 5:40–6:05pm, BBC1, 6 episodes, drama, classic, family, British, 19th century
BBCtv
Pr: John McRae
Dir: Derek Martinus
Wtr: Jeremy Paul
Based on Frances Hodgson Burnett
Cast: **Miss Minchin – Ruth Dunning**
Becky – Gaynor Hodgson
Sara Crewe – Deborah Makepeace
Mr. Carrisford – Peter Myers
Captain Crewe – Donald Pickering
Miss Amelia – Margery Withers

After her father leaves her at Miss Minchin's Select Seminary for Young Ladies, Sara Crewe suffers a dramatic reversal from wealth to poverty, being reduced to being a school scullery-maid before her fortunes again reverse and she is able to live like the princess visions of her imagination.

THE NEW ROAD

1 April 1973, Sunday, 5:20–6:05pm, BBC1, 5 episodes, drama, family, Scottish, 18th century
BBCtv/Scotland
Pr: Pharic Maclaren
Dir: Moira Armstrong
Wtr: Clifford Hanley
Based on Neil Munro
Cast: Janet Campbell – Maev Alexander
Aeneas Macmaster – David Ashton
Sandy Duncanson – John Grieve
The Highlander – Bill Henderson
Annabel Macmaster – Anne Kristen
Margaret Duncanson – Christine McKenna
The Muileach – David Mowat
Ninian Campbell – Tom Watson

Life in a remote Scottish village delivers more than its share of adventure for young Aeneas Macmaster, who is kidnapped and taken aboard a ship, rescued ultimately by loyal friend Ninian Campbell. Aeneas also discovers that his father was murdered by Sandy Duncanson for material gain which Duncanson could not obtain by fair means, and sets out in search of justice.

CHERI

19 April 1973, Thursday, 8:30–9:15pm, BBC2, 5 episodes, drama, French, 20th century
BBCtv
Pr: Martin Lisemore
Dir: Claude Whatham
Wtr: Michael Voysey
Based on Colette
Cast: **Chéri – Scott Antony**
Charlotte – Brenda Bruce
Rose – Betty Hardy
Léa – Yvonne Mitchell

Beautiful and worldly Léa, who is 49, has a four-year affair with irresponsible young Chéri, who has been brought up in the wealthy Parisian demimonde; her nearly-maternal affection turns into deep love, but Léa accepts with resignation the inevitable end of their relationship when Chéri leaves her to marry a woman closer to his own age.

A PICTURE OF KATHERINE MANSFIELD

1 May 1973, Tuesday, 9:25–10:15pm, BBC2, 6 episodes, drama, biographical, British, 20th century
BBCtv
Pr: Rosemary Hill
Dir: Alan Cooke
Wtr: Robin Chapman
Cast: John Middleton Murry – Jeremy Brett
L.M. – Annette Crosbie
Frieda Lawrence – Jacki Harding
Mrs. Beauchamp – Phyllida Law
Katherine Mansfield – Vanessa Redgrave
D.H. Lawrence – Michael Williams

The life story of unconventional writer and free spirit Katherine Mansfield, who was born in New Zealand but moved to London in 1906, where she became a renowned writer, before dying of tuberculosis in 1923.

In addition to telling the story of Mansfield's life, two of her short stories belonging to the period being examined were dramatized in each episode: *Psychology*, *The Garden Party*, *Germans at Meat*, *Something Childish but Very Natural*, *Je ne parle pas français*, *Sun and Moon*, *The Aloe*, *The Man Without a Temperament*, *Bliss*, *The Daughters of the Late Colonel*, *At the Bay*, and *Prelude*.

SCOTCH ON THE ROCKS

11 May 1973, Friday, 9:25–10:05pm, BBC1, 5 episodes, thriller, Scottish, 20th century
BBCtv/Scotland
Pr: Pharic Maclaren
Dir: Bob Hird
Wtr: James MacTaggart
Based on Douglas Hurd, Andrew Osmond
Cast: Sukey Dunmayne – Maria Aitken
John Mackie – John Cairney
Chief Con Blair – Iain Cuthbertson
Colonel Cameron – Clinton Greyn
Robert Duguid – Bill Henderson
Lord Thorganby – Cyril Luckham
James Henderson – Leonard Maguire
Brodie – Maurice Roeves
MacNair – Bill Simpson

In the late 1960s, a secretive group plots an action for an independent Scotland; it is up to the British Army, especially the special branch undercover unit, to control the nationalist rebels.

THE SONG OF SONGS

24 May 1973, Thursday, 8:30–9:25pm, BBC2, 5 episodes, drama, Austrian, 20th century
BBCtv
Pr: Martin Lisemore
Dir: Peter Wood
Wtr: Robert Muller
Based on Hermann Sudermann
Cast: Dr. Salmoni – Denholm Elliott
Count von Mertzbach – Charles Gray
Robert Horvath – David Griffin
Dr. Pieper – Richard Hurndall
Frau Czepanek – Doreen Mantle
Konrad – John McEnery
Richard Dehnicke – John Normington
Lilli Czepanek – Penelope Wilton

In Vienna, in the carefree years shortly before World War I, Lilli Czepanek searches for her ideal lover, finding him, she believes in Konrad . . . while still allowing herself to enjoy the protection of Richard Dehnicke.

SAM

12 June 1973, Tuesday, 9:00–10:00pm, ITV, 13 episodes, drama, British, 20th century
Granada Television
Pr: Michael Cox
Dir: Colin Cant, Les Chatfield, Richard Doubleday, Bill Gilmour, Alan Grint, Bill Podmore
Wtr: John Finch
Cast: Ethel Barraclough – Alethea Charlton
Dora Wilson – Barbara Ewing
Jack Barraclough – Michael Goodliffe
Frank Barraclough – James Hazeldine
Polly Barraclough – Maggie Jones
Toby Wilson – Frank Mills
Sam Wilson – Kevin Moreton
Alan Dakin – John Price
George Barraclough – Ray Smith

Sam Wilson's story begins in 1934, when

Sam is ten years old and his father has just deserted him and his mother Dora. They travel to Skellerton, the Yorkshire mining village where Dora had grown up, and Sam is raised amidst his extended maternal family. Over the next four years, Sam faces many changes in his life, including the loss of his mother, who dies while giving birth to Alan Dakin's child. Sam is sent to a charity school, but returns to Skellerton in 1938, and at the age of 14 goes into the pits . . . but the looming war in Europe threatens major upheaval for everyone.

Produced in three self-contained sets of 13 one-hour episodes, each covering a major span of years in the life of Sam Wilson, the early episodes of *Sam* were based on writer John Finch's own life. This first series won the TV Critics' award for the best series of 1973.

TWO WOMEN

28 June 1973, Thursday, 8:30–9:25pm, BBC2, 4 episodes, drama, Italian, 20th century
BBCtv
Pr: Martin Lisemore
Dir: Gareth Davies
Wtr: Ray Lawler
Based on Alberto Moravia
Cast: French Sergeant – Neville Barber
Vincenzo – Reg Lye
Concetta – Carmen Silvera
Rosetta – Jenny Twigge
Cesira – Margaret Whiting

In Rome in 1945, widow Cesira strains to make ends meet for herself and her daughter, managing to succeed even in the face of war . . . until she and Rosetta are brutally attacked by retreating Moroccan soldiers.

A PIN TO SEE THE PEEPSHOW

26 July 1973, Thursday, 8:30–9:25pm, BBC2, 4 episodes, drama, British, 20th century
BBCtv
Pr: Rex Tucker
Dir: Raymond Menmuir
Wtr: Elaine Morgan

Based on F. Tennyson Jesse
Cast: **Julia Almond – Francesca Annis**
Mrs. Almond – Mary Chester
Leonard Carr – John Duttine
Herbert Starling – Bernard Hepton
Mr. Almond – Ron Pember

When pretty Julia Almond leaves school in 1913, no one could predict that ten years later she would be facing the gallows, charged, along with her lover, Leonard Carr, with the death of her husband Herbert, and ultimately sentenced to death.

In addition to writing novels, F. Tennyson Jesse was a newspaper reporter; *A Pin to See the Peepshow* was based on the true-life murder of Percy Thompson in 1922, a crime for which his wife Edith and her lover Frederick Bywaters were tried and executed.

THE DONATI CONSPIRACY

14 September 1973, Friday, 9:25–10:15pm, BBC1, 3 episodes, thriller, British, contemporary
BBCtv
Pr: Morris Barry
Dir: Vere Lorrimer
Wtr: John Gould
Cast: Detective Sergeant Cole – Jonathan Adams
Donati – Michael Aldridge
Robert Sadler – Richard Beckinsale
Detective Chief Inspector Sandman – James Bree
Dent – Ian Gelder
Jane – Janet Key
Paul Frederick – Anthony Valentine

A suppositional look at a contemporary Britain which has somehow become a Fascist dictatorship. The mysterious figure of Paul Frederick holds the reins at the murder trial of Robert Sadler, where the outcome is determined more by political motivation than the truth or innocence of the defendant.

THE DRAGON'S OPPONENT

23 September 1973, Sunday, 8:15–9:05pm, BBC2, 4 episodes, drama, biographical, British, 20th century

BBCtv
Pr: Anthony Read
Dir: Gerald Blake
Wtr: Colin Morris
Cast: Cecil Howard – Mark Blackwell Baker
Greville Howard – Anton Darby
19th Earl of Suffolk – William Dexter
Margaret, Countess of Suffolk – Virginia McKenna
Jack Howard – Ronald Pickup
Dowager Countess of Suffolk – Margaret Rawlings

The life story of Charles Henry George Howard, known as "Jack," 20th Earl of Suffolk and 13th Earl of Berkshire. Picking up his life in 1914, Jack matures from a dissolute youth into a remarkable, heroic figure who dies in World War II at the age of 35.

JANE EYRE

27 September 1973, Thursday, 8:30–9:25pm, BBC2, 5 episodes, drama, classic, British, 19th century
BBCtv
Pr: John McRae
Dir: Joan Craft
Wtr: Robin Chapman
Based on Charlotte Brontë
Cast: **Jane Eyre – Sorcha Cusack**
Grace Poole – Zara Jaber
Mr. Rochester – Michael Jayston
Mrs. Fairfax – Megs Jenkins
Adele – Isabelle Rosin
Jane Eyre (as a child) – Juliet Waley

In the mid-1800s, orphaned Jane Eyre is hired to be governess at Thornfield Hall, but her involvement there becomes much more complicated when she falls in love with her brooding, mysterious employer, Mr. Rochester. Their romance is threatened by the discovery that Mr. Rochester is already married, but in the end fate at last intervenes kindly and the two are reunited.

POLLYANNA

7 October 1973, Sunday, 5:35–6:05pm, BBC1, 6 episodes, drama, classic, family, American, 20th century
BBCtv
Video: available in UK
Pr: John McRae
Dir: June Wyndham-Davies
Wtr: Joy Harington
Based on Eleanor H. Porter
Cast: **Pollyanna – Elizabeth Archard**
Timothy – Robert Coleby
Nancy – Paddy Frost
Jimmy Bean – Stephen Galloway
Mr. Pendleton – Ray McAnally
Aunt Polly – Elaine Stritch

Twelve-year-old orphan Pollyanna's ability to always see the bright side of things is challenged when she goes to live with her embittered Aunt Polly – but in the end no one can resist Pollyanna's philosophy of gladness.

THE TERRACOTTA HORSE

12 November 1973, Monday, 5:15–5:40pm, BBC1, 6 episodes, thriller, family, British/European, contemporary
BBCtv
Pr: Bill Sellars
Film Ed: Larry Toft
Wtr: Christopher Bond
Cast: Louis Meissner – Constantin De Goguel
Linda Jackson – Lindy Howard
Maggie Jackson – Kristine Howarth
Bob Jackson – Godfrey James
David Jackson – Patrick Murray
Hussein – Nadim Sawalha
Dan Walters – James Warwick

The Jackson family journeys to Morocco, bringing along a terracotta figurine of a horse, which becomes an integral part of an archeological discovery which may lead to the Holy Grail, but in the meantime leads to danger and intrigue for all involved.

HAWKEYE, THE PATHFINDER

18 November 1973, Sunday, 5:10–6:05pm, BBC1, 5 episodes, drama, American, 18th century
BBCtv
Pr: John McRae
Dir: David Maloney
Wtr: Alistair Bell, Allan Prior

Based on *The Pathfinder* by James Fenimore Cooper
Cast: Chingachgook – John Abineri
Sergeant Dunham – Windsor Davies
Jasper Western – William Ellis
Mabel Dunham – Jan Francis
Lieutenant Carter – Simon MacCorkindale
Pathfinder – Paul Massie
Uncle Cap – Patrick Troughton

In the American colonies in 1760, at the height of the Franco-British War, Mabel Dunham is helped on her journey to join her father, a British officer, by Hawkeye, the Pathfinder, who is in love with Mabel, but steps aside when he discovers that she loves another man.

LORD PETER WIMSEY: MURDER MUST ADVERTISE

30 November 1973, Tuesday, 9:25–10:15pm, BBC1, 4 episodes, mystery, British, 20th century
BBCtv
Pr: Richard Beynon
Dir: Rodney Bennett
Wtr: Bill Craig
Based on Dorothy L. Sayers
Cast: Major Milligan – Peter Bowles
Lord Peter Wimsey – Ian Carmichael
Cummings – Antony Carrick
Miss Parton – Caroline Dowdeswell
Chief Inspector Parker – Mark Eden
Withers – Alan Foss
Mr. Ingleby – John Hallam
Victor Dean – Robert Hamilton
Mr. Pym – Peter Pratt

A bright summer's afternoon at Pym's Publicity is ruined when young copywriter Victor Dean falls to his death down the spiral staircase . . . but was he actually pushed? It is up to urbane Lord Peter to find out, as he pseudonymously joins the advertising agency as a copywriter, then changes names once more to infiltrate the fast crowd in which Dean had travelled – but two more people are killed before the truth is finally revealed.

A RAGING CALM

7 January 1974, Monday, 9:00–10:00pm, ITV, 7 episodes, drama, British, contemporary
Granada Television
Pr: Brian Armstrong
Dir: June Howson, Gerry Mill
Wtr: Stan Barstow
Based on Stan Barstow
Cast: **Tom Simpkins – Alan Badel**
Horace Batchelor – John Collin
Norma Moffat – Diana Coupland
Kate Hart – Joanna Craig
Baden Roberts – Basil Dignam
Roger Coyne – Nigel Havers
Ted Moffat – John Pickles
Andrea Warner – Frances White
Philip Hart – Michael Williams
Shirley Moffat – Vicky Williams

In a seemingly quiet and orderly town in West Riding, widower Tom Simpkins has been having an affair for years with married Norma Moffat and is the father of Norma's daughter Shirley. When Norma's husband dies suddenly, Tom tries to become a part of her family, but is rejected by Shirley. Meanwhile, Tom's secretary, Andrea Warner, is involved with married man Philip Hart, who is Tom's rival in a local political campaign.

TOM'S MIDNIGHT GARDEN

7 January 1974, Monday, 5:15–5:40pm, BBC1, 3 episodes, drama, family, fantasy, British, contemporary
BBCtv
Pr: Dorothea Brooking
Designed by Myles Lang
Wtr: John Tully
Based on Philippa Pearce
Cast: **Tom Long – Nicolas Bridge**
Hatty Melbourne – Adrienne Byrne
Aunt Gwen – Myvanwy Jenn
Mrs. Bartholomew – Margot MacAlaster
Aunt Grace Melbourne – Anne Ridler
Uncle Alan – Charles West

When Tom Long goes to stay with his Aunt and Uncle, he is unhappily quarantined because of his brother Paul's illness, until he makes a strange and fascinating discovery late one night, thanks to the dreams of elderly Mrs. Bartholomew, stepping into a magical world which blends the present and the past.

DEATH OR GLORY BOY

13 January 1974, Saturday,
10:15–11:15pm, ITV, 3 episodes, drama, British, 20th century
Yorkshire Television
Pr: Peter Willes
Dir: Marc Miller
Wtr: Charles Wood
Cast: **David Parker – Christopher Blake**
Peter Putnum – Jonathan David
Tpr. Smiff – Philip David
Sergeant Walton – Jon Glover
Michael Marlowe – Martyn Jacobs
Squadron Sergeant-Major Hale – John F. Landry

In 1950 David Parker leaves his grammar school background and joins the Army as a regular soldier. The other men in his group are national servicemen who resent Parker, ostracizing and even beating him badly. But Parker retains his ambition to become an officer and sets out to prove he's the best soldier in his group, working and training hard – but that may not be enough to overcome the odds and the prejudice against him.

The first episode was broadcast as originally scheduled, but the remaining two were pre-empted for other programming. The entire serial was telecast on three Sundays beginning 10 March.

THE PALLISERS

19 January 1974, Saturday, 8:50–9:40pm, BBC2, 26 episodes, drama, classic, British, 19th century
BBCtv
Pr: Martin Lisemore
Dir: Hugh David, Ronald Wilson
Wtr: Simon Raven
Based on *Can You Forgive Her?*, *Phineas Finn The Irish Member*, *The Eustace Diamonds*, *Phineas Redux*, *The Prime Minister*, *The Duke's Children* by Anthony Trollope

Cast: Silverbridge – Anthony Andrews
Lizzie Eustace – Sarah Badel
Gerald – Michael Cochrane
Duke of Omnium – Roland Culver
Robert Kennedy – Derek Godfrey
Lord Fawn – Derek Jacobi
Burgo Fitzgerald – Barry Justice
Lady Glencora – Susan Hampshire
Plantagenet – Philip Latham
Violet Effingham – Mel Martin
Lady Laura Standish – Anna Massey
Phineas Finn – Donal McCann
Madame Max Goesler – Barbara Murray
Lady Mary – Kate Nicholls

The Palliser family saga, played out against the backdrop of the lives of Plantagenet Palliser and Glencora M'Cluskie Palliser, and those whom they meet over the course of their married life.

JOHN HALIFAX, GENTLEMAN

20 January 1974, Sunday, 5:15–6:05pm, BBC1, 5 episodes, drama, British, 18th–19th century
BBCtv
Pr: John McRae
Dir: Tristan de Vere Cole
Wtr: Jack Ronder
Based on Dinah Craik
Cast: Phineas Fletcher – Tony Calvin
Maud – Brenda Cavendish
John Halifax – Robert Coleby
John Halifax (as a boy) – Peter Duncan
Guy – Scott Fredericks
Louise – Barbara Kellermann
Abel Fletcher – John Phillips
Edwin – Christopher Ravenscroft
Ursula March – Gwen Taylor

In 1794, John Halifax arrives in county Gloucestershire to seek his fortune. As the years progress, John progresses from labourer to tradesman to businessman and, finally, to gentleman, meaning to pass all his success on to his two sons – but they are too busy quarrelling over Louise, with whom they are both in love.

CARRIE'S WAR

28 January 1974, Monday, 5:15–5:45pm,

BBC1, 5 episodes, drama, family, Welsh, 20th century
BBCtv
Exec. Pr: Anna Home
Dir: Paul Stone
Wtr: Marilyn Fox
Based on Nina Bawden
Cast: Albert Sandwich – Tim Coward
Hepzibah Green – Rosalie Crutchley
Carrie (as an adult) – Shirley Dixon
Miss Evans – Avril Elgar
Mr. Johnny – Matthew Guinness
Mr. Evans – Aubrey Richards
Nick Willow – Andrew Tinney
Carrie Willow – Juliet Waley

During World War II, Carrie Willow and her little brother Nick are evacuated from London to live in a Welsh mining village with strict Mr. Evans. When the children come upon Druid's Bottom, the house of housekeeper Hepzibah Green, they learn of a deadly curse which once hung over the house . . . and which, in the evil person of Mr. Evans, threatens to again be fulfilled. Carrie takes rash action against the curse, which she believes leads to the burning down of Druid's Bottom and the deaths of three people; 30 years later she returns to the area, having been haunted with guilt all these years, and discovers that in fact no one had been killed in the fire.

THE FORTUNES OF NIGEL

24 February 1974, Sunday, 5:10–6:05pm, BBC1, 5 episodes, drama, British, 17th century
BBCtv
Pr: John McRae
Dir: Peter Cregeen
Wtr: Alexander Baron
Based on Sir Walter Scott
Cast: Duke of Buckingham – Dallas Adams
Sir Nigel Olifaunt – Anthony Andrews
Lord Dalgarno – Murray Head
George Heroit – Simon Lack
King James I – Alfred Lynch
Charles, Prince of Wales – Mark Rogers
Margaret Ramsay – Nina Thomas
Richard Moniplies – Frank Wylie

During the reign of James I, Scottish nobleman Sir Nigel Olifaunt journeys to London to save his inheritance, finding many obstacles – and enemies – along the way. Sir Nigel meets Lord Dalgarno and soon is associated with the Royal Court, before obtaining his family's properties through the assistance of Richard Moniplies.

FALL OF EAGLES

15 March 1974, Friday, 9:25–10:15pm, BBC1, 13 episodes, drama, historical, German/Russian, 19th–20th century
BBCtv
Pr: Stuart Burge
Dir: Rudolph Cartier, David Cunliffe, Gareth Davies, James Ferman, Bill Hays, Michael Lindsay-Hogg, Donald McWhinnie, David Sullivan Proudfoot
Wtr: Keith Dewhurst, John Elliot, Trevor Griffiths, Elizabeth Holford, Ken Hughes, Troy Kennedy Martin, Robert Muller, Jack Pulman, David Turner, Hugh Whitemore.
Series created by John Elliot
Cast: Rasputin – Michael Aldridge
Franz Josef – Miles Anderson
Ratchkovsky – Michael Bryant
Glazkov – Tom Conti
Kaiser Wilhelm I – Maurice Denham
Krupskaya – Lynn Fairleigh
Kaiser Wilhelm II – Barry Foster
Edward VII – Derek Francis
Helphand – Michael Gough
Alexandra – Gayle Hunnicutt
Tsar Alexander III – Tony Jay
Narrator – Michael Hordern
Victoria – Gemma Jones
Bismark – Curt Jurgens
Tsar Nicholas II – Charles Kay
Elisabeth – Diane Keen
Trotsky – Michael Kitchen
Prince Frederick William – Denis Lill
Emperor Franz Josef – Laurence Naismith
Lenin – Patrick Stewart
Izvolski – Peter Vaughan

A chronicle of the collapse of the monarchies of Germany, Austria, Hungary and Russia, the battles over the Hapsburg empire, warring marital and political factions . . . and impending revolution and war as the new century begins. When the story opens, Franz

Josef (Kaiser Wilhelm I) has just married Princess Elisabeth; their son marries Victoria, the daughter of Great Britain's monarch. Just a few generations later the monarchy collapses when the heir, Archduke Ferdinand, is assassinated and Wilhelm is forced to abdicate; at the same time Russian Tsar Nicholas II and his family attempt to flee from the Bolsheviks.

SHOULDER TO SHOULDER

3 April 1974, Wednesday, 9:00–10:15pm, BBC2, 6 episodes, drama, historical, British, 20th century
BBCtv in association with Warner Bros. Television
Video: available in US
Pr: Verity Lambert
Dir: Moira Armstrong, Waris Hussein
Wtr: Douglas Livingstone, Alan Plater, Ken Taylor, Hugh Whitemore
Created by Midge MacKenzie, Verity Lambert, Georgia Brown
Cast: Emmeline Pathick-Lawrence – Sheila Allen
Annie Kenney – Georgia Brown
Sylvia Pankhurst – Angela Down
Lloyd George – Peter Geddis
Dr. Pankhurst – Michael Gough
Teresa Billington – Sheila Grant
Frederick Pethick-Lawrence – Ronald Hines
Keir Hardie – Fulton MacKay
Flora Drummond – Sally Miles
Lady Constance Lytton – Judy Parfitt
Emmeline Pankhurst – Sian Phillips
Dr. Ethel Smyth – Maureen Pryor
Christabel Pankhurst – Patricia Quinn

A chronicle of the Suffragette Movement in Great Britain, focusing notably on the Pankhurst family and their militant devotion to the cause. In 1903, Emmeline Pankhurst organizes the Women's Social and Political Union and, together with her daughters Christabel and Sylvia and other women from both the upper and working classes, fights for women's rights, risking arrest, physical and emotional pain, and even death, finally claiming success in 1919 when married and university-educated women get the right to vote, and complete victory in 1928 when suffrage is extended to all British women over the age of 21.

LORD PETER WIMSEY: THE NINE TAILORS

22 April 1974, Monday, 9:25–10:15pm, BBC1, 4 episodes, mystery, British, 20th century
BBCtv
Pr: Richard Beynon
Dir: Raymond Menmuir
Wtr: Anthony Steven
Based on Dorothy L. Sayers
Cast: Lady Wilbraham – Anne Blake
Mrs. Venables – Elizabeth Bradley
Lord Peter Wimsey – Ian Carmichael
Deacon – Keith Drinkel
Reverend Mr. Venables – Donald Eccles
Bunter – Glyn Houston
Sir Charles Thorpe – Desmond Llewellyn
Mary Deacon – Elizabeth Proud
Sir Hector Goffe – Anthony Roye
Inspector Frost – Robin Wentworth

In 1918, while attending a fashionable wedding in East Anglia, Lord Wimsey finds himself involved in solving a macabre murder which is itself connected to a crime Wimsey had witnessed himself 20 years earlier . . . and had long thought already solved.

SAM (second series)

16 May 1974, Thursday, 8:30–9:30pm, ITV, 13 episodes, drama, British, 20th century
Granada Television
Pr: Michael Cox
Dir: Les Chatfield, Alan Grint, Roland Joffe, Quentin Lawrence, Baz Taylor
Wtr: John Finch
Cast: Les Dakin – Peter Brown
David Ellis – Tom Conti
Jack Barraclough – Michael Goodliffe
Frank Barraclough – James Hazeldine
Sarah Corby – Jennifer Hilary
Sam Wilson – Mark McManus

Cassie Dent – Cherith Mellor
Toby Wilson – Frank Mills
Alan Dakin – John Price
George Barraclough – Ray Smith
Eileen Dakin – Dorothy White

Sam Wilson's story picks up in January, 1947. World War II has ended; Sam was exempt from service because he was a miner. Now a grown man, Sam leaves Skellerton and joins the Merchant Navy. He is away from home for several years; when he returns he comes into conflict with his grandfather and attempts to remain close with his half-brother, Les Dakin. He inherits some money from his father's family, offering him his first chance at independence and responsibility. In 1952 Sam, at another turning point in his life, marries middle-class Sarah, who has a child from a previous marriage.

THE INHERITORS

15 August 1974, Thursday, 8:30–9:30pm, ITV, 6 episodes, drama, British, contemporary
HTV
Pr: Wilfred Greatorex
Dir: Huw Davies, Henri Safran, Ian McNaughton
Wtr: Wilfred Greatorex, Ray Jenkins, Peter Draper
Cast: Jennie Garrett – Sarah Douglas
Meirion Ryder – Meredith Edwards
Michael Gethin – Peter Egan
Mackie – Richard Hurndall
Sally Neville – Jacqueline Hurst
Elliott Morris – Philip Madoc
Sefton Garrett – Bill Maynard
Alun Ryder – John Ogwen
James, Lord Gethin – Robert Urquhart
Eleanor – Heather Wright

The vast Gethin estate, which has been in the family for 600 years, is in danger of being broken up because of crushing death duties. Lord Gethin and his son Michael argue about what to do with their land. Lord Gethin leans towards a mining company which wants to exploit the land's copper reserves, but his son Michael is opposed to destroying the land and the lives of the people who have occupied it for generations. Successful businessman Alun Ryder, son of tenant farmer Meirion, is also determined to play a part in the estate's breakup, and joins forces with millionaire Sefton Garrett against the Gethins. Business interests and personal entanglements intensify the conflicts surrounding the ultimate disposition of the ancient land holdings.

THE HAGGARD FALCON

17 August 1974, Saturday, 8:25–9:15pm, BBC2, 4 episodes, thriller, Scottish, 16th century
BBCtv/Scotland
Pr: Pharic Maclaren
Dir: Mike Vardy
Wtr: Bill Craig
Cast: Moray – Victor Carin
Bothwell – Alec Heggie
Lethington – John Carlisle
Kirstie – Anne Kristen
Dominic Allardyce – Ian Ogilvy
Puddock – Alex McAvoy
Gillespie – Roddy McMillan
Mary, Queen of Scots – Mary Ann Reid
Gellie – Virginia Stark

In 1565, soldier of fortune Dominic Allardyce returns to Scotland after being in service to the French King . . . and soon finds himself involved in a plot to assassinate Mary, Queen of Scots.

THE STARS LOOK DOWN

4 September 1974, Thursday, 9:00–10:00pm, ITV, 13 episodes, drama, British, 20th century
Granada Television
Pr: Howard Baker
Dir: Roland Joffe, Alan Grint, Howard Baker
Wtr: Alan Plater
Based on A.J. Cronin
Cast: **Joe Gowlan – Alun Armstrong**
Sammy Fenwick – James Bate
Hughie Fenwick – Rod Culbertson
Stanley Millington – Geoffrey Davien
Richard Barras – Basil Dignam
Martha Fenwick – Avril Elgar
Hetty Todd – Adrienne Frank
Laura Millington – Valerie Georgeson

David Fenwick – Ian Hastings
Robert Fenwick – Norman Jones
Annie Macer – Anne Raitt
Arthur Barras – Christian Rodska
Jenny Sunley – Susan Tracy

In 1910, David Fenwick and Joe Gowlan leave the small northeast village of Sleescale to find work in Newcastle. David falls in love with and marries Joe's former girlfriend, Jenny Sunley. David works in the mines for Richard Barras, who ignores the dangerous situation in the pit, which leads to a deadly disaster when a flood traps a number of men underground. When World War I breaks out, David joins the army. Joe stays behind to run the steelworks where he now works, taking the opportunity to romance Laura, the wife of his absent boss. By the end of the War, both men's lives are irrevocably changed, both personally and professionally.

Cronin's novel was loosely based on his own experiences as a pit doctor in the 1920s. The serial was Granada's most ambitious production to date and took ten months to film.

SOUTH RIDING

16 September 1974, Monday, 9:00–10:00pm, ITV, 13 episodes, drama, British, 20th century
Yorkshire Television
Pr: James Ormerod
Dir: James Ormerod, Alastair Reid
Wtr: Stan Barstow
Based on Winifred Holtby
Cast: **Ald. Mrs. Beddows – Hermione Baddeley**
Midge Carne – Judi Bowker
Ald. Anthony Snaith – John Cater
Councillor Robert Carne – Nigel Davenport
Lydia Holly – Lesley Dunlop
Fred Mitchell – Milton Johns
Councillor Joe Astell – Norman Jones
Sarah Burton – Dorothy Tutin

In 1932, Saran Burton, a blacksmith's daughter, moves back to Yorkshire after attending university in London and becomes headmistress at the local girls' grammar school. Local city councillor and gentleman farmer Robert Carne attempts to maintain life in Yorkshire as it has always been, despite mounting financial and emotional pressures from the outside world. Over the next three years, the professional and personal lives of these two and the others in the community impact upon each other, culminating in a grand celebration of the Silver Jubilee of George V.

Winner, BAFTA Award, Best Drama Serial 1974.

HEIDI

20 October 1974, Sunday, 5:35–6:05pm, BBC1, 6 episodes, drama, classic, family, Swiss, 19th century
BBCtv
Video: available in UK
Pr: John McRae
Dir: June Wyndham-Davies
Wtr: Martin Worth
Based on Johanna Spyri
Cast: **Heidi – Emma Blake**
Brigitta – Kathleen Byron
Dete – Myra Frances
Clara – Chloe Franks
Peter – Nicholas Lyndhurst
Grandfather – Hans Meyer
Grandmother – Flora Robson

Orphaned Heidi is taken by her Aunt Dete to live with her grandfather on a remote mountain in Switzerland. Heidi learns to love living in the Alps, makes close friends with local goat boy Peter but is forced to leave her grandfather to live in the city and be a companion to a lonely crippled girl. Heidi is finally able to return to her grandfather, where the mountain air proves restorative to all.

NOTORIOUS WOMAN

3 November 1974, Sunday, 10:15–11:05pm, BBC2, 7 episodes, drama, biographical, French, 19th century
BBCtv in association with Warner Bros. Television
Pr: Pieter Rogers
Dir: Waris Hussein
Wtr: Harry W. Junkin
Cast: Alfred de Musset – Shane Briant

Frederic Chopin – George Chakiris
Gustave Flaubert – James Cossins
Marie Dorval – Sinead Cusack
Casimir Dudevant – Lewis Fiander
Aurore Dupin (George Sand) –
   Rosemary Harris
Prosper Merimée – Alan Howard
Franz Liszt – Jeremy Irons
Madame Dupin de Francueil –
   Cathleen Nesbit
Sophie Dupin de Francueil – Joyce
   Redman

The biography of Aurore Dupin, who left her husband and two children to live a most unconventional life in Paris as a journalist and novelist with a male pen name, George Sand, and was romantically involved with a number of men, highlighted by her eight-year affair with composer Frederic Chopin.

THE NEARLY MAN

4 November 1974, Tuesday,
9:00–10:00pm, ITV, 7 episodes, drama, British, contemporary
Granada Television
Pr: Jonathan Powell
Dir: John Irvin, Alan Grint
Wtr: Arthur Hopcraft
Based on play by Arthur Hopcraft
Cast: **Christopher Collinson – Tony Britton**
Millie Dutton – Katherine Fahy
Alice Collinson – Ann Firbank
Brian Griffin – John Leyton
Peter Richards – Ian McCulloch
Bernard King – Wilfred Pickles

Christopher Collinson, a Labour MP for over 15 years, has long been left on the back benches and is frustrated and cynical. He again seeks out the political limelight, a decision which affects both his political career and his marriage. Collinson and his wife Alice become estranged over his renewed ambition (and his involvement with university teacher Millie Dutton), and Alice is drawn to old friend Brian Griffin. As Collinson prepares to make a statement at the Labour Party Conference, he and Alice form an uneasy alliance, but all is threatened by disagreement between Collinson and his colleagues.

JENNIE, LADY RANDOLPH CHURCHILL

5 November 1974, Tuesday,
9:00–10:00pm, ITV, 7 episodes, drama, biographical, historical, British, 19th–20th century
Thames Television
Pr: Andrew Brown
Dir: James Cellan Jones
Wtr: Julian Mitchell
Cast: Winston Churchill (as a child) – Paul Ambrose
Count Kinsky – Jeremy Brett
George Cornwallis-West –
   Christopher Cazenove
Winston Churchill – Warren Clarke
Montie Porch – Charles Kay
Duchess of Marlborough – Rachel Kempson
Duke of Marlborough – Cyril Luckham
Leonie – Barbara Parkins
Mrs. Patrick Campbell – Sian Phillips
Lord Randolph Churchill – Ronald Pickup
Jennie – Lee Remick
Jack Churchill – Malcolm Stoddard
Prince of Wales – Thorley Walters

In 1873, spirited young American Jennie Jerome meets Lord Randolph Churchill, whom she soon marries. In the decades which follow, Jennie becomes the toast – and scandal – of two continents, charting her own independent path, while also involving herself closely in the political campaigns of her son, future prime minister Winston Churchill, until her death in London in 1921.

Portions of the program were produced at Blenheim, the ancestral estate of the Duke of Marlborough.

CAKES AND ALE

9 November 1974, Saturday, 8:05–9:00pm, BBC2, 3 episodes, drama, British, 20th century
BBCtv
Pr: Richard Beynon
Dir: Bill Hays
Wtr: Harry Green
Based on W. Somerset Maugham
Cast: Miss Fellowes – Barbara Atkinson
Rosie Gann – Judy Cornwell

Lord George Kemp – James Grout
Willie Ashenden – Michael Hordern
Alroy Kear – Peter Jeffrey
Edward Driffield – Mike Pratt

A satirical view of English literati, as Willie Ashenden looks back on the life of Victorian novelist Edward Driffield (who, despite Maugham's protests to the contrary, seems clearly modelled on Thomas Hardy), focusing mostly on the character of Driffield's first wife, beautiful, warm-hearted but unwise barmaid Rosie.

CHINESE PUZZLE

13 November 1974, Wednesday, 5:15–5:40pm, BBC1, 6 episodes, thriller, family, British, contemporary
BBCtv
Pr: Bill Sellars
Dir: Alan Bell
Wtr: Brian Finch
Cast: Martin Frazer – William Abney
**Robert Hardacre – Marcus Barclay
Wing Commander – William Fox**
Alison Frazer – Deborah Makepeace
Paul Jameson – Michael Tattersfield
China – Eric Young

A flying squadron holds its reunion at a pleasant country inn, but the festivities are interrupted when strange events begin to occur at a nearby unused airfield, and young friends Robert and Paul stumble unwittingly into a kidnapping and blackmail plot.

THE EARLY LIFE OF STEPHEN HIND

30 November 1974, Saturday, 8:10–9:05pm, BBC2, 3 episodes, drama, British, contemporary
BBCtv
Pr: William Slater
Dir: Timothy Combe
Wtr: Alexander Baron
Based on Storm Jameson
Cast: Sir Henry Chatteney – Roland Culver
Stephen Hind – Michael Kitchen
Lady Renee Chatteney – Beatrix Lehmann
Colette Hyde – Hildegard Neil
Olivia – Kate Nicholls
Stephen's mother – Maureen Pryor
Mary Duquesne – Nora Swinburne

Ambitious but poor Stephen Hind is secretary to Sir Henry Chatteney, helping to type and retype the pages of Sir Henry's autobiography. This access to wealth and power gives the unscrupulous Stephen the opportunity to meet influential men and (particularly) women. And so Stephen feels he is on his way . . . but the path is littered with intrigue, blackmail, and threats of legal action.

DAVID COPPERFIELD

1 December 1974, Sunday, 5:10–6:05pm, BBC1, 6 episodes, drama, classic, British, 19th century
BBCtv
Pr: John McRae
Dir: Joan Croft
Wtr: Hugh Whitemore
Based on Charles Dickens
Cast: Steerforth – Anthony Andrews
Betsey Trotwood – Patience Collier
Agnes Wickfield – Gail Harrison
Dan Peggotty – Ian Hogg
Uriah Heep – Martin Jarvis
David Copperfield (as a child) – Jonathan Kahn
Peggotty – Pat Keen
Little Emily – Katharine Levy
Mrs. Gummidge – Lala Lloyd
Mr. Micawber – Arthur Lowe
Dora Spenlow Copperfield – Beth Morris
Rosa Dartle – Jacqueline Pearce
Mrs. Micawber – Patricia Routledge
Mr. Murdstone – Gareth Thomas
David Copperfield – David Yelland

Following the death of his mother, young David Copperfield is dispatched by a cruel stepfather to London, where he lives with the poor yet cheerful Micawber family. David next journeys to the home of his great-aunt Betsey Trotwood, who becomes his guardian. After hard work, a tragic marriage to charming but frivolous Dora Spenlow and a series of trials and tribulations, David finds happiness with his first true love, Agnes Wickfield.

MELISSA

4 December 1974, Wednesday,
8:10–9:00pm, BBC1, 3 episodes, thriller,
British, contemporary
BBCtv
Pr: Morris Barry
Dir: Peter Moffatt
Wtr: Francis Durbridge
Cast: **Guy Foster – Peter Barkworth**
Paula Hepburn – Joan Benham
Dr. Swanley – Lyndon Brook
Felix Hepburn – Ronald Fraser
Mr. Antrobus – John Horsley
Don Page – Ray Lonnen
Melissa Foster – Moira Redmond
Detective Chief Inspector Carter – Philip Voss

An all-new (and colour) production of the Durbridge thriller first telecast in 1964, focusing on Guy Foster's entrapment in a web of intrigue and murder following the supposed death of his wife, Melissa.

Featured under the program banner of "Francis Durbridge presents . . . "

AN UNOFFICIAL ROSE

28 December 1974, Saturday,
8:30–9:20pm, BBC2, 4 episodes, drama,
British, 20th century
BBCtv
Pr: Ken Riddington
Dir: Basil Coleman
Wtr: Simon Raven
Based on Iris Murdoch
Cast: **Ann Peronett – Ann Bell**
Miranda – Adrienne Byrne
Hugh Peronett – Maurice Denham
Mildred Finch – Ruth Dunning
Felix Meecham – Derek Waring
Randall Peronett – John Woodvine

The quiet country life of the Peronett family is interrupted by the death of wife and mother Fanny . . . and the appearance at her funeral of two unexpected mourners. One of them is patriarch Hugh's ex-mistress, and his attempt to resume their relationship of old indirectly causes the estrangement of Hugh's son Randall from his wife Ann.

THE SECRET GARDEN

1 January 1975, Wednesday, 5:00–5:30pm,
BBC1, 6 episodes, drama, classic, family,
British, 20th century
BBCtv/Scotland
Video: available in UK, US
Pr: Dorothea Brooking
Dir: Katrina Murray
Wtr: Dorothea Brooking
Based on Frances Hodgson Burnett
Cast: **Mary Lennox – Sarah Hollis Andrews**
Dickon – Andrew Harrison
Ben Weatherstaff – Tom Harrison
Mrs. Medlock – Hope Johnston
Colin – David Patterson
Archibald Craven – John Woodnutt

Orphaned Mary Lennox goes to Misselthwaite Manor in the Yorkshire moors to live with her uncle, reclusive Archibald Craven and wheelchair-bound cousin, Colin. When Mary discovers the abandoned garden of Craven's dead wife, she works to transform it into a multi-colored, blooming glory, thereby bringing life back to the gloomy estate and its inhabitants.

THE CHANGES

6 January 1975, Monday, 5:20–6:00pm,
BBC1, 10 episodes, drama, family, British,
science fiction
BBCtv
Pr: Anna Home
Dir: John Prowse
Wtr: Anna Home
Based on Peter Dickinson
Cast: Chacha – Rafiq Anwar
Jonathan – Keith Ashton
Old Man – Bartlett Mullins
Grandmother – Sahab Qizilbash
Nicky – Vicky Williams

Young Nicky feels abandoned in a deserted city, but is taken in by a group of Sikhs, whom she joins in looking for a safe place to live. Cataclysmic change has beset the landscape – technology and machinery are generally hated, and people destroy cars, electricity pylons, and anything else they can get their hands on. In order to avoid persecution, Nicky must pretend to be in agreement with the "machine-breakers" and their philosophy.

ANNE OF AVONLEA

26 January 1975, Sunday, 5:10–6:05pm, BBC1, 6 episodes, drama, classic, family, British, 19th century
BBCtv
Pr: John McRae
Dir: Joan Craft
Wtr: Elaine Morgan
Based on L.M. Montgomery
Cast: Gilbert Blythe – Christopher Blake
Anne Shirley – Kim Braden
Roy Gardner – Anthony Forrest
Mr. Harrison – David Garfield
Marilla Cuthbert – Barbara Hamilton
Rachel Lynde – Madge Ryan
Jonas Blake – David Troughton

Anne Shirley, the heroine of *Anne of Green Gables*, has grown into a young woman. She teaches at the local school and dreams of meeting her ideal man. Anne's life revolves around the school, her life at home with her adoptive mother, Marilla Cuthbert, and her love for Gilbert Blythe.

THE HANGED MAN

15 February 1975, Saturday, 9:30–10:30pm, ITV, 8 episodes, thriller, British, contemporary
Yorkshire Television
Pr: Marc Miller, Edmund Ward
Dir: Marc Miller, Tony Wharmby
Wtr: Edmund Ward
Cast: **Lewis Burnett – Colin Blakely**
Elizabeth Hayden – Angela Browne
Charlie Galbraith – Alan MacNaughtan
Laura Burnett – Jane Seymour
John Quentin – Gary Watson
Alan Crowe – Michael Williams

Construction magnate Lewis Burnett pretends to be dead in order to track down the men who have made repeated attempts on his life. He re-lives his past to find out who might have hated him enough to want him out of the way for good. Contract killer John Quentin is the one presently gunning for Burnett, and when Burnett's daughter Laura returns to England, she, too, is in danger.

LATE CALL

1 March 1975, Saturday, 8:15–9:05pm, BBC2, 4 episodes, drama, British, contemporary
BBCtv
Pr: Ken Riddington
Dir: Philip Dudley
Wtr: Dennis Potter
Based on Angus Wilson
Cast: **Harold Calvert – Michael Bryant**
Mark Calvert – Nigel Crewe
Arthur Calvert – Leslie Dwyer
Judy Calvert – Rosalyn Elvin
Ray Calvert – Tim Morand
Sylvia Calvert – Dandy Nichols
Myra Longmore – Sarah Sutton

After they retire, unexpected circumstances force Sylvia and Arthur Calvert to move in with their widowed son Harold and his children, leading to a series of unexpected problems as Sylvia finds herself increasingly at odds with the inhabitants of her new community.

THE MASTER OF BALLANTRAE

9 March 1975, Sunday, 5:35–6:05pm, BBC1, 6 episodes, drama, classic, Scottish, 18th century
BBCtv
Pr: Martin Lisemore
Dir: Fiona Cumming
Wtr: Martin Worth
Based on Robert Louis Stevenson
Cast: **Henry Durie – Brian Cox**
Catherine – Jane Ferguson
Alison Graeme – Brigit Forsyth
James Durie – Julian Glover
Ephrain Mackellar – Fulton Mackay
Lord Durrisdeer – Bryden Murdoch

In 18th-century Scotland, a bitter, lifelong feud goes on between two brothers, decent Henry and unscrupulous James Durie. James, the Master of Ballantrae, is a dashing figure who travels the world as an adventurer; Henry, a more settled figure, wants nothing more than to remain at Durrisdeer, the ancestral home. When James is presumed killed at Culloden, Henry assumes the family title, marries his brother's intended, Alison . . . but when James returns several years later, his arrival proves in the end disastrous for all.

THE FIGHT AGAINST SLAVERY

19 March 1975, Wednesday, 9:25–10:20pm, BBC2, 6 episodes, drama, historical, British, 18th–19th century
BBCtv
Video: available in US
Pr: Christopher Ralling
Dir: Christopher Ralling
Wtr: Evan Jones
Cast: Colonel Lawson – Patrick Barr
Reverend John Newton – John Castle
William Wilberforce – David Collings
Charles James Fox – Ronald Lacey
David Lisle – Dinsdale Landen
William Knibb – Bryan Marshall
William Pitt – Ronald Pickup
Lord Mansfield – John Richmond
Thomas Clarkson – Gareth Thomas

A dramatic depiction of the development of the abolitionist movement in the British empire in the 18th century, beginning with Reverend John Newton's sermons on the horrors of slavery. In the West Indies the lawfulness of slavery is argued before the Lord Chief Justice in the famous Somerset case, and in 1787 Yorkshiremen William Wilberforce and Thomas Clarkson dedicate their lives to abolishing the slave trade.

A LEGACY

29 March 1975, Saturday, 8:20–9:10pm, BBC2, 5 episodes, drama, German, 20th century
BBCtv
Pr: Ron Craddock
Dir: Derek Martinus
Wtr: Robert Muller
Based on Sybille Bedford
Cast: Count Bernin – Robin Bailey
Caroline Trafford – Isla Blair
Sarah Merz – Claire Bloom
Eduard Merz – Jeremy Brett
Julius von Felden – John Fraser
Baron Felden – Hugh Griffith
Grandmama Merz – Irene Handl
Gottlieb – Richard Hurndall
Clara van Bernin – Angela Pleasence
Narrator – Flora Robson
Gustavus von Felden – Geoffrey Whitehead

An extraordinary legacy has a profound effect on two families linked by marriage at the turn of the century in the Kaiser's Germany.

EDWARD THE SEVENTH

1 April 1975, Tuesday, 9:00–10:00pm, ITV, 13 episodes, drama, biographical, historical, British, 19th–20th century
ATV Network
Pr: Cecil Clarke
Dir: John Gorrie
Wtr: David Butler, John Gorrie
Based on Sir Philip Magnus
Cast: Lillie Langtry – Francesca Annis
Queen Victoria – Annette Crosbie
H.H. Asquith – Basil Dignam
Benjamin Disraeli – John Gielgud
Prince Albert – Robert Hardy
W.E. Gladstone – Michael Hordern
Princess Vicky – Felicity Kendal
Dowager Empress Dagmar – Jane Lapotaire
Kaiser Wilhelm II – Christopher Neame
Alice Keppel – Moira Redmond
Princess Alexandra – Helen Ryan
Bertie – Charles Sturridge
Prince of Wales/King Edward VII – Timothy West

The story of King Edward VII, the son of Queen Victoria, who, before becoming monarch in 1902, spends 60 years as Bertie, the restless Prince of Wales. Bertie is repeatedly frustrated by his mother, who will not give him anything useful to do. He does organize the Queen's Golden Jubilee, but then the strength of the monarchy is threatened when he becomes involved in two scandals. When Bertie finally becomes King, he exhausts his strength working to maintain peace in Europe in the years leading up to World War I.

Timothy West's father, Lockwood West, played the role of this Prince of Wales in one of the most well-remembered episodes of the popular series *Upstairs, Downstairs* in 1972. Francesca Annis reprised her portrayal of Lillie Langtry in a serial about Langtry in 1978. Winner, BAFTA Award, Best Drama Serial 1975.

SAM AND THE RIVER

24 April 1975, Thursday, 5:15–5:40pm, BBC1, 6 episodes, drama, family, British, contemporary
BBCtv
Pr: Peggy Miller
Dir: Joe McGrath
Wtr: Peggy Miller
Cast: Paul Redmond – Mark Dignam
Patrick Flint – Harry Markham
Alan Flint – Bryan Marshall
Katie Leigh – Jo Rowbottom
Sam Leigh – Simon West

Sam Leigh lives in an old pub in the heart of London's docklands; the boy journeys up and down the Thames, finding more adventure than he had bargained for.

THE GIRLS OF SLENDER MEANS

3 May 1975, Saturday, 8:20–9:10pm, BBC2, 3 episodes, drama, British, 20th century
BBCtv
Pr: Martin Lisemore
Dir: Moira Armstrong
Wtr: Ken Taylor
Based on Muriel Spark
Cast: Judy Redwood – Jane Cussons
Nancy Riddle – Marilyn Finlay
Anne Baberton – Patricia Hodge
Nicholas Farrington – James Laurenson
Jane Wright – Miriam Margolyes
Dorothy Markham – Sarah Nash
Joanna Childe – Rosalind Shanks
Rudi Bittesch – Jack Shepherd
Selina Redwood – Mary Tamm
Narrator – Marjorie Westbury

In London in 1945, as World War II begins at last to wind down, the young ladies residing at the May of Teck Club continue to eke out their lives among poverty, ration coupons and questionable politics. Some years later, the mysterious death of a missionary in Haiti who knew the girls brings back memories of those times.

LOOKING FOR CLANCY

24 May 1975, Saturday, 8:10–9:00pm, BBC2, 5 episodes, drama, British, contemporary
BBCtv
Pr: Richard Beynon
Dir: Bill Hays
Wtr: Jack Pulman
Based on Frederic Mullally
Cast: **Dick Holt – Keith Drinkel**
Frank Clancy (as a child) – Steve Fletcher
Dick Holt (as a child) – Tommy Pender
Frank Clancy – Robert Powell
Penny Clancy – Catherine Schell

Frank Clancy and Dick Holt have been friends since their childhood in London's East End. As adults, they are both determined to succeed on Fleet Street, but the competitive circumstances have tragic results. Only Clancy, now a left-wing editor, survives, and he looks back on earlier, easier days, which seem all too far away.

SAM (third series)

2 June 1975, Monday, 8:00–9:00pm, ITV, 13 episodes, drama, British, 20th century
Granada Television
Pr: Michael Cox
Dir: Stephen Butcher, Les Chatfield, Michael Cox, Roland Joffe, Quentin Lawrence, Brian Mills
Wtr: John Finch
Cast: Tom Wilson (as a child) – Charles Booth
Liz Chadwick – Carol Drinkwater
Pat Barraclough – Jan Harvey
Sarah Wilson – Jennifer Hilary
Deborah Wilson (as a child) – Julie Horner
Chris Wilson – David Major
Sam Wilson – Mark McManus

Cassie Crossman – Cherith Mellor
Deborah Wilson – Veronica Roberts
Tom Wilson – Simon Rouse
Harry Carter – Michael Turner

In 1960, Sam Wilson is a manager at an engineering firm. He is settled in Golwick with his family, but domestic problems, including his own infidelity, threaten Sam's sense of security. Another shock takes place when Sam's long-lost father suddenly shows up on the scene, 30 years after he deserted Sam and his mother. Several years later, Sam's family is devastated when his stepson becomes a drug addict. His wife dies and Sam finds himself in 1973 alone, looking back on his entire life, and reflecting on how different he, and the world, used to be.

With the completion of the *Sam* saga, John Finch was the first television writer to produce 39 consecutive hour-long scripts about one set of characters.

FIVE RED HERRINGS

23 July 1975, Wednesday, 8:10–9:00pm, BBC1, 4 episodes, mystery, British, 20th century
BBCtv/Scotland
Pr: Bill Sellars
Dir: Robert Tronson
Wtr: Anthony Steven
Based on Dorothy L. Sayers
Cast: **Lord Peter Wimsey – Ian Carmichael**
Hugh Farran – Donald Douglas
Sergeant Dalziel – Michael Elder
Bunter – Glyn Houston
Matthew Gowan – Russell Hunter
Sandy Campbell – Ian Ireland
Sir Maxwell Jamieson – Robert James
John Ferguson – David McKail
Inspector MacPherson – Michael Sheard

Lord Wimsey, accompanied by faithful manservant Bunter, arrives in Scotland for what is meant to be a peaceful painting holiday . . . but takes an altogether different turn when they stumble upon the corpse of artist Sandy Campbell – a man who Wimsey soon discovers had offended nearly everyone in the village, which makes his investigation into Campbell's death all the more complicated.

MADAME BOVARY

22 September 1975, Monday, 9:00–9:55pm, BBC2, 4 episodes, drama, classic, French, 19th century
BBCtv
Pr: Richard Beynon
Dir: Rodney Bennett
Wtr: Giles Cooper
Based on Gustave Flaubert
Cast: **Emma Bovary – Francesca Annis**
L'heureux – John Cater
Charles Bovary – Tom Conti
Madame Bovary – Kathleen Helme
Rodolphe – Denis Lill
Guillaumin – Ivor Roberts
Homais – Ray Smith
Leon Dupuis – Brian Stirner

Emma Bovary's romantic dreams of marriage and fortune are shattered by the mundane realities of life with country doctor Charles. Emma's subsequent depression is abated first by flirtation with student Leon then an impassioned affair with rakish Rodolphe. Emma goes deeply into debt to placate her lover. When the affair ends, Emma's despair is overwhelming, leading to another, more serious involvement with Leon, both moral and financial bankruptcy and, ultimately, Emma's suicide.

THE HILL OF THE RED FOX

24 September 1975, Wednesday, 5:15–5:40pm, BBC1, 6 episodes, thriller, Scottish, contemporary
BBCtv/Scotland
Pr: Pharic Maclaren
Dir: Bob McIntosh
Wtr: Scot Finch
Based on Allan Campbell McLean
Cast: Major Cassell – Peter Copley
Murdo Beaton – Donald Douglas
Duncan Mor – Bernard Horsfall
Man with Blue Eyes – George Howell
Mother – Ellen McIntosh
Alasdair Cameron – Mark Rogers
Aunt Evelyn – Iris Russell

Alasdair Cameron travels from London

to Skye on holiday. When he receives a mysterious note from a stranger, Alasdair's journey becomes far more adventurous – and dangerous – than he could ever have imagined, involving rendezvous at remote Duntulm Castle, signal lights in the darkness, and a mysterious Man with Blue Eyes.

BALLET SHOES

4 October 1975, Sunday, 5:40–6:05pm, BBC1, 6 episodes, drama, family, British, 20th century
BBCtv
Video: available in US
Pr: John McRae
Dir: Timothy Combe
Wtr: John Wiles
Based on Noel Streatfeild
Cast: Donald Houghton – Patrick Godfrey
Nana – Barbara Lott
Pauline – Elizabeth Morgan
Posy – Sarah Prince
Mr. Simpson – Terence Skelton
Petrova – Jane Slaughter

In London in 1936, Pauline, Petrova and Posy, unrelated orphans who have been adopted by an eccentric archeology professor and raised as sisters, are sent to the Academy of Dancing and Stage Training to prepare for professional careers.

POLDARK

4 October 1975, Sunday, 7:25–8:15pm, BBC1, 16 episodes, drama, British, 18th–19th century
BBCtv
Video: available in UK, US
Pr: Morris Barry
Dir: Paul Annett, Christopher Barry, Kenneth Ives
Wtr: Peter Draper, Jack Pulman, Jack Russell, Paul Wheeler
Based on *Ross Poldark*, *Demelza*, *Jeremy Poldark* and *Warleggan* by Winston Graham
Cast: George Warleggan – Ralph Bates
Jud – Paul Curran
Ross Poldark – Robin Ellis
Mark Daniel – Martin Fisk
Francis Poldark – Clive Francis
Caroline Penvenen – Judy Geeson
Demelza – Angharad Rees
Verity Poldark – Norma Streader
Elizabeth Warleggan – Jill Townsend
Prudie – Mary Wimbush

In 1783, Captain Ross Poldark returns home to Cornwall from fighting in the American War of Independence to discover that his father has died, he has himself been reported dead and others have laid claim to his house, his family copper mines – and Elizabeth, the woman he was meant to marry. Ross struggles to regain all three, which leads to ten years of gallant adventures and a fierce feud with the rich and powerful Warleggans.

A second series of episodes involving Poldark and the re-kindling of his feud with George Warleggan began airing in September 1977.

PROMETHEUS: THE LIFE OF BALZAC

20 October 1975, Monday, 9:00–9:50pm, BBC2, 6 episodes, drama, biographical, French, 19th century
BBCtv
Pr: Richard Beynon
Dir: Joan Craft
Wtr: David Turner
Based on André Maurois
Cast: Zulma Carraud – Kate Coleridge
Honoré de Balzac – Nicky Henson
Madame Eve Henska – Nanette Newman
Madame Balzac – Helen Ryan
Victor Hugo – Peter Sallis
Comte de Berny – Barry Sinclair
Comtesee de Berny – Elizabeth Spriggs
Monsieur Balzac – William Squire

The life story of French writer Honoré de Balzac, one of the great figures of 19th-century French literature, starting as he first sets out, while in his 30s, to be a writer, finding fame and notoriety in Paris in the 1830s, until his death a mere 20 years later, after a life spent and overspent on grand living and loving.

THE LEGEND OF ROBIN HOOD

22 November 1975, Sunday, 5:00–5:55pm,
BBC1, 6 episodes, drama, classic,
adventure, 12th Century
BBCtv
Pr: George Gallaccio
Dir: Eric Davidson
Wtr: Alistair Bell
Cast: Will Scarlet – Miles Anderson
Little John – Conrad Asquith
Friar Tuck – Tony Caunter
Sheriff of Nottingham – Paul Darrow
Prince John – David Dixon
Richard I – Michael-John Jackson
Lady Marian – Diane Keen
Robin Hood – Martin Potter

The legendary outlaw hero and his band of Merry Men hold reign in Sherwood Forest while loyally defending King Richard I and holding their own against the evil Sheriff of Nottingham.

THE DOLL

25 November 1975, Tuesday,
8:05–9:00pm, BBC1, 3 episodes, thriller,
British, contemporary
BBCtv
Pr: Bill Sellars
Dir: David Askey
Wtr: Francis Durbridge
Cast: Max Lerner – Derek Fowlds
Peter Matty – John Fraser
Phyllis Du Salle – Anouska Hempel
Sir Arnold Wyatt – Cyril Luckham
Detective Inspector Seaton – John Pennington
Claude Matty – Geoffrey Whitehead

Publisher Peter Matty is on his way back from Geneva when he hears of an accident at sea and a quarrel having "something to do with a doll." The mystery takes those involved to Spain before Peter finally receives a letter which answers all his questions.

Featured under the program banner of "Francis Durbridge presents . . . "

MOLL FLANDERS

26 November 1975, Wednesday,
9:30–11:15pm, BBC2, 2 episodes, drama,
classic, British, 18th century
BBCtv
Pr: Cedric Messina
Dir: Donald McWhinnie
Wtr: Hugh Whitemore
Based on Daniel Defoe
Cast: Lady Verney – Diana Fairfax
Moll Flanders (Betty) – Julia Foster
Jemmy Earle – Kenneth Haigh
William Stubbs – Barry Jackson
Humphrey Oliver/Young Humphrey – Ian Ogilvy
Mrs. Oliver – Madge Ryan

Moll's picaresque 18th-century saga, best summed up in the novel's full title: *The Fortunes and Misfortunes of the Famous Moll Flanders, who was Born at Newgate, and during a Life of continued Variety for Threescore Years, besides her Childhood, was Twelve Year a Whore, five time a Wife (whereof once to her own Brother), Twelve Year a Thief, Eight Year a Transported Felon in Virginia, at last grew rich, liv'd Honest, and died a Penitent.*

NORTH AND SOUTH

1 December 1975, Monday, 9:00–9:50pm,
BBC2, 4 episodes, drama, British, 19th
century
BBCtv
Pr: Martin Lisemore
Dir: Rodney Bennett
Wtr: David Turner
Based on Mrs. Elizabeth Gaskell
Cast: Mr. Hale – Robin Bailey
Mrs. Hale – Kathleen Byron
Mrs. Thornton – Rosalie Crutchley
Margaret Hale – Rosalind Shanks
John Thornton – Patrick Stewart

When well-born but poor Margaret Hale moves North from London in the mid-1800s to live with her parents in Manchester, the sensitive young woman comes in conflict with brusque, strong-willed manufacturer John Thornton – but the two also find themselves strongly drawn to one another.

STATE OF EMERGENCY

4 December 1975, Thursday,

9:25–10:15pm, BBC1, 3 episodes, thriller, British, contemporary
BBCtv
Pr: Morris Barry
Dir: David Askey
Wtr: John Gould
Cast: Colonel Singleton – William Gaunt
Dent – Ian Gelder
Professor Donati – Michael Gwynn
Jane Frederick – Janet Key
Paul Frederick – Patrick Mower

This sequel to *The Donati Conspiracy* (1973) exhibits more far-reaching effects of a fictionalized, totalitarian future for Britain, leading to a nation on the brink of a bitter civil war. It is up to Paul Frederick to find the answers which will appease terrorists and bring forward an uneasy peace.

Writer John Gould died before completing *State of Emergency*; work on the script was completed by Hugh Whitemore.

HOW GREEN WAS MY VALLEY

29 December 1975, Monday, 9:00–9:50pm, BBC2, 6 episodes, drama, classic, British, 19th–20th century
BBCtv
Pr: Martin Lisemore
Dir: Ronald Wilson
Wtr: Elaine Morgan
Based on Richard Llewellyn
Cast: **Gwilym Morgan – Stanley Baker**
Iestyn Evans – Jeremy Clyde
Ifor Morgan – Norman Comer
Ianto Morgan – Keith Drinkel
Huw Morgan – Dominic Guard
Bronwen Morgan – Nerys Hughes
Angharad Morgan – Sue Jones-Davies
Beth Morgan – Sian Phillips
Young Huw – Rhys Powys
Mr. Elias – Aubrey Richards
Blodwen Evans – Sheila Ruskin
Reverend Mr. Gruffyd – Gareth Thomas

The Morgans have for generations lived and worked in the mines of the Rhondda Valleys of South Wales. As Huw, one of the youngest of Gwilym and Beth's children, comes of age, monumental changes take place which affect the world at large and the smaller universe of the Morgan family.

STRIKER

31 December 1975, Wednesday, 4:50–5:05pm, BBC1, 3 episodes, drama, family, British, contemporary
BBCtv
Pr: Anna Home
Dir: Colin Cant
Wtr: Kenneth Cope
Cast: Bomber – Keith Allingham
Harry – Joe Gladwin
Mr. Dyker – Geoffrey Hinsliff
Mr. Davies – Keith Marsh
Ben Dyker – Kevin Moreton

When Ben moves to the village of Brenton, it upsets the careful balance of the local football team.

THE PRINCE AND THE PAUPER

4 January 1976, Sunday, 4:55–5:25pm, BBC1, 6 episodes, drama, classic, family, British, 16th century
BBCtv
Designed by Kenneth Sharp
Dir: Barry Letts
Wtr: Richard Harris
Based on Mark Twain
Cast: Mother Canty – June Brown
Lord Sudbroke – Martin Friend
John Canty – Ronald Herdman
Archbishop Cranmer – Robert James
Tom Canty/Prince Edward – Nicholas Lyndhurst
Miles Hendon – Barry Stokes

Prince Edward, heir to the throne of King Henry VIII, impulsively changes place with poverty-stricken Tom Canty, who is his exact double. But the masquerade does not end as quickly as it should; the King dies, the Prince wanders the city in rags while Tom struggles with the responsibilities of royalty, and a boyish game quickly develops serious circumstances.

LIFE AND DEATH OF PENELOPE

7 January 1976, Wednesday, 9:00–10:00pm, ITV, 6 episodes, mystery, British, contemporary
Thames Television
Pr: Michael Chapman
Dir: Jonathan Alwyn, Peter Duguid, Kim Mills, David Wickes
Wtr: Ben Bassett, Philip Broadley, Ray Evans, Richard Harris
Cast: **Detective Chief Superintendent Lane – Antony Brown**
Evelyn Dyer – Gwen Cherrell
Sean McDermott – Prentice Hancock
Joe Finer – Don Hawkins
Tom Crispin – Richard Heffer
Nigel Priestman – Charles Keating
Detective Sergeant Fishlock – Matthew Long
Mr. Dyer – Alan MacNaughtan
Thames Division Sergeant – Colin Rix
Imogen – Bernice Stegers
Dr. Lewis-Clarke – Michael Turner

A young woman's body, identified as Penelope Dyer, is discovered in the Thames. C.I.D. detectives Lane and Fishlock then work backwards in time, trying to discover the kind of person Penelope was in life, which might account for the manner of her death. Her last days are closely re-constructed, her family, close friends, psychiatrist, and lover Tom Crispin all questioned. Due to their meticulous investigation, the detectives are able to identify Penelope's killer within just four days of her murder.

BOUQUET OF BARBED WIRE

9 January 1976, Friday, 9:00–10:00pm, ITV, 7 episodes, drama, British, contemporary
London Weekend Television
Video: available in UK, US
Pr: Tony Wharmby
Dir: Tony Wharmby
Wtr: Andrea Newman
Based on Andrea Newman
Cast: **Cassie Manson – Sheila Allen**
Gavin Sorenson – James Aubrey
Peter Manson – Frank Finlay
Sarah Francis – Deborah Grant
Prue Sorenson – Susan Penhaligon

Peter and Cassie Manson seem the picture of a happily-married couple . . . until a young American, Gavin Sorenson, intrudes into their lives. Gavin has married the Manson's daughter, Prue, and Peter strongly disapproves of the match. Gavin finds more acceptance from Cassie, with whom he becomes romantically involved. Peter, too, seeks consolation elsewhere, with his secretary Sarah. These personal conflicts build in tension and ultimately bring tragic results to the Mansons, when Prue dies following the birth of her daughter.

THE GLITTERING PRIZES

21 January 1976, Wednesday, 10:15–11:35pm, BBC2, 6 episodes, drama, British, 20th century
BBCtv
Pr: Mark Shivas
Dir: Waris Hussein, Robert Knights
Wtr: Frederic Raphael
Cast: **Adam Morris – Tom Conti**
Joyce Hadleigh Bradley – Angela Down
Alan Parks – John Gregg
Denis Porson – Nigel Havers
Barbara Hughes Morris – Barbara Kellermann
Gavin Pope – Dinsdale Landen
Bill Bourne – Clive Merrison
Tim Dent – Tim Pigott-Smith
Stephen Taylor – Eric Porter
Donald Davidson – David Robb
Lionel Morris – Leonard Sachs
Daniel Bradley – Malcolm Stoddard
Joann Case – Suzanne Stone
Mike Clode – Mark Wing-Davey

Set in the years 1952–1976, this drama traces the lives of a group of promising Cambridge graduates, with particular emphasis on Adam Morris, from his university years, where he mingles as the solitary Jew among the Christian upperclasses, through adulthood as a successful writer who, despite his personal and professional success, still questions what life has to offer.

KIZZY

21 January 1976, Wednesday,

5:15–5:45pm, BBC1, 6 episodes, drama, family, British, contemporary
BBCtv/Birmingham
Pr: Dorothea Brooking
Dir: Myles Lang
Wtr: John Tully
Based on *The Diddakoi* by Rumer Godden
Cast: Mrs. Cuthbert – Angela Browne
Prue Cuthbert – Melissa Docker
Kizzy – Vanessa Furst
Gran – Betty Hardy
Olivia Brooke – Anne Ridler
Admiral Twiss – John Welsh

Young Kizzy and her grandmother arrive in a village as part of a gypsy caravan. Kizzy and Gran hope to make it their permanent home, it is difficult to be accepted by the other inhabitants of the village, especially the schoolgirls who can be quite cruel to Kizzy. Things get even worse for Kizzy after her grandmother dies, until she is taken under wing by Admiral Twiss and local magistrate Olivia Brooke.

JUMBO SPENCER

9 February 1976, Monday, 5:15–5:40pm, BBC1, 5 episodes, drama, family, contemporary
BBCtv
Pr: Daphne Jones
Dir: Jeremy Swan
Wtr: Helen Cresswell
Cast: Maggots – Natalie Boyce
Mrs. Spencer – Helen Fraser
Mike – Huw Higginson
Mr. Spencer – Jim Smilie
Bill – Christopher Watts
Freckles – John Weavers
Jumbo Spencer – Mark Weavers

Jumbo Spencer comes up with an elaborate set of schemes for how he and his mates will spend their summer holiday, all aimed at raising the funds needed to build a new village hall.

THE FLIGHT OF THE HERON

29 February 1976, Sunday, 4:55–5:25pm, BBC1, 6 episodes, drama, Scottish, 18th century
BBCtv/Scotland
Pr: Pharic Maclaren
Dir: Alastair Reid
Wtr: Tom Wright
Based on D.K. Broster
Cast: Lachlan MacMartin – Joseph Blatchley
Keith Windham – Tom Chadbon
Dr. Archie Cameron – Michael Elder
Alison Grant – Estelle Kohler
Aunt Margaret – Eileen McCallum
Cameron of Lochiel – John Phillips
Ewen Cameron – David Rintoul
Sergeant Mackay – Gerard Slevin

Highlander Ewen Cameron and English Captain Keith Windham are sworn enemies at the battle of Culloden, the final stand of Bonnie Prince Charlie and his Jacobites, but a prophesy is made which foresees a flying heron bringing about a fateful meeting of the two men, who learn from each other and become wiser as a result of the experience.

OUR MUTUAL FRIEND

1 March 1976, Monday, 9:00–9:50pm, BBC2, 7 episodes, drama, classic, British, 19th century
BBCtv
Pr: Martin Lisemore
Dir: Peter Hammond
Wtr: Donald Churchill, Julia Jones
Based on Charles Dickens
Cast: Bradley Headstone – Warren Clarke
Rogue Riderhood – John Collin
Lizzie Hexam – Lesley Dunlop
Mrs. Boffin – Kathleen Harrison
Jenny Wren – Polly James
Mr. Venus – Ronald Lacey
Mrs. Wilfer – Patricia Lawrence
John Rokesmith – John McEnery
Mr. Boffin – Leo McKern
Mr. Wilfer – Ray Mort
Mortimer Lightwood – Andrew Ray
Mrs. Veneering – Liza Ross
Bella Wilfer – Jane Seymour

Money, in the form of the enormous Harmon fortune, rules the destiny of practically every character in this, Dickens' last completed novel, which begins with the discovery of a body in the Thames River – presumed to be that of the last Harmon heir John. Amiable former servant Mr. Boffin then inherits the fortune, but the lives of Boffin and his protégée, Bella Wilfer, change still more with the arrival on the scene of John Rokesmith . . . who is more than the mild-mannered secretary he initially appears to be.

ROCKY O'ROURKE

3 March 1976, Wednesday, 5:15–5:40pm, BBC1, 4 episodes, drama, family, British, contemporary
BBCtv
Pr: Anna Home
Dir: John Prowse
Wtr: Alan England
Based on *The Liverpool Cats* by Sylvia Sherry
Cast: Spadge – John Dalziel
 Nabber – James Hoey
 PC McMahon – Bernard Holley
 Rocky O'Rourke – Michael Mills
 Joey O'Rourke – Alan Pope
 Chick – Kenny Walker

While he awaits the release of his older brother Joey from prison, Rocky spends most of his time as part of a Liverpool gang, "the Cats." When Joey returns home, he gets Rocky involved in a series of dangerous exploits, and in the end Rocky must step away from his brother's less-than-benign influence and stand up for himself.

JOHN MACNAB

14 April 1976, Wednesday, 9:25–10:10pm, BBC1, 3 episodes, drama, British, 20th century
BBCtv/Scotland
Pr: Pharic Maclaren
Dir: Donald McWhinnie
Wtr: John Prebble
Based on John Buchan
Cast: Agatha Raden – Wendy Allnutt
 Lady Claybody – Lally Bowers
 Colonel Raden – Basil Dignam
 Lord Lamancha – Derek Godfrey
 John Palliser-Yeates – Bernard Horsfall
 Archie Roylance – Cavan Kendall
 Sir Edward Leithen – James Maxwell
 Wattie Lithgow – Roddy McMillan
 Lord Claybody – John Sharp
 Janet Raden – Susan Wooldridge

In the 1920s, three eminent members of the London upper-class establishment find that post-war life has lost its zest, and use the pseudonym "John Macnab" to find a cure for their boredom, challenging several landowners to keep them from poaching on their ground.

DANGEROUS KNOWLEDGE

19 May 1976, Wednesday, 8:30–9:00pm, ITV, 6 episodes, thriller, British, contemporary
Southern Television
Pr: Alan Gibson
Dir: Alan Gibson
Wtr: N.J. Crisp
Cast: **Roger Fane – Patrick Allen**
 Sanders – Ralph Bates
 Madame Lafois – Elizabeth Bergner
 Kirby – John Gregson
 Dr. Vincent – Robert Keegan
 Laura Marshall – Prunella Ransome
 Claire Kirby – Ruth Trouncer

A chance meeting between Laura Marshall and insurance agent Kirby (an ex-Army Intelligence agent) leads to romance and intrigue when a murdered body is discovered. Kirby's later discovery of government infiltration by the KGB involves Laura's stepfather, top government official Roger Fane, whose partner, Dr. Vincent, is accused by Kirby of working for the Soviets. But before Kirby can offer proof to Fane a key witness is killed, and Kirby himself is the chief suspect. Fane then must decide which man can be believed.

John Gregson, who played the lead role of Kirby, died of a heart attack before this show was aired.

ORDE WINGATE

16 July 1976, Friday, 9:25–10:35pm, BBC2, 3 episodes, drama, biographical, historical, British, 20th century
BBCtv
Pr: Innes Lloyd
Dir: Bill Hays
Wtr: Don Shaw
Cast: Brigadier Calvert – James Cosmo

Chaim Weizmann – Arnold Diamond
Senior Officer, Delhi – Denholm Elliott
Orde Wingate – Barry Foster
Palmer – Bernard Hepton
Lorna – Sheila Ruskin
General Wavell – Nigel Stock

The story of Orde Wingate, the charismatic, controversial leader of the Burma Expeditions of 1943–44.

LORNA DOONE

5 September 1976, Sunday, 5:00–5:55pm, BBC1, 5 episodes, drama, classic, British, 17th century
BBCtv
Pr: Barry Letts
Dir: Joan Craft
Wtr: B.R. Woodstock
Based on R.D. Blackmore
Cast: Sir Ensor Doone – Norman Henry
 Tom Faggus – Ian Hogg
 Mrs. Ridd – Rhoda Lewis
 Lorna Doone – Emily Richard
 John Ridd – John Sommerville
 Councellor Doone – Patrick Troughton
 Carver Doone – John Turner

The 17th-century story of the Exmoor feud between the Doone and Ridd families. The Doones kill John Ridd's father, so he hates them – but cannot keep himself from falling in love with Doone daughter Lorna, whom he ultimately discovers is actually the kidnapped child of a Scottish nobleman.

GANGSTERS

9 September 1976, Thursday, 9:55–10:45pm, BBC1, 6 episodes, thriller, British, contemporary
BBCtv/Birmingham
Pr: David Rose
Dir: Alastair Reid
Wtr: Philip Martin
Cast: Dermot Macavoy – Paul Antrim
 Malleson – Paul Barber
 Anne Darracott – Elizabeth Cassidy
 John Kline – Maurice Colbourne
 Rafiq – Saeed Jaffrey
 Khan – Ahmed Khalil
 Inspector Newbold – Ralph Lawton
 Sarah Gant – Alibe Parsons
 Sergeant Ede – Peter Simpson
 Sir George Jeavons – Robert Stephens

After the death of gangland leader Rawlinson, the Midland organizations in the white, Asian and West Indian underworlds search for a new leader. John Kline, a criminal figure suspected of Rawlinson's murder, is suddenly released from police custody . . . is he a serious contender for the position, or a police plant, working undercover with Pakistani security agent Khan?

A second *Gangsters* serial was produced in January 1978, with Ahmed Khalil and Maurice Colbourne reprising their roles as Khan and Kline.

I, CLAUDIUS

20 September 1976, Monday, 9:00–10:40pm (subsequent episodes aired from 9:00–9:55pm), BBC2, 12 episodes, drama, historical, Ancient Rome, 10 BC–AD 54
BBCtv in association with London Film Productions Ltd.
Video: available in UK, US
Pr: Martin Lisemore
Dir: Herbert Wise
Wtr: Jack Pulman
Based on Robert Graves
Cast: Tiberius – George Baker
 Nero – Christopher Biggins
 Augustus – Brian Blessed
 Posthumus – John Castle
 Narcissus – John Cater
 Herod – James Faulkner
 Pallas – Bernard Hepton
 Caligula – John Hurt
 Claudius – Derek Jacobi
 Drusilla – Beth Morris
 Drusus – Ian Ogilvy
 Livia – Sian Phillips
 Livilla – Patricia Quinn
 Macro – John Rhys Davies
 Germanicus – David Robb
 Calpurnia – Jo Rowbottom
 Sejanus – Patrick Stewart
 Antonia – Margaret Tyzack
 Agrippinia – Fiona Walker
 Julia – Frances White
 Messalina – Sheila White

Agrippinilla – Barbara Young

A history of the Roman Empire told by reluctant Emperor Claudius, fourth of the 12 Caesars, who sits down at the end of his life and writes of his reign as well as those of his three predecessors: his grandfather Augustus, who lived under the thumb of his treacherous wife Livia; Livia's son, Tiberius, who succeeds to power thanks to his mother's murderous ambition for him, and Caligula, Claudius' depraved nephew. Claudius, long considered an idiot due to his stutter, is in truth a wise man with an astute sense of history. He proves a shrewd emperor, but grows weary of rule and so marries his niece, Agrippinilla, in order to make her son his heir – Nero.

DICKENS OF LONDON

28 September 1976, Tuesday, 9:00–10:00pm, ITV, 13 episodes, drama, biographical, British, 19th century
Yorkshire Television
Pr: Marc Miller
Dir: Marc Miller
Wtr: Wolf Mankowitz
Cast: Mary Hogarth – Lois Baxter
Charles Dickens (as a boy) – Simon Bell
Catherine Hogarth Dickens – Adrienne Burgess
Mrs. Dickens – Diana Coupland
Maria Beadnell – Karen Dotrice
Charles Dickens/Mr. John Dickens – Roy Dotrice
Charles Dickens (as a young man) – Gene Foad
Dr. John Elliotson – Ben Kingsley
Edgar Allen Poe – Samuel Matthews
Mr. Tribe – John Slater

While on a promotional tour in New York, novelist Charles Dickens is taken ill; in his feverish state he thinks back across his life (and also envisions scenes from his fictional works). Dickens remembers his dismal childhood, dominated by his mercurial father, John, his first love for Maria Beadnell, his marriage to Catherine, his secret love for Catherine's sister Mary (who suddenly dies), and his developing success as a writer, which leads to the fateful trip to America.

In addition to playing Charles Dickens from the age of 35 through to his death at 58 and John Dickens as a middle-aged and elderly man, Dotrice also portrayed Dickens' character Daniel Quilp from *The Old Curiosity Shop* in one of the character's feverish fantasies.

KATY

10 October 1976, Sunday, 5:25–5:55pm, BBC1, 6 episodes, drama, family, American, 19th century
BBCtv
Pr: Barry Letts
Dir: Julia Smith
Wtr: Constance Cox
Based on *What Katy Did*, *What Katy Did At School* by Susan Coolidge
Cast: **Dr. Carr – Ed Bishop**
Elsie – Virginia Fiol
Cousin Helen – Toria Fuller
Aunt Izzie – Thomasine Heiner
Dorry – Scott Kunz
Katy Carr – Claire Walker

Motherless, irrepressible teenager Katy Carr has a knack for getting into trouble in New England in the 1870s, but gets far more than she bargained for when a fall renders her temporarily crippled. After recovering from the injury, Katy is a much more responsible young lady, but not quite proper enough for the staid atmosphere at the girls' school to which she is sent.

LITTLE LORD FAUNTLEROY

21 November 1976, Sunday, 5:00–5:30pm, BBC1, 6 episodes, drama, classic, family, British, 19th century
BBCtv
Pr: Barry Letts
Dir: Paul Annett
Wtr: Jack Gerson
Based on Frances Hodgson Burnett
Cast: **Cedric Errol – Glenn Anderson**
Dick Tipton – Paul D'Amato
Tom – Peter Hale
Minna – Carole Hayman
Mrs. Errol – Jennie Linden

Havisham – Preston Lockwood
Earl of Dorincourt – Paul Rogers
Mr. Hobbs – Ray Smith

The rags-to-riches story of young Cedric Errol, who lives with his impoverished widowed mother in New York. When news comes that Cedric is the rightful British Lord Fauntleroy he travels to England and is taken into the household of his father's wealthy relatives (who had disinherited him for marrying an American) – but the young boy so wins their hearts, especially that of his embittered grandfather, the Earl of Dorincourt, that the family ultimately opens its arms to Cedric's mother as well.

THE LADY OF THE CAMELLIAS

13 December 1976, Monday, 9:00–9:50pm, BBC2, 2 episodes, drama, classic, French, 19th century
BBCtv
Pr: Richard Beynon
Dir: Robert Knights
Wtr: Edmond Gosse
Based on Alexandre Dumas, fils
Cast: Olympe – Deborah Fallender
Armand Duval – Peter Firth
Gaston – James Hazeldine
Alexandre Dumas, fils – Garrick Hagon
Marguerite Gautier – Kate Nelligan
Comte de Nef – Brian Tully

Courtesan Marguerite Gautier is the rage of Paris in the 1840s, at the height of her popularity – when she succumbs, first to love, in the form of Armand Duval, and then to consumption.

THE PHOENIX AND THE CARPET

29 December 1976, Wednesday, 5:10–5:40pm, BBC1, 8 episodes, drama, family, British, 20th century
BBCtv
Pr: Dorothea Brooking
Dir: Clive Doig
Wtr: John Tully
Based on E.E. Nesbit
Cast: The Phoenix – Joe Barton/Richard Warner
Father – Edward Brooks
Jane – Jane Forster
Robert – Max Harris
Mother – Daphne Neville
Anthea – Tamzin Neville
Cyril – Gary Russell

A family living in Edwardian London experiences a series of magical events when they buy a second-hand carpet that turns out to have magic powers which transport the children to a variety of adventurous times and places.

ANOTHER BOUQUET

7 January 1977, Friday, 9:00–10:00pm, ITV, 7 episodes, drama, British, contemporary
London Weekend Television
Pr: John Frankau
Dir: John Frankau
Wtr: Andrea Newman
Cast: **Cassie Manson – Sheila Allen**
Gavin Sorenson – James Aubrey
Geoff Roberts – Eric Carte
Peter Manson – Frank Finlay
Sarah Roberts – Deborah Grant
Dr. Evan Lewis – Philip Madoc
Vicky – Elizabeth Romilly

Six months after the death of their daughter Prue, Cassie and Peter Manson are taking care of Prue's infant daughter, Eve. Prue's husband, Gavin, already has a new lady friend, Vicky, and does not appear overly interested in his daughter. Cassie is devoted to the baby's care, but there is much tension between Peter and Cassie. Peter is still involved with his secretary, Sarah, and when he learns that Cassie had had a brief entanglement with Gavin, he files for divorce. Sarah, though, has chosen to attempt a reconciliation with her own husband, and Peter finds himself alone.

Another Bouquet was Andrea Newman's original, written-for-television sequel to *Bouquet of Barbed Wire*, her novel which was serialized in January 1976.

ELEANOR MARX

10 January 1977, Monday, 9:00–10:00pm,

BBC2, 3 episodes, drama, biographical, British/Russian, 19th century
BBCtv
Pr: Louis Marks
Dir: Jane Howell
Wtr: Andrew Davies
Based on *The Life of Eleanor Marx 1855–1899: A Socialist Tragedy* by Chushichi Tsuzuki
Cast: Dr. Edward Aveling – Alan Dobie
Engels – Nigel Hawthorne
Frau Marx – Doreen Mantle
Karl Marx – Lee Montague
Eleanor Marx – Jennie Stoller

The story of Eleanor, the youngest daughter of Karl Marx, the only one of his six children to be born in England. Eleanor defied convention by living in a common-law marriage with Edward Aveling. Eleanor's dedication to her father's socialist cause is the driving force of much of her life, especially in the years between his death and her own. Her one personal dream, to be an actress, was destroyed by harsh criticism of her early efforts, and she died impoverished and unfulfilled when only 44.

HOLDING ON

16 January 1977, Sunday, 10:00–11:00pm, ITV, 6 episodes, drama, British, 20th century
London Weekend Television
Pr: Paul Knight
Dir: Raymond Menmuir, Gerry Mill
Wtr: Brian Phelan
Based on Mervyn Jones
Cast: **Charlie Wheelwright – Michael Elphick**
Ann Naylor Wheelwright – Patricia Franklin
Dora Wheelwright – Mary Healey
Bill Whitmarsh – Mark Moss
Ted Wheelwright – Gary Shall
Jack Wheelwright – Raymond Skipp
Vi – Kellie Twinn
Harry Wheelwright – Sam Williams
Charlie (as a child) – Barry Winch

Following the fortunes of the Wheelwright family over half a century in London's dockland, the drama opens in 1903 with stevedore Jack Wheelwright's sudden death, which leaves his widow Dora alone to raise Charlie and Vi. Charlie leaves school as soon as he is old enough to work on the docks, but in 1918 goes to fight in France. When he returns, Charlie, along with others, struggles through the depressed 1920s, finding himself in the forefront of the dockers' fight during the General Strike of 1926. Charlie works at the docks through World War II, but his wife Ann and sons Harry and Ted are evacuated. The family is reunited when the war ends. Neither of Charlie's sons works at the docks, so when he dies in 1970 the Wheelwright family tradition comes to a halt . . . as does the generations-old lifestyle of the London docks.

THIS YEAR NEXT YEAR

25 January 1977, Tuesday, 9:00–10:00pm, ITV, 13 episodes, drama, British, contemporary
Granada Television
Pr: Howard Baker
Dir: Bill Gilmour, Ken Grieve, Alan Grint, Richard Stroud, Ronald Wilson
Wtr: John Finch
Cast: Jack Shaw – Michael Elphick
Jim Shaw – Marc Harrison
Harry Shaw – Ronald Hines
Alan Williams – Michael Latimer
Carol Shaw – Sylvestra Le Touzel
Paula – Patricia Maynard
Kath Shaw – Julie Peasgood
Gentle Schofield Shaw – Anne Stallybrass
Liz Shaw – Virginia Stride
Tessa Shaw – Jill Summers
Ernest Shaw – Teddy Turner

When London businessman Harry Shaw unexpectedly loses his job, he moves his family out of the city and back to the Yorkshire Dales sheep farm where he spent his childhood. This adds new tension to Harry's already strained marriage to Liz, and his three children are ambivalent about the move as well. Harry's parents, Tessa and Ernest, make an uneasy transition after decades on the farm, and his brother Jack struggles to adjust to his new marriage to widowed Gentle Schofield. Further problems include Liz's affair with Harry's former business partner Alan Williams, and teenaged Kath's pregnancy. Some rifts are mended, others remain unresolved, and Harry must decide whether to stay on in the Dales or return and start anew in London.

ROB ROY

13 February 1977, Sunday, 4:55–5:25pm, BBC1, 6 episodes, drama, classic, adventure, Scottish, 18th century
BBCtv/Scotland
Pr: Pharic Maclaren
Dir: Bob Hird
Wtr: Tom Wright
Based on Sir Walter Scott
Cast: **Rob Roy – Andrew Faulds**
Rashleigh Osbaldistone – Anthony Higgins
Bailie Nicol Jarvie – Fulton Mackay
Osbaldistone – David Markham
Frank Osbaldistone – Robin Sachs
Morris – Jack Watson
Diana – Jane Wymark

Frank Osbaldistone returns home to Britain on his father's orders, his journey taking him from Bordeaux to London to Northumberland to Glasgow and beyond the Highland Line, to the land ruled by the legendary figure of romance and adventure, Rob Roy, leader of the McGregor clan. Frank must recover property stolen from his father by Rashleigh Osbaldistone, and enlists the aid of Rob Roy in doing so.

NICHOLAS NICKLEBY

27 March 1977, Sunday, 5:00–5:55pm, BBC1, 6 episodes, drama, classic, British, 19th century
BBCtv
Pr: Barry Letts
Dir: Christopher Barry
Wtr: Hugh Leonard
Based on Charles Dickens
Cast: Sir Mulberry Hawk – Anthony Ainley
Smike – Peter Bourke
Madeline Bray – Patricia Burke
Wackford Squeers – Derek Francis
Ralph Nickleby – Derek Godfrey
Frank Cheeryble – David Griffin
Nicholas Nickleby – Nigel Havers
Edwin Cheeryble – John Hewer
Newman Noggs – Robert James
Vincent Crummles – Freddie Jones
Charles Cheeryble – Raymond Mason
Mrs. Nickleby – Hilary Mason
Kate Nickleby – Kate Nicholls
Alfred Mantalini – Malcolm Reid
Madame Mantalini – Patricia Routledge
Miss LaCreevy – Patsy Smart

After the death of their father, Nicholas and Kate Nickleby are penniless and forced to turn to their greedy uncle Ralph for assistance, a cruel fate which brings them face-to-face with the harsh realities of life and work in early Victorian England. Nicholas flees from Ralph's tyranny, first to an even worse locale, as an instructor at the boys' academy operated by venal Wackford Squeers, where he meets and befriends the tragic Smike, who then accompanies Nicholas on his adventurous travels until both meet fateful ends.

ESTHER WATERS

10 April 1977, Sunday, 8:05–8:55pm, BBC2, 4 episodes, drama, British, 19th century
BBCtv
Pr: Richard Beynon
Dir: Jane Howell
Wtr: Douglas Livingstone
Based on George Moore
Cast: Mrs. Barfield – Jill Balcon
Mr. Barfield – Douglas Bisset
Fred Parsons – David Burke
Miss Peggy – Sarah Douglas
William Latch – James Laurenson
Esther Waters – Gabrielle Lloyd
Sarah – Alison Steadman

Esther Waters enters service as kitchen maid at the Woodview racing stable and is befriended by owner's wife Mrs. Barfield, who shares Esther's religious beliefs. Esther is seduced by footman William Latch, who then deserts her; she bears a son and marries Latch when he returns, but their union is beset with misfortune.

MURDER MOST ENGLISH

8 May 1977, Sunday, 9:30–10:20pm,
BBC2, 7 episodes, mystery, British, 20th century
BBCtv
Pr: Martin Lisemore
Dir: Ronald Wilson
Wtr: Richard Harris
Based on *The Flaxborough Chronicles* by Colin Watson
Cast: Mrs. Helen Carobleat – Caroline Blakiston
Miss Teatime – Brenda Bruce
PC – Christopher Driscoll
Doreen Periam – Lynn Farleigh
Sylvia Staunch – Gillian Martell
Gordon Periam – John Normington
Detective Inspector Purbright – Anton Rodgers
Rodney Gloss – Peter Sallis
Detective Sergeant Love – Christopher Timothy
Chief Constable Chubb – Moray Watson

Lincolnshire Detective Inspector Purbright searches for clues in four cases based on Watson's stories: *Hopjoy Was Here, Lonelyheart 4122, The Flaxborough Crab,* and *Coffin Scarcely Used.*

MAIDENS' TRIP

13 June 1977, Monday, 9:00–9:45pm,
BBC2, 3 episodes, drama, British, 20th century
BBCtv/Birmingham
Pr: Anthea Browne-Wilkinson
Dir: Moira Armstrong
Wtr: Thomas Ellice
Based on Emma Smith
Cast: **Charity – Liz Bagley**
Nanette – Tricia George
Maggie – Tina Heath
Sam Stevens – Derek Martin
Eli Blossom – John Salthouse
Vi Potter – Stella Tanner

During World War II, Maggie, Charity and Nanette work on a cargo boat on Grand Union Canal, operating a steel barge between London and Birmingham.

ROUGH JUSTICE

29 July 1977, Friday, 9:25–10:15pm, BBC1, 6 episodes, drama, British, contemporary
BBCtv
Pr: Morris Barry
Dir: Derrick Goodwin
Wtr: Simon Masters, Don Shaw
Cast: **Angela Conroy – Wendy Allnutt**
Simon Brooke – Colin Campbell
Ben Conroy – Clive Francis
Ellen Ross – Joy Harington
George Ross – Leon Sinden

Solicitors Ben and Angela Conroy work for Angela's father, George Ross, but idealistic Ben seeks to leave the prestigious firm to set up a Neighbourhood Law Centre where legal advice is available at no cost. In the conflict which ensues, Angela is caught in the middle between her husband and her father, and there seems no way to effect a positive end.

MARIE CURIE

16 August 1977, Tuesday, 9:00–9:55pm, BBC2, 5 episodes, drama, biographical, French, 19th century
BBCtv
Pr: Peter Goodchild
Dir: John Glenister
Wtr: Elaine Morgan
Cast: Irene Curie – Isabelle Amyes
Eve Curie – Gillian Bailey
Paul Langevin – Peter Birrel
Professor Sklodowski – Denis Carey
Pierre Curie – Nigel Hawthorne
Marie Curie – Jane Lapotaire

The life and work of Marie Curie, the Nobel Prize-winning discoverer of radium, beginning in 1886, when the young Polish woman leaves her homeland for France, where she meets scientist Pierre Curie, who becomes her partner in life and work. The rest is scientific history, ending with Marie's death at age 67 of radium-induced pernicious anemia.

Winner, BAFTA Award, Best Drama Serial 1977.

THE EAGLE OF THE NINTH

4 September 1977, Sunday, 5:45–6:15pm, BBC1, 6 episodes, drama, adventure, British, 2nd century
BBCtv/Scotland
Pr: Pharic Maclaren
Dir: Michael Simpson
Wtr: Bill Craig
Based on Rosemary Sutcliff
Cast: Drusillus – Bernard Gallagher
Guinhumara – Laura Graham
Marcus – Anthony Higgins
Hilarion – Matthew Long
Cradoc – Patrick Malahide
Marcus' father – Peter Whitbread

In approximately the year AD 117, the Ninth Legion marches north from Eboracum (the present-day site of York), to handle tribal uprisings in Caledonia. The Legion then disappeared without a trace. Marcus, whose father was a centurion with the Ninth, sets out in search of the Legion's standard, a Roman eagle, hoping to restore the lost honour of the legion, and his father.

LONDON BELONGS TO ME

6 September 1977, Tuesday, 9:00–10:00pm, ITV, 7 episodes, drama, British, 20th century
Thames Television
Pr: Paul Knight
Dir: Raymond Menmuir, Bill Hays
Wtr: Hugh Leonard
Based on Norman Collins
Cast: **Percy Boon – Terence Budd**
Mr. Josser – Derek Farr
Doris Josser – Fiona Gray
Connie Coke – Patricia Hayes
Henry Squales – Peter Jeffrey
Mrs. Josser – Julia McCarthy
Mr. Verriter – Arnold Peters
Mrs. Vizzard – Madge Ryan

In the late 1930s, as war clouds loom on the horizon, a group of disparate characters shares lodgings in a South London home under the ever-watchful gaze of landlady Mrs. Vizzard. When young Percy Boon is involved in an attempted car theft gone deadly-wrong, he becomes a murder suspect. The residents of 10 Dulcimer Street, led by retiree Mr. Josser, stand in support of Percy – but he is convicted and sentenced to death. Percy's neighbors band together to petition the courts for mercy, but larger issues overtake them all when World War II begins and London is set upon by the Blitz.

LOVE FOR LYDIA

9 September 1977, Friday, 9:00–10:00pm, ITV, 13 episodes, drama, British, 20th century
London Weekend Television
Video: available in US
Pr: Tony Wharmby
Dir: John Glenister, Piers Haggard, Christopher Hodson, Simon Langton, Michael Simpson, Tony Wharmby
Wtr: Julian Bond
Based on H.E. Bates
Cast: Blackie Johnson – Ralph Arliss
Edward Richardson – Christopher Blake
Tom Holland – Peter Davison
Nancy Holland – Sherrie Hewson
Alex Sanderson – Jeremy Irons
Aunt Juliana – Rachel Kempson
Aunt Bertie – Beatrix Lehmann
Lydia Aspen – Mel Martin

In 1929, 19-year-old heiress Lydia Aspen, who has been living with her aunts since the death of her father, is shy and inexperienced; but as she grows into womanhood Lydia has a significant, even tragic effect on the lives of four young men who fall under her spell – newspaper reporter Edward Richardson, married man Alex Sanderson, local farm boy Tom Holland, and Blackie Johnson, Lydia's chauffeur – and is herself doomed to perish at a young age from tuberculosis.

THE PEPPERMINT PIG

21 September 1977, Wednesday, 5:10–5:40pm, BBC1, 5 episodes, drama, family, British, 20th century
BBCtv
Pr: Anna Home
Dir: Paul Stone
Wtr: Julia Jones
Based on Nina Bawden

Cast: Theo – Ben Bethell
Lady March – Lally Bowers
Poll Greengrass – Lucy Durham-Matthews
Grandfather – Brian Hayes
George – David Parfitt
Lily – Sarah Prince
Emily Greengrass – Anne Stallybrass

The Greengrass family lives a peaceful life in Edwardian London, but then Poll and her mother Emily must move to rural Norfolk to live with relatives. Their purchase of a pig seems unremarkable at first, especially since "Johnnie" is the runt of the litter, but the animal's antics are quite notable and quickly make the Greengrasses the talk of the town.

ANNA KARENINA

25 September 1977, Sunday, 8:10pm–9:05pm, BBC2, 10 episodes, drama, classic, Russian, 19th century
BBCtv
Video: available in UK
Pr: Donald Wilson
Dir: Basil Coleman
Wtr: Donald Wilson
Based on Leo Tolstoy
Cast: Annushka – Marilyn Le Conte
Anna Karenina – Nicola Pagett
Karenin – Eric Porter
Seriozha – Paul Spurrier
Levin – Robert Swann
Captain Vronsky – Stuart Wilson

The doomed love story of wealthy married woman Anna Karenina and Captain Vronsky, whose open affair is seen as a breach of the social code. When Anna becomes pregnant, she is separated from her beloved son and she and Vronsky escape to Italy. But she cannot stay away from her roots and so Anna returns to St. Petersburg, where she is still considered an outcast. Her ensuing despair destroys her relationship with Vronsky and leads Anna to her fateful end under the wheels of a speeding train.

TREASURE ISLAND

16 October 1977, Sunday, 5:45–6:40pm, BBC1, 4 episodes, drama, classic, adventure, British, 18th century
BBCtv
Video: available in UK
Pr: Barry Letts
Dir: Michael E. Briant
Wtr: John Lucarotti
Based on Robert Louis Stevenson
Cast: Dr. Livesay – Anthony Bate
Black Dog – Christopher Burgess
Long John Silver – Alfred Burke
Ben Gunn – Paul Copley
Sarah Hawkins – Jo Kendall
Jim Hawkins – Ashley Knight
Daniel Hawkins – Terry Scully
Israel Hands – Patrick Troughton
Squire Trelawney – Thorley Walters
Billy Bones – Jack Watson

The swashbuckling classic of young Jim Hawkins, an ordinary boy propelled into a series of adventures across the high seas after he comes into possesion of a treasure map. Jim, Dr. Livesey and Squire Trelawney set out on the Hispaniola in search of Treasure Island, but their journey is threatened by a mutinous crew led by Long John Silver.

Anthony Bate reprises the role of Dr. Livesay, which he also played in the BBC's 1968 serial of *Treasure Island*.

HARD TIMES

25 October 1977, Tuesday, 9:00–10:00pm, ITV, 4 episodes, drama, classic, British, 19th century
Granada Television in association with WNET/13 New York
Video: available in UK, US
Pr: Peter Eckersley
Dir: John Irvin
Wtr: Arthur Hopcraft
Based on Charles Dickens
Cast: **Thomas Gradgrind – Patrick Allen**
Mrs. Sparsit – Rosalie Crutchley
Sissy Jupe – Michelle Dibnah
Stephen Blackpool – Alan Dobie
Rachael – Barbara Ewing
Captain James Harthouse – Edward Fox
Mrs. Gradgrind – Ursula Howells
Sleary – Harry Markham
Louisa Gradgrind – Jacqueline Tong

Josiah Bounderby – Timothy West
Tom Gradgrind – Richard Wren

In Dickens' story about the impact of the Industrial Revolution on the human spirit, Louisa Gradgrind has been forced by her father to lead a cold life devoid of emotion and enjoyment, culminating in her marriage to vulgar mill-owner Josiah Bounderby. A circus comes to town, offering Louisa her first glimpse of hope, laughter . . . and love. She meets and falls in love with amoral Captain James Harthouse, who entices Louisa to go away with him. When a desperate Louisa turns to her father for guidance, Gradgrind realizes at last how his harsh principles have affected the lives of those he loves. Can this be changed before it is too late?

The most expensive television drama made to date, *Hard Times* was co-produced by American public broadcasting network WNET – and aired in the US in May 1977, several months before its broadcast in Great Britain – the first instance of multi-national co-financing which would become very common in the 1980s and 1990s.

WHO PAYS THE FERRYMAN?

7 November 1977, Monday, 9:00–9:50pm, BBC2, 8 episodes, drama, British/Greek, contemporary
BBCtv
Pr: William Slater
Designed by Myles Lang
Wtr: Michael J. Bird
Cast: Annika Zeferis – Betty Arvanti
David Haldane – Bernard Brown
Matheos Noukakis – Takis Emmanuel
Alan Haldane – Jack Hedley
Duncan Neve – Patrick Magee
Ariadne – Marina Sirtis
Hebden – Jack Watson

Alan Haldane, who had served in the Greek resistance, returns to Crete after 30 years in England, to discover that he has an illegitimate daughter . . . and that a savage, decades-old vendetta awaits him as well.

THE CHILDREN OF THE NEW FOREST

13 November 1977, Sunday, 6:05–6:35pm, BBC1, 5 episodes, drama, family, British, 17th century
BBCtv
Pr: Barry Letts
Dir: John Frankau
Wtr: William Pointer
Based on Captain Frederick Marryat
Cast: Edith Beverley – Timandra Alwyn
Alice Beverley – Edwina Ashton
Judith Villiers – Caroline Blakiston
Humphrey Beverley – Arthur Campbell
Colonel Heatherstone – John Carson
Charles I – Jeremy Clyde
Patience Heatherstone – Rebecca Croft
Edward Beverley – Richard Gibson
Colonel Beverley – Andrew Lodge
Cromwell – Artro Morris
Jacob Armitage – Kendrick Owen
Lord Harcourt – Guy Slater

The Beverley children are caught in the middle of the battles between the Roundheads and the Cavaliers and are forced, after the death of their father and under constant threat of discovery and death, to hide out under the care of Jacob Armitage.

REBECCA OF SUNNYBROOK FARM

1 January 1978, Sunday, 5:40–6:10pm, BBC1, 4 episodes, drama, classic, family, American, 19th century
BBCtv
Pr: Barry Letts
Dir: Rodney Bennett
Wtr: Constance Cox
Based on Kate Douglas Wiggin
Cast: Miss Maxwell – Ingrid Bower
Jeremiah Cobb – Phil Brown
Aunt Miranda – Brenda Bruce
Rebecca Randall – Julia Lewis
Aunt Jane – Margery Mason
Adam Ladd – John Price
Emma Jane Perkins – Mandy Woodward

Rebecca goes to live with her two aunts

at Brick House, leaving behind the drudgery of an overcrowded, poverty-inflicted home for a life of comparative luxury. When adversity strikes again, Rebecca's aunts remain determined that, whatever the cost to themselves, Rebecca will continue her education – and so she does, ultimately graduating from Wareham Academy.

A TRAVELLER IN TIME

4 January 1978, Wednesday, 5:05–5:35pm, BBC1, 5 episodes, drama, fantasy, family, British, 16th–20th century
BBCtv
Pr: Anna Home
Dir: Dorothea Brooking
Wtr: Diana de Vere Cole
Based on Alison Uttley
Cast: Tabitha – Sarah Benfield
Aunt Tissie/Dame Cicely – Elizabeth Bradley
Mary, Queen of Scots – Heather Chasen
Francis Babington – Simon Gipps-Kent
Uncle Barnabas – Gerald James
Mistress Babington – Mary Maude
Penelope – Sophie Thompson

Young Penelope visits her uncle and aunt in Derbyshire. Their home had once belonged to an Elizabethan family, and Penelope magically finds herself travelling back in time, becoming involved in a plot to save Mary, Queen of Scots.

THE PRIME OF MISS JEAN BRODIE

22 January 1978, Sunday, 10:15–11:15pm, ITV, 8 episodes, drama, Scottish, 20th century
Scottish Television
Pr: Richard Bates
Dir: John Bruce, Mark Cullingham, Christopher Hodson, Tina Wakerell
Wtr: Jay Presson Allen, James Doran, William Pointer, Alick Rowe, Anna Stanley, Anthony Steven
Based on Muriel Spark
Cast: Sandy – Lynsey Baxter
Rose Stanley – Tracey Childs
Anna Pavlova – Andrea Durant
Giulia Cibelli – Romana Kaye
Jenny – Amanda Kirby
Jean Brodie – Geraldine McEwan
Mary MacGregor – Jean McKinley
George Jenkins – Robert Urquhart

In 1930, Miss Jean Brodie leaves Newcastle and journeys back to Scotland to take up a temporary post at the Marcia Blaine School for Girls. Her then-radical ideas inspire a number of students, whom Miss Brodie chooses as her protégées, and have a profound influence on these developing young women.

THE MAYOR OF CASTERBRIDGE

22 January 1978, Sunday, 8:05–8:55pm, BBC2, 7 episodes, drama, classic, British, 19th century
BBCtv
Video: available in UK
Pr: Jonathan Powell
Dir: David Giles
Wtr: Dennis Potter
Based on Thomas Hardy
Cast: **Michael Henchard – Alan Bates**
Mrs. Goodenough – Avis Bunnage
Donald Farfrae – Jack Galloway
Lucetta – Anna Massey
Elizabeth-Jane – Janet Maw
Susan – Anne Stallybrass

Michael Henchard quietly and anonymously returns to the Dorset countryside in the mid-1840s, where he becomes a successful merchant and the mayor of Casterbridge. But the true facts of his life are exposed when his long-estranged wife Susan and daughter appear, and it is revealed that Henchard had coldly sold Susan at auction when he learned she had been unfaithful to him. This revelation stuns the townspeople, and leads to Henchard's swift decline and death in bitterness and squalor.

HAWKMOOR

29 January 1978, Sunday, 5:20–6:10pm, BBC1, 5 episodes, drama, family, Welsh, 16th century
BBCtv/Wales
Pr: George P. Owen

Dir: Christopher King, George P. Owen
Wtr: Griffith Parry, created by Lynn Hughes
Cast: **Lady Joanne – Jane Asher**
Sir Tom – Meredith Edwards
Shanco – Godfrey James
Vicar Davyd – Philip Madoc
John Stedman – Jack May
Thomas Jones – John Ogwen
Young Stedman – Tom Owen
Agnes – Rachel Thomas

In the wild and lawless Welsh land that was Cardiganshire in the 16th century, the peasants, who are terrorized by brigands and under the thumb of ruthless landowners, turn for protection and justice to the mysterious folk hero Twm Sion Cati, who hides his true identity in order to protect his role.

WARRIOR QUEEN

20 February 1978, Monday, 4:45–5:15pm, ITV, 6 episodes, drama, British, 1st century
Thames Television
Pr: Ruth Boswell
Dir: Michael Custance, Neville Green
Wtr: Martin Mellett
Cast: Catus Decianus – Nigel Hawthorne
Tasca – Patti Love
Suetonius Paulinus – Stanley Meadows
Boudicca – Sian Phillips

The story of Boudicca, Queen of the ancient British Iceni tribe, who assumes its leadership after the death of her husband, Prasutagus. Boudicca then heads the revolt, in the first century AD, against the Romans, led by Suetonius Paulinus. Her rebellion extends across Southeast England, with the climactic battle taking place at Ratae (Leicester), where Boudicca is defeated and her troops massacred by the Roman forces.

PENNIES FROM HEAVEN

7 March 1978, Tuesday, 9:25–10:40pm, BBC1, 6 episodes, drama, musical/fantasy, British, 20th century
BBCtv
Pr: Kenith Trodd
Dir: Piers Haggard
Wtr: Dennis Potter

Cast: Tom – Hywel Bennett
Eileen – Cheryl Campbell
Accordion Man – Kenneth Colley
Joan Parker – Gemma Craven
Conrad Baker – Nigel Havers
Arthur Parker – Bob Hoskins
Headmaster – Freddie Jones
Blind Girl – Yolande Palfrey

In the depression-weary mid-1930s, travelling sheet-music salesman Arthur Parker escapes the drudgery of life both at home and on the road by immersing himself in the grand song lyrics he is selling. But reality intrudes all too painfully when Arthur becomes involved with struggling schoolteacher Eileen, an entanglement which leads to misadventure and tragedy, despite the sunny words of the popular tunes Arthur would much rather live by.

LAW AND ORDER

6 April 1978, Thursday, 9:00–10:20pm, BBC2, 4 episodes, drama, British, contemporary
BBCtv
Pr: Tony Garnett
Dir: Leslie Blair
Wtr: G.F. Newman
Cast: **Alex Gladwell – Ken Campbell**
Cathy Lynn – Dierdre Costello
Jack Lynn – Peter Dean
Clifford Harding – Alan Ford
Mr. English – Martin Gordon
Detective Inspector Fred Pyall – Derek Martin
Mickey Fielder – Roy Sone

Self-contained but connected episodes depict the criminal investigation process from four different points of view: *A Detective's* Tale outlines the lengthy process DI Fred Pyall goes through in solving a crime; *A Villain's* Tale offers the same story from the point-of-view of career thief Jack Lynn; *A Brief's* Tale focuses on solicitor Alex Gladwell, known for his crafty defense of seasoned criminals; and *A Prisoner's* Tale again picks up on Jack Lynn, who is now behind bars.

THE RITZ

24 April 1978, Friday, 9:30–10:20pm, BBC2, 6 episodes, drama, British, contemporary
BBCtv/Pebble Mill
Pr: Chris Parr
Dir: John Godber, Martin Shardlow
Wtr: John Godber
Based on *Bouncers*, a play by John Godber
Cast: Skodge – Andrew Dunn
Carol – Julia Ford
Veronica – Kate Layden
Eric – Richard James Lewis
Kenny – Andrew Livingstone
Chike – Paul Rider
Mad Mick – Richard Ridings

A chronicle of the first six nights of the operation of the Ritz disco, which has been purchased by naïve Eric and Veronica, who know nothing of the site's longstanding battle with rival disco owner Mad Mick, and so hire a trio of bouncers to protect their interests.

THE DEVIL'S CROWN

30 April 1978, Sunday, 9:00–9:55pm, BBC2, 13 episodes, drama, historical, British, 12th–13th century
BBCtv
Pr: Richard Beynon
Dir: Alan Cooke, Jane Howell, Ronald Wilson
Wtr: Jack Russell, Ken Taylor
Cast: Isabella – Lynsey Baxter
Empress Matilda – Brenda Bruce
Richard – Michael Byrne
Henry II – Brian Cox
John – John Duttine
Philip – Christopher Gable
Arthur – Simon Gipps-Kent
Louis – Charles Kay
Eleanor of Aquitaine – Jane Lapotaire
Henry – Kevin McNally
Thomas Becket – Jack Shepherd
Berengaria of Navarre – Zoe Wanamaker
Guy Diva – Alan Webb

The story of the ill-fated union between Henry II and Eleanor of Aquitaine, and the Plantagenet dynasty of the Middle Ages which follows, led first by son Richard the Lionhearted and, following his death, by youngest son John, who reigns from 1199 to 1216.

WILL SHAKESPEARE

13 June 1978, Tuesday, 9:00–10:00pm, ITV, 6 episodes, drama, biographical, British, 16th century
ATV Network
Pr: Cecil Clarke
Dir: Mark Cullingham, Robert Knights, Peter Wood
Wtr: John Mortimer
Cast: Earl of Essex – Keith Baxter
Queen Elizabeth – Patience Collier
William Shakespeare – Tim Curry
Dark Lady – Mary Fleminge
Hamnet Sadler – John McEnery
Christopher Marlowe – Ian McShane
Edward Alleyn – André Morrell
King James – Bill Paterson
Ingram Frizer – Simon Rouse

The life of William Shakespeare, beginning with Shakespeare's arrival in London, where he challenges Christopher Marlowe's reign as pre-eminent poet and playwright. Shakespeare's tumultuous personal life, including his fascination with the mysterious "Dark Lady," is the focus here, but the playwright also becomes involved with politics, acquainting himself with two monarchs.

OUT

24 July 1978, Monday, 9:00–10:00pm, ITV, 6 episodes, thriller, British, contemporary
Euston Films for Thames Television
Pr: Barry Hanson
Dir: Jim Goddard
Wtr: Trevor Preston
Cast: **Frank Ross – Tom Bell**
Pretty Billy Binns – Peter Blake
Tony McGrath – Brian Cox
Chris Cottle – Brian Croucher
Anne – Lynn Farleigh
Eddie Archer – Maurice O'Connell
Detective Inspector Bryce – Norman Rodway
Mr. Smith – Morgan Sheppard

Frank Ross is released from prison after

serving eight years for robbery. He is determined to find out who informed on him all those years ago, and tracks down his old cronies, but they offer few clues. Frank resumes a long-ago affair with Anne, but as he gets closer to the truth, Frank finds himself the target of professional killer Mr. Smith, hired by Frank's former associate Tony McGrath, to keep Frank from learning the identity of the informer.

DISRAELI, PORTRAIT OF A ROMANTIC

5 September 1978, Tuesday, 8:45–10:00pm, ITV, 4 episodes, drama, biographical, historical, British, 19th century
Independent Television/ATV Network
Pr: Cecil Clarke
Dir: Claude Whatham
Wtr: David Butler
Cast: Lord Lyndhurst – Mark Dignam
Count Alfred D'Orsay – Leigh Lawson
Queen Victoria – Rosemary Leach
Prince Albert – Jeremy Longhurst
Benjamin Disraeli – Ian McShane
Mary Anne – Mary Peach
Edward Lytton Bulwer – Brett Usher
Lady Blessing – Margaret Whiting

The story of Benjamin Disraeli, the British prime minister who ultimately becomes Queen Victoria's favorite politician. But first, the young Disraeli makes his climb through Parliament, gaining the respect of his peers with his progressive ideas. After a rakish youthful period, Disraeli finds happiness with his wife Mary Anne, to whom he is devoted until her death. With the monarch's supportive friendship to help him, Disraeli climbs to even higher diplomatic triumphs.

SEXTON BLAKE AND THE DEMON GOD

10 September 1978, Sunday, 5:55–6:25pm, BBC1, 6 episodes, mystery, British, 20th century
BBCtv
Pr: Barry Letts
Dir: Roger Tucker
Wtr: Simon Raven
Cast: Zigiana – Jacquey Chappell
Sexton Blake – Jeremy Clyde
Tinker – Philip Davis
Hubba Pasha – Derek Francis
Maremma Bey – Linal Haft
Mrs. Bardell – Barbara Lott
Cassandra – Natasha Parry

In London in 1927, dashing detective Sexton Blake investigates a mystery involving a stolen Egyptian mummy, an ancient curse, and a cult, led by the malevolent Hubba Pasha, that dabbles in human sacrifice.

The character of Sexton Blake first appeared in print in 1893; since then, nearly 200 writers have written of his exploits.

OFF TO PHILADELPHIA IN THE MORNING

12 September 1978, Wednesday, 9:25–10:25pm, BBC1, 3 episodes, drama, biographical, Welsh, 19th century
BBCtv/Wales
Pr: John Hefin
Designed by Julian Williams
Wtr: Elaine Morgan
Based on Jack Jones
Cast: Jane Parry – Connie Booth
Principal T.C. Edwards – Meredith Edwards
Henry Parry – Dafydd Hywell
Dick Llewellyn – Delme Bryn Jones
Joseph Parry – David Lyn
Sir William Sterndale Bennett – David Markham
Cathy Llewellyn – Fidelma Murphy
Lina Van Elyn – Sian Phillips
Anne Parry – Gaynor Morgan Rees
Daniel Parry – William Squire
Betty Parry – Rachel Thomas
Joseph Parry (as a child) – Gareth Ridgwell Whiley

The story of Welsh composer Joseph Parry who, after achieving a degree of fame outside his native country, returns home as a Professor of Music at the new University of Aberystwyth, which reels under his unconventional ways.

LILLIE

24 September 1978, Sunday, 8:15–9:15pm, ITV, 13 episodes, drama, biographical, British, 19th–20th century
London Weekend Television
Video: available in US
Pr: Jack Williams
Dir: John Gorrie, Christopher Hodson, Tony Wharmby
Wtr: David Butler, John Gorrie
Based on an idea by Mike Smith, *The Prince and the Lily* by James Brough
Cast: **Lillie Langtry – Francesca Annis**
Prince Louis of Battenburg – John Castle
Oscar Wilde – Peter Egan
Princess/Queen Alexandra – Ann Firbank
William LeBreton – Anthony Head
Prince of Wales – Denis Lill
Patsy Cornwallis-West – Jennie Linden
Queen Victoria – Sheila Reid
Edward Langtry – Anton Rodgers
Prince Rudolph – Patrick Ryecart
King Leopold – Derek Smith
Mrs. LeBreton – Peggy Ann Wood

The life and times of Lillie Langtry, the Jersey girl who is best remembered as the first openly acknowledged mistress of the Prince of Wales (later to be Edward VII). Born in 1853, a noted beauty even as a teenager, Lillie convinces her husband Edward to move to London, where she quickly becomes a social success . . . and a scandalous sensation. She is loved by, among others, Oscar Wilde, King Leopold of Belgium, and Prince Louis of Battenberg, Edward VII's nephew (and the father of Lillie's daughter). When she visits America, Lillie is as grand a success there as she has been in Britain. Despite her many escapades, her marriage survives, if in name only, until her husband's death in an insane asylum. Lillie's relationship with "Bertie" continues until his death, after which she sadly declines, becoming a mockery of her own legend, until her death in 1929.

A HORSEMAN RIDING BY

24 September 1978, Sunday, 7:15–8:05pm, BBC1, 13 episodes, drama, British, 20th century
BBCtv
Pr: Ken Riddington
Dir: Paul Ciappessoni, Philip Dudley, Alan Grint
Wtr: Alexander Baron, John Wiles, Arden Winch
Based on R.F. Delderfield
Cast: Sydney Codsall – Terence Budd
Will Codsall – David Delve
Grace Lovell Craddock – Fiona Gaunt
Simon Craddock – Adam Godley
Paul Craddock – Nigel Havers
John Rudd – Glyn Houston
Maureen O'Keefe – Gillian McCutcheon
James Grenfell – Frank Moorey
Claire Derwent Craddock – Prunella Ransome

City-bred Paul Craddock answers an advertisement in 1902 for land for sale in the Devonshire countryside, not realizing that his move to this interlinked and interdependent community will determine the path his life is to take over the next two decades.

WUTHERING HEIGHTS

24 September 1978, Sunday, 8:05–9:05pm, BBC2, 5 episodes, drama, classic, British, 19th century
BBCtv
Pr: Jonathan Powell
Dir: Peter Hammond
Wtr: Hugh Leonard, David Snodin
Based on Emily Brontë
Cast: **Catherine Earnshaw Linton – Kay Adshead**
Linton – Andrew Burleigh
Hindley – John Duttine
Catherine Linton – Cathryn Harrison
Ellen Dean – Pat Heywood
Heathcliff – Ken Hutchison
Mr. Lockwood – Richard Kay
Isabella – Caroline Langrishe
Edgar Linton – David Robb
Joseph – Brian Wilde
Hareton – David Wilkinson

The tragic, passionate love story of spoiled Catherine Earnshaw and stableboy Heathcliff. Catherine spurns him for well-to-do Edgar Linton, but her heart remains with Heathcliff, who himself becomes wealthy – and vengefully marries Edgar's sister Isabella. When Catherine is dying in childbirth, it is Heathcliff she turns to for a final farewell; Heathcliff's revenge continues into the next generation, when he forces a marriage between his son and Catherine's daughter. When Heathcliff finally dies, his ghost is seen wandering on the moors, reunited at last with his beloved.

THE LOST BOYS

11 October 1978, Wednesday,
9:25–10:55pm, BBC2, 3 episodes, drama, biographical, British, 19th–20th century
BBCtv
Pr: Louis Marks
Dir: Rodney Bennett
Wtr: Andrew Birkin
Cast: Sylvia Davies – Ann Bell
George Davies – Christopher Blake
Jack Davies – Osmund Bullock
Mary Hodgson – Anna Cropper
J.M. Barrie – Ian Holm
Peter Davies – Tom Kelly
Michael Davies – William Kelton
Mary Barrie – Maureen O'Brien
Nico Davies – David Parfitt
Arthur Llewellyn Davies – Tim Pigott-Smith
Gilbert Cannon – Brian Stirner

The story of the relationship between writer J.M. Barrie and the Llewellyn Davies family, beginning in 1897, a close acquaintance which not only sparks the writing of *Peter Pan*, but also has a profound affect on the lives of the five Davies sons – George, Jack, Peter, Michael and Nico – as the childless Barrie becomes their guardian following the deaths of their parents.

Each Davies son was played by three or four actors over the course of the drama; those noted portrayed the boys as young adults, towards the trilogy's conclusion; broadcast as part of *Play of the Week*.

HUNTINGTOWER

22 October 1978, Sunday, 6:05–6:35pm, BBC1, 6 episodes, mystery, Scottish, 20th century
BBCtv/Scotland
Pr: Pharic Maclaren
Dir: Bob Hird
Wtr: Edward Boyd
Based on John Buchan
Cast: Dougal – Iain Andrew
Old Bill – Neil Crossan
Wee Jaikie – Eric Cullen
Dickson McCunn – Paul Curran
James Loudon – Andrew Faulds
Peter Paterson – Alan Hunt
Saskia – Emma Jacobs
Tammas Yownie – John Keenan
John Heritage – Peter Settelen
Mrs. Morran – Jean Taylor Smith
Napoleon – Iain Stewart

The Gorbals Diehards, a group of amateur sleuths in Glasgow, led by retired grocer Dickson McCunn, band together to defeat an intricately organized and evil conspiracy which seeks to kidnap a refugee Russian princess. McCunn comes upon the princess in the dark tower and he and his group of Diehards become involved in a number of adventures before being able to rescue her.

THE HILLS OF HEAVEN

25 October 1978, Wednesday,
5:10–5:40pm, BBC1, 3 episodes, drama, family, British, 20th century
BBCtv
Pr: Angela Beeching
Dir: Eric Davidson
Wtr: Barry Collins
Based on John Farrimond
Cast: **Nancy Brindle – Katie Armstrong**
Billy Walsh – David Haddow
Charlie Drew – Peter Ma
Annie Walsh – Rowena Pa
Mick Mack – Malcolm Sproston

In this autobiographical story, set in the early 1930s, Billy, Nancy and Mick use the slag heaps of the Lancashire coalfields as their playground, which proves both exciting and dangerous for the children.

THE BIRDS FALL DOWN

29 October 1978, Sunday, 8:10–9:05pm, BBC2, 5 episodes, thriller, British/European, 20th century
BBCtv
Pr: Jonathan Powell
Dir: John Glenister
Wtr: Ken Taylor
Based on Rebecca West
Cast: Nikolai – George Coulouris
  Laura Rowan – Felicity Dean
  Chubinov – Peter Eyre
  Kamensky – John Normington
  Tania – Elizabeth Shepherd

At the turn of the century, Laura Rowan travels to Paris to visit her grandfather Nikolai, an exiled but still loyal member of the Tsar's court; while the two are travelling on a train Nikolai is confronted by an enemy of the Tsar who is searching for the truth about a purported double spy. This meeting catapults Laura into a world of jeopardy and revolutionary intrigue.

EDWARD & MRS. SIMPSON

8 November 1978, Wednesday, 9:00–10:00pm, ITV, 7 episodes, drama, historical, British, 20th century
Thames Television
Video: available in UK, US
Pr: Andrew Brown
Dir: Waris Hussein
Wtr: Simon Raven
Based on *Edward VIII* by Frances Donaldson
Cast: Queen Mary – Peggy Ashcroft
  Archbishop of Canterbury – Maurice Denham
  Edward – Edward Fox
  George V – Marius Goring
  Mrs. Simpson – Cynthia Harris
  Walter Monckton – Nigel Hawthorne
  Lady Diana Cooper – Patricia Hodge
  Ernest Simpson – Charles Keating
  Lady Thelma Furness – Cherie Lunghi
  Aunt Bessie Merryman – Jessie Matthews
  Duke of York – Andrew Ray
  Duchess of York – Amanda Reiss
  Major Alexander Hardinge – John Shrapnel
  Clement Attlee – Patrick Troughton
  Prime Minister Stanley Baldwin – David Waller

Spanning the years from 1928 to 1936 and telling the story of the Royal romance: Edward, Prince of Wales and a dashing society figure, meets Mrs. Wallis Simpson, a married American, in 1930. By 1934 they have fallen deeply in love, although she is still married. When George V dies in early 1936, Edward VIII ascends to the throne. Despite protests both public and private, Edward continues his relationship with Mrs. Simpson after her divorce. Edward reigns for just ten months and is never formally crowned King before he abdicates on 10 December 1936, refusing to buckle under national pressure to do without "the help and support of the woman I love."

Winner, BAFTA Award, Best Drama Serial 1978; winner, Emmy Award, Outstanding Limited Series 1979-1980.

THE MOON STALLION

15 November 1978, Wednesday, 5:10–5:40pm, BBC1, 6 episodes, drama, family, British, contemporary
BBCtv
Video: available in UK, US
Pr: Anna Home
Dir: Dorothea Brooking
Wtr: Brian Hayles
Cast: Sir George Mortenhurze – John Abineri
  Estelle – Caroline Goodall
  Professor Purwell – James Greene
  Green King – Michael Kilgarriff
  Paul – David Pullan
  Diana – Sarah Sutton

Professor Purwell, an archaeologist, is investigating the legend of King Arthur and the strange appearances of the mythical Moon Stallion. His work has the unexpected effect of leading his blind daughter Diana into mysteries and circumstances far removed from her own time.

PINOCCHIO

3 December 1978, Sunday, 6:10–6:40pm, BBC1, 4 episodes, drama, classic, family, fantasy

BBCtv
Video: available in UK
Designed by Kenneth Sharp; puppetmaster Barry Smith
Dir: Barry Letts
Wtr: Alec Drysdale
Based on Carlo Collodi
Cast: Cricket's voice/Zapporelli – James Berwick
Mr. Cat – Neil Fitzwilliam
Blue Fairy – Rhoda Lewis
Mr. Fox – Roy Macready
Voice of Pinocchio – Rosemary Miller
Geppetto – Derek Smith

The classic fable of the puppet Pinocchio who wishes to be a real boy, and the puppeteer Geppetto who loves him as if he were one, told with a combination of puppets and live actors.

THE MILL ON THE FLOSS

31 December 1978, Sunday, 5:20–5:50pm, BBC1, 8 episodes, drama, classic, British, 19th century
BBCtv
Pr: Barry Letts
Dir: Ronald Wilson
Wtr: James Andrew Hall
Based on George Eliot
Cast: **Tom Tulliver – Christopher Blake**
Bessy Tulliver – Judy Cornwell
Lucy Deane – Mona Durbridge
Maggie Tulliver – Pippa Guard
Philip Wakem – Anton Lesser
Stephen Guest – John Moulder-Brown
Tom Tulliver (as a child) – Jonathan Scott-Taylor
Maggie Tulliver (as a child) – Georgia Slowe
Mr. Tulliver – Ray Smith
Uncle Deane – John Stratton

Miller's daughter Maggie Tulliver defies her family and Victorian society when she follows the dictates of her heart. Maggie is loved by Philip Wakem, but their relationship is forbidden by Maggie's brother Tom, who holds a grudge against Wakem's father. Later Maggie falls in love with Stephen Guest, who is the fiancé of her cousin Lucy. But in the end, Maggie is bound forever with her brother, as the two are drowned together in a great flood.

THE APHRODITE INHERITANCE

3 January 1979, Wednesday, 8:05–9:00pm, BBC1, 8 episodes, thriller, British/Greek, contemporary
BBCtv
Pr: Andrew Osborn
Dir: Viktors Ritelis, Terence Williams
Wtr: Michael J. Bird
Cast: **Helene – Alexandra Bastedo**
Basileos – Brian Blessed
Martin Preece – Tony Doyle
Charalambos – Stefan Gryff
Barry Collier – Barry Halliday
Inspector Dimas – Godfrey James
Hellman – Paul Maxwell
David Collier – Peter McEnery
Eric Morrison – William Wilde

David Collier receives an urgent call to go to Cyprus; upon his arrival he quickly becomes involved with the mysterious and beautiful Helene, a relationship which leads to deadly intrigue for Collier and others on the island.

THE STRANGE AFFAIR OF ADELAIDE HARRIS

3 January 1979, Wednesday, 5:05–5:35pm, BBC1, 6 episodes, drama, British, 19th century
BBCtv
Exec. Pr: Anna Home
Dir: Paul Stone
Wtr: Robin Miller
Based on Leon Garfield
Cast: **Bostock – Matthew Beamish**
Mr. Brett – Timothy Davies
Dr. Bunnion – Derek Francis
Harris – Tim Harris
Tizzy Alexander – Amanda Kirby
Ralph Bunnion – Richard Wren

Harris and Bostock, pupils at Dr. Bunnion's Academy for Young Gentlemen, are continually making mischief, to the consternation of all, especially shy classics master Mr. Brett. When an attempted rape occurs, mischief gives way to more serious examination,

RUNNING BLIND

5 January 1979, Friday, 9:25–10:15pm, BBC1, 3 episodes, thriller, British, contemporary
BBCtv/Scotland
Pr: Bob McIntosh
Dir: William Brayne
Wtr: Jack Gerson
Based on Desmond Bagley
Cast: Slade – George Sewell
Vaslav Kennikin – Vladek Sheybal
Elin – Heida Steindorsdottir
Alan Stewart – Stuart Wilson

Former British Agent Alan Stewart is blackmailed by his old boss, Slade, to undertake what is allegedly a simple delivery job, but which turns out to be anything but simple; in fact, it is simply deadly and involves Alan and his lover Elin in a nightmare chase across Iceland.

TELFORD'S CHANGE

7 January 1979, Sunday, 7:15–8:30pm, BBC1, 10 episodes, drama, British, contemporary
BBCtv
Pr: Mark Shivas
Dir: Barry Davis
Wtr: Brian Clark
Cast: **Mark Telford – Peter Barkworth**
Tim Hart – Keith Barron
Jacques Dupont – Martin Benson
Maddox – Colin Douglas
Sylvia Telford – Hannah Gordon
Simon – Julian Holloway
Helen Stanton – Zena Walker

International bank manager Mark Telford grows weary of life in the fast lane, and takes a career step backwards, in the hope of finding personal fulfillment. Instead he finds intrigue, danger, and a serious threat to his marriage to Sylvia.

REBECCA

17 January 1979, Wednesday, 9:35–10:30pm, BBC2, 4 episodes, drama, classic, British, 20th century
BBCtv
Pr: Richard Beynon
Dir: Simon Langton
Wtr: Hugh Whitemore
Based on Daphne du Maurier
Cast: **Maxim de Winter – Jeremy Brett**
Mrs. de Winter – Joanna David
Colonel Julyan – Robert Flemyng
Jack Favell – Julian Holloway
Mrs. Danvers – Anna Massey
Frith – Hugh Morton

From the moment she arrives at Manderley, the family home of her new husband Maxim, the second Mrs. de Winter feels overshadowed by the presence of Maxim's dead first wife, Rebecca. The young woman, goaded by hostile housekeeper Mrs. Danvers, fears she will never be able to compete with her revered predecessor, but slowly the truth about Rebecca emerges, and it is anything but the idyllic series of images Mrs. de Winter had first envisioned.

FLAMBARDS

2 February 1979, Friday, 7:30–9:00pm (subsequent episodes aired from 8:00–9:00pm), ITV, 12 episodes, drama, British, 20th century
Yorkshire Television
Video: available in UK, US
Pr: Leonard Lewis
Dir: Lawrence Gordon Clark, Peter Duffell, Michael Ferguson, Leonard Lewis
Wtr: Alex Glasgow, William Humble, Alan Plater
Based on Kathleen Peyton
Cast: Dick – Sebastian Abineri
Tizzy – Paul Ahmet
Mark Russell – Steven Grives
Henry Russell – Edward Judd
Christine Parsons – Christine McKenna
William Russell – Alan Parnaby

Orphaned Christina Parson arrives at Flambards, the country house of her crippled uncle, Henry Russell, in 1909. She and cousins William and Mark all come of age in the ensuing years, sharing many experiences in an English countryside which seems balanced between two centuries. Mark is obsessed with riding, hunting and drinking, while

William becomes absorbed with the modern science of designing and flying airplanes. William and Christina eventually move together to London, and are married shortly before the outbreak of World War I. William is killed in battle in France, and Christina returns to Flambards, intending to run the estate. Mark Russell, along with William's former groom Dick, survive the war and they, too, come back to Flambards, where Mark and Christina must resolve decades-long personal conflicts.

THE SERPENT SON

7 March 1979, Wednesday, 9:25–11:00pm, BBC2, 3 episodes, drama, classic, Ancient Greece
BBCtv
Pr: Richard Broke
Dir: Bill Hays
Wtr: Kenneth McLeish, Frederic Raphael
Based on *The Oresteia Trilogy* by Aeschylus
Cast: **Athene – Claire Bloom**
Leader of the Old Men – Alfred Burke
Orestes – Anton Lesser
Kalchas – Patrick Magee
Kassandra – Helen Mirren
Apollo – John Nolan
Elektra – Maureen O'Brien
Priestess of Apollo – Natasha Parry
Leader of the Furies – Sian Phillips
Agamemnon – Denis Quilley
Klytemnestra – Diana Rigg
Kilissa – Flora Robson
Leader of the Women's Chorus – Billie Whitelaw

Aeschylus' dramatic trilogy of plays tells the gruesome history of the ancient royal house of Atreus, focusing on Queen Klytemnestra's adultery, her subsequent murder of her husband, and their son Orestes' execution-killing of his mother, after which he is pursued by the Furies, figures of conscience.

MALICE AFORETHOUGHT

15 March 1979, Thursday, 8:30–9:25pm, BBC2, 4 episodes, thriller, British, 20th century
BBCtv
Pr: Richard Beynon
Dir: Cyril Coke
Wtr: Philip Mackie
Based on Francis Iles
Cast: Sir Bernard Deverell – Michael Aldridge
William Chatford – David Ashford
Dr. Bickleigh – Hywel Bennett
Madeleine – Cheryl Campbell
Julia Bickleigh – Judy Parfitt
Sir Francis Lee-Bannerton – Thorley Walters

For the ten years of their marriage in the 1930s, Julia Bickleigh has selfishly bullied her meek (and, not incidentally, philandering) husband, and Dr. Bickleigh has not challenged the *status quo* . . . but that changes radically in just one moment, resulting in Bickleigh being arrested for his wife's murder.

MY SON, MY SON

18 March 1979, Sunday, 7:15–8:10pm, BBC1, 8 episodes, drama, British, 19th–20th century
BBCtv
Pr: Keith Williams
Dir: Peter Cregeen
Wtr: Julian Bond
Based on Howard Spring
Cast: Sheila O'Riorden – Kate Binchy
Maeve – Prue Clarke
Rory O'Riorden (as a child) – Matthew Dale
Captain Judas – Maurice Denham
Oliver Essex (as a child) – Stefan Gates
Dermot O'Riorden – Frank Grimes
Nellie Essex – Sherrie Hewson
Reverend Oliver – Cyril Luckham
Livia – Ciaran Madden
Rory O'Riorden – Gerard Murphy
Oliver Essex – Patrick Ryecart
William Essex – Michael Williams

In Manchester in the late 19th century, William Essex is taken in as a lodger into the O'Riorden household, where he develops a lifelong friendship with the O'Riorden's son Dermot. As the men grow older, William and Dermot place all their hopes on their own sons, Oliver and Rory.

KIDNAPPED

7 April 1979, Saturday, 6:15–6:45pm, ITV, 13 episodes, drama, classic, adventure, Scottish, 18th century
HTV in association with Tele-munchen
Pr: Peter Graham Scott
Dir: Jean Pierre Decourt, Bob Fuest
Wtr: Peter Graham Scott
Based on *Kidnapped* and *Catriona* by Robert Louis Stevenson
Cast: Prestangrange – Patrick Allen
David Balfour – Ekkehardt Belle
Bonnie Prince Charlie – Christopher Biggins
Catriona Drummond – Aude Landry
Ebenezer Balfour – Patrick Magee
Alan Breck – David McCallum
James of the Glens – Bill Simpson
Red Fox Campbell – Frank Windsor

Highlander Alan Breck secretly returns to Scotland. At the same time, David Balfour's travels to Scotland are interrupted when he is kidnapped aboard a slave ship bound for the American colonies. He is rescued by Alan, and the two are then pursued across the Scottish Highlands by Redcoats who wrongly accuse them of murder. The chase leads Alan and David to France and Holland. David meets and falls in love with Catriona, but before they can enjoy lasting happiness, David must repay Alan's favour and rescue his friend, whose life is in serious danger.

The serial was broadcast in Germany as *The Adventures of David Balfour* before being screened in Great Britain.

THE MOURNING BROOCH

17 April 1979, Tuesday, 9:40–10:30pm, BBC1, 3 episodes, thriller, British, contemporary
BBCtv/Scotland
Pr: Pharic Maclaren
Designed by Alex Gourlay
Wtr: Bill Craig
Cast: Gowrie Bannerman – Andrew Cruickshank
Jean Balfour – Gay Hamilton
Tessa Bannerman – Cyd Hayman
Ray Campion – Bryan Marshall
Inspector Napier – Tom Watson

Smooth operator Ray Campion arrives in town and quickly gets caught up in a series of chases with guys good and bad as he attempts to find his elusive quarry, wanted man Balfour. Trouble is, no one knows if Balfour is dead or alive, and it's up to Campion to find out.

MATILDA'S ENGLAND

18 April 1979, Wednesday, 9:40–10:40pm, BBC2, 3 episodes, drama, British, 20th century
BBCtv
Pr: Ann Kirch
Dir: Mark Cullingham
Wtr: William Trevor
Cast: Miss Pritchard – Georgine Anderson
Matilda Tyzack – Anna Calder-Marshall
Ralphie Gregary – Rowland Davies
Mr. Tyzack – Geoffrey Greenhill
Young Matilda – June Hooper
Mrs. Ashburton – Celia Johnson
Mr. Madden – Robert Lang
Mrs. Tyzack – Pat Keen

Matilda Tyzack grows from childhood in the 1930s to middle age in the 1950s in the Somerset countryside; her development is counterpointed with the disintegration of rural society around her.

CRIME AND PUNISHMENT

22 May 1979, Tuesday, 9:00–10:15pm, BBC2, 3 episodes, drama, classic, Russian, 19th century
BBCtv
Pr: Jonathan Powell
Dir: Michael Darlow
Wtr: Jack Pulman
Based on Fyodor Dostoevsky
Cast: **Raskolnikov – John Hurt**
Pawnbroker – Beatrix Lehmann
Marmeladov – Frank Middlemass
Sonia Marmeladovna – Yolande Palfrey
Katerina Ivanova – Sian Phillips
Lizaveta – Carinthia West
Porfiry Petrovich – Timothy West

In St. Petersburg in the 1860s, expelled, poverty-stricken student Raskolnikov puts his singular philosophical belief that truly great men are above the law in all ways to the ultimate test by murdering a nasty pawnbroker and her sister. In the end it is Raskolnikov who betrays himself to the authorities, as he has developed a new belief, thanks to Sonya, a strangely pious young prostitute: crime is a sin, and punishment will bring true redemption.

THE DEEP CONCERN

7 June 1979, Thursday, 9:25–10:15pm, BBC1, 6 episodes, thriller, British, contemporary
BBCtv/Birmingham
Pr: David Rose
Dir: Jonathan Alwyn, Richard Callanan
Wtr: Elwyn Jones
Cast: Jonathan Bross – Neil Cunningham
Colin Eadon – Ronald Hines
Wyn Lloyd – Bernard Lloyd
Detective Chief Inspector Donaldson – Bill Paterson
Carrie Stone – Beth Porter
Nigel Jackson – Tim Preece
Mary Eadon – Katharine Schofield

The guests at the Deep Corporation Conference arrive expecting lavish hospitality, end up instead confronting death, and ultimately plan an act of revenge.

THE MALLENS

10 June 1979, Sunday, 9:00–10:00pm, ITV, 7 episodes, drama, British, 19th century
Granada Television
Video: available in UK
Pr: Roy Roberts
Dir: Richard Martin, Brian Mills, Ronald Wilson
Wtr: Jack Russell
Based on *The Mallen Streak* by Catherine Cookson
Cast: Anna Brigmore – Caroline Blakiston
Constance Farrington – Julia Chambers
Donald Radlet – John Duttine
Barbara Farrington – Pippa Guard
Thomas Mallen – John Hallam
Dick Mallen – David Rintoul
Matthew Radlet – Ian Saynor

In 19th-century Northumberland, the family of Thomas Mallen, Squire of High Banks Hall, is involved in a series of scandals and romances. Mallen faces financial ruin, and is also confronted with the problems of his wastrel son Dick, and his illegitimate child Donald Radlet. Donald marries Constance Farrington, but she loves Donald's brother Matthew. Squire Mallen rapes Constance's sister Barbara, who dies in childbirth. By story's end, three generations have passed, many are dead, and few of those left alive are happy.

MURDER AT THE WEDDING

11 July 1979, Wednesday, 10:30–11:30pm, ITV, 4 episodes, mystery, British, contemporary
HTV
Pr: Leonard White
Dir: Peter Sasdy
Wtr: Bob Baker, Dave Martin
Cast: **Anne Russell – Barbara Ferris**
Mike Fulmer – James Hazeldine
Bigwood – David Lodge
Eric Russell – Cyril Luckham
Ken French – Alfred Lynch
William Appleyard – Bryan Marshall

Anne Russell and William Appleyard's happy preparations for their wedding day, overseen by Anne's wealthy father, are disrupted by the arrival of William's resentful children from his first marriage. The ceremony proceeds nevertheless, and the reception is in full swing . . . when a corpse is discovered in the grounds. As the police investigate the murder, it becomes apparent that everyone on the scene, including the blushing bride, has something to hide.

LOVE AMONG THE ARTISTS

31 July 1979, Tuesday, 9:00–10:00pm, ITV, 5 episodes, drama, British, 19th century
Granada Television
Pr: Howard Baker
Dir: Howard Baker, Marc Miller
Wtr: Stuart Latham
Based on George Bernard Shaw
Cast: Mrs. Herbert – Judy Campbell
Madge Brailsford – Jane Carr

Lettie Cairns – Joanna Dunham
Lady Geraldine Porter – Joan Greenwood
Adrian Herbert – Martyn Jacobs
Mary Sutherland – Geraldine James
Aurelie Szczymplica – Carolle Rousseau
Owen Jack – John Stride
John Hoskyn – Gary Watson

A Shavian look at London society in the 1870s, focusing on poverty-stricken Welsh composer Owen Jack, who arrives in London to teach piano, but is taken under wing by grande dame Lady Geraldine Porter, and soon becomes inextricably linked with members of high society, most closely independent-minded society girl Mary Sutherland.

A MOMENT IN TIME

4 September 1979, Tuesday, 8:30–9:00pm, BBC1, 4 episodes, drama, British, 20th century
BBCtv
Pr: Colin Tucker
Dir: Renny Rye
Wtr: Robin Chapman
Based on H.E. Bates
Cast: Catharine – Jill Balcon
Splodge – Robin Davies
Elizabeth – Alison Elliott
Bill – John Moulder-Brown
Tom – Michael Troughton
Harry – Benjamin Whitrow

In a small village in Kent during the summer of 1940, Elizabeth attempts to live the normal life of a young woman, but this proves impossible under the omnipresent cloud of World War II, which wreaks tragic havoc with Elizabeth's romance with a pilot.

Featured as part of the " . . . a love story" series.

PRINCE REGENT

4 September 1979, Tuesday, 9:15–10:15pm, BBC1, 8 episodes, drama, biographical, historical, British, 18th–19th century
BBCtv
Pr: Colin Tucker
Dir: Michael Simpson
Wtr: Ian Curteis, Reg Gadney, Nemone Lethbridge, Robert Muller
Cast: Charles James Fox – Keith Barron
Frances, Lady Jersey – Caroline Blakiston
William Pitt – David Collings
King George III – Nigel Davenport
George, Prince of Wales – Peter Egan
Frederick, Duke of York – Bosco Hogan
Princess Charlotte – Patsy Kensit
Princess Charlotte – Cherie Lunghi
Richard Sheridan – Clive Merrison
Isabella, Lady Hertford – Barbara Shelley
Princess Caroline – Dinah Stabb
Queen Charlotte – Frances White
Maria Fitzherbert – Susannah York

Beginning in 1782 with his coming-of-age at 21, and culminating with his ascendancy to the throne 37 years later, the biography of George Augustus Frederick, Prince of Wales, whose life was embroiled in much scandal, beginning with his secret marriage to widowed Roman Catholic Maria Fitzherbert, and climaxed with his attempt to unseat his seemingly mad father, King George III.

TINKER, TAILOR, SOLDIER, SPY

10 September 1979, Monday, 9:00–9:50pm, BBC2, 7 episodes, thriller, British, contemporary
BBCtv
Video: available in UK
Pr: Jonathan Powell
Dir: John Irvin
Wtr: Arthur Hopcraft
Based on John le Carré
Cast: Percy Alleline – Michael Aldridge
Jim Prideaux – Ian Bannen
Lacon – Anthony Bate
Ricki Tarr – Hywel Bennett
George Smiley – Alec Guinness
Toby Esterhase – Bernard Hepton
Peter Guillam – Michael Jayston
Control – Alexander Knox
Connie Sachs – Beryl Reid

Bill Haydon – Ian Richardson
Roy Bland – Terence Rigby
Inspector Mendel – George Sewell
Karla – Patrick Stewart
Roddy Martindale – Nigel Stock

Retired secret agent George Smiley is brought back into active service to track down an enemy infiltrator in the department where he was once the prize employee, which puts him in a series of delicate circumstances with those who had been his trusted friends and colleagues.

THE CAMERONS

26 September 1979, Wednesday, 10:00–10:50pm, BBC2, 6 episodes, drama, Scottish, 19th century
BBCtv/Scotland
Pr: Pharic Maclaren
Dir: Peter Moffatt
Wtr: Bill Craig
Based on Robert Crichton
Cast: Henry Selkirk – Graham Crowden
Maggie Drum – Morag Hood
Gillon Cameron – Malcolm Ingram
Walter Bone – Roddy McMillan
Mrs. Drum – Irene Sunters
Brothcock – Jack Watson
Tom Drum – Tom Watson

In Scotand in 1870, 16-year-old Maggie Drum sets out to find a husband. Big-hearted Highlander Gillon Cameron fits the bill, and in the decades to come the story of their life together unfolds, delivering joy, hardship, and seven children in the small Scottish mining community of Pitmungo.

THE LEGEND OF KING ARTHUR

7 October 1979, Sunday, 6:00–6:30pm, BBC1, 8 episodes, drama, classic, British, 6th century
BBCtv
Video: available in UK
Pr: Ken Riddington
Dir: Rodney Bennett
Wtr: Andrew Davies
Cast: Arthur (as a child) – Richard Austin
King Arthur – Andrew Burt
Queen Guinevere – Felicity Dean
Merlin – Robert Eddison
Mordred – Steve Hodson
Morgan le Fay (as a child) – Patsy Kensit
Morgan le Fay – Maureen O'Brien
Lancelot – David Robb

A new telling of the Arthurian legend, beginning with young Arthur's pulling of the sword Excalibur from the stone and ending with the downfall of Camelot following Queen Guinevere's ill-fated love affair with Lancelot.

PENMARRIC

12 October 1979, Friday, 8:05–9:00pm, BBC1, 12 episodes, drama, British, 19th–20th century
BBCtv
Video: available in UK
Pr: Ron Craddock
Dir: Derek Martinus, Tina Wakerell
Wtr: Julian Bond, John Prebble, Michael Robson, Anthony Seward, Jon Sommersby
Based on Susan Howatch
Cast: Michael Vincent – Peter Blake
Robert Yorke – Paul Darrow
Jan-Yves – Eric Deacon
Rebecca – Holly De Jong
Philip – Rupert Frazer
Helena – Fiona Gray
Janna Roslyn – Annabel Leventon
Isabella Clay – Deborah Makepeace
Simon Peter Roslyn – Gerard Ryder
Maud Penmar – Angela Scoular
Giles Penmar – Shaughan Seymour
Rose Parrish – Shirley Steedman
Mark Castallack – Martin C. Thurley

The multigenerational saga of the loves and hatreds of the families that live at the Cornwall estate of Penmarric, stretching from 1867 to 1940. Dominating the story is the tempestuous relationship between Janna Roslyn and Mark Castallack, which has ramifications for generations beyond them.

QUATERMASS

31 October 1979, Wednesday, 9:10–10:10pm, ITV, 3 episodes, science fiction, British, future

Thames Television/Euston Films
Video: available in UK, US
Pr: Ted Childs
Dir: Piers Haggard
Wtr: Nigel Kneale
Cast: Kickalong – Ralph Arliss
    Clare Kapp – Barbara Kellermann
    Kapp – Simon MacCorkindale
    Quatermass – John Mills
    Caraway – Paul Rosebury

Set in the not-too-distant future, legendary Professor Bernard Quatermass returns to London after years of seclusion in Scotland, to battle once again to save the world from a nightmare menace from space: aliens which are controlling the minds of young people and which are about to unleash an immobilizing death ray capable of destroying our planet.

Written by the original series creator, this was Quatermass' first reappearance since the legendary BBC serials of the 1950s.

TESTAMENT OF YOUTH

4 November 1979, Sunday,
10:15–11:10pm, BBC2, 5 episodes, drama, biographical, British, 20th century
BBCtv in association with London Film Productions Ltd.
Pr: Jonathan Powell
Dir: Moira Armstrong
Wtr: Elaine Morgan
Based on Vera Brittain
Cast: **Vera Brittain – Cheryl Campbell**
    Miss Penrose – Rosalie Crutchley
    Edward Brittain – Rupert Frazer
    Mr. Brittain – Emrys James
    Victor Richardson – Michael Troughton
    Mrs. Brittain – Jane Wenham
    Roland Leighton – Peter Woodward

The life story of Vera Brittain, beginning with her arrival at Oxford in 1915 at age 18. Vera's story focuses here on World War I; she leaves her studies to serve as a VAD nurse in London, Malta and France, and personally experiences the impact of the war as it changes the old values and established order of life in Great Britain for all time.

Winner, BAFTA Award, Best Drama Serial 1979.

THE ENCHANTED CASTLE

7 November 1979, Wednesday,
5:05–5:40pm, BBC1, 6 episodes, drama, family, British, 20th century
BBCtv
Exec. Pr: Anna Home
Dir: Dorothea Brooking
Wtr: Julia Jones
Based on E.E. Nesbit
Cast: **Eliza – Gill Abineri**
    Aunt – Sheila Beckett
    Cathy – Candida Beveridge
    Bailiff – Cavan Kendall
    Jimmy – Marcus Scott-Barrett
    Gerald – Simon Sheard
    Mabel – Georgia Slowe

Gerald, Cathy and Jimmy are looking for adventure when they set off to explore the woods, but get far more than they bargained for when they discover the Enchanted Castle. There the children are befriended by Mabel, the housekeeper's niece, who wears a magic ring which makes her invisible. Adventure follows adventure as the children try to control the magic, but it may be too powerful a force for the youngsters.

THE OLD CURIOSITY SHOP

9 December 1979, Sunday, 5:35–6:30pm, BBC1, 9 episodes, drama, classic, British, 19th century
BBCtv
Pr: Barry Letts
Dir: Julian Amyes
Wtr: William Trevor
Based on Charles Dickens
Cast: Mrs. Jarley – Margaret Courtenay
    Kit Nubbles – Christopher Fairbank
    Mrs. Jiniwin – Freda Jackson
    Sampson Brass – Colin Jeavons
    Little Nell – Natalie Ogle
    Mrs. Quilp – Sandra Payne
    Daniel Quilp – Trevor Peacock
    Dick Swiveller – Granville Saxton
    Grandfather – Sebastian Shaw

Little Nell, orphaned and devoted to her elderly Grandfather, becomes the pawn in a plot by lascivious money-lender Daniel Quilp, who plans to marry Nell when she becomes old enough. Nell and her grandfather then make a number of attempts to escape his evil clutches, but by the time a path to freedom is available, it is, tragically, too late for them both.

1980–1989

OUR JOHN WILLIE

2 January 1980, Wednesday, 5:10–5:40pm, BBC1, 5 episodes, drama, British, 19th century
BBCtv/Birmingham
Exec. Pr: Anna Home
Dir: Marilyn Fox
Wtr: Valerie Georgeson
Based on Catherine Cookson
Cast: **John Willie – David Burke**
Peter Talbot – Ian Cullen
Miss Peamarsh – Madeleine Cannon
Dan Potter – John Malcolm
Davy – Antony Manuel

Davy has always protected his frail brother John Willie, who is deaf and dumb since birth. Relying on his wits and resourcefulness to keep them both alive in the trying times of the mid-1800s, the brothers live in a deserted shed on the edge of Miss Peamarsh's land, and find themselves involved in her life in an unexpected manner when the reclusive eccentric takes kindly to the two scruffy orphans.

THE ASSASSINATION RUN

4 January 1980, Friday, 9:25–10:15pm, BBC1, 3 episodes, thriller, British, contemporary
BBCtv/Scotland
Video: available in UK, US
Pr: Bob McIntosh
Dir: Ken Hannam
Wtr: Jack Gerson
Cast: Vladimir Grigor – Sandor Eles
Bartlett – Leon Sinden
Mark Fraser – Malcolm Stoddard
Jill Fraser – Mary Tamm

Mark Fraser, who retired to the Scottish Highlands after working since university as a British Intelligence "eliminator," is forced back into service when his wife Jill is kidnapped and taken to Spain by KGB agent Vladimir Grigor.

FLESH AND BLOOD

8 January 1980, Tuesday, 9:25–10:20pm, BBC1, 10 episodes, drama, British, contemporary
BBCtv/Manchester
Pr: Bill Sellars
Dir: Terence Dudley
Wtr: John Finch
Cast: Sarah Brassington – Ann Firbank
Henry Brassington – Bill Fraser
Mabel Brassington – Thora Hird
Ross Brassington – Michael Jayston
Jim Turner – Nigel Stock
Max Brassington – John Stone

Although he is of an age to retire and has two sons and a son-in-law capable of taking over her business, Henry Brassington cannot seem to let go of the reins, which causes serious conflict for all involved.

BREAKAWAY: THE FAMILY AFFAIR

11 January 1980, Friday, 8:30–9:00pm, BBC1, 6 episodes, mystery, British, contemporary
BBCtv
Pr: Ken Riddington
Dir: Paul Ciappessoni
Wtr: Francis Durbridge
Cast: Hannah Harvey – Joan Benham
Bert Sinclair – Glyn Houston
Sam Harvey – Martin Jarvis
Larry Voss – Simon Oates
Jill Foster – Hilary Ryan
Peter Bradford – Paul Shelley

Detective Superintendent Sam Harvey plans to resign from the police force and pursue a career as a writer, but is forced to remain with Scotland Yard when his parents are murdered and Harvey is determined to solve the crime.

Featured under the program banner of "Francis Durbridge presents . . . "

PRIDE AND PREJUDICE

13 January 1980, Sunday, 9:35–10:30pm, BBC2, 5 episodes, drama, classic, British, 19th century
BBCtv in association with the Australian Broadcasting Commission
Video: available in UK, US
Pr: Jonathan Powell
Dir: Cyril Coke

Wtr: Fay Weldon
Based on Jane Austen
Cast: **Mr. Bingley – Osmund Bullock**
Caroline Bingley – Marsha Fitzalan
Jane Bennet – Sabina Franklyn
Elizabeth Bennet – Elizabeth Garvie
Kitty Bennet – Clare Higgins
Mrs. Bennet – Priscilla Morgan
Lydia Bennet – Natalie Ogle
Lady Catherine de Bourgh – Judy Parfitt
Mary Bennet – Tessa Peake-Jones
Mr. Collins – Malcolm Rennie
Charlotte Lucas Collins – Irene Richard
Mr. Darcy – David Rintoul
Mr. Wickham – Peter Settelen
Mr. Bennet – Moray Watson

When eligible bachelor Mr. Bingley comes to live at Netherfield, garrulous neighbour Mrs. Bennet sets her heart on his marrying one of her five single daughters (and so eventually he does), thus setting into motion the classic love story of Elizabeth Bennet and (Bingley's good friend) Mr. Darcy.

THE SPOILS OF WAR

27 January 1980, Sunday, 7:45–8:45pm, ITV, 7 episodes, drama, British, 20th century
Granada Television
Pr: Richard Everitt
Dir: Michael Custance, Richard Everitt, Bill Gilmour, Jonathan Wright Miller, Brian Mills, Charles Sturridge
Wtr: John Finch
Cast: **Mark Warrington – James Bate**
Helen Hayward – Avis Bunnage
Rosalynde Warrington – Jane How
Blake Hayward – Alan Hunter
Harry Hayward – Nat Jackley
Herta Wenkel – Katja Kersten
George Hayward – William Lucas
Peg Hayward – Emily Moore
Beth Warrington – Colette O'Neil
John Warrington – David Langton
Owen Hayward – Leslie Schofield

During the years 1945-1947, all of Great Britain must adjust to the end of World War II; for most, including the wealthy Warrington and working-class Hayward families of the Lake District, things will never be the same again. It would seem these two groups have no common ground, but after serving in the military together, Blake Hayward and Mark Warrington find themselves friends. Blake remains in Germany with the occupying forces and is drawn to German war widow Herta Wenkel; their affair produces a son. Upon returning home, Mark Warrington falls in love with Blake's sister Peg, formally joining the two families together when they marry.

GOD'S WONDERFUL RAILWAY

6 February 1980, Wednesday, 5:05–5:35pm, BBC1, 8 episodes, drama, family, British, 19th–20th century
BBCtv
Pr: Paul Stone
Dir: Fiona Cumming
Wtr: Avril Rowlands
Cast: Deborah – Anne Burns
George Grant – Colin Douglas
Andy Grant – Andrew Hughes
Robbie Grant – Gerard Kelly
Martha – Anne Kristen

A branch line of the Great Western Railway is constructed in the 1860s, disrupting lives in the peaceful countryside and having a significant impact on the lives of several generations of the Grant family.

BREAKAWAY: THE LOCAL AFFAIR

22 February 1980, Friday, 8:30–9:00pm, BBC1, 6 episodes, mystery, British, contemporary
BBCtv
Pr: Ken Riddington
Dir: Michael E. Briant
Wtr: Francis Durbridge
Cast: Scott Douglas – Ed Bishop
Rita Black – Sandra Bryant
Becky Royce – Judy Geeson
Sam Harvey – Martin Jarvis
Chief Superintendent Cooper – Jack McKenzie
Isabel Black – Vivien Merchant

Detective Superintendent Sam Harvey has just got over solving his parents' murder when he reluctantly returns to work at Market Cross on a new case, investigating the murder of Rita Black. He figures the routine will be an easy distraction, but things quickly become more complicated than he could ever have anticipated.

A sequel to *The Family Affair* which followed immediately after the first serial's conclusion; featured under the program banner of "Francis Durbridge presents . . . "

SWEET NOTHINGS

28 February 1980, Tuesday, 8:25–9:00pm, BBC1, 4 episodes, drama, British, contemporary
BBCtv/Scotland
Pr: Colin Tucker
Dir: Martyn Friend
Wtr: Ted Whitehead
Cast: **Tom Fearon – Tom Bell**
Mary Fearon – Lynn Farleigh
Susy Fearon – Kate Lock
Julia – Stephanie Turner

After 20 years of seeming wedded bliss, Tom and Mary Fearon's relationship suddenly shatters . . . but perhaps destiny will bring them together again.

Featured as part of the " . . . a love story" series.

THE FURTHER ADVENTURES OF OLIVER TWIST

2 March 1980, Sunday, 5:00–5:30pm, ITV, 13 episodes, drama, family, British, 19th century
ATV Network
Pr: Ian Fordyce
Dir: Ian Fordyce, Paul Harrison
Wtr: David Butler
Based on characters created by Charles Dickens; story idea by Hugh Leonard
Cast: Mr. Brownlow – Bryan Coleman
Artful Dodger – John Fowler
Mr. Bumble – Harold Innocent
Monks – Geoffrey Larder
Oliver Twist – Daniel Murray
Noah Claypoole – Leonard Preston
Mr. Grimwig – Derek Smith
Fagin – David Swift

Picking up where the Dickens classic ends, Oliver Twist has started a new life with his kindly guardian, Mr. Brownlow. Oliver endeavors to find proof of his origins, and, accompanied by the Artful Dodger, the boys find themselves once more in the clutches of the evil Fagin, who has managed to escape the hangman. Worse still, Oliver's half-brother Monks hatches a plot to ruin Oliver, who is sent to Newgate Prison. But Dodger comes to his rescue, helping to turn the tables on Oliver's enemies and securing his friend's freedom.

THE HISTORY OF MR. POLLY

2 March 1980, Sunday, 5:30–5:55pm, BBC1, 5 episodes, drama, British, 19th century
BBCtv
Pr: Barry Letts
Dir: Lovett Bickford
Wtr: James Andrew Hall
Based on H.G. Wells
Cast: Mrs. Johnson – Ann Beach
Platt – Peter Bourke
Mrs. Larkins – Fanny Carby
Mrs. Polly – Anita Carey
Mr. Johnson – Nigel Lambert
Alfred Polly – Andrew Sachs

Middle-class tradesman Alfred Polly is trapped in a life which never measures up to the greatness of his dreams. When he is presumed dead after a botched suicide attempt, Polly sets off for the countryside, where he decides to start his life anew, running a small country inn.

THERESE RAQUIN

23 March 1980, Wednesday, 9:00–9:55pm, BBC2, 3 episodes, drama, French, 19th century
BBCtv in association with London Film Productions Ltd.
Pr: Jonathan Powell
Dir: Simon Langton
Wtr: Philip Mackie
Based on Emile Zola
Cast: **Laurent – Brian Cox**
Camille Raquin – Kenneth Cranham
Thérèse Raquin – Kate Nelligan
Vidal – Alan Rickman

Madame Raquin – Mona Washbourne

Abandoned as a child, Thérèse Raquin grows up in the care of her aunt, and marries her delicate cousin, Camille. Her quiet, self-contained life is rocked by the arrival in Paris of Camille's friend, Laurent, who unleashes a lifetime of suppressed emotion and desire from within Thérèse, which leads to the murder of Camille, and the eventual suicide of Thérèse and Laurent.

A QUESTION OF GUILT

25 March 1980, Tuesday, 9:00–9:30pm, BBC2, 8 episodes, mystery, non-fiction, British, 19th century
BBCtv
Pr: Richard Beynon
Dir: Paul Annett
Wtr: Douglas Livingstone
Cast: **Samuel Kent – Joss Ackland**
Chief Inspector Whicher – Harry Andrews
Mary Ann Kent – Diana Beevers
Constance Kent – Prue Clarke
The Reverend Wagner – Ronald Hines
William Kent – Russell Lewis
Elizabeth Gough – Rosalind Lloyd
Elizabeth Kent – Eliza McClelland
Mrs. Kent – Amanda Murray

In June 1860, three-year-old Francis Kent is found brutally murdered. His 16-year-old stepsister Constance is charged with and tried for the crime, but ultimately is released on bond, the murder never officially solved.

THE SWISH OF THE CURTAIN

13 April 1980, Sunday, 6:10–6:40pm, BBC1, 4 episodes, drama, classic, family, British, 20th century
BBCtv
Pr: Barry Letts
Dir: Joan Craft
Wtr: Julia Jones
Based on Pamela Brown
Cast: Mrs. Potter-Smith – Mona Bruce
Nigel – Simon Cowell-Parker
Sandra – Sarah Greene
Viccy – Sally Jane Jackson
Lynette – Amanda Kirby
Bulldog – Ashley Knight
Jeremy – Dominic Savage
Roma Seymore – Dinah Sheridan
Maddy – Jayne Stevens

In an English seaside town in the late 1930s, seven stage-struck youngsters turn a disused old chapel into a theatre, with themselves as the resident Blue Door Theatre Company.

A QUESTION OF GUILT (2)

22 April 1980, Tuesday, 9:00–9:30pm, BBC2, 6 episodes, mystery, non-fiction, British, 18th century
BBCtv
Pr: Richard Beynon
Dir: Brian Farnham
Wtr: Ken Taylor
Cast: Mr. Blandy – Alfred Burke
Mary Blandy – Victoria Fairbrother
Dr. Addington – Charles Kay
Mrs. Blandy – Phyllida Law
Susan – Margery Mason
William Cranstoun – Alex Norton

In 1752, Mary Blandy is tried in Oxford for the murder of her father. At the same time, her lover, William Cranstoun, flees to the Continent, an act which leads many to question Mary's guilt, as the antipathy between Mr. Blandy and Cranstoun was no secret to anyone. Nevertheless, Mary is convicted and sentenced to death.

HANNAH

29 April 1980, Tuesday, 8:25–9:00pm, BBC1, 4 episodes, drama, British, 20th century
BBCtv
Pr: Colin Tucker
Dir: Peter Jefferies
Wtr: Lee Langley
Based on *Miss Mole* by E.H. Young
Cast: Mrs. Gibson – Kathleen Helme
Mrs. Riddings – Judi Maynard
Mr. Pilgrim – John Owens
Mr. Blenkinsop – Tim Pigott-Smith
Hannah Mole – Helen Ryan

Hannah Mole attempts to escape her scandalous past in the quiet village of

Radstowe, but constant reminders threaten her ability to move forward with a new life . . . and a new love interest.

Featured as part of the " . . . a love story" series.

BULL WEEK

1 May 1980, Thursday, 9:25–10:10pm,
BBC1, 6 episodes, drama, British, contemporary
BBCtv/Birmingham
Pr: Michael Wearing
Dir: Philip Dudley
Wtr: Ron Hutchinson
Cast: Fat Freddie Armadale – Dave Atkins
  Eddie Kowal – Philip Martin Brown
  Sanders – Forbes Collins
  Donna Kowal – Stephanie Fayerman
  Mr. Kowal – Czeslaw Grocholski
  Hilditch – Norman Jones
  Johnny Kowal – Mark McManus
  Danny Kowal – Terence Rigby

The day-by-day chronicle of one week at a Midlands factory – the "Bull Week" before the holiday shutdown, when workers look to earn large bonuses – focusing on the three Kowal brothers, who are deeply involved in the goings on there: Eddie and Danny Kowal, who work on the factory floor, and Johnny, shop steward of their union.

DOOM CASTLE

11 May 1980, Sunday, 6:10–6:40pm,
BBC1, 6 episodes, drama, British, 17th century
BBCtv/Scotland
Pr: Pharic Maclaren
Dir: Peter Moffatt
Wtr: Tom Wright
Based on Neil Munro
Cast: **Baron Lamond – Victor Carin**
  Cecile Favart – Nicola Forte
  Olivia – Valerie Fyfer
  Count Victor – Ian Saynor
  Simon Mactaggart – Paul Young

In the ten years since Bonnie Prince Charlie fled to France, Jacobites hold on to their hopes, and intrigue abounds on both sides of the Channel. Omens and warnings are given in both countries, with duelling action intertwined with secrecy before the final judgment occurs.

A QUESTION OF GUILT (3)

13 May 1980, Tuesday, 9:00–9:30pm,
BBC2, 8 episodes, mystery, non-fiction, British, 19th century
BBCtv
Pr: Richard Beynon
Dir: Carol Wiseman
Wtr: Douglas Livingstone
Cast: **Adelaide Bartlett – Marianne Borgo**
  Dr. Leach – Nigel Havers
  Reverend George Dyson – Bosco Hogan
  Mr. Bartlett – Frank Middlemass
  Edward Clarke, QC – Robert Stephens
  Sir Charles Russell – Thorley Walters
  Edwin Bartlett – Mark Wing-Davey

Frenchwoman Adelaide Bartlett marries Edwin Bartlett in an arranged union and is later charged with her husband's murder by chloroform poisoning. Also tried is the Reverend George Dyson, who provided Adelaide with chloroform just a few days before Bartlett's death. Dyson is ultimately discharged; Adelaide is not as lucky, but questions about her guilt remain unanswered.

THE MALLENS

29 May 1980, Thursday, 9:00–10:00pm,
ITV, 6 episodes, drama, British, 19th century
Granada Television
Video: available in UK
Pr: Roy Roberts
Dir: Mary McMurray, Brian Mills
Wtr: Jack Russell
Based on *The Mallen Girl*, *The Mallen Secret* by Catherine Cookson
Cast: Anna Brigmore – Caroline Blakiston
  Constance Radlet – June Ritchie
  Sarah Waite – Julie Shipley
  Barbara Mallen – Juliet Stevenson
  Michael Radlet – Gerry Sundquist
  Dan Bensham – Michael Thomas

The Mallen family saga continues with the stories of Michael Radlet, the illegitimate son of the late Matthew

Radlet and Constance Farrington Radlet (who was married to Matthew's brother Donald), and Barbara Mallen, the deaf, illegitimate daughter of the late Squire Thomas Mallen. Both Matthew and Barbara are unaware of the circumstances of their births; the two cousins are in love, but are forbidden to see one another. After being confronted with the bitter truth of her birth, Barbara enters into a loveless marriage with neighbor Dan Bensham. Michael, too, marries another. But Barbara and Michael meet up once again, and their love is rekindled . . . with tragic results.

THE SPOILS OF WAR (second series)

25 July 1980, Friday, 8:00–9:00pm, ITV, 6 episodes, drama, British, 20th century
Granada Television
Pr: James Brabazon
Dir: Michael Custance, Jonathan Wright Miller, Laurence Moody
Wtr: John Finch
Cast: **Mark Warrington – James Bate**
Ros Warrington – Jane How
Blake Hayward – Alan Hunter
Emil – David Kerr
John Warrington – David Langton
George Hayward – William Lucas
Peg Warrington – Emily Moore
Paula Brandt – Catherine Schell

The post-war adjustment of the Warrington and Hayward families continues in 1948. The families are still divided by class (George Hayward is John Warrington's employee at the Iron Works owned by Warrington), despite the marriage of Mark Warrington and Peg Hayward. Blake Hayward is reunited with his German son Emil, whose mother has died, but this complicates his romance with Ros Warrington. Both families' security is in jeopardy when the iron and steel industry is threatened with nationalization.

FAIR STOOD THE WIND FOR FRANCE

2 September 1980, Tuesday, 9:25–10:20pm, BBC1, 4 episodes, drama, British, 20th century
BBCtv
Pr: Colin Tucker
Dir: Martyn Friend
Wtr: Julian Bond
Based on H.E. Bates
Cast: **Franklin – David Beames**
O'Connor – John Flanagan
Father – Bernard Kay
Françoise – Cecile Paoli
Grandmother – Eileen Way

In 1942, Lancaster bomber Franklin crashes in France; as he recovers from his injuries, he becomes intensely involved with French country girl Françoise.

Featured as part of the " . . . a love story" series.

MACKENZIE

4 September 1980, Thursday, 9:25–10:55pm (subsequent episodes aired from 9:25–10:15), BBC1, 12 episodes, drama, British, 20th century
BBCtv
Pr: George Gallaccio
Dir: Kenny McBain
Wtr: Andrea Newman
Cast: Ruth Isaacs – Lynda Bellingham
Duncan Mackenzie – David Donaldson
Robert Mackenzie – Jack Galloway
Jamie Mackenzie (as a child) – Derek Gray
Lisa Isaacs (as a child) – Debra Langerman
George Kovacs – Richard Marner
Duncan Mackenzie (as a child) – Michael McLaughlin
Diana Crawley – Sheila Ruskin
David Isaacs – Toby Salaman
Jamie Mackenzie – Ewan Stewart
Lisa Mackenzie – Tracey Ullman
Jean Mackenzie – Kara Wilson

The 20-year chronicle, beginning in 1955, of the interrelationships between the Mackenzie, Isaacs and Kovacs families, focusing most intently on the relationship between Robert Mackenzie and his sons Jamie and Duncan.

WE, THE ACCUSED

10 September 1980, Wednesday,
9:25–10:15pm, BBC2, 5 episodes, drama,
British, 20th century
BBCtv
Pr: Jonathan Powell
Dir: Richard Stroud
Wtr: Julia Jones
Based on Ernest Raymond
Cast: **Detective Inspector Boltro – Iain Cuthbertson**
Myra Bawne – Angela Down
Sir Kenneth Eddy – Derek Farr
Sir Hayman Drewer – Charles Gray
Paul Presset – Ian Holm
Elinor Presset – Elizabeth Spriggs

In 1932, middle-aged, idealistic London schoolmaster Paul Presset, trapped in an unhappy marriage to selfish Elinor, falls in love with colleague Myra Bawne. When Elinor refuses to divorce him, Paul poisons and kills his wife, then continues his relationship with Myra. Detective Inspector Boltro suspects foul play in Elinor's death, and searches for Paul, who has fled with Myra, who stands by him loyally through to the end, when Paul is tried on murder charges and found guilty.

FLICKERS

17 September 1980, Wednesday,
9:00–10:00pm, ITV, 6 episodes, drama,
British, 20th century
ATV Network
Pr: Joan Brown
Dir: Cyril Coke
Wtr: Roy Clarke
Cast: **Corky Brown – Dickie Arnold**
Gwendoline Harper – Maxine Audley
Maud – Frances de la Tour
Arnie Cole – Bob Hoskins
Max Legendre – Granville Saxton

In the early days of the British film industry, Arnie Cole runs the struggling Travelling Bioscope Theatre, which journeys around the country renting halls to show moving pictures – but what he really wants to do is make comedy films. Arnold meets and marries sharp-tongued Maud, soon neglecting his wife as his new film company expands . . . but he moves too fast too soon and ultimately the whole endeavour blows up in Arnie's face.

A TALE OF TWO CITIES

5 October 1980, Sunday, 6:10–6:40pm,
BBC1, 8 episodes, drama, classic,
British/French, 18th century
BBCtv
Pr: Barry Letts
Dir: Michael E. Briant
Wtr: Pieter Harding
Based on Charles Dickens
Cast: Miss Pross – Vivien Merchant
Dr. Manette – Ralph Michael
Lucie Manette – Sally Osborn
Madame Defarge – Judy Parfitt
Charles Darnay/Sydney Carton – Paul Shelley
Mr. Lorry – Nigel Stock
Defarge – Stephen Yardley

During the French Revolution, jaded barrister Sydney Carton is in love with Lucie Manette, who in turns adores nobleman Charles Darnay (who bears an uncanny resemblance to Carton). When Darnay is sentenced to die on the guillotine, Carton unselfishly changes places with him, sacrificing himself to insure Lucie's happiness and thereby at last finding redemption and meaning in his life.

FORGIVE OUR FOOLISH WAYS

14 October 1980, Tuesday, 8:30–9:00pm,
BBC1, 4 episodes, drama, British, 20th century
BBCtv
Pr: Colin Tucker
Dir: Christopher King
Wtr: Reg Gadney
Cast: **Wolf Hahn – Hartmut Becker**
Christopher Lanyon – Ashley Clark
Vivien Lanyon – Kate Nelligan
Cameron Worrell – Tim Preece
David Senior – David Robb

In Yorkshire in 1946, the war is over, but many wounds remain unhealed. Vivien Lanyon's husband is still posted missing when she meets and becomes romantically involved with German prisoner-of-war Wolf Hahn, who is sent

TO SERVE THEM ALL MY DAYS

17 October 1980, Friday, 9:25–10:20pm, BBC1, 13 episodes, drama, British, 20th century
BBCtv
Pr: Ken Riddington
Dir: Ronald Wilson
Wtr: Andrew Davies
Based on R.F. Delderfield
Cast: **David Powlett-Jones – John Duttine**
Christine Forster – Susan Jameson
Alcock – Charles Kay
Ellie Herries – Patricia Lawrence
Sir Rufus Creighton – Cyril Luckham
Howarth – Alan MacNaughtan
Algy Herries – Frank Middlemass

David Powlett-Jones is invalided out of the Army and arrives in the mid-1920s at Bamfylde School, where his meeting with Headmaster Algy Herries alters the course of his life, as he becomes a dedicated teacher. Powlett-Jones suffers the trauma of losing his wife and children in a car accident, but then finds happiness with Christine Forster. Herries retires and Powlett-Jones does not see eye to eye with Alcock, the new headmaster, but does himself eventually become headmaster of Bamfylde.

LOVE IN A COLD CLIMATE

29 October 1980, Wednesday, 9:00–10:00pm, ITV, 8 episodes, drama, British, 20th century
Thames Television
Pr: Gerald Savory
Dir: Donald McWhinnie
Wtr: Simon Raven
Based on *The Pursuit of Love* and *Love in a Cold Climate* by Nancy Mitford
Cast: **Uncle Matthew – Michael Aldridge**
Sadie – Judi Dench
Emily Warbech – Diana Fairfax

to work in the area. The relationship is subject to many pressures from local people, and put to its greatest test when Wolf is repatriated to Germany.

Featured as part of the " . . . a love story" series.

Linda – Lucy Gutteridge
Lord Montdore – Richard Hurndall
Christian Talbot – Ralph Lawford
Lady Montdore – Vivian Pickles
Polly – Rebecca Saire
Boy Dougdale – Job Stewart
Davey Warbech – Michael Williams

An irreverent portrait of the English upper class between the two World Wars. Uncle Matthew oversees the goings on of Sadie and her children, with particular interest focused on young Linda's romantic escapades. Lord and Lady Montdore return from India with their daughter Polly, who marries widower Boy Dougdale. Linda marries Christian Talbot, and finds herself in Paris when war breaks out in 1939. She hastily returns to London. While the rest of her family spends the war years at Alconleigh, their country estate, Linda remains in London, where she becomes pregnant, ultimately dying in childbirth.

Loosely autobiographical, the character of eccentric Uncle Matthew is based on Mitford's father, the second Baron Redesdale.

OPPENHEIMER

29 October 1980, Wednesday, 9:25–10:20pm, BBC2, 7 episodes, drama, historical, American, 20th century
BBCtv
Pr: Peter Goodchild
Dir: Barry Davis
Wtr: Peter Prince
Cast: Isidor Rabi – Barry Dennen
Hans Bethe – Matthew Guinness
Jean Tatlock – Kate Harper
Lloyd Garrison – James Maxwell
General Kenneth Nichols – Christopher Muncke
Roger Robb – Philip O'Brien
General Leslie Groves – Manning Redwood
Kitty Harrison Oppenheimer – Jana Shelden
Edward Teller – David Suchet
Robert Oppenheimer – Sam Waterston
Robert Serber – Peter Whitman

Beginning in 1938, the story of the rise

and fall of physicist Robert Oppenheimer, who, once America becomes involved in World War II, leaves his teaching job in California to work, along with several other brilliant scientists, on developing the atomic bomb in Los Alamos, New Mexico. After the war, Oppenheimer's patriotism is brought into question by "red-baiters," and in 1953 Oppenheimer is stripped of his top-secret clearance status and must choose between resignation or facing a security hearing.

Winner, BAFTA Award, Best Drama Serial 1980.

THE WATERFALL

11 November 1980, Tuesday, 8:25–9:00pm, BBC1, 4 episodes, drama, British, contemporary
BBCtv
Pr: Colin Tucker
Dir: Peter Duffell
Wtr: Peter Duffell
Based on Margaret Drabble
Cast: Malcolm Gray – Stephen Boxer
James Otford – Robin Ellis
Jane Gray – Lisa Harrow
Lucy Otford – Caroline Mortimer

Poetess Jane Gray, pregnant with her second child, is abandoned by her husband, and she soon succumbs to despair and self-doubt. Shortly afterwards, she is visited by her cousin Lucy and Lucy's husband James, and within days she and James have embarked on a passionate affair which serves to redeem Jane's belief in hope and love.

Featured as part of the " . . . a love story" series.

THE GOOD COMPANIONS

14 November 1980, Friday, 9:00–10:00pm, ITV, 9 episodes, drama, musical, British, 20th century
Yorkshire Television
Pr: Leonard Lewis
Dir: Bill Hays, Leonard Lewis
Wtr: Alan Plater
Based on J.B. Priestley
Cast: Joe Brundit – John Blythe
Elizabeth Trant – Judy Cornwell
Jerry Jerningham – Simon Green
Mrs. Joe – Jo Kendall
Elsie Longstaff – Vivienne Martin
Jimmy Nunn – Frank Mills
Inigo Jollifant – Jeremy Nicholas
Morton Mitcham – Bryan Pringle
Jess Oakroyd – John Stratton

In 1930, Jess Oakroyd leaves his home and his dead-end job and impulsively goes into show business, joining a touring concert party which becomes known as The Good Companions. The trials and tribulations, romances and adventures of the group are chronicled in drama and music as they journey across England. Ultimately, the concert party breaks up, the individuals heading off on their separate ways . . . but of course going out with a song.

The music for *The Good Companions* was written by David Fanshawe.

THE LOST TRIBE

16 November 1980, Sunday, 8:05–9:05pm, BBC2, 6 episodes, drama, Scottish, 19th–20th century
BBCtv/Scotland
Pr: Pharic Maclaren
Dir: Tom Cotter
Wtr: Jack Ronder
Cast: Moshe Kaydan (as a child) – Frank Baker
Queenie – Miriam Margolyes
Moshe Kaydan – Bill Paterson
Mrs. Kaydan – Anne Raitt

In this fictionalized account of author Jack Ronder's own family, Lithuanian Jew Moshe Kaydan flees Russian pogroms and emigrates to Scotland in 1885. Planning at first to go to America, he instead settles in Edinburgh, where he establishes a family and survives as its patriarch until his death in 1955.

THE TALISMAN

30 November 1980, Sunday, 6:05–6:35pm, BBC1, 9 episodes, drama, classic, British, 12th century
BBCtv

Pr: Barry Letts
Dir: Richard Bramall
Wtr: Anthony Steven
Based on Sir Walter Scott
Cast: Amaury – Donald Burton
   Richard the Lionheart – Stephan Chase
   Edith – Lynn Clayton
   Montserrat – Richard Morant
   Berengaria – Joanne Pearce
   Sir Kenneth – Patrick Ryecart
   Ilderim – Damien Thomas
   De Vaux – Jack Watson

Sir Kenneth, Prince Royal of Scotland, one of a group of Crusaders who must deal with the treachery of friends and the nobility of enemies while fighting side by side in the Middle East with Richard the Lionheart, is entrusted with an historic amulet which is of great symbolic importance and able to cure illnesses and heal wounds.

MARIA MARTEN

28 December 1980, Sunday, 9:15–10:10pm, BBC2, 3 episodes, drama, British, 19th century
BBCtv
Pr: Richard Beynon
Dir: Jane Howell
Wtr: Douglas Livingstone
Cast: Ann Marten – Anne Carroll
   Mr. Corder – Tenniel Evans
   Maria Marten – Pippa Guard
   Mrs. Corder – Patricia Heneghan
   Emily Corder – Sylvestra le Touzel
   Bill – Kevin McNally
   Beauty Smith – Trevor Peacock
   Nancy Marten – Tilly Vosburgh
   Mr. Marten – Edgar Wreford

In Suffolk in 1826, rebellious farmer's son Bill meets Maria Marten, and their destinies become linked by tragedy and the "murder in the red barn."

THE HISTORY MAN

4 January 1981, Sunday, 10:20–11:10pm, BBC2, 4 episodes, drama, satire, British, contemporary
BBCtv/Birmingham
Video: available in UK

Pr: Michael Wearing
Dir: Robert Knights
Wtr: Christopher Hampton
Based on Malcolm Bradbury
Cast: Flora Beniform – Isla Blair
   Henry Beamish – Paul Brooke
   Annie Callendar – Laura Davenport
   Professor Marvin – Michael Hordern
   Barbara Kirk – Geraldine James
   Felicity Phee – Veronica Quilligan
   Howard Kirk – Antony Sher
   Myra Beamish – Maggie Steed

In 1972, progressive University of Watermouth sociology lecturer Howard Kirk, who had achieved fame and notoriety for his counterculture views during the 1960s, embarks on a new term, facing an era wherein the atmosphere has shifted from optimistic radicalism to despair.

THE HITCH-HIKER'S GUIDE TO THE GALAXY

5 January 1981, Monday, 9:00–9:30pm, BBC2, 6 episodes, science fiction, British, future
BBCtv
Video: available in UK, US
Pr: Alan Bell
Dir: Alan Bell
Wtr: Douglas Adams
Based on BBC Radio series by Douglas Adams
Cast: Vogon Captain – Martin Benson
   Trillian – Sandra Dickinson
   Ford Prefect – David Dixon
   Voice of the Book – Peter Jones
   Arthur Dent – Simon Jones
   Marvin – David Learner
   Mr. Prosser – Joe Melia
   Zaphod Beeblebrox – Mark Wing-Davey

Arthur Dent is informed by his best friend Ford Prefect that the world is about to end in 12 minutes; what's more, Ford confesses that he is an alien from the planet of Betelgeuse, and offers to whisk Arthur away to outer-space safety.

SONS AND LOVERS

14 January 1981, Wednesday,

9:25–10:20pm, BBC2, 7 episodes, drama, classic, British, 19th–20th century
BBCtv
Pr: Jonathan Powell
Dir: Stuart Burge
Wtr: Trevor Griffiths
Based on D.H. Lawrence
Cast: **Gertrude Morel – Eileen Atkins**
Walter Morel – Tom Bell
William Morel – Geoffrey Burridge
Clara Dawes – Lynn Dearth
Paul Morel – Karl Johnson
Miriam – Leonie Mellinger
Annie Morel – Amanda Parfitt
Baxter Dawes – Jack Shepherd
Paul Morel (as a child) – Tom and Luke Silburn

Lawrence's autobiographical novel about the lives of a Nottinghamshire mining family from 1875 to 1910 focuses on the emerging moral consciousness of Paul Morel, whose deep attachment to his mother inhibits his ability to commit to either of the women with whom he falls in love.

SECOND CHANCE

23 January 1981, Friday, 9:00–10:00pm, ITV, 6 episodes
Yorkshire Television, drama, British, contemporary
Video: available in US
Pr: Keith Richardson
Dir: Richard Handford, Gerry Mill
Wtr: Adele Rose
Cast: **Chris Hurst – Ralph Bates**
Jill Hurst – Kate Dorning
Martin Hurst – Mark Eadie
Trevor Fuller – Steven Grives
Kate Hurst – Susannah York

After 18 years of marriage and two children, Kate and Chris Hurst decide to end their marriage. Both must make adjustments in the months which follow, and it seems that Kate, who begins a new business venture, has an easier time coping with the changes. A year after the divorce Chris and Kate meet to discuss their feelings about the past and the future.

SENSE AND SENSIBILITY

1 February 1981, Sunday, 5:25–5:55pm, BBC1, 7 episodes, drama, classic, British, 19th century
BBCtv
Video: available in UK, US
Pr: Barry Letts
Dir: Rodney Bennett
Wtr: Alexander Baron, from an outline by Denis Constanduros
Based on Jane Austen
Cast: Robert Ferrars – Philip Bowen
Fanny Dashwood – Amanda Boxer
Lucy Steele – Julia Chambers
Marianne Dashwood – Tracey Childs
Sir John Middleton – Donald Douglas
Mrs. Dashwood – Diana Fairfax
John Dashwood – Peter Gale
Mrs. Jennings – Annie Leon
Edward Ferrars – Bosco Hogan
Elinor Dashwood – Irene Richard
Colonel Brandon – Robert Swann
John Willoughby – Peter Woodward

The Dashwood sisters and their mother lose the family home, due to an entailment to the late Mr. Dashwood's son from a former marriage. In their new surroundings the two sisters – romantic Marianne, who hungers for an emotional experience, and the more practical and collected Elinor – learn painful lessons when both suffer the pangs of love gone bad; true love finally triumphs when Elinor's sense gives way to sensibility, and Marianne's sensibility gives way to sense.

BREAK IN THE SUN

11 February 1981, Wednesday, 5:05–5:35pm, BBC1, 6 episodes, drama, family, British, contemporary
BBCtv
Exec. Pr: Anna Home
Dir: Roger Singleton-Turner
Wtr: Alan England
Based on Bernard Ashley
Cast: Sylvia Green – Catherine Chase
Patsy Bligh – Nicola Cowper
Eddie Green – Brian Hall
Mrs. Broadley – Kathleen Heath
Kenny Granger – Kevin Taffurelli
Jenny – Lindsay Walker

Patsy feels neglected by her mother and mistreated by her stepfather Eddie, and runs away from their London home, joining a group of amateur actors who are on a sailing barge on the Thames, heading for Margate, where Patsy had lived with her mother and kind landlady Mrs. Broadley.

THE LIFE AND TIMES OF DAVID LLOYD GEORGE

4 March 1981, Wednesday, 9:25–10:25pm, BBC2, 9 episodes, drama, biographical, historical, British, 19th–20th century
BBCtv/Cymru/Wales
Pr: John Hefin
Designed by Pauline Harrison
Wtr: Elaine Morgan
Cast: David Lloyd George (as a child) – Dylan Jones
Megan Lloyd George – Sue Jones-Davies
David Lloyd George – Philip Madoc
Herbert Henry Asquith – David Markham
Frances Stevenson – Kika Markham
Margaret Owen Lloyd George – Lisabeth Miles

The biography of Prime Minister Lloyd George, born in 1863 and raised in Wales by his widowed mother and bachelor uncle. At 27 he wins a Liberal seat in Parliament, and by 1906 is a Cabinet Minister, setting into motion a series of seemingly-radical proposals on behalf of the underprivileged, from whose ranks he had risen. Lloyd George serves as Prime Minister from 1916 to 1922, most notably directing British policies through World War I.

MY FATHER'S HOUSE

6 March 1981, Friday, 9:00–10:00pm, ITV, 7 episodes, drama, British, 20th century
Granada Television
Pr: June Howson
Dir: Alan Grint
Wtr: Paula Milne
Based on Kathleen Conlon
Cast: **Alec Blake – Terrence Hardiman**
Anna Blake – Judy Holt
Maurice Blake – Steven Mann
Olivia – Angela Morant
Aunt Kitty – Anne Reid
Celia Blake – Helen Ryan
Jake – Simon Shepherd

Set in the late Fifties and early Sixties, young Anna Blake's life is as tumultuous as the times around her. She learns that the man who raised her is not really her father, falls in love for the first time, and finally has the chance to resolve her past when she meets her natural father . . . but old wounds may prove too deep to forget or forgive.

A SPY AT EVENING

2 April 1981, Thursday, 9:25–10:15pm, BBC1, 4 episodes, thriller, British, contemporary
BBCtv
Pr: Ron Craddock
Dir: Ben Rea
Wtr: Dave Humphries
Based on Donald James
Cast: Mansfield – Patrick Allen
Tom Hart – James Laurenson
Jazz – Ciaran Madden
Virginia – Hildegard Neil
Dyson – John Patrick
Sir Richard Considine – John Paul

Dismissed Intelligence agent Tom Hart is determined to earn his job back, and becomes involved in a deadly confrontation between right- and left-wing extremists, attempting to discover the identity of an agency informant as a means to restore himself to the agency's good graces.

BREAD OR BLOOD

5 April 1981, Sunday, 10:00–10:40pm, BBC2, 5 episodes, drama, British, 19th century
BBCtv
Pr: Ruth Caleb
Dir: Peter Smith
Wtr: Peter Ransley
Based on *A Shepherd's Life* by W.H. Hudson
Cast: Harbutt – Milton Johns
Mary Jarvis – Carolyn Pickles
Ben Jarvis – Ian Redford

Isaac Bawcombe – Malcolm Storry
Mrs. Bawcombe – Sandra Voe

In 1816, Wiltshire shepherd Isaac Bawcombe battles against hunger; his father is gone and he must provide food for himself and his mother. Despite his religious principles, Isaac is driven to poach, which causes disagreement between Isaac and his good friend, free-thinking blacksmith Ben Jarvis, a conflict which comes to a violent head during the uprising of 1830.

THE NIGHTMARE MAN

1 May 1981, Friday, 8:20–8:50pm, BBC1, 4 episodes, thriller, Scottish, contemporary
BBCtv
Pr: Ron Craddock
Dir: Douglas Camfield
Wtr: Robert Holmes
Based on *Child of Vodyanoi* by David Wiltshire
Cast: Sergeant Carch – James Cosmo
Fiona Patterson – Celia Imrie
Colonel Howard – Jonathan Newth
Inspector Inskip – Maurice Roeves
Michael Gaffikin – James Warwick
Dr. Goudry – Tom Watson

Once the summer tourists return to the Scottish mainland, the island community of Inverdee prepares for the winter, but the lives of those remaining on the island are dramatically altered as Michael Gaffikin and Inspector Inskip investigate a deadly situation which seems to involve espionage or a monster-like creature at large on Inverdee . . . or both.

PRIVATE SCHULZ

6 May 1981, Wednesday, 9:35–10:25pm, BBC2, 6 episodes, drama, German, 20th century
BBCtv
Pr: Philip Hinchcliffe
Dir: Robert Chetwyn
Wtr: Jack Pulman
Cast: **Private Schulz – Michael Elphick**
Hitler – Garn Grainger
Major Neuheim – Ian Richardson
Solly – Cyril Shaps
Bertha Freyer – Billie Whitelaw

Based-on-fact story of Germany's World War II "Operation Bernhard," a bungled attempt to flood the British wartime economy with £500 million worth of counterfeit banknotes. Petty thief Schulz is released from jail and finds himself appointed to the post of confidential clerk to SS officer Major Neuheim in Counter-Espionage, where the plan is dreamed up and executed. When all is said and done, the war is over, the plan has failed, the Germans have lost, and Schulz, penniless and dispirited, makes a last-ditch attempt to see his efforts pay off.

THE SPOILS OF WAR (third series)

30 June 1981, Tuesday, 9:00–10:00pm, ITV, 7 episodes, drama, British, 20th century
Granada Television
Pr: James Brabazon
Dir: Tristan de Vere Cole, Bill Gilmour, Laurence Moody
Wtr: John Finch, Harry Kershaw
Cast: Mark Warrington – James Bate
Martha Blaze – Anita Carey
Keir Hayward – Ian Hastings
Ros Warrington – Jane How
Blake Hayward – Alan Hunter
Emil – David Kerr
Herta – Katja Kersten
John Warrington – David Langton
George Hayward – William Lucas
Paula Brandy – Catherine Schell
Richard Warrington – Malcolm Tierney

The post-World War II saga of the Warrington and Hayward families comes to a close in 1953, focusing on such romantic issues as the relationship between Keir Hayward, now a London journalist, and Martha Blaze, and the resolution of Blake Hayward's family life, once he learns that his German lover Herta is not dead after all.

A CHANCE TO SIT DOWN

10 July 1981, Friday, 8:25–9:00pm, BBC1, 4 episodes, drama, British, contemporary
BBCtv

Pr: Colin Shindler
Dir: Paul Ciappessoni
Wtr: Meredith Daneman
Based on Meredith Daneman
Cast: Dolly – Jean Anderson
Barbara Livesay – Jan Francis
Melissa – Cherry Gillespie
George – Del Henney
Jack – Alpo Pakarinen

Ballerina Barbara Livesay's promising career – and her marriage to George – is jeopardized by her relationship with Jack, the dynamic male star of the dancing company.

Featured as part of the " . . . a love story" series.

THE ROSE MEDALLION

7 August 1981, Friday, 8:10–9:00pm, BBC1, 3 episodes, thriller, British, contemporary
BBCtv
Pr: Ron Craddock
Dir: Peter Ellis
Wtr: John Foster
Based on James Grant
Cast: Chris Condoli – Robert Beatty
Selena Cantrell – Anna Nicholas
Stanley – Dave Prowse
Sergeant Ed Kusborski – Shane Rimmer
John Mason – George Roubicek
Harry – Donald Sumpter

Stanley's discovery of an old skeleton involves him and his cousin, private investigator Harry, in an intrigue which is further complicated by the somehow-connected arrival from America of a gangster, a lawyer, a beautiful woman and a surly New York detective.

THE MEMBER FOR CHELSEA

24 August 1981, Monday (subsequent episodes aired on Tuesday and Wednesday), 9:00–10:00pm, ITV, 3 episodes, drama, historical, British, 19th century
Granada Television
Pr: June Wyndham-Davies
Dir: John Gorrie
Wtr: Ken Taylor

Cast: **Christina Rogerson – Annette Crosbie**
Maye Smith – Eleanor David
Virginia Crawford – Felicity Dean
Sir Charles Dilke – Richard Johnson
Donald Crawford – Alan Rowe

In the summer of 1885, Victorian society is rocked by the intriguing "Three-in-a-Bed" sexual and political scandal involving Sir Charles Dilke, a leading member of the Liberal party who is widely tipped to succeed Gladstone as Prime Minister. The repercussions of Dilke's being named in the divorce of Virginia and Donald Crawford lead ultimately to the ruin of Dilke's political career.

STAY WITH ME TILL MORNING

28 August 1981, Friday, 9:00–10:00pm, ITV, 3 episodes, drama, British, contemporary
Yorkshire Television
Pr: Michael Glynn
Dir: David Reynolds
Wtr: John Braine
Based on John Braine
Cast: Joan Walker – Peggy Aitchison
Stephen Belgard – Keith Barron
Vicky Kelvedon – Kate Coleridge
Petronella Lendrick – Alison Elliott
Clive Lendrick – Paul Daneman
Robin Lendrick – Nanette Newman

As Clive Lendrick prepares to celebrate his 47th birthday he looks back over his adult life, spent in Yorkshire's prosperous West Riding. Lendrick's reflections lead to impulsive action and an extra-marital affair, which prove threatening to his marriage to Robin – who is doing some romantic exploring of her own, with Stephen Belgard, who has recently returned to his native Yorkshire. And so, by the time Lendrick decides to sort out his life, it is nearly too late.

THE FLAME TREES OF THIKA

1 September 1981, Tuesday, 8:30–9:30pm,

ITV, 7 episodes, drama, British, 20th century
Euston Films in association with Consolidated Productions for Thames Television
Video: available in UK, US
Pr: John Hawkesworth, Christopher Neame
Dir: Roy Ward Baker
Wtr: John Hawkesworth
Based on Elspeth Huxley
Cast: **Elspeth – Holly Aird**
Ian Crawfurd – Ben Cross
Hereward Palmer – Nicholas Jones
Mrs. Nimmo – Carol Macready
Tilly Grant – Hayley Mills
Lettice Palmer – Sharon Mughan
Robin Grant – David Robb

Huxley's autobiographical story opens in Kenya in 1913, when 11-year-old Elspeth and her parents, Tilly and Robin Grant, begin a new life when they move to the plains of Kenya, hoping to make their fortune growing coffee.

WINSTON CHURCHILL – THE WILDERNESS YEARS

6 September 1981, Sunday, 10:00–11:00pm, ITV, 8 episodes, drama, biographical, historical, British, 20th century
Southern TV
Pr: Richard Broke
Dir: Ferdinand Fairfax
Wtr: Ferdinand Fairfax, William Humble
Based on Martin Gilbert
Cast: Stanley Baldwin – Peter Barkworth
Winston Churchill – Robert Hardy
Randolph – Nigel Havers
Adolf Hitler – Gunter Meisner
Clementine – Sian Phillips
Neville Chamberlain – Eric Porter
Bernard Baruch – Sam Wanamaker
Sir Samuel Hoare – Edward Woodward

A chronicle of the ten years between the two World Wars, during which Winston Churchill is in danger of sinking into political oblivion. In 1929 he is Chancellor of the Exchequer and, it seems, at the height of his fame and influence. But the Wall Street stock exchange crash sends his personal fortune plummeting, and, with a change in government, Churchill finds himself out of political prominence. After a meeting with Adolf Hitler, who is on the brink of power, Churchill turns all his attention to the fight against Hitler, repeatedly warning the British government to see him as a serious threat. But as Hitler becomes stronger and stronger, it seems that no one is listening to Churchill. Chamberlain signs an agreement with Hitler . . . but the British people look towards Churchill as the countdown to war begins.

BLOOD MONEY

6 September 1981, Sunday, 9:35–10:05pm, BBC1, 6 episodes, thriller, British, contemporary
BBCtv
Pr: Gerard Glaister
Dir: Michael E. Briant
Wtr: Arden Winch
Cast: Captain Percival – Michael Denison
Irene Kohl – Juliet Hammond-Hill
Chief Superintendent Meadows – Bernard Hepton
Charles Vivian – Cavan Kendall
Rupert Fitzcharles – Grant Ashley Warnock
Danny Connors – Gary Whelan
James Drew – Stephen Yardley

Rupert Fitzcharles, whose father is Administrator General of the United Nations, is kidnapped from school by unidentified terrorists. It is then up to the authorities, under the leadership of Chief Superintendent Meadows, to rally all the technical resources of the police and Special Intelligence to rescue the boy.

THE DAY OF THE TRIFFIDS

10 September 1981, Thursday, 8:30–9:00pm, BBC1, 6 episodes, science fiction, British, contemporary
BBCtv
Pr: David Maloney
Dir: Ken Hannam
Wtr: Douglas Livingstone
Based on John Wyndham
Cast: Jack Coker – Maurice Colbourne
Bill Masen – John Duttine
Dr. Soames – Jonathan Newth
Miss Durrant – Perlita Neilson

Josella Payton – Emma Relph
John – Stephen Yardley

Farmer Bill Masen attempts to stop an invasion of biologically engineered, walking, intelligent flesh-eating plants called triffids, which can kill any human that gets in their way.

TRIPODS

15 September 1981, Saturday,
5:15–5:40pm, BBC1, 13 episodes
BBCtv, science fiction, British, future
Video: available in UK, US
Pr: Richard Bates
Dir: Christopher Barry, Graham Theakston
Wtr: Alick Rowe
Based on *The White Mountains* by John Christopher
Cast: **Henry Parker – Jim Baker**
Mrs. Parker – Lucinda Curtis
Mr. Parker – Michael Gilmour
Ozymandias – Roderick Horn
Duc de Sarlat – Robin Langford
Eloise – Charlotte Long
Beanpole – Ceri Seel
Will Parker – John Shackley

In the year 2089, alien "Tripod" machine-like creatures dominate the planet; they arrive in rural England to carry out a traditional ceremony which marks the transition from childhood to adulthood for 16-year-olds (and subsequent subservience to the Tripods) – but teenaged cousins Henry and Will Parker escape with their friend Beanpole on a journey to the White Mountains of Switzerland, where they help to begin a rebellion, in the hope of finding freedom from the extra-terrestrials' control.

FANNY BY GASLIGHT

24 September 1981, Thursday,
9:25–10:20pm, BBC1, 4 episodes, drama, British, 19th century
BBCtv
Pr: Joe Waters
Dir: Peter Jefferies
Wtr: Anthony Steven
Based on Michael Sadleir
Cast: Clive Seymour – Anthony Bate
Mrs. Hopwood – Susan Brown
Lucy Beckett – Julia Chambers
Lord Manderstoke – Michael Culver
Young Fanny – Sophie Kind
Captain Charles Tennant – David Robb
Fanny Hooper – Chloe Salaman
Harry Somerford – Peter Woodward
"Duke" Hopwood – Stephen Yardley

A sinister and hypocritical quarter of Victorian London is revealed in the story of Fanny Hooper, the illegitimate child of a farmer's daughter and a Yorkshire baronet; excluded from her rightful background by reason of her mother's low class, Fanny still is set apart from the corruption around her when she learns the truth of her birth, but a fateful love affair with Harry Somerford sets the course for the rest of her life.

GREAT EXPECTATIONS

4 October 1981, Sunday, 5:45–6:40pm,
BBC1, 12 episodes
BBCtv, drama, classic, British, 19th century
Video: available in US
Pr: Barry Letts
Dir: Julian Amyes
Wtr: James Andrew Hall
Based on Charles Dickens
Cast: Mr. Jaggers – Derek Francis
Miss Havisham – Joan Hickson
Wemmick – Colin Jeavons
Magwitch – Stratford Johns
Joe Gargery – Phillip Joseph
Estella – Patsy Kensit
Pip (as a child) – Graham McGrath
Herbert Pocket – Tim Munro
Uncle Pumblechook – John Stratton
Pip – Gerry Sundquist

Orphaned blacksmith's apprentice Pip's life is changed forever when he helps escaped convict Magwitch; unknown to Pip, Magwitch is the benefactor who finances Pip's transformation into a gentleman and is also the means of ultimately uniting Pip with Estella, whom Pip has loved since they were both small children.

BRIDESHEAD REVISITED

12 October 1981, Monday, 8:00–10:00pm (subsequent episodes aired on Tuesday from 9:00–10:00pm; final episode was also two hours long), ITV, 11 episodes
Granada Television, drama, British, 20th century
Video: available in UK, US
Pr: Derek Granger
Dir: Michael Lindsay-Hogg, Charles Sturridge
Wtr: John Mortimer
Based on Evelyn Waugh
Cast: **Sebastian Flyte – Anthony Andrews**
Celia Ryder – Jane Asher
Cara – Stephane Audran
Lady Marchmain – Claire Bloom
Edward Ryder – John Gielgud
Anthony Blanche – Nickolas Grace
Mr. Samgrass – John Grillo
Charles Ryder – Jeremy Irons
Brideshead – Simon Jones
Rex Mottram – Charles Keating
Cordelia Flyte – Phoebe Nicholls
Lord Marchmain – Laurence Olivier
Julia Flyte – Diana Quick
Nanny Hawkins – Mona Washbourne

In 1944, Army officer Charles Ryder finds himself stationed at Brideshead, the grand ancestral home of the aristocratic, catholic, Marchmain family, where he had spent his happiest days as a younger man. Being there once again takes Ryder back wistfully to his years at Oxford in the 1920s and his first meeting with dazzling, seductive Sebastian Flyte, the younger son of the Marchmains. From this moment on, Charles' life is changed forever, as he becomes intimately involved with not just Sebastian, but the rest of the Marchmain family as well.

The largest film serial to date for British television, production on *Brideshead Revisited* began in 1979. Castle Howard in Yorkshire served as Brideshead Castle. Winner, BAFTA Award, Best Drama Serial 1981.

THE BORGIAS

14 October 1981, Wednesday, 9:25–10:20pm, BBC2, 10 episodes, drama, historical, Italian, 15th–16th century
BBCtv
Pr: Mark Shivas
Dir: Brian Franham
Wtr: John Prebble, Ken Taylor
Cast: Giovanni Orsini – Joss Buckley
Giuliano della Rovere – Alfred Burke
Juan Borgia – George Camiller
Rodrigo Borgia – Adolfo Celi
Cesare Borgia – Oliver Cotton
Niccolo Machiavelli – Sam Dastor
Leonardo da Vinci – Malcolm Hayes
Lucrezia Borgia – Anne Louise Lambert
Paolo Orsini – Martin Potter

Rodrigo Borgia becomes Pope Alexander VI in 1492 through a corrupt mixture of bribery, blackmail and political cunning; two of his seven children, ambitious Cesare and (perhaps literally) poisonous Lucrezia, are more than a match for their father for similarly achieving their own goals.

WILFRED AND EILEEN

11 November 1981, Wednesday, 8:30–9:00pm, BBC1, 4 episodes, drama, British, 20th century
BBCtv
Pr: Colin Shindler
Dir: David Green
Wtr: Robin Chapman
Based on Jonathan Smith
Cast: Mr. Jenkins – Michael Aldridge
Eileen – Judi Bowker
Wilfred – Christopher Guard
Mr. Willett – Harold Innocent
Mrs. Willett – Rosemary Martin

Wilfred and Eileen are married in secret in 1914, but when Wilfred joins the London Rifle Brigade and is dispatched to France when war is declared, they are torn between their love for one another and an obligation to their country.

Featured as part of the " . . . a love story" series.

KESSLER

13 November 1981, Friday, 8:00–8:50pm, BBC1, 6 episodes, drama, European, contemporary
BBCtv

Pr: Gerard Glaister
Dir: Michael E. Briant
Wtr: John Brason
Cast: **Bauer – Alan Dobie**
　　　Natalie – Juliet Hammond-Hill
　　　Albert – Bernard Hepton
　　　Ruckert – Ralph Michael
　　　Monique – Angela Richards
　　　Ludwig Kessler – Clifford Rose
　　　Mical Rak – Nitza Saul

A group of Europeans, led by British officer Bauer, journeys to Brussels, where they endeavour to identify and unmask former SS Standartenfuhrer Ludwig Kessler, who is living there as a powerful and respected family and business man, his heinous past a deeply buried secret.

GULLIVER IN LILLIPUT

3 January 1982, Sunday, 5:15–5:45pm, BBC1, 4 episodes, drama, classic, satire, British, 18th century
BBCtv
Video: available in UK, US
Pr: Ron Craddock
Dir: Barry Letts
Wtr: Barry Letts
Based on *Gulliver's Travels* by Jonathan Swift
Cast: **Gulliver – Andrew Burt**
　　　King Golbasto – Jonathan Cecil
　　　Bolgolam – Godfrey James
　　　Flimnap – George Little
　　　Lady Bolgolam – Jenny McCracken
　　　Queen – Linda Polan
　　　Lady Flimnap – Elisabeth Sladen

Swift's satire on the follies of mankind, played out via Gulliver's shipwrecked adventures among the diminutive Lilliputians.

THE STORY OF THE TREASURE SEEKERS

6 January 1982, Wednesday, 5:05–5:35pm, BBC1, 6 episodes, drama, classic, family, British, 19th century
BBCtv
Pr: Paul Stone
Dir: Roger Singleton-Turner
Wtr: Julia Jones
Based on E.E. Nesbit

Cast: Noel Bastable – Jeremy Dimmick
　　　Albert-next-door – Piers Eady
　　　Dora Bastable – Lucinda Edmonds
　　　Oswald Bastable – Simon Hill
　　　Father – David Quilter
　　　Dicky Bastable – Christopher Reilly
　　　Alice Bastable – Jayn Rosamond
　　　Horace Octavius Bastable – Timothy Stark

The children in the Bastable family decide to search for treasure in order to help the family's finances, digging up the back garden and embarking on a series of novel adventures.

FAME IS THE SPUR

8 January 1982, Friday, 8:00–8:50pm, BBC1, 8 episodes, drama, British, 19th–20th century
BBCtv
Pr: Richard Beynon
Dir: David Giles
Wtr: Elaine Morgan
Based on Howard Spring
Cast: Gordon Stansfield – David Collings
　　　Tom Hannaway – George Costigan
　　　Ann Artingstall Shawcross – Joanna David
　　　Ellen Stansfield – Paola Dionisotti
　　　Polly – Susan Edmonstone
　　　Arnold Ryerson – David Hayman
　　　Lizzie – Phyllida Law
　　　Pen Muff – Julia McKenzie
　　　Hamer Shawcross – Tim Pigott-Smith

Three friends – Hamer, Arnold and Tom – who have grown up together in the slums of Manchester, come of age in 1877, each young man determined to improve his lot in life . . . and each man's path leading in a totally different direction. In the years that follow, Tom claws his way up the social ladder and is ultimately knighted; Arnold unselfishly serves the Trade Union movement; and Hamer exploits the Labour movement for the sake of his own ambitions, becoming a Cabinet Minister and ending up in the House of Lords.

KING'S ROYAL

10 January 1982, Sunday, 7:15–8:05pm, BBC1, 10 episodes, drama, Scottish, 19th century
BBCtv/Scotland
Pr: Geraint Morris
Dir: Andrew Morgan, David Reynolds
Wtr: Ewart Alexander, Michael Elder
Based on John Quigley
Cast: **Fergus King – Tom Bell**
Robert King – Eric Deacon
Morrison – Andrew Keir
Mrs. Veitch – Anne Kristen
Fiona Fraser – Heather Moray
Gwen Hoey – Sally Osborn
Rita King – Louise Ramsay
Tom Hoey – John Vine

In Victorian Glasgow, Fergus King has risen from youth as a poor orphan to an exalted position in society, but finds his respectability threatened from within his own family; a saga of guilt, skullduggery, traumatic childbirth and other disasters follows the lives of King's whisky-blending relatives.

A second series of eight episodes, extending the King characters beyond the novel's ending, was aired in July 1983.

THE BELL

13 January 1982, Wednesday, 9:25–10:15pm, BBC2, 4 episodes, drama, British, contemporary
BBCtv
Pr: Jonathan Powell
Dir: Barry Davis
Wtr: Reg Gadney
Based on Iris Murdoch
Cast: Peter Topglass – Edward Hardwicke
Michael Meade – Ian Holm
Toby Gashe – Michael Maloney
Noel Spens – Derrick O'Connor
Dora Greenfield – Tessa Peake-Jones
Bishop – Richard Pearson
Catherine Fawley – Trudie Styler
Paul Greenfield – James Warwick

A medieval bell, long lost at the bottom of a lake, is finally being replaced by the townspeople of Imber – at the same time that Dora Greenfield leaves her husband and journeys to Imber, where she and Toby Gashe secretly retrieve the ancient bell, an act which has startlingly dramatic repercussions.

STALKY & CO.

31 January 1982, Sunday, 5:15–5:45pm, BBC1, 6 episodes, drama, British, 19th century
BBCtv
Pr: Barry Letts
Dir: Rodney Bennett
Wtr: Alexander Baron
Based on Rudyard Kipling
Cast: **Stalky – Robert Addie**
M'Turk – Robert Burbage
Beetle – David Parfitt
Mr. Prout – John Sterland
Mr. King – John Woodnutt

Three boys at a late-Victorian public school – Stalky, M'Turk and Beetle (reputedly based on Kipling himself) – repeatedly out-think, out-fight and out-wit all their enemies, whether they be masters, prefects or classmates.

NANCY ASTOR

10 February 1982, Wednesday, 9:25–10:20pm, BBC2, 9 episodes, drama, biographical, historical, American/British, 19th–20th century
BBCtv in association with Time-Life Films
Pr: Philip Hinchcliffe
Dir: Richard Stroud
Wtr: Derek Marlowe
Cast: **Robert Gould Shaw – Pierce Brosnan**
Waldorf Astor – James Fox
Lord Revelstoke – Julian Glover
Nancy Langhorne Astor – Lise Harrow
Bobbie Shaw – Nigel Havers
Phyllis – Lise Hilboldt
Harry – William Hope
Margot Asquith – Rosalind Knight
Young Nancy – Anabelle Lanyon
Lord Curzon – T.P. McKenna
Chillie Langhorne – Dan O'Herlihy
Lizzie – Jana Shelden
Nanaire – Sylvia Syms
Philip Kerr – David Warner

The biography of Nancy Langhorne Astor, beginning in 1896. Born in Virginia, unhappily married at 17 to millionaire playboy Robert Gould Shaw, Nancy later achieves still more wealth and position via her second marriage to Waldorf Astor, and becomes, in 1919, the first woman to sit in British Parliament.

ALEXA

1 March 1982, Monday, 9:25–9:55pm, BBC1, 4 episodes, drama, British, contemporary
BBCtv
Pr: Colin Shindler
Dir: Laurence Moody
Wtr: Andrea Newman
Based on Andrea Newman
Cast: **Alexa – Isla Blair**
Paul – Christopher Blake
Mrs. King – Faith Brook
Christine – Joanna David
Robert – Gary Waldhorn

When journalist Alexa goes to visit her old friend Christine, Christine is delighted to see her . . . until Alexa embarks on an affair with Christine's husband, Paul.

Featured as part of the " . . . a love story" series.

LOVE IS OLD, LOVE IS NEW

25 March 1982, Thursday, 8:30–9:00pm, BBC1, 4 episodes, drama, British, contemporary
BBCtv
Pr: Colin Shindler
Dir: Alan Grint
Wtr: Paula Milne
Cast: **Katha – Jane Asher**
Martyn – James Fox
Steven – Philip Franks
Mo – Judy Holt

Martyn and Katha joined a commune in the 1960s, but ultimately leave because they want to start a family; the strains which follow their attempts to conceive a child threaten to destroy their relationship.

Featured as part of the " . . . a love story" series.

BADGER BY OWL-LIGHT

1 April 1982, Thursday, 9:25–10:15pm, BBC1, 3 episodes, thriller, British, contemporary
BBCtv/Scotland
Pr: Bob McIntosh
Dir: Bob McIntosh
Wtr: Edward Boyd
Cast: Hardekker – Bernard Horsfall
Peter Talion – Cavan Kendall
Sarah – Carole Mowlam
Esther – Heather Wright
David – James Wynn

After a bomb explosion in the middle of London, freelance hitman Peter Talion is hired to go to Scotland to investigate the secret cult responsible . . . and eliminate its leader.

A KIND OF LOVING

4 April 1982, Sunday, 9:00–10:00pm, ITV, 10 episodes, drama, British, 20th century
Granada Television
Pr: Pauline Shaw
Dir: Oliver Horsburgh, Gerry Mill, Jeremy Summers
Wtr: Stan Barstow
Based on *A Kind of Loving*, *The Watchers on the Shore*, *The Rigid True End* by Stan Barstow
Cast: Mrs. Brown – Constance Chapman
Mr. Brown – Robert Keegan
Mrs. Rothwell – Clare Kelly
Christine – Cherith Mellor
Mr. Rothwell – Fred Pearson
Donna Pennyman – Susan Penhaligon
Albert Conroy – Neil Phillips
Miriam Graham – Hilary Tindall
Ingrid Rothwell Brown – Joanne Whalley
Vic Brown – Clive Wood

The story of the life and loves of West Riding miner's son Vic Brown begins when he is an innocent 20-year-old in the late 1950s. Vic meets and marries Ingrid Rothwell, who is pregnant with his child. Several years later Vic accepts old chum

Albert Conroy's offer of a job in Essex. The experience opens up a whole new world for Vic, including romance with actress Donna Pennyman. His marriage to Ingrid ends, as does his affair with Donna. Vic finds great success in business in the years to come . . . but is still searching for happiness when his story comes to an end in 1973.

THE BRACK REPORT

6 April 1982, Tuesday, 9:00–10:00pm, ITV, 10 episodes, drama, British, contemporary
Thames Television
Pr: Richard Bates
Dir: Bill Bain, Alan Cooke, Gordon Flemyng
Wtr: John Elliot, Christopher Penfold, David Pinner, Bruce Stewart
Cast: **Harold Harlan – Robert Lang**
Andrei Tchenkov – Daniel Massey
Sarah Challen – Sue Robinson
Angela Brack – Jenny Seagrove
Paul Brack – Donald Sumpter

Scientist Paul Brack quits his job on a project at one of Britain's nuclear power stations after a falling out with his employers. He joins up with energy consultant Harold Harlan and writes a report on Britain's energy options. But the conclusions Brack reaches, such as promoting solar energy, bring him into conflict now with Harlan. The quest for the answer to the world's energy needs quickly takes on international significance, with the Brack Report at the center of the controversy. Paul Brack is caught in the middle, both professionally and personally, and he doubts that his radical suggestions will be able to bring about the desired changes in the world.

SHACKLETON

13 April 1982, Wednesday, 9:30–10:30pm, BBC2, 4 episodes, drama, historical, British, 20th century
BBCtv
Pr: John Harris
Dir: Martyn Friend
Wtr: Christopher Ralling
Cast: Lord Curzon – Anthony Bate
Emily Shackleton – Victoria Fairbrother
Sir John Scott-Keltie – Robert James
Frank Wild – David Rodigan
Ernest Shackleton – David Schofield
Captain Robert Scott – Neil Stacy
Roald Amundsen – Benjamin Whitrow

The story of Ernest Shackleton's quest to conquer the South Pole in the early years of the century, and the rivalry between him and fellow explorers Robert Scott and Roald Amundsen.

I REMEMBER NELSON

14 April 1982, Wednesday, 9:00–10:00pm, ITV, 4 episodes, drama, historical, British, 18th–19th century
Central Television
Pr: Cecil Clarke
Dir: Simon Langton
Wtr: Hugh Whitemore
Cast: Sir William Hamilton – John Clements
Lord Nelson – Kenneth Colley
William Blackie – Phil Daniels
Emma Hamilton – Geraldine James
Lady Nelson – Anna Massey
Rev. Edmund Nelson – Laurence Naismith
Captain Thomas Hardy – Tim Pigott-Smith

Lord Nelson returns to England a national hero after the Battle of the Nile. But his personal life is not nearly so triumphant, as he is embroiled in an extra-marital affair with Emma Hamilton. Nelson leaves his wife to live with Emma, but is ultimately called back into service. At the Battle of Trafalgar, Lord Nelson fights for his country one final time.

Each episode is told from the point of view of a different character: Lady Nelson, who relates the painful details of her husband's affair with Emma Hamilton; Sir William Hamilton, the cuckolded husband who loses his wife to Nelson; Captain Thomas Hardy, the loyal naval officer who accompanies Nelson to the Battle of Trafalgar; and young seaman William Blackie, part of the gun crew on the HMS Victory.

THE WOMAN IN WHITE

14 April 1982, Wednesday, 9:45–10:40pm, BBC2, 5 episodes, mystery, British, 19th century
BBCtv
Pr: Jonathan Powell
Dir: John Bruce
Wtr: Ray Jenkins
Based on Wilkie Collins
Cast: Count Fosco – Alan Badel
  Walter Hartright – Daniel Gerroll
  Anne Catherick – Deirdra Morris
  Marian Halcombe – Diana Quick
  Frederick Fairlie – Ian Richardson
  Laura Fairlie – Jenny Seagrove
  Sir Percival Glyde – John Shrapnel
  Professor Pesca – Milo Sperber

On his last night in London, Walter Hartright has a mysterious encounter with Anne Catherick, who he discovers bears a strong resemblance to Laura Fairlie, one of the students at his new teaching post in Cumberland. When Laura is abducted and forced to take Anne's place in an asylum, it is up to Hartright to find out what is happening, a quest which is tied into a secret kept by Laura's new husband, Sir Percival Glyde.

BIRD OF PREY

22 April 1982, Thursday, 9:25–10:20pm, BBC1, 4 episodes, thriller, British, contemporary
BBCtv/Birmingham
Pr: Michael Wearing
Dir: Michael Rolfe
Wtr: Ron Hutchinson
Cast: Detective Inspector Richardson – Jim Broadbent
  Louis Vacheron – Nicolas Chagrin
  Tony Hendersly – Jeremy Child
  Henry Jay – Richard Griffiths
  Anne Jay – Carole Nimmons
  Harry Tomkins – Roger Sloman

In the course of compiling a standard report, mid-level civil servant Henry Jay accidentally uncovers a massive, computer-based international financial conspiracy, and must hold his own against "Le Pouvoir," a vast, corrupt – and murderous – network of businessmen and politicians in order to protect his life, and that of his wife Anne.

Hutchinson's sequel, *Bird of Prey 2*, also featuring Henry Jay doing high-tech battle against Le Pouvoir, aired beginning 6 September 1984.

FROST IN MAY

19 May 1982, Wednesday, 9:30–10:55pm, BBC2, 4 episodes, drama, British, 20th century
BBCtv
Pr: Anne Head
Dir: Ronald Wilson
Wtr: Alan Seymour
Based on *Frost In May*, *The Lost Traveller*, *The Sugar House* and *Beyond The Glass* by Antonia White
Cast: Claude Batchelor – John Carson
  Archie Hughes-Follett – Daniel Day-Lewis
  Stephen Tye – Rupert Frazer
  Nanda – Patsy Kensit
  Marcus Gundry – James Laurenson
  Clara – Janet Maw
  Nell Crayshaw – Meg Wynn Owen
  Isobel Batchelor – Elizabeth Shepherd
  Mother Radcliffe – Elizabeth Spriggs
  Richard Crayshaw – Tim Woodward

Based on White's four autobiographical novels, the story chronicles a period of 15 years, beginning just after World War I, and tells the story of Clara Batchelor's struggles with religious and emotional issues. As young Nanda she goes to a strict convent school, is attracted to some elements of the religious life, but gradually finds herself rebelling more and more against what she sees as unreasonable restrictions on her freedom of thought; the adult Clara becomes an actress, has an unhappy marriage, several romantic escapades, and a dangerous descent into near-madness.

SOMETHING IN DISGUISE

30 June 1982, Wednesday, 9:00–10:00pm, ITV, 6 episodes, drama, British, contemporary
Thames Television

Pr: Moira Armstrong
Dir: Moira Armstrong
Wtr: Elizabeth Jane Howard
Based on Elizabeth Jane Howard
Cast: Alice Mount – Clare Clifford
Liz – Elizabeth Garvie
Oliver – David Gwillim
May Browne-Lacey – Ursula Howells
John Cole – Anton Rodgers
Leslie Mount – Barry Stanton
Herbert Browne-Lacey – Richard Vernon

When May and Herbert wed, it is the second marriage for both. Their union does not sit well with May's son and daughter, Liz and Oliver, or with Herbert's daughter Alice, who rushes into marriage herself. Couplings and uncouplings – marital and extra-marital – and black humor abound for this extended family as everyone seeks love and happiness . . . with generally disastrous results.

In adapting her novel for television, Howard updated the action from the 1960s to the 1980s, leaving the core of the story intact.

CLOUD HOWE

14 July 1982, Wednesday, 9:30–10:25pm, BBC2, 4 episodes, drama, Scottish, 20th century
BBCtv/Scotland
Pr: Roderick Graham
Dir: Tom Cotter
Wtr: Bill Craig
Based on Lewis Grassic Gibbon
Cast: Miss Ferguson – Jo Cameron Brown
Dalziel of Meiklebogs – Donald Douglas
Robert Colquohoun – Hugh Fraser
Chris Guthrie Colquohoun – Vivien Heilbron
Else Queen – Celia Imrie
Peter Peat – Hugh Martin

In rural Scotland strong-willed Chris Guthrie, who was widowed in World War I, remarries the idealistic minister of Segget, a mill town in the lowland valley south of Aberdeen.

The second part of Gibbons' *A Scots Quair* trilogy to be serialized (*Sunset Song* was broadcast in March 1971); Vivien Heilbron reprises her role as Chris Guthrie.

AN INSPECTOR CALLS

17 August 1982, Tuesday, 8:05–8:35pm, BBC1, 3 episodes, thriller, British, 20th century
BBCtv
Pr: Ronald Smedley
Dir: Michael Simpson
Wtr: J.B. Priestley
Cast: Sheila Birling – Sarah Berger
Mr. Birling – Nigel Davenport
Inspector Goole – Bernard Hepton
Eric Birling – David Sibley
Mrs. Birling – Margaret Tyzack
Gerald Croft – Simon Ward

Priestley's play is set in the North Midlands in 1912, where the careful, protected lives of industrial family the Birlings are upended by Inspector Goole's investigation into the death of a young girl, a circumstance which ultimately implicates everyone in the family.

COUSIN PHILLIS

5 September 1982, Sunday, 5:30–6:00pm, BBC1, 4 episodes, drama, British, 19th century
BBCtv
Pr: Ray Colley
Dir: Mike Healey
Wtr: Mike Healey
Based on Mrs. Elizabeth Gaskell
Cast: Margaret Holman – Georgine Anderson
Reverend Ebenezer Holman – Ian Bannen
Paul Manning – Dominic Guard
Phillis Holman – Anne Louise Lambert
Bessie Norton – Daphne Oxenford
Edward Holdsworth – Tim Woodward

In 1863, naive Paul Manning journeys via the new railway line to Hope Farm, where he and his friend, Edward Holdsworth, meet Paul's cousin, beautiful, self-assured Phillis Holman.

Phillis is strongly attracted to Edward, and Paul encourages her feelings, leaving Phillis devastated after Edward leaves, when she learns he has married someone else.

CLAIRE

9 September 1982, Thursday, 9:30–10:20pm, BBC1, 6 episodes, drama, British, contemporary
BBCtv
Pr: Ron Craddock
Dir: John Gorrie
Wtr: Alick Rowe
Cast: Emma Williamson – Jane Downs
  Claire Terson – Caroline Embling
  Pam Hunter – Lynn Farleigh
  Tony Hunter – William Gaunt
  Robert – Neil Nisbet

The Hunter family takes in foster child Claire, who has been in care for almost eight years; the several months that follow prove a difficult period of adjustment for all involved.

SMILEY'S PEOPLE

20 September 1982, Monday, 8:00–9:00pm, BBC2, 6 episodes, thriller, British, contemporary
BBCtv
Video: available in UK
Pr: Jonathan Powell
Dir: Simon Langton
Wtr: John Hopkins, John le Carré
Based on John le Carré
Cast: Madame Ostrakova – Eileen Atkins
   Oliver Lacon – Anthony Bate
   Mother Felicity – Rosalie Crutchley
   Detective Chief Superintendent – Michael Elphick
   Mikhel – Michael Gough
   George Smiley – Alec Guinness
   Toby Esterhase – Bernard Hepton
   The General – Curt Jurgens
   Grigoriev – Michael Lonsdale
   Lauder Strickland – Bill Paterson
   Otto Leipzig – Vladek Sheybal
   Karla – Patrick Stewart
   Oleg Kirov – Dudley Sutton

George Smiley returns once more to the "Circus" of government service, at the request of Oliver Lacon, to investigate the mystery surrounding the death of a Soviet General who was a double agent, an intrigue which involves Smiley in his final confrontation with long-time adversary Karla.

THE HOUND OF THE BASKERVILLES

3 October 1982, Sunday, 6:10–6:40pm, BBC1, 4 episodes, mystery, classic, British, 19th century
BBCtv in association with RCTV, Inc.
Pr: Barry Letts
Dir: Peter Duguid
Wtr: Alexander Baron
Based on Sir Arthur Conan Doyle
Cast: Beryl Stapleton – Kay Adshead
   Sherlock Holmes – Tom Baker
   Sir Charles Baskerville – John Boswall
   Sir Hugo Baskerville – Terry Forrestal
   Selden – Michael Goldie
   Stapleton – Christopher Ravenscroft
   Dr. Watson – Terence Rigby
   Sir Henry Baskerville – Nicholas Woodeson

The terrifying legend of a ghostly hound which stalks the Baskerville family has apparently found a real-life victim in Sir Charles Baskerville, who is mysteriously killed. Sir Henry seems destined to fall next . . . until the fateful intervention of Baker Street's finest, aided by his loyal friend Dr. Watson.

HARRY'S GAME

25 October 1982, Monday 9:00–10:00pm, (subsequent episodes aired on Tuesday and Wednesday), ITV, 3 episodes, thriller, British, contemporary
Yorkshire Television
Video: available in UK
Pr: Keith Richardson
Dir: Lawrence Gordon Clark
Wtr: Gerald Seymour
Based on Gerald Seymour
Cast: Minister of Defence – Denys Hawthorne
   Harry Brown – Ray Lonnen
   Theresa McCorrigan – Linda Robson
   Billy Downes – Derek Thompson

Commissioner of Police – Gary
  Waldhorn
Davidson – Benjamin Whitrow

After the brutal murder of a Cabinet Minister in London, British agent Captain Harry Brown is sent to Belfast on a secret search for a ruthless IRA assassin. Working undercover, Harry must strive to find the killer before he himself is exposed to the IRA.

BEAU GESTE

31 October 1982, Sunday, 6:10–6:40pm, BBC1, 8 episodes, drama, classic, adventure, British, 19th century
BBCtv
Pr: Barry Letts
Dir: Douglas Camfield
Wtr: Alistair Bell
Based on P.C. Wren
Cast: **Digby Geste – Anthony Calf**
  Young Digby – Robin Crane
  Young John – Paul Critchley
  Buddy – Barry Dennen
  Sergeat Major Lejaune – John Forgeham
  Young Beau – Paul Hawkins
  Hank – Christopher Malcolm
  John Geste – Jonathon Morris
  Major de Beaujolais – David Sumner
  Beau Geste – Benedict Taylor
  Lady Brandon – Wendy Williams

Wren's famous story of brotherly love, self-sacrifice and adventure in the French Foreign Legion begins when Major de Beaujolais leads a relief column to Fort Zinderneuf, where he encounters a baffling and macabre series of mysteries, involving the disappearance of the Blue Water sapphire and culminating in a mutiny at the Fort and a noble, final fight by the Legionnaires.

THE LIFE AND ADVENTURES OF NICHOLAS NICKLEBY

7 November 1982, Sunday, 7:00–9:00pm (final episode was three hours), Channel 4, 4 episodes, drama, classic, British, 19th century
Primetime Television in association with RM Productions
Video: available in US
Pr: Colin Callender
Dir: Jim Goddard
Wtr: David Edgar
Based on Charles Dickens
Cast: Wackford Squeers – Alun Armstrong
  Mr. Vincent Crummles – Christopher Benjamin
  Fanny Squeers – Suzanne Bertish
  Mrs. Nickleby – Jane Downs
  Madeline – Lucy Gutteridge
  Mrs. Squeers/Mrs. Crummles – Lila Kaye
  Mr. Mantilini – John McEnery
  Newman Noggs – Edward Petherbridge
  Nicholas Nickleby – Roger Rees
  Kate Nickleby – Emily Richard
  Smike – David Threlfall
  Ralph Nickleby – John Woodvine

Following the fortunes of Nicholas Nickleby and his sister, Kate, cast into a hostile English world by their cruel Uncle Ralph in the 1830s. Nicholas befriends the crippled Smike, and the two are friends until the end, which melds tragedy and triumph.

Based on and featuring the cast of the Royal Shakespeare Company production directed by Trevor Nunn and John Caird, in which 39 performers played more than 150 roles; only Roger Rees, as Nicholas, played a single part. This was the first multi-part drama to be broadcast on Channel 4, the first major drama to be made for the new network by an independent production company.

Winner, Emmy Award, Outstanding Limited Series 1982–1983.

THE BARCHESTER CHRONICLES

10 November 1982, Wednesday, 9:25–10:20pm, BBC2, 7 episodes, drama, British, 19th century
BBCtv
Video: available in UK
Pr: Jonathan Powell
Dir: David Giles
Wtr: Alan Plater
Based on *The Warden* and *Barchester Towers* by Anthony Trollope

Cast: John Bold – David Gwillim
Signora Madeline Neroni – Susan Hampshire
Archdeacon Grantly – Nigel Hawthorne
Bishop Grantly – Cyril Luckham
Eleanor Harding – Janet Maw
Mrs. Proudie – Geraldine McEwan
Susan Grantly – Angela Pleasence
Septimus Harding – Donald Pleasence
Obadiah Slope – Alan Rickman

One summer in the 1850s, Septimus Harding, the gentle and respected Warden of Hiram's Hospital in the cathedral city of Barchester, unwittingly becomes the central figure in a national scandal when the Church is accused of corruption and he is caught in the middle of a power struggle between bishop's wife Mrs. Proudie and nasty chaplain Obadiah Slope.

MR. RIGHT

4 January 1983, Tuesday, 9:25–9:55pm, BBC1, 4 episodes, drama, British, 20th century
BBCtv
Pr: Colin Shindler
Dir: Peter Smith
Wtr: Peter Prince
Based on *A Spring Of Love* by Celia Dale
Cast: **Raymond – David Hayman**
Esther – Carolyn Pickles
Gran – Liz Smith
Gloria – Gwyneth Strong
Terry – Ray Winstone

In 1956, Esther lives quietly in London with Gran, who despairs of Esther's ever finding a husband – until Esther meets Raymond. At first it appears that Raymond is every woman's dream come true, but Esther becomes increasingly suspicious of his odd behavior . . . which soon becomes dangerous and threatening.

Featured as part of the " . . . a love story" series.

THE FORGOTTEN STORY

9 January 1983, Sunday, 5:30–6:00pm, ITV, 6 episodes, drama, family, British, 19th century
HTV
Pr: Martin Schute
Dir: John Jacobs
Wtr: Arden Winch
Based on Winston Graham
Cast: Ned – George Camiller
Madge – Lila Kaye
Perry – Van Johnson
Patricia – Angharad Rees
Joe Veal – John Stratton
Anthony – Alexis Woutas

In the 1890s, 11-year-old Anthony is sent from the United States to live with his Uncle Joe Veal in the West England seaport of Falmouth. It's an exciting and frightening new world for Anthony, but the frights quickly become all too real when Joe suddenly dies and it seems Anthony is left alone and helpless in the grasp of those who want his uncle's fortune for themselves.

SKORPION

12 January 1983, Wednesday, 9:25–9:55pm, BBC1, 6 episodes, thriller, British, contemporary
BBCtv
Pr: Gerard Glaister
Dir: Michael Hayes
Wtr: John Brason
Based on story idea by Arden Winch
Cast: **Gabrielle – Marianne Borgo**
Captain Percival – Michael Denison
Chief Superintendent Franks – Terrence Hardiman
Inspector Clarke – Daniel Hill
Constant Delangre – Neville Jason
Chief Inspector Perry – Jack McKenzie
Agatha – Mary Wimbush

Chief Superintendent Franks investigates a mysterious plane crash on the Scottish moors, which is linked with a terrorist's assassination plot, and it is up to Franks and his associates to identify the assassin and stop him before he hits his target, a search which moves between Paris and London before the ultimate confrontation back in Scotland.

DOMBEY AND SON

16 January 1983, Sunday, 5:25 5:55pm, BBC1, 10 episodes, drama, classic, British, 19th century
BBCtv
Pr: Barry Letts
Dir: Rodney Bennett
Wtr: James Andrew Hall
Based on Charles Dickens
Cast: **Florence Dombey Gay – Lysette Anthony**
Paul – Barnaby Buik
Susan Nipper – Zelah Clarke
Major Bagstock – James Cossins
James Carker – Paul Darrow
Fanny Dombey – Patricia Donovan
Dombey – Julian Glover
Walter Gay – Max Gold
Captain Cuttle – Emrys James
Louisa Chick – Rhoda Lewis
Solomon Gills – Roger Milner
Edith Dombey – Sharon Mughan

Wealthy widowed Victorian merchant Dombey adores his son Paul and virtually ignores his daughter Florence. When Paul dies, Dombey turns not to his daughter, but to his selfish new wife Edith for comfort, and by the time he realizes the compounded errors of his ways it is nearly too late to make amends.

THE CLEOPATRAS

19 January 1983, Wednesday, 10:05–10:55pm, BBC2, 8 episodes, drama, historical, Ancient Egypt
BBCtv
Pr: Guy Slater
Dir: John Frankau
Wtr: Philip Mackie
Cast: Grypus – James Aubrey
Cleopatra Tryphaena – Amanda Boxer
Cleopatra Selene – Prue Clarke
Pot Belly – Richard Griffiths
Julius Caesar – Robert Hardy
Cleopatra IV – Sue Holderness
Chickpea – David Horovitch
Alexander I – Ian McNeice
Berenike – Pauline Moran
Cleopatra Thea – Caroline Mortimer
Mark Antony – Christopher Neame
Cleopatra – Michelle Newell
Cleopatra Tryphaena II – Emily Richard
Queen Cleopatra – Elizabeth Shepherd

A wry look at Alexandrian life under the rule of the Cleopatras, seven in all, covering the years 145–35 BC, beginning with Queen Cleopatra's marriage to her brother Pot Belly, which secures her ascension to the throne, and culminating in the ambitious, legendary figure who aspired to expand the Egyptian Empire across the world, but is perhaps best-known for her ill-fated romances with Julius Caesar and Mark Antony.

Michelle Newell plays the final Cleopatra and, in the opening episode, her great-grandmother.

THE CITADEL

20 January 1983, Thursday, 9:25–10:20pm, BBC1, 10 episodes, drama, British, 20th century
BBCtv
Pr: Ken Riddington
Dir: Peter Jefferies, Mike Vardy
Wtr: Don Shaw
Based on A.J. Cronin
Cast: **Andrew Manson – Ben Cross**
Dr. Page – Tenniel Evans
Sir Jenner Halliday – Michael Gough
Christine Barlow Manson – Clare Higgins
Mr. Hopper – Charles Kay
Charles Ivory – John Nettleton
Miss Cramb – Susan Porrett
Joe Morgan – David Pugh
Philip Denny – Gareth Thomas
Sir Robert Abbey – John Welsh

Young doctor Andrew Manson arrives in a Welsh mining town in the 1930s, full of enthusiasm to begin his career, but Andrew's ambitions soon outstrip the local possibilities, and he sacrifices ideals to material gain before learning – and losing – what is truly valuable in life.

THE HARD WORD

25 January 1983, Tuesday, 9:00–10:00pm, ITV, 6 episodes, drama, British, contemporary

Thames Television
Pr: Michael Chapman
Dir: Peter Hammond
Wtr: Geoffrey Case, John Finch
Cast: **David Wood – Ian Bannen**
Billy Clough – Duggie Brown
Vicky Clough – Sharon Duce
Sarah Wood – Lynn Farleigh
John Clough – Bob Keegan

Billy Clough resettles his family from the North to Kent, where he hopes to find work. At the same time, established executive David Wood's life is shattered when he unexpectedly loses his job. While seeming to be from different worlds, Billy and David and their families go through similar experiences as each man tries to chart a new path for himself.

NUMBER 10

13 February 1983, Sunday, 9:10–10:10pm, ITV, 7 episodes, drama, historical, British, 19th–20th century
Yorkshire Television
Pr: Margaret Bottomley
Dir: David Cunliffe, John Glenister, Alvin Rakoff, David Reynolds, Herbert Wise
Wtr: Terence Feely
Cast: **Duke of Wellington – Bernard Archard**
William Pitt the Younger – Jeremy Brett
Harriet Arbuthnot – Gabrielle Drake
Mrs. Gladstone – Celia Johnson
Frances Stevenson – Barbara Kellermann
Eleanor Eden – Caroline Langrishe
Asquith – David Langton
Margaret Lloyd George – Rhoda Lewis
William Ewert Gladstone – Denis Quilley
Disraeli – Richard Pasco
Ishbel MacDonald – Emma Piper
James Ramsay MacDonald – Ian Richardson
Lady Bradford – Elizabeth Sellars
David Lloyd George – John Stride
Mrs. Asquith – Dorothy Tutin
Queen Victoria – Zena Walker

Number 10 Downing Street first opened its doors to politicians in 1882. The lives of its first seven inhabitants, Prime Ministers Gladstone, MacDonald, Lloyd George, Duke of Wellington, Asquith, Disraeli, and Pitt, are examined, with emphasis on their personal rather than professional exploits.

THE MACHINE GUNNERS

23 February 1983, Wednesday, 5:10–5:35pm, BBC1, 6 episodes, drama, family, British, 20th century
BBCtv
Exec. Pr: Paul Stone
Dir: Colin Cant
Wtr: William Corlett
Based on Robert Westall
Cast: Rudi Gerlath – Jurgen Anderson
Audrey Parton – Debbie Breen
Nicky Nichol – Alastair Craig
Clogger Duncan – Andrew Craig
Cem Jones – Tony Saint
Chas McGill – Shaun Taylor
Headmaster – Des Young

In 1941, a group of youngsters in Tyneside sets out to do their bit for the war effort, and get more than they bargained for when they discover a machine gun . . . and befriend a German Luftwaffe pilot who crash lands in the region.

MY COUSIN RACHEL

7 March 1983, Monday, 8:30–9:25pm, BBC2, 4 episodes, drama, British, 19th century
BBCtv
Pr: Richard Beynon
Dir: Brian Farnham
Wtr: Hugh Whitemore
Based on Daphne du Maurier
Cast: **Cousin Rachel – Geraldine Chaplin**
Philip – Christopher Guard
Rainaldi – Charles Kay
Ambrose Ashley – John Shrapnel
Nick Kendall – John Stratton

On his annual winter trip abroad, Ambrose happens upon a distant relation, the Contessa Sangalletti – his cousin Rachel. Rachel and Ambrose marry, but he dies shortly afterwards, and the mysterious circumstances surrounding his death are investigated by another cousin,

Philip, who wonders whether or not Ambrose was poisoned by his seemingly sweet and sincere new bride.

WIDOWS

16 March 1983, Wednesday,
9:00–10:00pm, ITV, 6 episodes, thriller, British, contemporary
Thames Television
Video: available in UK
Pr: Linda Agran
Dir: Ian Toynton
Wtr: Lynda La Plante
Cast: Det. Inspector George Resnick – David Calder
Shirley Miller – Fiona Hendley
Dolly Rawlins – Ann Mitchell
Bella O'Reilly – Eva Mottley
Linda Perelli – Maureen O'Farrell

Dolly Rawlins, Linda Perelli and Shirley Miller are widowed when their husbands, members of a robbery gang, die while attempting to rob a security van. The three women band together and decide to carry out the robbery planned by the gang, using the notes left behind by the gang's leader. Unknown to them, the police are suspicious and carefully monitor their movements. But the women successfully pull off the robbery . . . and must then make their way out of the country with a suitcase stuffed with money.

A sequel to this serial was aired starting 3 April 1985, involving the women's adventures when they were tracked down by Dolly's husband, who had faked his own death; this time Dolly makes sure he dies for real, but in the process her two comrades also lose their lives and Dolly finds herself imprisoned on a murder charge . . . leaving behind a fortune in stolen diamonds.

DEATH OF AN EXPERT WITNESS

8 April 1983, Friday, 9:00–10:00pm, ITV, 7 episodes, mystery, British, contemporary
Anglia Television
Pr: John Rosenberg
Dir: Herbert Wise
Wtr: Robin Chapman
Based on P.D. James
Cast: Henry Kerrison – Ray Brooks
Domenica Howard – Meg Davies
Maxim Howarth – Barry Foster
Brenda Pridmore – Chloe Franks
Sir Charles Freeborn – Peter Howell
Adam Dalgliesh – Roy Marsden
Edwin Lorrimer – Geoffrey Palmer
Clifford Bradley – Andrew Ray
Stella Mawson – Fiona Walker

Detective Chief Superintendent Adam Dalgliesh is called to Norfolk to investigate the murder of a 19-year-old girl. Dalgliesh is aided by forensic biologist Edwin Lorrimer . . . who soon becomes the murderer's second victim. Dalgliesh's list of suspects grows with each question asked – and then yet another murder occurs. Raw nerves are exposed in the tight-knit community as Dalgliesh struggles to identify the killer in its midst.

Death of an Expert Witness marked the first television appearance of sensitive, poetry-writing crime solver Adam Dalgliesh.

THE FILE ON JILL HATCH

29 April 1983, Friday, 9:30–10:25pm, BBC2, 3 episodes, drama, British, contemporary
BBCtv
Pr: Alan Shallcross
Dir: Alastair Reid
Wtr: Kenneth Cavander
Cast: Jill – Penny Johnson
Carl – Joe Morton
Sheila – Frances Tomelty
Billy – Tim Woodward

Black American GI Carl marries Sheila, a white woman from Bristol, at the end of World War II. In the years that follow their lives and those of their respective family members interconnect in a number of ways, culminating with the sad, tragic life of their daughter Jill, all of this examined by Metropolitan Police officer Billy following the Brixton riots in 1981.

THE CONSULTANT

11 June 1983, Saturday, 10:10–11:00pm,
BBC1, 4 episodes, drama, British,
contemporary
BBCtv
Pr: Ron Craddock
Dir: Cyril Coke
Wtr: Alan Plater
Based on John McNeil
Cast: **Chris Webb – Hywel Bennett**
Harrington – Donald Burton
Alloway – Philip Jackson
Jake Kennedy – Jonathon Morris
Harvey – David Shaughnessy
Jennifer – Pamela Salem
Sir Neville Johnson – Geoffrey Toone

Chris Webb is determined to rise to the top in the competitive world of computer consultants; when he is hired to seek out fraud in a major bank's computer system he is drawn into a complicated network of deception, electronic blackmail and murder.

A MARRIED MAN

10 July 1983, Sunday, 9:15–10:30pm,
Channel 4, 4 episodes, drama, British,
contemporary
London Weekend Television
Video: available in US
Pr: John Davies
Dir: Charles Jarrott
Wtr: Derek Marlowe
Based on Piers Paul Read
Cast: Jilly Mascall – Tracey Childs
Henry Mascall – Clive Francis
Paula Gerrard – Lise Hilboldt
**John Strickland – Anthony Hopkins
Clare Strickland – Ciaran Madden**

Successful barrister John Strickland is at a midlife crossroads, discontented with both his marriage and his career. In a desperate attempt to change the pattern and return to the ideals of his youth, he rejoins the Labour Party and stands for Parliament. In the months that follow many changes do take place, in both Strickland's personal and professional lives . . . but in the end they have a disastrous impact on Strickland and those close to him.

THE MAD DEATH

16 July 1983, Saturday, 9:40–10:35pm,
BBC1, 3 episodes, thriller, British,
contemporary
BBCtv/Scotland
Video: available in US
Pr: Bob McIntosh
Dir: Robert Young
Wtr: Sean Hignett
Based on Nigel Slater
Cast: Tom Siegler – Ed Bishop
Miss Stonecroft – Brenda Bruce
Michael Hilliard – Richard Heffer
Norma Siegler – Valerie Holliman
Dr. Anne Maitland – Barbara Kellermann
Bill Stanton – Jimmy Logan
Johnny Dalry – Richard Morant

A pet cat, afflicted with rabies, is smuggled into Britain, and the disease spreads among the animal population – undetected by the general populace until the first human falls victim to the deadly disease. It is then up to a small group of medical professionals to attempt to stop the "mad death" before it becomes an epidemic.

GREY GRANITE

3 August 1983, Wednesday, 8:00–9:00pm,
BBC2, 3 episodes, drama, Scottish, 20th
century
BBCtv/Scotland
Pr: Roderick Graham
Dir: Tom Cotter
Wtr: Bill Craig
Based on Lewis Grassic Gibbon
Cast: Meg Watson – Maureen Carr
Stephen Selden – Paul Dalton
Chris Colquohoun – Vivien Heilbron
Ma Cleghorn – Eileen McCallum
Ewan Tavandale – Peter Raffan

Chris Colquohoun's son Ewan comes of age in the Scottish town of Duncairn.

The third and final instalment of Gibbon's *A Scots Quair* trilogy, following *Sunset Song* and *Cloud Howe*.

ONE SUMMER

7 August 1983, Sunday, 10:15–11:15pm, Channel 4, 5 episodes, drama, British, contemporary
Yorkshire Television
Pr: Keith Richardson
Dir: Gordon Flemyng
Wtr: Willie Russell
Cast: Kidder – James Hazeldine
**Icky Higson – Spencer Leigh
Billy Rizley – David Morrissey**

Billy and Icky, teenaged school chums from Liverpool, play truant during their final term. The boys then find themselves unexpectedly spending the summer in the Welsh countryside, where an all-too-brief idyllic few weeks changes the way the boys look at themselves and the world around them.

CALEB WILLIAMS

20 August 1983, Saturday, 10:15–11:40pm, Channel 4, 6 episodes, drama, British, 18th century
Tyne Tees Television in association with Tele-munchen
Pr: Ted Childs, Norton Romsey
Dir: Herbert Wise
Wtr: Robin Chapman
Based on *The Adventures of Caleb Williams (Or Things As They Are)* by William Godwin
Cast: **Jane – Chrissie Cotterill
Caleb Williams – Mick Ford
Falkland – Gunther Maria Halmer**
Mrs. Williams – Polly Hemingway
Tyrell – Stephen Rea
George Williams – Franz Rudnick

Young Caleb's father, an 18th-century estate worker, is hanged for murdering landowner Tyrell, although he is innocent. Grief-stricken Caleb goes to work for country squire Falkland, but most of his attention is directed to his determined search to clear his father's name . . . a search which ultimately leads to the front door of Falkland's manor.

KILLER

6 September 1983, Tuesday, 9:00–10:00pm, ITV, 3 episodes, thriller, Scottish, contemporary
Scottish Television
Pr: Robert Love
Dir: Laurence Moody
Wtr: Glen Chandler
Cast: Alison Taggart – Geraldine Alexander
Jean Taggart – Harriet Buchan
Detective Sergeant Peter Livingstone – Neil Duncan
Joe Ballantyne – Hugh Martin
Detective Chief Inspector Jim Taggart – Mark McManus
Superintendent Murray – Tom Watson

A murderer is loose in Glasgow, and a major police investigation is mounted to find the killer. The search is headed by top detective Jim Taggart, a tough local cop who has risen through the ranks. Working with Taggart is young "up-market" policeman Peter Livingstone, and although the two are different in many ways, they share an intense desire to find the killer before he strikes again.

Killer introduced the character of Jim Taggart, whose subsequent crime-solving exploits (beginning 2 July 1985) were simply titled *Taggart*, and who continued to make regular multi-part appearances (more than two dozen in all) until Mark McManus' death in June 1994; the final *Taggart* story, which was produced before McManus' death, aired beginning 11 January 1995.

THE GATHERING SEED

7 September 1983, Wednesday, 10:00–10:55pm, BBC2, 6 episodes, drama, British, 20th century
BBCtv
Pr: Colin Tucker
Dir: Tom Clegg
Wtr: Jim Allen
Cast: Jim Larkin – James Ellis
Kitty Henshaw – Brenda Fricker
Lizzie Scanlon – Christine Hargreaves
Sarah Goldman – Caroline Hutchison
Peggy Henshaw – Karen Meagher
Joe Henshaw (as a child) – David Philburn
Joe Henshaw – David Threlfall

Joe Henshaw turns 13 in Manchester in 1936; ten years later he comes of age, returning home after serving in the Army in World War II to find that the world has changed tremendously. Anything seems possible to the now-grown Joe, who becomes involved in workers' rights at the same time the Labour Party is victorious in national government.

A BROTHER'S TALE

9 September 1983, Friday, 9:00–10:00pm, ITV, 3 episodes, drama, British, contemporary
Granada Television
Pr: Pauline Shaw
Dir: Les Chatfield
Wtr: Stan Barstow
Based on Stan Barstow
Cast: **Gordon Taylor – Trevor Eve**
Eileen Taylor – Belinda Lang
Bonny Taylor – Kevin McNally
Lucy Browning – June Ritchie
John Pycock – Ivor Roberts

Flamboyant footballer Bonny Taylor, whose ebbing career is threatened by his turbulent private life, is suspended by his club and takes refuge with his brother Gordon and sister-in-law Eileen, teachers who live quietly in Yorkshire. Bonny's arrival disrupts the orderly pattern of Gordon and Eileen's lives, ultimately leaving what may be irreparable damage in its wake.

THE DARK SIDE OF THE SUN

13 September 1983, Tuesday, 9:25–10:20pm, BBC1, 6 episodes, mystery, British, contemporary
BBCtv
Pr: Vere Lorrimer
Dir: David Askey
Wtr: Michael J. Bird
Cast: Ismini Christoyannis – Betty Arvanti
Raoul Lavalliere – Peter Egan
Don Tierney – Patrick Mower
Anne Tierney – Emily Richard
David Bascombe – Christopher Scoular

Photographer Don Tierney arrives on the Greek island of Rhodes determined to unlock the secrets behind the mysterious, guarded castle overlooking the sea, unaware of the deadly, supernatural terror which lies waiting behind its walls. After Don's reported death, his wife Anne comes to the castle hoping to come to terms with her loss . . . and instead comes face to face herself with haunting secrets and images which may or may not be real, but which do pose a very real threat to her life.

THE OLD MEN AT THE ZOO

15 September 1983, Thursday, 9:30–10:20pm, BBC2, 5 episodes, drama, satire, British, 20th century
BBCtv
Pr: Jonathan Powell
Dir: Stuart Burge
Wtr: Troy Kennedy Martin
Based on Angus Wilson
Cast: Mr. Sanderson – Andrew Cruickshank
Dr. Edwin Leacock – Maurice Denham
Martha Carter – Toria Fuller
Emile Englander – Marius Goring
Lord Godmanchester – Robert Morley
Dr. Charles Langley-Beard – John Phillips
Sir Robert Falcon – Robert Urquhart
Simon Carter – Stuart Wilson
Matthew Price – Richard Wordsworth

Set in the a not-too-distant future, newly-appointed Secretary of the National Zoo Simon Carter is immediately presented with a crisis when Smokey the giraffe goes berserk. This sets into action a bizarre chain of events which satirically examine the British social and political structure, focusing on three fanatically eccentric old men who control the fortunes and futures of the zoo and those who work there.

JANE EYRE

9 October 1983, Sunday, 6:00–6:30pm, BBC1, 11 episodes, drama, classic, British, 19th century
BBCtv
Video: available in UK, US

Pr: Barry Letts
Dir: Julian Amyes
Wtr: Alexander Baron
Based on Charlotte Brontë
Cast: St. John Rivers – Andrew Bicknell
Bertha – Joolia Cappleman
Jane Eyre – Zelah Clarke
Mrs. Reed – Judy Cornwell
Mr. Rochester – Timothy Dalton
Grace Poole – Carol Gillies
Mrs. Fairfax – Jean Harvey
Jane Eyre (as a child) – Sian Pattenden
Richard Mason – Damien Thomas
Adele – Blanche Youinou

Neglected orphan Jane Eyre spends her childhood years at the Lowood School, eventually becoming a teacher there. The fiercely independent young woman leaves Lowood for a job as a governess at Thornfield, the remote estate of mysterious yet dashing Mr. Rochester; a passionate romance develops between them, but the lovers are separated for some time by circumstance and distance before they can be together.

BY THE SWORD DIVIDED

16 October 1983, Sunday, 7:45–8:40pm, BBC1, 10 episodes, drama, British, 17th century
BBCtv in association with Consolidated Productions
Pr: Brian Spiby
Dir: Brian Farnham, Henry Herbert
Wtr: Alexander Baron, John Hawkesworth, Jeremy Paul, Alfred Shaughnessy
Created by John Hawkesworth
Cast: Lucinda Lacey – Lucy Aston
Tom Lacey – Timothy Bentinck
Susan Protheroe – Judy Buxton
King Charles I – Jeremy Clyde
Will Saltmarsh – Simon Dutton
John Fletcher – Rob Edwards
Sir Martin Lacey – Julian Glover
Anne Lacey Fletcher – Sharon Mughan
Colonel Hannibal Marsh – Malcolm Stoddard

This romantic but historically authentic recreation of the English Civil War of the 1640s focuses on the conflict between the Royalist Laceys and their Parliamentary relatives. Shortly after the wedding of Anne Lacey to John Fletcher, the two families find themselves on opposing sides in the dispute, with dramatic ramifications.

GOOD BEHAVIOUR

28 October 1983, Friday, 9:25–10:25pm, BBC2, 3 episodes, drama, Irish, contemporary
BBCtv
Pr: Terry Coles
Dir: Bill Hays
Wtr: Hugh Leonard
Based on Molly Keane
Cast: Mrs. Brock – Judy Cornwell
Mother – Hannah Gordon
Aroon (as a child) – Henrietta Manktelow
Major – Daniel Massey
Aroon St. Charles – Joanna McCallum
Hubert – Timothy Sinclair

In middle age, Aroon St. Charles looks back on her childhood in the south of Ireland in the years before World War II, the discomfort and clumsiness she felt as a young girl reflected as well in the unhappy lives of the adults around her.

MANSFIELD PARK

6 November 1983, Sunday, 10:10–11:00pm, BBC2, 6 episodes, drama, classic, British, 19th century
BBCtv
Video: available in UK, US
Pr: Betty Willingale
Dir: David Giles
Wtr: Ken Taylor
Based on Jane Austen
Cast: Maria Bertram Rushworth – Samantha Bond
Henry Crawford – Robert Burbage
Julia Bertram – Liz Crowther
Fanny Price (as a child) – Katy Durham-Matthews
Edmund Bertram – Nicholas Farrell
Sir Thomas Bertram – Bernard Hepton
Fanny Price – Sylvestra Le Touzel
Mrs. Norris – Anna Massey
Lady Bertram – Angela Pleasence

Mary Crawford – Jackie Smith-Wood
Mr. Rushworth – Jonathan Stephens
Tom Bertram – Christopher Villiers

Fanny Price's life changes forever when she is removed from her impoverished Portsmouth home and taken to live with the Bertrams, her rich relations at Mansfield Park; she is patronized by several of her cousins, but befriended by clergyman Edmund Bertram, with whom she eventually finds lasting happiness.

SPYSHIP

9 November 1983, Wednesday,
8:05–9:00pm, BBC1, 6 episodes, thriller,
British, contemporary
BBCtv/Pebble Mill
Pr: Colin Rogers
Dir: Michael Custance
Wtr: James Mitchell
Based on Brian Haynes, Tom Keene
Cast: Sir Peter Hillmore – Michael Aldridge
Francis Main – Peter Eyre
Simon Tate – Paul Geoffrey
Evans – Phil Hynd
Suzy Summerfield – Lesley Nightingale
Erik Starvik – Bjorn Sundquist
Martin Taylor – Tom Wilkinson

In the Arctic waters off northern Norway, the military forces of NATO and the Soviet Union play a dangerous cat-and-mouse game of surveillance and counter-surveillance. At the same time, deep-sea trawlers of several nations set sail on fishing expeditions in the same waters; one such ship, the Caistor, which carries among others British journalist Martin Taylor, mysteriously disappears.

JOHNNY JARVIS

10 November 1983, Thursday,
9:25–10:15pm, BBC1, 6 episodes, drama,
British, contemporary
BBCtv
Pr: Guy Slater
Dir: Alan Dossor
Wtr: Nigel Williams
Cast: Mr. Jarvis – John Bardon
Jake – Maurice Colbourne
Mrs. Lipton – Diana Davies
Johnny Jarvis – Mark Farmer
Mrs. Jarvis – Catherine Harding
Stella – Johanna Hargreaves
Paul Turner – Alrick Riley
Alan Lipton – Ian Sears
Colonel – Nick Stringer

Beginning in 1977 and covering the next six years, an unlikely friendship develops between class clown Johnny Jarvis and introverted Alan Lipton, beginning in their last year at a comprehensive in Hackney, and following them through their early starts in the "real world."

CHESSGAME

23 November 1983, Wednesday,
9:00–10:00pm, ITV, 6 episodes, thriller,
British, contemporary
Granada Television
Pr: Richard Everitt
Dir: William Brayne, Ken Grieve, Roger Tucker
Wtr: John Brason, Murray Smith
Based on *The Labyrinth Makers*, *The Alamut Ambush* and *Colonel Butler's Wolf* by Anthony Price
Cast: Nick Hannah – Michael Culver
Faith Steerforth – Carmen Du Sautoy
Hugh Roskill – Robin Sachs
David Audley – Terence Stamp

David Audley, the head of a fictional branch of British security forces, investigates when the Soviets show an interest in the cargo aboard a newly-discovered wreck of a World War II aeroplane. Audley, an expert in Middle Eastern affairs, must figure out what is going on in time to salvage a top-level meeting which could lead to peace in the Middle East . . . or an international incident.

THE JEWEL IN THE CROWN

8 January 1984, Monday, 8:00–10:00pm (subsequent episodes aired Tuesdays 9:00–10:00pm), ITV, 14 episodes, drama, British, 20th century
Granada Television
Video: available in UK, US
Pr: Christopher Morahan
Dir: Christopher Morahan, Jim O'Brien

Wtr: Ken Taylor
Based on *The Raj Quartet* by Paul Scott
Cast: Barbie Batchelor – Peggy Ashcroft
Ahmed Kasim – Derrick Branche
Sophie Dixon – Warren Clarke
Nicky Paynton – Anna Cropper
Sergeant Guy Perron – Charles Dance
Mabel Layton – Fabia Drake
Teddie Bingham – Nicholas Farrell
Sarah Layton – Geraldine James
Lady Manners – Rachel Kempson
Aunt Fenny – Rosemary Leach
Nigel Rowan – Nicholas le Provost
Hari Kumar – Art Malik
Mohammed Ali Kasim – Zia Mohyeddin
Susan Layton – Wendy Morgan
Mildred Layton – Judy Parfitt
Ronald Merrick – Tim Pigott-Smith
Count Bronowsky – Eric Porter
Colonel Layton – Frederick Treves
Major Jimmy Clark – Stuart Wilson
Daphne Manners – Susan Wooldridge

An epic saga set against the backdrop of the last years of British rule in India in the mid-1940s, focusing on love, intrigue and tragedy among the English and Indians. At the centre are the women of the aristocratic Layton family, who find their lives taking a series of unexpected turns, Army intelligence Sergeant Guy Perron, sent to India as the Second World War draws to a close, and mercurial, somewhat depraved Ronald Merrick, former District Superintendent of Police, who cannot escape the after-effect of his brief relationship with Daphne Manners, an English nurse who was herself in love with Indian Hari Kumar, and whose rape echoes with profound consequences for many people.

Winner, BAFTA Award, Best Drama Serial 1984; winner, Emmy Award, Outstanding Limited Series 1984–1985.

STRANGERS AND BROTHERS

11 January 1984, Wednesday, 9:25–10:20pm, BBC2, 13 episodes, drama, British, 20th century
BBCtv
Pr: Philip Hinchcliffe
Dir: Jeremy Summers, Ronald Wilson
Wtr: Julian Bond
Based on C.P. Snow
Cast: Sir Hector Rose – Edward Hardwicke
Roy Calvert – Nigel Havers
Geoffrey Hollis – Richard Heffer
Roger Quaife – Anthony Hopkins
Charles March – Martyn Jacobs
Margaret Davidson Eliot – Cherie Lunghi
Martin Eliot – Stephen Riddle
Sheila Knight Eliot – Sheila Ruskin
Leonard March – Peter Sallis
Lewis Eliot – Shaughan Seymour

Lewis Eliot moves to London in 1927 to begin his law career, but is soon totally distracted by his infatuation with capricious Sheila Knight. Eliot marries Sheila, but their union is ill-fated; Eliot then leaves the bar to take a post at Cambridge. In the 40 years which follow, Eliot becomes entrenched in the Establishment while maintaining a left-wing philosophy, ultimately walking away from a successful career in Whitehall and becoming a successful writer.

Strangers and Brothers was in fact a series of 11 novels which Snow wrote between 1940 and 1970; Lewis Eliot is the one character who reappears throughout the books.

DIANA

12 January 1984, Thursday, 9:25–10:20pm, BBC1, 10 episodes, drama, British, 20th century
BBCtv
Pr: Ken Riddington
Dir: Richard Stroud, David Tucker
Wtr: Andrew Davies
Based on R.F. Delderfield
Cast: Uncle Reuben – Iain Anders
Rauol de Royden – Yves Beneyton
Mrs. Gayelorde-Sutton – Elizabeth Bennett
Uncle Luke – Fred Bryant
Jan (as a teenager) – Stephen J. Dean
Mr. Gayelorde-Sutton – Harold Innocent
Diana (as a teenager) – Patsy Kensit

Aunt Thirza – June Marlow
Jan – Kevin McNally
Diana Gayelorde-Sutton – Jenny Seagrove
Uncle Mark – Jack Watson

Orphaned teenager Jan arrives in Devon in the 1930s to live with his relatives, where he meets wealthy squire's daughter Diana. As the two come of age they fall deeply in love, but are separated time and again by fate and circumstance.

A FAMILY MAN

13 January 1984, Friday, 9:25–10:15pm, BBC2, 3 episodes, drama, British, contemporary
BBCtv/Bristol
Pr: Colin Rose
Dir: Colin Rose
Wtr: Ted Walker
Cast: Young William – Edward Barrett
Kate Robertson – Jean Heywood
William Robertson – Ian Hogg
Young Kate – Carol Leader
Young Bill – Lloyd McGuire
Bill Robertson – Tony Steedman

When William Robertson visits his father Bill, who is recovering from surgery, he learns that his father still has stored away an ancient motorcycle which is a near-mythic object from William's childhood; the discovery brings up a wellspring of Robertson family memories of years gone by.

GOODBYE MR. CHIPS

29 January 1984, Sunday, 5:15–5:45pm, BBC1, 6 episodes, drama, classic, British, 20th century
BBCtv
Pr: Barry Letts
Dir: Gareth Davies
Wtr: Alexander Baron
Based on James Hilton
Cast: Meldrum – George Baker
Daisy – Suzanne Halstead
Kemp – John Harding
Colley – Paul Hawkins
Max Staefel – Stephen Jenn
Mrs. Wickett – Anne Kristen
Mr. Chips – Roy Marsden
Katherine – Jill Meager
Branksome – Anthony Rowson

85-year-old Mr. Chipping ("Mr. Chips") looks back on his many years as schoolmaster at the Brookfield School, beginning with his first, nervous day on the job in the early years of the century; his reminiscences include his happy but brief marriage to Katherine, who tragically died in childbirth. A crusty and eccentric octogenarian, Chips' decency and humanism have given value not just to his own life, but over the decades to scores of young men as well.

THE BOY IN THE BUSH

9 February 1984, Thursday, 9:30–10:30pm, Channel 4, 4 episodes, drama, British, 19th century
Portman Productions, in association with the Australian Broadcasting Corporation
Pr: Geoff Daniels, Ian Warren
Dir: Rob Stewart
Wtr: Hugh Whitemore
Based on D.H. Lawrence and M.L. Skinner
Cast: Esau – Stephen Bisley
Tom – Jon Blake
Jack Grant – Kenneth Branagh
Mr. Grant – Don Reid
Lennie – Paul Smith
Monica – Sigrid Thornton

In 1882, 18-year-old Jack Grant is expelled from his English agricultural college and sent to Australia to live in the outback with his mother's family. At first Jack is miserable and isolated, but in time he learns valuable lessons about personal responsibility and developing trust, and falls deeply in love with Monica, one of his distant cousins.

THE ODD JOB MAN

11 February 1984, Saturday, 9:00–9:50pm, BBC1, 3 episodes, thriller, Scottish, contemporary
BBCtv/Scotland
Pr: Bob McIntosh
Dir: Tristan de Vere Cole
Wtr: N.J. Crisp
Cast: Major Drew – Ralph Bates
George Griffin – Jon Finch

Nancy – Polly Hemingway
Tauber – Wolf Kahler
Nick – Andrew McCulloch

Ex-SAS man George Griffin, who has been unable to settle into another kind of work, takes on private, SAS-style missions; his latest job, escorting a defecting Warsaw Pact Planning Officer across the East German border, has long-reaching effects which continue after Griffin returns to Scotland.

THE COUNTRY DIARY OF AN EDWARDIAN LADY

22 February 1984, Wednesday, 7:00–7:30pm, ITV, 12 episodes, drama, British, 19th–20th century
Central Television
Video: available in UK, US
Pr: Patrick Gamble
Dir: Dirk Campbell
Wtr: Dirk Campbell, Elaine Feinstein
Based on Edith Holden
Cast: Emma Holden – Elizabeth Choice
Ernest Smith – James Coombes
Edith Holden – Pippa Guard
Frank Mathews – Graham Padden
Evelyn – Allyson Rees

Exploring both the character of Edith Holden and the rural Warwickshire world she knew, Holden's life unfolds via a series of flashbacks, from her girlhood in the late 19th century until her mysterious drowning death in 1920, incorporating the day-to-day events of Holden's diary, as well as her poetry and prose.

MOONFLEET

22 February 1984, Wednesday, 5:10–5:40pm, BBC1, 6 episodes, drama, British, 18th century
BBCtv
Exec. Pr: Paul Stone
Dir: Colin Cant
Wtr: George Day
Based on J. Meade Falkner
Cast: Grace Maskew – Victoria Blake
Elzevir Block – David Daker
Sexton Ratsey – Bernard Gallagher
John Trenchard – Adam Godley
Magistrate Maskew – Ewan Hooper
Miss Jane Arnold – Hilary Mason

In the fishing village of Moonfleet in Dorset in the mid-1700s, many of the locals work at smuggling French alcohol into England, to the continued distress of Magistrate Maskew – but no one is prepared for the adventure and intrigue which follows young John Trenchard's search for the huge diamond which is thought to be part of the legend of Blackbeard.

DRIVING AMBITION

3 March 1984, Saturday, 9:00–9:55pm, BBC1, 8 episodes, drama, British, contemporary
BBCtv
Pr: Carol Robertson
Dir: Michael Simpson
Wtr: Paula Milne
Cast: **Jen Robinson – Anne Carroll**
Mick Robinson – Donald Gee
Ray Hewitt – Mark Kingston
Donna Hewitt – Rosemary Martin
Ken Lark – Gavin Richards

Housewives Donna and Jen, tired of being neglected by their sports-obsessed husbands, come up with an obsession of their own: Donna begins training to become a race car driver, with Jen (who does not even know how to drive) as her sideline mechanic. It seems an impossible dream, but the women are encouraged and sponsored by Ken Lark, a former racing driver turned garage mechanic.

WINTER SUNLIGHT

8 March 1984, Tuesday, 9:30–10:40pm, Channel 4, 4 episodes, drama, British, contemporary
Limehouse Productions
Pr: Susi Hush
Dir: Julian Amyes
Wtr: Alma Cullen
Cast: Jane – Polly Adams
Leo – Michael Burne
Jack – Derek Farr
Ernest – Derek Francis
Esme – Betty Marsden
Dorothy Ashford – Elizabeth Sellars

Dorothy Ashford's elderly parents separate, which seems to offer Dorothy the chance at last to strike out on her own . . . but she finds that independence presents as many if not more complications.

SWALLOWS AND AMAZONS FOREVER! – COOT CLUB

14 March 1984, Wednesday, 7:10–7:35pm, BBC2, 4 episodes, drama, family, British, 20th century
BBCtv
Pr: Joe Waters
Dir: Andrew Morgan
Wtr: Michael Robson
Based on *Coot Club* by Arthur Ransome
Cast: Pete – Jake Coppard
       Tom Dudgeon – Henry Dimbleby
       Dot Callum – Caroline Downer
       Jerry – Julian Fellowes
       Mrs. Barrable – Rosemary Leach
       Bill – Mark Page
       Joe – Nicholas Walpole
       Dick Callum – Richard Walton

A peaceful holiday on the Norfolk Broads in 1932 becomes an adventure when Dick and Dot Callum meet up with their aunt, Mrs. Barrable, Tom Dudgeon, and a group of local lads known as the "Death and Glory" boys.

MISSING FROM HOME

29 March 1984, Thursday, 9:25–10:15pm, BBC1, 6 episodes, drama, British, contemporary
BBCtv
Pr: Ron Craddock
Dir: Douglas Camfield
Wtr: Roger Marshall
Cast: **Allison Reynolds – Judy Loe**
      Tony Walters – Jonathan Newth
      Jason Reynolds – Edward Rawle-Hicks
      Barry Reynolds – Nigel Stewart

Allison Reynolds, content in her role as a wife and mother in Suffolk, must deal with her husband Jerry's sudden, unexplained disappearance; as the mystery of his "going missing" continues unsolved, Allison develops the strength to go forward on her own and also helps her two sons cope.

SWALLOWS AND AMAZONS FOREVER! – THE BIG SIX

11 April 1984, Wednesday, 7:00–7:30pm, BBC2, 4 episodes, drama, family, British, 20th century
BBCtv
Pr: Joe Waters
Dir: Andrew Morgan
Wtr: Michael Robson
Based on *The Big Six* by Arthur Ransome
Cast: Dr. Dudgeon – Colin Baker
       Mr. Farland – Andrew Burt
       Pete – Jake Coppard
       Tom Dudgeon – Henry Dimbleby
       Dot Callum – Caroline Downer
       Mrs. Barrable – Rosemary Leach
       Bill – Mark Page
       Harry Bangate – Patrick Troughton
       Joe – Nicholas Walpole
       Dick Callum – Richard Walton
       Constable Tedder – John Woodvine

Dick and Dot Callum return to Norfolk for another holiday, and are horrified to learn that their old friends, the "Death and Glory" boys, are suspected of criminal activity. Only Dick, Dot and Tom Dudgeon seem to believe they are innocent . . . and set out to unmask the real culprits.

SORRELL AND SON

6 June 1984, Wednesday, 9:00–10:00pm, ITV, 6 episodes, drama, British, 20th century
Yorkshire Television
Pr: Derek Bennett
Dir: Derek Bennett
Wtr: Jeremy Paul
Based on Warwick Deeping
Cast: Florence Palfrey – Stephanie Beacham
       Kit Sorrell – Peter Chelsom
       Kit Sorrell (as a child) – Paul Critchley
       Molly Pentreath – Sarah Neville
       Stephen Sorrell – Richard Pasco
       Fanny Garland – Prunella Ransome
       Dora Sorrell – Gwen Watford
       Mary Jewett – Debbie Wheeler

Set in the years between the two World Wars, this tale of love and duty focuses on Stephen Sorrell, who at the end of World War I finds himself unemployed and abandoned by his wife, Dora. Sorrell is left alone to bring up his young son, Kit, and he is determined to bring up the boy as a gentleman. Sorrell gets a job as a porter at the Pelican Hotel, and over the years he continues to work there, watching with pride as Kit grows up and becomes a successful surgeon.

A WINTER HARVEST

11 July 1984, Wednesday, 9:30–10:20pm, BBC2, 3 episodes, drama, British, contemporary
BBCtv/Bristol
BPr: Colin Godman
Dir: Colin Godman
Wtr: Jane Beeson
Cast: **Caroline Ashurst – Cheryl Campbell**
Tom – Mark Elliott
Martin – Roger McKern
Kitty – Deborah-Jane Sharpe
Vet – Victor Winding
Patrick Ashurst – Mark Wing-Davey

Caroline swaps urban life in London for a remote Dartmoor farmhouse when she falls in love with and marries Patrick Ashurst – but when Patrick falls ill it is up to Caroline to make difficult decisions and do much of the hard work the farm demands; surely country living is not the idyll she had envisioned.

THE INVISIBLE MAN

4 September 1984, Tuesday, 8:00–8:30pm, BBC1, 6 episodes, science fiction, classic, British, contemporary
BBCtv
Pr: Barry Letts
Dir: Brian Lighthill
Wtr: James Andrew Hall
Based on H.G. Wells
Cast: Teddy Henfrey – Jonathan Adams
The Invisible Man – Pip Donaghy
Dr. Samuel Kemp – David Gwillim
Sandy Wadgers – Roy Holder
Mrs. Hall – Lila Kaye
Thomas Marvel – Frank Middlemass
Mr. Hall – Ron Pember
The Reverend Bunting – Michael Sheard

The Invisible Man arrives as a stranger in the little village of Iping, where he turns his scientific brilliance to bad ends, uses his gift's power to destructive ends . . . and becomes a homicidal maniac who is invisible not only physically, but morally as well.

FREUD

14 September 1984, Friday, 9:25–10:25pm, BBC2, 6 episodes, drama, biographical, European, 19th–20th century
BBCtv
Pr: John Purdie
Dir: Moira Armstrong
Wtr: Carey Harrison
Cast: Martha Bernays – Helen Bourne
Anna Freud – Alison Key
Wilhelm Fliess – Anton Lesser
The Baroness – Miriam Margolyes
Jung – Michael Pennington
Sigmund Freud – David Suchet
Jacob Vreuer – David Swift

In 1939, the 83-year-old father of modern psychoanalysis, living his final years in London, looks back on his life, starting with his early experiences as a young doctor in Vienna. His recollections are interspersed with dramatizations of Freud's dreams, which illustrate his personal and intellectual development.

MORGAN'S BOY

11 October 1984, Thursday, 9:25–10:20pm, BBC1, 8 episodes, drama, Welsh, contemporary
BBCtv
Pr: Gerard Glaister
Dir: John Gorrie
Wtr: Alick Rowe
Cast: **Lee Turner – Martyn Hesford**
Sarah – Pippa Hinchley
Colin – Gary Oldman
Morgan – Gareth Thomas
Val Turner – Marjorie Yates

Reserved Welsh farmer Morgan, who lives in the remote Black Mountains, takes in his nephew from Manchester, Lee; after a difficult period of adjustment, a close relationship develops between the old-fashioned Morgan and the teenager, who is in some ways more worldly than his uncle.

THE PRISONER OF ZENDA

18 November 1984, Sunday, 6:00–6:30pm, BBC1, 6 episodes, drama, classic, adventure, European, 19th century
BBCtv
Pr: Barry Letts
Dir: Leonard Lewis
Wtr: James Andrew Hall
Based on Anthony Hope
Cast: Fritz von Tarlenheim – Nicholas Gecks
"Black" Duke Michael – George Irving
Antoinette de Mauban – Pauline Moran
Rupert of Hentzau – Jonathon Morris
Rudolf Rassendyll/King Rudolf – Malcolm Sinclair
Princess Flavia – Victoria Wicks
Colonel Sapt – John Woodvine

An impulsive visit to Ruritania at coronation time makes a dramatic change in the carefree life of wealthy and aristocratic Englishman Rudolf Rassendyll, who happens to be both cousin and double of the new King. When King Rudolf is drugged and kidnapped by enemy (and brother!) "Black" Michael shortly before his coronation, Rassendyll is asked to take his place. He does, and much adventure, intrigue and romance swiftly follow, before Rassendyll is able to secure his cousin's safe release.

THE BOX OF DELIGHTS

21 November 1984, Wednesday, 5:00–5:30pm, BBC1, 6 episodes, drama, family, British, 20th century
BBCtv
Video: available in UK
Pr: Paul Stone
Dir: Renny Rye
Wtr: Alan Seymour
Based on John Masefield
Cast: Maria Jones – Joanna Dukes
Kay Harker – Devin Stanfield
Abner Brown – Robert Stephens
Cole Hawlings – Patrick Troughton

On his way home from school for the Christmas holidays in the 1930s, Kay Harker encounters the mysterious travelling showman Cole Hawlings, who gives Kay his magical "Box of Delights," which takes the boy back into times past.

Winner, BAFTA Award, Best Children's Drama 1984.

THE SECRET SERVANT

6 December 1984, Thursday (subsequent episodes aired on Friday and Saturday), 9:25–10:25pm, BBC1, 3 episodes, thriller, British/European, contemporary
BBCtv/Scotland
Pr: Bob McIntosh
Dir: Alastair Reid
Wtr: Brian Clemens
Based on Gavin Lyall
Cast: George Harbinger – Harvey Ashby
Harry Maxim – Charles Dance
Agnes Algar – Jill Meager
Professor John Tyler – Dan O'Herlihy

SAS Major Harry Maxim is assigned the job of looking after nuclear strategist Professor John Tyler, who is traveling to Luxembourg to deliver a lecture. Unknown to Harry, Tyler has a dire secret in his past, one which is so threatening that agents both friendly and unfriendly will stop at nothing to uncover it, making Harry's task all the more difficult.

WYNNE AND PENKOVSKY

2 January 1985, Wednesday (subsequent episodes aired on Thursday and Friday), 9:25–10:20pm, BBC1, 3 episodes, drama, historical, British/Russian, 20th century
BBCtv
Video: available in UK
Pr: Innes Lloyd
Dir: Paul Seed
Wtr: Andrew Carr
Based on *Man From Moscow* by Greville Wynne
Cast: **Greville Wynne – David Calder**
Newson – Denys Hawthorne
Oleg Penkovsky – Christopher Rozycki

James – Frederick Treves
Sheila Wynne – Fiona Walker

In the years following World War II, British businessman Greville Wynne joins forces with high-ranking Soviet intelligence officer Oleg Penkovsky, who passes valuable information to the West; when they are discovered and tried by the KGB, Penkovsky is sentenced to death, and Wynne receives a stiff prison sentence, ultimately released in an exchange deal in 1964.

THE BEIDERBECKE AFFAIR

6 January 1985, Sunday, 8:45–9:45pm, ITV, 6 episodes, thriller, British, contemporary
Yorkshire Television
Pr: Anne W. Gibbons
Dir: David Reynolds, Frank W. Smith
Wtr: Alan Plater
Cast: **Trevor Chaplin – James Bolam**
Jill Swinburne – Barbara Flynn
Janey – Sue Jenkins
Detective Sergeant Hobson – Dominic Jephcott
Big Al – Terence Rigby
Mr. Carter – Dudley Sutton

Jazz buff and woodwork teacher Trevor Chaplin involves his colleague, English teacher Jill Swinburne, in the search for the mysterious woman who has given Chaplin a rare set of records by legendary jazzman Bix Beiderbecke – a quest which leads to comedy, mystery, and romance.

Plater wrote follow-up adventures for Trevor Chaplin and Jill Swinburne and their supporting players, the two-part *The Beiderbecke Tapes*, which was broadcast starting 13 December 1987, and the four-part *The Beiderbecke Connection*, which began airing 27 November 1988.

THE PICKWICK PAPERS

6 January 1985, Sunday, 5:25–5:55pm, BBC1, 12 episodes, drama, classic, British, 19th century
BBCtv
Video: available in UK
Pr: Barry Letts
Dir: Brian Lighthill
Wtr: Jack Davies
Based on Charles Dickens
Cast: Miss Witherfield – Shirley Cain
Sam Weller – Phil Daniels
Mr. Wardle – Colin Douglas
Rachael Wardle – Freda Dowie
Mr. Perker – Milton Johns
Mrs. Bardell – Jo Kendall
Tony Weller – Howard Lang
Mr. Jingle – Patrick Malahide
Mr. Winkle – Jeremy Nicholas
Mr. Snodgrass – Alan Parnaby
Mr. Pickwick – Nigel Stock
Mr. Tupman – Clive Swift
Serjeant Snubbin – John Woodnutt

Mr. Pickwick, his somewhat unprincipled servant Sam Weller, and his friends, the Corresponding Society of the Pickwick Club, travel by stagecoach through England, stopping in at a variety of inns and finding themselves involved with duels, cricket matches, runaways, and all sorts of assorted adventures, culminating in Mr. Pickwick's being unjustly accused and tried for breach of contract.

BY THE SWORD DIVIDED (2)

6 January 1985, Sunday, 8:15–9:10pm, BBC1, 10 episodes, drama, British, 17th century
BBCtv in association with Consolidated Productions
Pr: Jonathan Alwyn
Dir: Michael Custance, Brian Farnham, Diarmuid Lawrence
Wtr: Alexander Baron, Carey Harrison, John Hawkesworth, Jeremy Paul
Created by John Hawkesworth
Cast: Lady Lucinda Ferrar – Lucy Aston
Sir Thomas Lacey – Timothy Bentinck
Lord Edward Ferrar – Peter Birch
Hugh Brandon – Simon Butteriss
King Charles I – Jeremy Clyde
Goodwife Margaret – Rosalie Crutchley
John Fletcher – Rob Edwards
Rachel – Deborah Goodman
Oliver Cromwell – Peter Jeffrey
Frances Neville – Joanna McCallum
Anne Fletcher – Sharon Mughan
Sir Austin Fletcher – Bert Parnaby
Christopher Neame – Henry Snelling

Sir Ralph Winter – Robert Stephens
Major General Horton – Gareth Thomas
King Charles II – Simon Treves
Solicitor General – John Woodvine

Beginning where the earlier serial ended, Arnescoste Castle has passed from the Royalist Lacey family to the hands of Parliamentarian John Fletcher and his wife Anne, who was born a Lacey. The Civil War continues and finally ends, but many conflicts continue to pose a threat to Anne and John, culminating with John standing trial for regicide about the restoration of King Charles II.

ANNA OF THE FIVE TOWNS

9 January 1985, Wednesday, 9:00–9:55pm, BBC2, 4 episodes, drama, British, 19th century
BBCtv/Pebble Mill
Pr: Colin Rogers
Dir: Martyn Friend
Wtr: John Harvey
Based on Arnold Bennett
Cast: **Anna Tellwright – Linsey Beauchamp**
Mrs. Sutton – Anna Cropper
Henry Mynors – Peter Davison
Ephraim Tellwright – Emrys James
Titus Price – Edward Kelsey
Willie Price – Anton Lesser
Sarah Vodrey – Hilary Mason

In the dismal Potteries in the 1890s, Anna is the daughter of rich but miserly widower Ephraim Tellwright. When she turns 21, Anna finds herself entering a world from which she has been completely sheltered as a result of her Methodist upbringing – a world where money rules. She becomes engaged to marry Henry Mynors, but perhaps feels more drawn to Willie Price.

THE PRICE

10 January 1985, Thursday, 9:30–10:30pm, Channel 4, 6 episodes, thriller, British, contemporary
Astramead/RTE Presentation
Pr: Mark Shivas
Dir: Peter Smith
Wtr: Peter Ransley
Cast: **Geoffrey Carr – Peter Barkworth**
Richard Lefray – Hugh Fraser
Kate – Aingeal Grehan
Andrew – Nicholas Jones
Lansbury – Simon Jones
Clare – Susannah Reid
Frank Crossan – Derek Thompson
Frances Carr – Harriet Walter

English millionaire Geoffrey Carr's wife and stepdaughter are kidnapped in Ireland. Frustrated with the police's lack of progress and his inability to raise enough funds to pay the huge ransom demanded, Carr attempts to track down the kidnappers on his own.

CHARTERS AND CALDICOTT

10 January 1985, Thursday, 9:25–10:15pm, BBC1, 6 episodes, thriller, British, contemporary
BBCtv
Pr: Ron Craddock
Dir: Julian Amyes
Wtr: Keith Waterhouse
Based on characters created by Frank Launder and Sidney Gilliat
Cast: **Caldicott – Michael Aldridge
Charters – Robin Bailey**
Margaret Mottram – Caroline Blakiston
Grimes – Patrick Carter
Inspector Snow – Gerard Murphy
Jenny – Tessa Peake-Jones

The bumbling cricket buffs who first were introduced in *The Lady Vanishes* are older now, retired to country life for Charters and a Kensington flat for Caldicott. When a young girl is found murdered near the flat, the two old chums become embroiled in a criminal plot, finding their mannered ways a bit out of touch in the present day environment.

MAELSTROM

5 February 1985, Tuesday, 8:10–9:00pm, BBC1, 6 episodes, thriller, British/European, contemporary
BBCtv
Pr: Vere Lorrimer

Dir: David Maloney
Wtr: Michael J. Bird
Cast: Anders Bjornson – David Beames
Ingrid Nilsen – Edita Brychta
Anna Marie Jordahl – Susan Gilmore
Lars Nilsen – Christopher Scoular
Catherine Durrell – Tusse Silberg
Astrid Linderman – Ann Todd

A millionaire drowns and leaves a fortune to Catherine Durrell, whom he never met. Catherine travels from England to Norway to claim the inheritance and discover the truth behind the mysterious bequest, a journey which involves her with a Norwegian family which might know the answers which Catherine seeks . . . but at what cost to them all?

BLOTT ON THE LANDSCAPE

6 February 1985, Wednesday, 9:00–9:50pm, BBC2, 6 episodes, drama, satire, British, contemporary
BBCtv
Pr: Evgeny Gridneff
Dir: Roger Bamford
Wtr: Malcolm Bradbury
Based on Tom Sharpe
Cast: Ganglion – Geoffrey Bayldon
Dundridge – Simon Cadell
Sir Giles Lynchwood – George Cole
Lady Maud Lynchwood – Geraldine James
Mrs. Forthby – Julia McKenzie
Blott – David Suchet
Lord Leakham – John Welsh

A black comedy chronicling squirarchical MP Sir Giles Lynchwood's attempts to have a motorway built through Cleene Gorge, his wife's ancestral home, despite – or perhaps because of – her vociferous protests. With the aid of faithful gardener Blott, Lady Maud launches a counteroffensive; chilli powder and spiked beer are among the unlikely but deadly weapons used, as the conflict builds to a spectacular climax which finds Blott taking on the army single-handedly, armed only with 400 tins of baked beans.

COVER HER FACE

17 February 1985, Sunday, 8:30–9:30pm, ITV, 6 episodes, mystery, British, contemporary
Anglia Television
Pr: John Rosenberg
Dir: John Davies
Wtr: Robin Chapman
Based on P.D. James
Cast: Eleanor Maxie – Phyllis Calvert
Alice Liddell – Freda Dowie
Sir Reynold Price – Bill Fraser
Stephen Maxie – Rupert Frazer
Miss Molpas – Barbara Hicks
Adam Dalgliesh – Roy Marsden
Deborah Riscoe – Mel Martin
Sally Jupp – Kim Thomson
John Massingham – John Vine

Scotland Yard sleuth Adam Dalgliesh investigates the murder of a book club employee . . . who, Dalgliesh discovers, was running a drugs racket on the side. His investigation quickly centers on the Maxie household, where every family member seems to have his or her own secret. A number of other victims fall before Dalgliesh gets the vital information he needs to extract a confession from the killer.

THE LAST PLACE ON EARTH

18 February 1985, Monday, 8:30–10:00pm (subsequent episodes aired on Wednesdays from 9:00–10:00pm), ITV, 7 episodes, drama, historical, British/European, 20th century
Central Television
Video: available in US
Pr: Tim Van Rellim
Dir: Ferdinand Fairfax
Wtr: Trevor Griffiths
Based on *Scott and Amundsen* by Roland Huntford
Cast: Ernest Shackleton – James Aubrey
Helmer Hanssen – Jan Harstad
Sverre Hassel – Erick Hivju
Lt. Birdie Bowers – Sylvester McCoy
Dr. Bill Wilson – Stephen Moore
Captain Oates – Richard Morant
Roald Amundsen – Sverre Anker Ousdal
Petty Officer Evans – Pat Roach

Robert F. Scott – Martin Shaw
Fridtjof Nansen – Max Von Sydow
Kathleen Bruce Scott – Susan Wooldridge

British Captain Robert F. Scott and Norwegian Captain Roald Amundsen race to be the first to get to the South Pole. After several false starts, both men take off for the Antarctic in the winter of 1911. Amundsen, who carefully prepared for and planned his expedition, is the first to get within striking distance of the Pole, as Scott, who left much of the planning to others, is frustrated by equipment problems. Amundsen does, indeed, make it first to the South Pole; as he is already on his way home, Scott's team just arrives at the Pole, and then struggles to make it back. Tragically, virtually the entire British team, including Scott, succumbs, the last members dying just 11 miles short of safety.

SHROUD FOR A NIGHTINGALE

9 March 1985, Friday, 9:00–10:00pm, ITV, 5 episodes, mystery, British, contemporary
Anglia Television
Pr: John Rosenberg
Dir: John Gorrie
Wtr: Robin Chapman
Based on P.D. James
Cast: **Stephen Courtney-Briggs – Joss Ackland**
Mary Taylor – Sheila Allen
Jo Fallon – Eleanor David
Mavis Gearing – Liz Fraser
Martin Dettinger – Richard Marner
Adam Dalgliesh – Roy Marsden
Inspector John Massingham – John Vine
Delia Dettinger – Margaret Whiting

Chief Superintendent Adam Dalgliesh investigates the death of Martin Dettinger, who dies at Nightingale House, a nurse's training school. Dalgliesh's questions cut deep into the private lives of the students and staff, and information is held back, lies are told – and more murders take place before Dalgliesh is able to figure out whodunit.

WHO, SIR? ME, SIR?

12 March 1985, Tuesday, 5:10–5:35pm, BBC1, 6 episodes, drama, family, British, contemporary
BBCtv
Exec. Pr: Paul Stone
Dir: Colin Cant
Wtr: Jenny McDade
Based on K.M. Peyton
Cast: Gloria McTavish – Claire Callaghan
Headmaster – Anthony Dawes
Beans – Jimmy Demetriou
Nutty McTavish – Linda Frith
Gary – Kelly George
Sam – Ian Hastings
Mrs. McTavish – Josie Kidd
Jazz – Ashok Kumar
Mark Fountains-Abbott – Kevin Shaw
Hoomey – Nigel Stewart

The boys of Class 2C at Gasworks Comprehensive are all hopeless athletes, but find inspiration from Nutty McTavish, their non-playing (female!) captain when they must compete with a well-trained sports team from the local fee-paying school, Greycoats.

LATE STARTER

15 March 1985, Friday, 9:25–10:15pm, BBC1, 8 episodes, drama, British, contemporary
BBCtv
Pr: Ruth Boswell
Dir: Barry Davies, Nicholas Mallett
Wtr: Brian Clark
Cast: **Edward Brett – Peter Barkworth**
Mary Brett – Rowena Cooper
Simon Brett – Simon Cowell-Parker
Liz Weldon – Julia Foster
Helen Magee – Beryl Reid

Professor Edward Brett's private life and financial affairs both collapse on the very day he retires, and, penniless and abandoned by his wife Mary, he escapes to London in search of anonymity and, hopefully, employment.

OSCAR

26 March 1985, Tuesday, 9:00–9:50pm,

BBC2, 3 episodes, drama, biographical, British, 19th century
BBCtv
Pr: Carol Robertson
Dir: Henry Herbert
Wtr: John Hawkesworth
Cast: **Oscar Wilde – Michael Gambon**
Lord Alfred Douglas – Robin Lermitte
Bernard Shaw – Bryan Murray
Constance Wilde – Emily Richard
Marquis of Queensbury – Norman Rodway
Lillie Langtry – Catherine Strauss

The last, tragic years of writer Oscar Wilde, beginning with the scandalous revelation of his relationship with Alfred Douglas, the infamous trial and imprisonment which followed, and Wilde's subsequent demise.

BLEAK HOUSE

10 April 1985, Wednesday, 9:00–9:55pm, BBC2, 8 episodes, drama, classic, British, 19th century
BBCtv
Video: available in UK, US
Pr: John Harris, Betty Willingale
Dir: Ross Devenish
Wtr: Arthur Hopcraft
Based on Charles Dickens
Cast: **Sir Leicester Dedlock – Robin Bailey**
Esther Summerson – Suzanne Burden
Miss Flite – Sylvia Coleridge
Allan Woodcourt – Brian Deacon
Grandfather Smallweed – Charlie Drake
John Jarndyce – Denholm Elliott
Richard Carstone – Philip Franks
Krook – Bernard Hepton
Mr. Inspector Buckett – Ian Hogg
Ada Clare – Lucy Hornak
Harold Skimpole – T.P. McKenna
Mademoiselle Hortense – Pamela Merrick
William Guppy – Jonathan Moore
Jo – Chris Pitt
Lady Dedlock – Diana Rigg
Tulkinghorn – Peter Vaughan
Miss Barbary – Fiona Walker

Esther Summerson is called to London where she becomes acquainted with her guardian, John Jarndyce, for the first time, a meeting which alters the path of Esther's life forever when Jarndyce, who is involved in an ongoing, acrimonious lawsuit, entreats her to run Bleak House in his absence, an enterprise which leads to, among many other things, Esther's discovering her true parentage.

The first BBC Dickens adaptation to be shot entirely on film.

MAPP AND LUCIA

14 April 1985, Sunday, 8:15–9:15pm, Channel 4, 5 episodes, drama, British, 20th century
London Weekend Television
Pr: Michael Dunlop
Dir: Donald McWhinnie
Wtr: Gerald Savory
Based on E.F. Benson
Cast: **Georgie – Nigel Hawthorne**
Emmeline Lucas (Lucia) – Geraldine McEwan
Major Benjy Flint – Denis Lill
Elizabeth Mapp – Prunella Scales

It's the summer of 1930, and Mapp and Lucia are the social rivals of the small coastal village of Tilling. Under a thin veneer of etiquette and gentility, the two women battle for social prominence. The conflicts between them escalate, with Mapp and Lucia feared lost at sea after a particularly fierce encounter. But just as life in Tilling appears about to proceed without them, the women miraculously reappear, ready to resume their rivalry.

A second series of *Mapp and Lucia* episodes aired starting 3 May 1986.

THE DETECTIVE

10 May 1985, Friday, 9:25–10:15pm, BBC1, 5 episodes, thriller, British, contemporary
BBCtv
Pr: Sally Head
Dir: Don Leaver
Wtr: Ted Whitehead
Based on Paul Ferris
Cast: **Ken Crocker – Tom Bell**
David Marchwint – Michael Cochrane
Superintendent Wilf Penfield – Mark Eden
Linda Crocker – Victoria Fairbrother

Gordon Prokasky – Richard Fallon
Elsie Penfield – Alison Fiske
Detective Inspector Vera Harris – Vivienne Ritchie
Alison Crocker – Sasha Mitchell
Detective Assistant Commissioner Mars – Terence Rigby

While mounting a routine surveillance operation, Commander Ken Crocker stumbles upon evidence which suggests that a senior government minister is dangerously corrupt, a discovery which, if true, could pose a serious threat to the government. When his superiors are unwilling to act on his findings, the idealistic Crocker takes on the investigation himself . . . with startling, treacherous results.

JENNY'S WAR

3 June 1985, Monday, 9:00–10:00pm, ITV, 4 episodes, drama, American/British, 20th century
HTV
Video: available in UK, US
Pr: Peter Graham Scott
Dir: Steven Gethers
Wtr: Steven Gethers
Based on Jack Stoneley
Cast: Karl – Hartmut Becker
Jenny Baines – Dyan Cannon
Peter – Hugh Grant
Klein – Robert Hardy
Steinhardt – Patrick Ryecart
Eva – Elke Sommer
General Cutler – Richard Todd

American Jenny Baines, living in Bath in the early years of World War II, learns that her RAF son Peter has been shot down over Germany. Jenny decides to go to Germany to find out if Peter is still alive and, disguised as a man, is captured by the Gestapo and put in a prisoner-of-war camp – where she is reunited with Peter. Together, they make plans to escape.

Based on the true story of British woman Florence Barrington, who tracked down her son, Winston, to the German Stalag where he was being held during World War II.

FELL TIGER

24 July 1985, Wednesday, 8:00–8:50pm, BBC1, 6 episodes, drama, British, contemporary
BBCtv/Scotland
Pr: Bob McIntosh
Dir: Stephen Butcher, Roger Cheveley
Wtr: Christopher Green
Cast: Mal Fleet – Mark Drewry
Susan Harvey – Jan Harvey
Joe Borrow – David Hayman
Don Stanforth – Neil Phillips
Kath Borrow – Alyson Spiro

Mountaineer Joe Borrow returns from a dangerous Himalayan expedition and is hailed a national hero, but things are not nearly so grand at his home among the Lake District Fells, where Joe finds himself pulled to the breaking point both personally and professionally.

MURDER OF A MODERATE MAN

6 August 1985, Friday, 9:30–10:20pm, BBC1, 5 episodes, thriller, British, contemporary
BCtv/Pebble Mill in association with RAI
Video: available in US
Pr: John Bowen
Dir: Robert Tronson
Wtr: John Howlett
Cast: **Laleh – Susan Fleetwood**
Farshid – John Pierce-Jones
Parviz – Raad Rawi
Morgan Hunter-Brown – Denis Quilley
Annie – Fiona Victory

Morgan Hunter-Brown is assigned by Interpol to investigate when political prisoner Parviz is mysteriously released from a Middle Eastern prison camp and brought to England to testify against an Italian arms dealer.

MY BROTHER JONATHAN

12 August 1985, Monday, 9:00–9:50pm, BBC2, 5 episodes, drama, British, 20th century
BBCtv
Pr: Joe Waters

Dir: Anthony Garner
Wtr: James Andrew Hall
Based on Francis Brett Young
Cast: Edie Martyn – Caroline Bliss
  Jonathan Dakers – Daniel Day-Lewis
  Rachel Hammond – Barbara Kellermann
  Eugene Dakers – Mark Kingston
  Lloyd Moore – T.P. McKenna
  Lavinia Dakers – Helen Ryan
  Harold Dakers – Benedict Taylor

An accidental death begins a journey of recollection and reflection for Dr. Jonathan Dakers, who looks back upon his Edwardian upbringing, examining his relationship with his spoiled younger brother Harold, his romances with Edie and Rachel and the hard work which led to his career as a dedicated GP in an industrial town.

THE TRIPODS (2)

7 September 1985, Saturday, 5:20–5:50pm, BBC1, 12 episodes, science fiction, British BBCtv
Pr: Richard Bates
Dir: Christopher Barry, Bob Bladgen
Wtr: Christopher Penfold
Based on *The City of Gold and Lead* by John Christopher
Cast: **Henry Parker – Jim Baker**
  Fritz – Robin Hayter
  Albert – Simon Needs
  Ali Pasha – Bruce Purchase
  Beanpole – Ceri Seel
  Will Parker – John Shackley
  Master 468 – John Woodvine
  Julius – Richard Wordsworth

The continuing adventures of Will and Henry Parker and their friend Beanpole, who have successfully escaped the Tripods and travelled from England to join the Free Men in their Swiss mountain hideout. Now, along with new friend and ally Fritz, more is learned about the alien Masters' future plans for Earth, and Will and Fritz help devise a risky plan to overthrow the Tripods and free humankind from their evil domination.

TENDER IS THE NIGHT

23 September 1985, Monday, 9:30–10:25pm, BBC2, 6 episodes
BBCtv in association with Showtime/USA, drama, classic, American, 20th century
Video: available in UK
Pr: Betty Willingale
Dir: Robert Knights
Wtr: Dennis Potter
Based on F. Scott Fitzgerald
Cast: Devereux Warren – Edward Asner
  Franz Gregorovius – Jurgen Brugger
  Baby Warren – Kate Harper
  Abe North – John Heard
  Dr. Dohmler – Erwin Kohlund
  Mrs. Speers – Piper Laurie
  Nicole Warren Diver – Mary Steenburgen
  Dick Diver – Peter Strauss
  Rosemary Hoyt – Sean Young

In the late 1920s, American psychiatrist Dick Diver travels to Europe, where he meets, treats and subsequently marries beautiful, unstable heiress Nicole Warren; ironically, as Nicole's mental health improves, Dick's grasp on life deteriorates, eventually leading to his personal and professional downfall.

OLIVER TWIST

13 October 1985, Sunday, 6:00–6:30pm, BBC1, 12 episodes, drama, classic, British, 19th century
BBCtv/Pebble Mill
Video: available in US
Pr: Terrance Dicks
Dir: Gareth Davies
Wtr: Alexander Baron
Based on Charles Dickens
Cast: Rose – Lysette Anthony
  Bill Sikes – Michael Attwell
  Monks – Pip Donaghy
  Noah Claypole – Julian Firth
  Artful Dodger – David Garlick
  Nancy – Amanda Harris
  Mr. Bumble – Godfrey James
  Harry Maylie – Dominic Jephcott
  Mrs. Bumble – Miriam Margolyes
  Mr. Brownlow – Frank Middlemass
  Fagin – Eric Porter
  Oliver Twist – Ben Rodska
  Old Sally – Betty Turner

Beginning with his unfortunate birth in 1825, orphaned Oliver Twist finds himself thrust into the world alone and friendless. After fleeing a workhouse he is taken in by kindly Mr. Brownlow, but soon falls into the evil clutches of Fagin, who has a nefarious reason for keeping Oliver as part of his gang of young criminals. Much misfortune befalls the young boy before the truth of his past is finally revealed and his safe future can be assured.

OPERATION JULIE

4 November 1985, Monday (subsequent episodes aired on Tuesday and Wednesday), 9:00–10:00pm, ITV, 3 episodes, drama, non-fiction, British, 20th century
Tyne Tees Television in association with Chatsworth Television
Video: available in US
Pr: Malcolm Heyworth, Peter Holmans
Dir: Bob Mahoney
Wtr: Bob Mahoney, Gerry O'Hara, Keith Richardson
Based on Colin Pratt and Dick Lee
Cast: Rupert Creasey – John Ainley
  Detective Inspector Dick Lee – Colin Blakely
  Hugh Truscott – Michael Carter
  Kathleen Bates – Melanie Hughes
  Sergeant Julie Thompson – Lesley Nightingale

A dramatization of one of Britain's biggest drug hunts: in the 1970s, Detective Inspector Dick Lee headed an investigation, dubbed "Operation Julie," which broke up a worldwide, Britain-based LSD ring. In March, 1977, simultaneous raids across the country lead to dozens of arrests.

While the majority of the characters depicted here are true-life figures, only Dick Lee and Julie Thompson are identified by their real names.

EDGE OF DARKNESS

4 November 1985, Monday, 9:30–10:25pm, BBC2, 6 episodes, thriller, British, contemporary
BBCtv
Video: available in US
Pr: Michael Wearing
Dir: Martin Campbell
Wtr: Troy Kennedy Martin
Cast: Darius Jedburgh – Joe Don Baker
  Bennett – Hugh Fraser
  Pendleton – Charles Kay
  Harcourt – Ian McNeice
  Jerry Grogan – Kenneth Nelson
  Ronald Craven – Bob Peck
  Clemmy – Zoe Wanamaker
  James Godbolt – Jack Watson
  Emma Craven – Joanne Whalley
  Detective Chief Superintendent Ross – John Woodvine

When widowed Yorkshire detective Ronald Craven's daughter Emma is killed, Craven goes to London to investigate Emma's involvement in GAIA, a secret ecological group with ties to the worldwide nuclear arms race and the CIA (whose agent, Darius Jedburgh, helps Craven in his search for Emma's killer).

Winner, BAFTA Award, Best Drama Serial 1985.

THE BLACK TOWER

8 November 1985, Friday, 9:00–10:00pm, ITV, 6 episodes, mystery, British, contemporary
Anglia Television
Pr: John Rosenberg
Dir: Ronald Wilson
Wtr: William Humble
Based on P.D. James
Cast: **Maggie Hewson – Pauline Collins**
  Father Michael Baddeley – Maurice Denham
  Dr. Eric Hewson – Richard Heffer
  Helen Rainer – Heather James
  Wilfred Anstey – Martin Jarvis
  Grace Willison – Rachel Kempson
  Julius Court – Art Malik
  Adam Dalgliesh – Roy Marsden

Detective Chief Superintendent Dalgliesh, newly promoted to Commander and questioning the direction his life has taken, is recovering from an illness and hopes for a quiet, reflective recuperation – but a letter from old friend Father Baddeley summons

Dalgliesh to Toynton Grange, a nursing home on the Dorset coast. Instead of the peaceful visit he'd anticipated, Dalgliesh finds himself investigating first Baddeley's mysterious, sudden death, and then the questionable demise of several of the inhabitants of the Grange.

HEART OF THE HIGH COUNTRY

12 November 1985, Tuesday, 9:00–10:00pm, ITV, 6 episodes, drama, British, 19th century
Zenith Production for Central Television, in association with Phillips Whitehouse Television
Pr: Lloyd Phillips, Rob Whitehouse
Dir: Sam Pillsbury
Wtr: Elizabeth Gowans
Cast: Calvin Laird – Kenneth Cranham
    Ceci – Valerie Gogan
    Ginger – John Howard
    Bowen – David Letch

In the 1870s, English girl Ceci emigrates to New Zealand, one of the many "Petticoat Pioneers" who move to the distant colony. She arrives full of hope for a new life in a new land, but is quickly faced with more grim realities. Two marriages end in early widowhood, leaving Ceci alone to single-handedly run a large sheep station. After 15 years in the high country, Ceci moves to a coal mining town, where she resurrects an old tavern and slowly gains sympathy and support from the town's miners. Several years later, an underground explosion brings tragedy to the mining town, and Ceci returns to the high country, still seeking the happiness which has eluded her for too long.

STRIKE IT RICH!

4 January 1986, Saturday, 7:20–8:10pm, BBC1, 8 episodes, drama, British, contemporary
BBCtv
Pr: Joe Waters
Dir: Tom Cotter, David Maloney
Wtr: N.J. Crisp, Eric Paice
Devised by Joe Waters
Cast: Ken Stevenson – Tom Adams
    Susan Morgan – Sarah Collier
    David Morgan – Tom Georgeson
    Zelda – Susan Kyd
    Jeanette Mayne – Annabel Leventon
    Kelly – Robert McIntosh
    Tim Boyd – Ken Sharrock
    Stafford – Michael Siberry
    Jack Kingsley – John Stone
    Rick Pearce – Gary Tibbs
    Caroline Morgan – Sasha York

The Bentley News Agency experiences an unexpected windfall, which means that their shareholders, six in particular, who have never collected dividends, suddenly stand to become quite wealthy; their lives operate parallel to one another and also in tandem, as Bentley investigators seek them out with the good news.

ALICE IN WONDERLAND

5 January 1986, Sunday, 5:10–5:40pm, BBC1, 4 episodes, drama, classic, family, fantasy, British, 19th century
BBCtv
Pr: Terrance Dicks
Dir: Barry Letts
Wtr: Barry Letts
Based on Lewis Carroll
Cast: Knave of Hearts – Mark Bassenger
    White Rabbit – Jonathan Cecil
    Mad Hatter – Pip Donaghy
    Alice – Kate Dorning
    March Hare – Neil Fitzwilliam
    Queen of Hearts – Janet Henfrey
    Lewis Carroll – David Leonard
    Gryphon – Brian Miller
    King of Hearts – Brian Oulton
    Alice's Sister – Joanne Rolfe
    Dormouse – Elisabeth Sladen
    Mock Turtle – Roy Skelton
    Dodo – Ian Wallace

Magical adventures befall young Alice when she wanders away from a picnic (where family friend Lewis Carroll is telling stories to Alice and her sisters) and falls down a rabbit hole, encountering such well-known and loved figures as the White Rabbit, the Cheshire Cat, the Mad Hatter, the March Hare, and the infamous Queen of Hearts.

BLUEBELL

12 January 1986, Sunday, 7:45–8:35pm, BBC1, 8 episodes, drama, biographical, British, 20th century
BBCtv
Pr: Brian Spiby
Dir: Moira Armstrong
Wtr: Paul Wheeler
Cast: Paul Derval – Michael N. Harbour
Helen – Annie Lambert
Kurt Burnitz – Peter Machin
Aunt Mary – Carmel McSharry
Bluebell – Carolyn Pickles
Marcel Leibovici – Philip Sayer

Sickly orphan Margaret Kelly, brought up by her Aunt Mary in Liverpool in the 1920s, is encouraged to take up dancing to strengthen her limbs . . . and soon Margaret, now dubbed "Bluebell," is on the road with a Scottish touring group, a journey which takes her to Paris during the Nazi occupation and leads to the formation of the famous "Bluebell Girls" dancing troupe.

RUNNING SCARED

15 January 1986, Wednesday, 5:10–5:35pm, BBC1, 6 episodes, thriller, family, British, contemporary
BBCtv
Exec. Pr: Paul Stone
Dir: Marilyn Fox
Wtr: Bernard Ashley
Cast: Grandad – Fred Bryant
Uncle Frank – Tony Caunter
Narinda – Amarjit Dhillon
Charlie Elkin – Chris Ellison
Mick Prescott – Desmond McNamara
Paula Prescott – Julia Millbank
Dolly Prescott – Maureen Sweeney

Schoolgirl Paula Prescott is caught in the middle of a dangerous intrigue when she discovers a clue linking clever villain Charlie Elkin to an armed robbery.

DEAD HEAD

15 January 1986, Wednesday, 9:25–10:15pm, BBC2, 4 episodes, thriller, British, contemporary
BBCtv/Pebble Mill
Pr: Robin Midgley
Dir: Rob Walker
Wtr: Howard Brenton
Cast: Eldridge – George Baker
Caractacus – Norman Beaton
Jill – Susannah Bunyan
Hugo Silver – Simon Callow
Dana Cass – Lindsay Duncan
Detective Inspector Malcolm – Don Henderson
Eddie Cass – Denis Lawson

Small-time crook Eddie Cass gets in way over his head when he becomes innocently involved in a gruesome murder in the mold of Jack the Ripper's crimes.

HIDEAWAY

11 February 1986, Tuesday, 9:30–10:25pm, BBC1, 6 episodes, thriller, British, contemporary
BBCtv
Pr: Ron Craddock
Dir: Michael E. Briant
Wtr: Charlie Humphreys
Cast: Tracy Wright – Gabrielle Anwar
Ann Wright – Clare Higgins
Colin Wright – Ken Hutchison
Arnie – Harold Innocent
Robert Hammel – Jimmy Jewel
Detective Sergeant Albert Adams – Ron Moody
Terry Staples – Tony Selby
Tommy – Gary Whelan

London criminal Colin Wright decides to break with his past and escape to the country with his wife and daughter, taking with him the proceeds of a big diamond-smuggling deal . . . but he finds that getting away from it all isn't as easy as he'd hoped, as he is pursued by his former colleagues in the underworld.

BRAT FARRAR

16 February 1986, Sunday, 5:15–5:45pm, BBC1, 6 episodes, thriller, British, 20th century
BBCtv
Pr: Terrance Dicks
Dir: Leonard Lewis
Wtr: James Andrew Hall

Based on Josephine Tey
Cast: Eleanor Ashby – Dominique Barnes
Beatrice Ashby – Angela Browne
Brat Farrar/Simon Ashby – Mark Greenstreet
Alec Loding – Francis Matthews
George Ledingham – Frederick Treves

After World War II, Brat Farrar comes back to England without a job or money, but has the opportunity to change every aspect of his life when he takes on the identity of Simon Ashby, heir to a family estate . . . and also the target of a possibly deadly plot.

MR. PYE

2 March 1986, Sunday, 9:15–10:15pm, Channel 4, 4 episodes, drama, fantasy, British, contemporary
Landseer, in association with TSI Films
Pr: Judy Marle
Dir: Michael Darlow
Wtr: Donald Churchill
Based on Mervyn Peake
Cast: Kaka – Patricia Hayes
Mr. Pye – Derek Jacobi
Miss George – Betty Marsden
Tanty – Robin McCaffrey
Thorpe – Richard O'Callaghan
Miss Dredger – Judy Parfitt

Retired bank manager Harold Pye travels to the Channel Island of Sark, on a one-man crusade to bring love to the feuding islanders. Mr. Pye miraculously sprouts wings as he tries to do his good deeds, but when the local inhabitants prove unreceptive to his many kindnesses, horns grow from Mr. Pye's temples and his actions quickly swerve from goodness to evil.

THE DECEMBER ROSE

12 March 1986, Wednesday, 5:05–5:35pm, BBC1, 6 episodes, drama, British, 19th century
BBCtv
Pr: Paul Stone
Dir: Renny Rye
Wtr: Leon Garfield
Cast: Mrs. McDipper – Judy Cornwell

Tom Gosling – Tony Haygarth
Inspector Creaker – Ian Hogg
Hastymite – Patrick Malahide
Miranda McDipper – Cathy Murphy
Barnacle Brown – Courtney Roper-Knight
Roberts – Bill Wallis

Young, orphaned Victorian chimney sweep Barnacle Brown accidentally overhears a top secret meeting between a group of ill-meaning men and women, and, once they discover his presence, is on the run for his safety.

ZASTROZZI

13 April 1986, Sunday, 9:00–10:00pm, Channel 4, 4 episodes, drama, Italian, contemporary
Occam
Pr: David Lascelles, Lindsey C. Vickers
Dir: David G. Hopkins
Wtr: David G. Hopkins
Based on Percy Bysshe Shelley
Cast: Bianca – Maxine Audley
Matilda – Yvonne Bryceland
Zastrozzi – Geoff Francis
Verezzi – Mark McGann
Julia – Tilda Swinton

Based on Shelley's Gothic novel but produced as a contemporary tragi-comic romance, Verezzi, tormented by memories of his lost love Julia, who he believes is dead, is held captive by his sinister half-brother, Zastrozzi. Verezzi escapes from Zastrozzi's clutches, only to be taken prisoner again, this time by Matilda, who is obsessively in love with him. Julia, who is alive, embarks on a search for Verezzi . . . but will she be able to get him away from Matilda?

THE FOURTH FLOOR

14 April 1986, Monday (subsequent episodes aired on Tuesday and Wednesday), 9:00–10:00pm, ITV, 3 episodes, thriller, British, contemporary
Thames Television
Pr: Ian Toynton
Dir: Ian Toynton
Wtr: Ian Kennedy Martin

Cast: Detective Chief Inspector Haldane –
　　　Brian Cox
John Miller – Christopher Fulford
Jim Collis – Richard Graham
George Payne – Kenneth Haigh
　　Hanley – Derrick O'Connor
　　Monroe – Geoffrey Whitehead

Acting on an informer's tip, police arrest a heroin smuggler arriving at Heathrow airport. The series of arrests which follow threaten mobster George Payne's master crime plan, as detectives Collis and Miller come closer and closer to shutting down his entire operation.

KING OF THE GHETTO

1 May 1986, Thursday, 9:30–10:25pm,
BBC2, 4 episodes, thriller, British,
contemporary
BBCtv
Pr: W. Stephen Gilbert
Dir: Roy Battersby
Wtr: Farrukh Dhondy
Cast: Sammy – Ian Dury
　　　Raja – Ajay Kumar
　　　Timur Hussein – Zia Mohyeddin
　　　Matthew Long – Tim Roth
　　　Riaz – Aftab Sachak
　　　Sadie Deedes – Gwyneth Strong

Loner Matthew Long imposes himself into the Bengali community in London's East End, and a sociological power struggle develops when Long becomes an activist squatter up against businessman and "fixer" Timur Hussein.

A VERY PECULIAR PRACTICE

21 May 1986, Wednesday, 9:25–10:15pm,
BBC2, 7 episodes, drama, satire, British,
contemporary
BBCtv
Pr: Ken Riddington
Dir: David Tucker
Wtr: Andrew Davies
Cast: Ernest Hemmingway – John Bird
　　　Jock McCannon – Graham Crowden
　　　Dr. Stephen Daker – Peter Davison
　　　Rose Marie – Barbara Flynn
　　　Lyn Turtle – Amanda Hillward
　　　Bob Buzzard – David Troughton

Idealistic young doctor Stephen Daker's enthusiasm for his new job at the University Medical Practice is stilled when he meets his new colleagues, a manic group of feuding intellectuals who seem dedicated only to competing for attention and doing one another in.

Davison reprised his role as Stephen Daker in 1988 for seven more episodes, which saw him struggling with the responsibilities of his new job as head of the medical practice and problems in his personal life.

FIGHTING BACK

4 August 1986, Monday, 9:30–10:20pm,
BBC1, 5 episodes, drama, British,
contemporary
BBCtv/Pebble Mill
Pr: Chris Parr
Dir: Paul Seed
Wtr: Gareth Jones
Based on an idea by Victoria Hine
Cast: Neil Curran – Tony Carney
　　　Danny Hopkins – Malcolm Frederick
　　　Yvonne Sharpe – Cheryl Maiker
　　　Viv Sharpe – Hazel O'Connor
　　　Eddy Patel – Madhav Sharma
　　　Bruce Curran – Derek Thompson
　　　Gabriel – Larrington Walker

After 15 years in Liverpool, Viv Sharpe leaves her husband and returns to her childhood home of Bristol, now with her own children – but the re-adjustment is far from easy, the family is forced to live in a squat while Viv makes a valiant attempt to pull things together and improve the situation for herself, her children and the inner-city community.

TO HAVE AND TO HOLD

29 August 1986, Friday, 9:00–10:00pm,
ITV, 8 episodes, drama, British,
contemporary
London Weekend Television
Pr: Susi Hush
Dir: John Bruce
Wtr: Deborah Moggach
Cast: **Ann Fletcher – Marion Bailey**
　　　Ken Fletcher – Eamon Boland
　　　Doug – Alan Downer
　　　Irene – Elizabeth Morgan

Ollie Meadows – **Brian Protheroe**
Viv Meadows – **Amanda Redman**

Married sisters Ann Fletcher and Viv Meadows have always been very close. Ann is infertile and Viv, who already has two children of her own, offers to have a baby for Ann and her husband Ken. But instead of arranging for artificial insemination, Viv and Ken secretly make love, which has a devastating effect on both sisters' marriages.

THE MONOCLED MUTINEER

31 August 1986, Sunday, 9:05–10:20pm, BBC1, 4 episodes, drama, biographical, British, 20th century
BBCtv
Pr: Richard Broke
Dir: Jim O'Brien
Wtr: Alan Bleasdale
Based on William Allison and John Fairley
Cast: **Dorothy – Cherie Lunghi**
Charles Strange – Matthew Marsh
Percy Toplis – Paul McGann
Woodhall – Philip McGough
Brigadier General Andrew Graham Thomson – Timothy West
Young Percy – Tony Williams

The true story of British Army Private Percy Toplis, who leads a mutiny on the eve of the 1917 World War I Battle of Passchendaele. After the mutiny Toplis, who had been a petty thief before the War, flees to England, where a death sentence is hanging over him. He settles down and marries, but his past catches up with him in 1920 in a six-week manhunt, which ends in a shoot-out in the Lake District.

PARADISE POSTPONED

15 September 1986, Monday, 9:00–10:00pm, ITV, 11 episodes, drama, satire, British, 20th century
Euston Films for Thames Television
Pr: Jacqueline Davis
Dir: Alvin Rakoff
Wtr: John Mortimer
Cast: Lady Grace Fanner – Jill Bennett
Dr. Salter – Colin Blakely
Dorothy Simcox – Annette Crosbie
Agnes Salter – Eleanor David
Henry Simcox – Peter Egan
Reverend Simeon Simcox – Michael Hordern
Fred Simcox – Paul Shelley
Leslie Titmuss – David Threlfall
Sir Nicholas Fanner – Richard Vernon
Charlotte Fanner – Zoe Wanamaker

When Reverend Simeon Simcox dies, all are surprised when he leaves nothing to his widow and two sons; instead, everything goes to Tory minister Leslie Titmuss. As Simeon's sons – successful novelist and Hollywood screenwriter Henry and amiable country doctor Fred – try to explain their father's action, the story moves back in time, offering both an intimate family saga and an expansive portrait of England in the years following World War II.

The idea for *Paradise Postponed* was originally conceived for television, and developed concurrently as a novel by John Mortimer.

FIRST AMONG EQUALS

30 September 1986, Tuesday, 9:00–10:00pm, ITV, 10 episodes
Granada Television, drama, British, 20th century
Video: available in UK
Pr: Mervyn Watson
Dir: John Gorrie, Sarah Harding, Brian Mills
Wtr: Derek Marlowe
Based on Jeffrey Archer
Cast: Fiona Seymour – Jane Booker
Joyce Gould – Anita Carey
Charles Seymour – Jeremy Child
Elizabeth Kerslake – Joanna David
Simon Kerslake – James Faulkner
Louise Fraser – Diana Hardcastle
Andrew Fraser – David Robb
Alec Pimkin – Clive Swift
Raymond Gould – Tom Wilkinson

In October, 1964, four new MPs take their seats at Westminster. The new members – two Conservative and two Labour – are from widely different backgrounds, and as a Labour Government returns to power after 13 years in Opposition, they take their first steps on the Parliamentary ladder. Over the next 25 years, the four men fight their way to the top, challenging one another in the public arena, and coping with the private turmoils of their domestic lives.

THE LIFE AND LOVES OF A SHE DEVIL

8 October 1986, Wednesday, 9:25–10:25, BBC2, 4 episodes, drama, satire, British, contemporary
BBCtv
Pr: Sally Head
Dir: Philip Saville
Wtr: Ted Whitehead
Based on Fay Weldon
Cast: **Mary Fisher – Patricia Hodge**
Nurse Hopkins – Miriam Margolyes
Edna O'Brien – Edna O'Brien
Mrs. Fisher – Liz Smith
Ruth – Julie T. Wallace
Bobbo – Dennis Waterman

When her husband Bobbo leaves her for glamourous novelist Mary Fisher, devoted-yet-dowdy housewife Ruth is bent on revenge against them both, systematically devising a plan which takes some time and extraordinary means to accomplish . . . but in the end leads to the downfall of both Mary and Bobbo and Ruth's perverse triumph.

Winner, BAFTA Award, Best Drama Serial 1986.

DAVID COPPERFIELD

19 October 1986, Sunday, 5:50–6:20pm, BBC1, 10 episodes, drama, classic, British, 19th century
BBCtv
Pr: Terrance Dicks
Dir: Barry Letts
Wtr: James Andrew Hall
Based on Charles Dickens
Cast: Uriah Heep – Paul Brightwell
Aunt Betsey Trotwood – Brenda Bruce
Steerforth – Jeremy Brudenell
Mr. Micawber – Simon Callow
Mr. Murdstone – Oliver Cotton
Young David – David Dexter
Dora – Francesca Hall
David Copperfield – Colin Hurley
Mrs. Gummidge – Hilary Mason
Peggotty – Jenny McCracken
Agnes Wickfield – Natalie Ogle
Mr. Dick – Thorley Walters

Following the death of his mother and mistreatment by his stepfather Murdstone, David Copperfield is pretty much on his own, lodging at first with eccentric Mr. Micawber and his family then living with his Aunt Betsey Trotwood. After he's grown, David marries flighty Dora, and after her death he is reunited lovingly with childhood friend Agnes Wickfield.

LOST EMPIRES

24 October 1986, Friday, 8:30–10:00pm (subsequent episodes aired from 9:00–10:00pm), ITV, 7 episodes, drama, British, 20th century
Granada Television
Pr: June Howson
Dir: Alan Grint
Wtr: Ian Curteis
Based on J.B. Priestley
Cast: Cissie Mapes – Gillian Bevan
Nick Ollanton – John Castle
Julie Blane – Carmen Du Sautoy
Nancy Ellis – Beatie Edney
Richard Herncastle – Colin Firth
Tommy Beamish – Brian Glover
Otto Mergen – Alfred Marks
Harry Burrard – Laurence Olivier
Lily Farris – Pamela Stephenson

Richard Herncastle leaves the Yorkshire mill town of his youth to join his Uncle Nick's illusionist act. Moving through the music halls of Britain in the years before World War I, Richard is introduced to the hectic world of backstage life – and especially drawn to the women of the company, who offer the naïve young man his first experience of love. The music hall era, and life as Richard and the others know it, comes to a crashing end when the Great War begins, and Richard's story comes to its dramatic end on the battlefields of France.

THE CUCKOO SISTER

29 October 1986, Wednesday,
5:05–5:35pm, BBC1, 4 episodes, mystery, family, British, contemporary
BBCtv
Exec. Pr: Paul Stone
Dir: Marilyn Fox
Wtr: Julia Jones
Based on Vivien Alcock
Cast: Margaret Seton – Victoria Fairbrother
Anthony Seton – Michael N. Harbour
Kate Seton – Joanna Joseph
Rosie – Shelley Measures
Mrs. Trapp – Toni Palmer

Kate's older sister Emma had been kidnapped when just an infant, and Kate has always felt second best in her parents' hearts. When Rosie, a loud-mouthed Cockney girl suddenly appears on the scene with a letter claiming she is Kate's long-lost sister, no one knows whether or not this is true, and a search begins to determine Rosie's true identity.

THE SINGING DETECTIVE

16 November 1986, Sunday,
9:05–10:15pm, BBC1, 6 episodes, drama, mystery, musical, British, contemporary
BBCtv
Video: available in UK
Pr: John Harris, Kenith Trodd
Dir: Jom Amiel
Wtr: Dennis Potter
Cast: Philip Marlow (as a child) – Lyndon Davies
Philip Marlow – Michael Gambon
Mark Binney/Finney/Raymond – Patrick Malahide
Dr. Gibbon – Bill Paterson
Staff Nurse White – Imelda Staunton
Mrs. Marlow/Lili – Alison Steadman
Nicola – Janet Suzman
Nurse Mills – Joanne Whalley

Hack detective fiction writer Philip Marlow is bed-bound in hospital, suffering from severe psoriasis; tormented by the wartime childhood of his past and troubled by his future, he escapes into an elaborate crime-solving fantasy world involving the murder of a young woman, his hallucinations often accompanied by dance-band visions from the 1940s.

BREAKING UP

19 November 1986, Wednesday,
9:25–10:20pm, BBC2, 4 episodes, drama, British, contemporary
BBCtv
Pr: Sally Head
Dir: Stuart Burge
Wtr: Nigel Williams
Cast: **Mrs. Mailer – Eileen Atkins**
Mr. Posner – Alan Bennett
Tony Mailer – Tim Haynes
Mr. Mailer – Dave King
Clare – Gabrielle Lloyd
Marcia – Rosemary Martin

Gifted schoolboy Tony Mailer is dealing with all the angst of impending adolescence, and then has to deal with the breakup of his parents' marriage, brought about by his mother's discovery of his father's involvement with another woman.

THE CHILDREN OF GREEN KNOWE

26 November 1986, Wednesday,
5:00–5:35pm, BBC1, 4 episodes, mystery, family, British, 20th century
BBCtv
Pr: Paul Stone
Dir: Colin Cant
Wtr: John Stadelman
Based on Lucy M. Boston
Cast: **Tolly – Alec Christie**
Linnit – Polly Maberly
Boggis – George Malpas
Toby – Graham McGrath
Mrs. Oldknow – Daphne Oxenford
Mother Oldknow – Heather Ramsay
Alexander – James Trevelyan

Shortly before Christmas in the early 1950s, Tolly goes to stay with his great-grandmother, at her remote and mysterious house, Green Knowe. Over the fireplace hangs a picture of three children who grew up at Green Knowe in the 17th century, Toby, Linnit and Alexander; the elderly woman tells Tolly stories about these long-ago ancestors – and soon Tolly thinks he sees and hears them playing in the garden outside his window!

BLOOD RED ROSES

4 December 1986, Thursday,
9:30–10:30pm, Channel 4, 3 episodes,
drama, Scottish, 20th century
Freeway Films
Pr: Steve Clark-Hall
Dir: John McGrath
Wtr: John McGrath
Cast: Catriona – Dawn Archibald
       Bessie (as a child) – Louise Beattie
       Alex – Gregor Fisher
       Sandy – James Grant
       Bessie McGuigan – Elizabeth MacLennan

Back in Scotland after the death of her father, Bessie McGuigan looks back on her life in the north Highlands and Glasgow in the 1950s through the 1970s. It is a life characterized by battles, most notably those fought against the multi-national corporation that takes over the factory where she works and serves as a union representative. Despite strong opposition both at work and home, Bessie continues to fight on, determined to stand tall at every turn.

ALL PASSION SPENT

9 December 1986, Tuesday, 9:00–9:55pm, BBC2, 3 episodes, drama, British, 20th century
BBCtv
Pr: Colin Rogers
Dir: Martyn Friend
Wtr: Peter Buckman
Based on Vita Sackville-West
Cast: FitzGeorge – Harry Andrews
       William – Geoffrey Bayldon
       Lavinia – Faith Brook
       Carrie – Phyllis Calvert
       Herbert – Graham Crowden
       Bucktrout – Maurice Denham
       Kay – John Franklyn-Robbins
       Lady Slane – Wendy Hiller
       Edith – Hilary Mason
       Mabel – Antonia Pemberton

After the death of her husband, former Prime Minister and elder statesman Lord Slane, 85-year-old Lady Slane refuses to sit back and let her six children determine how she will spend what still remains of her life. For the first time she is free to live where and as she pleases . . . and she does just that, taking off on her own and discovering new places and new friends.

THE DIARY OF ANNE FRANK

4 January 1987, Sunday, 5:10–5:40pm, BBC1, 4 episodes, drama, biographical, Dutch, 20th century
BBCtv
Pr: Terrance Dicks
Dir: Gareth Davies
Wtr: Elaine Morgan
Based on Anne Frank
Cast: Miep Gies – Janet Amsbury
       Edith Frank – Elizabeth Bell
       Mr. Van Daan – Christopher Benjamin
       Margot Frank – Emma Harbour
       Otto Frank – Emrys James
       Peter Van Daan – Steven Mackintosh
       Anne Frank – Katherine Schlesinger
       Mr. Dussel – David Swift
       Mrs. Van Daan – Susan Tracy

The true story of the young Jewish girl who kept a diary chronicling her family's attempt to hide from the Nazis in an Amsterdam attic; they are successful for over two years, but ultimately their hideout is discovered and the Franks, along with Mr. Dussel and the Van Daan family, who were also in hiding with them, are transported to the Nazi death camps.

YESTERDAY'S DREAMS

9 January 1987, Friday, 9:00–10:00pm, ITV, 7 episodes, drama, British, contemporary
Central Independent Television
Pr: Chris Griffin
Dir: Ian Sharp
Wtr: Peter Gibbs
Cast: Kate – Frances Atkinson
       Don – Trevor Byfield
       Martin – Paul Freeman
       Diane – Judy Loe
       Matthew – Damien Lyne

Martin and Diane meet for the first time since their divorce seven years earlier. Memories and feelings are re-awakened, and both are torn between the past and the future. The situation becomes even more complicated when Diane gets a marriage proposal from suitor Don. Whom will she choose?

A SORT OF INNOCENCE

13 January 1987, Tuesday, 9:30–10:20pm, BBC1, 6 episodes, drama, British, contemporary
BBCtv
Pr: Ruth Boswell
Dir: John Gorrie
Wtr: Alick Rowe
Cast: Mark Fellowes – Michael Byrne
Elizabeth Fellowes – Cheryl Campbell
Eric Palmer – Kenneth Cranham
Tim Palmer – Neil Jeffery

Elizabeth Fellowes lives with her son, Tim and second husband Mark in a small Midlands cathedral town, where Tim sings in the choir. When Tim's voice breaks, it effects not only his standing in the choir, but is also mirrored in the disruption at home, where the presence of his drunken, reckless father, Eric, threatens every relationship in the family.

WHITE PEAK FARM

13 January 1987, Wednesday, 5:05–5:35pm, BBC1, 3 episodes, drama, family, British, contemporary
BBCtv
Exec. Pr: Paul Stone
Dir: Andrew Morgan
Wtr: Berlie Doherty
Cast: **Jeannie Tanner – Margery Bone**
Martin – Billy Fellows
Kathleen – Jan Graveson
John Tanner – John Hallam
Gran – Jean Heywood
Madge Tanner – Anne Raitt

Thirteen-year-old Jeannie Tanner doesn't understand why everyone in her family seems to have a secret and is especially perplexed when her grandmother suddenly decides to sell the Northumberland home the family has lived in for years and move to India.

A LITTLE PRINCESS

18 January 1987, Sunday, 4:30–5:00pm, ITV, 6 episodes, drama, classic, family, British, 19th century
London Weekend Television
Video: available in US
Pr: Colin Schindler
Dir: Carol Wiseman
Wtr: Jeremy Burnham
Based on Frances Hodgson Burnett
Cast: Becky – Natalie Abbott
Mr. Carrisford – Nigel Havers
Miss Minchin – Maureen Lipman
Miss Amelia – Miriam Margolyes
Sara Crewe – Amelia Shankley
Captain Crewe – David Telland

The riches-to-rags-to-riches story of Sara Crewe, a little girl raised by a loving father in India, then sent to a London boarding school. When her father dies, Sara loses her pampered standing at the school and is treated cruelly by headmistress Miss Minchin, but is ultimately rescued from her bleak circumstances by a mysterious benefactor.

Winner, BAFTA Award, Best Children's Drama 1987.

DEAD ENTRY

18 February 1987, Wednesday, 5:05–5:35pm, BBC1, 3 episodes, thriller, family, British, contemporary
BBCtv
Exec. Pr: Paul Stone
Dir: Margie Barbour
Wtr: Allan Baker
Cast: **Charlie – Duncan Baizley**
Richard Avery – Geoffrey Bateman
Susan Nelson – Frances Jeater
Daniel – Rhett Keen
Melissa – Lise-Ann McLaughlin

Friends Daniel and Charlie unwittingly become involved in a sea-faring mystery involving millionaire businessman Richard Avery, who is revealed to be a spy . . . but for which side?

HEART OF THE COUNTRY

25 February 1987, Wednesday,

9:25–10:25pm, BBC2, 4 episodes, drama, British, contemporary
BBCtv/Pebble Mill
Pr: Rogert Gregory
Dir: Brian Farnham
Wtr: Fay Weldon
Cast: Ben Harris – Christian Bale
　　　Flora – Rosalind Bennett
　　　Angus Patrick – David Buck
　　　Alice Harris – Sophie Cook
　　　Ros – Elizabeth Edmonds
　　　Jane Wandle – Ann Firbank
　　　Jean Patrick – Janet Key
　　　Harry Harris – Derek Merlin
　　　Natalie Harris – Susan Penhaligon
　　　Sonia – Jacqueline Tong
　　　Arthur Wandle – Derek Waring

Natalie Harris' husband has just run off with another, younger woman, leaving Natalie saddled with debts and two children; a variety of friends then offer advice on how to succeed with no man and no money, many of their suggestions double-handed and little of it useful.

This was novelist Weldon's first serial written directly for television.

A KILLING ON THE EXCHANGE

6 March 1987, Friday, 9:00–10:00pm, ITV, 6 episodes, thriller, British, contemporary
Anglia Television
Pr: John Rosenberg
Dir: Spencer Chapman
Wtr: Paul Ableman
Cast: Sir Max Sillman – Joss Ackland
　　　Detective Superintendent Lance Thorne – John Duttine
　　　Charles Makepeace – Michael Gough
　　　Millicent Thorne – Lesa Lockford
　　　Dan Maitland – Gavin O'Herlihy
　　　Isobel Makepeace – Sian Phillips
　　　John Field – Tim Woodward

When a leading merchant banker is murdered in the City, fellow banker John Field, who is fighting a takeover campaign, finds himself a prime suspect in the investigation being headed by Detective Superintendent Lance Thorne.

INTIMATE CONTACT

9 March 1987, Monday, 9:00–10:00pm, ITV, 4 episodes, drama, British, contemporary
Zenith Production for Central Television
Video: available in US
Pr: Chris Burt
Dir: Waris Hussein
Wtr: Alma Cullen
Cast: **Ruth Gregory – Claire Bloom**
　　　Nell Gregory – Abigail Cruttenden
　　　Bill Stanhope – Mark Kingston
　　　Clive Gregory – Daniel Massey
　　　Martin Gregory – David Phelan

The secure middle-class lifestyle of businessman Clive Gregory and his wife Ruth is shattered when Clive learns that he has AIDS, picked up from a sexual encounter with a female prostitute. As Clive bravely faces the inevitable, Ruth courageously comes to terms with his illness. She encounters hostility and ignorance from some old friends, but gains strength and new insight from the people she meets while campaigning for AIDS victims.

Intimate Contact was the first British television drama to deal with AIDS as a heterosexual virus.

THE HOUSEMAN'S TALE

21 March 1987, Saturday, 10:30–11:45pm, BBC1, 2 episodes, drama, British, contemporary
BBCtv/Scotland
Pr: Tom Kinninmont
Dir: Alastair Reid
Wtr: Colin Douglas
Based on Colin Douglas
Cast: Margaret Birss – Juliet Cadzow
　　　Dr. David Campbell – Colin Forsythe
　　　Nurse Joan Masson – Julie Graham
　　　Creech – Cyril Luckham
　　　Ted Main – Lawrie McNicol

A dramatized look at the first service year of young doctor David Campbell, as he deals with the ceaseless demands of being on the low end of the hospital hierarchy as a hospital houseman . . . but would much rather concentrate on alcohol and young nurses.

STRONG POISON

25 March 1987, Wednesday, 9:25–10:20pm, BBC2, 3 episodes, mystery, British, 20th century
BBCtv co-production with WGBH/Boston
Pr: Michael Chapman
Dir: Christopher Hodson
Wtr: Philip Broadley
Based on Dorothy L. Sayers
Cast: Norman Urquhart – Clive Francis
Bunter – Richard Morant
Lord Peter Wimsey – Edward Petherbridge
Chief Inspector Parker – David Quilter
Dowager Duchess – Margaretta Scott
Hannah Westlock – Tilly Vosburgh
Harriet Vane – Harriet Walter

In the 1920s, mystery writer Harriet Vane turns to urbane Lord Peter Wimsey for help when she is put on trial for and convicted of the poisoning death of her lover. Wimsey is determined to see Harriet set free, for not only is he convinced of her innocence, but he has quickly fallen in love with the charming, intelligent young woman.

This was the first of three productions of Sayers' mysteries which paired Wimsey with Harriet Vane.

HAVE HIS CARCASE

15 April 1987, Wednesday, 9:25–10:15pm, BBC2, 4 episodes, mystery, British, 20th century
BBCtv co-production with WGBH/Boston
Pr: Michael Chapman
Dir: Christopher Hodson
Wtr: Rosemary Anne Sisson
Based on Dorothy L. Sayers
Cast: Inspector Trethowan – Ray Armstrong
Mrs. Weldon – Rowena Cooper
Bunter – Richard Morant
Lord Peter Wimsey – Edward Petherbridge
Henry Weldon – Jeremy Sinden
Harriet Vane – Harriet Walter

While on a walking tour in the West Country, Harriet Vane stumbles across a blood-soaked corpse. Working with Lord Peter Wimsey, she discovers that the cause of death was not the suicide it initially appeared to be, and the two head off in search of a murderer – their first co-investigation.

THE EYE OF THE DRAGON

6 May 1987, Wednesday, 5:10–5:35pm, BBC1, 5 episodes, thriller, family, Welsh, contemporary
BBCtv/Wales
Pr: Allan Cook
Designed by Julian Williams
Wtr: Dyfed Glyn
Cast: Ianto Rees – Glan Davies
Robin Richards – Daniel Evans
Michael Richards – Iestyn Garlick
Gwen Richards – Lisabeth Miles
Sam Chan – Hugh Thomas
Mari Richards – Mali Tudno

Widowed Gwen Richards struggles to extend her family's mountain railway as a tourist attraction in the hills of Wales, but things get out of control when crooks use the railway as an escape route . . . and kidnap Gwen's children, Robin and Mari, to ensure their safe passage.

BROND

13 May 1987, Wednesday, 10:00–11:00pm, Channel 4, 3 episodes, thriller, Scottish, contemporary
Jam Jar Films
Pr: Paddy Higson
Dir: Michael Caton-Jones
Wtr: Frederic Lindsay
Cast: Margaret – Louise Beattie
Robert – John Hannah
Brond – Stratford Johns
Baxter – Sandy Neilson

Glasgow University student Robert witnesses a murder, but when the police come to investigate there is no body to be found. Brond, a mysterious and possibly sinister figure, appears on the scene, claiming to offer help to Robert . . . but soon afterwards Robert finds himself charged with murder and does not know whether or not Brond can be trusted.

GAUDY NIGHT

13 May 1987, Wednesday, 9:25–10:20pm, BBC2, 3 episodes, mystery, British, 20th century
BBCtv co-production with WGBH/Boston
Pr: Michael Chapman
Dir: Michael Simpson
Wtr: Philip Broadley
Based on Dorothy L. Sayers
Cast: Carrie Sadler – Eileen Bell
Dr. Baring – Sheila Burrell
Miss Chilperic – Nina Edwards
Miss Martin – Carol MacReady
Miss Hillyard – Charmian May
Bunter – Richard Morant
Lord Peter Wimsey – Edward Petherbridge
Harriet Vane – Harriet Walter

At a reunion of her Oxford college, Harriet Vane comes across a series of deadly acts of most unladylike vandalism and calls in her colleague (and beau) Lord Peter Wimsey for help in getting to the cause of the mysterious outrages. She also agrees to marry him once the mystery is solved.

PORTERHOUSE BLUE

3 June 1987, Wednesday, 10:00–11:00pm, Channel 4, 4 episodes, comedy, British, contemporary
Picture Partnership
Pr: Brian Eastman
Dir: Robert Knights
Wtr: Malcolm Bradbury
Based on Tom Sharpe
Cast: Mrs. Biggs – Paula Jacobs
Skullion – David Jason
Cornelius Carrington – Griff Rhys Jones
Sir Godber Evans – Ian Richardson
Dean – Paul Rogers
Zipser – John Sessions

When the master of Porterhouse, Cambridge University's most reactionary college, dies, head porter Skullion, the guardian of archaic college tradition for 45 years, fears that his position is threatened. And it is: newly-appointed master Sir Godber Evans announces his intention to thrust the college into the modern world. Conflicts and crises abound as Evans tries to implement his reforms – a task made more difficult when Skullion is dismissed and vows revenge.

LIZZIE'S PICTURES

3 June 1987, Wednesday, 9:25–10:25pm, BBC2, 4 episodes, drama, British, contemporary
BBCtv/Pebble Mill
Pr: Brenda Reid
Dir: Nicholas Renton
Wtr: Lesley Bruce
Cast: Tania – Amanda Boxer
Val – Victoria Fairbrother
Grace – Pam Ferris
Vernon – Richard E. Grant
Lizzie Dickinson – Lisa Harrow
Danny – Philip Jackson
Sandra – Sheila Ruskin
Angie – Melissa Simmonds
Jack Dickinson – Robert Stephens

Facing a mid-life crisis, photographer Lizzie leaves her husband Jack at home and heads to London, where she seeks out her old school friends and takes a series of telling pictures of the women, reflecting the paths their lives have taken, and learning valuable lessons about her own.

THE HONEY SIEGE

7 June 1987, Sunday, 4:30–5:00pm, ITV, 7 episodes, drama, family, British, 20th century
HTV
Pr: Derek Clark
Dir: John Jacobs
Wtr: David Martin
Based on *Le Chevalier Pierrot* by Gil Buhet
Cast: **Godfrey Green – Stephan Chase**
Pete Rainbow – Lyndon Davies
Feen Rainbow – Barbara Ewing
Phil Gattrell – Kevin Lloyd
Ben Rainbow – Brian Miller
Jenny – Natalie Morse
Phoebe Belham – Belinda Sinclair

This adaptation of the French novel sets its action in England in 1953, as the village of Crowker prepares, along with the rest of England, for the Coronation of

Elizabeth II. When someone destroys one of local schoolmaster Godfrey Green's beloved beehives and steals the honey, Green threatens to cancel his pupils' two-day holiday unless the culprit confesses. Protesting their innocence, the boys, led by Pete Rainbow, barricade themselves in the local castle, throwing the villagers' proposed celebration plans into confusion.

FLOODTIDE

14 June 1987, Sunday, 9:00–10:00pm, ITV, 7 episodes, thriller, British, contemporary
Granada Television
Pr: Steve Hawes
Dir: Tom Cotter
Wtr: Roger Marshall
Cast: Detective Inspector Brook – John Benfield
Isabel – Connie Booth
Tessa Waite – Gabrielle Dellal
Dany – Sybil Maas
Exton Waite – Roger Rowland
Ramsey – Philip Sayer
Lambert – Georges Trillat

When her cabinet minister father dies under suspicious circumstances, Tessa Waite seeks the help of Ramsey, an English doctor now out of the rat race and living in France. Ramsey reluctantly agrees to return to England and find out how Tessa's father died, and soon he has uncovered evidence of a cover-up conspiracy. In his quest for the truth, Ramsey discovers that Exton Waite was a cocaine addict killed by drug dealers. Ramsey quickly becomes a target, getting caught in the middle between an international drug network and an undercover police surveillance operation.

A second thriller serial about Ramsey was developed at the same time as *Floodtide* and aired beginning 8 January 1988, featuring many of the same characters and focusing on a showdown between Ramsey and drug trafficker/killer Lambert.

IMAGINARY FRIENDS

22 June 1987, Monday (subsequent episodes aired on Tuesday and Wednesday), 9:00–10:00pm, ITV, 3 episodes, drama, British, contemporary
Thames Television
Pr: Peter Sasdy
Dir: Peter Sasdy
Wtr: Malcolm Bradbury
Based on Alison Lurie
Cast: **Roger Zimmern – John Duttine**
Ed Novar – Ken Jones
Verena – Patricia Kerrigan
Felicity Coppard – Patsy Rowlands
Professor Tom McMann – John Stride
Elsie Novar – Billie Whitelaw

Professor McMann and his assistant Roger Zimmern set out to discover the truth about the Truth-Seekers, a bizarre religious sect whose members claim to be receiving guidance from prophetess Verena, a messenger from the planet Varna. Roger "joins" the Truth-Seekers, but, as he spends more time with Verena, he finds it difficult to determine just what is and is not real or true.

Lurie's novel was set in America but transposed by adaptor Bradbury to Norfolk.

BOOGIE OUTLAWS

3 July 1987, Thursday, 9:30–10:20pm, BBC2, 3 episodes, drama, British, science fiction
BBCtv/Pebble Mill
Pr: Carol Parks
Dir: Keith Godman
Wtr: Leslie Stewart
Cast: Boz – Nathan Airiss
Inspector Leesley – Isla Blair
Manfred Holt – Ian Hogg
Sergeant Cross – John Judd
Gladys – Claire Parker
Flash – David Schofield
Zoot – Chris Tummings
Pig – Andrew C. Watson

In a futuristic Britain where a curfew is enforced and the army helps the police keep the peace, a rock band and their roadie get caught up in dangerous intrigue when the band's drummer is arrested by the Territorial Army, and they take it upon themselves to rescue him.

WOLF TO THE SLAUGHTER

2 August 1987, Sunday, 7:45–8:45pm, ITV, 4 episodes, mystery, British, contemporary
TVS
Pr: John Davies
Dir: John Davies
Wtr: Clive Exton
Based on Ruth Rendell
Cast: **Detective Chief Inspector Wexford – George Baker**
Rupert Margolis – Nicholas Gecks
Mrs. Penistan – Jean Heywood
Ruby Branch – Carmel McSharry
Detective Inspector Burden – Christopher Ravenscroft
Detective Con Drayton – Robert Reynolds
Linda Grover – Kim Thomson
Anita Margolis – Harriet Thorpe

An anonymous letter announcing a young girl's murder is sent to Detective Chief Inspector Wexford, who has few other clues to work on in trying to locate the victim. When he finally does uncover the murder, the search for the killer proves equally frustrating.

VANITY FAIR

6 September 1987, Sunday, 5:50–6:25pm, BBC1, 16 episodes, drama, classic, British, 19th century
BBCtv
Pr: Terrance Dicks
Dir: Diarmuid Lawrence, Michael Owen Morris
Wtr: Alexander Baron
Based on William Makepeace Thackeray
Cast: **William Dobbin – Simon Dormandy**
Sir Pitt Crawley – Freddie Jones
Rawdon Crawley – Jack Klaff
Becky Sharp – Eve Matheson
Miss Crawley – Sian Phillips
Amelia Sedley Osborne – Rebecca Saire
Jos Sedley – James Saxon
George Osborne – Benedict Taylor

Shrewd orphan Becky Sharp is determined to make a proper place for herself in society. She marries aristocratic Rawdon Crawley, but he is cut off from his family, so her fortunes barely improve at all. Meanwhile, Becky's childhood friend Amelia Sedley marries officer George Osborne, who is killed in the Napoleonic conflict. Becky continues her ruthless attempts at self-promotion, but ultimately performs an unselfish act in order to ensure Amelia's happiness with William Dobbin, a comrade of George's who has long admired Amelia from afar.

FORTUNES OF WAR

11 October 1987, Sunday, 9:05–10:05pm, BBC1, 7 episodes, drama, British, 20th century
BBCtv
Video: available in UK, US
Pr: Betty Willingale
Dir: James Cellan Jones
Wtr: Alan Plater
Based on *The Balkan Trilogy* and *The Levant Trilogy* by Olivia Manning
Cast: **Guy Pringle – Kenneth Branagh**
Sasha Drucker – Harry Burton
Simon Boulderstone – Rupert Graves
Dobson – Charles Kay
Bella Niculesco – Caroline Langrishe
Nikko Niculesco – Vladimir Mirodan
Prince Yakimov – Ronald Pickup
Harriet Pringle – Emma Thompson
Inchcape – James Villiers

As World War II begins, newlyweds Guy and Harriet Pringle are in the midst of a journey across Europe, on their way to Bucharest, where Guy is to be a lecturer. In the four years that follow, they are caught on the far side of the German forces; their relationship is fraught with conflict, much of it having little to do with the tumultuous external circumstances surrounding them.

MY FAMILY AND OTHER ANIMALS

17 October 1987, Saturday, 6:25–6:55pm, BBC1, 10 episodes, drama, biographical, British, 20th century
BBCtv
Pr: Joe Waters
Dir: Peter Barber-Fleming
Wtr: Charles Wood
Based on Gerald Durrell
Cast: **Spiro – Brian Blessed**
Lawrence Durrell – Anthony Calf

Dr. Thoedore – Christopher Godwin
Mrs. Durrell – Hannah Gordon
Margo Durrell – Sarah-Jane Holm
Kralefsky – John Normington
Gerry Durrell – Darren Redmayne
George – Paul Rhys
Leslie Durrell – Guy Scantlebury

In 1935, widowed Mrs. Durrell and her four children follow a whim and leave England for the island of Corfu. For the next five years, until it is time for Gerry to head off to school back home, the setting is indeed idyllic and adventurous for the family, aided significantly by caring, overbearing taxi driver Spiro, who takes the Durrells under his wing.

A PERFECT SPY

4 November 1987, Wednesday,
9:25–10:25pm, BBC2, 7 episodes
BBCtv, thriller, British, 20th century
Video: available in US
Pr: Colin Rogers
Dir: Peter Smith
Wtr: Arthur Hopcraft
Based on John le Carré
Cast: Miss Dubber – Peggy Ashcroft
Mary Pym – Jane Booker
Makepeace Watermaster – Iain Cuthbertson
Mr. Muspole – Andy de la Tour
Magnus Pym – Peter Egan
Percy Loft – Jack Ellis
Syd Lemon – Tim Healy
Jack Brotherhood – Alan Howard
Dorothy Pym – Caroline John
Rick Pym – Ray McAnally
Magnus Pym (as a child) – Benedict Taylor
Axel – Rudiger Weigang

In the 1950s, spy Magnus Pym is on the run, hiding out in a seaside town where he had spent his childhood summers. In the familiar spot once again, he looks back on his life, how he got involved in the espionage business – going to all the right schools, passing as a perfect, proper English gentleman, but hiding the painful secret that his estranged father is a career criminal – a truth which has ultimately and ironically lead Pym back to where he began.

ALIENS IN THE FAMILY

18 November 1987, Wednesday,
5:10–5:35pm, BBC1, 6 episodes, science fiction, family, British, contemporary
BBCtv
Exec. Pr: Paul Stone
Dir: Christine Secombe
Wtr: Allan Baker
Based on Margaret Mahy
Cast: **Jacqueline – Sophie Bond**
Philippa – Clare Clifford
David – Rob Edwards
Lewis – Sebastian Knapp
Bond – Grant Thatcher
Dora – Clare Wilkie

Young Jacqueline is having a hard time adjusting to being with her father, new stepmother and step-siblings. She feels like an alien in the family – but that's nothing compared with the trying experiences of Bond, a genuine alien from the planet Galgonqua, who is being hunted by intergalactic enemies.

THE MARKSMAN

4 December 1987, Friday, 9:30–10:30pm, BBC1, 3 episodes, thriller, British, contemporary
BBCtv
Pr: Sally Head
Dir: Tom Clegg
Wtr: Ron Hutchinson
Based on Hugh C. Rae
Cast: Irwin – Michael Angelis
Hazel – Leslie Ash
Macfadden – Craig Charles
Doyle – James Ellis
Brown – Richard Griffiths
Weaver – David Threlfall

Professional criminal Weaver returns from self-imposed sunny exile in Spain to Liverpool to avenge the death of his young son. Enlisting the aid of some old comrades, Weaver tracks his son's murderers to Ireland.

THE CONTRACT

3 January 1988, Sunday (subsequent episodes aired on Monday and Tuesday), 9:00–10:00pm, ITV, 3 episodes

Yorkshire Television, thriller, British, contemporary
Video: available in UK
Pr: Keith Richardson
Dir: Ian Toynton
Wtr: Gerald Seymour
Cast: Professor Guttman – Hans Caninenberg
Henry Carter – Bernard Hepton
Erica Guttman – Brigitte Karner
Johnny Donoghue – Kevin McNally

When a top Soviet professor and his daughter wish to cross the East German border into the West, British Secret Intelligence hires "contract man" Johnny Donoghue, a German specialist, to sneak into East Germany and aid in the mission. But careful preparations go awry, and Donoghue must then single-handedly attempt to lead the professor and his daughter to freedom.

CAMPAIGN

6 January 1988, Wednesday, 9:25–10:15pm, BBC2, 6 episodes, drama, British, contemporary
BBCtv
Pr: Ruth Boswell
Dir: Brian Farnham
Wtr: Gerard MacDonald
Cast: Rose Thompson – Rosalind Bennett
Stephen Hallam – David Cardy
Sarah Copeland – Penny Downie
Warren Greenbank – John Fortune
Daniel Copeland – Robbie Engels

Advertising agency creative director Sarah Copeland feels a good deal of on-the-job pressure and sexist treatment as she sets out to get a political party's election advertising account, which would be a major feather in her professional cap – and is also put upon by problems at home, as her husband resents the time and energy she is putting into her career (and, by implication, withholding from him).

SMALL WORLD

24 January 1988, Sunday, 9:30–10:30pm, ITV, 6 episodes, comedy, American/British, contemporary

Granada Television
Pr: Steve Hawes
Dir: Robert Chetwyn
Wtr: Howard Schuman
Based on David Lodge
Cast: Hilary Swallow – Sarah Badel
Miss Maiden – Rachel Kempson
Persse McGarrigle – Barry Lynch
Angelica – Leonie Mellinger
Phillip Swallow – Stephen Moore
Morris Zapp – John Ratzenberger

Poet Persse McGarrigle arrives in England for a literary conference, and encounters a number of odd people – including fast-talking Professor Morris Zapp, prophetic Miss Maiden, and Angelica, with whom Persse falls deeply in love – who lead Persse on a series of adventures which take the sheltered, shy poet around the world, the journey climaxing at a glitzy literary conference in New York.

MOONDIAL

10 February 1988, Wednesday, 5:00–5:30pm, BBC1, 6 episodes, thriller, family, British, contemporary
BBCtv
Pr: Paul Stone
Dir: Colin Cant
Wtr: Helen Cresswell
Cast: Sarah – Helana Avellano
Kate – Joanna Dunham
Minty – Siri Neal
Tom – Tony Reid
John – Martin Sadler

Thirteen-year-old Minty is sent to stay with her grandmother, who lives in the gatehouse of a spooky 300-year-old Lincolnshire castle. A moondial on the castle grounds has mysterious powers, and it is there that Minty meets Tom and Sarah, children who lived at the castle hundreds of years ago. With them, Minty must do battle against timeless spirits, not all of them benign . . . one, in fact, being perhaps the devil himself.

THE FEAR

17 February 1988, Wednesday,

9:00–10:00pm, ITV, 5 episodes, drama, British, contemporary
Euston Films
Pr: Jacky Stoller
Dir: Stuart Orme
Wtr: Paul Hines
Cast: Marty – Jesse Birdsall
Carl Galton – Iain Glen
Linda – Susannah Harker
George Klein – Denis Lill
Tony Slater – Anthony Valentine

Ruthless Carl Galton is a successful young gangster, expanding his illegal businesses across London. His ambition puts Carl in direct conflict with powerful Tony Slater, and as his obsession with Slater grows, Carl becomes increasingly alienated from his wife Linda and best friend Marty. Marty is killed, Linda leaves Carl, and all that is left to him is the final confrontation with Tony Slater.

CROSSFIRE

15 March 1988, Tuesday, 9:40–10:30pm, BBC1, 5 episodes, thriller, British, contemporary
BBCtv
Pr: Ron Craddock
Dir: Ken Hannam
Wtr: John McNeil
Cast: **Freddie Ross – Eamon Boland**
Daisy Burke – Sean Caffrey
Eamon Duffy – Alan Devlin
Donal McCarthy – Tony Doyle
Collins – Aaron Harris
Sean Scanlon – John Keegan
Dermot Shea – Des McAleer
Kathy Ross – Lesley Nightingale
Clare – Hilary Reynolds

Special Branch computer expert Freddie Ross is sent to Belfast to aid RUC anti-terrorist operations in tracking down the identity of an IRA mole, but soon finds himself caught precariously in the middle of the goings on.

THIN AIR

8 April 1988, Friday, 9:30–10:20pm, BBC1, 5 episodes, thriller, British, contemporary
BBCtv
Pr: Caroline Oulton
Dir: Antonia Bird
Wtr: Peter Busby, Sarah Dunant
Cast: Zac – James Aubrey
Joe – Brian Bovell
Rachel Hamilton – Kate Hardie
Richard Hellier – Nicky Henson
Henry – Sam Kelly
Mark – Kevin McNally
Draeger – Clive Merrison
Samantha – Sarah Jane Morris
Haig – Robert Pugh

Urban Air radio reporter Rachel Hamilton is unwittingly caught up in a web of riverfront corruption as she investigates a colleague's murder which is somehow involved with development at the Docklands, ultimately flushing out the killer while doing a live broadcast.

SOPHIA AND CONSTANCE

13 April 1988, Wednesday, 9:25–10:15pm, BBC2, 6 episodes, drama, British, 19th–20th century
BBCtv
Pr: John Harris
Dir: Romey Allison, Hugh David
Wtr: John Harvey
Based on *The Old Wives' Tale* by Arnold Bennett
Cast: **Constance – Linsey Beauchamp**
Sophia – Katy Behean
Samuel Povey – Nigel Bradshaw
Mr. Critchlow – Alfred Burke
Old Constance – Phyllis Calvert
Old Sophia – Helen Cherry
Cyril – Philip Childs
Young Constance – Catherine Cusack
Young Sophia – Melissa Greenwood
Mr. Baines – John Scott Martin
Gerald Scales – Leonard Preston
Mrs. Baines – Patricia Routledge

In the Potteries town of Bursley, sisters Constance and Sophia Baines spend most of their lives at odds with one another – Sophia is headstrong and proud, while Constance is quiet and accepting – their experiences over the years taking them from the middle of the 19th century to the first decade of the 20th, and from England to Paris and back again, where they are finally reunited in old age.

TROUBLES

1 May 1988, Sunday, 9:30–11:30pm, ITV, 2 episodes, drama, Irish, 20th century
Little Production for London Weekend Television
Pr: Barry Blackmore
Dir: Christopher Morahan
Wtr: Charles Sturridge
Based on J.G. Farrell
Cast: Captain Bolton – Sean Bean
Brendan Archer – Ian Charleson
Mrs. Rappaport – Fabia Drake
Sarah Devlin – Emer Gillespie
Angela Spencer – Susannah Harker
Edward Spencer – Ian Richardson

In 1919, Major Brendan Archer, shell-shocked from the war, arrives at the Majestic Hotel in Ireland, owned by the father of his fiancée, Angela Spencer. The decaying hotel, like the family, has seen better days. Archer is looking for Angela, but instead finds himself drawn to her friend, Catholic Sarah Devlin. Later, Archer is embroiled in the escalating violence and bloodshed leading up to the formation of the Irish Free State.

MENACE UNSEEN

3 May 1988, Tuesday (subsequent episodes aired on Wednesday and Thursday), 9:00–10:00pm, ITV, 3 episodes, thriller, British, contemporary
Anglia Television
Pr: John Rosenberg
Dir: Paul Annett
Wtr: Alan Seymour
Cast: **Tessa Shriving – Judi Bowker**
Norma Trisk – Brenda Bruce
Duncan Free – Ian Ogilvy
Mark Hallstrom – Clarke Peters
Robert Shriving – Andrew Ray
Larry Knight – John Sessions

Computer consultant Duncan Free investigates the mysterious death of his business partner, Robert Shriving, and discovers that Shriving was involved in the misuse of vital databanks. Shriving's widow, Tessa, who had once been Duncan's lover, turns to Duncan for support, and together they search for the truth behind Shriving's death, a quest which puts them both in danger, and also re-kindles their feelings for one another.

ECHOES

25 May 1988, Wednesday, 10:00–11:00pm, Channel 4, 4 episodes, drama, Irish, 20th century
Working Title
Pr: Rebecca O'Brien
Dir: Barbara Rennie
Wtr: Barbara Rennie
Based on Maeve Binchy
Cast: Caroline Nolan – Alison Doody
Clare O'Brien – Siobhan Garahy
David Power – Robert Hines
Gerry Doyle – Stephen Holland
Angela O'Hara – Geraldine James
Clare (as a child) – Denise McCormick

Castlebay in the 1950s is a typical small Irish seaside town. Clare O'Brien, whose family just barely scrapes by, dreams of getting out. She is encouraged by her teacher, Angela O'Hara, to further her education, and gets a scholarship to university in Dublin. There she is re-introduced to David Powers, the well-to-do son of Castlebay's doctor. The two fall in love, but when they return to Castlebay, fate steps in with devastating results.

THE ONE GAME

4 June 1988, Saturday, 9:00–10:00pm, ITV, 4 episodes, thriller, British, contemporary
Central Television
Pr: Deirdre Deir
Dir: Mike Vardy
Wtr: John Brown
Devised by Tony Benet
Cast: **Nicholas Thorne – Stephen Dillon**
Jenny – Philippa Haywood
Magnus – Patrick Malahide
Fay – Kate McKenzie

Games tycoon Nicholas Thorne is forced to play a reality game invented by his former business partner Magnus, the creative genius who helped Thorne form his company – and whom Thorne then coldly cast aside. As the game is played out, Thorne's company loses a vast amount of money, his ex-wife Jenny is kidnapped and his life is jeopardized. Refusing to go to the police, Thorne and his girlfriend Fay follow clues leading Thorne to a confrontation with Magnus . . . where Thorne is forced to face his hidden past.

A VERY BRITISH COUP

19 June 1988, Sunday, 9:15–10:15pm, Channel 4, 3 episodes, thriller, British, contemporary
Skreba Films
Video: available in UK, US
Pr: Sally Hibbin, Ann Skinner
Dir: Mick Jackson
Wtr: Alan Plater
Based on Chris Mullin
Cast: Thompson – Keith Allen
　　　Wainwright – Geoffrey Beevers
　　　Browne – Alan MacNaughtan
　　　Harry Perkins – Ray McAnally
　　　Secretary of State – Shane Rimmer
　　　Cook – Marjorie Yates

Third-generation Sheffield steelworker and far left Labour idealist Harry Perkins is elected Prime Minister, and from the moment he takes office, powerful forces set to work against him. The media, the Civil Service, and British and American espionage forces all want to tame Harry's radical ideas, and when Perkins announces that he intends to remove American military bases and missiles from Britain, a dangerous plot is hatched to unseat him from office.

Winner, BAFTA Award, Royal Television Society Award, Best Drama Serial 1988.

A GUILTY THING SURPRISED

19 June 1988, Sunday, 8:15–9:15pm, ITV, 3 episodes, mystery, British, contemporary
TVS
Pr: Neil Zeiger
Dir: Mary McMurray
Wtr: Clive Exton
Based on Ruth Rendell
Cast: **Detective Chief Inspector Wexford – George Baker**
　　　Quentin Nightingale – Michael Jayston
　　　Georgina Villiers – Karen Meagher
　　　Elizabeth – Catherine Nielson
　　　Detective Inspector Burden – Christopher Ravenscroft
　　　Lionel Marriott – David Swift
　　　Denys Villiers – Nigel Terry

When Elizabeth Nightingale is murdered, her philandering husband Quentin is Wexford and Burden's immediate prime suspect, but the truth of the crime is actually connected to a terrible secret from the past which involves a complicated web of infidelity involving a number of people . . . including the victim herself.

FINAL RUN

10 July 1988, Sunday, 9:50–10:40pm, BBC2, 4 episodes, thriller, British, contemporary
BBCtv
Pr: Brenda Reid
Dir: Tim King
Wtr: Carol Bunyan
Original story by Ron Hutchinson
Cast: Courtney – Paul Jesson
　　　Dean – David Keane
　　　Grandma – Valerie Lilley
　　　Michael – Bryan Murray
　　　Mrs. Courtney – Eileen Nicholas
　　　Debbie – Geraldine O'Rawe
　　　Kate – Fiona Victory

Michael and Kate change their names and move to a new country to ensure freedom from their pursuers – a drastic decision which has a particularly traumatic effect on their son, Dean, who is unaware of the dangerous truth behind their circumstance.

STRANGE INTERLUDE

13 July 1988, Wednesday, 9:00–10:35pm, Channel 4, 3 episodes, drama, American, 20th century
HTV
Video: available in US
Pr: Philip Barry
Dir: Herbert Wise
Wtr: Robert Enders

Based on play by Eugene O'Neill
Cast: Gordon – Kenneth Branagh
  Dr. Edmund Darrell – David Dukes
  Madeleine Arnolds – Julie Eccles
  Professor Leeds – José Ferrer
  Mrs. Amos Evans – Rosemary Harris
  Sam Evans – Ken Howard
  Nina Leeds – Glenda Jackson
  Charles Marsden – Edward Petherbridge

After Nina Leeds' fiancé is killed in World War I, she has a nervous breakdown; when she later marries Sam Evans, it is a loveless match, Nina haunted by her fear of hereditary insanity in Sam's family. The psychological intrigues continue into the next generation, as Nina plots to control the life of her son Gordon (whose father is her former lover, Dr. Edmund Darrell, who had treated Nina after her breakdown).

WIPE OUT

2 August 1988, Tuesday, 9:00–10:00pm, ITV, 5 episodes, thriller, British, contemporary
Granada Television
Pr: Mervyn Watson
Dir: Michael Rolfe
Wtr: Richard Maher, Martin Stone
Cast: Khalid Aziz – Derrick Branche
  Clive Rawlinson – Tristram Jellinek
  Max Raines – Ian McElhinney
  Philip Benton – Ian McNeice
  Mike Reynolds – Catherine Neilson
  DI James Edmunds – Bill Stewart
  Doctor Fairling – Nigel Terry

Home Office Investigator Max Raines is charged with finding prison psychologist Fairling, who mysteriously vanished following a jail riot – an uprising that also resulted in the ritual murder of a warden. Raines' search uncovers a series of covert terrorist activities, and a number of other deaths occur before Raines is able to locate Fairling and eliminate the threat the terrorists pose.

THE FRANCHISE AFFAIR

25 September 1988, Sunday, 5:55–6:25pm, BBC2, 6 episodes, mystery, British, 20th century
BBCtv
Video: available in US
Pr: Terrance Dicks
Dir: Leonard Lewis
Wtr: James Andrew Hall
Based on Josephine Tey
Cast: **Mrs. Sharpe – Rosalie Crutchley**
  Inspector John Hallam – David Ellison
  Betty Kane – Kate Emma-Davies
  Mr. Heseltine – James Garbutt
  Nevil Bennet – Alex Jennings
  Bryan Murray – Kevin Macdermott
  Robert Blair – Patrick Malahide
  Marion Sharpe – Joanna McCallum
  Mrs. Wynn – Penelope Nice
  Detective Inspector Grant – John Vine

In the years following World War II, Betty Kane ruffles more than a few town feathers and sets into action a police investigation when she accuses Mrs. Sharpe and her daughter Marion of kidnapping her and forcing her to act as their servant – a charge which seems ludicrous at first . . . but then may turn out to be not so ridiculous after all.

In the first serialized version of *The Franchise Affair* in 1962, Rosalie Crutchley played the role of Marion Sharpe.

GAME, SET & MATCH

3 October 1988, Monday, 9:00–10:00pm, ITV, 13 episodes, thriller, British, contemporary
Granada Television
Pr: Brian Armstrong
Dir: Ken Grieve, Patrick Lau
Wtr: John Howlett
Based on Len Deighton
Cast: Bret Rensselaer – Anthony Bate
  Dicky Cruyer – Michael Culver
  Werner Volkmann – Michael Degen
  Gloria Kent – Amanda Donohoe
  Giles Trent – Hugh Fraser
  Bernard Samson – Ian Holm
  Erich Stinnes – Gottfried John
  Fiona Samson – Mel Martin
  Rolf Mauser – Michael Mellinger
  Frank Harrington – Frederick Treves
  Juri Roster – Ralf Wolter

Bernard Samson, once the most skilled British agent in Berlin, burned out on the job and now is safely behind a desk in London. But he is drawn back into the centre of things when he must trace a suspected traitor who might be jeopardizing the hidden Brahms Network of spies behind the Iron Curtain which Samson had himself set up. When it is revealed that the traitor is none other than Samson's wife, Fiona (who has defected to the KGB), the stakes climb even higher: Samson must not only find her, but prove his own loyalty as well.

A TASTE FOR DEATH

14 October 1988, Friday, 9:00–10:00pm, ITV, 6 episodes, mystery, British, contemporary
Anglia Television
Pr: John Rosenberg
Dir: John Davies
Wtr: Alick Rowe
Based on P.D. James
Cast: Father Barner – Oliver Ford Davies
Kate Miskin – Penny Downie
Emily Wharton – Avril Elgar
Barbara Berowne – Fiona Fullerton
Lady Ursula Berowne – Wendy Hiller
Sir Paul Berowne – Bosco Hogan
Evelyn Matlock – Gabrielle Lloyd
Adam Dalgliesh – Roy Marsden
Dominic Swayne – Matthew Marsh
Theresa Nolan – Rebecca Saire
Stephen Lampart – Simon Ward

In the midst of setting up Scotland Yard's new Sensitive Crimes Squad, Commander Adam Dalgliesh becomes involved in the bizarre death of Sir Paul Berowne, who had consulted Dalgliesh about a series of anonymous letters linking him to the drowning of an aspiring young actress. Still more killings follow as Dalgliesh's investigation continues, clues leading him to suspect someone within Berowne's own household.

FIRST BORN

30 October 1988, Sunday, 9:05–10:00pm, BBC1, 3 episodes, thriller, British, contemporary
BBCtv
Pr: Sally Head
Dir: Philip Saville
Wtr: Ted Whitehead
Based on *Gor Saga* by Maureen Duffy
Cast: **Edward Forester – Charles Dance**
Lancing – Philip Madoc
Nancy Knott – Rosemary McHale
Ann Forester – Julie Peasgood
Chris Knott – Peter Tilbury

Genetic scientist Edward Forester produces a mixed primate, half-human, half-gorilla; when his programme is cancelled and all experiments ordered destroyed, Forester cannot bring himself to kill the creature he has named Gordon ("Gor" for short) – but then is faced with the dilemma of how to hide the creature and still ensure its present and future safety.

THE CHRONICLES OF NARNIA: THE LION, THE WITCH AND THE WARDROBE

13 November 1988, Sunday, 5:40–6:10pm, BBC1, 6 episodes, drama, classic, family, fantasy, British, 20th century
BBCtv
Video: available in UK, US
Pr: Paul Stone
Dir: Marilyn Fox
Wtr: Alan Seymour
Based on C.S. Lewis
Cast: Professor – Michael Aldridge
Aslan – Ailsa Berk/William Todd-Jones
Susan – Sophie Cook
Peter – Richard Dempsey
White Witch – Barbara Kellermann
Mrs. Macready – Maureen Morris
Mr. Tumnus – Jeffrey Perry
Voice of Aslan – Ronald Pickup
Edmund – Jonathan R. Scott
Maugrim – Martin Stone
Lucy – Sophie Wilcox

Siblings Peter, Susan, Edmund and Lucy are evacuated from London in 1940, at the beginning of World War II. Staying with the eccentric Professor, the children discover an attic wardrobe through which they are transported to the magical and mysterious land of Narnia. Narnia is ruled by the evil White Witch, but the four children help fulfill an ancient prophecy which restores the reign of the true ruler of the land, the great lion Aslan.

CHRISTABEL

16 November 1988, Wednesday, 9:25–10:30pm, BBC2, 4 episodes
BBCtv, drama, biographical, British, 20th century
Video: available in US
Pr: Kenith Trodd
Dir: Adrian Shergold
Wtr: Dennis Potter
Based on *The Past Is Myself* by Christabel Bielenberg
Cast: Mrs. Burton – Ann Bell
    Peter Bielenberg – Stephen Dillon
    John – James Exell
    Nicky – Alastair Haley
    Christabel – Elizabeth Hurley
    Adam von Trott – Nigel Le Vaillant
    Mr. Burton – Geoffrey Palmer

In 1934, aristocratic Christabel goes against the wishes of her parents and marries German Peter Bielenberg. Christabel moves with him to Germany, and when war breaks out, they are trapped in Berlin, caught in the middle of the Nazi nightmare. Peter becomes involved in a plot to overthrow Hitler and is caught and sent to a concentration camp; Christabel sets out to save him, travelling across war-torn Berlin to the camp in Ravensbruck. Peter and Christabel survive the war and ultimately emigrate to Ireland.

THE RAINBOW

4 December 1988, Sunday, 9:20–10:20pm, BBC1, 3 episodes, drama, British, 20th century
BBCtv/Pebble Mill
Pr: Chris Parr
Dir: Stuart Burge
Wtr: Anne Devlin
Based on D.H. Lawrence
Cast: **Old Tom Brangwen – Tom Bell**
    Winifred Inger – Kate Buffery
    Uncle Tom – Jon Finch
    Anna – Jane Gurnett
    Gudrun – Clare Holman
    Ursula Brangwen – Imogen Stubbs
    Will Brangwen – Colin Tarrant
    Lydia Brangwen – Eileen Way
    Anton Skrebensky – Martin Wenner

Sixteen-year-old Ursula Brangwen lives with her multi-generational family in the Erewash Valley at the turn of the century, where memories of past generations continue to haunt those in the present. Adolescent Ursula rebels against her confining surroundings, her developing emotional independence and sexual identity expressed in her attraction to army cadet Anton Skrebensky, and her intense friendship with intellectual feminist Winifred Inger.

Ursula Brangwen's story is continued in Lawrence's classic novel, *Women in Love*.

THE WATCH HOUSE

7 December 1988, Wednesday, 5:05–5:35pm, BBC1, 3 episodes, thriller, British, contemporary
BBCtv/Newcastle
Pr: Brenda Ennis
Dir: Ian Keill
Wtr: William Corlett
Based on Robert Westall
Cast: Fiona – Lynette Davies
    Arthur – James Garbutt
    Mr. McGill – Benny Graham
    Anne – Diana Morrison
    Prudie – Sheri Shepstone
    Curator – Peter Van Gaver

Teenager Anne feels depressed and rebellious after her parents separate; when she is sent from London to the seaside, Anne is drawn to the mysterious Watch House, the abandoned home of the Garmouth Life Brigade. Anne begins to see scenes from the past, views of long-ago evil deeds . . . who is reaching out to her and what is it that they want?

THE DARK ANGEL

4 January 1989, Wednesday, 9:25–10:25pm, BBC2, 3 episodes
BBCtv, thriller, British, 19th century
Video: available in US

Pr: Joe Waters
Dir: Peter Hammond
Wtr: Don Macpherson
Based on *Uncle Silas* by Sheridan le Fanu
Cast: **Maud Ruthyn – Beatie Edney**
  Madame de la Rougierre – Jane Lapotaire
  Austin Ruthyn – Alan MacNaughtan
  Uncle Silas – Peter O'Toole
  Dr. Bryerly – Guy Rolfe
  Cousin Monica – Barbara Shelley
  Captain Oakley – Simon Shepherd
  Dudley Ruthyn – Tim Woodward

Young Victorian heiress Maud is captivated by a dynamic youthful portrait of her Uncle Silas – but in real life, Silas is old, embittered and evil. The nightmare begins for Maud with the arrival of dissipated governess Madame de la Rougierre . . . merely the beginning of Silas' sinister web of deception and terror.

TOM'S MIDNIGHT GARDEN

4 January 1989, Wednesday, 5:05–5:35pm, BBC1, 6 episodes, drama, family, fantasy, British, contemporary
BBCtv
Video: available in UK
Pr: Paul Stone
Dir: Christine Secombe
Wtr: Julia Jones
Based on Philippa Pearce
Cast: Aunt Gwen – Isabelle Amyes
  Mrs. Bartholomew – Renee Asherson
  Peter Long – Simon Fenton
  Tom Long – Jeremy Rampling
  Uncle Alan – Shaughan Seymour
  Hatty – Caroline Waldron

Tom's summer holiday is miserably interrupted when he is quarantined with his uncle and aunt in their small flat. But what he thinks will be a dull and unimaginative stay there is transformed into something else when he encounters a magical garden – which appears when elderly Mrs. Bartholomew's clock strikes 13! . . . and introduces Paul to people from the past, including his new friend Hatty.

BEHAVING BADLY

20 February 1989, Monday, 8:30–9:30pm, Channel 4, 4 episodes, drama, British, contemporary
Humphrey Barclay
Pr: Humphrey Barclay, Moira Williams
Dir: David Tucker
Wtr: Catherine Heath, Moira Williams
Based on Catherine Heath
Cast: Rebecca – Frances Barber
  Bridget Mayor – Judi Dench
  Giles – Douglas Hodge
  Mark Mayor – Ronald Pickup

After her husband leaves her for a younger woman, Bridget Mayor at first behaves as meekly and properly as she had before the divorce . . . but then realizes how isolated and unhappy she had been in that position, and decides to have a go at "behaving badly."

A QUIET CONSPIRACY

24 February 1989, Friday, 9:00–10:00pm, ITV, 4 episodes, thriller, British, contemporary
Anglia Television
Pr: John Rosenberg
Dir: John Gorrie
Wtr: Alick Rowe
Based on Eric Ambler
Cast: **Theo Carter – Joss Ackland**
  General Luther Novack – Mason Adams
  Valerie – Sarah Winman

Down-on-his-luck former journalist Theo Carter is pulled into the world of espionage and intrigue when he learns of a top-secret NATO project, code-named Daedalus, which is at the center of a strange conspiracy. Carter's discovery puts his and his daughter Valerie's lives in danger as he faces pressure from both NATO and the KGB to reveal what he knows.

THE JUSTICE GAME

7 April 1989, Friday, 9:30–10:20pm, BBC1, 4 episodes, thriller, Scottish, contemporary
BBCtv/Scotland
Pr: Peter Broughan

Dir: Norman Stone
Wtr: John Brown
Devised by Peter Broughan
Cast: Sir James Crichton – Joss Ackland
Brian Ash – Michael Culver
Jack Flynn – Iain Cuthbertson
Deborah – Roxanne Hart
Sandy Sadowski – Russell Hunter
Tim Forsythe – Michael Kitchen
Dominic Rossi – Denis Lawson
Kate Fielding – Diana Quick

Flamboyant criminal defense lawyer Dominic Rossi returns home to Glasgow after many years away in the States, and soon finds himself entangled in the deadly world of corporate criminals to whom the city now seems to belong.

THE REAL EDDY ENGLISH

11 April 1989, Tuesday, 10:00–11:00pm, Channel 4, 4 episodes, thriller, British, contemporary
North South Partnership
Pr: Colin McKeown, Martin Tempia
Dir: David Attwood
Wtr: Frank Cottrell-Boyce
Cast: Mrs. English – Beryl Cooke
Mrs. Holly – Meg Davies
Mad Bastard – Sue Devaney
Vicki – Cheryl Maiker
Eddy English – Stephen Persaud
Big Eddy – Frank Windsor

When Eddy English sets out to find the killers of his uncle Big Eddy, whom he idolized, he quickly gets in way over his head and is ensnared in a dangerous web of local politics and murderous intrigue.

SHALOM SALAAM

26 April 1989, Wednesday, 9:30–10:30pm, BBC2, 5 episodes, drama, British, contemporary
BBCtv/Pebble Mill
Pr: Chris Parr
Dir: Gareth Jones
Wtr: Gareth Jones
Cast: Candy – Buki Armstrong
Joe Aster – John Cater
Sarah Morris – Charlotte Cornwell
Hafiz Sattar – Ayub Khan Din
Jackie – Clare Holman
Mumtaz Sattar – Mamta Kaash
Sadiq Sattar – Zia Mohyeddin
Shehnaaz Sattar – Shahnaz Pakravan
Adam Morris – Toby Rolt
Meera – Janet Steel

Two families – one Jewish, one Muslim – find their lives intertwined in a number of ways, most poignantly in the star-crossed love affair between young Adam Morris and Mumtaz Sattar, who meet in 1983 at sixth-form college, and whose forbidden love develops over the following five years.

TAKE ME HOME

2 May 1989, Tuesday, 9:35–10:35pm, BBC1, 3 episodes, drama, British, contemporary
BBCtv
Pr: David Snodin
Dir: Jane Howell
Wtr: Tony Marchant
Cast: **Tom – Keith Barron**
Liz – Annette Crosbie
Martin – Reece Dinsdale
Kathy – Maggie O'Neill
Ray – Tim Preece

Craftsman Tom, who has been made redundant and now is driving a taxi, picks up young passenger Kathy one stormy night. Kathy is running from a row with her husband and turns to Tom for comfort; this meeting leads to another, and soon the two are having a passionate affair which seriously threatens both their marriages.

JUMPING THE QUEUE

12 May 1989, Friday, 9:30–10:50pm, BBC1, 2 episodes, drama, British, contemporary
BBCtv
Pr: Sally Head
Dir: Claude Whatham
Wtr: Ted Whitehead
Based on Mary Wesley
Cast: **Matilda Poliport – Sheila Hancock**
Huw Jones – Don Henderson
Tom – John Stride
Hugh Warner – David Threlfall

Widow Matilda, fearing that she is slowly going senile, decides to commit suicide. So she carefully prepares a final picnic, planning to drown herself afterwards – but before she has a chance to act on her plan, she meets fugitive murderer Hugh Warner, who is on the run from the police. Matilda postpones her plan, electing instead to help Warner, a decision which has profound consequences for them both.

A TALE OF TWO CITIES

21 May 1989, Sunday, 7:45–9:45pm, ITV, 3 episodes, drama, classic, British/French, 18th century
Granada Television/Dune
Video: available in UK, US
Pr: Roy Roberts
Dir: Philippe Monnier
Wtr: Arthur Hopcraft
Based on Charles Dickens
Cast: Dr. Manette – Jean-Pierre Aumont
Charles Darney – Xavier Deluc
Lucie Manette – Serena Gordon
Madame Defarge – Kathie Kriegel
Miss Pross – Anna Massey
Jarvis Lorry – John Mills
Sidney Carton – James Wilby

Dissolute solicitor Sidney Carton's tale of redemption is set against the backdrop of the French Revolution, as he ultimately sacrifices his life in exchange for that of aristocrat Charles Darnay, so as to protect the heart of the woman Sidney loves, Lucie Manette – who is devoted to Darnay.

RULES OF ENGAGEMENT

12 June 1989, Monday, 9:00–10:00pm, ITV, 6 episodes, thriller, British, contemporary
Futuremedia Production
Pr: Terence Williams
Dir: Robert Walker
Wtr: Graham Hurley
Cast: Joanna Goodman – Anna Calder-Marshall
Martin Goodman – Kenneth Cranham
Suzanne – Amanda Fawsett
Davidson – Derek Fowlds
Dave Gillespie – Karl Johnson
Annie McPhee – Cathy Tyson
Harry Cartwright – Rudolph Walker

Ex-marine Dave Gillespie investigates the public and private life of city controller Martin Goodman, uncovering an international web of greed, deception, and ruthless pursuit of power which threatens the lives of millions as an armed American nuclear submarine becomes disabled and drifts towards Russian territorial waters.

AFTER THE WAR

16 June 1989, Friday, 9:00–10:00pm, ITV, 10 episodes, drama, British, 20th century
Granada Television
Pr: Michael Cox, Sita Williams
Dir: John Glenister, John Madden, Nicholas Renton
Wtr: Frederic Raphael
Cast: Michael Jordan (as a child) – Nicolas Dastor
Joe Hirsch (as a child) – Nicholas Fletcher
Sally Raglan – Caroline Goodall
Manfred Hirsch – Henry Goodman
Annie Rose – Serena Gordon
Philippa Jordan – Ingrid Hafner
Rachel Jordan – Clare Higgins
Michael Jordan – Adrian Lukis
Ned Corman – Denis Quilley
Joe Hirsch – Robert Reynolds
Samuel Jordan – Anton Rodgers
David Lucas – Michael Siberry
Pierrette Levi – Almanta Suska
Irene Jameson – Susannah York

Michael Jordan and Joe Hirsch meet in 1942 as children, at a boarding school which has been evacuated to Devon during World War II. Both are Jewish, but Michael comes from the prosperous, assimilated middle class, while Joe is a refugee from Nazi-occupied Europe. In the decades which follow, they lose touch then meet again, also encountering each other's friends and families, lovers and wives, and build separate careers, Joe going into journalism and Michael becoming a successful writer.

TRAFFIK

22 June 1989, Thursday, 9:00–11:00pm (subsequent episodes aired on Monday

from 9:00–10:00pm), Channel 4, 5 episodes, drama, British, contemporary
Carnival Films
Video: available in US
Pr: Brian Eastman
Dir: Alastair Reid
Wtr: Simon Moore
Cast: **Helen – Lindsay Duncan**
Tariq Butt – Talat Hussain
Karl – George Kukura
Ulli – Fritz Muller-Scherz
Caroline – Julia Ormond
Jack Lithgow – Bill Paterson
Dieter – Tilo Pruckner
Fazal – Jamal Shah

British politician Jack Lithgow, head of the anti-drug cabinet, journeys to Pakistan, seeking to reduce production of the poppies which are processed into the opium which ends up, in part, on the streets of England (and in the veins of his daughter, Caroline). Lithgow's mission threatens the life and livelihood of local opium farmer Fazal, who must then turn to drug trafficker Tariq Butt for assistance. Meanwhile, in Germany, smuggler Helen reassesses the opulent lifestyle that years of dealing drugs has bought her; her life, and those of the others depicted here, illustrate the tense day-to-day goings on behind a major international drug trafficking operation.

Winner, BAFTA Award, Best Drama Series 1989.

CHELWORTH

9 July 1989, Sunday, 9:20–10:15pm, BBC1, 8 episodes, drama, British, contemporary
BBCtv
Pr: Jonathan Alwyn
Dir: Roger Bamford, Brian Farnham, Christopher Hodson, Robert Tronson
Wtr: Brian Thompson
Devised by John Hawkesworth and Brian Thompson
Cast: Barbara Chivers – Angela Browne
Rafe Hollingsworth – Geoffrey Chater
Charles Harper – Ronald Hines
Keith Shedden – Martin Jarvis
Michael Anstey Hincham – Peter Jeffrey
Virginia Anstey Hincham – Gemma Jones
Olivia Esholt – Phyllida Law
Patricia Anstey – Catherine Russell
Lord Toller – Sebastian Shaw
Ewan Chivers – John Stride
Peter Thornton – Gareth Thomas
Ronnie Esholt – James Villiers

The unexpected death of his older brother leaves Michael Anstey heir to the title of Earl of Hincham and the family estate, the much-neglected Chelworth. The initial plan is to dispose of the dilapidated stately home and acreage, but Michael soon becomes determined to restore Chelworth, and to reunite his family under one roof.

ANYTHING MORE WOULD BE GREEDY

26 July 1989, Wednesday, 9:00–10:00pm, ITV, 6 episodes, drama, British, contemporary
Anglia Television
Pr: John Rosenberg
Dir: Rodney Bennett
Wtr: Malcolm Bradbury
Cast: **Dennis Medlam – Robert Bathurst**
Anna – Sharon Holm
Mark – Matthew Marsh
Lynn – Alison Sterling
Peter – Martin Wenner

A serio-comic look at a group of young people from Cambridge, beginning in 1973 and tracing their personal and professional lives over the next ten years: Dennis becomes an MP, Peter a scientist, Mark and Anna marry . . . and Lynn ultimately publishes a racy "kiss-and-tell" book which reveals all about her Cambridge classmates.

ACT OF WILL

15 September 1989, Friday, 9:00–10:00pm, ITV, 4 episodes, drama, British, 20th century
Portman Production for Tyne Tees Television
Video: available in UK
Pr: Victor Glynn, Ian Warre
Dir: Don Sharp
Wtr: Jill Hyem
Based on Barbara Taylor Bradford

Cast: Jane Sedgewick – Lynsey Baxter
Miles Sutherland – Peter Coyote
Gwen – Serena Gordon
Christina – Elizabeth Hurley
Eliza Crowther – Jean Marsh
Vincent Crowther – Kevin McNally
Alex Newman – Stuart Milligan
Aunt Alicia – Judy Parfitt
Audra – Victoria Tennant

In a story based on the life of Bradford's mother, orphaned Audra and her brothers live with their unpleasant relatives in Yorkshire in the 1920s. Determined to be free, Audra studies nursing and also enters into an unhappy marriage to Vincent Crowther. Audra focuses her attention on her daughter Christina, who grows up to study art at the Royal Academy in London – but is distracted by her romance with married politician Miles Sutherland. After Audra's death, Christina moves to New York, where she attempts to put her life in England behind her . . . but memories continually intrude.

CONFESSIONAL

4 October 1989, Wednesday,
9:00–10:00pm, ITV, 4 episodes, thriller,
Irish, contemporary
Granada Television/Harmony Gold/Rete-Europa
Pr: Richard Everitt, Gordon Flemyng
Dir: Gordon Flemyng
Wtr: James Mitchell
Based on Jack Higgins
Cast: **Liam Devlin – Keith Carradine**
Thomas Kelly – Robert Lindsay
Pope – Anthony Quayle
Tanya Maslovskaya – Valentina Yakunina

Irish-American Liam Devlin is forced by British Intelligence to track down Irish-Russian assassin Thomas Kelly, whom Devlin had known as a child. Defecting Russian pianist Tanya helps Devlin in his search, but before Kelly can be arrested he escapes and embarks on his ultimate mission: a plan to assassinate the Pope.

NICE WORK

4 October 1989, Wednesday,
9:25–10:20pm, BBC2, 4 episodes, drama,
British, contemporary
BBCtv/Pebble Mill
Pr: Chris Parr
Dir: Christopher Menaul
Wtr: David Lodge
Based on David Lodge
Cast: Stuart Baxter – David Calder
Vic Wilcox – Warren Clarke
Marjorie Wilcox – Janet Dale
Brian Everthorpe – John Forgeham
Philip Swallow – Christopher Godwin
Robyn Penrose – Haydn Gwynne

Sexist, self-made engineering industrialist Vic Wilcox goes one-on-one with feminist academic Dr. Robyn Penrose when she reluctantly agrees to "shadow" Wilcox as part of a 1986 Industry Year initiative. Their relationship develops along parallel lines to the Victorian novels Robyn teaches at university; despite their many differences, the two grow close to one another.

Winner, Royal Television Society Award, Best Drama Serial 1989.

MOTHER LOVE

29 October 1989, Sunday, 9:05–10:00pm,
BBC1, 4 episodes, thriller, British, contemporary
BBCtv
Pr: Ken Riddington
Dir: Simon Langton
Wtr: Andrew Davies
Based on Domini Taylor
Cast: Ruth – Isla Blair
Angela – Fiona Gillies
George – James Grout
Alex – David McCallum
Helena – Diana Rigg
Kit – James Wilby

Helena's intense hatred for her ex-husband Alex is matched only by her obsessive love for their grown son Kit . . . and Helena will stop at nothing, including cold-blooded murder, to keep Alex from finding happiness and ensure she remains first in Kit's affections.

Winner, BAFTA Award, Best Drama Serial 1989.

SUMMER'S LEASE

1 November 1989, Wednesday, 9:25–10:20pm, BBC2, 4 episodes, drama, British, contemporary
BBCtv
Pr: Colin Rogers
Dir: Martyn Friend
Wtr: John Mortimer
Based on John Mortimer
Cast: Prince Tosti-Castelnuovo – Fyodor Chaliapin
Connie Tapscott – Annette Crosbie
Molly Pargeter – Susan Fleetwood
Haverford Downs – John Gielgud
Buck Kettering – Jeremy Kemp
Nancy Leadbetter – Rosemary Leach
Ken Corduroy – Denis Lill
Rosie Fortinbras – Mel Martin
Hugh Pargeter – Michael Pennington
William Fosdyke – Leslie Phillips
Nicholas Tapscott – Frederick Treves

The Pargeters set off for a month's holiday at a Tuscany villa, where Molly is determined to see that nothing disturbs her family's idyll, especially not the presence of her unpleasant father, aging journalist and rogue Haverford Downs. Her plans, however, go completely awry, and the trip to Tuscany ultimately changes the lives of all involved.

THE FREE FRENCHMAN

8 November 1989, Wednesday, 9:00–10:00pm, ITV, 6 episodes, drama, French, 20th century
Central Films/Films Ariane
Pr: Chris Burt
Dir: Jim Goddard
Wtr: Ted Whitehead
Based on Piers Paul Read
Cast: Captain Lutze – Hartmut Becker
Colonel Vivet – Bernard Bloch
Lucia – Katia Caballero
Madeleine – Corinne Dacla
Harry Jackson – Stephen Davies
Bertrand de Roujay – Derek de Lint
Jenny Trent – Beatie Edney
Nellie Planchet – Agnes Soral

In 1931, Catholic aristocrat Bertrand de Roujay is wed to Madeleine, but their union collapses at the advent of World War II. Bertrand joins the free French forces based in London, and serves courageously until he is captured by the Germans.

THE CHRONICLES OF NARNIA: PRINCE CASPIAN

19 November 1989, Sunday, 5:45–6:15pm, BBC1, 5 episodes, drama, classic, family, fantasy, British, 20th century
BBCtv
Video: available in UK, US
Pr: Paul Stone
Dir: Alex Kirby
Wtr: Alan Seymour
Based on C.S. Lewis
Cast: Aslan – Ailsa Berk/William Todd-Jones
Susan – Sophie Cook
Peter – Richard Dempsey
King Miraz – Robert Lang
Prince Caspian – Jean-Marc Perret
Voice of Aslan – Ronald Pickup
Edmund – Jonathan R. Scott
Eustace – David Thwaites
Lucy – Sophie Wilcox

Susan, Peter, Edmund and Lucy are summoned back to Narnia when Prince Caspian requests their help in restoring the magical land to its "Golden Age" when Aslan was the true ruler. After the old order is restored, the children prepare to leave, Susan and Peter bidding a final farewell to Narnia, as they have grown too old to ever come back again.

THE GINGER TREE

26 November 1989, Sunday, 9:05–10:05pm, BBC1, 4 episodes, drama, British, 20th century
BBCtv/NAK
Pr: Tim Ironside Wood
Dir: Anthony Garner
Wtr: Christopher Hampton
Based on Oswald Wynd
Cast: **Mary Mackenzie – Samantha Bond**
Baroness Aiko Onodera – Fumi Dan
Isabelle de Chamonpierre – Cecile Paoli

Richard Collingsworth – Adrian Rawlins
Count Kurihama – Daisuke Ryu

Love transcends national barriers as Scottish Mary Mackenzie journeys to Manchuria in 1903 to marry her fiancé, upper-crust military officer Richard Collingsworth. But Mary soon becomes disillusioned with her husband and finds herself involved in a passionate affair with Japanese nobleman Kurihama.

BLACKEYES

29 November 1989, Wednesday, 9:25–10:20pm, BBC2, 4 episodes, drama, British, contemporary
BBCtv
Pr: Rick McCallum
Dir: Dennis Potter
Wtr: Dennis Potter
Cast: Blackeyes – Gina Bellman
Maurice James Kingsley – Michael Gough
Jamieson – Colin Jeavons
Jeff – Nigel Planer
Jessica – Carol Royle
Detective Blake – John Shrapnel
Stilk – Nicholas Woodison

Elderly novelist Maurice James Kingsley writes a lurid novel, *Blackeyes* (dramatized here as a story-in-a-story), based on what his niece Jessica has told him about her modelling career, distorting her recollections into a work of near-pornography which becomes an unexpectedly huge success. Jessica is horrified by her uncle's unscrupulous actions and plans a suitable revenge.

THE CHRONICLES OF NARNIA: THE VOYAGE OF THE DAWN TREADER

24 December 1989, Sunday, 5:50–6:20pm, BBC1, 2 episodes, drama, classic, family, fantasy, British, 20th century
BBCtv
Video: available in UK, US
Pr: Paul Stone
Dir: Alex Kirby
Wtr: Alan Seymour
Based on C.S. Lewis
Cast: Princess – Gabrielle Anwar
Aslan – Ailsa Berk/William Todd-Jones/Tim Rose
Reepicheep – Warwick Davis
Voice of Aslan – Ronald Pickup
Edmund – Jonathan R. Scott
Eustace – David Thwaites
King Caspian – Samuel West
Lucy – Sophie Wilcox

Lucy, Edmund, and their arrogant cousin Eustace are magically pulled from their bedroom onto the sea-going Dawn Treader, where now-grown King Caspian is in search of the missing seven Lords of Narnia. They sail to the end of the earth before their mission is successfully completed; as Caspian readies to return to Narnia, he and Aslan bid a final farewell to Lucy and Edmund, who return with a humbled Eustace to the ordinary world.

1990–1994

LITTLE SIR NICHOLAS

3 January 1990, Wednesday, 5:10–5:35pm, BBC1, 6 episodes, drama, family, British, 19th century
BBCtv
Pr: Richard Callanan
Dir: Andrew Morgan
Wtr: David Benedictus
Based on Cecilia Anne Jones
Cast: **Sir Nicholas Tremaine – Max Beazley**
Lady Tremaine – Rachel Gurney
Margaret Tremaine – Louisa Haigh
Mere Annette – Jenny McCracken
Gerald Tremaine – Jonathan Norris
Mrs. Tremaine – Bernice Stegers
William Randle – Christopher Villiers

When young Nicholas Tremaine is presumed dead in a shipwreck, his rightful position as heir to a grand Cornish estate goes to another Tremaine boy; after being brought up in Brittany, Nicholas returns to Cornwall to reclaim his title, but he and the other family members have difficulty adjusting to his return.

ORANGES ARE NOT THE ONLY FRUIT

10 January 1990, Wednesday, 9:25–10:20pm, BBC2, 3 episodes, drama, British, contemporary
BBCtv
Pr: Phillippa Giles
Dir: Beeban Kidron
Wtr: Jeanette Winterson
Based on Jeanette Winterson
Cast: Small Jess – Emily Aston
Melanie – Cathryn Bradshaw
Jess – Charlotte Coleman
Pastor Finch – Kenneth Cranham
Mrs. Green – Freda Dowie
Mother – Geraldine McEwan
Katy – Tania Rodrigues
May – Elizabeth Spriggs
Doctor – David Thewlis
Elsie – Margery Withers

In this autobiographical novel, based on Winterson's own experiences in the Midlands in the 1960s, Jess is raised in Lancashire by her religiously fanatic adoptive Mother who trains Jess to devote herself to the Lord and keeps her isolated from other children; when, as a teenager, Jess falls in love with another young girl, Mother reacts strongly to what she feels is an unnatural passion.

Winner, BAFTA Award, Royal Television Society Award, Best Drama Serial 1990.

A SENSE OF GUILT

16 January 1990, Tuesday, 9:30–10:20pm, BBC1, 7 episodes, drama, British, contemporary
BBCtv
Pr: Simon Passmore
Dir: Bruce Macdonald
Wtr: Andrea Newman
Cast: Richard Murray – Jim Carter
Sally Hinde – Rudi Davies
Felix Cramer – Trevor Eve
Inge Murray – Malgoscha Gebel
Helen Irving – Lisa Harrow
Elizabeth Cramer – Morag Hood
Carey Hinde – Philip McGough

Self-centered novelist Felix Cramer returns to London after years abroad and in short order disrupts the social order of his circle of friends by seducing the teenage daughter of his best friend, social worker Richard Murray, but the young woman is just the first of Felix's latest romantic conquests.

BORDER WARFARE

10 February 1990, Saturday, 10:00–11:00pm, Channel 4, 3 episodes, drama, historical, Scottish, 16th–20th century
Freeway Films
Pr: David Brown
Dir: John McGrath
Wtr: John McGrath
Cast: **Irish Angus/Robert the Bruce/John Knox – Derek Anders**
Bon Accord – Dave Anderson
Elizabeth I/Isabel – Juliet Cadzow
Mary Queen of Scots/Edwina – Maria Miller
David I/Henry II – John Purcell
William Lyon/Henry VIII – Bill Riddoch

An epic telling of Scotland's stormy

relations with England, beginning with the story of Mary Queen of Scots, then moving on to the Gunpowder Plot, the controversial Act of Union and the riots which ensued, and concluding in the 1980s.

NEVER COME BACK

21 March 1990, Wednesday,
9:25–10:15pm, BBC2, 3 episodes, drama, British, 20th century
BBCtv
Pr: Joe Waters
Dir: Ben Bolt
Wtr: David Pirie
Based on John Mair
Cast: Mr. Poole – Timothy Bateson
Marcus – Jonathan Coy
Foster – James Fox
Anna Raven – Suzanna Hamilton
Desmond Thane – Nathaniel Parker

In 1939, aspiring novelist Desmond Thane, at loose ends, imagines himself suffering from boredom – until a chance meeting with mysterious Anna Raven quickly escalates into obsession, an attraction which embroils Thane in a wild and violent adventure which culminates in murder.

NOT A PENNY MORE, NOT A PENNY LESS

25 March 1990, Sunday, 7:15–8:05pm, BBC1, 4 episodes, drama, British, contemporary
BBCtv
Pr: Jacqueline Davis
Dir: Clive Donner
Wtr: Sherman Yellen
Based on Jeffrey Archer
Cast: Jill Albery – Jenny Agutter
Harvey Metcalfe – Edward Asner
Stephen Bradley – Ed Begley, Jr.
Charles – Jonathan Brook
David Kesler – Nicolas Colicos
Anne Summerton – Maryam D'abo
Saunders – Bill Hutchinson

Corrupt American millionaire Harvey Metcalfe sets up an office for his Spectra Oil in London, run by naïve and eager David Kesler – and plots a swindling scheme which nearly successfully drains the bank accounts of a number of wealthy victims.

THE GIFT

28 March 1990, Wednesday, 5:10–5:35pm, BBC1, 6 episodes, thriller, family, British, contemporary
Red Rooster Films for BBCtv
Pr: Linda James
Dir: Marc Evans, Red Saunders
Wtr: Anthony Horowitz
Based on Peter Dickinson
Cast: Dadda – Denys Graham
Nain – Cynthia Grenville
Penny Price – Emma-Louise Harrington
Sonia – Jodhi May
John Price – Jeff Rawle
Rita Price – Jacqueline Tong
Davy Price – Tat Whalley

After fourteen-year-old Davy is sent to Wales to stay with his grandparents, he discovers that he has inherited from his grandmother a strange, frightening, mind-reading power known as "the Gift."

THE GRAVY TRAIN

27 June 1990, Wednesday, 10:00–11:00pm, Channel 4, 4 episodes, drama, satire, British/European, contemporary
Portman Productions
Pr: Philip Hinchcliffe, Ian Warren
Dir: David Tucker
Wtr: Malcolm Bradbury
Cast: Delise – Amanda Mealing
Hilda – Judy Parfitt
Michael Spearpoint – Ian Richardson
Milcic – Alexei Sayle
Villeneuve – Jacques Sereys
Nadine – Almanta Suska
Hans-Joachim Dorfmann – Christoph Waltz

Hans-Joachim Dorfmann takes up a junior position at the EEC and is promoted to the odd position of supervisor of soft fruit, a circumstance which involves Hans in the transport of a convoy of rotting plums and leads to his

PORTRAIT OF A MARRIAGE

19 September 1990, Wednesday,
9:25–10:20pm, BBC2, 4 episodes, drama,
biographical, British, 20th century
BBCtv in association with WGBH/Boston, NZTV
Pr: Colin Tucker
Dir: Stephen Whittaker
Wtr: Penelope Mortimer
Based on Nigel Nicolson
Cast: Denys Trefusis – Peter Birch
Young Violet – Hannah Cresswell
Lady Sackville – Diana Fairfax
Harold Nicolson – David Haig
Young Vita – Nicola Hammett
Violet Keppel – Cathryn Harrison
Vita Sackville-West – Janet McTeer

In the 1920s, the marriage of novelist Vita Sackville-West and politician Harold Nicolson takes a number of unorthodox turns: first Harold tells Vita he is homosexual, then Vita begins a love affair with her childhood friend Violet Keppel. The women travel together to France; upon their return Vita finds herself the subject of gossip and scandal. Worse, Violet is pressured to marry, so the women elope, only to be tracked down by the men in their lives and convinced to end their relationship.

CENTREPOINT

8 October 1990, Monday, 10:00–11:00pm,
Channel 4, 4 episodes, thriller, British, contemporary
Rosso Productions
Pr: Franco Rosso, Joanna Smith
Dir: Piers Haggard
Wtr: Nigel Williams
Cast: Maria – Cheryl Campbell
Saskia – Abigail Cruttenden
Roland Wearing – Jonathan Firth
Nick – Murray Head
Dum Dum – Derrick O'Connor
Armstrong – Bob Peck
Claud – John Shrapnel

After ten years of believing his father discovery of the biggest bribery and corruption fraud in the Common Market's history.

Nick to be dead, Roland Wearing discovers that he is alive. But the reunion isn't as happy as it should be, and once Roland discovers that Nick's story about the past – which plays Nick as the innocent victim of betrayal at the hands of Roland's mother Maria and uncle Claud (Nick's brother) – is not the entire truth, father and son confront one another about what really is the truth, after all.

BLOOD RIGHTS

24 October 1990, Wednesday,
7:25–8:20pm, BBC2, 3 episodes, thriller, British, contemporary
BBCtv
Pr: Caroline Oulton
Dir: Lesley Manning
Wtr: Mike Phillips
Based on Mike Phillips
Cast: **Sammy Dean – Brian Bovell**
Roy – Akim Mogaji
Virginia – Hermione Norris
Winston – Dhobi Oparei
Grenville Barker – Struan Rodger
Tess Barker – Maggie Steed

Black journalist Sammy Dean is hired by prominent MP Grenville Barker to find Barker's kidnapped daughter Virginia. Unknown to both men, Virginia and her half-brother Roy are behind the kidnapping, as a way of extorting money from their father – but things get out of hand when Roy's associate Winston ups the ante, and the risk to all becomes quite real.

THE GREEN MAN

28 October 1990, Sunday, 9:05–10:00pm,
BBC1, 3 episodes, thriller, British, contemporary
BBCtv in association with Arts & Entertainment Network
Video: available in US
Pr: David Snodin
Dir: Elijah Moshinsky
Wtr: Malcolm Bradbury
Based on Kingsley Amis
Cast: Diana – Sarah Berger
Dr. Underhill – Michael Culver
Maurice Allington – Albert Finney

Jack – Nicky Henson
Gramps – Michael Hordern
Lucy – Josie Lawrence
Joyce – Linda Marlowe
Amy – Natalie Morse

On his 53rd birthday, alcoholic, womanizing hotel proprietor Maurice Allington is startled by the appearance of the ghost of Dr. Thomas Underhill, a 17th-century clergyman whose hauntings are part of the local lore. As Allingham attempts to unravel the mystery behind the visitations, he is drawn further and further into Underhill's web of evil thoughts and deeds.

DIE KINDER

14 November 1990, Sunday, 9:25–10:25pm, BBC2, 6 episodes, thriller, British/European contemporary
BBCtv in association with WGBH/Boston
Pr: Michael Wearing
Dir: Rob Walker
Wtr: Paula Milne
Cast: Alan Mitchell – Sam Cox
Karin Muller – Tina Engel
Lomax – Frederic Forrest
Crombie – Derek Fowlds
Sidonie Reiger – Miranda Richardson
Michael Reiger – Tommy Selby-Plewman
Sabine Reiger – Zara Warshal

After Sidonie's two children are kidnapped by her German ex-husband, Sidonie embarks on a desperate search to find them and bring them home, involving her in intrigue and terror, and leading from London to Germany and back to London.

THE CHRONICLES OF NARNIA: THE SILVER CHAIR

18 November 1990, Sunday, 5:45–6:15pm, BBC1, 6 episodes, drama, classic, family, fantasy, British, 20th century
BBCtv
Video: available in UK, US
Pr: Paul Stone
Dir: Alex Kirby
Wtr: Alan Seymour
Based on C.S. Lewis
Cast: **Puddleglum – Tom Baker**
Aslan – Ailsa Berk/William Todd-Jones
Glimfeather – Warwick Davis
Prince Rillian – Richard Henders
Green Lady/Queen of the Deep Realm – Barbara Kellermann
Young Caspian – Jean-Marc Perret
Aslan's Voice – Ronald Pickup
Jill – Camilla Power
King Caspian – Geoffrey Russell
Eustace – David Thwaites

Back at school after his adventures with his cousins, Eustace is transported again to Narnia, accompanied by schoolmate Jill, in order to find Prince Rillian, long-missing son of the now-aged King Caspian. Aided by Marshwiggle Puddleglum, the children's dangerous quest involves an encounter with the giants at Harfang Castle and capture in the underworld by the evil Queen of the Deep Realm. After finding and freeing the Prince, who is then crowned King, Jill and Eustace are sent home, the children's final farewell to the magical land of Narnia and its benevolent lion Aslan.

HOUSE OF CARDS

18 November 1990, Sunday, 9:00–10:00pm, BBC1, 4 episodes, thriller, satire, British, contemporary
BBCtv
Pr: Ken Riddington
Dir: Paul Seed
Wtr: Andrew Davies
Based on Michael Dobbs
Cast: Anne Collingride – Isabelle Amyes
Roger O'Neill – Miles Anderson
Elizabeth Urquhart – Diane Fletcher
Mattie Storin – Susannah Harker
Stamper – Colin Jeavons
Henry Collingridge – David Lyon
Francis Urquhart – Ian Richardson
Charles Collingridge – James Villiers

Set in a contemporaneous, not-too-distant future, treacherous, Machiavellian party Chief Whip Francis Urquhart will stop at nothing to see himself installed at No. 10 Downing Street, starting out by undermining the new Prime Minister . . . and eventually going so far as murder.

COME HOME CHARLIE AND FACE THEM

25 November 1990, Sunday,
9:05–10:20pm, ITV, 3 episodes, drama,
Welsh, 20th century
London Weekend Television
Pr: Sue Whatmough
Dir: Roger Bamford
Wtr: Alun Owen
Based on R.F. Delderfield
Cast: Delphine – Jennifer Calvert
      Gwladys – Sylvia Kay
      Charlie Pritchard – Tom Radcliffe
      Evan Rhys-Jones – Peter Sallis
      Ida – Mossie Smith
      Beppo – Jon Soresi

In North Wales in the Depression-hit 1930s, mild-mannered bank cashier Charlie Pritchard is seduced away from his humdrum existence by the lovely Delphine, who involves Charlie in a robbery plan. But Charlie suspects that Delphine and another cohort, Beppo, are planning to betray him and escape on their own after the robbery – and, having grown over the course of this experience, takes it upon himself to set things right.

DEVICES AND DESIRES

4 January 1991, Friday, 9:00–10:00pm, ITV,
6 episodes, mystery, British, contemporary
Anglia Television
Pr: John Rosenberg
Dir: John Davies
Wtr: Thomas Ellice
Based on P.D. James
Cast: Dr. Toby Gledhill – Harry Burton
      Miles Lessingham – Tom Chadbon
      Amy Camm – Nicola Cowper
      Hilary Robarts – Suzan Crowley
      Dr. Alex Mair – James Faulkner
      Chief Inspector Terry Rickards – Tony Haygarth
      Neil Pascoe – Robert Hines
      Alice Mair – Gemma Jones
      Adam Dalgliesh – Roy Marsden
      Caroline Amphlett – Helena Michell
      Teresa Blaney – Lisa Taylor
      Meg Dennison – Susannah York

Adam Dalgliesh is on leave near the North Norfolk coast, but soon is caught up in a series of murders which some local people believe are connected with the nearby Larksoken nuclear power station, run by ambitious Alex Mair. The killings appear to be the work of a serial killer referred to as the Whistler, but Dalgliesh comes to believe there may well be two killers at work, in an intrigue where computer sabotage, terrorism, and incest are revealed before all questions are answered.

PARNELL AND THE ENGLISHWOMAN

9 January 1991, Wednesday,
9:25–10:25pm, BBC2, 4 episodes, drama, biographical, historical, Irish, 19th century
BBCtv
Pr: Terry Coles
Dir: John Bruce
Wtr: Hugh Leonard
Cast: **Katharine O'Shea – Francesca Annis**
      Timothy Healy – Lorcan Cranitch
      Charles Stewart Parnell – Trevor Eve
      Mr. Gladstone – Robert Lang
      Justin McCarthy – T.P. McKenna
      Captain Willie O'Shea – David Robb
      Anna Steele – Sheila Ruskin

In 1880 Charles Stewart Parnell, one of the most charismatic politicians in the House, a champion of Home Rule, seems destined to do great things for Ireland and himself. But then he meets and falls in love with married Katharine O'Shea, and their romance and the scandal it provokes lead to his downfall, both politically and personally.

FIVE CHILDREN AND IT

9 January 1991, Wednesday, 5:10–5:35pm,
BBC1, 6 episodes, drama, family, fantasy,
British, 20th century
BBCtv
Video: available in UK
Pr: Richard Callanan
Dir: Marilyn Fox
Wtr: Helen Cresswell
Based on E.E. Nesbit
Cast: **Jane – Tamzen Audas**

Martha – Laura Brattan
Mother – Mary Conlon
Cyril – Simon Godwin
Anthea – Nicole Moway
Robert – Charlie Richards
Psammead's Voice – Francis Wright

While exploring in the sand, Jane, Cyril, Anthea, Robert and their baby brother discover "it," a Psammead sand fairy with the power to grant wishes. Their subsequent wishes at first bring much fun and adventure, but ultimately get the children into a ghastly mess – with no sign of the sand fairy to come to their rescue.

FOR THE GREATER GOOD

20 March 1991, Wednesday, 9:25–10:25pm, BBC2, 3 episodes, drama, British, contemporary
BBCtv
Pr: Kenith Trodd
Dir: Danny Boyle
Wtr: G.F. Newman
Cast: Naomi Balliol – Connie Booth
Charles Truman – Roy Dotrice
David West – David Harewood
Julian Brind – Nicholas Jones
Gillian Savage – Fiona Shaw
Dr. Peter Balliol – Martin Shaw
Sir Dennis Whites – Colin Welland

Set in the near future, Tory MP backbencher Peter Balliol, civil servant Gillian Savage and Home Secretary Charles Truman must weigh the dictates of conscience against career survival, as the government struggles to react to the combined crises of AIDS, prison riots and the threat of a police state.

PRIME SUSPECT

7 April 1991, Sunday (subsequent episodes aired on Monday), 9:05–11:05pm, ITV, 3 episodes, mystery, British, contemporary
Granada Television
Video: available in UK, US
Pr: Don Leaver
Dir: Christopher Menaul
Wtr: Lynda La Plante
Cast: **Detective Sergeant Bill Otley – Tom Bell**
Detective Chief Superintendent Michael Kernan – John Benfield
George Marlow – John Bowe
Detective Inspector Tony Muddyman – Jack Ellis
Detective Inspector Frank Burkin – Craig Fairbrass
Michael – Ralph Fiennes
Detective Chief Inspector Jane Tennison – Helen Mirren
Moyra Henson – Zoe Wanamaker
Detective Sergeant Terry Anson – Gary Whelan
Peter Rawlins – Tom Wilkinson

Detective Chief Inspector Jane Tennison has fought her way up the ranks at Scotland Yard and gets her first chance to head a murder inquiry when the detective in charge suddenly dies. Facing the open hostility of the men on her squad, most particularly from DS Bill Otley, Tennison has as much difficulty asserting her command and earning the trust of the other, male officers as solving the murders of a prostitute and another young woman.

Winner, BAFTA Award, Best Drama Serial 1991.

SLEEPERS

10 April 1991, Wednesday, 9:25–10:20pm, BBC2, 4 episodes, thriller, satire, British, contemporary
Cinema Verity Production for BBCtv
Pr: Caroline Gold
Dir: Geoffrey Sax
Wtr: John Flanagan, Andrew McCulloch
Cast: **Albert Robinson – Warren Clarke**
Bob Riley – John Flanagan
Andrei Zorin – Michael Gough
Jeremy Coward – Nigel Havers
Major Nina Grishina – Joanna Kanska

Ex-agents Jeremy Coward, now an investment banker, and brewery shop steward Albert Robinson are the unlikely pair assigned the task of investigating the sudden increase in KGB activity in the United Kingdom.

A PERFECT HERO

17 May 1991, Friday, 9:00–10:00pm, ITV, 6 episodes, drama, British, 20th century
Havahall Pictures and London Weekend Television
Pr: James Cellan Jones
Dir: James Cellan Jones
Wtr: Allan Prior
Based on Christopher Matthew
Cast: **Marjorie Fisher – Amanda Elwes**
Angus Meikle – James Fox
Bunty Morrell – Fiona Gillies
Hugh Fleming – Nigel Havers
Arthur Fleming – Bernard Hepton
Iris Fleming – Barbara Leigh-Hunt
Loretta Stone – Joanna Lumley
Julian Masters – Nicholas Pritchard
Tim Holland – Patrick Ryecart

Lady-killer Hugh Fleming leads a charmed life . . . until World War II begins. Hugh and his Cambridge friends immediately sign up in the RAF, but Hugh is terribly burnt in a Battle of Britain dogfight and undergoes extensive plastic surgery at the hands of expert Angus Meikle. Despite his painful recovery, Hugh is determined to return to the cockpit, and with the help of therapist Marjorie, whose interest in Hugh is more than strictly professional, he regains his strength, but whether he will ever fly again is still up in the air.

G.B.H.

6 June 1991, Thursday, 9:00–10:40pm, Channel 4, 7 episodes, drama, British, contemporary
GBH Films
Video: available in UK
Pr: Alan Bleasdale, David Jones
Dir: Robert Young
Wtr: Alan Bleasdale
Cast: Barbara Douglas – Lindsay Duncan
Michael Murray – Robert Lindsay
Laura Nelson – Dearbhla Molloy
Jim Nelson – Michael Palin
Dr. Jacobs – John Shrapnel
Mrs. Murray – Julie Walters
Franky Murray – Philip Whitchurch

Ambitious local politician Michael Murray comes in conflict with devoted headmaster Jim Nelson when a strike is called, but ultimately the two discover that they are both pawns in a game being played by higher powers.

Alan Bleasdale originally developed this story as a feature film, then attempted to turn it into a novel before re-formatting it for television.

SELLING HITLER

11 June 1991, Tuesday, 9:00–10:00pm, ITV, 5 episodes, drama, satire, non-fiction, British/German, contemporary
Euston Films
Pr: Andrew Brown
Dir: Alastair Reid
Wtr: Howard Schuman
Based on Robert Harris
Cast: Lord Dacre – Alan Bennett
Gina Heidemann – Alison Doody
Rupert Murdoch – Barry Humphries
David Irving – Roger Lloyd Pack
Gerd Heidemann – Jonathan Pryce
Conny Fischer – Alexei Sayle
Gerd Schulte Hillen – John Shrapnel
Edda Goering – Alison Steadman
Henri Hannen – Richard Wilson

German journalist Gerd Heidemann stumbles upon a diary written (or so he thinks) by Adolf Hitler, and convinces the editors of *Stern* magazine that they are on to the publishing coup of the century. The *Sunday Times* also contracts for exclusive rights to the diaries, which are ultimately revealed to be a forgery, to the embarrassment of the publications which had eagerly shelled out lots of money for them and heralded their authenticity.

THE REAL CHARLOTTE

16 June 1991, Sunday, 8:20–9:50pm, ITV, 3 episodes, drama, Irish, 19th century
Granada Television/Gandon Productions
Video: available in US
Pr: Niall McCarthy
Dir: Tony Barry
Wtr: Bernard McLaverty
Based on Martin Ross, Edith Somerville
Cast: Lambert – Patrick Bergin
Charlotte Mullen – Jeananne Crowley

Hawkins – Nicholas Hewetson
Christopher – Robin Lermitte
Francie Fitzpatrick – Joanna Roth

In Ireland in 1895, Francie Fitzpatrick lodges with her cousin, Charlotte Mullen, who disapproves when Francie falls in love with a penniless British officer. The conflict between the cousins continues after Francie's marriage, as Charlotte schemes to ruin Francie's husband, and it is up to Francie to come to his rescue.

CHIMERA

7 July 1991, Sunday, 9:00–10:00pm, ITV, 4 episodes, thriller, British, contemporary
Anglia Films
Video: available in UK
Pr: Lawrence Gordon Clark
Dir: Nick Gillott
Wtr: Stephen Gallagher
Based on Stephen Gallagher
Cast: Dr. Horsley – Gillian Barge
Dr. Jenner – David Calder
Hennessey – Kenneth Cranham
Nurse Tracy Pickford – Emer Gillespie
Alison Wells – Christine Kavanagh
Peter Carson – John Lynch

Following up on a lead from his girlfriend, journalist Peter Carson investigates the mysterious goings on at a top secret research clinic in Chimera where, unknown to the outside world, a half-man, half-ape creature has been genetically engineered . . . and after a violent, bloody rampage, breaks out, and is on the loose in the wilds of Cumbria. It's then up to Carson, aided by scientist Alison Wells, to get the truth out to the public.

MURDER IN EDEN

19 July 1991, Friday, 9:30–10:25pm, BBC1, 3 episodes, thriller, Irish, contemporary
BBCtv
Pr: Robert Cooper
Dir: Nicholas Renton
Wtr: Shane Connaughton
Based on *Bogmail* by Patrick McGinty
Cast: **Sergeant McGing – Alun Armstrong**
Canon Loftus – Ian Bannen
Tim Roarty – Tony Doyle
Kenneth Potter – Peter Firth
Susan – Tina Kelleher
Nora Hession – Tara MacGowran

The sleepy Irish fishing village of Glenkeel is rudely awakened by the grisly murder of barman Eales, whose body parts begin showing up around town. As Sergeant McGing attempts to solve the crime through conventional means, the self-named "Bogmailer" sends threatening letters to pub owner Tim Roarty, accusing him of the crime (Roarty is, in fact, guilty, having suspected Eales of seducing his daughter). Roarty decides the letters have been sent by Kenneth Potter, an Englishman new to the village, and plots to kill him, as McGing gets closer himself to the actual truth.

GREAT EXPECTATIONS

21 July 1991, Sunday, 7:45–8:45pm, ITV, 6 episodes, drama, classic, British, 19th century
HTV in association with Primetime Television
Video: available in US
Pr: Greg Smith
Dir: Kevin Connor
Wtr: John Goldsmith
Based on Charles Dickens
Cast: Herbert Pocket – Adam Blackwood
Pip – Anthony Calf
Young Pip – Martin Harvey
Magwitch – Anthony Hopkins
Mr. Jaggers – Ray McAnally
Mrs. Gargery – Rosemary McHale
Joe Gargery – John Rhys Davies
Miss Havisham – Jean Simmons
Estella – Kim Thomson

The saga of Pip, who is confronted early on by the menacing escaped convict Magwitch, but is rescued when mysterious Miss Havisham invites him to her home, where he meets the beautiful Estella. Later, Pip moves to London, where Herbert Pocket grooms him to become a gentleman, and where Pip finds himself aided by a mysterious benefactor whose generosity changes his life – but not necessarily for the better.

Jean Simmons had her feature film debut

in the role of Estella in the feature film of *Great Expectations* produced in 1946.

TITMUSS REGAINED

3 September 1991, Tuesday,
9:00–10:00pm, ITV, 3 episodes, drama, satire, British, contemporary
New Penny Production for Thames Television in association with WGBH/Boston
Pr: Jacqueline Davis
Dir: Martyn Friend
Wtr: John Mortimer
Based on John Mortimer
Cast: Ken Cracken – Peter Capaldi
 Joyce Timberlake – Holly De Jong
 Dot Curdle – Rosemary Leach
 Jenny Sidonia – Kristin Scott Thomas
 Dr. Fred Simcox – Paul Shelley
 Leslie Titmuss – David Threlfall

This sequel to *Paradise Postponed* finds Leslie Titmuss comfortably ensconced as the Conservative Minister for Housing, Ecological Affairs and Planning, better known as HEAP. Now widowed, Titmuss' relentless romantic pursuit of Jenny Sidonia nearly blinds him to the threat to the picturesque Rapstone Valley, where he has just bought a new estate, and which is in danger of falling prey to developers. In seeking to resolve the situation, Titmuss must choose between furthering his own career and helping his constituents.

THE MEN'S ROOM

25 September 1991, Wednesday,
9:25–10:15pm, BBC2, 5 episodes, drama, British, contemporary
BBCtv
Pr: David Snodin
Dir: Antonia Bird
Wtr: Laura Lamson
Based on Ann Oakley
Cast: Margaret – Charlotte Cornwell
 James – Patrick Drury
 Tessa Pascoe – Kate Hardie
 Jane Carleton – Mel Martin
 Mark Carleton – Bill Nighy
 Sally – Amanda Redman
 Swinhoe – Bill Stewart
 Charity Walton – Harriet Walter

A wicked tale of sex, marriage and betrayal spans the decade of the 1980s and focuses on the adulterous affair between Charity Walton and her new professor, Mark Carleton. The relationship ends both of their marriages, but it is several years before Charity and Mark make a serious commitment to one another . . . and even then it is threatened by Mark's attraction to the daughter of one of his colleagues.

JUTE CITY

27 October 1991, Sunday, 9:20–10:20pm, BBC1, 3 episodes, thriller, Scottish, contemporary
BBCtv
Pr: John Chapman
Dir: Stuart Orme
Wtr: David Kane
Cast: Sammy Kerr – Douglas Henshall
 Gabby – Jenny McCrindle
 Duncan Kerr – David O'Hara
 Caroline – Joanna Roth
 McMurdo – John Sessions

Bungling Scottish private detective McMurdo confronts strange and murderous goings on following ex-con Duncan Kerr's return home for his brother's wedding. When groom Sammy is murdered before the ceremony, Duncan sets out to solve the mystery, with McMurdo's help. The hapless private eye uncovers Sammy's shady business empire, involving the trafficking of illegal cargo . . . but will he survive to solve the crime?

THE GRAVY TRAIN GOES EAST

28 October 1991, Monday, 10:00–11:00pm, Channel 4, 4 episodes, drama, satire, British/European, contemporary
Portman Productions
Pr: Philip Hinchcliffe, Ian Warren
Dir: James Cellan Jones
Wtr: Malcolm Bradbury
Cast: **Katya Princip – Francesca Annis**
 Steadiman – Jeremy Child
 Hilda Spearpoint – Judy Parfitt
 Michael Spearpoint – Ian Richardson

Jean-Luc Villeneuve – Jacques
    Sereys
**Hans-Joachim Dorfmann –
Christoph Waltz**
Gianna Melchiori – Anita Zagaria

This sequel to *The Gravy Train* focuses on the fictitious Balkan state of Slaka, newly liberated from Communism. Romantic novelist Katya Princip is President, and she feverishly wants her country to join the European Community, a move which is blocked by Britain's pompous representative, Michael Spearpoint. Idealist Hans-Joachim Dorfmann, an officer with the World Bank, is dispatched east to Slaka to resolve the issue, and international havoc ensues.

CHILDREN OF THE NORTH

30 October 1991, Wednesday, 9:25–10:20pm, BBC2, 4 episodes, thriller, British/Irish, contemporary
BBCtv
Pr: Chris Parr
Dir: David Drury
Wtr: John Hale
Based on M.S. Power
Cast: **John Axton – Tony Doyle**
    Martin Deeley – Adrian Dunbar
    Kate – Michelle Fairley
    Arthur Apple – Michael Gough
    Shrapnell – Jonathan Hyde
    Seamus Reilly – John Kavanagh
    Colonel Mailer – Patrick Malahide

When two MI6 officers are killed near the border of Northern Ireland, it's up to Colonel Mailer and RUC Special Branch Officer John Axton to find the assassin and attempt to keep more killings from taking place. But the deaths have already set into action a chain of murder, intrigue and double-dealing between undercover elements of the British Army, RUC and IRA Provos.

Winner, Royal Television Society Award, Best Drama Serial 1991.

MERLIN OF THE CRYSTAL CAVE

17 November 1991, Sunday, 5:45–6:10pm, BBC1, 6 episodes, drama, fantasy, British, 6th century
Noel Gay Television
Video: available in US
Pr: Hilary Bevan Jones, Shaun Sutton
Dir: Michael Darlow
Wtr: Steve Bescoby
Based on books by Mary Stewart
Cast: Merlin (as a small boy) – Jody David
    Vortigern – Jon Finch
    Arthur – Sam Hails
    Galapas – Don Henderson
    Merlin (as a child) – Thomas Lambert
    Ralf – Trevor Peacock
    Ambrosius – Robert Powell
    Ninianne – Kim Thomson
    Merlin – George Winter

As Britain is divided by civil strife, Merlin the Enchanter comes of age and learns the ways and means of magic, ultimately clearing the path for Prince Arthur to take the throne as King and bring on the age of Camelot.

CLARISSA

27 November 1991, Wednesday, 9:25–10:30pm, BBC2, 3 episodes, drama, classic, British, 18th century
BBCtv in association with WGBH/Boston
Pr: Kevin Loader
Dir: Robert Bierman
Wtr: Janet Barron, David Nokes
Based on Samuel Richardson
Cast: Bella Harlowe – Lynsey Baxter
    Lovelace – Sean Bean
    Roger Solmes – Julian Firth
    Mrs. Sinclair – Cathryn Harrison
    Anna Howe – Hermione Norris
    Jack Belford – Sean Pertwee
    James Harlowe – Jonathan Phillips
    Lady Betty – Diana Quick
    Clarissa Harlowe – Saskia Wickham

Virginal and wilful 18th-century heiress Clarissa Harlowe seeks to escape marriage to the odious Roger Solmes, turning in desperation for protection to aristocratic rake Lovelace . . . whose own intentions are far from noble. Obsessed with seducing Clarissa, Lovelace "shelters" her in a London whorehouse, falsifies an engagement, drugs her, then finally resorts to rape, an act which ultimately leads to tragic ends for them both.

STANLEY AND THE WOMEN

28 November 1991, Thursday,
9:00–10:00pm, ITV, 4 episodes, drama, satire, British, contemporary
Central Films
Pr: Chris Burt
Dir: David Tucker
Wtr: Nigel Kneale
Based on Kingsley Amis
Cast: Rufus Hilton – Alun Armstrong
Susan Duke – Penny Downie
Bert Hutchinson – Michael Elphick
Nowell – Sheila Gish
Dr. Tish Collings – Geraldine James
Stanley Duke – John Thaw
Steve Duke – Samuel West

Newspaper advertising manager Stanley Duke seems to have it all – a good, reliable job, a loving second wife – and then all at once it falls apart: he is blamed for his son Steve's mental illness by both his first wife and the young man's (female) psychiatrist, his boss complains about his job performance, and wife Susan leaves him. At his breaking point, Stanley seeks to even the score.

GOODBYE CRUEL WORLD

6 January 1992, Monday, 9:00–10:00pm, BBC2, 3 episodes, drama, British, contemporary
BBCtv
Pr: David Snodin
Dir: Adrian Shergold
Wtr: Tony Marchant
Cast: **Roy Grade – Alun Armstrong**
Marjory – Brenda Bruce
Spector – Mick Ford
Barbara Grade – Sue Johnston
Cheevers – Will Knightley

The happily married lives of Barbara and Roy Grade suffer a crushing blow when Barbara is diagnosed with a rare, fatal muscle-wasting disease. In an attempt to deal with their grief, the Grades organize a charity for the condition, the Ways Disease Association, but are saddened still more when confronted with ambition, greed and possible fraud within the organization.

Winner, Royal Television Society Award, Best Drama Serial 1992.

A TIME TO DANCE

12 January 1992, Sunday, 9:05–10:05pm, BBC1, 3 episodes, drama, British, contemporary
BBCtv
Pr: Norman McCandlish
Dir: Kevin Billington
Wtr: Melvyn Bragg
Based on Melvyn Bragg
Cast: Joe Kennedy – Joseph Crilly
Bernadette Kennedy – Dervla Kirman
Angela Powell – Rosemary McHale
Andrew Powell – Ronald Pickup
Mrs. Kennedy – Anne Raitt
Jimmie – Stuart Wolfenden

Middle-aged bank manager Andrew Powell takes early retirement to care for his invalid wife. He meets 18-year-old Bernadette, a girl from the "wrong side" of the small Cumbrian town where they both live, and falls hopelessly in love with her. The chaos which ensues leads to the collapse of not only Andrew's marriage, but every aspect of his previously secure life.

THE CLONING OF JOANNA MAY

26 January 1992, Sunday, 9:05–10:35pm, ITV, 2 episodes, drama, British, contemporary
Granada Television
Pr: Gub Neal
Dir: Philip Saville
Wtr: Ted Whitehead
Based on Fay Weldon
Cast: Alice Morthampton – Helen Adie
Carl May – Brian Cox
Gina Herriot – Laura Eddy
Jane Jarvis – Emma Hardy
Joanna May – Patricia Hodge
Dr. Holly – Ian McNeice
Bethany – Siri Neal
Mavis – Billie Whitelaw

Divorcee Joanna May is already in the

throes of a middle-aged crisis when she learns that her former husband, wealthy and obsessive nuclear industrialist Carl, has used genetic engineering to create three clones of her. Joanna sets out in search of the clones, to protect them from Carl's lethal nature; but Carl has discovered that the young women are pale imitations of the real Joanna, "sow's ears from a silk purse" – although it is not his final foray into cloning.

UNDERBELLY

17 February 1992, Monday, 9:30–10:30pm, BBC2, 4 episodes, thriller, British, contemporary
Initial Production for BBCtv
Pr: Eileen Quinn
Dir: Nicholas Renton
Wtr: Peter Ransley
Based on Frank Kippax
Cast: Harry West – Michael Feast
       Stephen Crowe – David Hayman
       Jude Crowe – Christine Kavanagh
       Jack Preston – John McArdle
       Paul Manning – Tom Wilkinson

Successful property developer Stephen Crowe stands trial and is convicted on fraud charges. Hoping to spare his family and business from total ruin, Crowe turns for help to his friend Paul Manning, Junior Home Minister for Prisons. But Manning is in the midst of trying to control a rooftop prison protest; when it ends disastrously, Manning's professional life is also on the line. After Crowe is sent to prison, his wife Jude takes over the reins of the business; Manning pretends to help her, but really is planning to help turn the business over to one of Crowe's rivals. While behind bars, Crowe is caught in the middle of fellow inmate Jack Preston's escape plan at the moment a riot erupts at the prison.

THE OTHER SIDE OF PARADISE

22 February 1992, Saturday, 9:00–10:00pm, ITV, 4 episodes, drama, British, 20th century
Central Films in association with South Pacific Pictures and The Grundy Organization
Pr: Stanley Walsh
Dir: Renny Rye
Wtr: Denise Morgan
Based on Noel Barber
Cast: Edward Purvis – Hywel Bennett
       Paula Reid – Josephine Byrnes
       Chris Masters – Jason Connery
       Mana – Jay Lavea Laga'aia
       Aleena – Vivien Tan
       Doc Reid – Richard Wilson

In 1938 young Dr. Chris Masters must leave England after being involved in an accidental killing. He sets off for a remote South Seas island where he continues his work, often getting in trouble with the natives when he goes against island traditions. He also gets caught in the middle of a love triangle, between Paula Reid, the beautiful daughter of the island's doctor, and Aleena, an island Princess.

GROWING RICH

28 February 1992, Friday, 9:00–10:00pm, ITV, 6 episodes, drama, satire, British, contemporary
Anglia Television
Video: available in UK
Pr: Brian Farnham
Dir: Roger Gregory
Wtr: Fay Weldon
Cast: **Carmen – Rosalind Bennett**
      Tim – Jamie Foster
      Annie – Claire Hackett
      Laura – Caroline Harker
      Driver – Martin Kemp
      Woodie – Pearce Quigley
      Sir Bernard Bellamy – John Stride

Teenaged best friends Carmen, Laura and Annie dream of escaping from the rural rut of their life in East Anglia. The Devil, masquerading as suave chauffeur Driver, shows up and offers himself as the answer to the girls' dreams . . . but at what price? Driver chooses Carmen as a wife for his boss, offering good fortune for Carmen and her friends in exchange, but when she balks, Driver casts an evil spell over all three girls. In the several years that follow, each girl's life takes radical turns for both better and worse, and they ultimately join forces to give the Devil his due.

THE CAMOMILE LAWN

5 March 1992, Thursday, 9:00–11:00pm (subsequent episodes aired from 9:00–10:00pm), Channel 4, 4 episodes, drama, British, 20th century
A Zed Ltd. Production in association with the Australian Broadcasting Commission
Pr: Sophie Balhetchet, Glenn Wilhide
Dir: Peter Hall
Wtr: Ken Taylor
Based on Mary Wesley
Cast: Older Sophy – Claire Bloom
Max Erstweiler – Oliver Cotton
Richard Cuthbertson – Paul Eddington
Calypso – Jennifer Ehle
Polly – Tara Fitzgerald
Sophy – Rebecca Hall
Older Calypso – Rosemary Harris
Older Oliver – Richard Johnson
Helena Cuthbertson – Felicity Kendal
Hector/Hamish – Nicholas le Prevost
Older Polly – Virginia McKenna
Oliver – Toby Stephens
Walter – Ben Walden
Monika Erstweiler – Trudy Weiss

In 1939, five cousins spend time at an annual summer holiday at their aunt Helena Cuthbertson's home in Cornwall, their fun tempered by the tension of the impending war. After war breaks out, the lives of the Cuthbertsons and their friends and family are changed forever. Forty years later, the cousins meet again at the funeral of musician Max Erstweiler, a wartime refugee from Austria who had been befriended by the Cuthbertsons, an opportunity for reflection and reconciliation.

The Camomile Lawn marked theatrical director Peter Hall's first direction of a television serial; his daughter Rebecca played the role of Sophy.

THE OLD DEVILS

16 March 1992, Monday, 9:30–10:30pm, BBC2, 3 episodes, drama, Welsh, contemporary
BBCtv
Pr: Adrian Mourby
Dir: Tristram Powell
Wtr: Andrew Davies
Based on Kingsley Amis
Cast: **Rhiannon Weaver – Sheila Allen**
Gwen Cellan-Davies – Anna Cropper
Peter Thomas – James Grout
Malcolm Cellan-Davies – Bernard Hepton
Charlie Norris – Ray Smith
Muriel Thomas – Anne Stallybrass
Alun Weaver – John Stride

The Old Devils were students together in the 1950s, and this group of Welshmen now is older but not much wiser. When Rhiannon, the woman all the men loved 40 years ago, returns to Wales with her husband, television personality Alun, established patterns of living (and drinking) are turned upside down.

RESNICK: LONELY HEARTS

31 March 1992, Tuesday, 10:00–10:50pm, BBC1, 3 episodes, thriller, British, contemporary
Deco Productions for BBCtv
Pr: Colin Rogers
Dir: Bruce MacDonald
Wtr: John Harvey
Based on John Harvey
Cast: Detective Captain Diptak Patel – Paul Bazely
Detective Sergeant Lynn Kellogg – Kate Eaton
Superintendent Jack Skelton – Paul Jesson
John Benedict – John McGlynn
Detective Sergeant Graham Millington – David Neilson
Detective Captain Kevin Nicholls – Daniel Ryan
Rachel Chaplin – Fiona Victory
Detective Inspector Charlie Resnick – Tom Wilkinson

Unconventional Nottingham Detective Inspector Charlie Resnick has long neglected his personal life for his career, although he is attempting a relationship with social worker Rachel Chaplin. Resnick manages a team of young detectives, currently investigating the murder of a woman who at first seems to have been the victim of her former boyfriend's obsessive jealousy, but when another woman is found killed in the same way, it appears they may have a serial murderer on their hands – a killer who finds his victims through the lonely hearts column of the local newspaper.

A follow-up *Resnick* serial, *Rough Treatment*, was produced with the same lead characters and aired beginning 25 July 1993.

MR. WAKEFIELD'S CRUSADE

22 April 1992, Wednesday, 9:40–10:30pm, BBC2, 3 episodes, mystery, British, contemporary
BBCtv
Pr: Ruth Caleb
Dir: Angela Pope
Wtr: Paul Hines
Based on Bernice Rubens
Cast: **Luke Wakefield – Peter Capaldi**
　　　Mad Marion – Pam Ferris
　　　Porter – Richard Griffiths
　　　Sebastian – Geoff Little
　　　Richard – Michael Maloney
　　　Sandra – Miranda Richardson
　　　Connie – Mossie Smith

Oddball Luke Wakefield is drawn into a murder mystery when a man dies in front of him at the post office. Luke finds a letter in the dead man's pocket which implicates the man in the murder of his wife, Marion, and Luke becomes determined to unravel the details of her death. Unfortunately, these efforts lead Luke himself to be the suspect in a murder investigation. Complicating matters still further are Luke's infatuation with prostitute Sandra, whom he meets while searching for clues, and the return to London of his estranged wife, Connie.

FRANKIE'S HOUSE

9 May 1992, Saturday, 9:15–10:15pm, ITV, 4 episodes, drama, biographical, British, 20th century
Anglia Films in association with the Australian Broadcasting Commission
Video: available in UK
Pr: Matt Carroll, Eric Fellner
Dir: Peter Fisk
Wtr: Andy Armitage
Based on *Page After Page* by Tim Page
Cast: John Steinbeck, Jr. – Todd Boyce
　　　Danielle – Caroline Carr
　　　Sean Flynn – Kevin Dillon
　　　Kate Richards – Alexandra Fowler
　　　Tim Page – Iain Glen

A true-life drama, set in the years of the Vietnam War, and based on the life of English war photographer Tim Page. In 1964 Tim journeys to Vietnam and becomes close friends with correspondent Sean Flynn, whose father was famed movie star Errol Flynn. Page is quickly caught up in the whirlwind of life in a war zone. Another famous son, John Steinbeck, Jr., arrives to cover the war. Page is wounded and almost blinded, and decides to return to England. But he is lured back to Indochina by Flynn for one final, ill-fated sortie.

A FATAL INVERSION

10 May 1992, Sunday, 9:05–10:05pm, BBC1, 3 episodes, thriller, British, contemporary
BBCtv
Pr: Phillippa Giles
Dir: Tim Fywell
Wtr: Sandy Welch
Based on Ruth Rendell writing as Barbara Vine
Cast: Vivien – Julia Ford
　　　Adam – Douglas Hodge
　　　Rufus – Jeremy Northam
　　　Mary Gage – Clara Salaman
　　　DC Stretton – Michael Simkins
　　　Zosie – Saira Todd
　　　Shiva – Gordon Warnecke
　　　Inspector Winder – Nicholas Woodeson

In 1979, student friends Adam, Rufus, Shiva and Zosie secretly bury something in the grounds of Wyvis Hall – then vow never to see each other again. Years later, the hall is owned by different people, who unearth the bodies of a woman and a baby on the property. This news quickly reaches Adam and Rufus, both of whom are now successful and settled. But their present-day lives are threatened by the discovery, which also reunites them with Shiva and Zosie, as terrible secrets from the past are revealed.

ANGLO-SAXON ATTITUDES

12 May 1992, Tuesday, 8:30–10:00pm, ITV, 3 episodes, drama, British, 20th century
Euston Films
Pr: Andrew Brown
Dir: Diarmuid Lawrence
Wtr: Andrew Davies
Based on Angus Wilson
Cast: Lilian Portway – Helen Cherry
Young Dollie – Tara Fitzgerald
Young Gerald – Douglas Hodge
Young Lilian – Jane How
Gerald Middleton – Richard Johnson
Robin Middleton – Nicholas Jones
Inge Middleton – Elizabeth Spriggs
Dollie Stokesay – Dorothy Tutin

Archaeologist Gerald Middleton looks back 50 years to 1912 and the early years of his career, remembering most particularly the discovery of a medieval Bishop's tomb . . . and his love for young Dollie Stokesay. Trying to resolve issues surrounding his life at that time, Middleton embarks on a search for Dollie, and is finally able to discover the answers to his quest for the truth about the strange pagan idol found in the Bishop's tomb . . . and perhaps a second chance at love with Dollie.

Winner, BAFTA Award, Best Drama Serial 1992.

FRIDAY ON MY MIND

15 May 1992, Friday, 9:30–10:20pm, BBC1, 3 episodes, drama, British, contemporary
Portman Entertainment
Pr: Philip Hinchcliffe
Dir: Marc Evans
Wtr: Alick Rowe
Cast: Wing Commander Donague – David Calder
Sean Maddox – Christopher Eccleston
Toby – John Matthews
Louise – Maggie O'Neill
Sophie Maddox – Deborah Poplett

As the Gulf War looms in 1991, Louise's RAF pilot husband Peter is killed in training. Louise is devastated, but drawn out of her grief by Sean Maddox, an RAF officer assigned to offer help and guidance to Louise. Sean, who is married, falls deeply in love with Louise, but she is distracted from the affair when she learns that Peter's accident was caused by his own error, a mistake which might have occurred because of an argument she had had with him before he went out on the training exercise. Louise endeavours to end her relationship with Sean and devote her time to her son Toby, but finds this easier said than done.

NATURAL LIES

31 May 1992, Sunday, 9:05–10:00pm, BBC1, 3 episodes, thriller, British, contemporary
Lawson/London Films
Pr: Sarah Lawson
Dir: Ben Bolt
Wtr: David Pirie
Cast: **Maggie Fell – Sharon Duce**
James Towne – Denis Lawson
Beth – Judi Maynard
Andrew Fell – Bob Peck
Jo Scott – Arkie Whiteley

Advertising executive Andrew Fell is shattered when he learns that his first love, Beth, has died, an apparent suicide. Fell becomes obsessed with Beth's death and begins an investigation, which proves dangerous to him and his wife, Maggie. But he refuses to give up, determined to unearth the truth, ultimately discovering that Beth was murdered because of what she knew about dishonesty and corruption in the food industry. When Jo Scott, who had information Fell needed for his investigation, is murdered, Fell becomes a wanted man and is forced to jeopardize every element of his life to get at the truth.

THE GUILTY

8 June 1992, Monday (subsequent episodes aired on Tuesday), 9:00–10:00;

10:40–11:40pm, ITV, 4 episodes, thriller, British, contemporary
Central Films
Pr: Sarah Wilson
Dir: Colin Gregg
Wtr: Simon Burke
Cast: Inspector Brunskill – Al Ashton
Nicky Lennon – Caroline Catz
Lord Chancellor – Iain Cuthbertson
Sarah Vey – Eleanor David
Eddy Doyle – Sean Gallagher
Steven Vey – Michael Kitchen
Tommy – Lee Ross
Leo – Andrew Tiernan

Ruthless lawyer Steven Vey is in line for a highly-coveted seat as a high court judge, but an extra-marital dalliance and a past skeleton in his closet involving recently-released felon Eddy Doyle threaten the new position, and Vey will go to whatever means necessary to keep that from happening.

DOWNTOWN LAGOS

7 October 1992, Wednesday, 9:25–10:20pm, BBC2, 3 episodes, drama, British/African, contemporary
BBCtv
Pr: Fiona Finlay
Dir: Roger Michell
Wtr: Leigh Jackson
Cast: Alice Hughes – Kitty Aldridge
Elvis Afolabe – Maynard Eziashi
Ticker Dawson – Ursula Howells
Mungo Dawson – Anton Lesser
Scout Dawson – Frederick Treves
Hassan – Oke Wambu

Fastidious solicitor Mungo Dawson is tortured by nightmares of painful childhood memories; these visions intrude into daytime reality when Dawson takes on a Nigerian fraud case which merges his past and present.

THE SECRET AGENT

28 October 1992, Wednesday, 9:25–10:25pm, BBC2, 3 episodes, drama, classic, British, 19th century
BBCtv
Pr: Colin Tucker
Dir: David Drury
Wtr: Dusty Hughes
Based on Joseph Conrad
Cast: **Winnie Verloc – Cheryl Campbell**
Mr. Vladimir – Peter Capaldi
Stevie – Richard Stirling
Adolf Verloc – David Suchet
Margaret, Duchess of Chester – Janet Suzman

In London at the end of the 19th century, double agent Alfred Verloc is an anarchist who informs on his colleagues to both the British police and the Russian embassy. But new Russian secretary Vladimir blackmails him into attempting to blow up the Greenwich Observatory, which ends in personal disaster for Verloc, his dutiful wife Winnie, and Winnie's mentally retarded brother Stevie.

TELL TALE HEARTS

1 November 1992, Sunday, 9:25–10:10pm, BBC1, 3 episodes, thriller, British, contemporary
BBCtv
Pr: David Blair, Norman McCandlish
Dir: Thaddeus O'Sullivan
Wtr: Stephen Lowe
Cast: **Sally McCann – Brid Brennan**
Mike McCann – Martin Cochrane
Becky Wilson – Emma Fielding
Hilary Wilson – Morag Hood
Anthony Steadman – Bill Paterson
John Wilson – John Woodvine

Convicted child killer Anthony Steadman is released from prison after serving 17 years and given a new identity, but two women are determined to track him down: ambitious radio reporter Becky Wilson, who is haunted by events from her own childhood, and Sally McCann, whose daughter disappeared around the time of the murder and is convinced that Steadman also killed her child.

THE BORROWERS

8 November 1992, Sunday, 5:40–6:10pm, BBC1, 6 episodes, drama, family, fantasy, British, 20th century
Working Title Production for BBCtv
Video: available in UK, US
Pr: Grainne Marmion

Dir: John Henderson
Wtr: Richard Carpenter
Based on *The Borrowers*, *The Borrowers Afield* by Mary Norton
Cast: **Arrietty – Rebecca Callard**
George – Paul Cross
Aunt Lupy – Pamela Cundell
Eggletina – Victoria Donovan
Pod – Ian Holm
Uncle Hendreary – Stanley Lebor
Spiller – Daniel Newman
Mrs. Driver – Sian Phillips
Homily – Penelope Wilton

The Borrowers are 1/10th the size of regular people and have lived for generations in between the floors of a stately home belonging to full-sized humans. Pod, his wife Homily and their daughter Arietty "borrow" small items from above to furnish their apartment, always fearful of being spotted by those who live above . . . and when that does, indeed happen, they must leave their home and seek safe shelter with other Borrower relations, which means a dangerous journey in the larger-than-life outside world.

Winner, BAFTA Award, Best Children's Drama 1992, Royal Television Society Award, Best Children's Drama 1992. Author Mary Norton died on the final day of filming the serial.

THE LIFE AND TIMES OF HENRY PRATT

9 November 1992, Monday, 9:00–10:00pm, ITV, 4 episodes, drama, British, 20th century
Granada Television
Pr: Jenny Reeks
Dir: Adrian Shergold
Wtr: David Nobbs
Based on David Nobbs
Cast: Uncle Teddy – Alun Armstrong
Henry Pratt – Jack Deam
Paul Hargreaves – Christopher Haley
Ada Pratt – Barbara Marten
Auntie Doris – Maggie O'Neill
Ezra Pratt – Jeff Rawle
Cousin Hilda – Dinah Stabb

Born in Yorkshire in 1935, Henry Pratt, an only child, grows up during World War II. When the war ends, Henry must deal with his returning father's difficulties in re-adjustment. Both of Henry's parents die and he is cared for by his eccentric relatives, who send Henry to public school, where he makes several profound discoveries about himself, including that he is equally attracted to both men and women.

NICE TOWN

18 November 1992, Wednesday, 9:25–10:20pm, BBC2, 3 episodes, drama, British, contemporary
BBCtv
Pr: Hilary Salmon
Dir: Pedr James
Wtr: Guy Hibbert
Cast: **Paul Thompson – Philip Davis**
Jean Thompson – Doreen Mantle
Joe Thompson – Paul McGann
Frankie Thompson – Josette Simon
Linda Thompson – Gwyneth Strong
Bill Thompson – Allan Surtees

Joe Thompson, his wife Frankie and their young daughter return to England after several years abroad. Their homecoming is bittersweet for Joe's brother Paul and Paul's wife Linda, who are unable to have children of their own. Joe privately approaches Linda about being a secret sperm donor; after Linda has a baby girl the truth comes out, with catastrophic results.

THE BIG BATTALIONS

19 November 1992, Thursday, 9:00–10:00pm, Channel 4, 6 episodes, drama, British/African, contemporary
Carnival Production
Pr: Brian Eastman
Dir: Andrew Grieve
Wtr: Hugh Stoddart
Cast: **Edward Hoyland – Brian Cox**
Martha Hoyland – Jane Lapotaire
Lizzie Goodhew – Siobhan McCarthy
Alan Sturridge – Malcolm Sinclair
Cora Lynne – Loretta Swit

Edward Hoyland, the ambitious Archdeacon of Birmingham, schemes to become the new Bishop of the City. His wife Martha, a former missionary, must deal with their empty marriage, and decides to journey to Ethiopia to reopen several health centres. She is taken prisoner by rebels and Edward must travel there to negotiate for her release.

LOOK AT IT THIS WAY

22 November 1992, Sunday, 9:25–10:25pm, BBC1, 3 episodes, drama, satire, British, contemporary
BBCtv
Pr: Kevin Loader
Dir: Gavin Millar
Wtr: Justin Cartwright
Based on Justin Cartwright
Cast: **Tim Curtiz – David Dukes**
Steve – Jimmy Flint
Bernie Koppel – Lionel Jeffries
Simba Cochrane – Jimmy Jewel
Miles Goodall – Nathaniel Parker
Victoria Rolfe – Kristin Scott Thomas
Victoria's Mother – Fiona Walker

In London, American journalist Tim Curtiz becomes involved with advertising copywriter Victoria, whose ex-lover, disgraced yuppie banker Miles, finds himself involved in a questionable transaction which leads to Miles meeting a fateful end at the hands of a drug dealer and the paws of an escaped zoo lion.

FRAMED

27 November 1992, Friday, 9:00–10:00pm, ITV, 4 episodes, thriller, British, contemporary
Anglia Films in association with Arts & Entertainment Network
Pr: Guy Slater
Dir: Geoffrey Sax
Wtr: Lynda La Plante
Cast: Susan Jackson – Annabelle Apsion
Eddie Myers – Timothy Dalton
Lawrence Jackson – David Morrissey
Lola Del Moreno – Penelope Cruz Sanchez
George Minton – Ian Talbot
Detective Chief Inspector McKinnes – Timothy West

Detective Constable Lawrence Jackson is on holiday with his family in Spain when he spots former supergrass informer Eddie Myers, now living as Philip von Joel. Five years earlier, Myers had betrayed his underworld connections, then double-crossed the police. Myers is captured and extradited to London, to the delight of Detective Chief Inspector McKinnes, whose career had been devastated by Myers' earlier escape. Jackson is assigned to guard Myers, and an odd, seemingly-close relationship develops between the two, as Myers tries to convince Jackson to join with him in making a run for it, to collect the money he had stashed away five years ago.

THE BLACKHEATH POISONINGS

7 December 1992, Monday (subsequent episodes aired on Tuesday and Wednesday), 9:00–10:00pm, ITV, 3 episodes, mystery, British, 19th century
Central Television in association with WGBH/Boston
Pr: Stephen Smallwood
Dir: Stuart Orme
Wtr: Simon Raven
Based on Julian Symons
Cast: **Paul Vandervent – Christien Anholt**
Roger Vandervent – James Faulkner
Dr. Porter – Ronald Fraser
Isabel Collard – Christine Kavanagh
Robert Dangerfield – Patrick Malahide
George Collard – Ian McNeice
Harriet Collard – Judy Parfitt
Beatrice Vandervent – Julia St. John
Charlotte Collard – Zoe Wanamaker

In Victorian London, Paul Vandervent investigates his father Roger's mysterious death, unravelling a corrupt web of lies and deceit involving both his own seemingly-respectable family and the equally upstanding Collard family.

PRIME SUSPECT 2

15 December 1992, Tuesday (subsequent episodes aired on Wednesday),

9:00–10:00pm; 10:40–11:40pm, ITV,
4 episodes, mystery, British, contemporary
Granada Television in association with
WGBH/Boston
Video: available in UK, US
Pr: Paul Marcus
Dir: John Strickland
Wtr: Alan Cubitt
Devised by Lynda La Plante
Cast: Jason Reynolds – Matt Bardock
Esme Allen – Claire Benedict
Detective Chief Superintendent Mike
  Kernan – John Benfield
Detective Inspector Tony Muddyman
  – Jack Ellis
Detective Inspector Frank Burkin –
  Craig Fairbrass
Tony Allen – Fraser James
Sarah Allen – Jenny Jules
**Detective Chief Inspector Jane
Tennison – Helen Mirren**
Detective Sergeant Robert Oswalde
  – Colin Salmon
David Harvey – Tom Watson

DCI Jane Tennison, having won her battle against the chauvinism of her male colleagues, investigates a macabre case when a female skeleton is dug up in a garden in a racially-tense London neighborhood. Tennison's romantic involvement with black DS Robert Oswalde further complicates matters, as she finds her personal and professional worlds on a collision course.

Winner, Emmy Award, Outstanding Miniseries 1992-1993.

GALLOWGLASS

10 January 1993, Sunday, 9:05–10:00pm,
BBC1, 3 episodes, thriller, British,
contemporary
BBCtv
Pr: Phillippa Giles
Dir: Tim Fywell
Wr: Jacqueline Holborough
Based on Ruth Rendell as Barbara Vine
Cast: **Paul Garnet – John McArdle**
Jessica – Harriet Owen
Sandor – Paul Rhys
Joe – Michael Sheen
Nina – Arkie Whiteley

Joe is about to commit suicide, but is stopped by smooth talking but sadistic Sandor, who then insists that Joe is his "gallowglass" or loyal servant – and so must work with him on a plot to kidnap wealthy Nina. Paul Garnet is drawn into the psychological intrigue when the kidnappers abduct his daughter Jessica instead, forcing him to choose between her and Nina, for whom he works (and with whom he is in love).

THE MUSHROOM PICKER

3 February 1993, Wednesday,
9:25–10:30pm, BBC2, 3 episodes, comedy,
satire, British/Russian, contemporary
BBCtv
Pr: Estelle Daniel
Dir: Andy Wilson
Wtr: Liane Aukin
Based on Zinovy Zinik
Cast: **Clea – Lynsey Baxter**
Anthony – Simon Russell Beale
Margot – Lesley Manville
Tadeus – Andrew Sachs
Kostya – Nigel Terry

Naïve Londoner Clea goes to Moscow, where she is swept off her feet by mushroom picker Kostya. They marry and return to London, but Kostya is far from ready to settle down in suburbia. Clea doubts that Kostya is picking up just mushrooms on his frequent late-night forays, and the escalating tension threatens more than just their marriage.

LIPSTICK ON YOUR COLLAR

21 February 1993, Sunday, 9:00–10:00pm,
Channel 4, 6 episodes, drama, British, 20th
century
Whistling Gypsy Production
Video: available in UK
Pr: Dennis Potter, Alison Barnett, Rosemary Whitman
Dir: Renny Rye
Wtr: Dennis Potter
Cast: Sylvia Berry – Louise Germaine
Corporal Berry – Douglas Henshall
Uncle Fred – Bernard Hill
Lisa – Kymberley Huffman
Harold Atterbow – Roy Hudd
Major Church – Nicholas Farrell
Major Hedges – Clive Francis

Colonel Bernwood – Peter Jeffrey
Major Carter – Nicholas Jones
Private Hopper – Ewan McGregor
Lieutenant Colonel Trekker – Shane Rimmer
Aunt Vickie – Maggie Steed
Private Francis – Giles Thomas

Potter's characteristically skewed, semi-musical, semi-autobiographical look at Britain during the Suez Crisis of 1956: Army conscripts Hopper and Francis work in the War Office alongside staid officers who bristle over the Empire's imminent unravelling, while younger Britons seek to break the inhibiting shackles of pre-war conventions, turning to American social influences and contemporary music to form new generational attitudes.

MR. WROE'S VIRGINS

24 February 1993, Wednesday, 9:25–10:15pm, BBC2, 4 episodes, drama, British, 19th century
BBCtv
Pr: John Chapman
Dir: Danny Boyle
Wtr: Jane Rogers
Based on Jane Rogers
Cast: Dinah – Moya Brady
 Martha – Kathy Burke
 Leah – Minnie Driver
 Hannah – Kerry Fox
 Rachel – Catherine Kelly
 Rebekah – Ruth Kelly
 John Wroe – Jonathan Pryce
 Joanna – Lia Williams

In Lancashire in the 1830s, apocalyptic evangelist and self-styled prophet John Wroe arranges to have seven local virgins live with him to serve his household needs. The drama unfolds through the points-of-view of four of the virgins: spiritual Joanna, who wants only to serve devotedly as a missionary, but whom Wroe wants to bear his child; Leah, a beautiful temptress who seeks to claim Wroe as her own; forward-thinking socialist Hannah, with whom Wroe forms a strong intellectual and emotional bond; and Martha, a mute who has spent much of her life as a brutalized victim and is transformed through her time in Wroe's care.

Mr. Wroe's Virgins is based on a true set of circumstances which occurred in Ashton-Under-Lyme in the mid-19th century. Wroe was charged with sexually assaulting two of the young women in his household and fled to Australia. Nothing, however, is known of the seven virgins or their fate.

A YEAR IN PROVENCE

28 February 1993, Sunday, 8:25–8:55pm, BBC1, 12 episodes, comedy, British/French, contemporary
BBCtv in association with Arts & Entertainment Network
Video: available in UK, US
Pr: Ken Riddington
Dir: David Tucker
Wtr: Michael Sadler
Based on Peter Mayle
Cast: Antoine Rivière – Marcel Champel
 Colombani – Jean-Pierre Delage
 Amedée Clement – Jo Doumberg
 Annie Mayle – Lindsay Duncan
 Tony Havers – Alfred Molina
 Madame Hermonville – Annie Sinigalia
 Marcel – Bernard Spiegel
 Peter Mayle – John Thaw

Peter and Annie Mayle quit their jobs and leave England for the Luberon Valley of Provence, to spend a year living the "good life" in a 200-year-old stone farmhouse. Their hopes for peace and quiet are shattered by slow-moving workmen, odd neighbors, uninvited guests, and a variety of forms of culture clash.

GOGGLE EYES

24 March 1993, Wednesday, 9:25–10:05pm, BBC2, 4 episodes, drama, British, contemporary
Friday Productions for BBCtv
Pr: Georgina Abrahams
Dir: Carol Wiseman
Wtr: Deborah Moggach
Based on Anne Fine
Cast: **Gerald Faulkner – Alun Armstrong**

Rosie Killin – Lesley Manville
Helly – Alexandra Milman
Jude – Victoria Shalet
Kitty – Honeysuckle Weeks

Twelve-year-old Kitty avidly dislikes her mother Rosie's conventional new boyfriend Gerald, whom Kitty disdainfully refers to as Goggle Eyes. Kitty sets out to destroy the developing relationship, her vicious sabotage campaign coming to a surprising halt when Gerald unexpectedly saves Kitty from getting into trouble. But then Rosie and Gerald have a row and split up . . . and, strangely enough, Kitty doesn't find this cause for celebration.

YOU ME AND IT

28 March 1993, Sunday, 9:10–10:05pm, BBC1, 3 episodes, drama, British, contemporary
Wall to Wall
Pr: Alex Graham
Dir: Edward Bennett
Wtr: Andrew Payne
Cast: **Barbara Henderson – Suzanne Burden**
James Woodley – Stephen Dillane
Mike Enderby – Greg Hicks
Linda Enderby – Anna Patrick
Charlie Henderson – James Wilby

Charlie and Barbara Henderson seem to have it all: a happy marriage, good jobs, loyal friends, a nice home. But when they decide to have a baby they try unsuccessfully for 14 months to get pregnant. Reluctantly, Charlie and Barbara go to an infertility clinic, and find the high-tech mechanics of trying to get pregnant put a severe strain on their lives.

BODY AND SOUL

8 April 1993, Thursday, 9:00–10:00pm, ITV, 6 episodes, drama, British, contemporary
Red Rooster Films & TV Entertainment for Carlton Television
Pr: Jacky Stoller
Dir: Moira Armstrong
Wtr: Paul Hines, Jill Hyem
Based on Marcelle Bernstein

Cast: Walter Street – Patrick Allen
Daniel Stern – John Bowe
Sister Godric – Madeleine Christie
Hal – Gary Mavers
Lynn Gibson – Amanda Redman
Anna Gibson/Sister Gabriel – Kristin Scott Thomas
Mother Emmanuel – Dorothy Tutin
Stan Beattie – Anthony Valentine
Peggy – Sandra Voe

After 16 cloistered years in a convent as Sister Gabriel, Anna Gibson returns to her Yorkshire home when her brother, who heads the family's textile mill, suddenly dies. Anna decides to temporarily take charge of the mill, infuriating manager Stan Beattie, who plots the mill's downfall. The longer she stays out of the convent, the more torn Anna is between the secular and non-secular worlds.

LADY CHATTERLEY

6 June 1993, Sunday, 9:35–10:30pm, BBC1, 4 episodes, drama, British, 20th century
London Films/Global Arts production for BBCtv
Pr: Michael Haggiag
Dir: Ken Russell
Wtr: Michael Haggiag, Ken Russell
Based on *Lady Chatterley's Lover* by D.H. Lawrence
Cast: Hilda – Hetty Baynes
Oliver Mellors – Sean Bean
Mrs. Bolton – Shirley Anne Field
Donald Forbes – Breffni McKenna
Lady Constance Chatterley – Joely Richardson
Sir Michael Reid – Ken Russell
Sir Clifford Chatterley – James Wilby

Sir Clifford Chatterley returns home from World War I paralyzed, impotent, and embittered. His young wife Constance, to whom he was just briefly married before leaving for the War, endeavours to remain faithful to her husband – but is passionately and fatefully drawn to Mellors, the gamekeeper on the Chatterley estate.

TELLTALE

10 June 1993, Thursday, 9:00–10:00pm, ITV, 3 episodes, drama, British, contemporary
HTV Wales
Pr: Manny Wessels
Dir: Dewi Humphreys
Wtr: Ewart Alexander
Cast: Doreen Hodge – Rachel Davies
Detective Sergeant Paul Herbert – Nigel Harrison
Detective Sergeant Gavin Douglas – Bernard Hill
Billy Hodge – Robert Pugh
Jean Herbert – Melanie Walters

Habitual criminal Billy Hodge becomes a supergrass informer to avenge the group of thugs who attacked him and his wife.

AN EXCHANGE OF FIRE

6 July 1993, Tuesday, 10:00–11:40pm, Channel 4, 2 episodes, thriller, British/European, contemporary
Kestrel Films
Pr: Bill Shapter
Dir: Tony Bicat
Wtr: Tony Bicat
Cast: Oscar Karel – Ion Caramitru
Anne Shanks – Juliette Caton
Pavel Rhele – Frank Finlay
Michael Shanks – James Fleet
President Slajek – Tom Wilkinson
Olga Slajek – Clare Woodgate

Heroism and hatred collide on the streets of London and Prague as Eastern European President Slajek sends his daughter Olga to London on a publicity-seeking mission, in the hopes of saving his government from collapse. Instead, though, Olga and media figure Michael Shanks become involved with ruthless London-based terrorist leader Pavel Rhele, whose actions – which include kidnapping – threaten Slajek both politically and personally.

LOVE AND REASON

1 September 1993, Wednesday, 9:25–10:30pm, BBC2, 3 episodes, drama, satire, British, contemporary
BBCtv
Pr: Hilary Salmon
Dir: Carol Wilks
Wtr: Ron Rose
Cast: **Lou Larson – Phyllis Logan**
Mel Lynch – Barbara Marten
Phil Spencer – Kevin McNally
Arthur Milne – Jack Watson
George Douglass – Tom Watson

Outspoken MP Lou Larson is a rising star in the Labour Party, but her past, which is a deeply-held secret, could threaten her political future, and Lou is having a hard time keeping the facts from the tabloids and the Party, and soon must choose between her head and her heart.

Labour politicians Neil Kinnock and Clare Short appeared as themselves in the serial.

CRACKER

27 September 1993, Monday, 9:00–10:00pm, ITV, 2 episodes, thriller, British, contemporary
Granada Television
Pr: Gub Neal
Dir: Michael Winterbottom
Wtr: Jimmy McGovern
Cast: **Fitz – Robbie Coltrane**
Detective Sergeant Beck – Lorcan Cranitch
Kelly – Adrian Dunbar
Detective Chief Inspector Bilborough – Christopher Eccleston
Judith Fitzgerald – Barbara Flynn
Simon Appleby – John Grillo
Anne Appleby – Kika Markham
Mark Fitzgerald – Kieran O'Brien
Detective Sergeant Penhaligon – Geraldine Sommerville

Brilliant criminal psychologist Fitz often creates as many problems as he solves (both at work and at home), given his saber-sharp tongue and his compulsive gambling and drinking. Nevertheless, he is called in by the police when a woman is murdered on a train; the prime suspect in the case is amnesiac Kelly, who remembers nothing of the murder and less about his own identity.

This drama, titled "The Mad Woman in the Attic", introduced the character of

Fitz, who continued in subsequent months to solve a number of two- and three-part crimes. More episodes aired in 1995.

TALES OF THE CITY

28 September 1993, Tuesday, 9:00–11:05pm, Channel 4, 5 episodes, drama, American, 20th century
Propaganda/Working Title Production for Channel 4 in association with American Playhouse and KQED/San Francisco
Video: available in US
Pr: Alan Poul
Dir: Alastair Reid
Wtr: Richard Kramer
Based on Armistead Maupin
Cast: Jon Fielden – William Campbell
Michael Tolliver – Marcus D'Amico
Norman Neal Williams – Stanley De Santis
Anna Madrigal – Olympia Dukakis
Frannie Halcyon – Nina Foch
Dede Halcyon Day – Barbara Garrick
Beauchamp Day – Thomas Gibson
Brian Hawkins – Paul Gross
Mary Ann Singleton – Laura Linney
Archibald Anson Gidde – Ian McKellen
Edgar Halcyon – Donald Moffat
Mona Ramsey – Chloe Webb
D'orothea Wilson – Cynda Williams

In a harmonious San Francisco in the 1970s, 28 Barbary Lane is home to an assortment of lovelorn hetero- homo- and bi-sexual tenants and their friends, enemies, lovers and spouses, including the newest arrival, naïve Midwesterner Mary Ann Singleton, all overseen by bohemian landlady Anna Madrigal, who greets all new arrivals with some of her homemade marijuana.

Winner, BAFTA Award, Royal Television Society Award, Best Drama Serial 1993.

THE SCARLET AND THE BLACK

31 October 1993, Sunday, 9:05–10:25pm, BBC1, 3 episodes, drama, classic, French, 19th century
BBCtv
Pr: Rosalind Wolfes
Dir: Ben Bolt
Wtr: Stephen Lowe
Based on Stendhal
Cast: Napoleon – Christopher Fulford
Monsieur de Renal – Martin Jarvis
Abbe Pirard – Stratford Johns
Madame de Renal – Alice Krige
Julien Sorel – Ewan McGregor
Marquis de la Mole – T.P. McKenna
Mathilde – Rachel Weisz

In France in the mid-1800s, the ideological struggle between the republican Liberals and the Ultra-Royalists who support Charles X comes to life in the story of ambitious Julien Sorel, a carpenter's son who is determined to rise through the ranks of both the army (the "scarlet") and the church (the "black") – while at the same time making his way to the heart of society, where he seduces the most eligible young women of Paris . . . and even a few ineligible ones, most notably Madame de Renal, the wife of the local mayor who employs Julien.

THE BUDDHA OF SUBURBIA

3 November 1993, Wednesday, 9:25–10:30pm, BBC2, 4 episodes, drama, British/Indian, contemporary
BBCtv
Pr: Kevin Loader
Dir: Roger Michell
Wtr: Hanif Kureishi, Roger Michell
Based on Hanif Kureishi
Cast: **Karim Amir – Naveen Andrews**
Margaret Amir – Brenda Blethyn
Auntie Jean – Janet Dale
Eva Kay – Susan Fleetwood
Charlie Kay – Steven Mackintosh
Uncle Ted – John McEnery
Jamila – Nisha Nayar
Changez – Harish Patel
Eleanor – Jemma Redgrave
Haroom Amir – Roshan Seth
Matthew Pyke – Donald Sumpter

In London in the 1970s, teenager Karim Amir, son of an English mother and an Indian father, finds his life turned upside down first when his Muslim-turned-Buddhist father, Haroom, becomes a guru, and then when Karim becomes a successful actor, travelling to New York to star in a play. But Karim ultimately decides to return to London, only to find that in his absence things and people have changed considerably, leaving him to reflect on both the past and the future.

THE BORROWERS (2)

14 November 1993, Sunday, 5:35–6:05pm, BBC1, 6 episodes
Working Title Production for BBCtv, drama, family, fantasy, British, 20th century
Video: available in UK
Pr: Grainne Marmion
Dir: John Henderson
Wtr: Richard Carpenter
Based on *The Borrowers Afloat*, *The Borrowers Aloft* by Mary Norton
Cast: **Arrietty – Rebecca Callard**
Ditchley – Ben Chaplin
George – Paul Cross
Aunt Lupy – Pamela Cundell
Eggletina – Victoria Donovan
Pod – Ian Holm
Miss Menzies – Gemma Jones
Mr. Platter – Robert Lang
Uncle Hendreary – Stanley Lebor
Ilrick – Ross McCall
Spiller – Daniel Newman
Mrs. Platter – Judy Parfitt
Mrs. Driver – Sian Phillips
Mr. Potts – Richard Vernon
Homily – Penelope Wilton

Little people (1/10th the size of real people) Pod, Homily, and daughter Arrietty have left their home upon being discovered and now continue to "borrow" things humans have no further use for to make a new home for themselves and other Borrower relations in a model village built by a retired railwayman.

TO PLAY THE KING

21 November 1993, Sunday, 9:05–10:00pm, BBC1, 4 episodes, thriller, British, contemporary
BBCtv
Pr: Ken Riddington
Dir: Paul Seed
Wtr: Andrew Davies
Based on Michael Dobbs
Cast: Sarah Harding – Kitty Aldridge
David Mycroft – Nicholas Farrell
Elizabeth Urquhart – Diane Fletcher
Mattie Storin – Susannah Harker
Tim Stamper – Colin Jeavons
Chloe Carmichael – Rowena King
King – Michael Kitchen
Prime Minister Francis Urquhart – Ian Richardson
Princess Charlotte – Bernice Stegers
Lord Quillington – Frederick Treves

In this sequel to *House of Cards* Francis Urquhart, having fulfilled his scheme to become Prime Minister, is uneasy over his memories of Mattie, the journalist he murdered to assure his political rise, and faces criticism from a caring and honourable new monarch who is appalled by Urquhart's heartless, materialistic policies. But, once having achieved power, Urquhart is determined to hold onto it – whatever nefarious means it may take – and seething antagonism develops between the two, ripening into an all-out confrontation.

A WOMAN'S GUIDE TO ADULTERY

29 November 1993, Monday, 9:00–10:00pm, ITV, 3 episodes, drama, British, contemporary
Hartswood Films/Carlton Television
Video: available in UK
Pr: Beryl Vertue
Dir: David Hayman
Wtr: Frank Cottrell Boyce
Based on Carol Clewlow
Cast: **Paul – Sean Bean**
Jo – Amanda Donohoe
Michael – Adrian Dunbar
Jennifer – Fiona Gillies
Helen – Ingrid Lacey
Martin – Ian McElhinney
David – Neil Morrissey
Rose – Theresa Russell
Ray – Danny Webb

Four women in their early thirties – photographer Rose, political agent Jo, art lecturer Jennifer, and advertising executive Helen – become involved with men who are committed elsewhere.

ALL OR NOTHING AT ALL

3 December 1993, Friday, 9:00–10:00pm, ITV, 3 episodes, drama, British, contemporary
London Weekend Television
Pr: Brian Eastman
Dir: Andrew Grieve
Wtr: Guy Andrews
Cast: Marion – Pippa Guard
  Leo Hopkins – Hugh Laurie
  Giles – Bob Monkhouse
  Rebecca – Caroline Quentin
  Duncan – Steve Steen
  Jane – Jessica Turner

Leo Hopkins seems to have it all: a charming, wealthy wife, loving children, a wide circle of friends, and a secure financial career in the City. But he remains unsatisfied, a con man at heart, addicted to horse racing, and in an attempt to make things still better gambles everything he has, with tragic consequences.

STARK

8 December 1993, Wednesday, 9:25–10:20pm, BBC2, 3 episodes, drama, satire, British/Australian, science fiction
BBCtv
Pr: David Parker, Michael Wearing, Timothy White
Dir: Nadia Tass
Wtr: Ben Elton
Based on Ben Elton
Cast: **CD – Ben Elton**
  Sly Morgan – Colin Friels
  Rachel – Jacqueline McKenzie
  Zimmerman – Derrick O'Connor
  Karen – Fiona Press
  Walter – Bill Wallis

English writer Colin Dobson (CD), a stranger to any cause except his own, becomes unwittingly involved in Australia with a rag-tag ecological group's struggle to delay the coming of Armageddon, which seems surely on its way when a group of businessmen, led by billionaire Sly Morgan, attempt to take over Aboriginal land because the earth is about to be asphyxiated by industrial pollution.

PRIME SUSPECT 3

19 December 1993, Sunday (subsequent episodes aired Monday), 9:00–11:00pm, ITV, 4 episodes, mystery, British, contemporary
Granada Television in association with WGBH/Boston
Video: available in UK
Pr: Paul Marcus
Dir: David Drury
Wtr: Lynda La Plante
Cast: Detective Sergeant Bill Otley – Tom Bell
  Detective Chief Superintendent Kernan – John Benfield
  Vera Reynolds – Peter Capaldi
  John Kennington – Terence Harvey
  Edward Parker-Jones – Ciaran Hinds
  Jessica Smithy – Kelly Hunter
  Detective Chief Inspector Jane Tennison – Helen Mirren
  James Jackson – David Thewlis
  Detective Inspector Brian Dalton – Andrew Woodall

While investigating the suspicious death of a rent boy, DCI Jane Tennison uncovers a paedophile ring which implicates people in some very high places – including higher-ups in the police department. Pressured to put a hasty, convenient end to her search for the truth, Tennison instead focuses on her pursuit of squeaky-clean social worker Edward Parker-Jones.

Winner, BAFTA Award, Best Drama Serial 1994; winner, Emmy Award, Oustanding Miniseries 1993–1994. At this writing, three more *Prime Suspect* mysteries are being planned, with the format changing from multi-parters to two-hour-long telefilms.

SMOKESCREEN

2 January 1994, Sunday, 4:55–5:25pm, BBC1, 6 episodes, drama, British, 20th century
Red Rooster Production for BBCtv
Video: available in UK

Pr: Jill Green
Dir: Giancarlo Gemin
Wtr: James Andrew Hall
Based on Elsie McCutcheon
Cast: Gertie – Anita Dobson
   Albert Gold – Peter Guinness
   Vicky Sheringham – Kate Hardie
   Sidney Greenaway – Sean Murray
   Harry Gallant – Michael Sanderson
   Chip Gallant – Sam Townend
   Chrissie Gallant – Sally Walsh
   Frank Sheringham – Timothy West
   Sara Bean – Paula Wilcox

In 1907, Frank Sheringham is an eccentric, enterprising film-maker who dreams of developing a film industry in northern England and involves an entire industrial town – especially the three Gallant children – in his vicious rivalry with sleazy theatre owner Albert Gold.

MIDDLEMARCH

12 January 1994, Wednesday, 9:00–10:25pm (subsequent episodes from 9:30–10:30pm), BBC2, 6 episodes, drama, classic, British, 19th century
BBCtv in association with WGBH/Boston
Video: available in UK
Pr: Louis Marks
Dir: Anthony Page
Wtr: Andrew Davies
Based on George Eliot
Cast: **Dorothea Brooke Casaubon – Juliet Aubrey**
   Rev. Farebrother – Simon Chandler
   Fred Vincy – Jonathan Firth
   Arthur Brooke – Robert Hardy
   Celia Brooke – Caroline Harker
   Dr. Tertius Lydgate – Douglas Hodge
   Peter Featherstone – Michael Hordern
   Nicholas Bulstrode – Peter Jeffrey
   Rev. Edward Casaubon – Patrick Malahide
   Mayor Vincy – Stephen Moore
   Rosamund Vincy Lydgate – Trevyn McDowell
   Mary Garth – Rachel Power
   Will Ladislaw – Rufus Sewell
   Sir James Chettam – Julian Wadham

A new age of reform is dawning in England in 1829, and its effects are being felt in the town of Middlemarch, especially by young idealists such as Dorothea Brooke and Dr. Tertius Lydgate. But marriage puts a crimp in both of their visions, as Dorothea is locked in a passionless union with stiff Edward Casaubon and Lydgate suffers the whims of his shallow, materialistic wife Rosamund.

An enormous endeavour harkening back to the "glory days" of the BBC classic serials, production took 30 weeks to film in locations ranging from Lincolnshire to Rome and cost £6 million.

HEADHUNTERS

16 January 1994, Sunday, 9:10–10:00pm, BBC1, 3 episodes, drama, British, contemporary
BBCtv
Pr: Andy Park
Dir: Simon Langton
Wtr: Doug Lucie
Cast: **Sally Hall – Francesca Annis**
   Roddy Metcalfe – Jeremy Child
   Malcolm Standish – Iain Cuthbertson
   Barbara Levy – Eleanor David
   Simon Hall – James Fox
   Sammy – Alex Norton
   Roger Garrison – Danny Webb

Corporate headhunter Simon Hall is the best in the business, but he begins to develop a conscience and questions the ruthless ways which have gotten him to the top. Furthermore, he's not nearly as successful at home: his wife, Sally, a best-selling novelist, is thinking of leaving him. Simon's personal suffering begins to have an effect on his professional life, and things quickly seem to be breaking down on all fronts.

DANDELION DEAD

6 February 1994, Sunday, 8:20–10:20pm, ITV, 2 episodes, drama, non-fiction, British, 20th century
London Weekend Television
Pr: Patrick Harbinson
Dir: Mike Hodges
Wtr: Michael Chaplin
Cast: Chief Inspector Crutchett – Don Henderson

Davies – Bernard Hepton
**Major Herbert Armstrong –
Michael Kitchen**
Katharine Armstrong – Sarah Miles
Marion Glassford-Gale – Diana Quick
Connie Davies – Lesley Sharp
Vaughan – Robert Stephens
Oswald Martin – David Thewlis
Eleanor Armstrong – Chloe Tucker
Tom Hincks – Peter Vaughan

Based on true events which occurred in the early 1920s, solicitor Major Herbert Armstrong purchases arsenic weedkiller to combat the dandelions ruining his garden. Several months later, Armstrong's overbearing wife Katharine dies after a long, unexplained illness. There is no suspicion of foul play, but then Armstrong's business rival, Oswald Martin, is suddenly taken ill, and an examination shows he has been poisoned with arsenic. Mrs. Armstrong's body is exhumed, and the Major is tried for murder, found guilty, and executed.

CALLING THE SHOTS

15 February 1994, Tuesday, 9:30–10:50pm, BBC1, 2 episodes, thriller, British, contemporary
BBCtv in association with WGBH/Boston
Pr: David Snodin
Dir: Ross Devenish
Wtr: Laura Lamson
Cast: Angela – Adie Allen
Charlie – John Benfield
Caroline – Kelly Clark
Michael – Jonathan Cullen
Paul – Cyril Nri
Brian Summers – James Purefoy
Maggie Donnelly – Lynn Redgrave
Nick – Jack Shepherd
Atima – Rita Wolf

Tough-as-nails television journalist Maggie Donnelly, under pressure to deliver ratings, does a story about an alleged rapist which seems to lead its subject to commit suicide. Maggie then finds the tables frighteningly turned when, after years of turning the cameras on others, her own privacy is invaded by an unknown stalker who seems to know Maggie's every move.

THE RECTOR'S WIFE

3 March 1994, Thursday, 10:00–11:05pm, Channel 4, 4 episodes, drama, British, contemporary
Talisman Films
Video: available in UK, US
Pr: Alan Wright
Dir: Giles Foster
Wtr: Hugh Whitemore
Based on Joanna Trollope
Cast: Patrick O'Sullivan – Miles Anderson
Peter Bouverie – Jonathan Coy
Flora Bouverie – Lucy Dawson
Jonathan Byrne – Stephen Dillane
Anna Bouverie – Lindsay Duncan
Luke Bouverie – Simon Fenton
Eleanor Ramsay – Pam Ferris
Daniel Byrne – Ronald Pickup
Laura Marchant – Joyce Redman
Marjorie Richardson – Prunella Scales
Colonel Richardson – Frederick Treves

When Anna Bouverie's minister husband Peter fails to get his promotion to archdeacon, she embarks on a small but significant rebellion, taking a job in a supermarket in order to pay for her daughter's education. The local ramifications far exceed Anna's modest action; her relations with Peter deteriorate and Anna is drawn to another man. In the end, Anna stands alone, but it is a triumphant moment for her, as she has finally achieved the freedom and independence she has craved for so long.

GRUSHKO

24 March 1994, Thursday, 9:30–10:25pm, BBC1, 3 episodes, thriller, Russian, contemporary
Mark Forstater production for BBCtv
Pr: Nicky Lund
Dir: Tony Smith
Wtr: Philip Kerr, Robin Mukherjee
Cast: **Colonel Yevgeni Grushko – Brian Cox**
Nikolai – Dave Duffy
Bosenka – Paul Freeman
Tanya – Amanda Mealing
Andrei – Stephen McGann
Sasha – Cathy White

Yevgeni Grushko, in charge of the Mafia

Investigations Division of the St. Petersburg police force, must fight not just the organized crime figures, but also the councillors, politicians and businessmen who have their hands in gangland's pockets. While investigating two brutal murders, he uncovers horrifying evidence about nuclear waste and possible mass radiation.

A PINCH OF SNUFF

9 April 1994, Saturday, 10:30–11:30pm, ITV, 3 episodes, mystery, British, contemporary
Yorkshire Television
Pr: Emma Hayter
Dir: Sandy Johnson
Wtr: Robin Chapman
Based on Reginald Hill
Cast: Sergeant Wield – Christopher Fairbank
    Chief Superintendent Andy Dalziel – Gareth Hale
    Dr. Gilbert Haggard – Freddie Jones
    Emma Shorter – Julia Lane
    Jack Shorter – John McGlynn
    Detective Inspector Peter Pascoe – Norman Pace
    Ray Crabtree – Malcolm Storry

Detective Inspector Pascoe and his boss, Chief Superintendent Andy Dalziel, reluctantly join forces to investigate the violent murder of the owner at a private cinema club.

THE CINDER PATH

17 April 1994, Sunday, 8:00–9:00pm, ITV, 3 episodes, drama, British, 20th century
World Wide International Television/Festival Films for Tyne Tees Television
Video: available in UK, US
Pr: Ray Marshall
Dir: Simon Langton
Wtr: Alan Seymour
Based on Catherine Cookson
Cast: Mary MacFell – Rosalind Ayres
    Edward MacFell – Tom Bell
    Ginger Slater – Antony Byrne
    Arthur Benton – Ralph Ineson
    Victoria Chapman MacFell – Catherine Zeta Jones
    Nellie Chapman – Maria Miles
    Polly Benton – Madelaine Newton
    Charlie MacFell – Lloyd Owen
    Betty MacFell – Victoria Scarborough

In 1913, mild-mannered Charlie MacFell is bullied by his brutal father, wealthy Northumberland farmer Edward, into marrying faithless Victoria Chapman, when in fact it is Victoria's sister, Nellie, for whom Charlie has genuine feelings. But personal conflicts seem to take a backseat to world affairs when Charlie is called to action on the Western Front during World War I, until his fateful confrontation with long-time nemesis Ginger Slater, who had once been a hired hand on the MacFell farm.

THE DWELLING PLACE

8 May 1994, Sunday, 8:00–9:00pm, ITV, 3 episodes, drama, British, 19th century available in UK
World Wide International Television/Festival Films for Tyne Tees Television
Video: available in UK
Pr: Ray Marshall
Dir: Gavin Millar
Wtr: Gordon Hann
Based on Catherine Cookson
Cast: **Lord Fischel – James Fox**
    Rose Turnbull – Julie Hesmondhalgh
    Clive Fischel – Edward Rawle-Hicks
    Matthew Turnbull – Ray Stevenson
    Cunningham – Philip Voss
    Cissie Brodie – Tracy Whitwell

In rural Northumberland in the 1830s, 16-year-old Cissie Brodie fights to keep her younger brothers and sisters from the workhouse. The orphaned Brodies take refuge in a cave on the moors. When Cissie is raped by drunken aristocrat Clive Fischel, she becomes pregnant but loses custody of her son to Clive's father, Lord Fischel. When Clive returns to the area after an extended absence, he attempts to make amends to Cissie, who is also aided by Matthew Turnbull, who has loved Cissie for years.

FAMILY

8 May 1994, Sunday, 9:35–10:25pm, BBC1, 4 episodes, drama, Irish, contemporary

BBCtv
Pr: Andrew Eaton
Dir: Michael Winterbottom
Wtr: Roddy Doyle
Cast: Leanne Spencer – Gemma Butterly
Nicola Spencer – Neili Conroy
Fats – John Cronin
Tony – Darren Kenny
Ray Harris – Des McAleer
Charlo Spencer – Sean McGinley
Paula Spencer – Ger Ryan
John Paul Spencer – Barry Ward

In a working-class Dublin suburb, Charlo Spencer rules his wife and children with a mixture of fear and violence, his erratic behaviour pushing them all to the breaking point and ultimately causing Paula to throw Charlo out.

Each episode is told from a different point of view: Charlo, 13-year-old son John Paul, 16-year-old daughter Nicola, and Paula.

LITTLE NAPOLEONS

7 June 1994, Tuesday, 10:00–11:05pm, Channel 4, 4 episodes, drama, British, contemporary
Picture Palace Productions
Pr: Malcolm Craddock
Dir: Rob Walker
Wtr: Michael Abbensetts
Cast: **N.K. Edwards – Norman Beaton**
Angus – Niall Buggy
Edward Feathers – Simon Callow
Vijad Shaw – Saeed Jaffrey
Judith Silver – Lesley Manville

Rival solicitors N.K. Edwards and Vijay Shaw are both invited to stand for election as Labour candidates to their local inner-London borough council. In addition to their own fierce (and funny) conflicts, the racist leader of the Conservatives, Edward Feathers, always stands ready to take advantage of their rivalry.

LOVE ON A BRANCH LINE

12 June 1994, Sunday, 9:10–10:00pm, BBC1, 4 episodes, drama, British, 20th century

Theatre of Comedy/D.L. Taffner UK Ltd./New Penny Production for BBCtv
Pr: Jacqueline Davis
Dir: Martyn Friend
Wtr: David Hobbs
Based on John Hadfield
Cast: Lady Flamborough – Maria Aitken
Professor Pollux – Graham Crowden
Belinda – Abigail Cruttenden
Chloe – Cathryn Harrison
Jasper Pye – Michael Maloney
Quirk – Stephen Moore
Lord Flamborough – Leslie Phillips
Miss Mounsey – Amanda Root
Matilda – Charlotte Williams

In the 1950s, stiff, proper London Civil Servant Jasper Pye is sent to East Anglia to report on a long-forgotten government department housed in Arcady Hall, the magnificent stately home of eccentric Lord Flamborough, his semi-detached wife, and three decidedly odd daughters.

MASTER OF THE MOOR

2 September 1994, Friday, 9:00–10:00pm, ITV, 3 episodes, mystery, British, contemporary
Blue Heaven
Pr: Neil Zeiger
Dir: Marc Evans
Wtr: Trevor Preston
Based on Ruth Rendell
Cast: Detective Inspector Manciple – George Costigan
Lyn Whalby – Emma Croft
Stephen Whalby – Colin Firth
Nick – John Michie
Dadda Whalby – Robert Urquhart

Stephen Whalby is drawn to the eeriness that is Dartmoor, considers himself "master of the moor," and walks its twisting paths daily. When Whalby discovers the body of a young woman one day, the once-popular moor is quickly deserted by most, which at first somewhat pleases Whalby, as it makes the moors more his than ever. But he is soon haunted by premonitions of murder and is also suspected by Detective Inspector Manciple of committing the recent crime, so Whalby must search deep into his memories to discover the truth of the present . . . and the past.

FAITH

7 September 1994, Wednesday (subsequent episodes aired on Thursday), 9:00–10:00; 10:40–11:40pm, ITV, 4 episodes, thriller, British, contemporary
Central Television
Pr: Colin McKeown
Dir: John Strickland
Wtr: Simon Burke
Cast: Jeff Wagland – Keith Allen
Pat Harbinson – Connie Booth
Peter John Moreton – Michael Gambon
Nick Simon – John Hannah
Holly Moreton – Susannah Harker
Jane Moreton – Gemma Jones
Matthew Sheridan – Struan Rodger

Ruthless, ambitious MP Peter John Moreton lands at the centre of a political arms deal cover-up, while at the same time trying to keep the wraps on a personal sex scandal. His daughter Holly (who has an axe to grind with her callous father) becomes romantically involved with tabloid journalist Nick Simon, and Simon uses information he has obtained from Holly to write a story which could expose all of Moreton's dirty dealings, ignoring the dire consequences which threaten to follow the story's publication.

SEAFORTH

9 October 1994, Sunday, 8:30–10:05pm (subsequent episodes aired from 9:00–9:50pm), BBC1, 9 episodes, drama, British, 20th century
BBCtv
Pr: Eileen Quinn, Alan J. Wands
Dir: Stuart Burge, Martyn Friend, Peter Smith
Wtr: Peter Ransley
Cast: John Stacey – Ciaran Hinds
Richard Austen – Richard Huw
Diana Stacey – Diana Kent
Sarah Wickham – Rosemary Martin
Larry Field – Sean Murray
Bri Longman – Raymond Pickard
Bob Longman – Linus Roache
Sal Longman – Heather Tobias
Paula Wickham – Lia Williams

The rags-to-riches saga of ambitious working-class ne'er-do-well Bob Longman begins in the fictional Yorkshire town of Seaforth in 1943; during a bombing blackout he meets decent, innocent middle-class Paula Wickham, a chance encounter which sets off a chain of intense events both romantic and violent. By war's end, Bob and Paula are married and Bob is well on his way to material prosperity . . . and marital havoc, given his involvement with Diana Stacey. But these concerns pale when Bob is arrested for murder.

As we went to press, plans for production of the second series of *Seaforth* episodes (the story was originally outlined to span 50 years and three generations before its ultimate conclusion) had not yet been confirmed by the BBC.

MARTIN CHUZZLEWIT

7 November 1994, Monday, 9:00–10:30pm (subsequent episodes aired from 9:30–10:30pm), BBC2, 6 episodes, drama, classic, British, 19th century
BBCtv
Video: available in UK, US
Pr: Chris Parr
Dir: Pedr James
Wtr: David Lodge
Based on Charles Dickens
Cast: Jonas Chuzzlewit – Keith Allen
Mrs. Lupin – Lynda Bellingham
Charity Pecksniff – Emma Chambers
Tom Pinch – Philip Franks
Old Chuffey – John Mills
Mark Tapley – Steve Nicolson
Montague Tigg – Pete Postlethwaite
Anthony Chuzzlewit/Old Martin Chuzzlewit – Paul Scofield
Mrs. Gamp – Elizabeth Spriggs
Mercy Pecksniff – Julia Sawalha
Mary Graham – Pauline Turner
Young Martin Chuzzlewit – Ben Walden
Seth Pecksniff – Tom Wilkinson

The destinies of the brothers Chuzzlewit – Old Martin and Anthony – are tied to the fortunes and misfortunes, both personal and financial, of subsequent generations, the focus most pointedly on Young Martin Chuzzlewit. Estranged from his grandfather, due to his attachment to orphaned Mary Graham, Martin sets sail for America to seek his fortune, finally returning to England to face his destiny and his family – which has been embroiled in its own share of adventures and intrigues.

CROCODILE SHOES

10 November 1994, Thursday,
9:30–10:25pm, BBC1, 7 episodes, drama, British, contemporary
Big Boy/Red Rooster Films Productions for BBCtv
Pr: Peter Wolfes
Dir: David Richards
Wtr: Jimmy Nail
Cast: Rex Hall – Brian Capron
Alan Clarke – Christopher Fairbank
Emma Shepperd – Melanie Hill
Caroline Carrison – Alex Kingston
Carmel Cantrell – Amy Madigan
Jed Shepperd – Jimmy Nail
Snotter – Vince Pellegrino
Ade Lynn – James Wilby
Lou Benedetti – Burt Young

Aspiring Newcastle songwriter/performer Jed Shepperd thinks his big break has come when his "demo" cassette attracts the interest of London recording executive Ade Lynn, but, unknown (at first) to Jed, Ade has fallen on hard times and is more desperate for a break than Jed. Ade becomes Jed's manager, Jed quits his factory job, and the two journey from London to Nashville in their quest for the musical holy grail – but success is easier to dream about than achieve, especially since Ade's involvement with drugs and thugs threatens to destroy everything, just as Jed's record is about to be released.

FINNEY

17 November 1994, Thursday,
9:00–10:00pm, ITV, 6 episodes, drama, British, contemporary
Zenith Production for Tyne Tees Television
Pr: Nigel Stafford-Clark
Dir: David Hayman
Wtr: David Kane
Cast: Bobo Junior – Christopher Fairbank
Mary – Lynn Farleigh
McDade – David Hayman
Lena – Melanie Hill
Suzie – Angela Lonsdale
Louis Souter – John McArdle
Finney – David Morrissey
Carol – Pooky Quesnel
Tucker – Clive Russell
Tom – Andy Serkis
Bobo Senior – John Woodvine

Jazz musician Finney returns to his Newcastle home following the gangland slaying of his mobster father Tucker. Finney, the single law-abiding member of his family, wants only to live in peace, reconcile with his estranged wife Carol and open his own jazz club, but his brother Tom remains involved with underworld figures and his sister Lena is out for bloody revenge against the rival Simpson family, which she holds responsible for her father's death.

Some of the characters in *Finney* were featured in the 1987 feature film *Stormy Monday*, also produced by Nigel Stafford-Clark, but the television programme is meant to take place before the events of the film, acting as something of an after-the-fact "prequel".

THE WIMBLEDON POISONER

11 December 1994, Sunday,
9:10–10:35pm, BBC1, 2 episodes, drama, satire, British, contemporary
BBCtv
Pr: Linda Agran
Dir: Robert Young
Wtr: Nigel Williams
Based on Nigel Williams
Cast: Detective Inspector Russell Rush – Philip Jackson
Dr. Donald Templeton – Larry Lamb
Henry Farr – Robert Lindsay
Karim Jackson – Art Malik
Elinor Farr – Alison Steadman

Mild-mannered solicitor Henry Farr endeavours to murder his difficult wife Elinor, but has a hard time accomplishing the task; instead he manages to eliminate a number of his neighbours, which rouses the suspicions of police Detective Inspector Russell Rush.

LITTLE LORD FAUNTLEROY

1 January 1995, Sunday, 4:55–5:25pm, BBC1, 6 episodes, drama, classic, family, British, 19th century
BBCtv
Video: available in UK
Pr: Richard Callanan
Dir: Andrew Morgan
Wtr: Julian Fellowes
Based on Frances Hodgson Burnett
Cast: **Lord Dorincourt – George Baker**
Cedric Errol – Michael Benz
Mrs. Errol – Betsy Brantley
Havisham – John Castle
Hobbs – David Healy
Dick – Truan Munro
Lady Fauntleroy – Bernice Stegers

Young Cedric Errol, who lives with his impoverished, widowed mother in New York, is discovered to be the wealthy, titled Lord Fauntleroy, heir to Britain's Dorincourt Castle. Cedric is brought to England, where he is separated from his mother. But Cedric's embittered grandfather, Lord Dorincourt, is ultimately charmed and softened by the good-natured, innocent young boy, so much so that his American mother is welcomed into the family fold.

ELIDOR

4 January 1995, Wednesday, 5:10–5:35pm, BBC1, 6 episodes, drama, adventure, family, fantasy, British, contemporary
Screen First for BBCtv
Pr: Paul Madden, Mairede Thomas
Dir: John Reardon
Wtr: Don Webb
Based on Alan Garner
Cast: Frank Watson – David Beckett
Helen – Suzanne Crowshaw
Gwen Watson – Noreen Kershaw
Lead Warrior – Renny Krupinski
Sibyl – Valerie Lilley
Nicholas – Gavin J. Morris
Malebron – Stevan Rimkus
David – Alexander Trippier
Roland – Damian Zuk

In Manchester, Roland and his siblings explore a ruined church, where Roland hears and sees strange figures . . . which he discovers have journeyed from the land of Elidor, whose evil forces are attempting to break through to our world. Instead, the children find themselves in Elidor, pursued by evil warriors who follow even when the youngsters are able to escape and return home.

THE GLASS VIRGIN

6 January 1995, Friday, 9:00–10:00pm, ITV, 3 episodes, drama, British, 19th century
World Wide International Television/Festival Films for Tyne Tees Television
Pr: Ray Marshall
Dir: Sarah Hellings
Wtr: Alan Seymour
Based on Catherine Cookson
Cast: **Manuel Mendoza – Brendan Coyle**
Young Annabella – Samantha Glenn
Betty Watford – Jan Graveson
Edmund Lagrange – Nigel Havers
Rosina – Christine Kavanagh
Annabella Lagrange – Emily Mortimer
Mr. Carpenter – Fred Pearson
Lady Constance – Sylvia Syms
Jessie – Denise Welch

In the late 19th century, 17-year-old Annabella Lagrange runs away from her life of luxury at Redford Hall after her cruel, autocratic father Edmund tells her the sordid truth of her birth: she is the illegitimate daughter of Edmund and local prostitute Jessie. Annabella is accompanied on her travels by Manuel Mendoza, her father's Irish groom; on her journey Annabella discovers true love, accepts the truth about herself, and prepares to start a new life, but finds she must return to Redford Hall to resolve things with her father before she can move on.

TEARS BEFORE BEDTIME

8 January 1995, Sunday, 9:40–10:30pm, BBC1, 4 episodes, drama, comedy, British, contemporary
BBCtv
Exec. Pr: Caroline Oulton, Michael Wearing

Dir: Tristram Powell
Wtr: Sandy Welch
Cast: Maureen – Louise Beattie
Sarah Baylis – Samantha Bond
Lisa – Nicola Cowper
Katherine – Julie Cox
Stuart Freeman – Richard Hope
Ben Farlow – Peter Howitt
Beattie Freeman – Lesley Manville
Teresa Turner – Veronica Quilligan
David Baylis – Adrian Rawlins
Hugo Freeman – Guy Wiltcher

Three seemingly-secure couples – Sarah and David, Beattie and Stuart, and Teresa and Jimmy – find their lives turned upside down when they attempt to find (and keep) nannies to take care of their young children.

SIGNS AND WONDERS

16 January 1995, Monday, 9:30–10:30pm, BBC2, 4 episodes, drama, British, contemporary
BBCtv
Pr: Elaine Steel
Dir: Maurice Phillips
Wtr: Michael Eaton
Cast: Diamond – James Earl Jones
Stephen Palmore – Michael Maloney
Claire Palmore – Jodhi May
Cornelius Van Damm – Donald Pleasence
Brother Nahum – David Rasche
Elizabeth Palmore – Prunella Scales
Reverend Timothy Palmore – David Warner
Sherry Rossen – Debra Weston
Father Mercy – Ric Young

Reverend Timothy Palmore and his wife Elizabeth face a personal and spiritual crisis when their daughter Claire falls in with the World Mercy Mission, a religious cult in Los Angeles. By the time Claire is rescued and successfully de-programmed, everyone in the family has endured his or her own major predicament.

THE BUCCANEERS

5 February 1995, Sunday, 9:05–10:25pm (subsequent episodes aired from 9:05–10:00pm), BBC1, 5 episodes, drama, American/British, 19th century
BBCtv
Pr: Philip Saville
Dir: Philip Saville
Wtr: Maggie Wadey
Based on Edith Wharton
Cast: Idina Hatton – Jenny Agutter
Miss Jacqueline March – Connie Booth
Virginia St. George – Alison Elliott
Julius, Duke of Trevenick – James Frain
Nan St. George – Carla Gugino
Duchess of Trevenick – Sheila Hancock
Lizzy Elmsworth – Rya Kihlstedt
Sir Helmsley Thwaite – Michael Kitchen
Lord Brightlingsea – Dinsdale Landen
Lady Brightlingsea – Rosemary Leach
Laura Testvalley – Cherie Lunghi
Conchita Closson – Mira Sorvino
Lord Seadown – Mark Tandy
Lord Richard Marable – Ronan Vibert
Guy Thwaite – Greg Wise

After failing to find social acceptance in their own homeland, four wealthy, free-spirited young American women travel to England in the 1870s, in hopes of finding love, marriage and entry into British society. They all do marry, but ultimately their naïve dreams are squelched by the repressive realities before them, as the young women make the painful discovery that the price of sophistication is often their native sense of freedom.

BLOOD AND PEACHES

13 February 1995, Monday, 9:00–10:15pm, BBC2, 2 episodes, drama, British, contemporary
Waller Film Company
Pr: Peter Waller
Dir: Charles Beeson
Wtr: Martin Sadofski
Cast: **Sue – Jayne Ashbourne**
Gary – Jason Done
Sunil – Ravi Kapoor
Steve – Stuart Laing

Nan – Rosemary Leach

Bradford teenagers Sue and Steve have been close friends for years, but now find their relationship taking on a romantic turn; their new-found joy, though, is cut tragically short, and also painfully counterpointed with the racial tension in their community.

HEARTS AND MINDS

16 February 1995, Thursday, 10:00–11:05pm, Channel 4, 4 episodes, drama, British, contemporary
Witz End and Alamo Productions
Pr: Tara Prem, David Wimbury
Dir: Stephen Whittaker
Wtr: Jimmy McGovern
Cast: Sahira – Trina Ali
    Joanna – Pauline Black
    Drew McKenzie – Christopher Eccleston
    Shotton – Peter Halliday
    Trevor – David Harewood
    Mo – Sara Mair-Thomas
    Alex – Ian McElhinney
    Emma – Lynda Steadman

Idealistic student teacher Drew McKenzie arrives at a Liverpool comprehensive school, where he sets out on the difficult task of transmitting his love of poetry to his sullen, disaffected students, the endeavour compounded by the open hostility he encounters from his fellow teachers.

THE GAMBLING MAN

26 February 1995, Sunday, 7:45–8:45pm, ITV, 3 episodes, drama, British, 19th century
Festival Films/World Wide International TV Production for Tyne Tees Television
Pr: Ray Marshall
Dir: Norman Stone
Wtr: T.R. Bowen
Based on Catherine Cookson
Cast: **Rory Connor – Robson Green**
    John George Armstrong – David Haddow
    Frank Nickle – Bernard Hill
    Victor Pittie – Sammy Johnson
    Lizzie O'Dowd – Anne Kent
    Charlotte Kean – Sylvestra Le Touzel
    Jimmy Connor – Dave Nellist
    Janie Waggett – Stephanie Putson

In the South Shields slums in the 1870s, ambitious rent collector and gambler Rory Connor strives to rise above his humble origins and achieve middle-class respectability. Rory does accomplish this end, but the path is fraught with betrayal and catastrophe for Rory and those around him.

SHE'S OUT

6 March 1995, Monday, 9:00–10:00pm, ITV, 6 episodes, thriller, British, contemporary
Cinema Verity
Pr: Verity Lambert
Dir: Ian Toynton
Wtr: Lynda La Plante
Cast: Connie Stephens – Zoe Heyes
    Ester Freeman – Linda Marlowe
    Kathleen O'Reilly – Maggie McCarthy
    Dolly Rawlins – Ann Mitchell
    Angela Dunn – Indra Ove
    Julia Lawson – Anna Patrick
    Detective Chief Inspector Ron Craigh – Hugh Quarshie
    Detective Sergeant Mike Withey – Adrian Rawlins
    Gloria Radford – Maureen Sweeney
    Audrey Withey – Kate Williams

A decade has passed since Dolly Rawlins organized a group of *Widows* (see listing for 16 March 1983) to commit a robbery originally planned by their late husbands. Dolly is just now getting out of prison, and she hopes to lay claim to a hidden fortune in stolen diamonds, planning to go straight and use the funds to set up a children's home. But six female ex-convicts greet Dolly upon her release, each with her own idea of what to do with the riches, and Dolly's good intentions are replaced by a plan for one more spectacular robbery.

BAND OF GOLD

12 March 1995, Sunday, 9:00–10:00pm,

ITV, 6 episodes, thriller, British, contemporary
Granada Television
Pr: Tony Dennis
Dir: Richard Standeven
Wtr: Kay Mellor
Cast: Joyce – Rachel Davies
Anita – Barbara Dickson
George – Tony Doyle
Gina – Ruth Gemmell
Rose – Geraldine James
Curly – Richard Moore
Tracy – Samantha Morton
Inspector Newall – David Schofield
Steve – Ray Stevenson
Carol – Cathy Tyson

Several prostitutes – young mother Gina, old hand Rose, still-dreamy Anita and hard-boiled Carol – find their livelihood, and their lives, in jeopardy when they are caught in the middle of a murder investigation.

THE CHOIR

19 March 1995, Sunday, 9:05–10:25 pm, BBC1, 5 episodes, drama, British, contemporary
BBCtv
Pr: Peter Cregeen
Dir: Ferdinand Fairfax
Wtr: Ian Curteis
Based on Joanna Trollope
Cast: Felicity Troy – Jane Asher
Bridget Cavendish – Richenda Carey
Leo Beckford – Nicholas Farrell
Hugh Cavendish – James Fox
Sally Ashworth – Cathryn Harrison
Bishop Robert Young – John Standing
Frank Ashworth – Peter Vaughan
Alexander Troy – David Warner
Henry Ashworth – Anthony Way

The seeming serenity at Aldminster Cathedral actually masks a den of intrigue, betrayal and hypocrisy, focusing on Hugh Cavendish and Alexander Troy, dean and headmaster of the Cathedral school. Further complicating matters are the Cathedral's rundown buildings, which are in need of costly repair. The ensuing cash crisis threatens the survival of the choir, but the arrival of an outstanding boy soprano changes the fortunes of many in the cathedral close.

VANITY DIES HARD

24 March 1995, Friday, 9:00–10:00pm, ITV, 3 episodes, mystery, British, contemporary
Blue Heaven Productions
Pr: Neil Zeiger
Dir: Alan Grint
Wtr: Julian Bond
Based on Ruth Rendell
Cast: **Alice Whittaker – Eleanor David**
Dr. Harry Blunde – Peter Egan
Andrew Fielding – Mark Frankel
Nesta Drage – Jane Gurnett
Justin Whittaker – Leslie Phillips
Hugo Whittaker – Arthur White

Plain Alice Whittaker's unexpected and seemingly-hasty marriage to teacher Andrew Fielding, who has just recently arrived in the village, seems to be somehow connected with the sudden disappearance of Alice's best friend Nesta Drage . . . and the suspicion of murder.

INDEX OF
TITLES OF SERIALS

£1,000,000 Bank Note, The	93
"A" For Andromeda	57
Act of Will	242
Adventures of Ben Gunn, The	32
Adventures of Peter Simple, The	21
Adventures of Tom Sawyer, The	50
After Many A Summer	87
After The War	241
Alexa	188
Alexander Graham Bell	73
Alice In Wonderland	217
Aliens In The Family	231
All Or Nothing At All	273
All Passion Spent	224
Ambassadors, The	72
Amelia	55
Andromeda Breakthrough, The	61
Angel Pavement	28, 86
Anglo-Saxon Attitudes	263
Ann Veronica	67
Anna Karenina	149
Anna of The Five Towns	210
Anne of Avonlea	132
Anne of Green Gables	6, 112
Another Bouquet	144
Anything More Would Be Greedy	242
Aphrodite Inheritance, The	158
Ask For King Billy	42
Assassin, The	24
Assassination Run, The	169
Badger By Owl-Light	188
Ballet Shoes	136
Band of Gold	282
Barbara In Black	60
Barchester Chronicles, The	193
Barnaby Rudge	52
Bat Out of Hell	82
Battle of St. George Without, The	98
Beau Geste	193
Behaving Badly	239
Beiderbecke Affair, The	209
Bel Ami	107
Bell, The	187
Benbow and The Angels	14
Big Battalions, The	265
Big M, The	86
Big Pull, The	61
Big Spender, The	77
Bird of Prey	190
Birds Fall Down, The	157
Black Arrow, The	29, 117
Black Brigand, The	18
Black Tower, The	216
Black Tulip, The	19, 103
Blackeyes	245
Blackheath Poisonings, The	266
Blakes, The	16
Bleak House	41, 213
Blood and Peaches	281
Blood Money	183
Blood Red Roses	224
Blood Rights	251
Blott On The Landscape	211
Bluebell	218
Body and Soul	269
Boogie Outlaws	229
Border Warfare	249
Borgias, The	185
Borrowers, The	264
Borrowers (2), The	272
Bouquet of Barbed Wire	139
Box of Delights, The	208
Boy In The Bush, The	204
Brack Report, The	189
Brat Farrar	218
Bread Or Blood	180
Break In The Sun	179
Breakaway: The Family Affair	169
Breakaway: The Local Affair	170
Breaking Point	81
Breaking Up	223
Brideshead Revisited	185
Broken Horseshoe, The	5
Brond	227
Broome Stages	81
Brother's Tale, A	200
Brothers Karamazov, The	71
Buccaneers, The	281
Buddenbrooks	76
Buddha of Suburbia, The	271
Budds of Paragon Row, The	36
Bull Week	173
By The Sword Divided	201
By The Sword Divided (2)	209
Cabin In The Clearing, The	11, 35
Cakes and Ale	129
Caleb Williams	199
Calling The Shots	275
Camerons, The	164
Camomile Lawn, The	261
Campaign	232
Captain Moonlight – Man of Mystery	31, 48
Carrie's War	124
Casanova	110
Centrepoint	251
Champion Road	32
Chance of Thunder, A	59
Chance To Sit Down, A	181
Changes, The	131
Charters and Caldicott	210
Chelworth	242
Chem. Lab. Mystery, The	64
Chéri	119
Chessgame	202
Children of Green Knowe, The	223
Children of The New Forest, The	15, 69, 150
Children of The North	258
Chimera	256
Chinese Puzzle	130
Choir, The	283
Christ Recrucified	96
Christabel	238
Chronicles of Narnia	
The Prince Caspian	244
The Lion, The Witch and The Wardrobe	237
The Silver Chair	252
Voyage of The Dawn Treader	245
Cinder Path, The	276
Citadel, The	53, 195
Claire	192
Clarissa	258
Clayhanger	77
Clementina	11
Cleopatras, The	195
Clochemerle	112
Cloning of Joanna May, The	259
Cloud Howe	191
Cold Comfort Farm	91

TITLES OF SERIALS

Come Home Charlie and Face Them	253	Diary of Samuel Pepys, The	30	Fell Tiger	214
Confessional	243	Dickens of London	143	Fifth Form At St. Dominic's, The	54
Consultant, The	198	Die Kinder	252	Fight Against Slavery, The	133
Contenders, The	96	Dimension of Fear	63	Fighting Back	220
Contract To Kill	74	Disraeli, Portrait of A Romantic	154	File On Jill Hatch, The	197
Contract, The	231	Doll, The	137	Final Run	235
Count of Monte Cristo, The	70	Dombey and Son	96, 195	Finney	279
Country Diary of An Edwardian Lady, The	205	Donati Conspiracy, The	121	Firm of Girdlestone, The	32
Cousin Bette	107	Doom Castle	173	First Among Equals	221
Cousin Phillis	191	Downtown Lagos	264	First Born	237
Cover Her Face	211	Dr. Jekyll and Mr. Hyde	20	First Churchills, The	97
Cracker	270	Dragon's Opponent, The	121	Fish	118
Cranford	117	Driving Ambition	205	Five Children and It	253
Crime and Punishment	161	Dwelling Place, The	276	Five Names For Johnny	26
Crime of The Century, The	21			Five Red Herrings	135
Crime On Our Hands	13	Eagle of The Ninth, The	148	Flambards	159
Crimson Ramblers, The	18	Early Life of Stephen Hind, The	130	Flame Trees of Thika, The	182
Crocodile Shoes	279	Echoes	234	Flesh and Blood	169
Crossfire	233	Edge of Darkness	216	Flickers	175
Crying Down The Lane	59	Edward & Mrs. Simpson	157	Flight of The Heron, The	89, 140
Cuckoo Sister, The	223	Edward The Seventh	133	Floodtide	229
Curtain of Fear	70	Eleanor Marx	144	Flower of Evil	57
		Electrode 93	23	For The Greater Good	254
Dancers In Mourning	39	Elidor	280	For Whom The Bell Tolls	76
Dancing Bear, The	12	Elizabeth R	106	Forgive Our Foolish Ways	175
Dandelion Dead	274	Elusive Pimpernel, The	95	Forgotten Story, The	194
Dangerous Game, The	32	Emma	47, 114	Forsyte Saga, The	82
Dangerous Knowledge	141	Enchanted Castle, The	165	Fortunes of Nigel, The	125
Daniel Deronda	102	Enemy of The State, An	76	Fortunes of War	230
Dark Angel, The	238	Epilogue To Capricorn	42	Fourth Floor, The	219
Dark Island, The	62	Epitaph For A Spy	8, 64	Framed	266
Dark Number, The	82	Escape of R.D.7, The	58	Franchise Affair, The	61, 236
Dark Side of The Sun, The	200	Esther Waters	71, 146	Frankie's House	262
David Copperfield	20, 78, 130, 222	Eugénie Grandet	77	Free Frenchman, The	244
Day of The Triffids, The	183	Eustace Diamonds, The	39	Freud	207
Days of Vengeance, The	49	Exchange of Fire, An	270	Friday On My Mind	263
Dead Entry	225	Explorer, The	15	Frontier Drums	56
Dead Head	218	Eye of The Dragon, The	227	Frost In May	190
Death Is A Good Living	79	Eyeless In Gaza	108	Further Adventures of Oliver Twist, The	171
Death of A Ghost	49			Further Adventures of The Musketeers	84
Death of An Expert Witness	197	Fair Stood The Wind For France	174		
Death Or Glory Boy	124	Faith	278	G.B.H.	255
Death To The First Lady	19	Fall of Eagles	125	Gallowglass	267
December Rose, The	219	Fame Is The Spur	186	Gamble For A Throne	58
Deep Concern, The	162	Family	276	Gambler, The	89
Desperate People, The	64	Family At War, A		Gambling Man, The	282
Destination Downing Street	23	first series	102	Game of Murder, A	79
Detective, The	213	second series	104	Game, Set & Match	236
Devices and Desires	253	third series	109	Gangsters	142
Devil's Crown, The	153	Family Man, A	204	Garry Halliday	36
Devil-In-The-Fog	91	Fanny By Gaslight	184	Gathering Seed, The	199
Diana	203	Farewell To Arms, A	78	Gaudy Night	228
Diary of Anne Frank, The	224	Fatal Inversion, A	262	Gentle Falcon, The	13
		Fathers and Sons	109		
		Fear, The	232		

TITLES OF SERIALS

Gentle Killers, The	22
Germinal	101
Gift, The	250
Ginger Tree, The	244
Girl In A Black Bikini	83
Girls of Slender Means, The	134
Glass Virgin, The	280
Glittering Prizes, The	139
God's Wonderful Railway	170
Goggle Eyes	268
Golden Bowl, The	114
Golden Girl	50
Golden Spur, The	39
Good Behaviour	201
Good Companions, The	177
Good Wives	33
Goodbye Cruel World	259
Goodbye Mr. Chips	204
Gordon Honour, The	15
Gravelhanger	12
Gravy Train, The	250
Gravy Train Goes East, The	257
Great Expectations	37, 83, 184, 256
Green Man, The	251
Grey Granite	198
Growing Rich	260
Grushko	275
Guilty Thing Surprised, A	235
Guilty, The	263
Gulliver In Lilliput	186
Haggard Falcon, The	127
Handful of Thieves, A	97
Hanged Man, The	132
Hannah	172
Happy and Glorious	6
Hard Times	149
Hard Word, The	195
Harry's Game	192
Have His Carcase	227
Hawkeye, The Pathfinder	122
Hawkmoor	151
Headhunters	274
Heart of Midlothian, The	80
Heart of The Country	225
Heart of The High Country	217
Hearts and Minds	282
Heidi	10, 38, 128
Heidi Grows Up	13
Heir of Skipton, The	9
Heiress of Garth	75
Here Lies Miss Sabry	50
Hereward The Wake	76
Herries Chronicle, The	50
Hideaway	218
Hilda Lessways	38
Hill of The Red Fox, The	135
Hills of Heaven, The	156
History Man, The	178
History of Mr. Polly, The	40, 171
Hit and Run	72
Hitch-Hiker's Guide To The Galaxy, The	178
Holding On	145
Hole In The Wall, The	116
Holly	115
Honey Siege, The	35, 228
Horseman Riding By, A	155
Hound of The Baskervilles, The	192
House of Cards	252
House Under The Water, The	54
Houseman's Tale, The	226
How Green Was My Valley	47, 138
Huckleberry Finn	4
Hunchback of Notre Dame, The	79
Huntingtower	25, 156
Hurricane	56
I Remember Nelson	189
I, Claudius	142
Idiot, The	78
Imaginary Friends	229
Imperial Palace	94
Infamous John Friend, The	37
Inheritors, The	127
Inspector Calls, An	191
Intimate Contact	226
Intruder, The	111
Invisible Armies, The	30
Invisible Man, The	207
It's Murder, But Is It Art?	113
Ivanhoe	101
Jane Eyre	17, 64, 122, 200
Jennie, Lady Randolph Churchill	129
Jenny's War	214
Jewel In The Crown, The	202
Jo's Boys	36
Joe and The Gladiator	106
John Halifax, Gentleman	124
John Macnab	141
Johnny Jarvis	202
Johnny, You're Wanted!	11
Joyous Errand	23
Jude The Obscure	105
Judith Paris	69
Jumbo Spencer	140
Jumping The Queue	240
Justice Game, The	239
Jute City	257
Katy	62, 143
Kenilworth	22, 92
Kessler	185
Kidnapped	6, 20, 65, 161
Killer	199
Killing On The Exchange, A	226
Kind of Loving, A	188
King of The Ghetto	220
King's Royal	187
Kipps	52
Kizzy	139
Lady Chatterley	269
Lady of The Camellias, The	144
Last Chronicle of Barset, The	35
Last Man Out, The	62
Last of The Mohicans, The	105
Last Place On Earth, The	211
Late Call	132
Late Starter	212
Law and Order	152
Leave It To Todhunter	33
Legacy, A	133
Legend of Death	75
Legend of King Arthur, The	164
Legend of Robin Hood, The	137
Les Misérables	87
Letters From The Dead	94
Life and Adventures of Nicholas Nickleby, The	193
Life and Death of Penelope	139
Life and Loves of A She Devil, The	222
Life and Times of David Lloyd George, The	180
Life and Times of Henry Pratt, The	265
Lillie	155
Lion, The Witch and The Wardrobe, The	85
Lipstick On Your Collar	267
Little Lord Fauntleroy	26, 143, 280
Little Napoleons	277
Little Princess, A	119, 225
Little Red Monkey	7
Little Sir Nicholas	249
Little Women	3, 31, 104
Lizzie's Pictures	228
London Belongs To Me	148
Long Way Home, The	48
Look At It This Way	266
Looking For Clancy	134
Lord Peter Wimsey	
Clouds of Witness	114
Murder Must Advertise	123

Nine Tailors, The	126	
Unpleasantness At The Bellona Club, The	118	
Lord Raingo	79	
Lorna Doone	65, 142	
Lost Boys, The	156	
Lost Empires	222	
Lost King, The	33	
Lost Tribe, The	177	
Love Among The Artists	162	
Love and Mr. Lewisham	37, 115	
Love and Reason	270	
Love For Lydia	148	
Love In A Cold Climate	176	
Love Is Old, Love Is New	188	
Love On A Branch Line	277	
Machine Breakers, The	24	
Machine Gunners, The	196	
Mackenzie	174	
Mad Death, The	198	
Mad O'Haras, The	33	
Madame Bovary	66, 135	
Maelstrom	210	
Magnolia Street	55	
Maidens' Trip	147	
Malice Aforethought	160	
Mallens, The	162, 173	
Man Called Harry Brent, A	73	
Man Dog	111	
Man In The Iron Mask, The	92	
Man In The Mirror, The	78	
Man of Straw	112	
Man Who Finally Died, The	40	
Man Who Sold Death, The	29	
Man Who Was Hunting Himself, The	115	
Man Who Was Two, The	22	
Mansfield Park	201	
Mapp and Lucia	213	
Maria Marten	178	
Marie Curie	147	
Marksman, The	231	
Married Man, A	198	
Martin Chuzzlewit	66, 278	
Mary Barton	67	
Mask For Alexis, A	41	
Massingham Affair, The	69	
Master of Ballantrae, The	61, 132	
Master of The Moor	277	
Matilda's England	161	
Matter of Degree, A	49	
Mayor of Casterbridge, The	151	
McCreary Moves In	27	
Melissa	67, 131	

Member For Chelsea, The	182	
Men's Room, The	257	
Menace Unseen	234	
Merlin of The Crystal Cave	258	
Middlemarch	91, 274	
Midnight Men, The	68	
Mill On The Floss, The	73, 158	
Mind of The Enemy, The	74	
Missing From Home	206	
Moll Flanders	137	
Moment In Time, A	163	
Money Man, The	31	
Monocled Mutineer, The	221	
Monsters, The	63	
Moon Stallion, The	157	
Moondial	232	
Moonfleet	205	
Moonstone, The	40, 111	
More Than Robbery	30	
Morgan's Boy	207	
Mother Love	243	
Motive For Murder	24	
Moulded In Earth	75	
Mourning Brooch, The	161	
Mr. Pye	219	
Mr. Right	194	
Mr. Wakefield's Crusade	262	
Mr. Wroe's Virgins	268	
Mulberry Accelerator, The	15	
Murder At The Wedding	162	
Murder In Eden	256	
Murder Most English	147	
Murder of A Moderate Man	214	
Music and Macaroni	14	
My Brother Jonathan	214	
My Cousin Rachel	196	
My Family and Other Animals	230	
My Father's House	180	
My Friend Charles	18	
My Son, My Son	160	
Mystery of Edwin Drood, The	51	
Naked Lady, The	39	
Nana	93	
Nancy Astor	187	
Napoleon and Love	113	
Natural Lies	263	
Nearly Man, The	129	
Never Come Back	250	
New Road, The	119	
Nice Town	265	
Nice Work	243	
Nicholas Nickleby	27, 88, 146	
Night Train To Surbiton	72	
Nightmare Man, The	181	

No Cloak – No Dagger	65	
No Wreath For The General	51	
North and South	80, 137	
Not A Penny More, Not A Penny Less	250	
Notorious Woman	128	
Number 10	196	
Odd Job Man, The	204	
Odd Man, The	52	
Off To Philadelphia In The Morning	154	
Old Curiosity Shop, The	63, 165	
Old Devils, The	261	
Old Men At The Zoo, The	200	
Old Wives' Tale, The	70	
Oliver Twist	59, 215	
One Game, The	234	
One Summer	199	
Operation Diplomat	7	
Operation Fantail	58	
Operation Julie	216	
Oppenheimer	176	
Opportunity Murder	18	
Oranges Are Not The Only Fruit	249	
Orde Wingate	141	
Ordeal of Richard Feverel, The	69	
Oscar	212	
Other Man, The	20	
Other Side of Paradise, The	260	
Our John Willie	169	
Our Mutual Friend	34, 140	
Out	153	
Outbreak of Murder	62	
Owl Service, The	98	
Pallisers, The	124	
Paradise Makers, The	83	
Paradise Postponed	221	
Paradise Walk	54	
Parbottle Speaking	60	
Parnell and The Englishwoman	253	
Passenger, The	109	
Pen of My Aunt, The	48	
Penmarric	164	
Pennies From Heaven	152	
Peppermint Pig, The	148	
Pere Goriot	90	
Perfect Hero, A	255	
Perfect Spy, A	231	
Persuasion	53, 107	
Phoenix and The Carpet, The	144	
Pickwick Papers, The	7, 209	
Picture of Katherine Mansfield, A	120	
Pilgrim's Progress, The	88	

TITLES OF SERIALS

Pin To See The Peepshow, A	121
Pinch of Snuff, A	276
Pinocchio	157
Place of Execution, A	10
Plateau of Fear	57
Pocket Lancer, The	37, 58
Point Counter Point	89
Poison Island	75
Poldark	136
Pollyanna	122
Porterhouse Blue	228
Portrait of A Lady, The	88
Portrait of A Marriage	251
Portrait of Alison	14
Possessed, The	94
Precious Bane	24
Pretenders	113
Price, The	210
Pride and Prejudice	5, 29, 86, 169
Prime of Miss Jean Brodie, The	151
Prime Suspect	254
Prime Suspect 2	266
Prime Suspect 3	273
Prince and The Pauper, The	16, 138
Prince Regent	163
Prior Commitment, The	95
Prisoner of Zenda, The	208
Private Schulz	181
Prometheus: The Life of Balzac	136
Puck of Pook's Hill	4
Quatermass	164
Quatermass and The Pit	35
Quatermass Experiment, The	10
Quatermass II	16
Queen's Champion	32
Queen's Traitor, The	86
Question of Guilt, A	172
Question of Guilt, A (2)	172
Question of Guilt, A (3)	173
Quiet Conspiracy, A	239
Racketty Street Gang, The	56
Raging Calm, A	123
Railway Children, The	3, 22, 90
Rainbow City	85
Rainbow, The	238
Ramshackle Road	92
Ransom For A Pretty Girl	80
Real Charlotte, The	255
Real Eddy English, The	240
Rebecca	159
Rebecca of Sunnybrook Farm	150
Rebel Heiress, The	34
Rector's Wife, The	275

Redgauntlet	41
Reluctant Bandit	72
Resnick: Lonely Hearts	261
Resurrection	93
Rex Milligan	18
Riddle of The Red Wolf, The	30
Ring Out An Alibi	71
Rise and Fall of César Birotteau, The	74
Ritz, The	153
River Flows East, The	63
Roads To Freedom, The	104
Rob Roy	55, 146
Robin Hood	8
Rocky O'Rourke	141
Rose Medallion, The	182
Rough Justice	147
Royalty, The	27
Rules of Engagement	241
Run To Earth	30
Runaway Summer, The	109
Running Blind	159
Running Scared	218
Rupert of Hentzau	66
Sam	120
Sam (second series)	126
Sam (third series)	134
Sam and The River	134
Sara Crewe	4, 23
Scarf, The	36
Scarlet and The Black, The	74, 271
Schirmer Inheritance, The	26
Scobie In September	94
Scoop	116
Scotch On The Rocks	120
Seaforth	278
Search For The Nile, The	108
Second Chance	179
Secret Agent, The	85, 264
Secret Garden, The	5, 47, 131
Secret Kingdom, The	48
Secret Servant, The	208
Selling Hitler	255
Sense and Sensibility	105, 179
Sense of Guilt, A	249
Sentimental Education	103
Serpent Son, The	160
Seven Little Australians	9
Sexton Blake and The Demon God	154
Shackleton	189
Shadow of The Tower, The	111
Shalom Salaam	240
She's Out	282

Sheep's Clothing	51
Shoulder To Shoulder	126
Shroud For A Nightingale	212
Signs and Wonders	281
Silas Marner	67
Silver Swan, The	7
Silver Sword, The	28, 108
Singing Detective, The	223
Sinister Street	95
Six Faces	116
Six Proud Walkers, The	13, 60
Six Wives of Henry VIII, The	101
Skorpion	194
Sleeper, The	68
Sleepers	254
Small House At Allington, The	51
Small World	232
Smiley's People	192
Smokescreen	273
Smuggler's Bay	68
Solo For Canary	34
Something In Disguise	190
Song of Songs, The	120
Sons and Lovers	178
Sophia and Constance	233
Sorrell and Son	206
Sort of Innocence, A	225
South Riding	128
Space School	17
Spanish Farm, The	90
Special Project Air	97
Spindoe	84
Splendid Spur, The	47
Spoils of Poynton, The	103
Spoils of War, The	
first series	170
second series	174
third series	181
Spy At Evening, A	180
Spyship	202
St. Ives	17, 49, 83
Stalky & Co.	187
Stand By To Shoot	9
Stanley and The Women	259
Stark	273
Stars Look Down, The	127
State of Emergency	137
Stay With Me Till Morning	182
Story of The Treasure Seekers, The	9, 186
Strange Affair of Adelaide Harris, The	158
Strange Interlude	235
Strange World of Planet X, The	19
Stranger In The City	60

Stranger On The Hills, A	101	Thursday's Child	117	Waterfall, The	177
Stranger On The Shore	57	Time of Day, A	28	Way We Live Now, The	95
Strangers and Brothers	203	Time To Dance, A	259	We, The Accused	175
Strauss Family, The	115	Tinker, Tailor, Soldier, Spy	163	Web	28
Strictly Personal	8	Titmuss Regained	257	Weir of Hermiston	119
Strike It Rich!	217	To Have and To Hold	220	What Maisie Knew	90
Striker	138	To Play The King	272	White Peak Farm	225
Strong Poison	227	To Serve Them All My Days	176	White Rabbit, The	87
Summer's Lease	244	Tom Brown's Schooldays	110	Who Pays The Ferryman?	150
Sunset Song	106	Tom's Midnight Garden	123, 239	Who, Sir? Me, Sir?	212
Swallows and Amazons	65	Traffik	241	Wide, Wide World, The	12
Swallows and Amazons Forever! – Coot Club	206	Traveller In Time, A	151	Wideawake	25
		Treasure Island	3, 26, 93, 149	Widow of Bath, The	38
Swallows and Amazons Forever! – The Big Six	206	Treasure Seekers, The	54	Widows	197
		Tripods	184	Wilfred and Eileen	185
Sweet Nothings	171	Tripods (2), The	215	Will Shakespeare	153
Swish of The Curtain, The	172	Triton	55, 91	Wimbledon Poisoner, The	279
Sword of Honour	82	Trollenberg Terror, The	21	Windmill Family, The	12
		Troubles	234	Winston Churchill – The Wilderness Years	183
Take A Pair of Private Eyes	79	Truth About Melandrinos, The	31		
Take Me Home	240	Two Women	121	Winter Harvest, A	207
Tale of Two Cities, A	25, 73, 175, 241			Winter Sunlight	205
Tales of The City	271	Underbelly	260	Wipe Out	236
Talisman, The	177	Unofficial Rose, An	131	Witch Hunt	84
Taste For Death, A	237			Witch Wood	68
Tears Before Bedtime	280	Vanity Dies Hard	283	Witch's Daughter, The	108
Teckman Biography, The	11	Vanity Fair	21, 88, 230	Wives and Daughters	110
Telford's Change	159	Very British Coup, A	235	Wolf To The Slaughter	230
Tell Tale Hearts	264	Very Peculiar Practice, A	220	Woman In White, The	81, 190
Telltale	270	Viaduct, The	118	Woman's Guide To Adultery, A	272
Tenant of Wildfell Hall, The	94	Vice Versa	59	Woodlanders, The	102
Tender Is The Night	215	Victoria Regina	71	Woodstock	118
Terracotta Horse, The	122	Villette	25, 103	World of Tim Frazer, The	53
Testament of Youth	165	Visitors, The	114	Wuthering Heights	87, 155
The Mushroom Picker	267	Voodoo Factor, The	42	Wynne and Penkovsky	208
Thérèse Raquin	171				
Thin Air	233	Walk A Crooked Mile	56	Year In Provence, A	268
This Way For Murder	85	Wanderer, The	38	Yesterday's Dreams	224
This Year Next Year	145	War and Peace	116	You Me and It	269
Three Golden Nobles	42	Warden, The	3	Young Lady From London, The	42
Three Hostages, The	5	Warrior Queen	152		
Three Musketeers, The	14, 81	Watch House, The	238	Zastrozzi	219
Thunder In The West	27	Watch The Birdies	80		

INDEX OF
ORIGINAL WORKS
when titles changed

Adventures of Caleb Williams (Or Things As They Are), The	199
Adventures of Huckleberry Finn	4
Age of Reason, The	104
Alamut Ambush, The	202
Balkan Trilogy, The	230
Barchester Towers	193
Beyond The Glass	190
Big Six, The	206
Bogmail	256
Borrowers, The	265
Borrowers Afield, The	265
Borrowers Afloat, The	272
Borrowers Aloft, The	272
Bouncers	153
Brigand, The	18
Can You Forgive Her?	124
Catriona	65, 161
Chevalier Pierrot, Le	35, 228
Child of Vodyanoi	181
Children, The Duke's	124
City of Gold and Lead, The	215
Clayhanger	38, 77
Colonel Butler's Wolf	202
Coot Club	206
Detectives In Togas	30
Diddakoi, The	140
Duke's Children, The	124
Edward VIII	157
Eldorado	95
Elusive Pimpernel, The	95
Eustace Diamonds, The	124
Family at Misrule, The	9
Flaxborough Chronicles, The	147
Frost In May	190
Good Wives	104
Gor Saga	237
Gulliver's Travels	186
Hilda Lessways	38, 77
In Chancery	82
Iron In The Soul	104
Jeremy Poldark	136
Jo's Boys	36
Kidnapped	65, 161
Labyrinth Makers, The	202
Lady Chatterley's Lover	269
Levant Trilogy, The	230
Life of Eleanor Marx 1855–1899: A Socialist Tragedy, The	145
Little Men	36
Little Princess, A	4, 23
Little Women	104
Liverpool Cats, The	141
Lost Traveller, The	190
Love in a Cold Climate	176
Mallen Girl, The	173
Mallen Secret, The	173
Mallen Streak, The	162
Man From Moscow	208
Man of Property, The	82
Men At Arms	82
Minister, The Prime	124
Miss Mole	172
Mistress Nancy Molesworth	34
Moonfleet	68
Nicholas and The Woolpack	101
Old Wives' Tale, The	233
Oresteia Trilogy, The	160
Ovington's Bank	75
Page After Page	262
Past Is Myself, The	238
Pathfinder, The	123
Phineas Finn The Irish Member	124
Phineas Redux	124
Prime Minister, The	124
Pursuit of Love, The	176
Raj Quartet, The	203
Reprieve, The	104
Rigid True End, The	188
Rogue Herries	50
Ross Poldark	136
Scott and Amundsen	211
Seven Little Australians	9
Shepherd's Life, A	180
Spring Of Love, A	194
Story of the Treasure Seekers, The	54
Sugar House, The	190
These Twain	77
To Let	82
Trial And Error	33
Twenty Years After	84
Uncle Silas	239
Warden, The	193
Warleggan	136
What Katy Did	62, 143
What Katy Did At School	62, 143
White Mountains, The	184

INDEX OF
SERIAL WRITERS
adaptors or screenplay writers

Abbensetts, Michael 277	Bowers, Raymond 18, 30, 50	Clark, Brian 159, 212
Ableman, Paul 226	Boyce, Frank Cottrell 272	Clarke, Roy 175
Alexander, Ewart 187, 270	Boyd, Eddie 82	Clarke, Thomas 58
Allen, Eric 48	Boyd, Edward 13, 52, 156, 188	Clemens, Brian 208
Allen, Jay Presson 151	Boyer, Carole 113	Coburn, Anthony 69, 75
Allen, Jim 199	Brabazon, James 104	Cole, Diana de Vere 151
Andrews, Guy 273	Bradbury, Malcolm 211, 228, 229, 242, 250, 251, 257	Collins, Barry 156
Armitage, Andy 262		Connaughton, Shane 256
Ashley, Bernard 218	Bragg, Melvyn 259	Constanduros, Denis 37, 67, 72, 90, 103, 104, 105, 109, 113, 114, 179
Ashman, Susan 11, 14, 35	Braine, John 182	
Aukin, Liane 267	Brason, John 186, 194, 202	
	Brenton, Howard 218	Cooper, Giles 8, 66, 76, 78, 82, 87, 135
Baker, Allan 225, 231	Broadley, Philip 139, 227, 228	
Baker, Bob 113, 162	Brooking, Dorothea 3, 9, 14, 22, 47, 54, 56, 131	Cope, Kenneth 138
Baron, Alexander 84, 85, 93, 101, 102, 103, 104, 108, 109, 125, 130, 155, 179, 187, 192, 201, 204, 209, 215, 230		Corlett, William 196, 238
	Brown, J. Potter 18	Cottrell-Boyce, Frank 240
	Brown, John 234, 240	Cox, Constance 17, 21, 24, 27, 29, 31, 33, 36, 39, 40, 41, 50, 59, 61, 62, 63, 64, 65, 66, 67, 69, 73, 82, 143, 150
Barr, Robert 62	Brown, Pamela 6, 9, 12, 34	
Barron, Janet 258	Bruce, Lesley 228	
Barry, Michael 74, 81	Buckeridge, Anthony 18	
Barstow, Stan 102, 123, 128, 188, 200	Buckman, Peter 224	Craig, Bill 94, 95, 107, 123, 127, 148, 161, 164, 191, 198
Bassett, Ben 139	Bunyan, Carol 235	
Beeson, Jane 207	Burke, Simon 264, 278	Craig, Laurie 82
Bell, Alistair 73, 80, 104, 108, 122, 137, 193	Burnham, Barbara 53	Cresswell, Helen 140, 232, 253
	Burnham, Jeremy 225	Crisp, N.J. 116, 141, 204, 217
Bell, E.J. 41, 48, 55	Busby, Peter 233	Cross, Beverley 101
Benbrook, Ivan 113	Butler, David 115, 133, 154, 155, 171	Cross, John Keir 25, 51
Benedictus, David 249		Cubitt, Alan 267
Bennett, Margot 39, 77	Campbell, Dirk 205	Cullen, Alma 205, 226
Bentley, Phyllis 9, 24	Campbell, Patrick 33	Cummings, P.D. 37
Bescoby, Steve 258	Canning, Victor 68, 70, 74, 81, 85	Curteis, Ian 163, 222, 283
Bicat, Tony 270	Capon, Naomi 21	Curzon, St. John 23
Bird, Michael J. 150, 158, 200, 211	Carpenter, Richard 265, 272	
Birkin, Andrew 156	Carr, Andrew 208	D'Abbes, Ingram 29
Black, Ian Stuart 80	Carr, David 32	Dallas, Ian 17, 21, 23
Black, Peter 35	Carr, John Dickson 51	Daneman, Meredith 182
Blackburn, Eileen 14	Cartwright, Justin 266	Davies, Andrew 145, 164, 176, 203, 220, 243, 252, 261, 263, 272, 274
Blake, Justin 36	Case, Geoffrey 196	
Blatchley, John 29	Cavander, Kenneth 197	Davies, Jack 209
Bleasdale, Alan 221, 255	Chandler, Glen 199	Davis, Desmond 6
Bond, Christopher 122	Chaplin, Michael 274	Day, George 205
Bond, Julian 116, 148, 160, 164, 174, 203, 283	Chapman, John 72	de Gray, Alice 5
	Chapman, Robin 84, 108, 115, 120, 122, 163, 185, 197, 199, 211, 212, 276	Deans, Marjorie 39, 51
Borer, Mary Cathcart 54		Degas, Brian 80
Bowen, John 118	Christie, Robert 7	Delderfield, R.F. 32
Bowen, T.R. 282	Churchill, Donald 140, 219	Devlin, Anne 238
		Dewhurst, Keith 125

292

SERIAL WRITERS 293

Dhondy, Farrukh	220	
Dickinson, Peter	111	
Doherty, Berlie	225	
Doran, James	151	
Douglas, Colin	226	
Doyle, Roddy	277	
Draper, Peter	127, 136	
Drysdale, Alec	158	
Dudley, Terence	63	
Duffell, Peter	177	
Dunant, Sarah	233	
Durbridge, Francis	5, 7, 11, 14, 18, 20, 28, 36, 53, 64, 67, 73, 79, 82, 109, 131, 137, 169, 170	
East, Michael	28	
Eaton, Michael	281	
Edgar, David	193	
Elder, Michael	187	
Ellice, Thomas	147, 253	
Elliot, John	57, 61, 77, 85, 101, 111, 125, 189	
Ellison, John	109	
Elton, Ben	273	
Enders, Robert	235	
England, Alan	141, 179	
Evans, Eynon	71	
Evans, Ray	139	
Exton, Clive	52, 53, 230, 235	
Fairfax, Ferdinand	183	
Feely, Terence	196	
Feinstein, Elaine	205	
Fellowes, Julian	280	
Fellows, Malcolm Stuart	57	
Felton, Felix	11, 14, 35	
Finch, Brian	130	
Finch, John	102, 104, 109, 120, 126, 134, 145, 169, 170, 174, 181, 196	
Finch, Scot	135	
Fitzgerald, Penelope	12	
Flanagan, John	254	
Ford, Gordon	17	
Foster, John	109, 182	
Fox, Marilyn	125	
Frazer, Evelyn	63, 72	
Fry, Christopher	94	
Furnival, Robert	109	
Gadney, Reg	163, 175, 187	
Gallagher, Stephen	256	
Galton, Ray	112	
Garfield, Leon	219	
Garner, Alan	98	
Gates, Tudor	80	

Georgeson, Valerie	169	
Gerson, Jack	143, 159, 169	
Gethers, Steven	214	
Gibbs, Peter	224	
Gielgud, Val	12	
Gilbert, Michael	21, 25, 74	
Glasgow, Alex	159	
Glyn, Dyfed	227	
Godber, John	153	
Goddard, David	34, 42	
Goldsmith, John	256	
Gorrie, John	133, 155	
Gosse, Edmond	144	
Gotfurt, Frederick	71	
Gould, John	111, 121, 138	
Gould, Robert	61	
Gowans, Elizabeth	217	
Greatorex, Wilfred	127	
Green, Christopher	214	
Green, Harry	71, 87, 102, 105, 129	
Greenwood, Walter	48	
Greifer, Lewis	22, 26, 28, 40, 42	
Griffiths, Trevor	125, 179, 211	
Haggiag, Michael	269	
Haisman, Mervyn	111	
Hale, John	86, 106, 258	
Hall, James Andrew	158, 171, 184, 195, 207, 208, 215, 218, 222, 236, 274	
Hammond, Peter J.	92	
Hampton, Christopher	178, 244	
Hanley, Clifford	119	
Hann, Gordon	276	
Harding, Pieter	175	
Hardy, Lindsay	41, 56, 68, 78	
Harington, Joy	3, 6, 10, 13, 20, 26, 38, 65, 122	
Harper, Barbara S.	58	
Harris, Richard	138, 139, 147	
Harrison, Carey	207, 209	
Harvey, John	210, 233, 261	
Hastings, Michael	108	
Hawkesworth, John	93, 95, 183, 201, 209, 213	
Hayes, Peter	56	
Hayles, Brian	75, 157	
Healey, Mike	191	
Healy, Ben	117	
Heath, Catherine	239	
Hibbert, Guy	265	
Hignett, Sean	198	
Hill, Rosemary	36	
Hines, Paul	233, 262, 269	
Hobbs, David	277	

Hodgson, Sheila	48, 57, 60	
Holborough, Jacqueline	267	
Holford, Elizabeth	77, 125	
Holmes, Robert	181	
Holt, Estelle	15, 19	
Home, Anna	106, 131	
Hopcraft, Arthur	129, 149, 163, 213, 231, 241	
Hopkins, David G.	219	
Hopkins, John	40, 49, 59, 89, 192	
Horowitz, Anthony	250	
Howard, Elizabeth Jane	191	
Howlett, John	214, 236	
Hoyle, Fred	57, 61	
Hughes, Dusty	264	
Hughes, Ken	34, 76, 125	
Hughes, Lynn	152	
Humble, William	159, 183, 216	
Humphreys, Charlie	218	
Humphries, Dave	180	
Hurley, Graham	241	
Hutchinson, Ron	173, 190, 231	
Hyde, Kenneth	26, 53	
Hyem, Jill	242, 269	
Jackson, Leigh	264	
James, Horace	85	
Jenkins, Ray	127, 190	
Jones, Elwyn	162	
Jones, Evan	133	
Jones, Gareth	220, 240	
Jones, Julia	112, 140, 148, 165, 172, 175, 186, 223, 239	
Junkin, Harry W.	128	
Kane, David	257, 279	
Kay, Ada F.	25	
Kelsall, Moultrie R.	89	
Kerr, Judith	25	
Kerr, Philip	275	
Kershaw, H.V.	102	
Kershaw, Harry	181	
Kester, Max	8	
Key, Peter	19, 21	
Kneale, Nigel	10, 16, 35, 165, 259	
Knox, Penelope	4, 23	
Kramer, Richard	271	
Kureishi, Hanif	271	
La Plante, Lynda	197, 254, 266, 273, 282	
Lamson, Laura	257, 275	
Lancashire, Geoffrey	104	
Langley, Lee	172	
Latham, Keith	58	

Latham, Stuart	162	
Lawler, Ray	96, 107, 114, 121	
Le Carré, John	192	
Lehman, Leo	78	
Lejeune, C.A.	6, 11	
Leonard, Hugh	83, 87, 88, 94, 96, 103, 111, 146, 148, 155, 201, 253	
Lethbridge, Nemone	86, 163	
Letts, Barry	186, 217	
Levy, Muriel	16	
Lewis, Hilda	13	
Lindsay, Frederic	227	
Lingstrom, Freda	34	
Livingstone, Douglas	77, 126, 146, 172, 173, 178, 183	
Lodge, David	243, 278	
Lowe, Stephen	264, 271	
Lucarotti, John	63, 149	
Lucie, Doug	274	
MacCormick, Iain	31	
MacDonald, Gerard	232	
Mackie, Philip	113, 160, 171, 195	
Macpherson, Don	239	
MacTaggart, James	120	
Maher, Richard	236	
Mahoney, Bob	216	
Mankowitz, Wolf	143	
Marchant, Tony	240, 259	
Marlowe, Derek	108, 187, 198, 221	
Marshall, Roger	206, 229	
Martin, Dave	113, 162	
Martin, David	228	
Martin, Ian Kennedy	94, 219	
Martin, Philip	142	
Martin, Troy Kennedy	125, 200, 216	
Maschwitz, Eric	7	
Mason, Edward J.	49, 57, 62	
Masters, Donald	14	
Masters, Simon	147	
McCarty, Nick	101	
McCulloch, Andrew	254	
McDade, Jenny	212	
McGovern, Jimmy	270, 282	
McGrath, John	224, 249	
McLaverty, Bernard	255	
McLeish, Kenneth	160	
McLoughlin, Maurice	11	
McNeil, John	233	
Mellett, Martin	152	
Mellor, Kay	283	
Merwin, W.S.	4	
Michell, Roger	271	
Miller, Brian	101	
Miller, Peggy	134	
Miller, Robin	158	
Miller, Stanley	91	
Milne, Paula	180, 188, 205, 252	
Mitchell, James	202, 243	
Mitchell, Julian	106, 107, 111, 129	
Moggach, Deborah	220, 268	
Moore, Simon	242	
Morgan, Alison	118	
Morgan, Denise	260	
Morgan, Elaine	49, 60, 64, 67, 102, 121, 132, 138, 147, 154, 165, 180, 186, 224	
Morris, Colin	72, 122	
Morris, Jean	101	
Morrison, Arthur	116	
Mortimer, John	153, 185, 221, 244, 257	
Mortimer, Penelope	251	
Mukherjee, Robin	275	
Muller, Robert	93, 107, 112, 120, 125, 133, 163	
Nail, Jimmy	279	
Newman, Andrea	139, 144, 174, 188, 249	
Newman, G.F.	152, 254	
Nicholson, Paul	113	
Nobbs, David	265	
Nokes, David	258	
O'Donnell, Peter	79	
O'Hara, Gerry	216	
Oughton, Winifred	3	
Owen, Alun	253	
Paice, Eric	217	
Pain, Nesta	31	
Parish, James	20, 31	
Parry, Griffith	152	
Paul, Jeremy	79, 119, 201, 206, 209	
Payne, Andrew	269	
Peacock, John	111	
Penfold, Christopher	189, 215	
Pertwee, Michael	8, 50	
Phelan, Brian	145	
Phillips, Lennox	90, 103	
Phillips, Mike	251	
Pinner, David	189	
Pirie, David	250, 263	
Plater, Alan	126, 127, 159, 177, 193, 198, 209, 230, 235	
Pleat, Susan	104	
Plummer, Peter	111	
Pointer, William	150, 151	
Potter, Dennis	110, 132, 151, 152, 215, 223, 238, 245, 267	
Powell, Jonathan	109	
Powell, Lester	22, 86	
Power, Rhoda	16	
Prebble, John	101, 106, 141, 164, 185	
Preston, Trevor	85, 88, 153, 277	
Priestley, J.B.	191	
Prince, Peter	176, 194	
Pringle, Eric	113	
Prior, Allan	55, 122, 255	
Pulman, Jack	76, 88, 96, 114, 116, 125, 134, 136, 142, 161, 181	
Pursall, David	113	
Purser, Philip	104	
Ralling, Christopher	189	
Ransley, Peter	180, 210, 260, 278	
Raphael, Frederic	139, 160, 241	
Raven, Simon	89, 95, 124, 131, 154, 157, 176, 266	
Rawlinson, A.R.	30, 37, 40, 51, 55, 65	
Rawlinson, Brian	111	
Ray, Rene	19	
Rennie, Barbara	234	
Richards, Alun	111, 115	
Richardson, Keith	216	
Ridge, Antonia	35	
Riley, Douglas	23	
Robinson, Christopher	113	
Robson, Michael	164, 206	
Roddick, John	42, 83	
Rodger, Ian	106	
Roe, Ivan	59	
Rogers, Jane	268	
Rogers, Martin C.	113	
Ronder, Jack	104, 124, 177	
Rose, Adele	179	
Rose, Ron	270	
Ross, Duncan	39, 65	
Ross, Sutherland	57	
Rowe, Alick	151, 184, 192, 207, 225, 237, 239, 263	
Rowlands, Avril	170	
Russell, Jack	136, 153, 162, 173	
Russell, Ken	269	
Russell, Roy	109	
Russell, Willie	199	
Sadler, Michael	268	
Sadofski, Martin	281	
Sands, Leslie	102	

Sangster, Jimmy	24	
Savory, Gerald	213	
Schuman, Howard	232, 255	
Scott, Peter Graham	161	
Seddon, Jack	113	
Seward, Anthony	164	
Seymour, Alan	190, 208, 234, 237, 244, 245, 252, 276, 280	
Seymour, Gerald	192, 232	
Shaughnessy, Alfred	10, 201	
Shaw, Don	141, 147, 195	
Sheldon, Kevin	31	
Shepstone, Vere	4	
Simpson, Alan	112	
Sisson, Rosemary Anne	69, 73, 97, 101, 106, 110, 111, 227	
Skene, Anthony	115	
Smith, A.C.H.	113	
Smith, Murray	202	
Snodin, David	155	
Sommersby, Jon	164	
Stadelman, John	223	
Stanley, Anna	151	
Steven, Anthony	65, 70, 74, 76, 81, 82, 92, 110, 114, 118, 126, 135, 151, 178, 184	
Stevenson, John	104	
Stewart, Bruce	189	
Stewart, Leslie	229	
Stoddart, Hugh	265	
Stone, Martin	236	
Stuart, Bob	68, 75	
Sturridge, Charles	234	
Sutton, Shaun	15, 32, 38, 48, 54, 58, 62
Taylor, Ken	126, 134, 153, 157, 172, 182, 185, 201, 203, 261
Thomas, Adrian	35
Thomas, Barry	47, 54, 75
Thompson, Brenda R.	3
Thompson, Brian	242
Thorne, Ian	101, 111
Tilsley, Vincent	20, 22, 27, 47, 63, 78, 79, 82
Took, Barry	117
Trevor, William	161, 165
Tucker, Rex	17, 42, 49, 55, 60, 70, 84, 87, 88, 91
Tully, John	98, 117, 118, 123, 140, 144
Turner, David	64, 80, 86, 90, 91, 93, 101, 104, 125, 136, 137
Tutaev, David	47
Twigge, Tom	15
Vance, Leigh	22
Verner, Gerald	19
Voysey, Michael	27, 38, 52, 53, 70, 81, 87, 91, 95, 110, 117, 119
Wade, Richard	12
Wadey, Maggie	281
Walker, Ted	204
Wallis, Cedric	3, 5, 29
Ward, Edmund	132
Waterhouse, Keith	210
Webb, Don	280
Webber, C.E.	7, 28, 30, 32, 38, 42, 50, 54, 56, 59
Weir, David	109
Welch, Sandy	262, 281
Weldon, Fay	170, 226, 260
Wheeler, Paul	136, 218
White, Jon Manchip	84
Whitehead, Ted	171, 213, 222, 237, 240, 244, 259
Whitemore, Hugh	106, 111, 125, 126, 130, 137, 159, 189, 196, 204, 275
Wildeblood, Peter	71
Wiles, John	12, 109, 136, 155
Williams, Ben	97
Williams, Moira	239
Williams, Nigel	202, 223, 251, 279
Willis, Ted	49, 57, 62
Wilson, Donald	9, 13, 15, 27, 51, 60, 66, 68, 82, 97, 149
Winch, Arden	83, 155, 183, 194
Winterson, Jeanette	249
Wood, Charles	124, 230
Woodstock, B.R.	142
Woolf, Dennis	96
Worth, Martin	128, 132
Wright, Josephine Smith	26
Wright, Tom	119, 140, 146, 173
Yeldham, Peter	80
Yellen, Sherman	250

INDEX OF
AUTHORS OF ORIGINAL WORKS
adapted for television

Aeschylus	160
Alcock, Vivien	223
Alcott, Louisa May	3, 14, 31, 33, 36, 104
Allingham, Margery	40, 49
Allison, William	221
Ambler, Eric	8, 26, 64, 239
Amis, Kingsley	251, 259, 261
Anstey, F.	59
Archer, Jeffrey	221, 250
Ashford, Jeffrey	72
Ashley, Bernard	179
Austen, Jane	5, 29, 47, 53, 86, 105, 107, 114, 170, 179, 201
Bagley, Desmond	159
Baker, Margaret J.	14
Balzac, Honoré de	74, 77, 90, 107
Barber, Noel	260
Barstow, Stan	123, 188, 200
Bates, H.E.	148, 163, 174
Bawden, Nina	97, 108, 110, 125, 148
Bedford, Sybille	133
Bennett, Arnold	38, 70, 77, 79, 95, 210, 233
Bennett, Margot	39
Benson, E.F.	213
Berkeley, Anthony	33
Bernstein, Marcelle	269
Bielenberg, Christabel	238
Binchy, Maeve	234
Blackmore, R.D.	65, 142
Boston, Lucy M.	223
Bradbury, Malcolm	178
Bradford, Barbara Taylor	242
Bragg, Melvyn	259
Braine, John	182
Brittain, Vera	165
Brontë, Anne	94
Brontë, Charlotte	17, 25, 64, 103, 122, 201
Brontë, Emily	87, 155
Broster, D.K.	89, 140
Brough, James	155
Brown, Pamela	172
Brown, Ron	118
Buchan, John	6, 25, 68, 141, 156
Buhet, Gil	35, 228
Bunyan, John	88
Burnett, Frances Hodgson	4, 5, 23, 26, 47, 119, 131, 143, 225, 280
Carroll, Lewis	217
Cartwright, Justin	266
Chevallier, Gabriel	112
Christopher, John	184, 215
Clewlow, Carol	272
Colette	119
Collins, Norman	148
Collins, Wilkie	40, 81, 111, 190
Collodi, Carlo	158
Conan Doyle, Sir Arthur	32, 192
Conlon, Kathleen	180
Conrad, Joseph	85, 264
Cookson, Catherine	106, 162, 169, 173, 276, 280, 282
Coolidge, Susan	62, 143
Cooper, James Fenimore	105, 123
Cowan, Maurice	101
Craik, Dinah	124
Crichton, Robert	164
Cronin, A.J.	53, 127, 195
Dale, Celia	194
Dane, Clemence	81
Daneman, Meredith	182
de Maupassant, Guy	107
Deeping, Warwick	206
Defoe, Daniel	137
Deighton, Len	236
Delderfield, R.F.	32, 155, 176, 203, 253
Dickens, Charles	7, 20, 25, 27, 34, 37, 41, 51, 52, 59, 63, 66, 73, 78, 83, 89, 96, 130, 140, 146, 149, 165, 175, 184, 193, 195, 209, 213, 215, 222, 241, 256, 278
Dickinson, Peter	131, 250
Dobbs, Michael	252, 272
Donaldson, Frances	157
Dostoevsky, Fyodor	71, 78, 89, 94, 161
Douglas, Colin	226
Drabble, Margaret	177
du Maurier, Daphne	159, 196
Duffy, Maureen	237
Dumas, Alexandre	14, 18, 19, 70, 81, 84, 92, 103
Dumas, Alexandre (fils)	144
Durrell, Gerald	230
Eliot, George	67, 73, 91, 102, 158, 274
Ellis, E.S.	11, 35
Elton, Ben	273
Evers, L.H.	56
Fairley, John	221
Falkner, J. Meade	68, 205
Farrell, J.G.	234
Farrimond, John	156
Ferris, Paul	213
Fielding, Henry	55
Fine, Anne	268
Fitzgerald, F. Scott	215
Flaubert, Gustave	66, 103, 135
Frank, Anne	224
Gallagher, Stephen	256
Galsworthy, John	82
Garfield, Leon	91, 158
Garner, Alan	98, 280
Garnett, Henry	58
Garnett, Mrs. R.S.	37
Gaskell, Mrs. Elizabeth	67, 80, 110, 117, 137, 191
Gibbon, Lewis Grassic	107, 191, 198
Gibbons, Stella	91
Gielgud, Val	12
Gilbert, Martin	183
Godber, John	153
Godden, Rumer	140
Godwin, William	199
Golding, Louis	55
Graham, Winston	136, 194
Grant, James	182
Graves, Robert	142
Greenwood, Walter	48
Grierson, Edward	70

AUTHORS OF ORIGINAL WORKS

Hadfield, John	277
Hammond, P.J.	116
Hardy, Thomas	102, 105, 151
Harnett, Cynthia	101
Harris, Robert	255
Harvey, John	261
Haynes, Brian	202
Heath, Catherine	239
Hemingway, Ernest	76, 78
Higgins, Jack	243
Hill, Reginald	276
Hilton, James	204
Hocking, Joseph	34
Holden, Edith	205
Holtby, Winifred	128
Hopcraft, Arthur	129
Hope, Anthony	66, 208
Housman, Laurence	6, 71
Howard, Elizabeth Jane	191
Howatch, Susan	164
Hudson, W.H.	180
Hughes, Thomas	110
Hugo, Victor	79, 87
Huntford, Roland	211
Hurd, Douglas	120
Huxley, Aldous	87, 89, 108
Huxley, Elspeth	183
Iles, Francis	160
James, Donald	180
James, Henry	72, 88, 90, 103, 114
James, P.D.	197, 211, 212, 216, 237, 253
Jameson, Storm	130
Jesse, F. Tennyson	121
Jones, Cecilia Anne	249
Jones, Jack	154
Jones, Mervyn	145
Jones, Philip	80
Kazantzakis, Nikos	96
Keane, Molly	201
Keene, Tom	202
Kingsley, Charles	76
Kipling, Rudyard	4, 187
Kippax, Frank	260
Kureishi, Hanif	271
Kyle, Elizabeth	30
La Plante, Lynda	267
Lawrence, D.H.	179, 204, 238, 269
Le Carré, John	163, 192, 231
Le Fanu, Sheridan	239
Lee, Dick	216

Lewis, C.S.	85, 237, 244, 245, 252
Lewis, Hilda	13
Llewellyn, Richard	47, 138
Lodge, David	232, 243
Lurie, Alison	229
Lyall, Gavin	208
Lynch, Patricia	34
Mackenzie, Compton	96
Magnus, Sir Philip	133
Mahy, Margaret	231
Mair, John	250
Mann, Heinrich	112
Mann, Thomas	76
Manning, Olivia	230
Marryat, Captain Frederick	15, 21, 69, 150
Marshall, Bruce	87
Masefield, John	208
Mason, A.E.W.	11
Mather, Berkley	63
Matthew, Christopher	255
Maugham, W. Somerset	129
Maupin, Armistead	271
Maurois, André	136
Mayle, Peter	268
McCutcheon, Elsie	274
McGinty, Patrick	256
McLean, Allan Campbell	135
McMinnies, Mary	114
McNeil, John	198
McNeill, Janet	98
Meredith, George	69
Mitford, Nancy	176
Montgomery, L.M.	6, 112, 132
Moore, George	71, 146
Moravia, Alberto	121
Mortimer, John	244, 257
Mottram, R.H.	90
Mullally, Frederic	134
Mullin, Chris	235
Munro, Neil	119, 173
Murdoch, Iris	131, 187
Nesbit, E.E.	3, 9, 22, 54, 90, 144, 165, 186, 253
Newman, Andrea	139, 188
Nicolson, Nigel	251
Nobbs, David	265
Norton, Mary	265, 272
O'Neill, Eugene	236
Oakley, Ann	257
Orczy, The Baroness	95
Osmond, Andrew	120

Page, Tim	262
Parish, James	58
Peake, Mervyn	219
Pearce, Philippa	123, 239
Pepys, Samuel	30
Peyton, K.M.	212
Peyton, Kathleen	159
Phillips, Mike	251
Porter, Eleanor H.	122
Power, M.S.	258
Pratt, Colin	216
Price, Anthony	202
Price, Christine	42
Priestley, J.B.	29, 86, 177, 222
Quigley, John	187
Quiller-Couch, Arthur	47, 75
Rae, Hugh C.	231
Ransome, Arthur	65, 206
Raymond, Ernest	175
Read, Piers Paul	198, 244
Reed, Talbot Baines	54
Rendell, Ruth	230, 235, 262, 267, 277, 283
Richardson, Samuel	258
Rogers, Jane	268
Ross, Martin	255
Rubens, Bernice	262
Sabatini, Rafael	33
Sackville-West, Vita	224
Sadleir, Michael	184
Sartre, Jean-Paul	104
Sayers, Dorothy L.	114, 118, 123, 126, 135, 227, 228
Scott, Paul	203
Scott, Sir Walter	22, 41, 55, 80, 92, 101, 118, 125, 146, 178
Serraillier, Ian	28, 108
Seymour, Gerald	192
Sharpe, Tom	211, 228
Shaw, George Bernard	162
Shelley, Percy Bysshe	219
Sherry, Sylvia	141
Sindall, Marjorie A.	36
Skinner, M.L.	204
Slater, Nigel	198
Smith, Emma	147
Smith, Jonathan	185
Snow, C.P.	203
Somerville, Edith	255
Spark, Muriel	134, 151
Spring, Howard	160, 186
Spyri, Johanna	10, 38, 128

Stendhal	74, 271	
Stevenson, Robert Louis	3, 6, 17,	
20, 26, 29, 49, 61, 65, 84, 93, 117,		
119, 132, 149, 161		
Stewart, Mary	258	
Stoneley, Jack	214	
Streatfeild, Noel	117, 136	
Sudermann, Hermann	120	
Sutcliff, Rosemary	148	
Swift, Jonathan	186	
Symons, Julian	266	
Taylor, Domini	243	
Tey, Josephine	61, 219, 236	
Thackeray, William Makepeace		
21, 88, 230		
Tilsley, Frank	33	
Todd, Lyon	73	
Tolstoy, Leo	93, 116, 149	
Townsend, John Rowe	111	
Treece, Henry	42	
Tritten, Charles	13	

Trollope, Anthony	3, 35, 39, 51, 95, 193
Trollope, Joanna	275, 283
Tsuzuki, Chushichi	145
Turgenev, Ivan	109
Turner, Ethel S.	9
Twain, Mark	4, 16, 50, 93, 138
Uttley, Alison	151
Vaughan, Richard	75
Vine, Barbara	262, 267
Wain, John	96
Walpole, Hugh	50, 69
Warner, Susan	12
Watson, Colin	147
Waugh, Evelyn	82, 117, 185
Webb, Mary	24
Weldon, Fay	222, 259
Wells, H.G.	37, 40, 52, 67, 115, 171, 207
Wesley, Mary	240, 261

West, Rebecca	157
Westall, Robert	196, 238
Weyman, Stanley J.	75
Wharton, Edith	281
White, Antonia	190
Wiggin, Kate Douglas	150
Williams, Nigel	279
Wilson, Angus	132, 200, 263
Wiltshire, David	181
Winterfield, Henry	30
Winterson, Jeanette	249
Wren, P.C.	193
Wright, Alison	16
Wylie, Denis	23
Wynd, Oswald	244
Wyndham, John	183
Wynne, Greville	208
Young, E.H.	172
Young, Francis Brett	54, 215
Zinik, Zinovy	267
Zola, Emile	93, 101, 171

INDEX OF
PRODUCERS

Abrahams, Georgina — 268
Acton-Bond, Brandon — 86
Agran, Linda — 197, 279
Allen, Douglas — 7, 20, 27, 34, 37, 40, 52, 60, 63, 64, 65, 66, 67, 68, 69, 70, 71, 72, 73, 74, 76, 77, 78, 79, 80
Alwyn, Jonathan — 209, 242
Amyes, Julian — 18, 51
Armstrong, Brian — 123, 236
Armstrong, Moira — 191
Atkins, Ian — 6

Baker, Howard — 107, 127, 145, 162
Bakewell, Michael — 82
Balhetchet, Sophie — 261
Barclay, Humphrey — 239
Barnett, Alison — 267
Barry, Christopher — 65
Barry, Michael — 81
Barry, Morris — 121, 131, 136, 138, 147
Barry, Philip — 235
Bates, Richard — 151, 184, 189, 215
Beeching, Angela — 156
Bell, Alan — 178
Bell, Brian — 63
Bennett, Derek — 206
Beynon, Richard — 114, 118, 123, 126, 129, 134, 135, 136, 144, 146, 153, 159, 160, 172, 173, 178, 186, 196
Blackmore, Barry — 234
Blair, David — 264
Blake, Gerald — 70
Bleasdale, Alan — 255
Boswell, Ruth — 152, 212, 225, 232
Bottomley, Margaret — 196
Bowen, John — 214
Brabazon, James — 174, 181
Brett, Leonard — 13, 24
Broke, Richard — 160, 183, 221
Bromly, Alan — 14, 18, 20, 28, 31, 36, 53, 64, 67, 68, 73, 74, 75, 76, 77, 78, 79, 80, 81, 82, 83, 84, 85, 86
Brooking, Dorothea — 3, 5, 9, 13, 14, 16, 18, 22, 26, 33, 37, 47, 50, 54, 56, 62, 64, 98, 117, 118, 123, 131, 140, 144

Broughan, Peter — 239
Brown, Andrew — 129, 157, 255, 263
Brown, David — 249
Brown, Joan — 175
Brown, Pamela — 3, 6, 9, 12, 14, 16
Browne-Wilkinson, Anthea — 147
Bryant, Peter — 97
Burge, Stuart — 125
Burnham, Barbara — 25, 29
Burt, Chris — 226, 244, 259
Burton, Hal — 33
Burton, John Nelson — 22, 42

Caleb, Ruth — 180, 262
Callanan, Richard — 249, 253, 280
Callender, Colin — 193
Capon, Naomi — 4, 9, 12, 15, 19, 21, 23, 29, 32, 33, 39
Carlisle, Harry — 49, 57, 62
Carroll, Matt — 262
Cartier, Rudolph — 10, 16, 35, 68
Chapman, John — 257, 268
Chapman, Michael — 139, 196, 227, 228
Chapman, Robin — 84
Childs, Ted — 165, 199
Chovil, Claire — 118
Clark, Derek — 228
Clark, Lawrence Gordon — 256
Clark-Hall, Steve — 224
Clarke, Cecil — 133, 153, 154, 189
Coles, Terry — 201, 253
Colley, Ray — 191
Collin, Reginald — 113
Conroy, David — 80, 81, 85, 86, 87, 88, 89, 90, 91, 92, 93, 94, 95, 96, 101, 102, 104, 116
Cook, Allan — 227
Cooper, Robert — 256
Cox, Michael — 104, 109, 115, 120, 126, 134, 241
Craddock, Malcolm — 277
Craddock, Ron — 133, 164, 180, 181, 182, 186, 192, 198, 206, 210, 218, 233
Craft, Joan — 50
Cregeen, Peter — 283
Croft, Peter — 117

Currier-Briggs, Michael — 91

Daniel, Estelle — 267
Daniels, Geoff — 204
Daniels, Vivian A. — 55
Davies, John — 198, 230
Davis, Desmond — 6
Davis, Jacqueline — 221, 250, 257, 277
Deir, Deirdre — 234
Dennis, Tony — 283
Dews, Peter — 38
Dicks, Terrance — 215, 217, 218, 222, 224, 230, 236
Doubleday, Richard — 102, 104
Dromgoole, Patrick — 113
Dudley, Terence — 61
Dunlop, Michael — 213

Eastman, Brian — 228, 242, 265, 273
Eaton, Andrew — 277
Eckersley, Peter — 149
Elliot, John — 61, 85
Ennis, Brenda — 238
Evans, Robert — 18
Everitt, Richard — 170, 202, 243

Farnham, Brian — 260
Fawcett, Eric — 41
Fellner, Eric — 262
Finlay, Fiona — 264
FitzGerald, Prudence — 59
Flemyng, Gordon — 243
Foa, George R. — 34, 61, 63
Fordyce, Ian — 171
Forsyth, Matthew — 4
Frankau, John — 144

Gallaccio, George — 137, 174
Gamble, Patrick — 205
Garnett, Tony — 152
Gatward, James — 94
Gibbons, Anne W. — 209
Gibson, Alan — 141
Gibson, Chloe — 22, 30, 37, 48, 55
Gilbert, W. Stephen — 220
Giles, Phillippa — 249, 262, 267
Glaister, Gerard — 25, 39, 62, 109, 183, 186, 194, 207

299

300 PRODUCERS

Glynn, Michael 182
Glynn, Victor 242
Goddard, David 30, 32, 34, 42, 47, 51, 58
Godman, Colin 207
Gold, Caroline 254
Goodchild, Peter 147, 176
Graham, Alex 269
Graham, Roderick 106, 191, 198
Granger, Derek 185
Greatorex, Wilfred 127
Green, Jill 274
Gregory, Rogert 226
Gridneff, Evgeny 211
Griffin, Chris 224
Gruffydd, Dafydd 47, 54, 75

Haggiag, Michael 269
Halfpenny, Tony 42
Hammond, Barbara 24, 36, 48, 54
Hanson, Barry 153
Harbinson, Patrick 274
Harington, Joy 3, 6, 8, 10, 11, 13, 20, 26, 31, 36, 38, 56, 64
Harris, John 189, 213, 223, 233
Harrison, John 40, 49
Harrison, Stephen 8, 35, 59
Hawes, Steve 229, 232
Hawkesworth, John 183
Hayes, Michael 57
Hayter, Emma 276
Head, Anne 190
Head, Sally 213, 222, 223, 231, 237, 240
Hefin, John 154, 180
Heyworth, Malcolm 216
Hibbin, Sally 235
Higson, Paddy 227
Hill, Rosemary 120
Hinchcliffe, Philip 181, 187, 203, 250, 257, 263
Holmans, Peter 216
Home, Anna 106, 111, 118, 125, 131, 138, 141, 148, 151, 157, 158, 165, 169, 179
Howson, June 180, 222
Hurn, Douglas 15
Hush, Susi 205, 220

Jacobs, John 29
James, Linda 250
James, Norman 57
Jones, Daphne 140
Jones, David 255
Jones, Hilary Bevan 258

Jones, James Cellan 255

Kinninmont, Tom 226
Kirch, Ann 161
Knight, John 19, 23, 27
Knight, Paul 145, 148

Lambert, Peter 23
Lambert, Verity 126, 282
Lane, Arthur 19
Lascelles, David 219
Latham, Stuart 26
Lawrence, Jordan 111
Lawrence, Quentin 19, 21, 22, 26, 28, 40, 42
Lawson, Sarah 263
Leaver, Don 254
Leeston-Smith, Michael 51
Letts, Barry 142, 143, 146, 149, 150, 154, 158, 165, 171, 172, 175, 178, 179, 184, 187, 192, 193, 195, 201, 204, 207, 208, 209
Lewis, Leonard 159, 177
Lisemore, Martin 102, 103, 105, 107, 108, 109, 110, 112, 114, 115, 119, 120, 121, 124, 132, 134, 137, 138, 140, 142, 147
Livingstone, Douglas 77
Lloyd, Innes 141, 208
Loader, Kevin 258, 266, 271
Logan, Campbell 3, 5, 17, 21, 24, 27, 39, 47, 53, 65, 66, 67, 68, 70, 73, 75, 76, 78, 83, 86, 87, 88, 90, 92, 93, 95, 96, 101
Lonsdale, Pamela 85
Lorrimer, Vere 200, 210
Love, Robert 199
Lund, Nicky 275
Lyon-Shaw, W. 7

Maclaren, Pharic 18, 61, 94, 95, 107, 119, 120, 127, 135, 140, 141, 146, 148, 156, 161, 164, 173, 177
Madden, Paul 280
Mahoney, Brian 89
Maloney, David 183
Marcus, Paul 267, 273
Marks, Louis 145, 156, 274
Marle, Judy 219
Marmion, Grainne 264, 272
Marsh, Ronald 50
Marshall, Ray 276, 280, 282
McCallum, Rick 245
McCandlish, Norman 259, 264
McCarthy, Niall 255

McIntosh, Bob 159, 169, 188, 198, 204, 208, 214
McKeown, Colin 240, 278
McRae, John 91, 97, 101, 103, 104, 105, 108, 110, 111, 112, 116, 117, 118, 119, 122, 124, 125, 128, 130, 132, 136
Messina, Cedric 137
Midgley, Robin 218
Miller, Brian 92, 101
Miller, Marc 132, 143
Miller, Peggy 134
Mills, Michael 112, 116
Milroy, Vivian 4
Moodie, Douglas 11
Morahan, Christopher 202
Morris, Geraint 187
Mourby, Adrian 261
Muir, Graeme 113

Neal, Gub 259, 270
Neame, Christopher 183

O'Brien, Rebecca 234
O'Donovan, Desmond 27, 30, 32
Ormerod, James 58, 128
Osborn, Andrew 21, 29, 33, 158
Oulton, Caroline 233, 251, 280
Owen, George P. 151

Park, Andy 274
Parker, David 273
Parks, Carol 229
Parr, Chris 153, 220, 238, 240, 243, 258, 278
Passmore, Simon 249
Phillips, Lloyd 217
Plummer, Peter 98, 111
Potter, Dennis 267
Poul, Alan 271
Powell, Jonathan 129, 151, 155, 157, 161, 163, 165, 169, 171, 175, 179, 187, 190, 192, 193, 200
Prem, Tara 282
Purdie, John 207

Quinn, Eileen 260, 278

Rakoff, Alvin 10, 11
Ralling, Christopher 108, 133
Read, Anthony 122
Reeks, Jenny 265
Reid, Brenda 228, 235
Reid, David 77, 115
Rellim, Tim Van 211

PRODUCERS

Richardson, Keith 179, 192, 199, 232
Richardson, Tony 6
Richman, Stella 116
Riddington, Ken 131, 132, 155, 164, 169, 170, 176, 195, 203, 220, 243, 252, 268, 272
Roberts, Roy 162, 173, 241
Robertson, Carol 205, 213
Robins, John 65
Rod, David E. 56
Rogers, Colin 202, 210, 224, 231, 244, 261
Rogers, Pieter 128
Romsey, Norton 199
Rose, Colin 204
Rose, David 142, 162
Rosenberg, John 197, 211, 212, 216, 226, 234, 237, 239, 242, 253
Rosso, Franco 251
Russell, Paddy 69, 72

Salmon, Hilary 265, 270
Sasdy, Peter 229
Saville, Philip 20, 281
Savory, Gerald 176
Schindler, Colin 225
Schute, Martin 194
Scott, Peter Graham 53, 161, 214
Sears, Bryan 8, 13, 72
Sellars, Bill 116, 122, 130, 135, 137, 169
Shallcross, Alan 197
Shapter, Bill 270
Shaw, Pauline 188, 200
Sheldon, Kevin 17, 25, 31, 35, 39, 41, 48, 55, 57, 60
Shindler, Colin 182, 185, 188, 194
Shivas, Mark 101, 110, 139, 159, 185, 210
Skinner, Ann 235

Slater, Guy 195, 202, 266
Slater, William 130, 150
Smallwood, Stephen 266
Smedley, Ronald 191
Smith, Greg 256
Smith, Joanna 251
Snodin, David 240, 251, 257, 259, 275
Spiby, Brian 201, 218
Stafford-Clark, Nigel 279
Steel, Elaine 281
Sterling, William 81, 84
Stoller, Jacky 233, 269
Stone, Paul 170, 186, 196, 205, 208, 212, 218, 219, 223, 225, 231, 232, 237, 239, 244, 245, 252
Sutton, Shaun 9, 15, 25, 28, 30, 32, 37, 40, 48, 54, 58, 62, 258

Taylor, Eric 41, 59
Tempia, Martin 240
Thomas, David J. 49, 60
Thomas, Mairede 280
Toynton, Ian 219
Travers, Ronald 101
Trodd, Kenith 152, 223, 238, 254
Tucker, Colin 163, 171, 172, 174, 175, 177, 199, 251, 264
Tucker, Rex 7, 11, 14, 15, 17, 31, 35, 38, 42, 55, 60, 121

Vance, Dennis 9, 12, 50
Verney, Guy 57, 63
Vertue, Beryl 272
Vickers, Lindsey C. 219
Voytek 88

Waller, Peter 281
Walsh, Stanley 260
Wands, Alan J. 278

Ward, Edmund 132
Warre, Ian 242
Warren, Ian 204, 250, 257
Waters, Joe 184, 206, 214, 217, 230, 239, 250
Watson, Mervyn 221, 236
Wearing, Michael 173, 178, 190, 216, 252, 273, 280
Webster, Martyn C. 5, 7
Wessels, Manny 270
West, Richard 34, 36, 49
Wharmby, Tony 139, 148
Whatmough, Sue 253
Whitaker, Ayton 12
White, Leonard 113, 162
White, Timothy 273
Whitehouse, Rob 217
Whitman, Rosemary 267
Wildeblood, Peter 71
Wilhide, Glenn 261
Willes, Peter 124
Williams, Arthur 71
Williams, Jack 52, 155
Williams, Keith 160
Williams, Moira 239
Williams, Sita 241
Williams, Terence 241
Willingale, Betty 201, 213, 215, 230
Wilson, Donald 82, 97, 149
Wilson, Sarah 264
Wiltshire, Gerald 58
Wimbury, David 282
Wolfes, Peter 279
Wolfes, Rosalind 271
Wood, Tim Ironside 244
Woolf, Dennis 96
Wright, Alan 275
Wyndham-Davies, June 182

Zeiger, Neil 235, 277, 283

INDEX OF
DIRECTORS*

Acton-Bond, Brandon 13, 65, 69, 75, 81	Boyle, Danny 254, 268	Cole, Tristan de Vere 92, 124, 181, 204
Allison, Romey 233	Brady, Morris 52	Coleman, Basil 131, 149
Alwyn, Jonathan 113, 139, 162	Bramall, Richard 178	Collin, Reginald 113
Amiel, Jom 223	Brayne, William 159, 202	Combe, Timothy 130, 136
Amyes, Julian 6, 165, 184, 201, 205, 210	Brett, Leonard 24	Connor, Kevin 256
	Briant, Michael E. 149, 170, 175, 183, 186, 218	Cooke, Alan 120, 153, 189
Annett, Paul 136, 143, 172, 234	Bridges, Alan 71, 78, 83, 87	Cooper, John 13, 17, 21, 25, 33, 38, 39
Armstrong, Moira 103, 107, 111, 119, 126, 134, 147, 165, 191, 207, 218, 269	Broadhouse, Lawrence 11, 20, 23, 26, 27, 28, 30, 33, 59	Cotter, Tom 177, 191, 198, 217, 229
	Bromly, Alan 67, 68, 73, 79, 82, 86	Cox, Michael 102, 134
Askey, David 137, 138, 200	Brooking, Dorothea 64, 151, 157, 165	Craft, Joan 63, 66, 69, 73, 78, 86, 88, 91, 96, 108, 112, 116, 122, 132, 136, 142, 172
Attwood, David 240	Browne-Wilkinson, Anthea 111	
	Bruce, John 151, 190, 220, 253	
Bain, Bill 113, 189	Bundy, Stephen 6, 15, 17, 21, 24, 29, 37, 40, 41, 53, 55, 58, 59	Cregeen, Peter 125, 160
Baker, Howard 107, 127, 162		Croft, Joan 102, 130
Baker, Roy Ward 183	Burge, Stuart 20, 179, 200, 223, 238, 278	Cullingham, Mark 110, 151, 153, 161
Bamford, Roger 211, 242, 253		Cumming, Fiona 132, 170
Barber-Fleming, Peter 230	Burnley, Fred 108, 113	Cunliffe, David 125, 196
Barbour, Margie 225	Butcher, David 54, 75	Currier-Briggs, Michael 91
Barnes, Edward 62	Butcher, Stephen 134, 214	Custance, Michael 152, 170, 174, 202, 209
Barry, Christopher 65, 67, 68, 79, 83, 84, 115, 136, 146, 184, 215		
	Caldwell, Peter 111	
Barry, Michael 74, 80, 81	Callanan, Richard 162	Dale, Philip 26
Barry, Tony 255	Camfield, Douglas 80, 81, 87, 181, 193, 206	Darlow, Michael 161, 219, 258
Battersby, Roy 220		David, Hugh 80, 84, 92, 96, 105, 110, 114, 117, 124, 233
Bayldon, Oliver 98	Campbell, Dirk 205	
Beeson, Charles 281	Campbell, Martin 216	Davidson, Eric 137, 156
Bell, Alan 130, 178	Cant, Colin 120, 138, 196, 205, 212, 223, 232	Davies, Barry 212
Bennett, Derek 113, 206		Davies, Gareth 107, 110, 115, 121, 125, 204, 215, 224
Bennett, Edward 269	Capon, Naomi 94, 101	
Bennett, Rodney 123, 135, 137, 150, 156, 164, 179, 187, 195, 242	Cartier, Rudolph 68, 125	Davies, Huw 127
	Caton-Jones, Michael 227	Davies, John 77, 93, 101, 102, 107, 116, 211, 230, 237, 253
Bicat, Tony 270	Chapman, Spencer 112, 226	
Bickford, Lovett 171	Chatfield, Les 104, 109, 120, 126, 134, 200	Davis, Barry 159, 176, 187
Bierman, Robert 258		Decourt, Jean Pierre 161
Billington, Kevin 259	Chetwyn, Robert 181, 232	Delacey, Terry 113
Bird, Antonia 233, 257	Cheveley, Roger 214	Devenish, Ross 213, 275
Bladgen, Bob 215	Chinn, Desmond 69, 101	Dilly, John 94
Blair, Leslie 152	Ciappessoni, Paul 155, 169, 182	Diss, Eileen 13, 22, 25, 31, 32, 40, 42
Blake, Darrol 111	Clark, Lawrence Gordon 159, 192	
Blake, Gerald 66, 70, 75, 78, 79, 83, 85, 90, 95, 122	Clayton, Harold 67	Doig, Clive 144
	Clegg, Tom 199, 231	Donner, Clive 250
Boisseau, David 113	Clements, John 13	Dossor, Alan 202
Bolt, Ben 250, 263, 271	Coke, Cyril 84, 160, 169, 175, 198	Doubleday, Richard 102, 109, 120

* Includes 'designers' when no director is listed

302

DIRECTORS 303

Dowling, Patrick 35
Dromgoole, Patrick 113
Drury, David 258, 264, 273
Dudley, Philip 97, 132, 155, 173
Dudley, Terence 169
Duffell, Peter 159, 177
Duguid, Peter 84, 139, 192
Duncan, Douglas 62

Elliot, John 85
Ellis, Peter 182
Evans, Graham 96
Evans, Marc 250, 263, 277
Evans, Robert 19
Everitt, Richard 170

Fairfax, Ferdinand 183, 211, 283
Farnham, Brian 172, 196, 201, 209, 226, 232, 242
Federer, Henry 51
Ferguson, Michael 82, 89, 91, 109, 159
Ferman, James 31, 125
Fisk, Peter 262
Fitzgerald, Prudence 111
Flemyng, Gordon 52, 189, 199, 243
Florence, Edwin 24
Fordyce, Ian 171
Foster, Giles 275
Foster, Gordon 31
Fox, Marilyn 169, 218, 223, 237, 253
Franham, Brian 185
Frankau, John 53, 144, 150, 195
Friend, Martyn 171, 174, 189, 210, 224, 244, 257, 277, 278
Fuest, Bob 161
Fywell, Tim 262, 267

Garner, Anthony 215, 244
Gemin, Giancarlo 274
Gethers, Steven 214
Gibson, Alan 141
Giles, David 70, 82, 88, 93, 97, 105, 109, 115, 151, 186, 193, 201
Gillott, Nick 256
Gilmour, Bill 120, 145, 170, 181
Glaister, Gerard 65
Glenister, John 101, 110, 114, 147, 148, 157, 196, 241
Godber, John 153
Goddard, Jim 153, 193, 244
Godman, Colin 207
Godman, Keith 229
Goodwin, Derrick 147

Gorrie, John 133, 155, 182, 192, 207, 212, 221, 225, 239
Gourlay, Alex 161
Graham, Roderick 106
Green, David 185
Green, Neville 152
Gregg, Colin 264
Gregory, Roger 260
Grieve, Andrew 265, 273
Grieve, Ken 145, 202, 236
Grint, Alan 120, 126, 127, 129, 145, 155, 180, 188, 222, 283

Haggard, Piers 148, 152, 165, 251
Hall, Peter 261
Hammond, Peter 59, 70, 74, 76, 79, 81, 87, 91, 93, 140, 155, 196, 239
Handford, Richard 179
Hannam, Ken 169, 183, 233
Harding, Sarah 221
Harding, Terry 113
Harrison, Paul 171
Harrison, Pauline 180
Harvey, Patrick 8
Harvey, Tim 94
Hatts, Clifford 35
Hayes, Michael 194
Hayman, David 272, 279
Hays, Bill 125, 129, 134, 141, 148, 160, 177, 201
Healey, Mike 191
Hellings, Sarah 280
Henderson, John 265, 272
Henry, Richard 14, 15, 30, 37, 55, 56
Herbert, Henry 201, 213
Hills, Eric 85
Hird, Bob 104, 109, 120, 146, 156
Hodges, Mike 274
Hodson, Christopher 148, 151, 155, 227, 242
Home, Anna 106, 118
Hopkins, David G. 219
Horne, Donald 13, 18
Horsburgh, Oliver 188
Howard, Gillian 113
Howell, Jane 145, 146, 153, 178, 240
Howson, June 102, 123
Humphreys, Dewi 270
Hunt, Richard 72
Hussein, Waris 126, 128, 139, 157, 226

Imison, Michael 67, 76
Irvin, John 129, 149, 163
Ives, Kenneth 136

Jackson, Mick 235
Jacobs, John 194, 228
James, Norman 49, 57, 61, 63
James, Pedr 265, 278
Jarrott, Charles 198
Jefferies, Peter 172, 184, 195
Joffe, Roland 126, 127, 134
Johnson, Sandy 276
Jones, Gareth 240
Jones, James Cellan 71, 72, 74, 76, 79, 82, 88, 95, 104, 108, 114, 129, 230, 255, 257
Jones, Tim 102, 104

Keill, Ian 238
Kemp-Welch, Joan 111
Kidron, Beeban 249
King, Christopher 152, 175
King, Tim 235
Kirby, Alex 244, 245, 252
Knapman, Frederick 5, 14, 25, 29, 32, 34, 36, 38, 42, 48, 51, 54, 55, 58
Knight, John 27
Knights, Robert 139, 144, 153, 178, 215, 228

Lane, Arthur 19
Lang, Myles 123, 140, 150
Langton, Simon 148, 159, 171, 189, 192, 243, 274, 276
Latham, Stuart 52, 71
Lau, Patrick 236
Lawrence, Charles 19, 50
Lawrence, Diarmuid 209, 230, 263
Lawrence, Quentin 19, 21, 22, 26, 28, 109, 126, 134
Lawton, Mark 51
Learoyd, Barry 12, 33
Leaver, Don 63, 113, 213
Leeston-Smith, Michael 68
Letts, Barry 97, 138, 158, 186, 217, 222
Lewis, Leonard 159, 177, 208, 218, 236
Lighthill, Brian 207, 209
Lindsay-Hogg, Michael 125, 185
Lingwood, Tom 42
Logan, Campbell 5, 86
Lorrimer, Vere 121

Macdonald, Bruce 249, 261
Macdonald, David 12
MacGowan, Robert 56, 60
Madden, John 241
Mahoney, Bob 216

Mahoney, Brian	89	
Mallett, Nicholas	212	
Maloney, David	101, 103, 105, 108, 118, 122, 211, 217	
Manning, Lesley	251	
Marquand, Richard	108	
Marshall, Stewart	15, 36, 47, 49, 64	
Martin, Richard	77, 80, 104, 106, 109, 162	
Martinus, Derek	90, 103, 119, 133, 164	
Mason, Ronald	50	
McBain, Kenny	174	
McGrath, Joe	134	
McGrath, John	224, 249	
McIntosh, Bob	135, 188	
McKenzie, David	95	
McMurray, Mary	173, 235	
McNaughton, Ian	127	
McWhinnie, Donald	82, 106, 125, 137, 141, 176, 213	
Menaul, Christopher	243, 254	
Menmuir, Raymond	121, 126, 145, 148	
Michell, Roger	264, 271	
Mill, Gerry	102, 104, 109, 123, 145, 179, 188	
Millar, Gavin	266, 276	
Miller, Brian	92	
Miller, Jonathan Wright	170, 174	
Miller, Marc	124, 132, 143, 162	
Mills, Brian	115, 134, 162, 170, 173, 221	
Mills, Kim	57, 139	
Moffatt, Peter	111, 131, 164, 173	
Monnier, Philippe	241	
Moody, Laurence	174, 181, 188, 199	
Morahan, Christopher	202, 234	
Morgan, Andrew	187, 206, 225, 249, 280	
Morris, Michael Owen	230	
Morris, Stanley	61	
Moshinsky, Elijah	251	
Murray, Katrina	131	
Murray-Leach, Roger	116	
Nadolny, Sylva	56	
Nash, Robin	57	
Newbury, Barry	62	
Newell, Cormac	84	
O'Brien, Jim	202, 221	
O'Sullivan, Thaddeus	264	
Orme, Stuart	233, 257, 266	
Ormerod, James	104, 128	
Ornadel, Cyril	115
Osborn, Andrew	29
Owen, George P.	152
Oxley, Roy	14, 18, 20, 28, 36, 39, 41, 53, 56, 59, 64
Page, Anthony	274
Peacock, Margaret	38
Pemberton, Reece	40
Phillips, Maurice	281
Pillsbury, Sam	217
Pinfield, Mervyn	61, 63
Plummer, Peter	98
Podmore, Bill	120
Pope, Angela	262
Pople, Jim	56
Potter, Dennis	245
Potter, Peter	115
Powell, Tristram	261, 281
Proudfoot, David Sullivan	125
Prowse, John	131, 141
Radford, Lionel	61
Rakoff, Alvin	8, 196, 221
Ralling, Christopher	108, 133
Rea, Ben	180
Reardon, John	280
Reid, Alastair	116, 128, 140, 142, 197, 208, 226, 242, 255, 271
Reid, David	77, 115
Rennie, Barbara	234
Renton, Nicholas	228, 241, 256, 260
Reynolds, David	182, 187, 196, 209
Richards, David	279
Ridge, Mary	110
Ritelis, Viktors	158
Roberts, Marilyn	30, 32, 35
Robillard, Chris	101
Roland, Gordon	14, 16, 17, 23, 25
Rolfe, Michael	190, 236
Rose, Colin	204
Russell, Ken	269
Russell, Paddy	70, 72, 74, 75, 86, 90, 95, 104, 109, 111
Rye, Renny	163, 208, 219, 260, 267
Safran, Henri	127
Sasdy, Peter	87, 94, 103, 162, 229
Saunders, Peter	65
Saunders, Red	250
Saville, Philip	20, 222, 237, 259, 281
Sax, Geoffrey	254, 266
Secombe, Christine	231, 239
Seed, Paul	208, 220, 252, 272
Shardlow, Martin	153
Sharp, Don	242
Sharp, Ian	224
Sharp, Kenneth	138, 158
Shaw, Colin	71
Shedden, Eric	42
Sheppard, Guy	18, 34, 39
Shergold, Adrian	238, 259, 265
Shortman, Daphne	51
Simpson, Michael	148, 163, 191, 205, 228
Singleton-Turner, Roger	179, 186
Smith, Frank W.	209
Smith, Julia	73, 90, 143
Smith, Peter	180, 194, 210, 231, 278
Smith, Tony	275
Spence, Susan	26, 31, 32, 36, 38, 39, 42, 48, 54, 58
Spencer, Rex	22, 23, 31
Standage, Helen	85
Standeven, Richard	283
Stewart, Rob	204
Stone, Norman	240, 282
Stone, Paul	111, 125, 148, 158
Strickland, John	267, 278
Stroud, Richard	145, 175, 187, 203
Sturridge, Charles	170, 185
Summers, Jeremy	188, 203
Swan, Jeremy	140
Symonds, Vic	40
Tass, Nadia	273
Taylor, Alan	47, 49, 60
Taylor, Baz	104, 109, 126
Taylor, Eric	27, 34
Taylor, Fanny	22, 30, 33, 34, 37, 41, 48, 51, 55
Taylor, Stephen	15, 16, 31
Theakston, Graham	184
Thorpe, Antony	117
Toynton, Ian	197, 219, 232, 282
Tronson, Robert	23, 135, 214, 242
Tucker, David	203, 220, 239, 250, 259, 268
Tucker, Rex	64, 66, 69, 73, 76, 77, 78, 83, 89, 93, 96
Tucker, Roger	154, 202
Tyrer, Bertram	19
Vardy, Mike	127, 195, 234
Verney, Guy	27
Voytek	88
Wakerell, Tina	119, 151, 164
Walker, Rob	218, 241, 252, 277
Waller, Anthony	24

DIRECTORS

Warrender, Valerie	113	Williams, Julian	154, 227	Winterbottom, Michael	270, 277
Wharmby, Tony	132, 139, 148, 155	Williams, Keith	111	Wise, Herbert	106, 112, 142, 196, 197, 199, 235
Whatham, Claude	16, 106, 119, 154, 240	Williams, Terence	116, 158	Wiseman, Carol	173, 225, 268
Whitbread, Oscar	104	Wilmot, Richard	18, 27, 35, 48, 54	Wood, Peter	120, 153
White, Leonard	113	Wilson, Andy	267	Wyndham-Davies, June	122, 128
Whittaker, Stephen	251, 282	Wilson, Ronald	114, 118, 124, 138, 145, 147, 153, 158, 162, 176, 190, 203, 216		
Wickes, David	139			Yates, Michael	23
Wilks, Carol	270	Wiltshire, Gerald	60	Young, Robert	198, 255, 279

INDEX OF
PLAYERS

Abbott, Natalie 225
Abineri, Gill 165
Abineri, John 56, 105, 108, 123, 157
Abineri, Sebastian 159
Abney, William 130
Ackland, Joss 78, 79, 84, 116, 172, 212, 226, 239, 240
Adams, Dallas 125
Adams, Jill 25
Adams, Jonathan 91, 121, 207
Adams, Mason 239
Adams, Polly 86, 97, 205
Adams, Tom 217
Addie, Robert 187
Adie, Helen 259
Adrian, Max 59, 71, 89
Adshead, Kay 155, 192
Agutter, Jenny 90, 250, 281
Ahmet, Paul 159
Ainley, Anthony 146
Ainley, John 216
Aird, Holly 183
Airiss, Nathan 229
Aitchison, Peggy 182
Aitken, Maria 120, 277
Alan, Pamela 11
Aldridge, Kitty 264, 272
Aldridge, Michael 6, 15, 31, 61, 121, 125, 160, 163, 176, 185, 202, 210, 237
Alexander, Geraldine 199
Alexander, Jean 111
Alexander, Maev 119
Alexander, Terence 25, 36, 60, 75, 118
Ali, Trina 282
Alison, Dorothy 28
Alkin, John 114
Allen, Adie 275
Allen, Keith 235, 278
Allen, Patrick 82, 141, 149, 161, 180, 269
Allen, Sheila 126, 139, 144, 212, 261
Allingham, Keith 138
Allison, Bart 90
Allnutt, Wendy 107, 141, 147
Alwyn, Timandra 150

Alyn, Glen 13
Ambrose, Paul 129
Amsbury, Janet 224
Amyes, Isabelle 147, 239, 252
Anders, Derek 107, 111, 249
Anders, Iain 203
Anderson, Daphne 39, 40, 53
Anderson, Dave 249
Anderson, Gene 21, 24, 41
Anderson, Georgine 161, 191
Anderson, Glenn 143
Anderson, Jean 3, 22, 65, 76, 84, 109, 182
Anderson, Jurgen 196
Anderson, Margaret 9, 29
Anderson, Martyn 16
Anderson, Michael 32
Anderson, Miles 125, 137, 252, 275
Anderson, Rona 51
Anderson, Rosemarie 30
Andre, Annette 73
Andrew, Iain 156
Andrews, Anthony 124, 125, 130, 185
Andrews, David 75
Andrews, Harry 77, 172, 224
Andrews, Naveen 271
Andrews, Sarah Hollis 131
Angelis, Michael 231
Anholt, Christien 266
Anholt, Tony 113
Annis, Francesca 73, 83, 121, 133, 135, 155, 253, 257, 274
Anthony, Jane 111
Anthony, Lysette 195, 215
Anthony, Michael 21
Antony, Scott 119
Antrim, Paul 142
Antrobus, Yvonne 90
Anwar, Gabrielle 218, 245
Anwar, Rafiq 131
Appleby, Basil 8
Apsion, Annabelle 266
Archard, Bernard 68, 69, 75, 196
Archard, Elizabeth 122
Archibald, Dawn 224
Arden, Curtis 113
Aris, Doreen 56

Arkwright, Nigel 32, 34, 38, 42, 47, 48, 52, 58
Arliss, Ralph 148, 165
Armstrong, Alun 127, 193, 256, 259, 265, 268
Armstrong, Buki 240
Armstrong, Katie 156
Armstrong, Ray 227
Arnatt, John 18, 20
Arne, Peter 23, 85
Arnold, David 118
Arnold, Dickie 175
Arnold, Elsie 64
Arrighi, Nike 80
Arthure, Richard 69
Arthy, Judith 87
Arvanti, Betty 150, 200
Ash, Leslie 231
Ashbourne, Jayne 281
Ashby, Harvey 208
Ashcroft, Peggy 157, 203, 231
Asher, Jane 71, 73, 152, 185, 188, 283
Asherson, Renee 6, 239
Ashford, David 160
Ashton, Al 264
Ashton, David 119
Ashton, Edwina 150
Ashton, Keith 131
Ashton, Warwick 19
Ashwin, Michael 11, 24
Asner, Edward 215, 250
Asquith, Conrad 137
Aston, Emily 249
Aston, Lucy 201, 209
Atkins, Coral 102, 104, 109
Atkins, Dave 173
Atkins, Eileen 38, 70, 179, 192, 223
Atkinson, Barbara 129
Atkinson, Frances 224
Attwell, Michael 215
Aubrey, James 139, 144, 195, 211, 233
Aubrey, Juliet 274
Audas, Tamzen 253
Audley, Maxine 22, 42, 80, 83, 90, 175, 219
Audran, Stephane 185

PLAYERS

Aumont, Jean-Pierre	241	
Austin, Carol	116	
Austin, Richard	164	
Avellano, Helana	232	
Aylmer, David	4, 23	
Aylward, Derek	11, 35, 40	
Ayres, Robert	15	
Ayres, Rosalind	276	
Aza, Graham	59	
Baddeley, Angela	66, 96	
Baddeley, Hermione	128	
Baddeley, John	118	
Badel, Alan	21, 29, 70, 123, 190	
Badel, Sarah	91, 114, 124, 232	
Bagley, Liz	147	
Bailey, Edmund	81	
Bailey, Gillian	90, 108, 117, 147	
Bailey, John	23	
Bailey, Marion	220	
Bailey, Robin	22, 63, 133, 137, 210, 213	
Bailie, David	80	
Baizley, Duncan	225	
Baker, Colin	107, 111, 116, 206	
Baker, Frank	177	
Baker, George	31, 66, 70, 142, 204, 218, 230, 235, 280	
Baker, Jim	184, 215	
Baker, Joe Don	216	
Baker, Mark Blackwell	122	
Baker, Stanley	17, 138	
Baker, Terry	31, 34	
Baker, Tom	192, 252	
Balcon, Jill	146, 163	
Bale, Christian	226	
Balfour, Michael	30, 47, 72	
Ball, Vincent	24	
Banks, Spencer	108	
Bannen, Ian	163, 191, 196, 256	
Bannerman, Celia	86	
Barber, Frances	239	
Barber, Neville	121	
Barber, Paul	142	
Barclay, Marcus	130	
Bardock, Matt	267	
Bardon, John	202	
Barge, Gillian	256	
Barkworth, Peter	97, 109, 131, 159, 183, 210, 212	
Barlow, Thelma	101	
Barnes, Dominique	219	
Barr, Patrick	6, 11, 14, 133	
Barrett, Edward	204	
Barrett, Ray	71	
Barrett, Sean	34	
Barrie, John	71	
Barron, John	78, 81	
Barron, Keith	159, 163, 182, 240	
Barrow, Ernest	3	
Barry, June	79, 82	
Bartok, Eva	68	
Barton, Joe	144	
Barton, Margaret	31	
Baskett, Ann	5	
Bassenger, Mark	217	
Bastedo, Alexandra	158	
Bate, Anthony	31, 78, 81, 84, 86, 87, 93, 101, 109, 149, 163, 184, 189, 192, 236	
Bate, James	127, 170, 174, 181	
Bateman, Geoffrey	225	
Bates, Alan	151	
Bates, James	111	
Bates, Ralph	102, 136, 141, 179, 204	
Bateson, Timothy	21, 41, 250	
Bathurst, Robert	242	
Bauer, David	72	
Baxter, Keith	153	
Baxter, Lois	116, 143	
Baxter, Lynsey	151, 153, 243, 258, 267	
Bayldon, Geoffrey	81, 211, 224	
Bayliss, Peter	66	
Baynes, Hetty	269	
Bazely, Paul	261	
Bazely, Sally	19	
Beach, Ann	171	
Beacham, Stephanie	86, 103, 113, 206	
Beale, Simon Russell	267	
Beames, David	174, 211	
Beamish, Matthew	158	
Bean, Sean	234, 258, 269, 272	
Beaton, Norman	218, 277	
Beattie, Louise	224, 227, 281	
Beatty, Robert	182	
Beauchamp, Linsey	210, 233	
Beaumont, Robert	7	
Beavis, Ivan	117	
Beazley, Max	249	
Bebb, Richard	23, 54	
Beck, James	54, 117	
Becker, Hartmut	175, 214, 244	
Beckett, David	280	
Beckett, Sheila	165	
Beckinsale, Richard	121	
Beeny, Christopher	62	
Beevers, Diana	172	
Beevers, Geoffrey	235	
Begley, Ed Jr.	250	
Behean, Katy	233	
Beint, Michael	118	
Bell, Ann	64, 76, 131, 156, 238	
Bell, Eileen	228	
Bell, Elizabeth	97, 112, 224	
Bell, Gordon	19	
Bell, Keith	94	
Bell, Simon	143	
Bell, Tom	153, 171, 179, 187, 213, 238, 254, 273, 276	
Belle, Ekkehardt	161	
Bellingham, Lynda	174, 278	
Bellman, Gina	245	
Benda, C. Kenneth	117	
Benedict, Claire	267	
Beneyton, Yves	203	
Benfield, John	229, 254, 267, 273, 275	
Benfield, Sarah	151	
Benham, Joan	131, 169	
Benjamin, Christopher	193, 224	
Bennett, Alan	223, 255	
Bennett, Elizabeth	203	
Bennett, Hywel	78, 152, 160, 163, 198, 260	
Bennett, Jill	25, 221	
Bennett, John	50, 65, 71, 102, 109	
Bennett, Rosalind	226, 232, 260	
Benson, George	110	
Benson, Martin	159, 178	
Bentinck, Timothy	201, 209	
Bentley, John	8	
Benz, Michael	280	
Berger, Sarah	191, 251	
Bergin, Patrick	255	
Bergman, Jonathan	48	
Bergner, Elizabeth	141	
Berk, Ailsa	237, 244, 245, 252	
Berkeley, Ballard	29, 33	
Bernard, Carl	27, 65, 66, 77	
Bernard, Nicolette	48	
Bertish, Suzanne	193	
Berwick, James	158	
Bethell, Ben	149	
Bettenay, Geoffrey	56	
Bevan, Gillian	222	
Beveridge, Candida	165	
Bicknell, Andrew	201	
Bidmead, Stephanie	91, 104	
Biggins, Christopher	142, 161	
Bikel, Theodore	11	
Binchy, Kate	160	
Binns, Pamela	29	
Birch, Derek	26

PLAYERS

Birch, Peter	209, 251	
Bird, John	220	
Birdsall, Jesse	233	
Birrel, Peter	147	
Bishop, Ed	143, 170, 198	
Bishop, Edward	88	
Bisley, Stephen	204	
Bisset, Douglas	146	
Black, Isobel	68, 74, 85	
Black, Pauline	282	
Blackman, Honor	8	
Blackwell, Douglas	58, 60	
Blackwell, Patrick	29	
Blackwood, Adam	256	
Blair, Isla	133, 178, 188, 229, 243	
Blake, Anne	126	
Blake, Christopher	124, 132, 148, 156, 158, 188	
Blake, Emma	128	
Blake, Gerald	18	
Blake, Grey	8	
Blake, Jon	204	
Blake, Katharine	63	
Blake, Peter	153, 164	
Blake, Rosemary	77	
Blake, Victoria	205	
Blakely, Colin	95, 132, 216, 221	
Blakiston, Caroline	65, 82, 110, 147, 150, 162, 163, 173, 210	
Blatchley, Joseph	140	
Blessed, Brian	81, 84, 142, 158, 230	
Blethyn, Brenda	271	
Blick, Newton	52	
Bliss, Caroline	215	
Bloch, Bernard	244	
Blomfield, Derek	21, 53	
Bloom, Claire	133, 160, 185, 226, 261	
Blythe, John	177	
Blythe, Peter	84	
Bogdan, Paul	58	
Bolam, James	209	
Boland, Eamon	220, 233	
Bond, Derek	10	
Bond, Gary	83	
Bond, Jane	86	
Bond, Philip	50, 56, 70	
Bond, Samantha	201, 244, 281	
Bond, Sophie	231	
Bone, Margery	225	
Bone, Stephen	110	
Bonney, John	58	
Booker, Jane	221, 231	
Boot, Gladys	61	
Booth, Charles	134	

Booth, Connie	154, 229, 254, 278, 281	
Booty, Jill	35	
Borgo, Marianne	173, 194	
Borisenko, Don	80	
Boswall, John	192	
Boty, Pauline	74	
Bould, Beckett	11, 24	
Bourke, Peter	146, 171	
Bourne, Helen	207	
Bovell, Brian	233, 251	
Bowe, John	254, 269	
Bowen, Debbie	114	
Bowen, Philip	179	
Bowen, Trevor	102, 104	
Bower, Ingrid	150	
Bowers, Lally	25, 141, 149	
Bowker, Judi	128, 185, 234	
Bowler, Norman	94	
Bowles, Peter	123	
Bown, John	75	
Boxer, Amanda	179, 195, 228	
Boxer, Stephen	177	
Boyce, Natalie	140	
Boyce, Todd	262	
Boyd, Beth	98	
Boyd, Paula	65	
Boyd, Tony	91	
Boyle, Catherine	50	
Brack, Philip	108	
Braden, Kim	112, 132	
Bradley, Elizabeth	102, 126, 151	
Bradshaw, Cathryn	249	
Bradshaw, Nigel	233	
Brady, Moya	268	
Branagh, Kenneth	204, 230, 236	
Branche, Derrick	203, 236	
Brantley, Betsy	280	
Brassett, Stephen	98	
Brattan, Laura	254	
Brayshaw, Edward	69, 73, 81, 84	
Bree, James	31, 121	
Breen, Debbie	196	
Brennan, Brid	264	
Brennan, Kevin	41	
Brennan, Sheila	30, 112	
Brent, Renate	14	
Breslin, John	59, 61, 70	
Brett, Jeremy	81, 92, 120, 129, 133, 159, 196	
Briant, Shane	128	
Bridge, Nicolas	123	
Brightwell, Paul	222	
Britt, Leo	36	
Britton, Tony	20, 60, 67, 129	

Broadbent, Jim	190	
Brodrick, Susan	89	
Bromly, Alan	3	
Brook, Faith	116, 188, 224	
Brook, Jonathan	250	
Brook, Lyndon	28, 70, 71, 89, 131	
Brook-Jones, Elwyn	37	
Brooke, Paul	178	
Brooking, John	39	
Brooks, Edward	144	
Brooks, Ray	197	
Brooks, Victor	20, 24, 75, 86	
Brooks, Vivian	101	
Brosnan, Pierce	187	
Brough, Arthur	49	
Brown, Antony	139	
Brown, Barbara	27, 51	
Brown, Bernard	52, 56, 73, 150	
Brown, Duggie	196	
Brown, Georgia	104, 126	
Brown, Jo Cameron	191	
Brown, John	77	
Brown, June	138	
Brown, Pamela	116	
Brown, Peter	126	
Brown, Phil	150	
Brown, Philip Martin	173	
Brown, Susan	184	
Browne, Angela	62, 90, 132, 140, 219, 242	
Browne, Jennifer	22	
Browne, Laidman	18, 26, 51	
Bruce, Brenda	119, 147, 150, 153, 198, 222, 234, 259	
Bruce, Mona	103, 109, 172	
Brudenell, Jeremy	222	
Brugger, Jurgen	215	
Bryans, John	93, 96, 107	
Bryant, Anthony	18	
Bryant, Fred	203, 218	
Bryant, Michael	83, 86, 104, 125, 132	
Bryant, Sandra	170	
Bryceland, Yvonne	219	
Brychta, Edita	211	
Buchan, Harriet	199	
Buck, David	78, 118, 226	
Buck, Pamela	48	
Buckley, Denise	87	
Buckley, Joss	185	
Buckley, Keith	87, 108	
Budd, Terence	148, 155	
Buffery, Kate	238	
Buggy, Niall	277	
Buik, Barnaby	195	
Bull, Peter	7, 21, 42	

… PLAYERS 309

Bullock, Osmund 156, 170	Caldicott, Richard 40, 59	Carter, Patrick 210
Bunnage, Avis 112, 151, 170	Caldwell, Zoe 50	Carteret, Anna 69
Bunyan, Susannah 218	Calf, Anthony 193, 230, 256	Carvic, Heron 48
Burbage, Robert 187, 201	Callaghan, Claire 212	Case, Gerald 9, 31
Burden, Hugh 35, 69	Callard, Rebecca 265, 272	Casimir, Golda 55
Burden, Suzanne 213, 269	Callow, Simon 218, 222, 277	Cassidy, Elizabeth 142
Burfield, Kim 96	Calvert, Jennifer 253	Cast, Edward 41, 60
Burger, Elizabeth 108	Calvert, Phyllis 31, 33, 211, 224, 233	Castaldini, Anne 38, 42, 69
Burgess, Adrienne 143	Calvin, Tony 124	Castle, Ann 90
Burgess, Christopher 149	Cameron, Gay 59	Castle, John 133, 142, 155, 222, 280
Burke, Alfred 149, 160, 172, 185, 233	Cameron, Kate 31, 33, 36	Cater, John 83, 85, 103, 128, 135,
Burke, David 79, 102, 115, 146, 169	Camiller, George 185, 194	142, 240
Burke, Kathy 268	Campbell, Arthur 150	Caton, Juliette 270
Burke, Patricia 146	Campbell, Cheryl 152, 160, 165, 207,	Cattouse, Nadia 56
Burleigh, Andrew 155	225, 251, 264	Catz, Caroline 264
Burn, Jonathan 82	Campbell, Colin 4, 102, 104, 147	Caunter, Tony 137, 218
Burne, Michael 205	Campbell, Judy 162	Cavan, Barbara 30, 50, 73
Burnham, Jeremy 66, 80	Campbell, Ken 152	Cavendish, Brenda 124
Burns, Anne 170	Campbell, William 271	Cawdron, Robert 91
Burrell, Richard 28	Caninenberg, Hans 232	Cazenove, Christopher 129
Burrell, Sheila 33, 63, 101, 228	Cannon, Dyan 214	Cecil, Jonathan 186, 217
Burridge, Geoffrey 179	Cannon, Madeleine 169	Celi, Adolfo 185
Burring, Jeremy 94	Capaldi, Peter 257, 262, 264, 273	Cellier, Peter 24
Burt, Andrew 164, 186, 206	Cappleman, Joolia 201	Chadbon, Tom 140, 253
Burt, Oliver 7, 9, 30, 31	Capron, Brian 279	Chagrin, Nicolas 92, 190
Burton, Donald 104, 116, 178, 198	Caramitru, Ion 270	Chakiris, George 129
Burton, Harry 230, 253	Carby, Fanny 171	Chaliapin, Fyodor 244
Bushell, Anthony 35	Cardy, David 232	Challis, Jean 98
Butler, Richard 115	Carell, Annette 37, 41	Chamberlain, Cyril 9
Butterfield, Cherrald 108	Carey, Anita 171, 181, 221	Chamberlain, Richard 88
Butteriss, Simon 209	Carey, Denis 147	Chambers, Emma 278
Butterly, Gemma 277	Carey, Richenda 283	Chambers, Julia 162, 179, 184
Buxton, Judy 201	Cargill, David 69	Champel, Marcel 268
Byfield, Trevor 224	Cargill, Patrick 15, 32, 33, 40, 48,	Chandler, Simon 274
Byrne, Adrienne 111, 123, 131	58, 62	Chaplin, Ben 272
Byrne, Antony 276	Caridia, Michael 36	Chaplin, Geraldine 196
Byrne, Michael 153, 225	Carin, Victor 107, 127, 173	Chapman, Constance 188
Byrnes, Josephine 260	Carlin, John 81	Chapman, Edward 21, 29
Byron, John 5	Carlisle, John 127	Chapman, Marian 3
Byron, Kathleen 114, 128, 137	Carmichael, Ian 114, 118, 123, 126,	Chappell, Jacquey 154
	135	Charles, Craig 231
Caballero, Katia 244	Carney, Tony 220	Charleson, Ian 234
Caddick, Edward 89	Carr, Caroline 262	Charlesworth, John 15
Cadell, Jean 12	Carr, Jane 162	Charlton, Alethea 81, 120
Cadell, Simon 211	Carr, Maureen 198	Chase, Catherine 179
Cadzow, Juliet 226, 249	Carradine, Keith 243	Chase, Stephan 110, 178, 228
Caffrey, James 94	Carrell, Annette 76	Chasen, Heather 53, 151
Caffrey, Sean 233	Carrick, Antony 123	Chater, Geoffrey 24, 242
Cain, Shirley 209	Carroll, Anne 178, 205	Chelsom, Peter 206
Cairncross, James 30	Carson, John 59, 70, 76, 83, 96,	Cherrell, Gwen 139
Cairney, John 41, 50, 60, 61, 120	114, 150, 190	Cherry, Helen 19, 30, 33, 233, 263
Cairns, Adrian 102	Carson, Violet 33, 38	Chesnakov, Alexis 68
Calder, David 197, 208, 243, 256,	Carte, Eric 144	Chester, Mary 121
263	Carter, Jim 249	Child, Jeremy 190, 221, 257, 274
Calder-Marshall, Anna 161, 241	Carter, Michael 216	Childs, Philip 233

Childs, Tracey	151, 179, 198	
Chitty, Erik	7	
Choice, Elizabeth	205	
Christie, Alec	223	
Christie, Helen	67, 110	
Christie, Julie	57	
Christie, Madeleine	82, 269	
Church, Tony	22	
Churchill, Diana	79	
Churchill, Donald	42	
Churchman, Ysanne	3	
Clark, Ashley	175	
Clark, Kelly	275	
Clarke, Prue	160, 172, 195	
Clarke, Warren	129, 140, 203, 243, 254	
Clarke, Zelah	195, 201	
Claughton, Peter	48	
Clay, Nicholas	58	
Clay, Peter	80	
Clay, Rachel	64	
Clayton, Lynn	178	
Clements, John	189	
Clifford, Clare	191, 231	
Clifford, Jefferson	26	
Clifford, Peggyann	63	
Cloughton, Peter	35	
Clyde, Jeremy	138, 150, 154, 201, 209	
Clyne, Fiona	12	
Cochran, Barbara	12	
Cochrane, Martin	264	
Cochrane, Michael	124, 213	
Coke, Peter	11, 12	
Colbourne, Maurice	8, 35, 54, 142, 183, 202	
Cole, David	31, 33, 36, 47	
Cole, George	211	
Cole, Paul	30	
Coleby, Robert	122, 124	
Coleman, Bryan	18, 36, 171	
Coleman, Charlotte	249	
Coleman, Richard	32, 57, 63, 94	
Coleridge, Kate	136, 182	
Coleridge, Sylvia	86, 213	
Colicos, Nicolas	250	
Colin, Ian	10, 54	
Colley, Kenneth	152, 189	
Collier, Patience	130, 153	
Collier, Sarah	217	
Collin, John	123, 140	
Collings, David	85, 94, 133, 163, 186	
Collins, Brendan	69	
Collins, Forbes	173	
Collins, Jonathan	54	
Collins, Kenneth	36	
Collins, Pauline	216	
Coltrane, Robbie	270	
Comer, Norman	138	
Compton, Fay	39, 91	
Conlon, Mary	254	
Connell, Maureen	19	
Connell, Miranda	51	
Connery, Jason	260	
Connor, Kenneth	4	
Conor, Joseph	27	
Conroy, Neili	277	
Conti, Tom	89, 125, 126, 135, 139	
Cook, Sophie	226, 237, 244	
Cook, Vera	16	
Cooke, Ann	17	
Cooke, Beryl	110, 240	
Cooklin, Shirley	15	
Cookson, Georgina	114	
Coombes, James	205	
Cooper, Betty	32	
Cooper, George A.	54, 67	
Cooper, Rowena	212, 227	
Copeland, James	80	
Copley, Paul	149	
Copley, Peter	63, 95, 135	
Coppard, Jake	206	
Coppen, Hazel	89	
Cornwell, Charlotte	240, 257	
Cornwell, Judy	63, 129, 158, 177, 201, 219	
Corri, Adrienne	14, 18, 42, 78, 108, 109, 113	
Cosmo, James	80, 141, 181	
Cossins, James	129, 195	
Costa, Michael da	96	
Costello, Dierdre	152	
Costigan, George	186, 277	
Cotterill, Chrissie	199	
Cotton, Oliver	185, 222, 261	
Cotts, Campbell	33	
Coulouris, George	93, 157	
Counsell, Elizabeth	87	
Couper, Barbara	10	
Coupland, Diana	123, 143	
Courage, Carolyn	115	
Court, Hazel	22	
Courtenay, Margaret	54, 107, 165	
Courtney, Nicholas	80	
Coward, Tim	125	
Cowell-Parker, Simon	172, 212	
Cowper, Nicola	179, 253, 281	
Cox, Brian	132, 153, 171, 220, 259, 265, 275	
Cox, Julie	281	
Cox, Martin	35	
Cox, Michael Graham	63	
Cox, Sam	252	
Coxell, Amanda	65	
Coy, Jonathan	250, 275	
Coyle, Brendan	280	
Coyote, Peter	243	
Cracknell, Leonard	20, 51	
Craig, Alastair	196	
Craig, Andrew	196	
Craig, Joanna	123	
Crane, Robin	193	
Cranham, Kenneth	171, 217, 225, 241, 249, 256	
Cranitch, Lorcan	253, 270	
Craven, Gemma	152	
Crawford, Andrew	105	
Crawford, Anne	8, 13, 15, 18	
Craze, Sarah	104	
Crean, Patrick	29	
Cree, Patricia	30	
Cresswell, Christopher	9	
Cresswell, Hannah	251	
Crewe, Nigel	132	
Crilly, Joseph	259	
Critchley, Paul	193, 206	
Croft, Colin	26	
Croft, Emma	277	
Croft, Peter	13	
Croft, Rebecca	150	
Cronin, John	277	
Cropper, Anna	67, 74, 90, 95, 111, 118, 156, 203, 210, 261	
Crosbie, Annette	87, 101, 120, 133, 182, 221, 240, 244	
Cross, Ben	183, 195	
Cross, Gerald	28, 53, 66	
Cross, Hugh	64, 85	
Cross, Paul	265, 272	
Crossan, Neil	156	
Croucher, Brian	153	
Croucher, Derek	58	
Croucher, Roger	58, 76	
Croudson, Michael	3	
Crowden, Graham	23, 164, 220, 224, 277	
Crowley, Jeananne	255	
Crowley, Suzan	253	
Crowshaw, Suzanne	280	
Crowther, Elizabeth	85	
Crowther, Liz	201	
Cruickshank, Andrew	15, 32, 39, 41, 161, 200	

PLAYERS 311

Crutchley, Rosalie	61, 70, 72, 73, 83, 91, 94, 101, 106, 125, 137, 149, 165, 192, 209, 236	
Cruttenden, Abigail	226, 251, 277	
Cuby, Joseph	56	
Cuka, Frances	70	
Culbertson, Rod	127	
Cullen, Anne	9	
Cullen, Eric	156	
Cullen, Ian	65, 169	
Cullen, Jonathan	275	
Culver, Michael	184, 202, 236, 240, 251	
Culver, Roland	110, 117, 124, 130	
Cundell, Pamela	265, 272	
Cunliffe, Ronald	63	
Cunningham, Dan	15	
Cunningham, Neil	162	
Curram, Roland	93	
Curran, Paul	68, 136, 156	
Currie, Finlay	87, 89	
Curry, Julian	86	
Curry, Tim	153	
Curtis, Lucinda	184	
Curzon, George	53, 59	
Cusack, Catherine	233	
Cusack, Cyril	112, 114	
Cusack, Sinead	117, 129	
Cusack, Sorcha	122	
Cushing, Peter	5, 8	
Cussons, Jane	134	
Cuthbertson, Alan	22, 42	
Cuthbertson, Iain	110, 120, 175, 231, 240, 264, 274	
D'abo, Maryam	250
d'Albie, Julian	67
D'Amato, Paul	143
D'Amico, Marcus	271
Dacla, Corinne	244
Daine, Lois	67
Daker, David	205
Dale, Eileen	67
Dale, Janet	243, 271
Dale, Matthew	160
Dalton, Paul	198
Dalton, Timothy	201, 266
Dalziel, John	141
Damon, Stuart	93
Dan, Fumi	244
Dance, Charles	203, 208, 237
Dane, Ellen	38
Daneman, Paul	34, 47, 53, 81, 182
Daniel, Jennifer	52, 68, 73
Daniels, Phil	189, 209
Daniely, Lisa	13
Darby, Anton	122
Darrow, Paul	137, 164, 195
Dastor, Nicolas	241
Dastor, Sam	185
Davenport, Laura	178
Davenport, Nigel	66, 128, 163, 191
David, Eleanor	182, 212, 221, 264, 274, 283
David, Hugh	31, 49
David, Joanna	105, 116, 159, 186, 188, 221
David, Jody	258
David, Jonathan	124
David, Michael	25
David, Philip	124
Davien, Geoffrey	127
Davies, D.L.	71
Davies, David	28, 29, 34, 75
Davies, Diana	202
Davies, Glan	227
Davies, Henry	19
Davies, Howell	3
Davies, John Rhys	142, 256
Davies, Lyndon	223, 228
Davies, Lynette	238
Davies, Meg	197, 240
Davies, Oliver Ford	237
Davies, Petra	7, 21, 47, 50, 67
Davies, Rachel	270, 283
Davies, Robin	163
Davies, Rowland	107, 110, 161
Davies, Rudi	249
Davies, Rupert	16, 32, 116
Davies, Stephen	244
Davies, Sylvia	31
Davies, Timothy	158
Davies, Windsor	123
Davion, Alex	79
Davis, Carol	110
Davis, Philip	154, 265
Davis, Warwick	245, 252
Davison, Peter	148, 210, 220
Dawes, Anthony	212
Dawson, Lucy	275
Day, Diana	12, 31
Day-Lewis, Daniel	190, 215
Deacon, Brian	115, 213
Deacon, Eric	164, 187
Deam, Jack	265
Dean, Felicity	157, 164, 182
Dean, Isabel	10, 52, 105
Dean, Peter	152
Dean, Stephen J.	203
Dearman, Glyn	12
Dearth, John	53
Dearth, Lynn	179
Deebank, Felix	61
Degen, Michael	236
De Goguel, Constantin	122
Dejey, Sarah-Juliette	96
De Jong, Holly	164, 257
de la Tour, Andy	231
de la Tour, Frances	175
Delage, Jean-Pierre	268
Delamain, Aimee	59
Delgado, Roger	14, 52
de Lint, Derek	244
Dellal, Gabrielle	229
Deluc, Xavier	241
Delve, David	155
de Marney, Terence	65
Demetriou, Jimmy	212
Dempsey, Martin	91
Dempsey, Richard	237, 244
Dench, Judi	38, 176, 239
Denham, Maurice	29, 125, 131, 157, 160, 200, 216, 224
Denison, Michael	183, 194
Dennen, Barry	176, 193
Dentith, Edward	80
Denzil, Caroline	9
Derby, Brown	41, 89
De Santis, Stanley	271
Desmond, Robert	9
de Souza, Edward	25, 73
Devaney, Sue	240
Devereux, W. Thorp	10
Devlin, Alan	233
Devlin, William	10, 14, 18, 20, 22, 32, 59
de Wolff, Francis	81
Dexter, David	222
Dexter, William	61, 72, 84, 122
Dhillon, Amarjit	218
Diamond, Arnold	142
Dibnah, Michelle	149
Dickens, Robert	6
Dickins, Anne	29
Dickinson, Sandra	178
Dickson, Barbara	283
Diffring, Anton	94
Dignam, Basil	4, 84, 106, 107, 109, 111, 123, 127, 133, 141
Dignam, Mark	38, 63, 74, 77, 104, 134, 154
Dillane, Stephen	269, 275
Dillon, Kevin	262
Dillon, Stephen	234, 238
Dimbleby, Henry	206

Dimmick, Jeremy 186
Din, Ayub Khan 240
Dinsdale, Reece 240
Dionisotti, Paola 186
Dixon, David 102, 104, 137, 178
Dixon, Jill 33, 34
Dixon, Shirley 125
Dobie, Alan 9, 29, 32, 33, 93, 116, 145, 149, 186
Dobson, Anita 274
Docker, Melissa 140
Dodd, Pearson 36
Dodimead, David 103
Dodson, Eric 48
Doherty, Robert 89
Donaghy, Pip 207, 215, 217
Donaldson, David 174
Done, Jason 281
Donohoe, Amanda 236, 272
Donovan, Patricia 195
Donovan, Victoria 265, 272
Doody, Alison 234, 255
Doonan, Anthony 26
Doran, Sonny 9
Dormandy, Simon 230
Dorning, Kate 179, 217
Dotrice, Karen 113, 143
Dotrice, Michele 58, 62, 63, 87, 91
Dotrice, Roy 95, 112, 143, 254
Douglas, Angela 87
Douglas, Colin 15, 16, 32, 42, 58, 67, 102, 104, 109, 159, 170, 209
Douglas, Donald 41, 55, 68, 91, 135, 179, 191
Douglas, Howard 63
Douglas, Sarah 127, 146
Doumberg, Jo 268
Dowdeswell, Caroline 123
Dowie, Freda 209, 211, 249
Down, Angela 104, 116, 126, 139, 175
Downer, Alan 220
Downer, Caroline 206
Downie, Penny 232, 237, 259
Downing, Ernest 9
Downing, Wilfrid 9
Downs, Jane 29, 192, 193
Doyle, Tony 158, 233, 256, 258, 283
Drake, Charlie 213
Drake, Fabia 27, 53, 72, 117, 203, 234
Drake, Gabrielle 196

Dresdel, Sonia 13, 20, 51, 80, 92, 110
Drewry, Mark 214
Drinkel, Keith 96, 102, 126, 134, 138
Drinkwater, Carol 134
Driscoll, Christopher 147
Driscoll, Patricia 20
Driver, Minnie 268
Drummond, David 17
Drury, Patrick 257
Duce, Sharon 196, 263
Duering, Carl 11, 24
Duffy, Dave 275
Dukakis, Olympia 271
Dukes, David 236, 266
Dukes, Joanna 208
Dunbar, Adrian 258, 270, 272
Duncan, Archie 4, 82
Duncan, David 3
Duncan, Lindsay 218, 242, 255, 268, 275
Duncan, Neil 199
Duncan, Peter 124
Dundas, David 90, 119
Dunham, Joanna 109, 163, 232
Dunlop, Lesley 128, 140
Dunn, Andrew 153
Dunn, Clive 26
Dunn, Geoffrey 71
Dunning, Jessica 39
Dunning, Ruth 119, 131
Dunrich, Brenda 28, 35
Durant, Andrea 151
Durbridge, Mona 158
Durham-Matthews, Katy 201
Durham-Matthews, Lucy 149
Dury, Ian 220
Du Sautoy, Carmen 202, 222
Duttine, John 121, 153, 155, 162, 176, 183, 226, 229
Dutton, Simon 201
Dwyer, Leslie 132
Dyall, Valentine 3, 26, 91
Dyce, Hamilton 74, 84, 85, 91
Dyneley, Peter 50
Dyrenforth, James 26
Dyson, Noel 4

Eadie, Mark 179
Eady, Piers 186
Eagles, Leon 103
Earl, Clifford 61
Earlle, Freddie 112
East, Robert 114

Eaton, Kate 261
Eccles, Donald 59, 114, 126
Eccles, Julie 236
Eccleston, Christopher 263, 270, 282
Eddington, Paul 261
Eddison, Robert 39, 164
Eddy, Laura 259
Eden, Mark 84, 114, 118, 123, 213
Edmett, Nicky 35
Edmonds, Elizabeth 226
Edmonds, Lucinda 186
Edmonstone, Susan 186
Edney, Beatie 222, 239, 244
Edwards, Alan 16
Edwards, Dennis 13
Edwards, Dorothy 98
Edwards, Glynn 66, 76, 84
Edwards, Graveley 6
Edwards, Hilton 20, 37
Edwards, Mark 104
Edwards, Maudie 19
Edwards, Meredith 49, 117, 127, 152, 154
Edwards, Nina 228
Edwards, Rob 201, 209, 231
Egan, Peter 91, 127, 155, 163, 200, 221, 231, 283
Eggar, Samantha 55
Ehle, Jennifer 261
Elder, Michael 135, 140
Eles, Sandor 42, 169
Elgar, Avril 125, 127, 237
Elkin, Clifford 51
Elliott, Alison 163, 182, 281
Elliott, Denholm 77, 120, 142, 213
Elliott, Mark 207
Ellis, Jack 231, 254, 267
Ellis, Jacqueline 31
Ellis, James 199, 231
Ellis, June 64, 103
Ellis, Patrick 32
Ellis, Robin 105, 106, 107, 112, 136, 177
Ellis, William 123
Ellison, Chris 218
Ellison, David 236
Elphick, Michael 145, 181, 192, 259
Elton, Ben 273
Elvin, Rosalyn 132
Elwes, Amanda 255
Embling, Caroline 192
Emma-Davies, Kate 236
Emmanuel, Takis 150
Endersby, Clive 73
Engel, Susan 86

Engel, Tina	252	
Engels, Robbie	232	
English, Patricia	89	
Eugeniou, George	31	
Evans, Clifford	59	
Evans, Daniel	227	
Evans, Edith	89	
Evans, Edward	60	
Evans, Eynon	47, 71	
Evans, Islwyn Maelor	47	
Evans, Jessie	49	
Evans, Nicholas	91	
Evans, Tenniel	97, 178, 195	
Eve, Trevor	200, 249, 253	
Everest, Barbara	3, 17	
Ewing, Barbara	120, 149, 228	
Exell, James	238	
Eyre, Peter	157, 202	
Eziashi, Maynard	264	
Fahy, Katherine	129	
Fairbank, Christopher	165, 276, 279	
Fairbrass, Craig	254, 267	
Fairbrother, Victoria	172, 189, 213, 223, 228	
Fairclough, Fred	25, 47	
Fairfax, Diana	30, 41, 47, 52, 137, 176, 179, 251	
Fairleigh, Lynn	125	
Fairley, Michelle	258	
Falconer, Vari	10	
Fallender, Deborah	144	
Fallon, Richard	214	
Farebrother, Violet	74	
Farell, Claude	61	
Farleigh, Lynn	115, 147, 153, 171, 192, 196, 279	
Farmer, Mark	202	
Farmer, Suzan	78	
Farr, Derek	148, 175, 205	
Farrell, Nicholas	201, 203, 267, 272, 283	
Farrington, Kenneth	47	
Faulds, Andrew	65, 146, 156	
Faulkner, James	142, 221, 253, 266	
Fawsett, Amanda	241	
Fay, Sheila	110	
Faye, Janina	50, 104, 113	
Fayerman, Stephanie	173	
Fearn, Sheila	77	
Feast, Michael	260	
Feller, Catherine	18, 29	
Fellowes, Julian	206	
Fellowes, Robert	118	

Fellows, Billy	225	
Fenton, Simon	239, 275	
Ferguson, Gillian	47	
Ferguson, Jane	132	
Fernald, Karin	74, 80	
Ferrer, José	236	
Ferris, Barbara	162	
Ferris, Pam	228, 262, 275	
Fiander, Lewis	86, 129	
Field, Shirley Anne	269	
Fielding, Emma	264	
Fiennes, Ralph	254	
Finch, Jon	204, 238, 258	
Finch, Scot	60	
Finlay, Frank	87, 110, 139, 144, 270	
Finlay, Marilyn	134	
Finn, Christine	35, 72	
Finn, Edwin	56	
Finney, Albert	251	
Fiol, Virginia	143	
Firbank, Ann	22, 33, 107, 129, 155, 169, 226	
Firth, Colin	222, 277	
Firth, Jonathan	251, 274	
Firth, Julian	215, 258	
Firth, Peter	144, 256	
Fisher, Gregor	224	
Fisk, Martin	136	
Fiske, Alison	104, 214	
Fitzalan, Marsha	170	
Fitzgerald, Tara	261, 263	
Fitzgerald, Walter	13	
Fitzwilliam, Neil	158, 217	
Flanagan, John	174, 254	
Fleet, James	270	
Fleetwood, Susan	214, 244, 271	
Fleming, Ian	9, 20	
Fleming, Lucy	86	
Fleming, Tom	31, 41, 55, 119	
Fleminge, Mary	153	
Flemyng, Robert	88, 159	
Fletcher, Diane	95, 103, 114, 252, 272	
Fletcher, Nicholas	241	
Fletcher, Steve	134	
Flint, Jimmy	266	
Flood, Gerald	57, 110	
Flynn, Barbara	102, 104, 109, 209, 220, 270	
Flynn, Eric	101, 117	
Foad, Gene	143	
Foch, Nina	271	
Ford, Alan	152	
Ford, Julia	153, 262	

Ford, Mick	199, 259	
Forgeham, John	193, 243	
Forrest, Anthony	132	
Forrest, Frederic	252	
Forrest, John	27	
Forrestal, Terry	192	
Forster, Jane	144	
Forsyth, Brigit	115, 132	
Forsythe, Colin	226	
Forte, Nicola	173	
Fortune, John	232	
Foss, Alan	123	
Foster, Barry	27, 37, 125, 142, 197	
Foster, Dudley	82, 113	
Foster, Jamie	260	
Foster, Julia	137, 212	
Foster, Maude	96	
Fowlds, Derek	79, 137, 241, 252	
Fowler, Alexandra	262	
Fowler, John	171	
Fox, Edward	88, 149, 157	
Fox, James	187, 188, 250, 255, 274, 276, 283	
Fox, Kerry	268	
Fox, William	64, 76, 130	
Frain, James	281	
Frampton, Rufus	108	
France, Dawson	5	
Frances, Myra	128	
Francis, Clive	91, 105, 136, 147, 198, 227, 267	
Francis, Derek	48, 58, 60, 68, 84, 86, 89, 91, 125, 146, 154, 158, 184, 205	
Francis, Geoff	219	
Francis, Jan	112, 123, 182	
Francis, Raymond	11	
Frank, Adrienne	127	
Frankel, Mark	283	
Franklin, Patricia	145	
Franklyn, Sabina	170	
Franklyn, William	51, 65, 70	
Franklyn-Robbins, John	96, 105, 111, 224	
Franks, Chloe	128, 197	
Franks, Philip	188, 213, 278	
Fraser, Bill	78, 169, 211	
Fraser, Helen	96, 140	
Fraser, Hugh	191, 210, 216, 236	
Fraser, John	6, 92, 133, 137	
Fraser, Liz	212	
Fraser, Ronald	82, 131, 266	
Fraser, Shelagh	102, 104	
Frazer, Alison	101	
Frazer, Rupert	164, 165, 190, 211	

PLAYERS

Frederick, Malcolm	220
Fredericks, Scott	124
Freeman, Paul	224, 275
French, Leslie	37, 47, 61
Fricker, Brenda	199
Friels, Colin	273
Friend, Martin	138
Frith, Linda	212
Frost, Paddy	122
Fryer, Patricia	4
Fuerst, Tamara	95
Fulford, Christopher	220, 271
Fuller, Toria	143, 200
Fullerton, Fiona	237
Furse, Judith	52
Furst, Joseph	68
Furst, Vanessa	140
Fusek, Vera	26
Fyfer, Valerie	173
Gable, Christopher	153
Gabriel, John	62
Gale, Gillian	15
Gale, Peter	179
Gale, Richard	63
Gallagher, Bernard	148, 205
Gallagher, Sean	264
Gallie, Kay	105
Galloway, Jack	151, 174
Galloway, Stephen	122
Gambon, Michael	213, 223, 278
Garahy, Siobhan	234
Garbutt, James	106, 108, 236, 238
Gardner, Jimmy	95, 118
Garfield, David	71, 132
Garlick, David	215
Garlick, Iestyn	227
Garner, Laurie	26
Garrick, Barbara	271
Garrie, John	87
Garth, David	19
Garvie, Elizabeth	170, 191
Garwood, Patricia	14
Gastoni, Lisa	52
Gates, Stefan	160
Gaunt, Fiona	116, 155
Gaunt, William	94, 115, 138, 192
Gaussen, Nora	3
Gearon, Valerie	77, 89, 107, 110
Gebel, Malgoscha	249
Gecks, Nicholas	208, 230
Geddis, Peter	126
Gee, Donald	205
Geeson, Judy	136, 170
Gelder, Ian	121, 138
Gemmell, Ruth	283
Geoffrey, Paul	202
George, Kelly	212
George, Susan	65
George, Tricia	147
Georgeson, Tom	217
Georgeson, Valerie	111, 127
Germaine, Louise	267
Gerroll, Daniel	190
Gibbs, Sheila Shand	3, 9, 16, 19, 20, 37, 63
Gibson, Richard	150
Gibson, Thomas	271
Gielgud, John	133, 185, 244
Gifford, Alan	63, 72
Gifford, Wendy	78, 103
Gilbert, Henry	80
Gill, John	60, 89
Gill, Peter	49
Gillespie, Cherry	182
Gillespie, Emer	234, 256
Gillies, Carol	201
Gillies, Fiona	243, 255, 272
Gilmore, Denis	60
Gilmore, Susan	211
Gilmour, Michael	184
Gipps-Kent, Simon	117, 151, 153
Gish, Sheila	259
Gittins, Chris	38
Gladwin, Joe	138
Glazer, Karen	38
Glen, Iain	233, 262
Glen, John	10
Glenn, Libby	95
Glenn, Samantha	280
Glover, Brian	222
Glover, Jon	124
Glover, Julian	132, 187, 195, 201
Goacher, Denis	49
Goddard, Willoughby	12, 59
Godfrey, Anne	48
Godfrey, Derek	124, 141, 146
Godfrey, Michael	80
Godfrey, Patrick	136
Godley, Adam	155, 205
Godsell, Vanda	55
Godwin, Christopher	231, 243
Godwin, Doran	114
Godwin, Simon	254
Goettinger, Lislott	8
Gogan, Valerie	217
Gold, Max	195
Goldie, Michael	192
Goldie, Wyndham	10
Golding, Dennis	87
Goodall, Caroline	157, 241
Goodliffe, Michael	21, 33, 78, 90, 102, 120, 126
Goodman, Deborah	209
Goodman, Henry	241
Goodman, Tim	105
Goodwin, Harold	35
Goolden, Richard	20
Goorney, Howard	101
Gordon, Alan	6
Gordon, Bruce	16, 34
Gordon, Dorothy	40
Gordon, Hannah	78, 92, 94, 159, 201, 231
Gordon, John N.	26
Gordon, Martin	152
Gordon, Serena	241, 243
Goring, Marius	157, 200
Gostelow, Gordon	71, 89
Gouge, Kenneth	58
Gough, Kenneth	54
Gough, Michael	70, 86, 93, 108, 125, 126, 192, 195, 226, 245, 254, 258
Gover, Michael	68
Grace, Nickolas	185
Graham, Benny	238
Graham, Clive	92, 101
Graham, Denys	250
Graham, Julie	226
Graham, Laura	61, 148
Graham, Michael	94
Graham, Richard	220
Grainger, Garn	181
Grant, Deborah	139, 144
Grant, Hugh	214
Grant, James	107, 224
Grant, Richard E.	228
Grant, Sheila	89, 126
Grant, Susan Lyall	29
Graves, Diana	11
Graves, Rupert	230
Graveson, Jan	225, 280
Gray, Charles	120, 175
Gray, Derek	174
Gray, Elspet	11
Gray, Fiona	148, 164
Gray, Willoughby	6
Grazebrook, Sarah	117
Green, Danny	25
Green, Gerard	14
Green, Nigel	85, 86
Green, Robson	282
Green, Simon	177
Greene, James	157

PLAYERS

Greene, Sarah	172
Greene, William	63
Greenhill, Geoffrey	161
Greenlaw, Verina	91
Greenstreet, Mark	219
Greenwood, Joan	163
Greenwood, Melissa	233
Greenwood, Rosamund	24
Gregg, John	139
Gregg, Olive	38
Gregson, John	141
Grehan, Aingeal	210
Grenville, Cynthia	250
Grey, Monica	16
Greyn, Clinton	120
Grieve, John	95, 119
Griffin, David	120, 146
Griffith, Hugh	16, 112, 133
Griffith, Kenneth	76, 112
Griffiths, Lucy	24
Griffiths, Richard	190, 195, 231, 262
Grillo, John	185, 270
Grimes, Frank	160
Grinling, Amanda	57
Grist, Paul	91, 109
Grives, Steven	159, 179
Grocholski, Czeslaw	173
Gross, Paul	271
Grout, James	130, 243, 261
Gryff, Stefan	158
Guard, Christopher	78, 83, 185, 196
Guard, Dominic	138, 191
Guard, Philip	64
Guard, Pippa	158, 162, 178, 205, 273
Gudrun, Ann	37
Gugino, Carla	281
Gugolka, John	97
Guidotti, Stewart	31
Guinness, Alec	163, 192
Guinness, Matthew	125, 176
Guinness, Peter	274
Gurnett, Jane	238, 283
Gurney, Rachel	9, 40, 62, 88, 95, 249
Gurney, Sharon	89, 91, 95
Gutteridge, Lucy	176, 193
Gwillim, David	191, 193, 207
Gwillim, Jack	92
Gwynn, Michael	37, 75, 138
Gwynne, Haydn	243
Gynt, Greta	23

Hackett, Claire	260
Haddow, David	156, 282
Hafner, Ingrid	241
Haft, Linal	154
Hagan, George	55, 117
Hagon, Garrick	144
Haig, David	251
Haigh, Kenneth	108, 137, 220
Haigh, Louisa	249
Hails, Sam	258
Haines, Brian	3
Haines, Patricia	72
Hale, Elvi	60, 101, 107
Hale, Gareth	276
Hale, Georgina	115
Hale, Peter	143
Hales, Jennifer	33
Haley, Alastair	238
Haley, Christopher	265
Hall, Brian	179
Hall, Francesca	222
Hall, Harvey	33, 36, 60
Hall, Rebecca	261
Hallam, John	123, 162, 225
Halliday, Barry	158
Halliday, Peter	57, 61, 282
Halmer, Gunther Maria	199
Halstead, Robin	112
Halstead, Suzanne	204
Hamilton, Barbara	112, 132
Hamilton, Gabrielle	110, 117
Hamilton, Gay	65, 79, 80, 84, 161
Hamilton, George	78
Hamilton, Robert	123
Hamilton, Suzanna	250
Hammett, Nicola	251
Hammond-Hill, Juliet	183, 186
Hampshire, Susan	61, 62, 82, 88, 97, 124, 194
Hampton, Richard	86
Hancock, Christopher	112
Hancock, Prentice	139
Hancock, Sheila	117, 240, 281
Handford, Leslie	28
Handl, Irene	26, 133
Hankin, Douglas	16
Hannah, John	227, 278
Hansard, Paul	14
Hansen, Joachin	71
Hanslip, Ann	10, 11, 35
Harbour, Emma	224
Harbour, Michael N.	218, 223
Hardcastle, Diana	221
Hardie, Jane	3, 17, 53

Hardie, Kate	233, 257, 274
Hardiman, Terrence	180, 194
Harding, Catherine	202
Harding, Jacki	120
Harding, John	204
Hardmuth, Paul	19
Hardwick, Paul	82, 90
Hardwicke, Edward	114, 187, 203
Hardy, Betty	50, 62, 69, 73, 119, 140
Hardy, Emma	259
Hardy, Laurence	48, 67, 94
Hardy, Robert	20, 62, 102, 106, 133, 183, 195, 214, 274
Harewood, David	254, 282
Hargreaves, Christine	199
Hargreaves, David	114
Hargreaves, Johanna	202
Harington, Joy	147
Harker, Caroline	260, 274
Harker, Susannah	233, 234, 252, 272, 278
Harper, Gerald	68, 73, 79
Harper, Kate	176, 215
Harrington, Emma-Louise	250
Harris, Aaron	233
Harris, Amanda	215
Harris, Cynthia	157
Harris, Max	144
Harris, Nesta	71
Harris, Robert	63
Harris, Rosemary	129, 236, 261
Harris, Tim	158
Harrison, Andrew	131
Harrison, Cathryn	155, 251, 258, 277, 283
Harrison, Gail	130
Harrison, Kathleen	140
Harrison, Marc	145
Harrison, Nigel	270
Harrison, Tom	131
Harrow, Lisa	177, 228, 249
Harrow, Lise	187
Harstad, Jan	211
Hart, Diane	15
Hart, Roxanne	240
Harvey, Jan	134, 214
Harvey, Jean	83, 201
Harvey, John	79
Harvey, Martin	256
Harvey, Terence	273
Hasse, Camilla	67
Hastings, Ian	128, 181, 212

PLAYERS

Havers, Nigel 123, 139, 146, 152, 155, 173, 183, 187, 203, 225, 254, 255, 280
Hawdon, Robin 116
Hawkins, Don 139
Hawkins, Frank 22
Hawkins, Paul 193, 204
Hawkins, Peter 24, 26, 49
Hawser, Gillian 92, 96
Hawthorne, Denys 192, 208
Hawthorne, Nigel 145, 147, 152, 157, 194, 213
Hawtrey, Marjory 37
Hay, Philip 31
Haye, Helen 5
Hayes, Brian 90, 149
Hayes, Elton 47
Hayes, Malcolm 185
Hayes, Melvyn 28, 59
Hayes, Patricia 148, 219
Haygarth, Tony 219, 253
Hayman, Carole 143
Hayman, Cyd 112, 161
Hayman, David 186, 194, 214, 260, 279
Haynes, Tim 223
Hayter, James 25, 35, 40
Hayter, Robin 215
Haywood, Alan 52
Haywood, Philippa 234
Hazeldine, James 120, 126, 144, 162, 199
Hazell, Carol 111
Head, Anthony 155
Head, Murray 125, 251
Healey, Mary 103, 145
Healy, David 280
Healy, Tim 231
Heard, Daphne 81
Heard, John 215
Heath, Eira 52
Heath, Joan 103
Heath, Kathleen 179
Heath, Tina 147
Heathcote, Thomas 21, 35
Hedley, Jack 53, 150
Hedley, Maurice 51, 90
Heffer, Richard 139, 198, 203, 216
Heggie, Alec 127
Heilbron, Vivien 107, 112, 118, 191, 198
Heiner, Thomasine 143
Heinz, Gerard 64
Helme, Kathleen 135, 172
Helsby, Eileen 81

Hemingway, Polly 199, 205
Hempel, Anouska 137
Hempson, Peter 47, 56
Henders, Richard 252
Henderson, Bill 89, 119, 120
Henderson, Don 218, 240, 258, 274
Henderson, Jane 17
Hendley, Fiona 197
Heneghan, Patricia 51, 178
Henfrey, Janet 217
Henley, Drewe 87
Henney, Del 182
Henry, Martha 102
Henry, Norman 142
Henry, Victor 97
Henshall, Douglas 257, 267
Henson, Basil 116
Henson, Elizabeth 11
Henson, Nicky 136, 233, 252
Hepton, Bernard 90, 92, 95, 101, 106, 121, 142, 163, 183, 186, 191, 192, 201, 213, 232, 255, 261, 275
Herbert, Rachel 84, 114
Herdman, Ronald 138
Herley, Randal 7
Hesford, Martyn 207
Hesmondhalgh, Julie 276
Hewer, John 146
Hewetson, Nicholas 256
Hewing, Mary 36
Hewlett, Arthur 93
Hewson, Sherrie 148, 160
Heyes, Zoe 282
Heywood, Jean 204, 225, 230
Heywood, Pat 155
Hicks, Barbara 211
Hicks, Greg 269
Hickson, Joan 27, 52, 94, 184
Higgins, Anthony 146, 148
Higgins, Clare 170, 195, 218, 241
Higginson, Huw 140
Hignett, Mary 36
Higson, David 24
Hilary, Jennifer 81, 126, 134
Hilboldt, Lise 187, 198
Hill, Bernard 267, 270, 282
Hill, Charles 74
Hill, Daniel 194
Hill, Jacqueline 23, 60
Hill, Melanie 279
Hill, Simon 186
Hiller, Wendy 112, 224, 237
Hills, Gillian 98, 110
Hillwood, Amanda 220

Hinchley, Pippa 207
Hinds, Ciaran 273, 278
Hines, Frazer 28, 30, 32, 68, 70
Hines, Robert 234, 253
Hines, Ronald 106, 126, 145, 162, 172, 242
Hines, Roy 25, 33
Hinsliff, Geoffrey 138
Hird, Thora 169
Hitchman, Michael 48
Hivju, Erick 211
Hodge, Douglas 239, 262, 263, 274
Hodge, Patricia 134, 157, 222, 259
Hodgson, Gaynor 119
Hodson, Steve 164
Hoey, James 141
Hogan, Bosco 163, 173, 179, 237
Hogarth, David 118
Hogg, Ian 130, 142, 204, 213, 219, 229
Holden, Jan 52
Holden, Michael 98
Holder, Owen 30
Holder, Roy 64, 207
Holderness, Sue 195
Holland, Mary 26, 34
Holland, Stephen 234
Holley, Bernard 141
Holliman, Valerie 112, 198
Holloway, Julian 159
Holm, Ian 113, 156, 175, 187, 236, 265, 272
Holm, Sarah-Jane 231
Holm, Sharon 242
Holman, Clare 238, 240
Holme, Thea 3, 53, 89
Holt, Judy 180, 188
Home, Sally 84, 96
Hood, Morag 107, 116, 164, 249, 264
Hooper, Ewan 205
Hooper, June 161
Hope, Richard 281
Hope, William 187
Hopkins, Anthony 116, 198, 203, 256
Hordern, Michael 125, 130, 178, 221, 252, 274
Horgan, Patrick 13
Horn, Roderick 184
Hornak, Lucy 213
Horne, David 7, 30, 41

PLAYERS

Horner, Julie	134	
Horner, Penelope	90	
Horovitch, David	195	
Horsfall, Bernard	40, 48, 49, 101, 135, 141, 188	
Horsley, John	19, 131	
Horton, Helen	12, 61	
Hoskins, Bob	152, 175	
Houston, Donald	8	
Houston, Glyn	47, 62, 83, 114, 126, 135, 155, 169	
How, Jane	170, 174, 181, 263	
Howard, Alan	129, 231	
Howard, Arthur	113	
Howard, John	217	
Howard, Ken	236	
Howard, Lindy	122	
Howard, Ronald	22	
Howarth, Jack	33	
Howarth, Kristine	122	
Howe, George	7, 13, 34, 76, 93	
Howell, George	135	
Howell, Peter	197	
Howells, Ursula	12, 23, 107, 149, 191, 264	
Howitt, Peter	281	
Howlett, Noel	33, 40, 50	
Hudd, Roy	267	
Hudson, Tim	32, 60	
Huffman, Kymberley	267	
Hughes, Andrew	170	
Hughes, Hazel	25	
Hughes, Melanie	216	
Hughes, Nerys	138	
Hughes, Peter	40	
Hulme, Bryan	33	
Humphries, Barry	255	
Hunnicutt, Gayle	114, 125	
Hunt, Alan	156	
Hunt, Dudley	54, 56	
Hunter, Alan	170, 174, 181	
Hunter, Kelly	273	
Hunter, Russell	135, 240	
Huntley, Raymond	7, 28, 56	
Huntley-Wright, Betty	97	
Hurley, Colin	222	
Hurley, Elizabeth	238, 243	
Hurndall, Richard	62, 81, 83, 84, 113, 120, 127, 133, 176	
Hurren, Bonnie	93	
Hurst, Jacqueline	127	
Hurt, John	142, 161	
Hussain, Talat	242	
Hussey, John	34	
Hutchinson, Bill	250	
Hutchinson, Stuart	24	
Hutchinson, Wendy	25	
Hutchison, Caroline	199	
Hutchison, Ken	155, 218	
Huw, Richard	278	
Hyde, Jemma	52	
Hyde, Jonathan	258	
Hyde, Kenneth	19	
Hynd, Phil	202	
Hywell, Dafydd	154	
Ibbs, Ronald	37	
Imrie, Celia	181, 191	
Ineson, Ralph	276	
Ingham, Barrie	67	
Ingram, Malcolm	164	
Innes, George	88	
Innocent, Harold	63, 171, 185, 203, 218	
Ipale, Aharon	96	
Ireland, Ian	135	
Irons, Jeremy	129, 148, 185	
Irvine, Andrew	30	
Irvine, Robert	6, 7	
Irving, George	208	
Isbister, Claire	41	
Ives, Kenneth	105	
Jaber, Zara	122	
Jackley, Nat	170	
Jackson, Barry	137	
Jackson, Dan	117	
Jackson, Freda	165	
Jackson, Glenda	106, 236	
Jackson, Michael-John	137	
Jackson, Nancie	93, 101	
Jackson, Philip	198, 228, 279	
Jackson, Sally Jane	172	
Jacobi, Derek	112, 115, 124, 142, 219	
Jacobs, Anthony	19, 34, 60, 66, 116	
Jacobs, David	3	
Jacobs, Emma	156	
Jacobs, Martyn	124, 163, 203	
Jacobs, Paula	228	
Jaeger, Frederick	51, 55, 78, 104, 113	
Jaffe, Carl	55	
Jaffrey, Saeed	142, 277	
James, Emrys	75, 165, 195, 210, 224	
James, Fraser	267	
James, Gerald	26, 151	
James, Geraldine	163, 178, 189, 203, 211, 234, 259, 283	
James, Godfrey	122, 152, 158, 186, 215	
James, Gwyn	14	
James, Heather	216	
James, Horace	85	
James, Polly	140	
James, Robert	55, 115, 135, 138, 146, 189	
James, Sidney	21	
Jameson, Pauline	103	
Jameson, Susan	176	
Jarvis, Martin	82, 89, 104, 112, 130, 169, 170, 216, 242, 271	
Jason, David	228	
Jason, Neville	194	
Jay, Tony	125	
Jayston, Michael	122, 163, 169, 235	
Jeater, Frances	225	
Jeavons, Colin	37, 41, 51, 64, 78, 111, 165, 184, 245, 252, 272	
Jeffery, Neil	225	
Jeffrey, Leonard	31	
Jeffrey, Peter	103, 106, 130, 148, 209, 242, 268, 274	
Jeffries, Lionel	266	
Jellinek, Tristram	66, 89, 236	
Jenkins, Clare	101	
Jenkins, Megs	4, 122	
Jenkins, Nigel	54	
Jenkins, Sue	209	
Jenn, Myvanwy	123	
Jenn, Stephen	204	
Jennings, Alex	236	
Jephcott, Dominic	209, 215	
Jephcott, Sam	35	
Jesson, Paul	235, 261	
Jewel, Jimmy	218, 266	
Jewesbury, Edward	33	
John, Caroline	231	
John, Errol	54, 85	
John, Gottfried	236	
John, Julia St.	266	
Johns, Harriette	41	
Johns, Mervyn	33	
Johns, Milton	105, 111, 128, 180, 209	
Johns, Stratford	184, 227, 271	
Johnson, Celia	161, 196	
Johnson, Karl	179, 241	
Johnson, Michael	111	
Johnson, Noel	57, 61, 82, 85	
Johnson, Penny	197	

Johnson, Richard	5, 9, 42, 182, 261, 263	Kavanagh, Christine	256, 260, 266, 280	Kensit, Patsy	163, 164, 184, 190, 203
Johnson, Sammy	282	Kavanagh, John	258	Kent, Anne	282
Johnson, Van	194	Kavanagh, Patrick	84	Kent, Diana	278
Johnston, Oliver	63	Kay, Bernard	81, 85, 174	Kenton, Mary	65
Johnston, Sue	259	Kay, Charles	125, 129, 153, 172, 176, 195, 196, 216, 230	Kermack, Paul	61
Johnstone, Hope	131			Kerr, David	174, 181
Jones, Alan	118	Kay, Richard	155	Kerridge, Mary	77
Jones, Barry	66	Kay, Sylvia	253	Kerrigan, Patricia	229
Jones, Catherine Zeta	276	Kaye, Lila	78, 108, 193, 194, 207	Kerry, James	97
Jones, Delme Bryn	154	Kaye, Romana	151	Kershaw, Noreen	280
Jones, Dwyryd Wyn	16	Kaye, Stubby	87	Kersten, Katja	170, 181
Jones, Dylan	180	Keane, David	235	Key, Alison	207
Jones, Emrys	40, 74	Keating, Charles	139, 157, 185	Key, Janet	121, 138, 226
Jones, Freddie	91, 93, 146, 152, 230, 276	Keegan, Bob	196	Khalil, Ahmed	142
		Keegan, John	233	Kidd, Josie	212
Jones, Gemma	85, 92, 103, 125, 242, 253, 272, 278	Keegan, Robert	141, 188	Kihlstedt, Rya	281
		Keen, Diane	125, 137	Kilgarriff, Michael	39, 157
Jones, Griff Rhys	228	Keen, Malcolm	27, 48, 55	Kind, Sophie	184
Jones, James Earl	281	Keen, Pat	130, 161	King, Dave	223
Jones, Ken	229	Keen, Rhett	225	King, Diana	36
Jones, Maggie	120	Keenan, John	156	King, Rowena	272
Jones, Mark	101, 104	Keir, Andrew	68, 70, 90, 107, 187	Kingsley, Ben	143
Jones, Mary	15			Kingston, Alex	279
Jones, Meurig	17	Kelland, John	78	Kingston, Mark	205, 215, 226
Jones, Nicholas	183, 210, 254, 263, 268	Kelleher, Tina	256	Kirby, Amanda	151, 158, 172
		Kellermann, Barbara	124, 139, 165, 196, 198, 215, 237, 252	Kirman, Dervla	259
Jones, Norman	86, 128, 173			Kitchen, Michael	125, 130, 240, 264, 272, 275, 281
Jones, Peter	3, 72, 178	Kelly, Catherine	268		
Jones, Simon	178, 185, 210	Kelly, Clare	188	Klaff, Jack	230
Jones, Tegid Wyn	16	Kelly, Elizabeth	115	Klouda, Anthony	54
Jones-Davies, Sue	138, 180	Kelly, Gerard	170	Knapp, Sebastian	231
Jordan, Desmond	51	Kelly, Hugh	10	Kneale, Patricia	36, 57
Jordan, Kerry	67	Kelly, Kevin	30	Knight, Ashley	149, 172
Joseph, Joanna	223	Kelly, Ruth	268	Knight, David	41, 109
Joseph, Phillip	184	Kelly, Sam	233	Knight, Esmond	27, 52, 57, 107
Joye, Janet	4	Kelly, Tom	156	Knight, Rosalind	27, 66, 187
Judd, Edward	89, 159	Kelsall, Moultrie	52	Knightley, Will	259
Judd, John	229	Kelsey, Edward	210	Knox, Alexander	18, 163
Judd, Leslie	38	Kelton, William	156	Kohler, Estelle	140
Jules, Jenny	267	Kemp, Jason	106, 111	Kohlund, Erwin	215
Junkin, John	82, 117	Kemp, Jeremy	74, 244	Kossoff, David	8
Jurgens, Curt	125, 192	Kemp, Martin	260	Kriegel, Kathie	241
Justice, Barry	69, 73, 124	Kempner, Brenda	116	Krige, Alice	271
Justin, John	39	Kempson, Rachel	106, 111, 129, 148, 203, 216, 232	Kriss, Peter	66, 73
				Kristen, Anne	82, 119, 127, 170, 187, 204
Kaash, Mamta	240	Kendal, Felicity	102, 133, 261		
Kahler, Wolf	205	Kendall, Cavan	22, 24, 36, 42, 95, 141, 165, 183, 188	Krupinski, Renny	280
Kahn, Jonathan	130			Kukura, George	242
Kane, Marvin	18	Kendall, Jo	96, 105, 149, 177, 209	Kumar, Ajay	220
Kanska, Joanna	254	Kendrick, Bryan	32	Kumar, Ashok	212
Kapoor, Ravi	281	Kennedy, Cheryl	113	Kunz, Scott	143
Karner, Brigitte	232	Kennedy, Fiona	108	Kyd, Susan	217
Kasket, Harold	14	Kenny, Darren	277	Kydd, Sam	7, 79
Kaufmann, Maurice	37, 42			Kyle, Leslie	16

Lacey, Catherine	116	
Lacey, Ingrid	272	
Lacey, Ronald	133, 140	
Lack, Simon	125	
Laga'aia, Jay Lavea	260	
Laing, Stuart	281	
Lake, Alan	97	
Lamb, Charles	117	
Lamb, Larry	279	
Lambert, Anne Louise	185, 191	
Lambert, Annie	218	
Lambert, Diana	23, 34	
Lambert, Jack	25	
Lambert, Nigel	38, 171	
Lambert, Thomas	258	
Lamden, Derek	83	
Lamont, Duncan	10, 18, 20	
Land, Anthony	9	
Landen, Dinsdale	37, 133, 139, 281	
Lander, Eric	17, 53	
Landone, Alice	3	
Landry, Aude	161	
Landry, John F.	124	
Lane, Julia	276	
Lane, Matthew	17	
Lang, Belinda	200	
Lang, Howard	209	
Lang, Robert	161, 189, 244, 253, 272	
Langerman, Debra	174	
Langford, David	26	
Langford, Robin	117, 184	
Langova, Sylva	23	
Langrishe, Caroline	155, 196, 230	
Langton, David	23, 56, 92, 94, 114, 170, 174, 181, 196	
Lansbury, Kate	86	
Lanyon, Anabelle	187	
Lapotaire, Jane	115, 133, 147, 153, 239, 265	
Larder, Geoffrey	171	
Large, Paul	62	
Latham, Philip	40, 54, 92, 124	
Latimer, Hugh	117	
Latimer, Michael	145	
Laurenson, James	109, 111, 134, 146, 180, 190	
Laurie, Hugh	273	
Laurie, John	6, 11, 20, 108	
Laurie, Piper	215	
Laurimore, Jon	89	
Law, Phyllida	120, 172, 186, 242	
Lawford, Ralph	176	
Lawrence, Delphi	40, 60	
Lawrence, Josie	252	
Lawrence, Patricia	140, 176	
Lawrence, Shirley	51	
Lawson, Denis	218, 240, 263	
Lawson, Gerald	17	
Lawson, Leigh	154	
Lawson, Sarah	21, 75	
Lawton, Ralph	142	
Layden, Kate	153	
Leach, Rosemary	104, 154, 203, 206, 244, 257, 282	
Leader, Carol	204	
Leake, Barbara	97	
Leaman, Graham	112	
Learner, David	178	
Leaver, Philip	8	
le Bars, Jeanne	57, 60	
Lebor, Stanley	265, 272	
Le Conte, Marilyn	149	
Lee, Annabelle	33, 36, 40	
Leech, Richard	34, 64, 78, 80, 91	
Leggatt, Alison	70	
Lehmann, Beatrix	77, 88, 130, 148, 161	
Lehmann, Carla	6	
Leigh, Spencer	199	
Leigh-Hunt, Barbara	108, 255	
Leigh-Hunt, Ronald	50	
Leith, Audine	73	
Lennard, Philip	8	
Lennie, Angus	85	
Leno, Charles	63	
Leon, Annie	179	
Leonard, David	217	
Le Prevost, Nicholas	261	
Lermitte, Robin	213, 256	
Leslie, Barbara	38, 58	
Leslie, Bethel	72	
Lesser, Anton	158, 160, 207, 210, 264	
Letch, David	217	
Le Touzel, Sylvestra	145, 178, 201, 282	
Letts, Barry	16, 24, 28, 29, 32, 33, 38, 40, 48, 51, 58, 62	
Letts, Pauline	34, 71	
Le Vaillant, Nigel	238	
Leventon, Annabel	164, 217	
Levy, Katharine	130	
Lewis, Julia	150	
Lewis, Rhoda	142, 158, 195, 196	
Lewis, Richard James	153	
Lewis, Russell	172	
Leyton, John	129	
Lill, Denis	125, 135, 155, 233, 244	
Lilley, Valerie	235, 280	
Lincoln, Mary	4	
Lind, Gillian	5, 27, 67	
Linden, Jennie	143, 155	
Linder, Cec	35	
Lindholm, Maureen	57	
Lindo, Olga	20, 24, 78	
Lindsay, Helen	24, 37, 63	
Lindsay, Robert	243, 255, 279	
Linehan, Barry	86, 93, 108, 112	
Lines, Graham	92	
Lingard, Dennis	106	
Linney, Laura	271	
Lipman, Maureen	225	
Lister, Clement	12	
Lister, Renny	52, 64, 70	
Little, Geoff	262	
Little, George	70, 186	
Littleton, David	98	
Littleton, Kenneth	98	
Liversidge, June	87	
Livesay, Bernard	25	
Livesay, Peggy	7, 23	
Livesay, Roger	92	
Livingstone, Andrew	153	
Llewellyn, Desmond	27, 54, 126	
Llewellyn, Raymond	98	
Lloyd, Anne	75	
Lloyd, Bernard	162	
Lloyd, Gabrielle	146, 223, 237	
Lloyd, Kevin	228	
Lloyd, Lala	130	
Lloyd, Rosalind	110, 172	
Lloyd, Tracey	60	
Lock, Kate	171	
Locke, Philip	78, 88	
Lockford, Lesa	226	
Lockhart, Calvin	83	
Lockwood, Julia	10, 13, 60	
Lockwood, Margaret	27	
Lockwood, Preston	144	
Loder, John	19, 24	
Lodge, Andrew	150	
Lodge, David	162	
Lodge, Ruth	40	
Loe, Judy	118, 206, 224	
Logan, Jimmy	198	
Logan, Phyllis	270	
Lohr, Marie	36	
Long, Adele	9	
Long, Charlotte	184	
Long, Matthew	139, 148	
Longden, John	29	
Longdon, Terence	37, 81, 85	
Longhurst, Jeremy	154	
Longworth, Eric	77	

PLAYERS

Lonnen, Ray	131, 192
Lonsdale, Angela	279
Lonsdale, Michael	192
Lord, Justine	64
Lorimer, Carole	3, 4, 6
Lorimer, Shirley	6
Lorne, Constance	93
Lorraine, Paul	36
Lott, Barbara	5, 24, 136, 154
Lott, David	65
Love, Patti	152
Lovell, Dyson	88
Lovell, Roderick	18
Lowe, Arthur	113, 130
Lowe, Barry	52
Lucas, William	19, 21, 33, 37, 49, 57, 95, 170, 174, 181
Luckham, Cyril	62, 65, 67, 68, 74, 86, 90, 95, 120, 129, 137, 160, 162, 176, 194, 226
Luckie, Michael	56
Lukis, Adrian	241
Lumley, Joanna	255
Lunghi, Cherie	157, 163, 203, 221, 281
Lye, Reg	121
Lyn, David	154
Lynch, Alfred	76, 125, 162
Lynch, Barry	232
Lynch, John	256
Lynch, Sean	32
Lyndhurst, Nicholas	128, 138
Lyne, Damien	224
Lyon, David	252
Ma, Peter	156
Maas, Sybil	229
Maberly, Polly	223
MacAlaster, Margot	123
Macarthur, Edith	107, 119
MacCarthy, Karin	112
MacCorkindale, Simon	123, 165
Macdermott, Kevin	236
MacDonald, Stephen	68
MacGowran, Tara	256
Macgregor, Barry	4, 9, 42
Machin, Peter	218
Macintosh, Kenneth	8
Mackay, Fulton	68, 126, 132, 146
Mackenzie, Mary	40
Mackerrel, Vivian	87
Mackey, Beatrix	57, 60
Mackintosh, Steven	224, 271
MacLennan, Elizabeth	80, 224
MacLeod, Kenneth	9
MacLeod, Robert	84
MacNaughtan, Alan	87, 110, 132, 139, 176, 235, 239
Macrae, Duncan	66
Macready, Carol	183, 228
Macready, Roy	158
Macready, Susan	92
Madden, Ciaran	105, 160, 180, 198
Madden, Peter	56
Madigan, Amy	279
Madoc, Philip	70, 75, 89, 105, 118, 127, 144, 152, 180, 237
Magee, Patrick	50, 150, 160, 161
Maguire, Leo	20, 25
Maguire, Leonard	41, 66, 89, 119, 120
Maguire, Michael	17, 26, 30
Maiker, Cheryl	220, 240
Mair-Thomas, Sara	282
Major, David	134
Makepeace, Deborah	119, 130, 164
Malahide, Patrick	148, 209, 219, 223, 234, 236, 258, 266, 274
Malcolm, Christopher	193
Malcolm, John	169
Malik, Art	203, 216, 279
Maloney, Michael	187, 262, 277, 281
Malpas, George	223
Manahan, Sheila	48
Mango, Alec	31
Manktelow, Henrietta	201
Mann, Steven	180
Manning, Henry	77
Mansi, John	14
Mansi, Louis	81
Mantez, Dolores	56
Mantle, Doreen	120, 145, 265
Manuel, Antony	169
Manville, Lesley	267, 269, 277, 281
Marden, Peter	54
Margolyes, Miriam	134, 177, 207, 215, 222, 225
Markham, David	3, 5, 23, 67, 81, 146, 154, 180
Markham, Harry	134, 149
Markham, Kika	73, 116, 180, 270
Markham, Petra	69
Marks, Alfred	222
Marle, Arnold	31
Marlow, June	204
Marlowe, Anthony	18
Marlowe, Linda	252, 282
Marlowe, William	87
Marmont, Patricia	26
Marner, Richard	174, 212
Marriott-Watson, Nan	64, 66
Marsden, Betty	7, 205, 219
Marsden, Roy	88, 197, 204, 211, 212, 216, 237, 253
Marsh, Carol	27
Marsh, Jean	243
Marsh, Keith	138
Marsh, Matthew	221, 237, 242
Marsh, Reginald	86
Marshall, Alex	105
Marshall, Bryan	84, 88, 94, 103, 104, 107, 133, 134, 161, 162
Marshall, Juliet	97
Marson, Ania	114
Martell, Gillian	147
Marten, Barbara	265, 270
Martin, Derek	147, 152
Martin, Hugh	191, 199
Martin, John Scott	233
Martin, Mel	107, 109, 124, 148, 211, 236, 244, 257
Martin, Rosemary	185, 205, 223, 278
Martin, Vivienne	29, 177
Martins, Orlando	4
Maryott, Susan	30, 36, 55
Mason, Hilary	27, 47, 146, 205, 210, 222, 224
Mason, James	108
Mason, Margery	150, 172
Mason, Raymond	146
Massey, Anna	124, 151, 159, 189, 201, 241
Massey, Daniel	104, 114, 189, 201, 226
Massie, Paul	123
Masters, Donald	31
Matheson, Eve	230
Matthews, A.E.	27
Matthews, Francis	17, 55, 62, 219
Matthews, Jessie	157
Matthews, John	263
Matthews, Samuel	143
Maude, Mary	151
Maur, Meinhart	8
Maureen, Mollie	117
Mavers, Gary	269
Maw, Janet	151, 190, 194
Maxwell, James	76, 79, 88, 111, 114, 141, 176
Maxwell, Lois	72
Maxwell, Paul	158
Maxwell, Roger	10, 13

May, Bunny	14	
May, Charmian	228	
May, Jack	21, 29, 53, 152	
May, Jodhi	250, 281	
May, Julie	118	
Maybank, Carole	7	
Maynard, Bill	127	
Maynard, Judi	172, 263	
Maynard, Patricia	105, 145	
Mayne, Ferdy	57	
Mayock, Peter	55	
McAleer, Des	233, 277	
McAnally, Ray	84, 122, 231, 235, 256	
McArdle, John	260, 267, 279	
McAvoy, Alex	127	
McCaffrey, Robin	219	
McCall, Ross	272	
McCallum, David	39, 47, 161, 243	
McCallum, Eileen	140, 198	
McCallum, Joanna	201, 209, 236	
McCann, Donal	124	
McCarthy, Julia	148	
McCarthy, Maggie	282	
McCarthy, Neil	52, 60, 83	
McCarthy, Siobhan	265	
McClelland, Eliza	172	
McCorkindale, Donald	17	
McCormick, Denise	234	
McCowen, Alec	29, 37, 73	
McCoy, Sylvester	211	
McCracken, Jenny	186, 222, 249	
McCrindle, Jenny	257	
McCulloch, Andrew	205	
McCulloch, Ian	89, 108, 129	
McCutcheon, Gillian	155	
McDermot, Neil	90	
McDermott, Brian	67	
McDowall, Betty	19, 28, 49, 57, 62	
McDowell, Trevyn	274	
McElhinney, Ian	236, 272, 282	
McEnery, John	120, 140, 153, 193, 271	
McEnery, Peter	77, 158	
McEwan, Geraldine	13, 151, 194, 213, 249	
McGann, Mark	219	
McGann, Paul	221, 265	
McGann, Stephen	275	
McGee, Henry	79	
McGinley, Sean	277	
McGlynn, John	261, 276	
McGough, Philip	221, 249	
McGrath, Graham	184, 223	
McGregor, Ewan	268, 271	
McGuire, Lloyd	204	
McHale, Rosemary	237, 256, 259	
McIntire, Janet	64	
McIntosh, Ellen	31, 135	
McIntosh, Robert	217	
McIntyre, Duncan	9	
McKail, David	135	
McKechnie, James	6	
McKellen, Ian	78, 271	
McKelvey, John	102, 104, 109	
McKenna, Breffni	269	
McKenna, Christine	119, 159	
McKenna, T.P.	187, 213, 215, 253, 271	
McKenna, Virginia	122, 261	
McKenzie, Jack	170, 194	
McKenzie, Jacqueline	273	
McKenzie, Julia	186, 211	
McKenzie, Kate	234	
McKern, Leo	140	
McKern, Roger	207	
McKinley, Jean	151	
McLaughlin, Lise-Ann	225	
McLaughlin, Michael	174	
McManus, Mark	126, 134, 173, 199	
McMillan, Roddy	41, 55, 66, 68, 82, 127, 141, 164	
McMurray, Edward	85	
McNally, Kevin	153, 178, 200, 204, 232, 233, 243, 270	
McNamara, Desmond	218	
McNeice, Ian	195, 216, 236, 259, 266	
McNicol, Lawrie	226	
McShane, Ian	87, 153, 154	
McSharry, Carmel	59, 218, 230	
McTeer, Janet	251	
Meadows, Stanley	152	
Meager, Jill	204, 208	
Meagher, Karen	199, 235	
Mealing, Amanda	250, 275	
Measor, Beryl	36	
Measures, Shelley	223	
Meier, Michael	56	
Meillon, John	59	
Meisner, Gunter	183	
Melia, Joe	178	
Mellinger, Leonie	179, 232	
Mellinger, Michael	10, 236	
Mellor, Cherith	127, 135, 188	
Melly, Andree	31	
Melvin, Murray	86	
Merchant, Vivien	170, 175	
Merlin, Derek	226	
Merrall, Mary	49	
Merrick, Pamela	213	
Merrick, Simon	24	
Merrison, Clive	139, 163, 233	
Merrow, Jane	65	
Merton, Zienia	110	
Mervyn, William	13, 59, 73, 75	
Meyer, Hans	128	
Michael, Ralph	53, 78, 175, 186	
Michaels, Sandra	22, 37	
Michell, Helena	253	
Michell, Keith	101	
Michie, John	277	
Middlemass, Frank	161, 173, 176, 207, 215	
Middleton, Anna	66	
Middleton, Noelle	17	
Mileham, Mark	54	
Miles, Bernard	3, 26	
Miles, Lisabeth	180, 227	
Miles, Maria	276	
Miles, Sally	126	
Miles, Sarah	275	
Miles, Vanessa	102	
Mill, Callum	95, 119	
Mill, Robert	76	
Millbank, Julia	218	
Miller, Brian	217, 228	
Miller, Joan	6, 76	
Miller, Maria	249	
Miller, Rosemary	21, 50, 158	
Milligan, Stuart	243	
Millross, Raymond	102	
Mills, Frank	97, 120, 127, 177	
Mills, Hayley	183	
Mills, John	165, 241, 278	
Mills, Michael	141	
Milman, Alexandra	269	
Milner, Roger	195	
Milton, Ernest	6	
Mirodan, Vladimir	230	
Mirren, Helen	107, 160, 254, 267, 273	
Mitchell, Ann	197, 282	
Mitchell, Charlotte	107	
Mitchell, Leslie	118	
Mitchell, Sasha	214	
Mitchell, Yvonne	119	
Moffat, Donald	271	
Moffatt, John	32, 88	
Mogaji, Akim	251	
Mohyeddin, Zia	87, 203, 220, 240	
Molina, Alfred	268	
Molinas, Richard	23	
Molloy, Dearbhla	255	
Monaghan, Leonard	35	

Monkhouse, Bob		273
Montague, Lee		145
Moody, Jeanne		96
Moody, Ron		218
Moody, Ronald		12
Moon, Georgina		112
Moore, Emily		170, 174
Moore, Harry		28
Moore, Jonathan		213
Moore, Richard		283
Moore, Stephen		118, 211, 232, 274, 277
Moore, William		96
Moorey, Frank		155
Moran, Pauline		195, 208
Morand, Sylvester		116
Morand, Tim		132
Morant, Angela		180
Morant, Richard		110, 118, 178, 198, 211, 227, 228
Moray, Heather		187
More, Kenneth		79, 82, 87, 116
Morell, Andre		35
Moreton, Kevin		120, 138
Morgan, Anita		49
Morgan, Charles		101
Morgan, Elizabeth		136, 220
Morgan, Garfield		116
Morgan, Priscilla		170
Morgan, Terence		30
Morgan, Wendy		203
Moriarty, Paul		115
Morison, Elsie		7
Morley, Donald		22, 23
Morley, Robert		200
Morrell, André		153
Morris, Artro		150
Morris, Aubrey		57, 95
Morris, Beth		130, 142
Morris, Deirdra		190
Morris, Edna		40
Morris, Gavin J.		280
Morris, Jonathon		193, 198, 208
Morris, Lana		27, 34, 39, 51, 60, 65, 70, 82
Morris, Mary		62
Morris, Maureen		237
Morris, Sarah Jane		233
Morris, Vernon		30
Morris, Wolfe		104
Morrison, Diana		238
Morrissey, David		199, 266, 279
Morrissey, Neil		272
Morse, Barry		114
Morse, Natalie		228, 252
Mort, Patricia		71
Mort, Ray		140
Mortimer, Caroline		90, 177, 195
Mortimer, Emily		280
Morton, Clive		12, 36, 110, 118
Morton, Hugh		159
Morton, Joe		197
Morton, Samantha		283
Moss, Mark		145
Mottley, Eva		197
Moulder-Brown, John		91, 158, 163
Mount, Peggy		11
Mowat, David		119
Moway, Nicole		254
Mower, Patrick		67, 80, 138, 200
Mowlam, Carole		54, 188
Mughan, Sharon		183, 195, 201, 209
Muller, Endre		38
Muller-Scherz, Fritz		242
Mullins, Bartlett		131
Muncke, Christopher		176
Munro, Janet		94
Munro, Tim		184
Munro, Truan		280
Murch, Polly		107
Murdoch, Bryden		62, 132
Murphy, Anthony		110
Murphy, Cathy		219
Murphy, Fidelma		154
Murphy, Gerard		160, 210
Murphy, Pixie		9
Murray, Amanda		172
Murray, Barbara		39, 58, 124
Murray, Bryan		52, 213, 235
Murray, Daniel		171
Murray, Patrick		122
Murray, Sean		274, 278
Murray, Stephen		18, 28, 36, 106
Myers, Peter		119
Nail, Jimmy		279
Naismith, Laurence		125, 189
Nash, Sarah		134
Nayar, Nisha		271
Neal, Siri		232, 259
Neame, Christopher		111, 113, 133, 195
Needs, Simon		215
Neil, Hildegard		95, 130, 180
Neilson, Catherine		236
Neilson, David		261
Neilson, Perlita		39, 47, 183
Neilson, Sandy		227
Neilson-Terry, Phyllis		29
Nelligan, Kate		144, 171, 175
Nellist, Dave		282
Nelson, Kenneth		216
Nesbit, Cathleen		129
Nettles, John		104, 109
Nettleton, John		106, 195
Neve, Suzanne		56, 68, 77, 88, 107
Neville, Daphne		144
Neville, John		97
Neville, Sarah		206
Neville, Tamzin		144
Newark, Derek		118
Newell, Joan		11
Newell, Michelle		195
Newell, Patrick		56, 78, 110
Newlands, Anthony		18, 22, 56, 57, 70
Newman, Daniel		265, 272
Newman, Nanette		136, 182
Newport, Karen		102
Newport, Michael		93
Newth, Jonathan		113, 181, 183, 206
Newton, Daphne		34
Newton, Madelaine		276
Neylin, James		34
Nice, Penelope		236
Nicholas, Anna		182
Nicholas, Eileen		235
Nicholas, Jeremy		177, 209
Nicholls, Anthony		14, 63
Nicholls, Kate		124, 130, 146
Nicholls, Phoebe		185
Nichols, Dandy		64, 132
Nicholson, Audrey		49
Nicholson, Nora		24
Nicols, Rosemary		67, 81, 109
Nicolson, Steve		278
Nielson, Catherine		235
Nielson, Claire		95
Nightingale, Lesley		202, 216, 233
Nighy, Bill		257
Nimmo, Dudy		25
Nimmons, Carole		190
Nisbet, Neil		192
Noakes, John		74
Nolan, John		102, 160
Nolan, Victoria		13
Normington, John		120, 147, 157, 231
Norris, Hermione		251, 258
Norris, Jonathan		249
North, Caroline		98
Northam, Jeremy		262
Norton, Alex		172, 274
Norton, Martin		76
Nossek, Ralph		29
Nri, Cyril		275

PLAYERS 323

Nunnerley, Lesley 102, 104, 109
Nye, Pat 90

O'Brien, Edna 222
O'Brien, Kieran 270
O'Brien, Maureen 156, 160, 164
O'Brien, Philip 176
O'Callaghan, Richard 219
O'Casey, Roland 21
O'Connell, Maurice 153
O'Connor, Derrick 187, 220, 251, 273
O'Connor, Hazel 220
O'Connor, Sarah 38, 54
O'Conor, Joseph 14, 72, 73, 79, 83, 90, 94, 116
O'Farrell, Maureen 197
O'Hara, David 257
O'Herlihy, Dan 187, 208
O'Herlihy, Gavin 226
O'Leary, Bryon 69
O'Neil, Colette 84, 88, 170
O'Neill, Maggie 240, 263, 265
O'Rawe, Geraldine 235
O'Sullivan, Richard 26
O'Toole, Peter 239
Oates, Simon 169
Ogilvy, Ian 103, 112, 127, 137, 142, 234
Ogle, Natalie 165, 170, 222
Ogwen, John 127, 152
Okun, Alun 7
Oldman, Gary 207
Oliver, Donald 39
Olivier, Laurence 185, 222
Oparei, Dhobi 251
Ormond, Julia 242
Osborn, Andrew 13, 15, 34, 39
Osborn, Sally 175, 187
Osborne, Joy 60
Oscar, Henry 24, 64
Oulton, Brian 117, 217
Ousdal, Sverre Anker 211
Ove, Indra 282
Owen, Bill 93
Owen, Christopher 111
Owen, Glyn 21, 24, 94, 103
Owen, Harriet 267
Owen, Kendrick 150
Owen, Lloyd 276
Owen, Meg Wynn 61, 63, 71, 190
Owen, Tom 152
Owens, John 172
Owens, Richard 105
Oxenford, Daphne 191, 223

Pa, Rowena 156
Pace, Norman 276
Pack, Roger Lloyd 255
Packer, Tina 78
Padden, Graham 205
Padwick, Anne 38
Page, Katharine 30
Page, Mark 206
Pagett, Nicola 113, 149
Pairie, Elspeth 62
Pakarinen, Alpo 182
Pakravan, Shahnaz 240
Palfrey, Yolande 152, 161
Palin, Michael 255
Palk, Anna 70, 84
Palmer, Edward 89
Palmer, Geoffrey 197, 238
Palmer, Richard 26, 54, 58
Palmer, Toni 223
Paoli, Cecile 174, 244
Parfitt, Amanda 179
Parfitt, David 149, 156, 187
Parfitt, Judy 73, 78, 86, 103, 126, 160, 170, 175, 203, 219, 243, 250, 257, 266, 272
Parker, Althea 117
Parker, Anthony 68
Parker, Claire 229
Parker, Nathaniel 250, 266
Parkins, Barbara 129
Parnaby, Alan 159, 209
Parnaby, Bert 209
Parr, Katherine 49
Parr, Melanie 69
Parrish, Clifford 70, 117
Parry, Natasha 70, 154, 160
Parsons, Alibe 142
Parsons, Nicholas 72
Partington, Frank 48
Pasco, Richard 40, 81, 196, 206
Pastell, George 28, 73
Patch, Wally 40
Patel, Harish 271
Paterson, Bill 153, 162, 177, 192, 223, 242, 264
Patrick, Anna 269, 282
Patrick, John 180
Pattenden, Sian 201
Patterson, David 131
Paul, Betty 9
Paul, John 38, 65, 84, 110, 180
Payne, Laurence 14, 21, 78
Payne, Sandra 165
Peach, Mary 82, 154
Peacock, Trevor 165, 178, 258

Peake-Jones, Tessa 170, 187, 210
Pearce, Jacqueline 130
Pearce, Joanne 178
Pearce, Sally 14
Pearce, Timothy 55
Pearson, Fred 188, 280
Pearson, Lloyd 21, 52
Pearson, Richard 27, 34, 39, 41, 49, 51, 66, 92, 97, 187
Peasgood, Julie 145, 237
Peck, Bob 216, 251, 263
Peck, Brian 27, 67
Peel, David 21, 37, 55
Peisley, Frederick 110
Pellegrino, Vince 279
Pember, Ron 121, 207
Pemberton, Antonia 224
Pender, Tommy 134
Penhaligon, Susan 114, 139, 188, 226
Penn, Dallia 76, 78, 80, 83
Pennell, Nicholas 71, 74, 81, 83
Pennington, John 137
Pennington, Michael 92, 207, 244
Percy, Esme 12
Perret, Jean-Marc 244, 252
Perrins, Leslie 49
Perry, Jeffrey 237
Perry, Morris 22, 70, 74, 84
Persaud, Stephen 240
Pertwee, Sean 258
Peters, Arnold 148
Peters, Clarke 234
Peters, Lorraine 31
Peters, Timothy 114
Petherbridge, Edward 193, 227, 228, 236
Phelan, David 226
Phethean, David 40, 75
Philburn, David 199
Phillips, Conrad 26, 79, 86
Phillips, Dorothea 117
Phillips, Gregory 60
Phillips, John 21, 41, 66, 68, 73, 75, 89, 96, 124, 140, 200
Phillips, Jonathan 258
Phillips, Leslie 244, 277, 283
Phillips, Neil 188, 214
Phillips, Redmond 36, 53
Phillips, Sian 126, 129, 138, 142, 152, 154, 160, 161, 183, 226, 230, 265, 272
Phillpotts, Ambrosine 78
Pickard, Raymond 278
Pickering, Donald 118, 119

Pickering, Roland	96	
Pickles, Carolyn	180, 194, 218	
Pickles, John	123	
Pickles, Vivian	82, 86, 106, 176	
Pickles, Wilfred	129	
Pickup, Ronald	122, 129, 133, 230, 237, 239, 244, 245, 252, 259, 275	
Pierce-Jones, John	214	
Pigott-Smith, Tim	139, 156, 172, 186, 189, 203	
Piper, Emma	196	
Piper, Frederick	71	
Pitney, Wemsley	8	
Pitt, Chris	213	
Planer, Nigel	245	
Platt, Sydonie	50	
Platt, Victor	26, 28	
Pleasance, Pat	28, 37	
Pleasant, Gordon	38	
Pleasence, Angela	101, 133, 194, 201	
Pleasence, Donald	36, 194, 281	
Plowright, Joan	4	
Polan, Linda	186	
Pollock, Ellen	58	
Pollon, Christine	110	
Poole, Michael	56	
Pooley, Olaf	12	
Pope, Alan	141	
Poplett, Deborah	263	
Porrett, Susan	195	
Porter, Beth	162	
Porter, Eric	83, 139, 149, 183, 203, 215	
Porter, Nyree Dawn	66, 69, 83	
Postlethwaite, Pete	278	
Potter, Carole	82, 84	
Potter, Martin	137, 185	
Powell, Robert	103, 105, 134, 258	
Power, Camilla	252	
Power, Rachel	274	
Powys, Rhys	138	
Prador, Irene	95	
Praid, Mark	105	
Pratt, Elaine	64	
Pratt, Mike	74, 130	
Pratt, Peter	123	
Pravda, George	23, 33, 36, 70, 78, 85, 96	
Pravda, Hana	64	
Preece, Tim	79, 101, 162, 175, 240	
Presle, Micheline	112	
Press, Fiona	273	
Preston, Leonard	171, 233	
Price, Dennis	13, 20	
Price, John	120, 127, 150	
Primrose, Dorothy	10	
Prince, Sarah	136, 149	
Pringle, Bryan	76, 177	
Pritchard, Nicholas	255	
Prochnik, Bruce	59	
Protheroe, Brian	221	
Proud, Elizabeth	126	
Provost, Nicholas le	203	
Prowse, Dave	182	
Pruckner, Tilo	242	
Pryce, Jonathan	255, 268	
Pryor, Maureen	29, 36, 48, 126, 130	
Pugh, David	195	
Pugh, Robert	233, 270	
Pullan, David	157	
Purcell, John	249	
Purcell, Roy	82	
Purchase, Bruce	77, 215	
Purdy, Susan	50	
Purefoy, James	275	
Purnell, Louise	77	
Purvis, Ken	106	
Putson, Stephanie	282	
Pyne, Natasha	67	
Pyott, Keith	65	
Qizilbash, Sahab	131	
Quarshie, Hugh	282	
Quayle, Anthony	243	
Quayle, John	3	
Quentin, Caroline	273	
Quentin, John	66, 84, 108, 118	
Quesnel, Pooky	279	
Quick, Diana	96, 113, 185, 190, 240, 258, 275	
Quigley, Godfrey	59, 74, 102	
Quigley, Pearce	260	
Quilley, Denis	40, 64, 77, 160, 196, 214, 241	
Quilligan, Veronica	178, 281	
Quilter, David	186, 227	
Quinn, Patricia	126, 142	
Radcliffe, Tom	253	
Radd, Ronald	26, 89	
Raffan, Peter	198	
Raghan, Michael	118	
Raglan, James	5, 11, 13, 14	
Raglan, Robert	16, 28, 72	
Raikes, Robert	16	
Raine, Gillian	18	
Raitt, Anne	128, 177, 225, 259	
Rampling, Jeremy	239	
Ramsay, Heather	223	
Ramsay, Louise	187	
Ramsden, Angela	28	
Ransome, Prunella	92, 141, 155, 206	
Ranson, Robin	36	
Rasche, David	281	
Ratcliffe, Martin	97	
Rathbone, Nigel	116	
Ratzenberger, John	232	
Ravenscroft, Christopher	124, 192, 230, 235	
Rawi, Raad	214	
Rawle, Jeff	250, 265	
Rawle-Hicks, Edward	206, 276	
Rawlings, Margaret	122	
Rawlins, Adrian	245, 281, 282	
Ray, Andrew	140, 157, 197, 234	
Ray, Philip	21	
Raymond, Gary	66, 79, 90, 96	
Raymond, Ronnie	33, 50, 56	
Rea, Stephen	199	
Redford, Ian	180	
Redgrave, Corin	89, 94	
Redgrave, Jemma	271	
Redgrave, Lynn	275	
Redgrave, Vanessa	78, 120	
Redman, Amanda	221, 257, 269	
Redman, Joyce	21, 77, 129, 275	
Redmayne, Darren	231	
Redmond, Moira	90, 131, 133	
Redwood, Manning	176	
Reed, Annemarie	102	
Reed, Myrtle	40	
Reed, Oliver	39	
Rees, Allyson	205	
Rees, Angharad	95, 136, 194	
Rees, Gaynor Morgan	154	
Rees, John	75	
Rees, Llewellyn	24, 85	
Rees, Roger	193	
Reeves, Kynaston	33, 39	
Reid, Anne	180	
Reid, Beryl	163, 212	
Reid, Don	204	
Reid, Malcolm	146	
Reid, Mary Ann	127	
Reid, Sheila	155	
Reid, Susannah	210	
Reid, Tony	232	
Reid, Trevor	42	
Reilly, Christopher	186	
Reiss, Amanda	157	
Relph, Emma	184	
Relton, William	77	
Remick, Lee	129	

Rennie, Hilary	10	
Rennie, Malcolm	170	
Reynalds, David	95	
Reynolds, Dorothy	76	
Reynolds, Hilary	233	
Reynolds, Malcolm	95	
Reynolds, Robert	230, 241	
Rhodes, Christopher	12	
Rhys, Paul	231, 267	
Rich, Gary	105	
Richard, Emily	142, 193, 195, 200, 213	
Richard, Irene	170, 179	
Richard, Josee	8	
Richards, Angela	103, 186	
Richards, Aubrey	125, 138	
Richards, Charlie	254	
Richards, Gavin	205	
Richardson, Charles	6	
Richardson, Ian	108, 164, 181, 190, 196, 228, 234, 250, 252, 257, 272	
Richardson, Isla	9	
Richardson, Jeremy	108	
Richardson, Joely	269	
Richardson, Miranda	252, 262	
Richfield, Edwin	92, 96, 98	
Richmond, Anthony	35	
Richmond, John	22, 117, 133	
Richmond, Susan	13	
Rickman, Alan	171, 194	
Riddle, Stephen	203	
Riddoch, Bill	249	
Rider, Paul	153	
Ridings, Richard	153	
Ridler, Anne	18, 71, 123, 140	
Ridley, Arthur	3, 7	
Rigby, Arthur	8	
Rigby, Terence	164, 173, 192, 209, 214	
Rigg, Carl	90	
Rigg, Diana	160, 213, 243	
Riley, Alrick	202	
Rimkus, Stevan	280	
Rimmer, Shane	182, 235, 268	
Rintoul, David	119, 140, 162, 170	
Ripper, Michael	35	
Ritchie, June	75, 90, 173, 200	
Ritchie, Vivienne	214	
Rix, Colin	139	
Roach, Pat	211	
Roache, Linus	278	
Robb, David	139, 142, 155, 164, 175, 183, 184, 221, 253	
Robbins, Michael	88	
Robert, Harold	41	
Roberts, Christian	112
Roberts, Ewan	66
Roberts, Ivor	135, 200
Roberts, J.H.	4
Roberts, Nancy	5
Roberts, Veronica	135
Robertson, Annette	101, 102
Robillard, Elizabeth	113
Robinson, Alan	27
Robinson, John	5, 17, 51
Robinson, Robert	97
Robinson, Sue	189
Robson, Flora	78, 128, 133, 160
Robson, Linda	192
Robson, Zuleika	85
Roche, Zhivila	107, 110
Rodger, Struan	251, 278
Rodgers, Anton	63, 95, 147, 155, 191, 241
Rodgers, Ilona	66
Rodigan, David	189
Rodrigues, Tania	249
Rodska, Ben	215
Rodska, Christian	128
Rodway, Norman	70, 153, 213
Roeves, Maurice	89, 94, 104, 111, 120, 181
Rogers, Mark	125, 135
Rogers, Mitzi	86
Rogers, Paul	144, 228
Roland, Jeanne	79
Rolfe, Guy	39, 239
Rolfe, Joanne	217
Rollett, Raymond	3, 19, 27, 37
Rollings, Gordon	117
Rolt, Toby	240
Romilly, Elizabeth	144
Ronane, John	76, 101
Root, Amanda	277
Roper, Brian	5
Roper-Knight, Courtney	219
Rosamond, Jayn	186
Rose, Clifford	118, 186
Rose, Tim	245
Rosebury, Paul	165
Rosin, Isabelle	122
Rosmer, Milton	5
Ross, Hector	7
Ross, Lee	264
Ross, Liza	140
Rossington, Norman	104, 108, 110
Rossiter, Leonard	80
Roth, Joanna	256, 257
Roth, Tim	220
Roubicek, George	182
Rouse, Simon	135, 153
Rousseau, Carolle	163
Routledge, Patricia	71, 130, 146, 233
Rouvel, Catherine	112
Rowbottom, Jo	104, 134, 142
Rowe, Alan	71, 74, 182
Rowe, Frances	15, 36
Rowland, Roger	229
Rowlands, Patsy	70, 90, 229
Rowsell, Janet	39
Rowson, Anthony	204
Roye, Anthony	126
Roylance, Nicholas	69
Royle, Carol	245
Rozycki, Christopher	208
Ruddock, John	19
Rudnick, Franz	199
Rush, Louise	102
Ruskin, Sheila	111, 138, 142, 174, 203, 228, 253
Russell, Billy	75, 91
Russell, Catherine	242
Russell, Clive	279
Russell, Gary	144
Russell, Geoffrey	252
Russell, Iris	41, 135
Russell, Ken	269
Russell, Mairhi	25
Russell, Theresa	272
Russell, William	17, 27, 49, 55, 64, 81
Ryan, Daniel	261
Ryan, Ger	277
Ryan, Helen	133, 136, 172, 180, 215
Ryan, Hilary	169
Ryan, Jacqueline	34
Ryan, Madge	132, 137, 148
Ryder, Gerard	164
Rye, Ann	78
Ryecart, Patrick	155, 160, 178, 214, 255
Ryu, Daisuke	245
Sachak, Aftab	220
Sachs, Andrew	60, 75, 171, 267
Sachs, Leonard	4, 139
Sachs, Robin	146, 202
Sadler, Martin	232
Sagar, Anthony	62, 113
Saint, Tony	196
Saire, Rebecca	176, 230, 237
Salaman, Chloe	184
Salaman, Clara	262
Salaman, Toby	174

Salem, Pamela	198	
Salew, John	30	
Sallis, Peter	9, 30, 39, 55, 60, 64, 136, 147, 203, 253	
Salmon, Colin	267	
Salthouse, John	147	
Samson, Ivan	7, 11	
Sanchez, Penelope Cruz	266	
Sanderson, Joan	38, 58	
Sanderson, Michael	274	
Sarruf, Valerie	70	
Saul, Nitza	186	
Saunders, Elizabeth	5	
Saunders, Stuart	21	
Savage, Dominic	172	
Savile, David	86, 107, 116	
Sawalha, Julia	278	
Sawalha, Nadim	122	
Saxon, James	230	
Saxton, Granville	165, 175	
Sayer, Philip	218, 229	
Sayle, Alexei	250, 255	
Saynor, Ian	162, 173	
Sbath, Jocelyne	97	
Scales, Prunella	5, 47, 213, 275, 281	
Scantlebury, Guy	231	
Scarborough, Victoria	276	
Schaller, Jody	101	
Schell, Catherine	108, 113, 134, 174, 181	
Schlesinger, Katherine	224	
Schofield, David	189, 229, 283	
Schofield, Katharine	93, 162	
Schofield, Leslie	170	
Schofield, Peter	108	
Scofield, Paul	278	
Scott Thomas, Kristin	269	
Scott, Alex	34, 66, 97	
Scott, Delene	50	
Scott, Harold	15	
Scott, Joan	97	
Scott, Jonathan R.	237, 244, 245	
Scott, Margaretta	25, 106, 227	
Scott-Barrett, Marcus	165	
Scott-Patton, Lindsay	54	
Scott-Taylor, Jonathan	158	
Scoular, Angela	83, 87, 164	
Scoular, Christopher	200, 211	
Scully, Terry	91, 149	
Seagrove, Jenny	189, 190, 204	
Sears, Ian	202	
Seaton, Derek	96	
Seel, Ceri	184, 215	
Seely, Tim	51	
Segal, Jeffrey	118	
Selby, Nicholas	80, 106, 111	
Selby, Tony	218	
Selby-Plewman, Tommy	252	
Sellars, Elizabeth	196, 205	
Selwyn, Louis	84, 115	
Sereys, Jacques	250, 258	
Serkis, Andy	279	
Sessions, John	228, 234, 257	
Seth, Roshan	271	
Seton, Bruce	10	
Settelen, Peter	156, 170	
Sevretan, Lance	10	
Sewell, George	159, 164	
Sewell, Rufus	274	
Seymour, Jane	115, 132, 140	
Seymour, Shaughan	164, 203, 239	
Shackley, John	184, 215	
Shah, Jamal	242	
Shalet, Victoria	269	
Shall, Gary	145	
Shand, Ian	58	
Shankley, Amelia	225	
Shanks, Rosalind	134, 137	
Shaps, Cyril	29, 181	
Sharkey, James	40, 48	
Sharma, Madhav	220	
Sharman, Marigold	111	
Sharp, Anthony	18	
Sharp, John	69, 141	
Sharp, Lesley	275	
Sharp, Richard	42	
Sharpe, Deborah-Jane	207	
Sharplin, John	28	
Sharrock, Ken	217	
Shaughnessy, David	198	
Shaw, Barnaby	116	
Shaw, Fiona	254	
Shaw, Kevin	212	
Shaw, Martin	212, 254	
Shaw, Maxwell	20, 22, 42	
Shaw, Sebastian	50, 165, 242	
Shawzin, Barry	24	
Sheard, Michael	135, 207	
Sheard, Simon	165	
Sheen, Michael	267	
Shelden, Jana	176, 187	
Shelley, Barbara	34, 66, 163, 239	
Shelley, Frank	47	
Shelley, Joanna	108	
Shelley, Paul	89, 169, 175, 221, 257	
Shepherd, Elizabeth	41, 53, 55, 76, 157, 190, 195	
Shepherd, Jack	134, 153, 179, 275	
Shepherd, Simon	180, 239
Sheppard, Morgan	153
Shepstone, Sheri	238
Sher, Antony	178
Shergold, Adrian	111
Sheridan, Dinah	172
Sherrier, Julian	102
Sherwin, Derrick	50
Sheybal, Vladek	159, 192
Shingler, Helen	14
Shipley, Julie	173
Shipp, Stephen	98
Shrapnel, John	106, 157, 190, 196, 245, 251, 255
Shumway, Phyllis	6
Siberry, Michael	217, 241
Sibley, David	191
Sidney, Derek	56
Sieman, Frank	51
Silberg, Tusse	211
Silburn, Luke	179
Silburn, Tom	179
Silvera, Carmen	121
Sim, Alastair	91
Simkins, Michael	262
Simmonds, Melissa	228
Simmons, Jean	256
Simon, Josette	265
Simons, William	13, 14
Simpson, Bill	120, 161
Simpson, Diana	91
Simpson, Peter	142
Sinclair, Barry	136
Sinclair, Belinda	228
Sinclair, Hugh	27, 29
Sinclair, Malcolm	208, 265
Sinclair, Timothy	201
Sinden, Donald	51
Sinden, Jeremy	227
Sinden, Leon	147, 169
Singer, Campbell	16
Singh, Yasmin	96
Singleton, Anthony	36
Singleton, Dudley	35
Sinigalia, Annie	268
Sirtis, Marina	150
Skelton, Roy	217
Skelton, Terence	136
Skillan, George	12
Skinner, Keith	91
Skinner, Martin	97
Skipp, Raymond	145
Sladen, Elisabeth	186, 217
Slater, Daphne	5, 17, 24, 53, 92, 106

Slater, Guy 150
Slater, John 11, 143
Slaughter, Jane 136
Slevin, Gerard 140
Sloman, Roger 190
Slowe, Georgia 158, 165
Smart, Patsy 146
Smer, Derek 34, 47
Smilie, Jim 140
Smith, Brian 38
Smith, Derek 155, 158, 171
Smith, Fred 50
Smith, Herbert 5
Smith, Jean Taylor 156
Smith, Liz 194, 222
Smith, Mossie 253, 262
Smith, Paul 204
Smith, Ray 54, 71, 75, 120, 127, 135, 144, 158, 261
Smith, Ursula 106
Smith, Valerie 17
Smith-Wood, Jackie 202
Snelling, Henry 209
Sofiano, Jayne 94
Solon, Ewen 11, 16, 35, 41
Sommer, Elke 214
Sommerville, Geraldine 270
Sommerville, John 142
Sone, Roy 15, 152
Soral, Agnes 244
Soresi, Jon 253
Sorvino, Mira 281
Southworth, John 4
Spaull, Colin 37, 38, 47
Spencer, Harvey 72
Spencer, Marian 29, 107
Spenser, David 6, 56
Spenser, Jeremy 4, 6
Sperber, Milo 190
Spiegel, Bernard 268
Spiro, Alyson 214
Spriggs, Elizabeth 136, 175, 190, 249, 263, 278
Sproston, Malcolm 156
Sproule, Peter 97
Spurrier, Paul 149
Squire, William 29, 38, 47, 54, 88, 117, 136, 154
Stabb, Dinah 163, 265
Stacy, Neil 189
Stallybrass, Anne 87, 94, 101, 115, 145, 149, 151, 261
Stamp, Terence 202
Standing, John 97, 283
Stanfield, Devin 208

Stanhope, Warren 8
Stanton, Barry 191
Stark, Timothy 186
Stark, Virginia 127
Stassino, Paul 26, 60
Staunton, Imelda 223
Steadman, Alison 146, 223, 255, 279
Steadman, Lynda 282
Steed, Maggie 178, 251, 268
Steedman, Shirley 164
Steedman, Tony 76, 86, 88, 204
Steel, Janet 240
Steele, Richard 106
Steen, Steve 273
Steenburgen, Mary 215
Stegers, Bernice 139, 249, 272, 280
Steindorsdottir, Heida 159
Stephen, Susan 3
Stephens, Jonathan 202
Stephens, Peter 30
Stephens, Robert 142, 173, 208, 210, 228, 275
Stephens, Roy 72
Stephens, Toby 261
Stephenson, Pamela 222
Sterke, Jeannette 33
Sterland, John 187
Sterling, Alison 242
Steuart, David 61, 80
Stevens, Jayne 172
Stevens, Vi 13
Stevenson, Juliet 173
Stevenson, Ray 276, 283
Stewart, Bill 236, 257
Stewart, Ewan 174
Stewart, Iain 156
Stewart, Job 176
Stewart, Nigel 206, 212
Stewart, Patrick 125, 137, 142, 164, 192
Stewart, Sophie 89
Stirling, Helen 4
Stirling, Richard 264
Stirner, Brian 135, 156
Stock, Nigel 65, 77, 142, 164, 169, 175, 209
Stoddard, Malcolm 129, 139, 169, 201
Stokes, Barry 138
Stoller, Jennie 145
Stone, John 16, 23, 169, 217
Stone, Martin 237
Stone, Suzanne 139

Stoney, Kevin 64
Storry, Malcolm 181, 276
Stott, Judith 72
Stratton, John 35, 49, 93, 94, 104, 158, 177, 184, 194, 196
Strauss, Catherine 213
Strauss, Peter 215
Streader, Norma 136
Streatfeild, Noel 54
Streather, Paul 18
Stride, John 74, 163, 196, 229, 240, 242, 260, 261
Stride, Virginia 145
Stringer, Nick 202
Stritch, Elaine 122
Strong, Gwyneth 194, 220, 265
Strong, Veronica 76
Stronge, Helen 117
Strotheide, Mike 50
Stuart, Grahame 19
Stuart, John 3, 17
Stubbs, Imogen 238
Sturridge, Charles 133
Styler, Trudie 187
Suchet, David 176, 207, 211, 264
Sullivan, Elliott 112
Summerfield, Eleanor 72
Summers, Jill 145
Sumner, David 77, 84, 193
Sumner, Geoffrey 7, 8, 12
Sumpter, Donald 182, 189, 271
Sundquist, Bjorn 202
Sundquist, Gerry 173, 184
Sunters, Irene 164
Surtees, Allan 265
Suska, Almanta 241, 250
Sutton, Dudley 192, 209
Sutton, Sarah 132, 157
Sutton, Shaun 11
Suzman, Janet 77, 79, 223, 264
Swann, Robert 149, 179
Sweeney, Maureen 218, 282
Sweeney, Norman 98
Swift, Clive 96, 209, 221
Swift, David 76, 116, 171, 207, 224, 235
Swinburne, Nora 51, 130
Swinton, Tilda 219
Swit, Loretta 265
Sydney, Derek 73
Sylvester, Ingrid 28
Sylvester, William 26
Syms, Sylvia 82, 187, 280

Taffurelli, Kevin 179

Tafler, Sydney	22, 29	
Talbot, Ian	266	
Talfrey, Hira	49	
Tamm, Mary	134, 169	
Tan, Vivien	260	
Tandy, Mark	281	
Tanner, Stella	147	
Tarrant, Colin	238	
Tate, John	83	
Tate, Reginald	10	
Tattersfield, Michael	130	
Taunton, Sarah	86	
Taylerson, Marilyn	88, 92	
Taylor, Amelia	104	
Taylor, Benedict	193, 215, 230, 231	
Taylor, Elaine	96	
Taylor, Gladys	54	
Taylor, Gwen	124	
Taylor, Lisa	253	
Taylor, Shaun	196	
Taylor, Siobhan	65	
Telland, David	225	
Tennant, Victoria	243	
Terry, Nigel	235, 236, 267	
Textor, Stella	56	
Thatcher, Grant	231	
Thaw, John	82, 259, 268	
Thesiger, Ernest	23	
Thewlis, David	249, 273, 275	
Thomas, Damien	178, 201	
Thomas, Gareth	130, 133, 138, 195, 207, 210, 242	
Thomas, Giles	268	
Thomas, Henley	47	
Thomas, Hugh	227	
Thomas, Kristin Scott	257, 266	
Thomas, Michael	173	
Thomas, Nina	125	
Thomas, Rachel	47, 152, 154	
Thomas, Talfryn	84	
Thompson, Derek	192, 210, 220	
Thompson, Emma	230	
Thompson, Eric	29	
Thompson, Ian	20, 77, 102, 109	
Thompson, Sophie	151	
Thomsett, Sally	90	
Thomson, Hilary	61	
Thomson, Kim	211, 230, 256, 258	
Thorne, Angela	102	
Thorne, Kenneth	25	
Thornett, Kenneth	37, 42	
Thornton, Sigrid	204	
Thorpe, Harriet	230	
Thorpe-Bates, Peggy	32, 59, 61, 69	
Threlfall, David	193, 199, 221, 231, 240, 257
Thurley, Martin C.	164
Thwaites, David	244, 245, 252
Tibbs, Gary	217
Tiernan, Andrew	264
Tierney, Malcolm	181
Tilbury, Peter	237
Tilley, David	20
Tillinger, John	72
Tilvern, Alan	52
Timothy, Christopher	147
Tindall, Hilary	188
Tingwell, Charles	76
Tinney, Andrew	125
Tobias, Heather	278
Tobin, June	61, 74
Todd, Ann	211
Todd, Richard	214
Todd, Saira	262
Todd-Jones, William	237, 244, 245, 252
Togni, Suzanne	78
Tomelty, Frances	197
Tong, Jacqueline	149, 226, 250
Toone, Geoffrey	52, 80, 198
Townend, Sam	274
Townley, Toke	32, 61
Townsend, Jill	114, 136
Tracey, Jill	39
Tracy, Susan	128, 224
Travers, Bill	65
Treagear, Frank	116
Trevelyan, James	223
Treves, Frederick	76, 90, 203, 209, 219, 236, 244, 264, 272, 275
Treves, Simon	210
Trevor, Austin	75
Trillat, Georges	229
Trippier, Alexander	280
Troughton, David	132, 220
Troughton, Michael	163, 165
Troughton, Patrick	6, 8, 11, 20, 24, 32, 34, 36, 39, 40, 47, 63, 65, 68, 74, 101, 104, 109, 123, 142, 149, 157, 206, 208
Trouncer, Ruth	141
Tucker, Burnell	64
Tucker, Chloe	275
Tudno, Mali	227
Tully, Brian	144
Tully, David	117
Tummings, Chris	229
Turleigh, Veronica	61
Turner, Anna	33
Turner, Betty	215
Turner, Bridget	93
Turner, Jessica	273
Turner, John	142
Turner, Michael	135, 139
Turner, Pauline	278
Turner, Simon	108, 110, 111
Turner, Stephanie	171
Turner, Stephen	104
Turner, Teddy	145
Turner, Valerie	14
Tutin, Dorothy	101, 128, 196, 263, 269
Twigge, Jenny	121
Twinn, Kellie	145
Tyrrell, Norman	69
Tyson, Cathy	241, 283
Tyzack, Margaret	19, 29, 37, 83, 97, 107, 142, 191
Ullman, Tracey	174
Urquhart, Robert	39, 127, 151, 200, 277
Usher, Brett	96, 154
Usher, Elaine	32
Valentine, Anthony	15, 18, 121, 233, 269
Valmere, Lila	72
van der Burgh, Margot	37, 50
Van Gaver, Peter	238
Van Gyseghem, André	28, 49, 55, 103, 108
Vanne, Marda	25, 34, 39
Varley, Beatrice	38, 52
Vassiliou, Monica	96
Vaughan, Peter	59, 63, 83, 85, 93, 125, 213, 275, 283
Vaughan-Scott, Edward	39
Veasay, Frank	85
Ventham, Wanda	80
Verner, Jimmy	9
Vernon, Richard	52, 53, 57, 60, 62, 191, 221, 272
Vibert, Ronan	281
Victory, Fiona	214, 235, 261
Villiers, Christopher	202, 249
Villiers, James	82, 97, 230, 242, 252
Vine, John	187, 211, 212, 236
Voe, Sandra	181, 269
Von Sydow, Max	212
Vosburgh, Tilly	178, 227
Voss, Philip	131, 276
Waddington, Patrick	25

PLAYERS   329

Wadham, Julian		274
Wainwright, John		66
Waite, Charles		117
Walden, Ben		261, 278
Waldhorn, Gary		188, 193
Waldron, Caroline		239
Waley, Juliet		122, 125
Walker, Amanda		80
Walker, Claire		117, 143
Walker, Fiona	105, 142, 197, 209,	213, 266
Walker, Kenny		141
Walker, Larrington		220
Walker, Lindsay		179
Walker, Rudolph		241
Walker, Zena	34, 53, 116, 159, 196	
Wallace, Elizabeth		85
Wallace, Ian		217
Wallace, Julie T.		222
Waller, David		157
Waller, Paul		85
Wallis, Bill		219, 273
Wallis, Francis		98
Walpole, Nicholas		206
Walsh, Dermot		19, 22
Walsh, Sally		274
Walter, Harriet	210, 227, 228, 257	
Walters, Hugh		89
Walters, Julie		255
Walters, Melanie		270
Walters, Thorley	107, 129, 149, 160,	173, 222
Walton, Richard		206
Waltz, Christoph		250, 258
Wambu, Oke		264
Wanamaker, Sam		183
Wanamaker, Zoe	153, 216, 221,	254, 266
Ward, Barry		277
Ward, Georgina		86, 89
Ward, Margaret		18
Ward, Simon	82, 104, 191, 237	
Wardroper, James		112
Waring, Derek		16, 131, 226
Warnecke, Gordon		262
Warner, David		187, 281, 283
Warner, Fern		66
Warner, Richard		22, 144
Warnock, Grant Ashley		183
Warre, Michael		23, 25
Warren, Barry		68
Warren, Kenneth J.		117
Warshal, Zara		252
Warwick, James		122, 181, 187
Warwick, Richard		97, 105, 111

Washbourne, Mona		172, 185
Waterman, Dennis		85, 222
Waterston, Sam		176
Watford, Gwen	20, 28, 74, 81, 206	
Watling, Jack		13
Watson, Andrew C.		229
Watson, Gary	63, 82, 132, 163	
Watson, Greta		29
Watson, Jack	146, 149, 150, 164,	178, 204, 216, 270
Watson, John H.		32
Watson, Malcolm		29
Watson, Mary		20
Watson, Moray	10, 51, 67, 147, 170	
Watson, Tom	68, 119, 161, 164,	181, 199, 267, 270
Watts, Christopher		140
Watts, Gwendolyn		71
Watts, Victoria		42, 47
Way, Ann		90
Way, Anthony		283
Way, Eileen		14, 174, 238
Weaver, Elizabeth		63
Weavers, John		140
Weavers, Mark		140
Webb, Alan		153
Webb, Chloe		271
Webb, Danny		272, 274
Webb, Julie		17
Webster, Mary		28, 40, 85
Webster, Paddy		21
Weeks, Honeysuckle		269
Weeks, Ingeborg		12
Weigang, Rudiger		231
Weiss, Trudy		261
Weisz, Rachel		271
Welch, Denise		280
Welland, Colin		254
Wells, Jerold		37
Welsh, John	62, 63, 74, 83, 88, 104,	110, 112, 118, 140, 195, 211
Wenham, Jane		165
Wenner, Martin		238, 242
Wennink, Michael		87
Wentworth, John	75, 101, 107	
Wentworth, Robin		126
West, Carinthia		161
West, Charles		123
West, Lockwood	4, 5, 14, 36, 67	
West, Norma		95, 111
West, Samuel		245, 259
West, Simon		134
West, Timothy	53, 133, 150, 161,	221, 266, 274
Westbrook, John		27, 97

Westbury, Marjorie		134
Weston, David		75
Weston, Debra		281
Westwood, Patrick		21
Whalley, Joanne	188, 216, 223	
Whalley, Tat		250
Wheeler, Debbie		206
Whelan, Gary	183, 218, 254	
Whiley, Gareth Ridgwell		154
Whitbread, Peter		148
Whitchurch, Philip		255
White, Alan		28, 58
White, Arthur		283
White, Cathy		275
White, Dorothy		127
White, Frances	123, 142, 163	
White, Jeremy		31
White, Meadows		27, 32
White, Sheila		142
Whitehead, Geoffrey	133, 137, 220	
Whitehead, Jane		14
Whitelaw, Billie	5, 113, 160, 181,	229, 259
Whiteley, Arkie		263, 267
Whiteley, Thelma		77
Whiting, Margaret	115, 121, 154, 212	
Whitman, Peter		176
Whitrow, Benjamin	163, 189, 193	
Whitsun-Jones, Paul	12, 14, 16, 25,	38
Whittingham, Sheila		89
Whitwell, Tracy		276
Wickham, Saskia		258
Wicks, Victoria		208
Wilby, James	241, 243, 269, 279	
Wilcox, Paula		274
Wilcox, Sophie	237, 244, 245	
Wild, Katy		51, 58
Wilde, Brian	14, 67, 73, 155	
Wilde, Colette		70
Wilde, William		158
Wilding, April		60
Wilkie, Clare		231
Wilkinson, David		155
Wilkinson, Tom	202, 221, 254,	260, 261, 270, 278
Willard, Edmund		6
Williams, Charlotte		277
Williams, Christopher		54
Williams, Cynda		271
Williams, Derek		64
Williams, Frank		87
Williams, Ieuan Rhys		76
Williams, Kate		282
Williams, Kit		75

Williams, Leonard	56	Wolter, Ralf	236	Wright, Jennifer	39, 58
Williams, Lia	268, 278	Wolveridge, Carol	12, 24	Wyatt, Tessa	104
Williams, Michael	120, 123, 132, 160, 176	Wong, Anna May	43	Wyce, Hilary	48, 54
		Wood, Clive	188	Wyldeck, Martin	11
Williams, Richard	54	Wood, Georgie	4	Wylie, Frank	125
Williams, Sam	145	Wood, John	52, 74	Wymark, Jane	146
Williams, Tony	221	Wood, Peggy Ann	155	Wymark, Patrick	29
Williams, Vicky	123, 131	Woodall, Andrew	273	Wyngarde, Peter	25, 32, 42, 66
Williams, Victoria	103	Woodbridge, George	28	Wynn, James	188
Williams, Wendy	39, 81, 193	Woodburn, Eric	19	Wynne, Michael	86
Willis, Jerome	41, 118	Woodeson, Nicholas	192, 262	Wyse, John	4
Willman, Noel	92	Woodgate, Clare	270		
Wills, Annika	58	Woodison, Nicholas	245	Yakunina, Valentina	243
Willys, Anneke	16, 22	Woodnutt, John	18, 24, 32, 34, 35, 58, 131, 187, 209	Yang, Lian-Shin	28
Wilmer, Douglas	19, 30			Yannis, Michael	5
Wilsher, Barry	70	Woods, Aubrey	40	Yardley, Julian	54
Wilson, Anthony	32	Woodthorpe, Peter	79	Yardley, Stephen	175, 183, 184
Wilson, Donald	36	Woodville, Catherine	51, 59	Yates, Marjorie	207, 235
Wilson, Jennifer	27	Woodvine, John	84, 106, 131, 193, 206, 208, 210, 215, 216, 264, 279	Yates, Pauline	42, 103
Wilson, Kara	69, 96, 174			Yeldham, Lyn	110
Wilson, Manning	30, 64, 74	Woodward, Edward	56, 82, 183	Yelland, David	130
Wilson, Neil	48	Woodward, Mandy	150	York, Michael	83
Wilson, Richard	255, 260	Woodward, Peter	165, 179, 184	York, Sasha	217
Wilson, Stuart	115, 149, 159, 200, 203	Woodward, Tim	190, 191, 197, 226, 239	York, Susannah	163, 179, 241, 253
				Youinou, Blanche	201
Wiltcher, Guy	281	Woofe, Eric	104, 115	Young, Arthur	17
Wilton, Penelope	120, 265, 272	Wooland, Norman	12, 26	Young, Barbara	143
Wimbush, Mary	136, 194	Wooldridge, Susan	113, 141, 203, 212	Young, Burt	279
Winch, Barry	145			Young, Des	196
Winding, Victor	207	Woolf, Gabriel	55	Young, Eric	130
Windsor, Frank	161, 240	Woolf, Henry	60	Young, Felicity	57
Wing, Anna	109	Woolfe, Betty	16	Young, Gladys	13, 34
Wing-Davey, Mark	139, 173, 178, 207	Woolgar, Jack	85, 90, 111	Young, Jeremy	82, 84
		Wordsworth, Richard	16, 25, 27, 200, 215	Young, Joan	6
Winman, Sarah	239			Young, Paul	107, 119, 173
Winmill, Joan	8	Workman, Charles	25	Young, Raymond	47
Winstone, Ray	194	Worth, Harry	117	Young, Ric	281
Winter, George	258	Worth, Helen	97	Young, Sean	215
Winton, Roger	26	Woutas, Alexis	194	Younger, Shane	65
Wise, Greg	281	Wreford, Edgar	178		
Withers, Margery	117, 119, 249	Wren, Richard	150, 158	Zagaria, Anita	258
Wolf, Rita	275	Wright, Francis	254	Zuk, Damian	280
Wolfenden, Stuart	259	Wright, Heather	127, 188		

INDEX OF
GENRES

adventure   3, 6, 8, 14, 17, 20, 26, 29, 32, 33, 39, 49, 55, 62, 65, 81, 83, 84, 93, 117, 118, 137, 146, 148, 149, 161, 193, 208, 280
allegory, religious   88
American   3, 4, 11, 12, 31, 33, 35, 36, 50, 62, 72, 76, 78, 88, 90, 104, 105, 114, 122, 143, 150, 176, 215, 235, 271
American/British   87, 93, 187, 214, 232, 281
Australian   9, 56
Austrian   115, 120
biographical   6, 15, 30, 31, 71, 73, 81, 87, 97, 106, 110, 111, 113, 115, 120, 121, 128, 129, 133, 136, 141, 143, 145, 147, 153, 154, 155, 156, 163, 165, 180, 183, 187, 207, 213, 218, 221, 224, 230, 238, 251, 253, 262
+ British   3–42, 47–98, 101–111, 113–165, 169–245, 249–270, 272–283
British/African   264, 265
British/Australian   273
British/European   21, 42, 62, 68, 79, 116, 122, 157, 208, 210, 211, 250, 252, 257, 270
British/French   17, 25, 49, 73, 83, 175, 241, 268
British/German   255
British/Greek   150, 158
British/Indian   271
British/Irish   258
British/Italian   72
British/Russian   145, 208, 267
Canadian   6, 112
Century
   1st   152
   2nd   148
   6th   164, 258
   6th–20th   15
   11th   76
   12th   8, 101, 137, 177
   12th–13th   153
   14th   42
   14th–15th   13
   15th   9, 29, 39, 79, 101, 111, 117
   15th–16th   185
   16th   16, 22, 32, 86, 92 101, 106, 127, 138, 151, 153
   16th–20th   151, 249
   17th   14, 15, 19, 27, 30, 47, 58, 65, 68, 69, 81, 84, 92, 103, 113, 118, 125, 142, 150, 173, 201, 209
   17th–20th   7
   18th   3, 6, 8, 11, 18, 20, 25, 26, 32, 33, 35, 41, 50, 52, 55, 61, 65, 68, 73, 80, 89, 91, 93, 95, 97, 105, 110, 119, 122, 132, 137, 140, 146, 149, 161, 172, 175, 186, 199, 205, 241, 258
   18th–19th   81, 124, 133, 136, 163, 189
   19th   3, 4, 5, 6, 7, 9, 10, 12, 13, 14, 15, 17, 20, 21, 23, 24, 25, 26, 27, 29, 31, 32, 34, 35, 36, 37, 38, 39, 40, 41, 47, 49, 50, 51, 52, 53, 54, 55, 56, 58, 59, 62, 63, 64, 66, 67, 69, 70, 71, 73, 74, 75, 76, 77, 78, 80, 81, 83, 85, 86, 87, 88, 89, 90, 91, 93, 94, 95, 96, 101, 102, 103, 104, 105, 107, 108, 109, 110, 111, 112, 113, 114, 115, 116, 117, 119, 122, 124, 128, 130, 132, 135, 136, 137, 140, 143, 144, 145, 146, 147, 149, 150, 151, 154, 155, 158, 161, 162, 164, 165, 169, 171, 172, 173, 178, 179, 180, 182, 184, 186, 187, 190, 191, 192, 193, 194, 195, 196, 200, 201, 204, 208, 209, 210, 213, 215, 217, 219, 222, 225, 230, 238, 249, 253, 255, 256, 264, 266, 268, 271, 274, 276, 278, 280, 281, 282
   19th–20th   47, 70, 82, 125, 129, 133, 138, 155, 156, 160, 164, 170, 177, 179, 180, 186, 187, 196, 205, 207, 233
   20th   3, 5, 8, 22, 24, 25, 28, 33, 37, 38, 47, 48, 53, 55, 58, 61, 62, 65, 67, 68, 72, 76, 78, 79, 82, 85, 86, 87, 89, 90, 91, 95, 96, 102, 104, 106, 108, 109, 110, 114, 115, 116, 117, 118, 119, 120, 121, 122, 123, 124, 125, 126, 127, 128, 129, 131, 133, 134, 135, 136, 139, 141, 144, 145, 147, 148, 151, 152, 154, 155, 156, 157, 159, 160, 161, 163, 165, 170, 172, 174, 175, 176, 177, 180, 181, 183, 185, 188, 189, 190, 191, 194, 195, 196, 198, 199, 200, 202, 203, 204, 206, 208, 211, 213, 214, 215, 216, 218, 221, 222, 223, 224, 227, 228, 230, 231, 234, 235, 236, 237, 238, 241, 242, 244, 245, 250, 251, 252, 253, 255, 260, 261, 262, 263, 264, 265, 267, 269, 271, 272, 273, 274, 276, 277, 278
§ classic   3, 4, 5, 6, 7, 8, 9, 10, 13, 14, 16, 17, 18, 19, 20, 21, 22, 23, 25, 26, 27, 29, 31, 33, 34, 35, 36, 37, 38, 39, 40, 41, 47, 49, 50, 51, 52, 53, 54, 55, 59, 61, 63, 64, 65, 66, 67, 70, 71, 72, 73, 74, 76, 78, 79, 80, 81, 82, 83, 84, 85, 86, 87, 88, 89, 90, 91, 92, 93, 95, 96, 101, 103, 104, 105, 107, 109, 100, 111, 112, 114, 116, 117, 118, 119, 122, 124, 128, 130, 131, 132, 135, 137, 138, 140, 142, 143, 144, 146, 149, 150, 151, 155, 157, 158, 159, 160, 161, 164, 165, 169, 172, 175, 177, 179, 184, 186, 192, 193, 195, 200, 201, 204, 207, 208, 209,

+ denotes story setting/main characters
§ adaptation of classic work

213, 215, 217, 222, 225, 230, 237, 241, 244, 245, 252, 256, 258, 264, 271, 274, 278, 280
comedy   18, 59, 112, 116, 228, 232, 267, 268, 280
¶ contemporary   5, 7, 8, 9, 10, 11, 12, 13, 14, 15, 16, 18, 19, 20, 21, 22, 23, 24, 25, 26, 27, 28, 29, 30, 31, 32, 33, 34, 35, 36, 38, 39, 40, 41, 42, 48, 49, 50, 51, 52, 53, 54, 56, 57, 58, 59, 60, 62, 63, 64, 65, 67, 68, 70, 71, 72, 73, 74, 75, 76, 77, 78, 79, 80, 81, 82, 83, 84, 85, 86, 92, 94, 95, 96, 97, 98, 106, 109, 111, 113, 115, 116, 118, 121, 122, 123, 127, 129, 130, 131, 132, 134, 135, 137, 138, 139, 140, 141, 142, 144, 145, 147, 150, 152, 153, 157, 158, 159, 161, 162, 163, 169, 170, 171, 173, 177, 178, 179, 180, 181, 182, 183, 185, 187, 188, 189, 190, 192, 194, 195, 197, 198, 199, 200, 201, 202, 204, 205, 206, 207, 208, 209, 210, 211, 212, 213, 214, 216, 217, 218, 219, 220, 222, 223, 224, 225, 226, 227, 228, 229, 230, 231, 232, 233, 234, 235, 236, 237, 238, 239, 240, 241, 242, 243, 244, 245, 249, 250, 251, 252, 253, 254, 255, 256, 257, 258, 259, 260, 261, 262, 263, 264, 265, 266, 267, 268, 269, 270, 271, 272, 273, 274, 275, 276, 277, 278, 279, 280, 281, 282, 283
drama   3–42, 47–98, 101–165, 169–226, 228–230, 232–235, 237–245, 249–283
Dutch   224
Egypt, Ancient   195
European   12, 28, 38, 57, 66, 68, 108, 185, 207, 208
family   3, 4, 5, 6, 7, 9, 10, 12, 13, 14, 15, 16, 17, 18, 21, 22, 23, 26, 28, 30, 31, 32, 35, 36, 37, 38, 42, 47, 48, 54, 56, 57, 58, 59, 60, 62, 63, 64, 65, 69, 85, 90, 92, 97, 98, 101, 104, 108, 110, 111, 112, 116, 117, 118, 119, 122, 123, 125, 128, 130, 131, 132, 134, 136, 138, 140, 141, 143, 144, 148, 150, 151, 156, 157, 165, 170, 171, 172, 179, 186, 194, 196, 206, 208, 212, 217, 218, 223, 225, 227, 228, 231, 232, 237, 239, 244, 245, 249, 250, 252, 253, 264, 272, 280
fantasy   85, 123, 151, 157, 217, 219, 237, 239, 244, 245, 252, 253, 258, 264, 272, 280
French   14, 19, 31, 33, 35, 66, 70, 74, 77, 79, 81, 84, 87, 90, 92, 93, 95, 101, 103, 104, 107, 112, 113, 119, 128, 135, 136, 144, 147, 171, 244, 271
German   76, 112, 133, 181
German/Russian   125
Greece, Ancient   160
Greek   96
historical   6, 13, 55, 71, 73, 97, 101, 106, 108, 111, 113, 125, 126, 129, 133, 141, 142, 153, 154, 157, 163, 176, 180, 182, 183, 185, 187, 189, 195, 196, 208, 211, 249, 253
Irish   33, 201, 234, 243, 253, 255, 256, 276
Italian   14, 110, 121, 185, 219
musical   177, 223
musical/fantasy   152
mystery   7, 9, 14, 18, 19, 20, 22, 23, 24, 25, 28, 30, 33, 36, 38, 40, 48, 49, 51, 56, 61, 62, 64, 71, 75, 79, 81, 109, 111, 114, 118, 123, 126, 135, 139, 147, 154, 156, 162, 169, 170, 172, 173, 190, 192, 197, 200, 211, 212, 216, 223, 227, 228, 230, 235, 236, 237, 253, 254, 262, 266, 267, 273, 276, 277, 283
non-fiction   58, 172, 173, 216, 255, 274
Rome, Ancient   30, 142
Russian   71, 78, 89, 93, 94, 109, 116, 149, 161, 275
satire   89, 178, 186, 200, 211, 220, 221, 222, 250, 252, 254, 255, 257, 259, 260, 266, 267, 270, 273, 279
science fiction   10, 16, 17, 19, 23, 35, 57, 58, 61, 63, 131, 164, 178, 183, 184, 207, 215, 229, 231, 273
Scottish   6, 20, 25, 30, 55, 61, 62, 65, 68, 73, 80, 89, 94, 95, 106, 108, 119, 120, 127, 132, 135, 140, 146, 151, 156, 161, 164, 177, 181, 187, 191, 198, 199, 204, 224, 227, 239, 249, 257
Spanish   18
Swiss   10, 13, 38, 128
thriller   5, 7, 8, 10, 11, 12, 13, 15, 18, 20, 21, 22, 23, 24, 26, 27, 29, 30, 31, 34, 39, 40, 41, 42, 48, 49, 50, 51, 52, 53, 56, 57, 59, 60, 62, 63, 64, 65, 67, 68, 69, 70, 72, 73, 74, 75, 76, 77, 78, 79, 80, 81, 82, 83, 84, 85, 86, 92, 94, 95, 97, 98, 111, 113, 115, 116, 120, 121, 122, 127, 130, 131, 132, 135, 137, 138, 141, 142, 153, 157, 158, 159, 160, 161, 162, 163, 169, 180, 181, 182, 183, 188, 190, 191, 192, 194, 197, 198, 199, 202, 204, 208, 209, 210, 213, 214, 216, 218, 219, 220, 225, 226, 227, 229, 231, 232, 233, 234, 235, 236, 237, 238, 239, 240, 241, 243, 250, 251, 252, 254, 256, 257, 258, 260, 261, 262, 263, 264, 266, 267, 270, 272, 275, 278, 282
Welsh   47, 60, 71, 75, 98, 118, 125, 151, 154, 207, 227, 253, 261

¶ set at time programme was produced